*The publisher gratefully acknowledges the generous
contribution to this book provided by the
General Endowment Fund of the Associates of
the University of California Press.*

City for Sale

City for Sale

The Transformation of San Francisco

REVISED AND UPDATED EDITION

CHESTER HARTMAN with Sarah Carnochan

University of California Press

Berkeley   Los Angeles   London

University of California Press
Berkeley and Los Angeles, California

University of California Press, Ltd.
London, England

Library of Congress Cataloging-in-Publication Data

Hartman, Chester W.
    City for sale : the transformation of San Francisco / Chester
Hartman, with Sarah Carnochan.
        p.   cm.
    Rev. ed. of: The transformation of San Francisco / Chester Hartman.
    1984.
    Includes bibliographical references (p.) and index.
    ISBN 0-520-08605-8 (pbk. : alk. paper).
    1. Urban renewal—California—San Francisco.   2. City planning—
California—San Francisco.   3. San Francisco (Calif.)   I. Carnochan,
Sarah.   II. Hartman, Chester W. Transformation of San Francisco.
III. Title.
HT177.S38 H36   2002
307.76'09794'6109045—dc21   2001007072

Manufactured in the United States of America

10   09   08   07   06   05   04   03   02
10   9   8   7   6   5   4   3   2   1

The paper used in this publication meets the minimum requirements of
ANSI/NISO Z39.48-1992 (R 1997) (*Permanence of Paper*). ♾

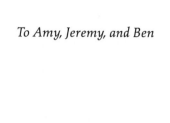

To Amy, Jeremy, and Ben

Contents

Preface

For a city as politically fascinating and world renowned as San Francisco, it is surprising how little exists in the way of book-length scholarly literature focused solely on the city's recent history. Fred Wirt's 1974 *Power in the City: Decision Making in San Francisco*, Allan Jacobs's 1978 *Making City Planning Work*, Richard DeLeon's 1992 *Left Coast City: Progressive Politics in San Francisco*, Stephen McGovern's 1998 *The Politics of Downtown Development: Political Cultures in San Francisco and Washington, D.C.*, and the 1998 collection *Reclaiming San Francisco: History, Politics, Culture*, edited by James Brook, Chris Carlsson, and Nancy J. Peters (see also their related CD-ROM, *Shaping San Francisco: A Multimedia Excavation of the Lost History of San Francisco*, 2d ed.), along with my 1984 *The Transformation of San Francisco*, stand out as the few examples. Thus, when that book went out of print several years ago, I could not resist the temptation to update and reissue it. That I no longer live in San Francisco (although I still own a home there) turned out to be both an advantage and a disadvantage. The downside is obvious. But a combination of regular trips back, constant contacts with old friends and activist colleagues, and regular consultation of the city's newspapers (now easily accessed via the Internet) gave me a basic understanding of how the various strands of my earlier history have developed in the dozen and a half subsequent years. To provide the additional detail needed, I was fortunate to recruit Sarah Carnochan, then a lawyer with the Tenderloin Housing Clinic and currently a doctoral student in social work at UC-Berkeley, who spent many weeks, at different periods of the rewrite, under my direction, tracking down the various items I needed for the new edition and writing up this new material. For my final writing push, she was joined by Art Armstrong, a San Francisco State graduate student, to provide answers to the many lingering research questions, large and small. It is no cliché to say this book would not be possible without their first-rate work. My correspondence and personal interviews with key actors over the past years, by phone and in the course of trips back to the city, provided additional material, and I am pleased to acknowledge their help below. The positive spin on how my removal to Washington, D.C., in the early eighties was a plus is the way that distance can often provide a useful overview of developments, once one no longer is mired in details and day-to-day involvement, as I was during the 1970s. My frequent use and citation of accounts from the dailies I now read—the *Washington Post* and *New York Times*, papers that regularly report on this most interesting of U.S. cities—reflect a recognition that such capsulized, reflective analyses often provide more insightful coverage of political and cultural developments than is to be found in the day-to-day coverage of the local press; these "foreign" sources also provide a filtering device of sorts as to which San Francisco happenings are of larger interest to the rest of country.

My account of development politics in San Francisco is in large part that of a participant-observer and resident of the city from 1970 to 1980. The stand on development issues embodied in this book has been shaped by the direct and indirect roles I played in many of the events chronicled here: as a staff member of the National Housing Law Project (cocounsel in the Yerba Buena Center [YBC] displacees' historic litigation opposing the illegal displacement activities of the San Francisco Redevelopment Agency) from 1970 to 1974; as a member (appointed by TOOR [Tenants and Owners in Opposition to Redevelopment], the displaced residents' organization) of the Relocation Appeals Board established in 1970 as part of the federal court decree resolving TOOR's suit against the City and Redevelopment Agency; as an organizer of the 1974–75 effort to reshape the Yerba Buena Center project via litigation and creation of the Citizens Committee on Yerba Buena Center; as coplaintiff in the final, 1978 financing suit against YBC; as an organizer of the November 1978 ballot initiative requiring landlords to pass on to their tenants their Proposition 13 property tax windfalls; as cochair (with Charles Lamb, president of Local 2, Hotel and Restaurant Employees Union) of San Franciscans for Affordable Housing, the coalition that placed the comprehensive housing reform initiative on the November 1979 city ballot; and as an activist in many of the city's housing and neighborhood struggles, such as those around the International Hotel and Goodman Building. This long-term and intimate involvement in the politics of the city has permitted greater depth of understanding, as well as greater access to information and actors, than would otherwise have been possible.

Having a publishing contract with University of California Press and a massive pile of documentation needed for the rewrite, all I needed was a few solid weeks of writing time, something I was simply unable, for far too many years, to find, given my position as executive director of a small national public interest organization. Thus, I jumped at the invitation to return to the University of North Carolina—where I had taught for a year right after leaving San Francisco—as the Cecil B. Sheps Visiting Fellow in Social Justice. Over a four-week period during March and April 1997, I went to Chapel Hill three to four days a week and put in often sixteen-hour days absorbing the new material and creating new text. I am extremely grateful to Bill Rohe and his staff at UNC's Center for Urban and Regional Studies for their hospitality, support, and fellowship (in both senses), and to Dr. Sheps for creating this award. And as well, I am indebted to various Chapel Hill-ers— Jane and Adam Stein, Anita and Paul Farel, especially—who put me up and put up with me during this stay and made it so pleasant. But alas, time ran out before I could finish the book in 1997, as I needed to heed importunities from family and office to return. And so the manuscript once again lay in boxes—this kind of writing not being something I can do in dribs and drabs. Then in 1999, the hidden hand that so often has dropped into my life, and comes as close as anything to challenging my atheism with a belief that someone up there likes me, struck—this time in the form of an invitation to apply for a stay at a writers' refuge in Point Reyes Station, California, an hour north of San Francisco. I applied, went there for two weeks in mid-July, and shortly afterward was able to turn an updated manuscript in to UC Press. The Mesa Refuge, created by Peter Barnes and Leyna Bernstein, is a magnificent concept and execution: Point Reyes is heaven on earth (counteratheism again); the Mesa Refuge is set up and equipped with such care and sensitivity as to make life and writing there as supportive as possible. Those readers of this book who also are writers—especially those, like me, who are not full-time writers—will know what a precious gift it is to have the time and proper environment—away from regular work, from family (*pace* Amy, Jeremy, Ben), from everything except the project one needs to do—to concentrate solely on *writing*. Thank you, Peter and Leyna.

This revised edition is actually the third iteration of a project that began with my 1974 book *Yerba Buena: Land Grab and Community Resistance in San Francisco* (Glide Publications), written while I was on the staff of the National Housing Law Project. I then expanded the scope of the earlier treatment to deal with citywide development politics and impacts (*The*

Transformation of San Francisco, Rowman and Allanheld, 1984). This revised edition takes that broader treatment up through early 2002.

Each book incorporates text from and builds on the prior work, and in all stages there have been great numbers of people who have helped: supplying information, drafting materials, reviewing drafts, typing drafts (in the old, precomputer days), providing hospitality, and assisting this technoklutz with word-processing problems. My list of acknowledgments therefore is extremely long (*Yerba Buena* alone, a collective effort, had sixteen "with" coauthors), perhaps of Guinness length (and likely still overlooks a few folks who should be acknowledged). Nonetheless, it is important and appropriate to list—and thus to thank—them all. The following megalist is simply alphabetical and does not distinguish among who assisted with which book, how much, and in what way; it is offered with the standard caveat that responsibility for the final product is mine alone:

Gerald Adams, Donald Andeini, Phyllis Andelin, Frank Anderson, Carl Anthony, Gaynell Armstrong, Jim Augustino, Alvin Averbach, Linda Avery, Larry Badiner, Buck Bagot, Carol Baker, John Bardis, Charlotte Barham, William R. Barnes, Stephen Barton, Robert Begley, Nancy Belden, Harold Bell, Bruce Bernhard, Jessica Bernstein, Marsha Berzon, Stephen Berzon, Melissa Best, Sue Bierman, Dian Blomquist, Michael Bodaken, Tiffany Bohee, Leo Borregard, Charlotte Brady, David Bratton, Gray Brechin, David Brigode, William Brinton, Harry Britt, Keli'i Brown, Evelyn Bruce, Bruce Brugmann, Simeon Bruner, Kevin Carew, Chris Carlsson, Willard Carpenter, Suzanne Caster, Jerry Cauthen, Adelaide Chen, Gordon Chin, Sandy Close, Gene Coleman, Sara Colm, Kathleen Connell, Tom Conrad, Roger Crawford, Anna Creighton, John Crew, Kelley Cullen, Henry Dakin, Lisa Dancer, Josephine de Jesus, Richard DeLeon, Paul Deutsch, Robert DeVries, Steve Dietz, Philip Dochow, Catherine Dodd, Jim DuPont, Alvin Duskin, Stephen Dutton, Lauren Dzubak, John Elberling, Arnold Ellis, Elizabeth Ellis, Mike Estrada, Jim Faye, Mary Filippini, Amy Fine, Frank Fitch, Jeffrey Freed, Jon Garfield, Judy Gerritts, David Glaser, Armando Gomez, Robert Goodman, Rachel Gosiengfiao, Ruth Gottstein, Fiona Gow, Claire Greensfelder, Susan Griffin, Mary Grogan, Richard Gryziec, Ted Gullicksen, David Gurin, Joy Hackel, Barbara Halliday, Michael Harney, Neil Hart, Lauren Hauptman, Amanda Hawes, Robert Herman, Barbara Herzig, Dale Hess, Sue Hestor, Anita Hill, Steven Hill, Melvin Holli, Richard Hongisto, Lorraine Honig, Victor Honig, Karen Hull, John Igoe, Bradford Inman, Jonas Ionin, William Issel, Kim Jackson, Allan Jacobs, John Jacobs, Garrett Jenkins, Sharon Johnson, Andrea Jones, David Jones, Tom Jones, Alan Kay, Dennis Keating, Robert Kessler, Marshall Kilduff, Tony Kilroy, Marsha Kimmel, John King,

J. Anthony Kline, John Kriken, Michael Krinsky, Joe LaTorre, Rachel Lederman, Clarence Lee, Susan Lee, Alison Leff, Richard LeGates, Eva Levine, Dan Levy, Robert Levy, Joel Lipski, Suzanna Locke, Alejandra Lopez-Fernandini, Dean Macris, David Madway, Michael Mann, Sandra Marks, Dennis Marshall, Polly Marshall, Rob McBride, Deena McClain, Jim McCormick, Michael McGill, Patrick McGrew, Paul Melbostad, Ann Meyerson, Spencer Michels, Mike Miller, Earl Mills, John Mollenkopf, David Moon, Betsy Morris, Jack Morrison, Brian Murphy, Michael Narvid, Amy Neches, Jill Nelson, Thai-An Ngo, Judith Nies, Ira Nowinski, Rai Okamoto, Mitchell Omerberg, Patsy Oswald, Kay Pachtner, Sandra Paik, Bradford Paul, Bruce Pettit, Ken Phillips, Catherine Pickering, Kay Pilger, G. Bland Platt, Katherine Porter, Denise Rivera Portis, David Prowler, Theresa Rabe, Tim Redmond, James Reed, Marcia Rosen, Lee Rosenthal, Paula Rosenthal, Matthew Ross, Gayle Rubin, Jana Rumminger, Bill Rumpf, Lois Salisbury, John Sanger, Helen Sause, Crichton Schacht, Alan Schlosser, Martha Senger, Randy Shaw, Matthew Sheridan, Frank Shipe, Les Shipnuck, Jim Shoch, Joseph Sickon, Richard Sklar, Moira So, Rebecca Solnit, Ron Sonnenshine, Sean Spear, Alan Stein, Fred Stout, Walt Streeter, Allan Temko, Juli Tolleson, Cheryl Towns, Charles Turner, William Bennett Turner, Kim Vaugeois, Nancy Walker, Paul Wartelle, Stanley Weigel, Mike Weiss, Calvin Welch, Frances Werner, George Williams, Sherry Williams, Fred Wirt, Stephen Wirtz, Bill Witte, Sidney Wolinsky, Susan Wong, Lee Woods, Gerald Wright, and Barbara Ziller.

At UC Press, Monica McCormick, Suzanne Knott, Julie Mori, and Hillary Hansen were very helpful throughout. Greatest kudos go to Ellen Browning, my copyeditor, whose competence, intelligence, and attention to detail were remarkable, and who actually was *fun* to work with—the kind of claim I'll bet few authors can make. Teri Grimwood employed her usual competence in assisting me with the indexing.

Finally, my thanks to the wonderful San Francisco Mime Troupe, whose recent play, "City for Sale"—about gentrification and the city's housing crisis—provided the title for this book.

CHESTER HARTMAN

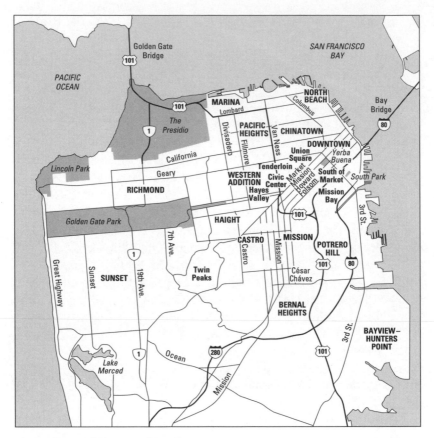

Map 1. City and County of San Francisco.

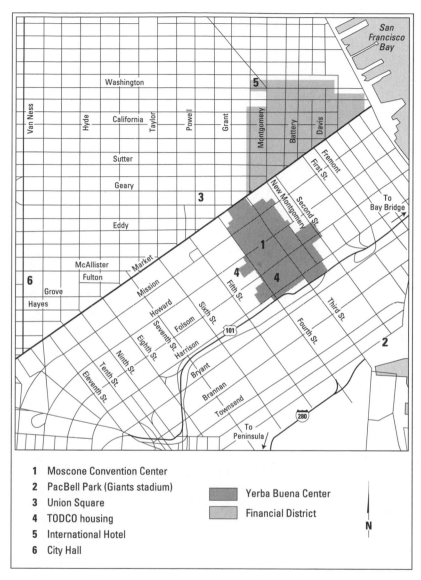

1 Moscone Convention Center
2 PacBell Park (Giants stadium)
3 Union Square
4 TODCO housing
5 International Hotel
6 City Hall

Yerba Buena Center
Financial District

Map 2. Downtown San Francisco.

1 | The Larger Forces

San Francisco is perhaps the most unique and exhilarating of the nation's cities. A typical valentine, this from veteran *New York Times* reporter R. W. Apple Jr., sings the theme: "More than any other, this is the city that Americans fantasize about. No one leaves his heart in Salt Lake City."[1]* The city's location, views, cultural and political avant-gardism, lifestyle, beauty, weather, topography, and history have given it the slightly hyperbolic label of "everyone's favorite city," if not to live in, at least to visit. *Condé Nast Traveler* magazine has three times declared San Francisco the world's most desirable tourist destination.

San Franciscans' aberrations, idiosyncrasies, and cutting-edge social policies are legendary, often the subject of national news stories, many front-pagers: legitimizing domestic partnership arrangements; limiting high-rise development (see chapter 12); enacting numerous official boycotts and making other municipal foreign-policy forays; instituting the country's toughest pesticide ban; setting safety standards for video display terminals; permitting cannabis buyers' clubs for medicinal use of marijuana; banning workplace drug tests; forbidding pizza and other food deliverers from "redlining" neighborhoods;[2] placing far-out propositions on City† ballots, such as whether a police officer can walk his beat with a ventriloquist dummy[3] and whether cab drivers can wear striped shirts; throwing for a powerful local political consultant a salacious, sadomasochistic fiftieth birthday party attended by

*This book contains two types of notes. Numbered notes begin on page 403; notes with symbols appear at the foot of the page.

†When capitalized, "City" refers to San Francisco's government.

1

the mayor, district attorney, and several city council members (in San Francisco, Board of Supervisors, as the city is a county as well);[4] taking over the downtown streets with bicycles ridden by members of the Critical Mass movement (see figure 7b);[5] extending health insurance to cover sex-change operations for municipal employees;[6] appointing a transsexual to the City's Human Rights Commission;[7] passing an ordinance making it illegal to discriminate against a person based on "size" (known colloquially as "the fat ordinance," although it applies to skinny people as well);[8] agreeing—a compromise to the alternative of making it a historic landmark, as called for in a seven-thousand–signature petition—that the Doggie Diner will, for five years, keep in place a truly gross seven-foot-high dachshund head (topped with a chef's toque), following which the head will become City property;[9] running "john schools" for first offenders violating antiprostitution laws;[10] and representing prostitutes and body piercers by unions (the latter by the United Food and Commercial Workers, no less).[11]

Among San Francisco's traditionally strong features has been enormous population diversity (racially, the city's late 1990s population of 790,000 was 41 percent white, 33 percent Asian/Pacific Islander, 16 percent Latino/Hispanic, and 10 percent black; the Asian/Pacific Islander and Latino/Hispanic categories embrace a wide variety of countries of origin) and its well-defined districts and neighborhoods. San Francisco has always had a rambunctious quality to it, an unmistakable spirit, a sense that people truly care about their city. Residents are conscious of being at once part of a neighborhood and of a world community. There is a real awareness of the city's past and its architectural heritage. And for the most part, there is an astonishing toleration of diversity and experimentalism living side by side with great traditionalism and conservatism.

The city has always experienced a tension between the forces of rapid change and continuation of tradition—from the Gold Rush days through the 1906 earthquake and World War II and on into the modern period. The most recent era of change is captured eloquently in the city's transformed skyline, one of the most recognizable features of which is the Transamerica pyramid, shown in this book's cover photograph. Behind that dramatic infusion of steel, concrete, and glass of the later photo lurk profound changes that threaten to destroy what the city has been for one and a half centuries. The sense of human scale is breaking down, along with the disappearance of sunlight and replacement of bay and ocean breezes with skyscraper-induced winds downtown. The city is rapidly becoming a city of have-a-lots and have-nots, with the working-class and lower-middle-class population being pushed out. Class (although not race) diversity is disappearing; it has become hard to find niches where idiosyncratic residential, commercial, and cultural life can flourish, and segregation by neighborhoods, classes, and races is increasing. There is a pervasive sense that much of what is good in San Francisco is on its way out. Things can get pushed only so far before they are irretrievably lost.

The focus and central motor of this transformation of San Francisco is the downtown and what it does for and to the city and region. Geographically, downtown has been dramatically expanding outward as well as upward. And the impact of that expansion—economically, socially, politically, culturally—suffuses the entire city and its people.

One of the most far-reaching consequences of this downtown expansion has been the profound change in the city's economic activity and employment base. Blue-collar jobs are out, white-collar jobs are in. Although total employment in the city rose substantially during the 1960s and 1970s (even with total population falling nearly 10 percent in the same period), jobs in the manufacturing and wholesale trade sectors dropped sharply in numbers—and even more as a proportion of total employment—and were replaced by jobs in the real estate, insurance, retail trade, office, and financial sectors. By the mid-1970s, San Francisco was second only to New York City among U.S. cities as a center of international commerce and banking.[12] By the mid-1990s, only 15 percent of the city's total workforce of 513,300 fell into the category, "production, construction, operating, materials handling" (the blue-collar jobs), while 8 percent were "managers and administrative occupations"; 25 percent were "professional, paraprofessional, technical"; 11 percent were "sales and related occupations"; 24 percent were "clerical, administrative support"; and 16 percent were "service occupations."[13]

The surge in white-collar employment is expressed in office construction: From 1960 through 1981, 30 million square feet of office buildings were added. During that period, the average annual increase in office space rose rapidly from 573,000 square feet in the five-year period 1960–64; to 1,631,400 square feet in 1970–74; to 2,156,500 square feet in just the two-year period 1980–81. By that time, San Francisco was second only to Boston in its ratio of office space to population.[14] In 1986, rampant "Manhattanization" eventually produced a popular rebellion against uncontrolled downtown development, in the form of a voter-approved annual limit of 950,000 square feet of large-scale office projects (as discussed in chapter 12), although cyclical shifts in the economy have determined actual construction activity. In early 1999, approximately 1.6 million square feet of office space was under construction; 600,000 square feet had been approved but were not yet under construction; and 2.2 million square feet was under review.[15] This metamorphosis of San Francisco stems from the city's evolving role in the nation's corporate economy—a growth spurred by World

War II and accelerated by the Korean and Vietnam conflicts in the 1950s and 1960s.

The Pacific Rim

West Coast cities have always been the launching points for U.S. advances into the Pacific region, and Pacific wars and conquests have provided a powerful stimulus to their economic growth. The West Coast has profited not only by serving as a base for the shipment of war-related personnel and goods but also by reaping the larger corollary spoils of war. The growing number of U.S. allies and neocolonies through World War II and the Korean conflict provided growing Pacific markets for North American corporations and financial institutions. The Vietnam War and its high-level technology led to an annual influx of billions of federal dollars into the West Coast, stimulating a boom in electronics, aerospace, and related industries. New trade markets thus developed in the United States and throughout the immense region known as the Pacific Rim, defined in 1970 by Rudolph Peterson, president of the Bank of America:

> When I speak of the Pacific Rim, I am putting the broadest possible construction on the term—the western coasts of South America, Central America, our own continent, and extending beyond Australia and the Far East to India. There is no more vast or rich area for resource development or trade growth in the world today than this immense region, and it is virtually our own front yard. . . . Were we California businessmen to play a more dynamic role in helping trade development in the Pacific Rim, we would have giant, hungry new markets for our products and vast new profit potentials for our firms.[16]

The significance to San Francisco of Asian trade alone was described in a 1970 Wells Fargo Bank report: "Geographically, San Francisco is a natural gateway for this country's ocean-going and air-borne commerce with the Pacific area nations. Trade with Asian nations is gaining in importance especially relative to Europe. . . . The most important stimulus to San Francisco's economic base has been the increasing U.S. involvement in this century in Asian geopolitics with the concurrent buildup in armament production . . . and large gains in foreign trade."[17] More recent openings to China have made San Francisco a leading U.S. gateway for goods to and from the country containing one-fourth of the world's population.[18] This is a fitting role for the city with one of the largest Chinese-origin populations of any city outside Asia.[19]

America's efforts to exploit the Pacific's "hungry new markets" and "vast new profit potentials" have led to the steadily expanding growth of San Francisco as a powerful corporate and service center for Pacific Rim trade. The city is now (or, until the recent mergers and acquisitions mania, has been) headquarters for such corporate giants as Chevron (formerly Standard Oil of California), Southern Pacific, Transamerica Corporation, Crown Zellerbach, McKesson (formerly Foremost-McKesson), the Potlatch Corporation (formerly Potlatch Forests), Levi Strauss, Del Monte Foods, the Bechtel Group, Pacific Telesis (formerly Pacific Telephone and Telegraph), Pacific Gas and Electric, Utah International, Genstar, the Gap, the Natomas Corporation, Charles Schwab, Macromedia, Williams-Sonoma, and the Di-Giorgio Corporation. Among the major financial institutions now or until recently (in some instances departed as a result of the constantly changing merger scene) headquartered in San Francisco are Bank of America (recently merged with NationsBank and as of this writing by far the country's largest bank in terms of assets), Wells Fargo, Crocker National Bank, First Republic Bank, Golden State Bancorp, and UnionBancal. The rapidly moving corporate centralization, which has been going on since the 1980s, has important implications for San Francisco. A 1987 *San Francisco Chronicle* feature reported that "in recent years, 20 of the city's top 50 corporate headquarters have left town after merging with outside firms,"[20] and an October 5, 1988, *San Francisco Bay Guardian* report on "Who Owns San Francisco" lamented (a trifle hyperbolically), "San Francisco is rapidly becoming a branch-office town, a franchise city owned and operated by somebody in an office far away." Particularly worrisome has been the recent Bank of America merger, because BofA CEO David Coulter wound up the number two man to NationsBank CEO Hugh McColl; this led to predictions that the money action would be in Charlotte, not San Francisco—employment, too, as middle management moved to the region with the lower living cost.[21] In mid-2000, Bank of America announced it was eliminating some ten thousand jobs, bringing to thirty-four thousand the number of such job "restructurings" since its September 1998 merger with NationsBank.[22]

Regional Planning

The increasing importance of San Francisco and the Bay Area in the domestic economy and international trade and military relations created the need to develop and organize the area into specialized, coordinated functions. Bay Area business leaders first learned the value of regional planning for efficient economic organization during World War II, through the

wartime Metropolitan Defense Committee. Composed of political appointees and influential citizens, mainly businessmen, MDC was the Bay
Area's first regional planning agency. It was responsible for fire prevention,
law enforcement, health, safety, and transportation, and it made regionwide
decisions affecting workers' housing and the location of industrial facilities.
MDC's main drawback was bickering among competing local interests,
which by 1944 had paralyzed operations and led to a cutoff in federal funding.[23] If regionalism was to work, it had to be based on forces much more
substantial than petty politics. Still, MDC established a working model for
later, more sophisticated modes of regional coordination and planning.

The Bay Area Council

The Metropolitan Defense Committee led to the formation in 1944 of the
Bay Regional Council, in 1945 renamed the Bay Area Council. BAC is the
organized muscle of the region's corporate power structure, a private regional government whose purpose is to coordinate and plan functions especially important to the efficient conduct of business throughout the entire Bay Area. As a University of California study phrased it, "The Council
has served as an influential 'private chamber of commerce' . . . and has been
an important force in creating an environment amenable to big business in
the Bay Area."[24] The council summed up its function in its 1992–93 report
as follows: "The nearly 300 corporate members of the Bay Area Council
share the belief that business can and should play a major role in shaping
public policy in the San Francisco Bay Area."

To ensure that amenable environment, BAC was organized around the
corporations and financial institutions that dominated the West's economy.
Six of these—Bank of America, American Trust Company, Standard Oil of
California, Pacific Gas and Electric, U.S. Steel, and the Bechtel Corporation—
each pledged ten thousand dollars annually to start BAC operations. Its ini-
tial board of directors were top executives from Pacific Gas and Electric, U.S.
Steel, Bechtel, the Southern Pacific Railroad, Foremost-McKesson, and the
Central Bank of Oakland.[25]

BAC's work focused primarily on transportation and industrial location.
By sponsoring studies, issuing reports, and holding conferences, it pushed
for development of airports, freeways, and bridges, which were laid out in
master plans it published and lobbied for. BAC also published industrial location surveys and directories that helped distribute the various economic
functions "rationally" throughout the region. Thus, the East Bay is the locus
for heavier industry, chemicals, and petroleum and also serves as the re-

gional transportation hub. The Peninsula and South Bay are areas for light manufacturing, electronics, and the aerospace industry. Alameda, Contra Costa, and San Mateo Counties support recent secondary office development. San Francisco is the center for administration, finance, consulting, and entertainment. An elaborate network of freeways and the Bay Area Rapid Transit (BART) system link all sectors of this regional economic unit to its administrative heart, the city (*pace* Oakland).

BAC was the primary planner and lobbyist for this rail system: "BART was a BAC product," Brown University sociologist J. Allen Whitt wrote in the pithy conclusion of his 1982 book.[26] The function of the BART system is to carry suburban workers from Contra Costa, Alameda, and San Mateo Counties into the downtown center. Within San Francisco, BART has only four stations outside downtown and lacks service to vast areas of the city, including most of its lower-income population. Upper-income suburbs such as Orinda and Lafayette have BART stations; the city's low-income African American ghetto, Hunters Point, has none. The study cited above concludes: "BART was designed to serve . . . the preservation and growth of the central city and the protection of corporate investments there. The prime initiators and supporters of BART were the giant corporations located in San Francisco."[27] These large corporations were the principal contributors to the $792 million BART general obligation bond issue referendum campaign of 1962. The referendum passed only because a last-minute change in state law allowed approval by three-fifths rather than two-thirds of the voters and permitted application of that figure to the entire three-county total rather than requiring each county to be tallied individually.

BAC is vitally interested in nourishing the growth of San Francisco as the brains and heart of this regional economic unit. As one of the few studies of its operations notes, "The policy-makers of the Council are primarily officers of large corporations located in San Francisco."[28] Sociologist Whitt observes, "Business groups such as the Bay Area Council espouse centralized urban growth, particularly in downtown San Francisco. In the first place, many of the businesses represented on the BAC own large blocks of land and expensive buildings [there] whose value would increase with rising land prices. . . . Banks and other financial firms have direct interests too since they hold millions of dollars in mortgages on central city offices."[29]

Downtown Expansion

If San Francisco was to be increasingly a regional, national, and international service center, its central business district had to expand in area. As one executive put it, "The people who run these [financial and corporate] centers want all their services, the people they work with—advertisers, attorneys, accountants—around them. It's a complete part of the way we do business in this country."[30]

As far back as the 1950s, planners saw, correctly, that the city's relatively small office district could not accommodate the number of buildings that would be required in the coming decades. However, there were obstacles to further development. Expansion westward was impossible: In that direction lay the city's prime retail and hotel area, plus difficult, hilly topography. To the north lay the internally strong residential communities of Chinatown and North Beach and more hills. To the east, the bay limited expansion to the small area occupied by the city's wholesale produce market. If there was to be a substantial increase in the central office district, it would have to be to the south, across 120-foot-wide Market Street, traditionally the city's "Great Divide" and "a physical and psychological barrier to the orderly development of South of Market."[31] The South of Market area offered hundreds of acres of flat land with low-density use, low land prices, and, to the corporate eye, expendable people and businesses.

Necessary, then, was to take a massive parcel of downtown land, evict its occupants, demolish the existing structures, and convert the land to the desired uses. A land-use transformation of this magnitude requires careful preparation, specialized skills, and, most important, a legal and political base of operations. The federal-local urban renewal program, introduced by Congress in the 1949 Housing Act, with its powers of eminent domain, land cost and land clearance subsidies, and battery of planners and other technicians, was the ideal vehicle for downtown expansion. The easier move eastward would be accomplished first via the Golden Gateway renewal project, replacing the produce market with an office headquarters and prestigious residential complex. But the "block-busting" wedge for the more substantial and critical expansion southward across Market Street would be the highly controversial, problematic, and costly redevelopment scheme to be known as Yerba Buena Center.

The Blyth-Zellerbach Committee

Because urban redevelopment must be carried out on the local level by local bodies, the regional structure and image of BAC were inappropriate; a local committee involving BAC members would be more effective. That group was the Blyth-Zellerbach Committee, formed in 1956 by Charles Blyth, a prominent stockbroker and director of the Hewlett-Packard electronics firm, Crown-Zellerbach Corporation, and the Stanford Research Institute. Joining Blyth was J. D. Zellerbach, the pulp and paper magnate. They and their brethren made up a group the Chamber of Commerce bluntly described as "San Francisco's most powerful business leaders, whose purpose is to act in concert on projects deemed good for the City."[32]

The immediate impetus to form the committee was the redevelopment potential of the city's wholesale produce market just east of the financial district. The colorful market area, with its stalls, narrow passageways, and early-morning shouting and human bustle, was run-down and congested to the point of inefficiency. Business and political figures were placing enormous pressure on the wholesalers to move to an outlying location.

Among those interested in undertaking a massive development plan for the area was William Zeckendorf of Webb and Knapp, the mammoth New York development firm. In late 1955, Zeckendorf offered the City $250,000 in planning funds, with the proviso that if the City adopted his plan, he would have the right to purchase 75 percent of the land, and that if he and the City could not agree on a price and the land was awarded to another developer, the successful bidder would have to reimburse Webb and Knapp for its planning costs. To forestall this move by Eastern money and ensure development of the area in accord with local corporate interests, the Blyth-Zellerbach Committee immediately made a gift of twenty-five thousand dollars to the City Planning Department for an "objective" evaluation of the produce market situation. Several months later it made a second gift for a similar amount.[33] According to Blyth, no personal interest was involved: "We're just a group of fellows devoted to San Francisco."[34] Virtually every one of the fellows, however, was also a member of the BAC executive board.[35]

A key element of the committee's operation was its low profile. A *Business Week* article stated, "Zellerbach and his collaborators have no bylaws, no written policy, no executive director, and keep no minutes. They regard the absence of such organizational trappings as prerequisite to their operations." The explanation for this lack of record keeping was that the committee thus avoided "the epithetical label of big business control."[36] Insofar as possible, this group, representing powerful corporate interests, adopted a style and posture that would enable it to achieve common goals without risking public exposure and criticism. And as *Business Week* also noted, "It is the corporations, really, rather than the executives, that comprise the B-Z Committee." Thus, when Charles Blyth died, he was replaced by Roy L. Shurtleff of Blyth and Company, and when Mark Sullivan retired, he was replaced by Carl O. Lindeman, Sullivan's successor as president of Pacific Telephone and Telegraph.

The committee's intervention in the produce market question served to force Zeckendorf out of the picture and led to the plan that ultimately became the Golden Gateway, a fifty-one-acre luxury residential and corporate headquarters zone. The project, begun in 1959, included the Embarcadero Center (a five-block high-rise office and hotel complex), the Alcoa Building, assorted shops, and a mass of pedestrian platforms and outdoor sculpture—all built with federal and local urban renewal subsidies. By 1999, more than twelve hundred luxury apartments and townhouse units had been built, with monthly rents of $1,325 to $2,495 for studio apartments, $1,725 to $3,650 for two-bedroom apartments, and $3,250 to $4,695 for townhouses. A private swimming and tennis club for residents occupies a key site near the waterfront. Sales prices for the low-rise condominium units ranged from $500,000 to more than $1 million. The committee's work thus paid off handsomely in terms of developing a plan for the produce market consistent with corporate interests and at the same time benefiting local investors.

SPUR

While the Blyth-Zellerbach Committee served its purpose of stimulating plans for San Francisco redevelopment, its covert character had limitations. Corporate interests needed a group that could more openly take definitive positions and actions; this would be particularly important as drawing-board proposals came up for public approval and the search for funds began. The first step toward creation of such a group occurred in early 1959 when the committee sponsored and paid for a report on the city's redevelopment program by Philadelphia city planning consultant Aaron Levine, an action widely publicized and praised by the newspapers, as was the resulting report. Levine's unsurprising conclusions were that San Francisco was far behind other large cities in redevelopment, badly in need of leadership and improved staff for its redevelopment agency, and in need of substantial support from the business community for its redevelopment program. In his words, "The Blyth-Zellerbach Committee is the logical group in San Francisco to assume this role."[37] The Levine report led the committee to father the San Francisco Planning and Urban Renewal Association (SPUR—which, two decades later, cognizant of the bad odor associated with urban "renewal," changed the "R" word to "Research"). SPUR was devised to openly generate more "citizen" (meaning business) support for urban renewal in San Francisco.

SPUR's initial financing came entirely from the committee and related business interests. The committee originally pledged thirty thousand dollars a year and after three years committed itself to funding half the SPUR budget, the other half to come from membership dues and private institutions. It maintained its central support of SPUR until 1982, its annual contribution $118,000 by that time. Although formal committee support was withdrawn, "The corporate members of the B-Z Committee continue to contribute to SPUR as they have in the past."[38]

Several SPUR directors were, of course, from either the Blyth-Zellerbach Committee or the Bay Area Council. For example, SPUR's first board chairman was Jerd Sullivan, a BAC trustee, director of both Crocker-Citizens Bank and Del Monte Properties, and vice president of the Fairmont Hotel Company. SPUR's 1960–61 chairman was John Merrill, a board member of the San Francisco Redevelopment Agency 1957–59, a director of the B-Z Committee and of the Chamber of Commerce, president of an engineering research firm, and a director of both the Arthur D. Little Company and Pacific Telephone and Telegraph. John Hirten, SPUR's first executive director, was a trustee of BAC. Another director was William Zellerbach.

SPUR immediately focused on redevelopment south of Market Street. According to the February 13, 1960, *San Francisco Examiner:*

> The Planning and Urban Renewal Association took dead aim on the "most blighted area in San Francisco" yesterday with a project for coordinated private-public redevelopment of the South of Market St. district.
> Calling together civic and business leaders as a "steering committee," association chairman Jerd F. Sullivan Jr. announced [that] a preliminary plan would be worked up for clearing the slums out of an area roughly bounded by Fourth, Minna, Hawthorne and Harrison Sts.

Throughout 1960, SPUR worked closely with the San Francisco Redevelopment Agency (SFRA), holding meetings with businessmen and influential citizens who favored downtown commercial redevelopment. In December 1960, Mayor George Christopher designated SPUR the City's official Citizens' Advisory Committee, a body required under federal urban renewal law. Shortly thereafter, this "citizens' group" gave its required approval, and the mayor formally requested SFRA to undertake South of Market urban renewal.

Ben Swig's Dream

SPUR's entry into planning for South of Market redevelopment in reality took the form of reviving a proposal put forward six years earlier by one of the city's more fabulous proposers and disposers, Ben Swig.

Benjamin Harrison Swig was a Bostonian who, already wealthy from dealings in hotels and real estate, moved to San Francisco in the 1940s.[39] A model of the self-made man, he had amassed a fortune through real estate and land speculation in the 1920s and 1930s. Although hit hard by the Depression, Swig had kept wheeling and dealing, concentrating on land brokerage for such chain-store developments as Kress, Woolworth, and JCPenney. He emerged a partner in a large New York real estate firm and with a reputation as a "super-broker" who often conducted twenty to thirty deals simultaneously. By the end of World War II, Swig and his partner, J. D. Weiler, were considered the biggest individual real estate dealers in the country.

Within a short time after his arrival in San Francisco, Swig acquired the prestigious Fairmont Hotel atop Nob Hill, as well as the St. Francis and Bellevue hotels and other valuable downtown properties. He cultivated powerful friends and soon became a major Democratic Party fundraiser and contributor. (It was said in San Francisco that "You can't be elected dogcatcher here without his blessing.")[40] Besides holding wealth and power, he was a philanthropist *par excellence* and by 1954 was in a position to assume that San Franciscans would listen when he spoke.

What Swig was speaking about in 1954 was his vision of massive clearance and commercial redevelopment South of Market, soon dubbed "The San Francisco Prosperity Plan." It covered four large blocks and called for constructing a convention center, sports stadium, high-rise office buildings, and parking for seven thousand cars. Swig enlarged the grand scheme in 1955 by adding two adjacent blocks and inserting thereon a transportation terminal, a large luxury hotel with convention facilities, an auditorium and theater, moving sidewalks, a shopping center with a network of malls and fountains like Manhattan's Rockefeller Center, and parking increased to sixteen thousand cars.

With characteristic energy, Swig moved into action, mobilizing resources behind the scheme. He found some support among city politicians, then embarked upon winning over businessmen by speaking before numerous civic and business organizations such as the Chamber of Commerce and the prestigious Commonwealth Club. Yet even with substantial support from political and business figures and from the newspapers, Swig's plan ran into trouble. Its major flaw was that neither he nor any of his friends controlled the site of the proposed development. Without the land, the scheme was only so much paper. Here, as in many similar situations, the ideal solution seemed to be the urban renewal program, but the program was available only for "blighted" areas, and, according to the City Planning Department, Swig's original four blocks did not qualify.

One large area South of Market had been approved earlier as a possible urban renewal project. Known as Area D, it was farther from Market Street and the central business district and thus less attractive to private developers than the blocks Swig proposed. City planning director Paul Oppermann had studied the Swig area and reported that two of the four original blocks were only 10 percent blighted. Oppermann determined that to use urban renewal to erect the center in these blocks would be a perversion of the program's purpose, and he recommended that development of Swig's area be left to the private market. Mayor George Christopher—a Republican, whereas Swig and his allies were mostly Democrats—tended to agree with Oppermann, compounding Swig's obstacles. A small businessman, Christopher was not an enthusiastic supporter of large-scale urban renewal during his first term (1956–59).

Swig, however, was relentless. To encourage the City to designate his six blocks eligible for renewal, he even made one of his many charitable donations, this one to the San Francisco Redevelopment Agency to finance preliminary planning studies. The agency accepted but later returned the donation. According to the agency's new board chairman, a young, dynamic downtown lawyer named Joseph Alioto, the study's purpose was "to find the most expeditious way of declaring the area of Mr. Swig's interest a blighted area."[41] Swig's claims about the public benefits of his "San Francisco Prosperity Plan" and the justification for using government aids were somewhat weakened by his statement that "This is a straight business proposition. . . . I think I'm going to make a lot of money out of it, or I wouldn't be spending all this time on it."[42]

Swig also had been instrumental in bringing William Zeckendorf to the city to stimulate grand thoughts about South of Market development. (Zeckendorf proved far more interested in the produce market area, as previously noted, and began to operate independently of Swig.) In December 1955, Swig, Zeckendorf, and Alioto were able to convince the Board of Supervisors to redraw the boundaries of Area D to include Swig's original four blocks, in effect approving the Redevelopment Agency's similar action the previous October. ("I don't care what Oppermann's conclusions are," said Alioto.)[43]

Swig even went so far as to offer to loan the agency the $12 million he estimated it would need for land acquisition costs, thereby substituting himself for the federal urban renewal agency, should the latter turn out to be uncooperative about approving his plans.[44] Oppermann, however, maintained his strong opposition to the Swig plan. Swig was incensed by the planner's attitude and told a Kiwanis Club luncheon, "Private capital knows a great deal better than city planners. I say to our city fathers, 'Stop planning, stop thinking, but go out and do something right away.' "[45]

In the end, however, Swig had to capitulate to the combined opposition of the Christopher administration, Oppermann, and, last, the federal urban renewal agency, which was cool to the plan and did not have an abundance of grant money to hand out. By late 1956, Ben Swig's dream was for all immediate purposes dead.

The Planning Commission and Board of Supervisors subsequently removed the blight designation from half of Area D in order to allow a group of landowners within the area to try to put together a plan of their own. Oppermann, with the unenthusiastic concurrence of the Redevelopment Agency, prepared an industrial spot clearance renewal plan for that part of Area D labeled most blighted. But there was little dynamism behind this plan, and although the supervisors adopted it in mid-1957, it was rejected a few months later by the federal urban renewal agency—effectively freezing redevelopment South of Market for several years. In the long run, although Swig's initial plan was not adopted, it set the course for succeeding plans for South of Market redevelopment: to begin renewal in the area closest to the central business district, irrespective of "blight" conditions; to rely primarily on the bulldozer approach to renewal; and to construct in the area a massive convention-sports-office center.

In the mid-1950s, the corporate powers of the Bay Area had not yet mobilized themselves to plan fully for their future needs and to establish the necessary apparatus to carry out their plans. In terms of background, operating style, and economic position, Ben Swig was not an integral part of the region's corporate power structure. As powerful and dynamic an individual as he was, he could not unite the forces necessary to pull off his scheme for South of Market redevelopment. Ben Swig failed to realize his original dream, but once the need for expansion of the financial district into the area South of Market was to be embraced by the broader group, his plan would be revived, this time with the necessary government and private support and intervention to make it a reality. Swig and his sons were to continue to play a role in some aspects of the project, but the driving force would pass to others' hands.

2 | Superagency and the Redevelopment Booster Club

Ben Swig's dream and corporate San Francisco's plans needed the official backing of the City and the federal government. Financing and assembling land for massive downtown redevelopment is an enormous undertaking, and unguided individual developers might create a patchwork of small projects, more a hindrance than a help in changing the face of the city. The task required government to step in, take land by eminent domain, furnish central direction and guidelines, and provide the financial incentives to guarantee appropriate investment by private developers.

As the body shaped to achieve these ends, the San Francisco Redevelopment Agency (SFRA) is far more than just another government department or regulatory body; it is a "superagency" with broad-ranging political and economic powers that reflect the full authority of the state apparatus. As Frederick Wirt notes:

> Like its counterparts in other cities, SFRA is a compound of public and private powers that provides a touch of the corporate state to local government in America. It can make and implement its own plans, move people from one section of town to another, arrange massive sums for financing, condemn property, and promote all its wonders. Traditional controls of public power, so endemic in American government, run a little thin with these agencies.[1]

The SFRA was established in 1948 in anticipation of passage by Congress of the 1949 Housing Act, which introduced the urban renewal program. Like redevelopment bodies in general, SFRA is a semiautonomous entity with vast independent legal, financial, and technical powers and resources. Its commissioners are appointed by the mayor and confirmed by the Board of Supervisors. During the heyday of urban renewal—the 1960s and first half of the 1970s—the agency had access to massive sums of federal funds; between 1959 and 1971, it was able to secure $128 million in federal urban renewal dollars for the city. Its relative freedom from local control and its direct access to federal money tended to reduce city hall control over its activities. Its large technical staff developed an exclusive familiarity with the complex arcana of federal urban renewal statutes and administrative regulations. It is able to issue its own bonds. It has and extensively uses the power of eminent domain, and even when such power is not directly used, that lurking presence often creates "willing" sellers.

During most of its first decade, SFRA's operations and importance were limited, as evidenced by a small and not very talented staff, generally uninspired appointments to its governing board, and frequent squabbles both internally and with federal urban renewal officials. Urban renewal was new, and direction and support from Washington was less than optimal. According to one account, even in the late 1950s the agency staff was "riddled with political hacks."[2] This tone was set during the term of Mayor Elmer Robinson (1952–55). The agency secretary at that time was a man who had threatened to oppose Robinson in the 1951 election but withdrew on promise of an agency position; another board member was a private detective known as Robinson's "hatchet man" on the agency. Internal dissension ran high and culminated in the summary firing of Executive Director James Lash in 1953, which brought anguished cries from the city's "good government" advocates as well as from the newspapers. Lash's successor was Eugene Riordan, the retiring director of City Property, a "gentlemen of the old school but with no evident qualifications for so demanding a post."[3]

Throughout the 1950s, federal urban renewal officials were highly critical of the agency, its staff, and its leadership. The August 28, 1957, *Examiner* reported that "M. Justin Herman, regional administrator of the Housing and Home Finance Agency, which controls federal funds for redevelopment projects, accused the agency of 'the most cumbersome and costly' handling of funds of any city in the U.S." Within the city, the agency was criticized from several quarters. The mutual acrimony between the agency and the City Planning Department was well known. In mid-1956, Mayor George Christopher asked agency chairman Joseph Alioto to resign, calling him an "obstructionist," referring to controversy over the agency's difficulties in putting together a plan to relocate the produce market.[4]

Mayor Christopher entered office wary of massive renewal schemes and resisted the Swig plan for South of Market. But eventually the efforts of the Blyth-Zellerbach Committee and its powerful offspring, the San Francisco Planning and Urban Renewal Association (SPUR), turned him into an enthusiastic supporter of redevelopment. Christopher simply could not ignore the urging of the city's corporate representatives, especially at election time. Another factor was the changing face of San Francisco into a "city of color," with increasing African, Asian, and Latino populations. It was becoming apparent that urban renewal could be used to displace the city's minorities and recapture the centrally located residential areas they had inherited after whites moved out, an opportunity not lost on Christopher, who reflected the attitudes of the city's Anglo-European politicians and small businessmen.

The wheels were set in motion for a revitalized Redevelopment Agency when Alioto announced in August 1958 that for business reasons he was resigning as chair, and two months later Executive Director Riordan, nearing seventy, announced his forthcoming retirement. The Blyth-Zellerbach Committee's Levine report and its formation of SPUR in early 1959 then provided the necessary impetus for reshaping the agency. In January 1959, Mayor Christopher appointed as Alioto's successor Everett Griffin, a retired chemical company president and former Chamber of Commerce director. According to the January 13, 1959, *Examiner*, "Christopher said he had never met Griffin. . . . But he said the executive was highly recommended to him by members of the Blyth-Zellerbach committee of financiers."

The appointment of agency commissioners revealed a good deal about the overlapping roles played by these powerful people in the city's economy as public figures ostensibly devoted to serving the general welfare. Christopher's original nominee for the agency chair was an up-and-coming state assemblyman named Caspar Weinberger, but the nomination was withdrawn when the city attorney ruled that a conflict of interest might be involved, since Weinberger's law firm represented several wholesale produce firms being relocated to make room for the agency's Golden Gateway project. Weinberger thereupon was named to chair SPUR's executive committee. Three months later, Christopher appointed Walter Kaplan, secretary-treasurer of the Emporium, a large downtown department store, to the agency board. Kaplan succeeded John Merrill, who had asked to be replaced, because he owned property in the Golden Gateway area that he did not want to sell. Merrill then was named to chair SPUR.

But by far the most significant step taken by Mayor Christopher in his newfound commitment to redevelopment was his April 1959 announcement that M. Justin Herman would become executive director of the San Francisco Redevelopment Agency.

Justin Herman

Until his death in 1971, Justin Herman was official and corporate San Francisco's chief architect, major spokesman, and operations commander for the transformation of whole sections of the city. People formed two distinct opinions about him from his activities in these roles. In the downtown high-rise office buildings, banks, and city hall, he was Saint Justin, while in the Western Addition housing projects and the streets of the Mission barrio he was the "white devil." "Negroes and the other victims of a low income generally regard [Herman] as the arch villain in the black depopulation of the city," wrote Thomas Fleming in 1965 in the *Sun-Reporter*, the newspaper of the city's black community.[5]

Herman was a talented and experienced administrator, well acquainted with the problems of urban renewal, and a man with useful connections inside the federal government. From 1951 until his appointment to head the SFRA, he was administrator of the San Francisco Regional Office of the Housing and Home Finance Agency (predecessor of the U.S. Department of Housing and Urban Development), responsible for its activities in the western states. Herman's SFRA appointment was based on his familiarity with and strong criticism of the city's redevelopment program during the 1950s, his knowledge of and ability to circumvent federal red tape, and above all his commitment to the kind of downtown urban renewal pressed for by the Bay Area Council, the Blyth-Zellerbach Committee, and SPUR.

As a condition to accepting the position, Herman wanted complete discretion to reconstitute the agency by appointing new staff and developing new methods of operation. He also made it clear that he would tolerate no interference from other City agencies. Mayor Christopher granted these conditions, and Herman set to work establishing the new superagency.

His command brought rapid results. SFRA soon became a powerful force with a staff of several hundred (compared to sixty in the pre-Herman era), a battery of consultants, close working relations with the mayor's office, and control over eight renewal projects and tens of millions of dollars in federal subsidies. The agency's professional and political competence under Herman was well reflected in its staff composition, which consisted of expert planning, design, and financing specialists on the one hand and a raft of political appointees on the other. All of these changes resulted in an extremely large staff and staggering administrative costs. A 1972 HUD report showed that the San Francisco Redevelopment Agency, with 462 employees, had a staff nearly three times as large as Pittsburgh's agency and nearly twice as large as Boston's, even though each of these cities had more redevelopment projects and disbursed far larger sums of grant money than did San Francisco.[6]

The role and character of the agency's board also changed under Herman. Its commissioners were in effect representatives of the agency's organized constituency. Significant businessmen such as Walter Kaplan and Everett Griffin were later joined by James Folger, president of Folger Coffee Company (and a Bay Area Council founder), and James B. Black Jr., son of the president of Pacific Gas and Electric and himself a U.S. Steel executive. Within a few years, representatives of organized labor were also appointed to the board. As expected, these business and labor leaders warmly supported Herman's SFRA policies, which assured his success in steering his programs through San Francisco's political and bureaucratic structure. Under his leadership, the SFRA became a powerful and aggressive army out to capture as much downtown land as it could: not only the Golden Gateway and South of Market but also Chinatown, the Tenderloin (a decidedly not upscale area north of Market), and the port. Under the rubric of "slum clearance" and "blight removal," the agency turned to systematically sweeping out the poor, with the full backing of the city's power elite.

Beyond his qualifications as administrator, planner, and knowledgeable navigator of federal channels, Herman was a monument builder who approached his job like a classical entrepreneur. In many ways he was Ben Swig's counterpart in the public sector, and it is not surprising that the two men were close associates and friends. Herman was more than a redevelopment administrator: He was an enthusiastic proponent of plans to remake San Francisco. Toward this end he used every trick, technique, and legal loophole that could be mustered, and when established procedures did not work, he devised new methods, stretching the laws whenever necessary.[7] (In his published memoirs, the city's planning director from 1967 to 1974, Allan Jacobs, characterized Herman as "devious.")[8] He was a man of incredible energy, tenacity, and political talent. Those who knew him well regarded him as tough, a perfectionist, someone who relished controversy, a man who wanted to leave his mark on the world through tangible achievements. With respect to South of Market development, he was able—despite labor's early qualms about the project—to weld together the necessary coalition of downtown business and labor by appealing to their common interest in higher sales and more jobs, which he promised would result from increased downtown land values.

Tourists and Conventions

A principal driving force behind the transformation of the city is the growth of tourism and conventioneering, now loosely labeled "San Francisco's number one industry." This sector comprises hotels, restaurants, retail stores, sports and other entertainment events, taxis, tour vehicles, transportation companies, and the suppliers to all these entities. Central to the success of all is the city's ability to attract large conventions, trade shows, and sporting events.

In the early 1960s, the city's facilities for these events were quite limited. They consisted of the City-owned Civic Auditorium and Brooks Hall complex in the downtown Civic Center, the state-owned Cow Palace, and the meeting rooms in major hotels. The Civic Auditorium contains a seven-thousand-seat arena. Brooks Hall is a medium-sized (ninety thousand square feet) exhibition area, but its fourteen-foot ceilings are low by trade-show standards and the floor space is broken up by supporting pillars. The Cow Palace is a much larger hall, with some 315,000 square feet of usable exhibition space and a 16,500-seat arena, but it has major drawbacks—too few meeting rooms, its considerable distance from downtown, and a shortage of nearby restaurants and hotels. The central objection to the Cow Palace was well expressed by a former Convention & Visitors Bureau (CVB) president, who stated, "The trouble with the Cow Palace is . . . [i]t doesn't bring any business downtown."[9]

Forces were beginning to line up behind South of Market redevelopment, and the convention industry moved to ensure that the project would include a convention center with the large, modern exhibit space and ample meeting facilities that could increase the city's convention business and situate it downtown. The Redevelopment Agency had in hand the project that was to break through the traditional development barrier and move the financial district across Market Street. They christened it "Yerba Buena Center," a project whose epicenter was to be the new convention facility.

The most active promotion of Yerba Buena Center and its public facilities came from the San Francisco Convention & Visitors Bureau—crucial in marshaling support for both the center and the Redevelopment Agency. The bureau plays a dual role, representing the private tourism industry and acting as a quasi-official agent for the City. It grew out of an advisory committee appointed by Mayor Christopher and headed by J. D. Zellerbach, of Blyth-Zellerbach fame. The committee's task was to reorganize and enlarge the city's tourism and convention promotional functions. Once a reorganization plan was submitted, Zellerbach appointed Richard Swig, Ben's son, and Albert E. Schlesinger to carry it out. On Schlesinger's recommendation, the Board of Supervisors in 1961 enacted a 3 percent hotel room occupancy tax to support an aggressive and centralized tourism promotion agency, and when the CVB finally was formed in 1963, Schlesinger was named to head it. (Schlesinger in the 1950s had been president of the Downtown Association, then chaired the mayor's Tourism and Commerce Committee. He would later become a central figure in the first private development group named to build Yerba Buena Center.)

Under the slogan "In the business of keeping San Francisco in business," the bureau, with more than twenty-two hundred member businesses, in 2000 had an annual budget of $15.7 million, over half of which came from assigned hotel tax receipts (roughly half of the hotel tax traditionally has gone to the CVB). Membership dues accounted for only 12 percent of the bureau's budget.[10] By far the greater part of the budget was devoted to convention sales and promotion rather than promotion of tourism (to "wholesale" rather than "retail" visitor trade).

The bureau has grown markedly over the past decades, from a $1.2 million budget in 1972–73 to its current figure. Several years ago, the bureau engineered a fixed percentage of the hotel tax take rather than have its money allocated by the City's chief administrative officer as part of an overall Publicity and Advertising Fund disbursed to cultural groups as well. This assures it of an allocation that will increase annually at a substantial rate as the number of hotel rooms and hotel room rates rise.

The bureau walks a thin line between the public and private sectors. As a *San Francisco Bay Guardian* article noted:

> [It uses] this tax windfall as a cheap way to advertise and promote their private members. For example: their brochures, maps and free information on where to eat, drink, sleep, shop and sightsee in the city's vacationland "recommend" the very same restaurants, hotels, stores and galleries of their member businesses. . . . Smaller eating or entertainment spots, many with the real flavor of San Francisco, don't get plugs because they can't afford the membership. . . . [T]he Bureau releases

dates and information on upcoming conventions only to its private members."[11]*

In the past, the Board of Supervisors' budget analyst, Harvey Rose, raised complaints that the City had no control over the operations and pay scales of the CVB staff, despite the extent to which these operations and salaries are paid for with City taxes.[12] But the CVB has been able to retain its independence, and, as noted above, the move giving it an automatic "take" from hotel tax revenues further insulates it from normal budgetary scrutiny by the city's elected officials. Until not too long ago, the CVB's board lacked any significant ethnic and gender diversity; in 1984, the bureau had only five minority members on its forty-five-person board of directors, and that was a very recent, and pressured, change.† A decade and a half later, things were only somewhat better: Of the CVB's fifty-two 1998–99 directors, twelve (23 percent) were not white; of the eight active past chairmen/ 1998–99 ex-officio directors, only one was not white; and there were no minorities among the bureau's senior staff (president, executive vice president, division heads). Also among the underrepresented was organized labor's strong presence in the city's highly unionized hotel industry: Only one of the CVB's fifty-two board members was from a labor union—Local 16 of the International Alliance of Theatrical Stage Employees.[13]

The CVB supported all of Justin Herman's redevelopment projects. Not surprisingly, the convention and tourism industry wanted to see certain "blight" and certain elements in the population removed from downtown San Francisco in order to create more genial surroundings for tourists and conventions. Yerba Buena Center represented an urban renewal project ideally suited to the needs of the CVB. Not only did it remove from the down-

---

*The CVB, which now receives more than $7 million annually in City tax subsidies, places its calendar and the long-range edition of its annual schedule (listing dates of upcoming conventions for many years into the future) on file at the San Francisco Public Library, under the condition that it may be viewed only behind the reference desk and may not be copied.

†A 1987 *Examiner* feature about then-Supervisor Doris Ward noted, "A few years ago, when she learned that the City's Convention & Visitors Bureau had no minority members on its board, Ward walked into then–chief administrative officer Roger Boas's office and said, 'The Bureau gets millions from the City's Hotel Tax Fund and there's not one minority member on its board. You'd better color up that board, and fast, or you're not getting another dime.' " Bill Mandel, "Doris Ward Races to Finish First Somewhere over the Rainbow," *San Francisco Examiner*, 22 March 1987.

town people who in its eyes ought not to be seen by conventioneers and tourists, but it also was to provide modern, enlarged convention facilities.

One of the bureau's principal promotional activities for YBC in the mid-1960s was a tour of convention centers in other cities. On the tour were important City officials, business and union representatives, architects, and contractors, who predictably concluded that San Francisco was no longer competitive in convention and sports facilities and that developing Yerba Buena Center was critical to the city's future economic health: If something was not done, San Francisco would face losing conventions and meetings to other cities, such as Las Vegas, Anaheim, Los Angeles, New Orleans, Chicago, and Dallas, where facilities were newer, larger, and more comfortable.

The problematic question of whether such a facility would actually enhance the city's convention business, and, if so, whether the increased business would be sufficient to warrant a huge expenditure of public funds, is discussed in chapter 9. Three things may be said with certainty, however. First, since San Francisco inherently is probably the most attractive and popular city in the United States, conventioneers would exert enormous pressure on their organizations to include it in their regular rotation, independent of how modern and centrally located the city's convention facilities are. Second, statistics and trends on the number of conventions and convention attendees going to the city have in the past fluctuated independently of this variable. And, third, the issue is one on which conclusive, objective evaluation is inherently difficult, as the relevant data were and are controlled by advocates of a new publicly funded convention center: The CVB and its member businesses are the source of virtually all information on convention planning and impacts, and they guard and manipulate this information in their own self-interest. *Los Angeles Times* columnist Robert A. Jones observed about this local controversy, "Unfortunately, discussion of the visitor industry can get as cloudy as the San Francisco sky. Much of the public information is dated and soft. . . . And the numbers that are readily available come from boosters."[14]

The hotel industry—organized as the Hotel Council of San Francisco, formerly the Hotel Employers Association—understandably is the most dominant membership group within the bureau. Thirteen of the CVB's 1998–99 board members were hotel senior executives. Virtually every major hotel is or recently has been represented on the bureau's board of directors: The 1998–99 board had representatives from the San Francisco Marriott, the Handlery Union Square, the Crowne Plaza, the Radisson

Miyako, Hotel Nikko, Victorian Inn, the Fairmont, the Canterbury, the Grand Hyatt, Mansions Hotel, Pan Pacific, and the Argent.

The hotel owners' interests in Yerba Buena Center were, naturally, to increase hotel occupancy through added convention business. Conventioneers' average spending far exceeds that of tourists. Hotel construction has been booming in San Francisco. In 1959, the city had fewer than thirty-three hundred first-class hotel rooms; by 1970, the number was nine thousand; and by 1999, there were more than thirty thousand. While much of the new hotel construction was described in 1973 as "in large measure . . . keyed to the . . . completion of . . . Yerba Buena Center,"[15] in addition to earlier hyperbolic rhetoric such as that of the Hilton Hotel's Henri Lewin— "If that convention center gets killed, we get killed. At least 50 percent of the hotels in this city will go out of business"[16]—in fact, the hotels have done quite well; and the ups and downs in their occupancy rates have had little to do with whether a new convention center existed or not. The hotel owners were eager to have the public pay for a new facility, in the hope that it would increase their business.

The Alioto Touch

The nature of urban renewal and political timetables is such that a redevelopment scheme and administrator will usually have a lifespan considerably greater than the tenure of most elected officials. Plans and partial construction of Yerba Buena Center have spanned the political lives of eight mayors— George Christopher, John Shelley, Joseph Alioto, George Moscone, Dianne Feinstein, Art Agnos, Frank Jordan, and Willie Brown. How many additional mayors will come and go before Yerba Buena Center is completed remains to be seen.

Joseph L. Alioto did not fall from the sky, but in the closing months of the 1967 mayoral campaign it looked that way to many San Franciscans. Incumbent John Shelley, a former state legislator, U.S. congressman, and AFL-CIO leader, had been elected mayor in 1963 over conservative businessman Harold Dobbs, owner of the Mel's Drive-In restaurant chain, which had received considerable notoriety earlier that year as the target of militant civil rights demonstrations against the restaurants' lily-white hiring policies. Shelley's term as mayor had not been a time of brotherhood and goodwill. As in many large cities, the mid-1960s was a period of racial confrontation in San Francisco. Militant civil rights campaigns achieving nationwide publicity were launched against luxury hotels, automobile dealers, and other discriminatory employers. Many of the "riots" of the mid-sixties were related to actual and proposed people-removing redevelopment activity in the city's Mission, Bayview–Hunters Point, and Western Addition–Fillmore ghettos.

The Western Addition A-1 urban renewal project in particular was singled out for neighborhood opposition. The project was part of a longer-range development scheme for the city's central African American and Japanese ghettos. It involved widening Geary Boulevard—the main thoroughfare connecting central San Francisco with the northwestern part of the city, the Richmond District—into an eight-lane highway and surrounding it with new construction. Some four thousand families were moved out during the 1960s, virtually none of whom were able to move back.[17] The area now consists of high-rise apartments and condominiums, new office buildings and churches, a Japanese Cultural and Trade Center, and some middle-income housing—all where low-income black and Japanese families once made their homes. Symbolically, the agency's new fortress-like headquarters building was built on a site adjacent to the new Geary Expressway.

Civil rights groups issued strong statements opposing the project; the Redevelopment Agency and Board of Supervisors were vilified at their hearings on the project; people sat in at the mayor's office and in front of bulldozers.[18] John Shelley's background and instincts produced in him a concern for and sympathy with the protestors, but in action he vacillated. At first he opposed the project, asked for delays, and raised questions about relocation. In 1966, over Justin Herman's opposition, he appointed to the agency board the militant president of the NAACP, Dr. Joseph Wellington, a vocal renewal opponent. But eventually Shelley backed the project.

Shelley also vacillated on Yerba Buena Center, questioning the expenses and priorities involved; nonetheless, he announced his support. He expressed unhappiness with the growing strength and independence of the Redevelopment Agency, a denunciation triggered by Justin Herman's unilateral abolition of the job of agency secretary, a post that traditionally had been the mayor's appointment in order to place his own "watchdog" in the agency.[19] In an effort to undercut Herman, Shelley announced he was not reappointing Herman's agency board chairman, Everett Griffin. The October 27, 1966, *Examiner* labeled this "a public slap on the wrist [to] the agency's real power, Executive Director M. Justin Herman." In his stead, Shelley appointed a close personal friend and political neophyte, Francis Solvin, a Coast Guard hearing officer. Shelley's off-and-on opposition to redevelopment, combined with serious community protests, resulted in a six-to-five Board of Supervisors vote upholding the Latino Mission District's opposition to a neighborhood renewal program, and an unprecedented six-to-two vote asking the agency to halt its follow-up Western Addition A-2 project (a resolution Shelley then vetoed). Justin Herman and his renewal program were on the ropes. The same *Examiner* article, entitled "City Hall and the Slum Dragon," began: "The San Francisco Redevelopment Agency is in trouble. In the Mission they call it a plague. In city hall they charge it with a power grab. Citizen groups have banded together to curb its powers. Young priests and ministers are charging the redevelopers with utter disregard for the fate of the poor."

Mayor Shelley's ambivalence on the redevelopment issue was one of the principal factors underlying the "dump Shelley" movement initiated by the city's ruling elite. Shelley had begun to organize his reelection effort. Harold Dobbs was once again running his law-and-order campaign, this time with considerably greater chance of success in the dominant white community as a result of backlash from the Hunters Point uprising earlier in the year and other African American rebellions. Liberal supervisor Jack Morrison wanted to run but would not oppose his friend Shelley. Early public opinion polls indicated Dobbs would make a very strong showing against Shelley.

In late August 1967, a meeting was arranged at the Fairmont Hotel by Vernon Kaufman, a San Francisco clothing manufacturer and later Joseph Alioto's campaign manager. Present were representatives of downtown interests, including Ben Swig and Cyril Magnin, department store owner and financier, head of the Port Commission, and prime mover behind the proposed Embarcadero City project (the entire eighty-block north waterfront area, from Fisherman's Wharf to the Ferry Building), whose principal element, a 550-foot U.S. Steel tower, so enraged conservationists that the project was blocked in a bitter political battle.[20] Also present were such political influentials as William Coblentz, a University of California regent, and former mayor Elmer Robinson. According to some accounts, at least one important labor representative (from the International Longshoremen's and Warehousemen's Union–ILWU) was also present.[21] The subject was city hall politics.

On September 8, 1967, just two months before election day, Shelley held a dramatic press conference to announce he was dropping out of the race, citing as his reasons poor health and exhaustion. Exactly one and a half hours later, Joseph Alioto held a press conference (at Ben Swig's Fairmont Hotel) announcing his candidacy. Charges and rumors of dirty politics inevitably flew thick and fast. Congressman Phillip Burton, leader of the liberal wing of the city's Democratic Party, declared, "Truthfully, it smacks to me like a deal." Noting the extraordinary timing of the two announcements, Burton expressed what most San Franciscans also must have thought: "I can't believe this just happened."[22] A few days later, Jack Morrison announced his own candidacy. A political ally of Burton and clearly the Shelley replacement liberal Democrats would have preferred, Morrison stated (a trifle optimistically, as events turned out): "The events of the past four days indicate to me that the few downtown financial tycoons are making a last desperate grasp for political power in San Francisco. . . . I think . . . there was a conviction in the minds of a few fat cats . . . that Shelley could not win. I think there were discussions and arrangements made. I think this would have occurred whether or not Mayor Shelley had a crisis in health."[23]

In breaking the story of Shelley's withdrawal, the September 8, 1967, *Examiner* confirmed reports that "Alioto, Shelley and former Mayor Robinson met in the back room of Shelley's office on Tuesday night [three days before the announcement]. One source said that when Shelley and Alioto emerged, 'they were both smiling.' " The September 8, 1967, *Chronicle* noted that "Alioto, a highly successful lawyer, who represents California's rice growers and some other important business accounts, is considered a much stronger 'downtown' candidate than Shelley."

Indeed, the downtown interests had apparently pulled the necessary strings and provided the necessary grease. Immediately following Alioto's announcement, Vernon Kaufman announced, "We will have all the money we need to elect Joseph Alioto."[24] A scant four days later, a group of Alioto backers, including "big financial interests" that had supported Mayor Shelley, and the mayoral bid of state senator Eugene McAteer before his death the previous spring, were brought together at the Fairmont Hotel at a meeting hosted by Ben Swig "that raised a cool $203,500 for Joseph Alioto's war chest in exactly 45 minutes."[25] As for Shelley, several reliable sources indicated a "payoff" was involved. According to the September 7, 1967, *Examiner:* "There were reports from City Hall sources that members of the San Francisco 'establishment' were planning to get together a 'retirement fund' for Shelley, who is not personally wealthy." The October 31, 1967, *Bay Guardian* reported that the deal to have Shelley step down had originally been made with McAteer: "The package at the time, a key McAteer source said, was $125,000 to be paid to a future employer over a five-year period to employ Shelley in a comfy post until his government pension came due. Shelley in return would throw his support to McAteer. Employers under discussion: Stanford Research Institute, Arthur D. Little Co. and friendly unions like laborers local 261."

To no one's surprise, Shelley endorsed Alioto rather than Morrison. And following an extended recuperation period, Shelley was in fact appointed by Mayor Alioto as the city's lobbyist in Sacramento, a job initially paying twenty-five thousand dollars a year plus a healthy expense account. Shelley held this position until his death in 1974.

Joe Alioto came from a well-established Bay Area family, having many branches involved in Fisherman's Wharf restaurants, real estate, finance, and law. He was a highly successful plaintiff's antitrust lawyer, a multimillionaire, and very active in politics behind the scenes until his dramatic emergence at center stage in September 1967. He previously held only non-elective public office in the city, first as a member of the Board of Education (1948–54) and its president (1952–53), later chairing the Redevelopment Agency. In the latter capacity, he showed himself a firm supporter of downtown renewal, although the agency was not very productive under his tenure. As *Examiner* columnist Dick Nolan wrote at the time of the swirl over Ben Swig's "San Francisco Prosperity Plan," "Alioto is dreaming the dream even more ardently—or at least more eloquently—than B. Swig hisself."[26]

Labeled "a conservative Democrat," Alioto had been cochairman of former state senator Eugene McAteer's mayoral drive and a major figure in John Shelley's 1963 campaign. Not averse to helping Republicans, particularly in San Francisco's nominally nonpartisan elections, Alioto also had handled George Christopher's mayoral campaign and was one of the key backers of Republican U.S. Senator Thomas Kuchel. His close relationship with the Shelley and McAteer organizations paid off in 1967. According to the September 9, 1967, *Chronicle:* "Alioto . . . has found himself in a position to collect some major political IOU's. He withdrew from the mayor's race in 1963 in Shelley's favor, with at least a tacit understanding that some day he would like to have Shelley reciprocate." And he had no trouble picking up McAteer's organization and financial support.

Alioto had two major problems to overcome in the two months between his announcement and election day: first, as the *Examiner* put it, "to the man on the street he is probably largely unknown";[27] second, as the candidate of the downtown establishment he needed working-class appeal in a town where labor was extremely powerful and in an election where Jack Morrison, a man who had received labor's endorsement in his three previous supervisorial races, was running against him. As Daniel Del Carlo, head of the Building Trades Council, understated it, "After all, Alioto isn't very well known in the labor movement."[28]

Alioto's lack of public visibility was overcome by an extremely well-run and well-financed campaign and by the candidate's forceful and effective personality. And the "labor problem" was overcome by convincing organized labor that it was in their interest to support Alioto, based on what he could and would do for them, and on the argument that Morrison could not win and to throw labor's support to Morrison would result only in giving the election to the reactionary Dobbs. A study of San Francisco politics notes:

> Labor was . . . instrumental in the shift to Joseph Alioto. . . . There [were] explicit signs of implicit trade-offs between the mayor's office and the unions, particularly the Building and Construction Trades Council and the longshoremen. In his 1967 and 1971 elections, Alioto received the benefit of labor's campaign workers and fund-raising. . . . In return, unions received help in major strikes in the form of mediation by the mayor, sympathetic police in cases of picketing, and zealous efforts to attract construction projects with their attendant jobs.
>
> There were appointments from labor's ranks, giving them access and visibility.[29]

The key unions in Alioto's drive were two of the city's largest: Local 10 of the ILWU and Local 261 of the Laborers International, AFL-CIO. Both unions had large minority memberships, the ILWU being mostly black, and the Laborers having a strong position among Spanish-speaking workers in the Mission District. The ILWU gave Alioto additional access to the black community through the Baptist Ministers Union, one of the earliest black organizations to support him. According to Jack Morrison, "The ILWU did more to elect Alioto than anyone. . . . They gave him a liberal cachet and allowed him to get the black vote."[30] The Laborers Union, through its Mission-based caucus, the Centro Social Obrero, a major neighborhood political force, and through the Centro's influence over the Mexican-American Political Association (MAPA), gave Alioto a powerful base of support within the city's large Spanish-speaking population. It also gave him substantial financial backing, secured as political contributions from the union's members, many of whom, as recent, and sometimes illegal, immigrants from Central and South America, often had to submit to high initiation fees, dues, and special assessments. Other large and important unions such as the Department Store Employees and the Metal Trades and Industrial Union Council also supported Alioto, and although he was just shy of the two-thirds majority needed for AFL-CIO Central Labor Council endorsement, he clearly managed to win labor to his side.

To explain why union support went to Alioto when he had not been closely identified with labor and when Morrison was clearly more sympathetic to labor, the *Chronicle*'s labor reporter, Dick Meister, writing in the September 20, 1967, edition, cited these factors: (1) the timing and rapidity of Alioto's move, which caught Morrison and Burton off guard; (2) the fact that Alioto was making more liberal noises than had been expected; (3) Alioto's friendship with AFL-CIO secretary-treasurer George Johns (the two men had served together on the Board of Education, and Alioto had been campaign committee chair for Johns's unsuccessful 1961 Board of Supervisors race); and (4) Alioto's tactic of using the support of a few key ILWU leaders who had been close to Shelley as a wedge to win over the membership. "Perhaps the most important reason," wrote Meister, "was indicated when Alioto walked into the ILWU [endorsement] meeting on Monday night surrounded by several of Shelley's former campaign aides. It was a graphic demonstration that the men around the man who is San Francisco's first labor mayor in a half century . . . know whom they want to inherit his position." The outcome of this joint downtown-labor push was a victory for Alioto, who received 106,000 votes to Dobbs's 90,000 and Morrison's 40,000.

Labor's support was rewarded immediately by appointments to influential City posts and in the long run by construction and other types of jobs for its members.[31] An ILWU Local 10 official was appointed to Alioto's cabinet. ILWU International president Harry Bridges was appointed to the San Francisco Port Commission. Hector Rueda of the Elevator Construction Workers Union was appointed to the Planning Commission. Bill Chester of ILWU was made president of the Bay Area Rapid Transit system (BART). In late 1969, the San Francisco Redevelopment Agency awarded the ILWU a choice lot in the Western Addition A-2 redevelopment area to build its world headquarters. Local 261 also received its rewards: The head of the Centro Social Obrero was appointed to the mayor's cabinet; the local's president went on the Housing Authority board; and a leader of MAPA was appointed by the mayor to fill a vacancy on the Board of Supervisors, another to the Board of Education. Local 261 soon after received a contract to build "miniparks" on various SFRA properties, with the pilot project located next to the local president's house. Alioto's most crucial political link to the ILWU and the labor movement generally, Dave Jenkins, received a patronage post in 1968 as "labor consultant" to the Redevelopment Agency. The controversial and highly influential Jenkins remained on the agency payroll until the late 1970s, receiving a total of $188,000 for his nine years of part-time employ.[32] Alioto also appointed ILWU representative Wilbur Hamilton to the SFRA board. Within a few months, Hamilton applied for and got an SFRA staff job as manager of the Western Addition A-2 project, a move reportedly engineered by Justin Herman. Alioto thereupon replaced Hamilton on the board with Joe Mosley, another ILWU representative. (Mosley resigned the position in 1976, after being indicted by a federal grand jury for attempted extortion in connection with the agency's Hunters Point project; he eventually received a one-year jail sentence and twenty-thousand-dollar fine.)[33]

At the same time that Alioto appointed Hamilton to the agency board, he appointed Michael J. Driscoll, a mortuary owner whose daughter married Alioto's son. Alioto's appointment of his extended family members, close friends, and business associates to City posts was a standing joke in San Francisco: For example, he appointed his campaign manager and press secretary to key Redevelopment Agency posts, his wife to the War Memorial Trustees, his wife's nephew to a staff job in the mayor's office, an associate of his law firm to the Civil Service Commission, his brother-in-law to the Port Commission, a close friend as Port Director, his cousin to the Fire Commission and later to the Civil Service Commission, his sister to the Landmarks Preservation Advisory Board, and two cousins and a real estate partner to the five-person nonprofit corporation that at one point was intended to build a sports arena in Yerba Buena Center.

Joe Alioto's election appeared to signal the change in the fortunes of the city's redevelopment program that the business-union coalition desired. Alioto immediately named as his deputy for development John Tolan Jr., assistant administrator of HUD's Western Region, a long-time friend from college days, a close friend of Justin Herman, and the son of a former East Bay congressman. At a news conference, held fittingly at Ben Swig's Fairmont Hotel, Alioto pledged his support for the Yerba Buena Center development. "Plans for a grandiose cultural and sports center in the South-of-Market area 'will go forward quickly' in the new City administration, Mayor-elect Joseph L. Alioto said yesterday," reported the January 4, 1968, *Chronicle.* On the same day, Chamber of Commerce president Cyril Magnin vowed to do something to further a downtown sports arena in Yerba Buena Center. Alioto then went to Washington to seek additional federal money for YBC and the Western Addition A-2 project. "It looks like the tide is turning for us," Justin Herman predicted confidently.[34] On March 20, 1968, in a story headed "Alioto Gives His Blessing to Herman," the *Examiner* wrote: "Mayor Alioto has reaffirmed his confidence in M. Justin Herman, the controversial executive director of the Redevelopment Agency. . . . The praise which Alioto heaped on Herman also appeared to be the Mayor's way of telling those leaders of the Negro community who've been demanding the ouster of the redevelopment boss that nothing is further from his mind."

Labor's Turn Toward YBC

Organized labor's strong backing of Joe Alioto in 1967, followed by its strong backing for Yerba Buena Center, was a dramatic reversal of its original stance toward the project. Businesses in the South of Market area were highly unionized, and when redevelopment plans first came to light, the San Francisco Central Labor Council, AFL-CIO, opposed them on the basis that the development would displace thousands of blue-collar jobs and replace them with nonunion clerical and service workers.

In the early and mid-1960s, labor leadership generally had expressed great reservations about the type of economic development being pushed by the Bay Area Council, the Blyth-Zellerbach Committee, and SPUR. The April 14, 1963, *Chronicle* reported a statement issued by local AFL-CIO and Teamster leaders, which asserted: "It may suit the purpose of some to make San Francisco a financial and service center, but it destroys the jobs of working people and weakens the City's economic foundations."

In the November 3, 1965, Official Bulletin of the San Francisco Labor Council, Secretary-Treasurer George Johns took a broad look at the YBC project, the Redevelopment Agency, and the interests served by urban renewal in San Francisco. It was the first truly incisive public critique of this downtown development:

> Speculative real estate operators . . . seem to have taken over the planning functions of our City. . . .
>
> Convention halls and sports arenas have their place. But the loss of millions of square feet of industrial space can only extend unemployment, suffering and poverty. . . . A redevelopment program is certainly needed there [South of Market]. However . . . a rehabilitation and conservation program makes far better sense than the program of massive clearance. . . .
>
> Certain politically important persons consider the clearance program in Yerba Buena as the beginning of the redevelopment of 1100 industrially zoned acres South of Market. With the support and blessings of the [Redevelopment] agency, they are ready to kick industry out of San Francisco. . . .
>
> In addition to the many workers who will lose their jobs, we wonder if the policy makers of this City have thought of the social and economic effect on over 3,000 single persons, a third of them aged, who will be

displaced in the area without realistic provision for relocation. Displacement can mean higher rents and out of the way locations. The hardship such conditions will impose on senior citizens is obvious enough to anyone still sensitive to human needs. . . .

Yet citizens who oppose a policy of rezoning light industry right out of the City are considered "obstructionists." Obstructionism, in fact, has generally become a dirty word for anyone bucking the policies of the redevelopment agency. But isn't it the agency that is really obstructing? Aren't they obstructing efforts to retain industry and therefore jobs in San Francisco by moving away from the preservation and expansion of industrial zoning that is so necessary if we are to maintain the economic balance of this City and the continuance of job opportunities?

What they are not obstructing are the special interests of certain groups. The Agency and Mr. Herman must be reminded of their obligations to the rest of the citizens of San Francisco. The Yerba Buena issue is a good place to start.

But as time passed, and the various pieces began falling into place, pressures began building within and outside labor ranks for a reversal of labor's position on YBC. The politics of the Alioto campaign and election was one major element in the switch. Justin Herman and other SFRA representatives courted labor leaders, trying to convince them that the loss of blue-collar jobs and the transformation of the city into a white-collar administrative center was inevitable and that labor could reap certain gains from this process. In a short time, the conversion was complete.

Within the Labor Council, it was the Building and Construction Trades Council (BCTC) that carried the day for YBC. The conversion of downtown San Francisco into the administrative and financial headquarters of the West—particularly through the massive BART system and the Golden Gateway project—had been good for the various construction industry trades and locals. By the mid-1960s, the BCTC was a backer not just of Yerba Buena Center but also of any planned construction that would provide employment for members of its affiliated unions. This included the proposed 550-foot U.S. Steel high-rise on the waterfront and a proposed freeway through Golden Gate Park, both of which earned the hostility of the general populace because of the loss of recreational space and scenic views. But as a representative of the BCTC said regarding Yerba Buena Center, "We are in favor of building with no respect to where it is and how it is."[35] For many San Francisco workers the quest for construction jobs was vital to survival. The redevelopment master plan for the city was displacing thousands of jobs, and it was not likely that unemployed blue-collar workers would find employment in white-collar jobs.

> [U]nion leaders usually agree to whatever projects are proposed by busi-
> ness—just as long as the projects provide jobs. . . . It . . . has been rare for
> union leaders to question financial returns promised to business from
> proposed projects; they merely agree they should be as large as possible
> to maximize the share granted their members. . . . Unions merely react
> to the doings of others, occasionally forcing them to alter their plans
> after they have been unveiled but usually playing only the role of im-
> portant supporter.
>
> A critic put it this way: The unions are an arm of the downtown es-
> tablishment, playing pretty much of an establishment game. They stand
> by while business dictates the course of San Francisco and, as long as
> they get theirs, they don't rock the boat.[36]

Along with the construction trades, the Bartender and Culinary Workers and Cooks unions, which had much to gain from more hotel and entertainment facilities, joined the chorus of YBC supporters. The ILWU's strong
support of the project was at least partially explainable by the union's concerns for its future. The ILWU has a historic reputation as one of the most
progressive unions in the country, having readily taken such stands as supporting the Civil Rights movement and opposing the Vietnam War. With
growing mechanization of the West Coast docks, the ILWU was forced to
face the prospect of slowly dying or merging with a larger union, such as
the International Longshoremen's Association, dominant on East Coast and
Gulf docks, or the Teamsters, who were handling increasing quantities of
containerized cargo. ILWU leadership therefore saw it in their best interest
to generate more jobs by backing business and political forces determined
to advance San Francisco and the Bay Area as a service and trading hub for
the Pacific Rim. As union membership declined, the old guard in leadership
moved to protect its position by becoming a direct participant in the city's
political machine and thus consolidated its power around the union's
steadily employed members.

Labor support for clearance in South of Market was not without its irony.
Many of the area's retired residents had once been active union members,
organizers, and even officials, and were supplementing their Social Security
with union pensions. Yet the union leaders were insensitive to the plight of
the older men, classifying them as "winos and bums." As one union leader
put it: "They poor-mouth a lot, but under our system the residents can't remain. A few can't hold up progress."

But more than a few were doing their best to hold up "progress." The
South of Market residents were to form an organization called Tenants and
Owners in Opposition to Redevelopment (TOOR) to fight for their rights
in the face of the displacement threat (see chapter 4). Organized labor's

break with its former constituency and membership, and its new ties to the Alioto administration and its downtown growth policies, led it to go so far as to file a "friend of the court" brief defending the Redevelopment Agency against charges of inadequate relocation brought in federal court by the South of Market residents.

The Media

The downtown interests found the main outlet for pro-development propaganda in San Francisco's major daily newspapers, the morning *Chronicle* and the (until recently) afternoon *Examiner.** As political scientist Frederick Wirt noted in his 1974 study of decision making in San Francisco, "neither [the *Examiner*] nor the *Chronicle* is regarded by professional analysts as distinguished."[37] And University of California, Berkeley, geographer Dick Walker, in his 1990 political economy analysis of the Bay Area, refers to the *Chronicle*'s "persistent mediocrity."[38] (In more recent years, however, the *Examiner* won a number of journalism awards, and the quality of its local reporting was of a relatively high caliber.) Both papers have been avid supporters of redevelopment schemes, especially YBC, and SPUR, the Swigs, Justin Herman, and other project proponents have had no difficulty in getting maximum coverage of their positions.

San Francisco's dailies, like virtually all major newspapers, have numerous threads binding them to the area's corporate, financial, and political leadership. In the case of Yerba Buena Center, the *Chronicle*'s and *Examiner*'s stakes were also more direct. Headquarters for both papers directly adjoin the project area. As large landowners, both newspapers stood to gain financially from the substantial increase in land values triggered by the YBC project. A 1981 study of the *Examiner*'s and *Chronicle*'s real estate holdings reported that "between them the newspapers control . . . 36 parcels . . . near or directly adjacent to the three superblocks of the YBC development." The total assessed value of the forty parcels owned by the papers, citywide, was

*On local development and political issues the two papers have been editorially almost indistinguishable. A *Bay Guardian* feature referred to "the long pattern of the two papers backing the same candidates and taking the same positions on basic power-structure issues. In virtually every major election since the two papers formed a monopoly joint-operating agreement in 1965, the *Ex* and *Chron* endorsements have been all but identical. And, often, the two papers' news coverage of key issues and important elections has shown the same pattern as the endorsements." See Tim Redmond, "The Importance of Being Harry," *San Francisco Bay Guardian,* 15 April 1987.

$46 million. "With YBC about to boom, this land is being quickly transmuted into 'brown gold,' " the study concluded.[39]

Dozens of editorials supporting Yerba Buena Center have appeared in the two dailies over the past three decades. Both papers extolled the claims of SPUR and the Convention & Visitors Bureau and heaped praise on the Redevelopment Agency. An unfounded and wildly exaggerated CVB statement about loss of revenues from convention activity was duly reproduced in a March 16, 1972, *Examiner* editorial, which proclaimed, "San Francisco has definitely lost $40 million [of] convention business this year.... By 1976 the annual loss will reach $80 million." A 1972 SPUR report on the city's redevelopment program received similar treatment: "SPUR is characteristically independent in expertise and outlook," the May 2, 1972, *Chronicle* solemnly stated, in support of that organization's incredible conclusion that "in all the years of its operations, the Redevelopment Agency has never failed to provide adequately for residents who were forced to seek new quarters." "This extraordinary record," the editorial continued, "has been verified by painstaking study which showed that the agency has relocated some 2,633 families and more than 400 individuals without once violating federal rules for 'safe, decent, and sanitary housing' for relocated persons." This conclusion relied totally on the agency's own reports and ignored both the mass of contrary evidence and the numerous persons unaided by the agency who were left to their own devices in locating new residences. An earlier *Examiner* editorial, published on November 14, 1969, right after TOOR had filed its eventually winning relocation suit (see chapter 5), asserted: "The Redevelopment Agency is proceeding with meticulous care and compassion in relocating residents of the Yerba Buena area."*

Taking the occasion of Justin Herman's death to plug YBC, the *Examiner*'s September 1, 1971, editorial eulogy ended with these words: "The day that Mr. Herman died he was fighting to protect the grand, unified design of the big Yerba Buena Center project south of Market. No memorial to him

---

*Herbert Gans's reports about press coverage of Boston's notorious West End urban renewal project showed marked parallels with the Yerba Buena Center story: "The Boston press not only favored the redevelopment of the West End in repeated and enthusiastic editorials, but also covered the news only from the point of view of the Redevelopment Authority. Press releases or interviews with officials about the West End were never complemented by the West Enders' version of the situation, or, indeed, by their feelings about the matter. Features, moreover, depicted the West End as a vice-ridden set of hovels in which respectable human beings could not be expected to live, thus insulting the West Enders and making them feel like outcasts." See Herbert Gans, *The Urban Villagers*, rev. ed. (New York: The Free Press, 1982), 172.

could be finer than a determination by city hall to move ahead strongly on that distinguished enterprise." On the same day, the *Chronicle* editorialized: "The only thing that ever stopped [Herman] was the poverty lawsuit that ground the Yerba Buena project to a halt. It once drew from him a remark that was a key to his single-minded drive and determination. 'A litigation attorney,' he said, 'can do nothing in the social field. We can.' The truth of this remark will, we think, ultimately prevail and become one of his monuments in San Francisco."

Each of the papers used any incident involving the project to publish optimistically headlined editorials, such as "The Way Cleared for Yerba Buena" (*Chronicle*, March 29, 1972), "Hopeful News on Yerba Buena" (*Examiner*, June 9, 1972), "Help for Yerba Buena" (*Chronicle*, August 9, 1972), "Yerba Buena Looks Up" (*Chronicle*, February 29, 1972). The overall impact of such editorializing was to help create a stampede effect, pushing the project forward with little regard for the consequences. Editorial advocacy even entered the letters column. When San Francisco assemblyman (later congressman, then again assemblyman, and still later state senator) John Burton wrote the *Examiner* (November 16, 1971) regarding responsibility for a hotel fire in the YBC area, the following gratuitous, disparaging note was appended to his published letter: "Assemblyman Burton has feuded with the Redevelopment Agency for years.—Editor."

Attacks on the South of Market residents and denigrations of their struggle were commonplace. An editorial in the January 26, 1970, *Chronicle* put forth the following position on statutory rights: "In our assessment of the public interest, redevelopment should be allowed and encouraged to go forward undisrupted by harassing litigation." Commenting on a HUD grant of $12 million to cover South of Market relocation costs, a June 29, 1972, *Examiner* editorial noted that the "much belabored Yerba Buena may get off the ground—always assuming the absence of further harassing suits which have added millions of dollars to construction costs. By the way, shouldn't those who file suits like that be held accountable in some degree for the damage their delays inflict?" In a June 11, 1971, *Examiner* editorial, YBC opponents were put down as "ideologues," and in the same editorial the paper went on to state, with breathtaking class arrogance and factual misstatement, about South of Market residents: "Neither do we believe that such people should have the right—in the absence of some compelling reason deeply rooted in the public good—to delay and quite possibly kill a major public project of profound importance to the economic well-being of a city that is not really their home community, that they have built no stake in, that they make no attempt to adorn, and to which they are on the whole an unsought burden."

In an earlier day—before the residents became troublesome by demanding their rights—the *Examiner* had a different view of those who lived in the YBC area and urged more charitable treatment. Its February 24, 1964, editorial stated: "We share Mayor Shelley's concern over one important phase of the project. The area contains 3,165 single residents. These are not drifting derelicts. They are for the most part aged persons living in old hotels on small pensions. They will have to be resettled. Into the task must go as much compassion as energy."

Distortions abounded: Commenting on the TOOR lawsuit that led a federal court to enjoin the project and impose a settlement requiring the Redevelopment Agency to provide some two thousand permanent subsidized low-rent replacement units (see chapter 5), the *San Francisco Progress*'s June 26, 1974, editorial mounted this incredible reading of the events:

> Most of the settlements have resulted in some kind of personal gain for the plaintiff, but very little for the public. For example, an outfit known as Tenants and Owners Opposed to Redevelopment [sic] (TOOR) held things up in the Yerba Buena center under the premise of protecting the residents who would be thrown out in the street with no place to live. The settlement included several units of senior citizens housing. The developers? TOOR, of course. And who is going to pay the higher cost of constructing the units? The senior citizen tenants.

News coverage and columnists in the dailies tended to be more informative and independent, but the papers often used "features" and "human interest" stories, sometimes supplied by the Redevelopment Agency, to distort the plight of area residents. One such story in the December 1, 1971, *Chronicle* transmitted directly, without investigation, the Redevelopment Agency's claims that an "illegal hippie commune" was threatening the project with loss of an $8 million office building and two thousand new permanent jobs. As it turned out, the three individuals under attack were living and working in an $85-per-month storefront they had completely renovated for residency and a carpentry workshop, were legally protected by a federal court order, and were understandably reluctant to move until the agency could find the comparable quarters they were entitled to by law. However, it was enough to associate "hippie" and "commune" with the well-developed image of "bums" and "degenerates" housed in South of Market flophouses.

Another story of this character, headlined "The High Cost of Don and His Dog," appeared in the April 1, 1971, *Chronicle*, also clearly designed to put pressure on "holdouts" to move. The story involved agency attempts to remove the last three residents from the Daton Hotel, since keeping it open was allegedly costing seven thousand dollars monthly. The focus was on

Don Caldwell, his dog Tammey, and his "dogged obstinacy" in bringing his case before the Relocation Appeals Board established by the federal court to protect the rights of displacees. The severely crippled Caldwell had refused agency relocation offers because they all involved climbing hills or stairs or living in places with inadequate fire exits. The story had its intended effect. The *Chronicle* story produced "a rash of death threats. . . . The day before, he (Caldwell) said, he received a special delivery letter saying: 'May God punish you that you may pray to die.' The threat, plus four telephoned warnings taken by hotel clerks, 'scared me to death,' said Caldwell, bursting into tears."[40]

A similar story from the February 9, 1970, *Examiner,* reporting on the only remaining resident of the Colorado Hotel, who was at the time under the protection of a federal court order forbidding his eviction, began: "At the cost of $2000 a month the government is providing 24-hour doorman service for a Skid Row resident." Another *Chronicle* story (October 23, 1972), headlined "One Man's Battle with Yerba Buena," focused on TOOR chairman Peter Mendelsohn, presenting him as a crazed senior citizens' power activist, living in the past and personally holding up the development of YBC.

Not at all irrelevant to the ease with which public agencies and officials can have their stories appear in the daily papers and the frequency with which the official viewpoint dominates news accounts is the career path of journalists, from those who report news to those who create and manipulate it. Numerous examples exist in San Francisco of newspaper writers moving to more lucrative positions inside the establishment. To name a few: Mel Wax, formerly a *Chronicle* reporter and moderator of "Newsroom"—a critically praised news program that once brought the city's public television station, KQED-TV, national attention—became press secretary to Mayor George Moscone and remained as Mayor Dianne Feinstein's press secretary; Wes Willoughby, the SFRA assistant director for Public Affairs, and Hadley Roff, deputy mayor in the Feinstein and Agnos administrations, formerly were reporters for the now-defunct *San Francisco News–Call Bulletin;* William O'Brien, a former *Examiner* reporter, was press secretary to Mayor Alioto; Tom Eastham, former executive editor of the *Examiner,* was press secretary to Feinstein; W. E. Barnes, a former political writer for the *Examiner,* became a freelancer, with the city's new convention center one of his clients; Eileen Maloney (E. Cahill when she was a reporter for the now-defunct twice-weekly *San Francisco Progress*) became Mayor Art Agnos's press secretary.

Recently, there was a shakeup in the city's newspaper world. In 2000 the Hearst Corporation, owner of the *Examiner,* bought the *Chronicle* for $660 million in a dramatic and fun-filled San Francisco saga. The two papers had

entered a joint operating agreement in 1965 covering business and printing functions (an arrangement subsequently authorized and codified by
Congress for widespread use in the Newspaper Preservation Act of 1970)
designed to save both papers money and ensure their continuance. At the
time, the two papers had about equal circulation, but three decades later, the
afternoon *Examiner*'s circulation was only one-fourth that of its morning
rival. (All over the country, afternoon papers had been losing out to morning papers, in large part due to competition from evening television news.)
The joint operating agreement was due to expire in 2005, and the *Chronicle* had no intention of renewing it. The New York–based Hearst Corporation (owner of many other newspapers as well as such magazines as *Cos-
mopolitan* and *Popular Mechanics*) then offered to purchase the *Chronicle*
from its San Francisco–based family owners (owner of local television station KRON and Chronicle Books, as well as newspapers in Illinois and Massachusetts), sparking a series of controversies. The immediate concern in
many quarters was that San Francisco would be left with just one (English-
language) daily, the fate of many large U.S. cities. There was little interest
in purchasing the *Examiner* until a deal emerged involving the Fang family, publisher of the thrice-weekly, free *Independent Asian Week* and other
community newspapers, as well as owners of a large printing business and
other enterprises. The sale occurred in late 2000, but not without a series of
attempted roadblocks. Justice Department approval was needed in order to
secure exemption from antitrust laws.* There was talk of a City lawsuit to
block the sale if no one would buy the *Examiner*, and both the City's district attorney and the state attorney general had begun investigating the
sale for possible antitrust violations. Clint Reilly, a rejected bidder and political consultant who had spent $4 million of his own money in a losing
1999 mayoral bid against Willie Brown (see chapter 11), brought suit—represented by none other than Joseph M. Alioto, son of the ex-mayor—
alleging violation of federal antitrust laws.[41] Reilly lost his suit, but it caused
quite a stir when the trial brought out the fact that *Examiner* editor/pub-
lisher Timothy O. White "testified that he offered Mayor Willie Brown favorable editorials in exchange for the mayor's support of Hearst's plan to
buy the *San Francisco Chronicle*."[42] The admission elicited loud and public

---

*In accordance with the 1970 Newspaper Preservation Act, the Justice Depart-
ment must approve joint operating agreements and has power to allow them to be
dissolved. In the past decade and a half, the department has permitted dissolution of
these agreements in fifteen cities, and in each case, the morning paper has survived
while the afternoon paper went out of business. See Lane Williams, "Clint Reilly
Sues to Halt Purchase of Chronicle," *San Francisco Examiner*, 12 January 2000.

protests from *Examiner* as well as *Chronicle* reporters and led to White's suspension. A subsequent report lent credence to his admission: "A Bay Area media watchdog group says it found a 'subtle but troubling shift' in the *Examiner's* editorial page treatment of Mayor Willie Brown in the two months after publisher Timothy O. White offered the mayor favorable editorials in exchange for Brown's support of the Hearst Corporation's bid to buy the *Chronicle.*"[43] There was no doubt that Mayor Brown was pushing hard for the Fang purchase, in part because he probably genuinely wanted San Francisco to remain a two-newspaper town but also because the Fangs have been strong Brown allies.

The sale went through, and on November 21, 2000, the *Examiner* (old version) published its final edition, 135 years after it had begun.* The new *Examiner*, which began printing the next day under its new publisher, Ted Fang (later fired by his mother and replaced by his brother, James), became a morning paper put out six times a week (no Sunday edition yet) and is now a low-budget operation, relying on a very tiny (non-union) news staff and lots of stringers and syndication and news services: "a minimalist cost structure . . . an experiment in how cheaply a daily newspaper can be produced."[44] The Hearst Corporation, as part of the deal, guaranteed that all *Examiner* employees would have jobs with the *Chronicle* for at least a year, and virtually the entire 220-person staff accepted the offer. Exactly one year later the *Chronicle* laid off 220 workers. The "purchase" provided Fang (via Pan Asia Venture Capital, the family company) with a $66 million subsidy over three years (having paid only a symbolic $100 for the *Examiner* and its various properties), but as someone familiar with newspaper economics put it, "in newspaper terms it is a pittance."[45]

The paper's early performance hit some pretty low notes, with lots of embarrassing glitches. In its maiden edition, a front-page story jumped to a full-page ad; a front-page photo of the mayor and Giants' manager Dusty Baker was "so out of focus it looked like a video game screen of 10 years ago. And, in what may have turned out to be a blessing in disguise, the paper

---

*An interesting historical angle was caught in the *New York Times* account of the sale: "That the fight to save the *Examiner* should end with Mr. Fang's ownership represented a sweet, if belated, justice for the Chinese community reviled in its pages a century ago. Thomas C. Leonard, the associate dean of the Graduate School of Journalism at the University of California at Berkeley, said: 'The exquisite piece of irony here is that both the Chronicle and the *Examiner* got their start playing into the strong anti-Asian period in California in the 1880s. I think that to find more than a century later that the key to their business plans is an enterprising Chinese family—that's a real story about America.' " Felicity Barringer and Evelyn Nieves, "The San Francisco Examiner Is Sold by Hearst to a Local Newspaper Owner," *New York Times*, 8 March 2000.

delivered only half of its 100,000 copies." Other regular goofs included mis-
spellings of the paper's date and the names of its managing editor and associate editor and headlines left in midair: "The International Olympic
Committee Selects the," "Miami (2–3) Opened Its Home." Changing type-
faces, crammed layouts, and weird choices of front-page stories (e.g., a
reprint of a *Baltimore Sun* article about a Cecil County, Maryland, dispute
on whether to ban dodge-ball from the school curriculum) also marred the
start-up period.[46] By the end of the paper's first month, the managing editor, executive editor, and editorial page editor had been replaced.[47]

In his lawsuit challenging the sale to the Fangs, Clint Reilly alleged that
the transaction was nothing but a "sham." According to the Reilly/Alioto
brief, Ted Fang was earning $500,000 a year and receiving a $500,000 bonus
as the *Examiner*'s publisher.[48] This is not just the contention of a failed
suitor. The *New York Times* gave the interpretation credence in one of its
early reports on the proposed sale: "[S]ome critics say Hearst's deal with
Mr. Fang is a sham, meant to save off antitrust action by the Justice Department while limiting Hearst's costs and shielding the *Chronicle* from serious competition."[49] Time will tell. Perhaps the Fang-owned *Examiner* will
prove a huge success to the public as well as to Fang financially. Or it may
go down the tubes after a few years, the Fang family having risked no
money and pocketed a chunk of the $66 million pot-sweetener, and the
Hearst Corporation having secured a lucrative newspaper monopoly for itself, in the process avoiding the appearance of antitrust violations.*

The electronic media have played a supportive role in the transforma-
tion of San Francisco as well, frequently airing radio and television edito-
rials with titles such as, "Yerba Buena Is Key" (KGO-TV, July 5–11, 1971),
"Economic Disaster Threatens" (KGO-TV, December 6–12, 1971), and
"Time to Expedite Yerba Buena" (KFAX, January 9, 1973). Redevelopment
Agency handouts were likewise parroted, and the agency routinely praised.
"The Redevelopment Agency is aware that unsympathetic displacement of
people isn't fair play. And we choose to believe it's been responsive to the

*The sale immediately produced an antitrust lawsuit of another type: Fricke-
Parks Press, a longtime rival of the Fang family's printing operation, Grant Print-
ing, accused the family of using the newspaper purchase subsidy to drive Fricke-
Parks out of business by underbidding for printing contracts at prices lower than
the cost of raw materials. See Christine Hanley, "New Examiner Publisher Ted Fang
Sued for Alleged Antitrust Violations," Associated Press, 11 October 2000. The suit
was settled when the Hearst Corporation (but not the *Examiner*) agreed to pay
Fricke-Parks $250,000 in return for dismissal of the suit. See Dan Evans and Nina
Wu, "Examiner Free and Clear in Printer's Conspiracy Suit," *San Francisco Exam-
iner*, 25 May 2001.

rights of affected residents," said KPIX-TV on June 12–14, 1970—just a few months before the federal court chose to believe the residents' claims to the contrary. In a flurry of alliterative indignation, radio station KCBS (January 11–16, 1972) editorialized: "Federally financed lawyers have worked feverishly to frustrate the project which, ironically, is mainly funded by federal tax dollars. Somehow, that seems less than reasonable."

The media tie-in to the tourism-convention industry was acknowledged (and discounted) in an editorial by KPIX area vice president Louis S. Simon, which began: "Although I'm president-elect of the Convention & Visitors Bureau, vitally interested in this subject, I am speaking today solely on behalf of KPIX and our editorial board."

These entities, then—the large corporations and financial institutions, the hotels and other downtown businesses, the Convention & Visitors Bureau, city hall, the major labor unions, the daily newspapers and other media—were the principal members of the redevelopment booster club and cheerleading squad who provided the public support for planning and building Yerba Buena Center and for the broader transformation of San Francisco.

3 | The Assault on South of Market

In 1961, with Justin Herman firmly in the saddle, the San Francisco Redevelopment Agency began the official assault on South of Market by filing for a federal urban renewal survey and planning grant. While outlining a redevelopment study area slightly larger than that in Ben Swig's 1955 plan, the application moved the site closer to Market Street and also omitted the segment the City Planning Department had identified as the most blighted blocks. Changing the project area boundaries was neither capricious nor scientific: The agency determined and gerrymandered the boundaries in response to real estate values and the demands of the politically influential. As the *Wall Street Journal* later noted (May 27, 1970):

> It's clear that the redevelopment agency considerably broadened the meaning of the designation "blight" in order to achieve the current boundaries. Ironically, the project now bears a remarkable resemblance to a plan first suggested in 1954 by Benjamin Swig, prominent Democrat and owner of the prestigious Fairmont Hotel on Nob Hill. However, Mr. Swig's "San Francisco Prosperity Plan" was rejected by the redevelopment and planning agency in 1956 on the grounds that it "perverted" the basic reason for redeveloping the area.

The revised boundaries were well suited to benefit adjacent owners, whose land values could be expected to skyrocket as a result of the renewal project. These beneficiaries included some of the more powerful and influential individuals and concerns in the city: Ben Swig, Pacific Telephone and Telegraph (later renamed Pacific Telesis), Standard Oil (later renamed Chevron), Litton Systems, United California Bank, the Emporium, the

Hearst Corporation (then publisher of the *Examiner*), the *San Francisco Chronicle*, and others. Noteworthy is the case of the Emporium department store, then located on the south side of Market between Fourth and Fifth, adjacent to the new redevelopment area. Emporium secretary-treasurer Walter Kaplan also chaired the Redevelopment Agency board and was president of the City-sponsored Fifth and Mission Garage Corporation. Under the redevelopment plan, Mr. Kaplan's garage was to expand to Fourth and Mission, to better serve Mr. Kaplan's Emporium customers, via land made available through Mr. Kaplan's Redevelopment Agency.

The application sailed through the Board of Supervisors and on to the federal government. The Housing and Home Finance Agency in October 1962 approved a $600,000 planning grant. With federal moneys in hand and Swig's conception of a sports-office-convention complex in mind, all survey and planning efforts were directed toward total clearance.

The Swig family reentered the YBC picture that same year when Ben's son Melvin became part-owner, with Albert Schlesinger, of the city's professional basketball and hockey teams. Melvin Swig hired the architecture firm Skidmore, Owings & Merrill to draw up schematics of a revised Yerba Buena Center plan, focused around an indoor sports arena and convention center. According to Swig, "I was after Justin to get something going arena-wise and conventionwise. . . . I went to see Justin with a plan for a sports arena in Yerba Buena. And he liked the idea very much."[1]

SFRA had hired its own planning consultant firm, Livingston and Blayney, and they maintained close contacts with the business community. As the February 21, 1964, *Chronicle* reported, "The consultants planned closely with civic leaders and businessmen, many of whom have already expressed interest in the proposals and will serve on a committee created by [Mayor] Shelley to evaluate it."

There was important input from outside consultants, but Justin Herman's general strategy was to keep all planning within his own agency and wherever possible circumvent the City Planning Commission, whose staff could not be relied upon for properly supportive studies. Although California law directs the City Planning Commission to decide project boundaries and devise a preliminary plan, then–planning director James McCarthy described his agency's role in YBC planning as only "the tail of the kite." Incredibly, the commission first saw the YBC redevelopment plan upon its completion when SFRA asked for the planners' approval. The commission expressed strong resentment at SFRA for having bypassed the City's official planning staff and taking its approval for granted.[2] Agency assistant director Robert Rumsey later told the commission, "I respectfully suggest that you leave the decision to the Board of Supervisors. I doubt that Mr. McCarthy could find a staff capable of evaluating our planning."[3]

Another tactic in the agency's modus operandi throughout the protracted planning and approval period was to use the tentativeness of its plans as a way of manipulating, maneuvering, and remaining in control. Thus, initially, at the time of applying for the federal planning grant, the agency asked approval of its preliminary plan on the basis that it was not binding; criticism was deflected and dismissed through agency assurances that all redevelopment plans were tentative, serving only to point directions, and that there would be ample opportunity to change plans before they became final. When the agency and its planning consultants completed their final redevelopment scheme in 1964, it asked approval on the basis that the plan was really nothing more than a detailed elaboration of the preliminary version.

But there was still a good deal of public confusion about Justin Herman's plans for the YBC. At first, the agency gave assurances that it was not intending a massive clearance project: According to the February 28, 1961, *Chronicle*, "As Herman foresaw the project, it would require razing only a quarter of the existing structures. . . . Herman cautioned against regarding the projected demolition in terms of 'vast, cleared blocks.' " Herman later said, "We will keep what's rehabilitable, and raze the rest."[4]

As the February 1, 1966, *Examiner* was to note: "The Redevelopment Agency itself is definitely not blameless for some of the confusion and discontent among property owners. When the agency asked the supervisors in 1961 to designate the South of Market redevelopment area, it listed as its major aims 'spot clearance' and 'extensive conservation techniques.' " However, the project as developed by the agency during the years 1962–65 retained only 15 percent of the buildings originally on the site, and the Central Blocks portion was totally cleared, except for St. Patrick's Church. (The pastor of St. Patrick's, Msgr. Vincent McCarthy, praised the project mightily: "I think Yerba Buena is the greatest thing to come along. When it's built I won't have to stand in the center of Mission Street on Sundays and apologize for the heart of San Francisco.")[5]

The Redevelopment Agency unveiled its plans for the South of Market area in early 1964, and, after making some revisions, applied to the Housing and Home Finance Agency for the urban renewal grant reservation. In June 1965, the federal agency announced a $19.6 million grant for the project. The agency board approved the plan unanimously (with Walter Kaplan tactfully abstaining). In January 1966, the Planning Commission likewise approved the plan unanimously. And in April the Board of Supervisors approved it by a nine-to-two vote (Supervisors Jack Morrison and George Moscone in opposition).

These rapid-fire approvals were the result of extensive lobbying on the part of the Swigs, Herman, Schlesinger, and others, as public and "civic" representatives fell in line behind the plan. Albert Schlesinger of the Convention & Visitors Bureau, along with Herman and one of the Swigs, talked with each of the supervisors individually. According to Schlesinger, the plan went through the board "like shooting fish."

Some opposition voices made themselves heard during the hearings. Labor representatives, as noted above, were upset over the lack of industrial reuse in the area and the loss of blue-collar jobs. Official data would later show that between 1960 and 1970 manufacturing employment in San Francisco decreased by 19 percent.[6] Herman promised at least 25 percent of the land in the YBC area would be devoted to industry.[7] Social workers, ministers, and representatives of the City's Human Rights Commission appeared, carrying petitions with several hundred names, to register protest over the lack of relocation housing. The agency conveniently sidestepped the controversial issue of how to relocate four thousand low-income persons. Herman promised that he would be able to get federal relocation money when it was needed and emphasized that the plan was flexible within its basic outlines. The February 22, 1966, *Chronicle* reported that "Herman, responding to a question from Supervisor Terry Francois, said some of the old hotels in the 87-acre area might possibly be rehabilitated instead of demolished." The opposition was weak and unorganized, however, and Justin Herman knew how to respond to their concerns, at least verbally. But the project in its final form contained few industrial uses, and Herman turned down the residents' later proposal to rehabilitate some of the hotels.

The Nonsupervising Supervisors

Justin Herman's handling of the Board of Supervisors during the Yerba Buena hearings was typical of Redevelopment Agency relations with other City agencies. As the city's elected legislative body, the supervisors hold crucial powers in the renewal process because they must approve plans before the federal government will release funds reserved for a project. Since supervisors work only part time and lack the necessary staff to investigate or evaluate proposed renewal plans, the SFRA was able to overwhelm the board with a mass of data and federal administrative regulations.

Among the important tools used by Herman over the next several years to "snow" the supervisors, and the public in general, were feasibility studies commissioned to show that federal urban renewal was absolutely necessary for redevelopment of the YBC area; that redevelopment would have to be total, rather than mere spot clearance; that projected demand for office space and shopping facilities would support large-scale new construction; and that the development as a whole would show a profit.[8]

Such studies provide technical information on which to base rebuilding and relocation plans but in large part also serve to legitimize those actions by giving them the aura of objectivity and even necessity. If surveys show overwhelming evidence of "blight," then clearance and removal appear logical. If economic feasibility studies show that certain uses are "needed" while others are "infeasible," then it's obvious what the land-reuse plan must be. The various federal and local bodies that must approve Redevelopment Agency plans, as well as the public, have little basis to quarrel with the reams of reports by the agency and outside consultants on which a final plan is based.

Consultants' reports inevitably seemed to reflect the thinking of the Redevelopment Agency. Rarely were such reports commissioned out of a real desire to amass facts and outside advice for the purpose of making policy decisions. Rather, consultants selected were those who could be relied upon to share the agency's views, and it was the rare outside consultant who would risk losing future contracts by producing a report sharply different from what was known to be the desired outcome (see chapter 4, n. 24).[9]

Confusion and ignorance as to the technical details were only part of the problem. More basic was that the supervisors did not really concern themselves with the results of the city's massive redevelopment projects unless there was extensive public opposition. From their point of view, if the project was held out as costless to the city, fully paid for by federal funds or project-generated revenues, as Herman constantly assured, then there was no reason to dig too deeply into the proposal.

Until the late 1970s, when, for a short period, supervisors were elected from neighborhood districts in which they lived (see chapter 11), supervisors for the most part resided in the city's wealthier neighborhoods, such as St. Francis Wood, Pacific Heights/Marina, and Nob Hill. Their social and business ties were to the downtown, with the contributions necessary to run $75,000–$150,000 campaigns—the going rate at the time, current costs being along the order of $250,000 (for an office that until 1983 paid only $9,600 a year—raised in that year to $23,924 and again in 1998 to the current level, $37,585)—providing the glue that cemented the link.[10]

At least two supervisors in the 1968–73 period had direct interest in seeing the Yerba Buena project completed. Robert Mendelsohn was an employee of Lawrence Halprin and Associates, landscape architect for YBC (and also had been a Redevelopment Agency official, 1961–64). Supervisor Peter Tamaras owned the Tamaras Supply Company, which provided janitorial services and supplies to most major downtown hotels. Other supervisors have held interests in some aspect of citywide development through real estate and business activities, employment by downtown interests, or union ties. With few exceptions, the board was a willing supporter of plans for downtown renewal and other redevelopment projects.

The Board of Supervisors' approval of the Yerba Buena Center plan in April 1966 gave the agency and downtown corporate and financial interests the go-ahead they had been seeking since the late 1950s. While actual land clearance and relocation of South of Market residents was still a year or two off, the agency could now sell the plan to the public.

HUD

The Board of Supervisors was not the only government entity that failed to exercise control over the evolution of the project. Their posture of ceding effective responsibility to private interests and to the agency, and their unwillingness and inability to marshal evaluation independent of special interests and redirect the project, were matched or exceeded by the U.S. Department of Housing and Urban Development.[11]

Created in 1965 to give cabinet status to the Housing and Home Finance Agency, HUD evolved essentially as a conduit of funds to local agencies. As its legislative mandate to control projects developed, its philosophy and staff capacity did not keep pace. HUD staff tended to favor large-scale downtown development. Its personnel moved back and forth between HUD and local government agencies and private companies undertaking this type of development. And HUD staff subordinated themselves to local initiative. It is significant that Justin Herman moved *up* to the directorship of the San Francisco Redevelopment Agency from his position as regional director of the HHFA with jurisdiction over all HHFA activity (only part of which was urban renewal) for the entire western United States. HUD's deference to SFRA was related to the fact that the SFRA staff by the late 1960s was approximately five times greater than that of HUD's entire regional office.

High staff turnover, combined with a cadre of "deadwood," left HUD with a staff lacking the capacity to control the more stable and technically competent staffs of large redevelopment agencies such as SFRA. Within

HUD, the enormous paper flow involved in project approval was distributed among a range of highly specialized technicians' offices over a very long period of time; overall assessment of the project was almost nonexistent. Prior to neighborhood protest and litigation, the YBC relocation plan was processed and approved in isolation from the rest of the project, and the federal agency routinely signed approvals as to the project's legality. Only after the deficiencies in HUD's supervisory role became so blatant as to embarrass the department publicly did it intervene in the project.

Urban Design: Form Follows Finance

In December 1966, the Redevelopment Agency and HUD signed the urban renewal loan and grant contract making available the federal funds reserved for YBC, and by July 1967, site preparation commenced. Properties and buildings were purchased and condemned, design plans prepared, and the search for a developer launched. All efforts focused on the Central Blocks, the twenty-one acres of YBC bounded by Third, Fourth, Market, and Folsom Streets, which were to contain the convention and sports facilities. The surrounding sixty-six acres would primarily contain office buildings on some two dozen parcels, and their design would be handled by developers and their architects once the central lode of public facilities had been fixed in place.

It was Justin Herman's decision to produce a detailed urban design plan for the Central Blocks as soon as possible, before selecting a developer— rather than follow the more usual urban renewal practice of having developers bid on a plan and then hire their own designers. He felt this would give him more control over the project, for in theory it meant that the Redevelopment Agency, not the developer, would be in charge of locating the facilities and establishing their configuration. Herman resolved to retain as much control over the project as he could, for as long as possible, knowing that once the developer entered the scene, practical considerations of profitability and capability would begin to determine its details. He also wanted a visually striking project, stemming from both his own interest in design quality and his desire to attract adequate financing and prestigious developers from outside the Bay Area.

To head the Central Blocks urban design team, Herman chose the internationally known Japanese architect Kenzo Tange; and to ensure a functionalist approach, local inputs, city hall contacts, and high-quality landscape design for the extensive malls and plazas, he teamed Tange with local architects John Bolles and Gerald McCue and landscape architect Lawrence

Halprin. As planning for YBC moved ahead, however, it became clear that rather than the design dictating the behavior of the developer, the financial needs of both the City and the private developer would dictate the design.

This design team was named in January 1968 and unveiled its product in June 1969 with great fanfare. (Fittingly, the unveiling took place at the annual luncheon of the Convention & Visitors Bureau hosted by Richard Swig, the bureau's president.) It was a beautiful package designed to impress the public and attract a major developer. Since the basic decisions and guidelines for the YBC Central Blocks design had already been set in the earlier work of SFRA's planning consultant, Livingston and Blayney, the design team's task was to fit all the facilities into twenty-one acres and accommodate such bulky structures as the exhibition hall, sports arena, and parking garages.

The urban design team's plan provided for a 350,000-square-foot exhibition hall, a 14,000-seat sports arena, an 800-room hotel, a 2,200-seat theater, an Italian Cultural and Trade Center, parking for 4,000 cars, an airlines terminal, four office buildings, shops, restaurants, pedestrian malls, and landscaped plazas. Most prominent visually in the plan were two massive multistory parking structures, while the convention center was placed underground. These "unique visual elements" (a representation of which was used by the SFRA as its logo for the YBC project) well symbolized the financial importance of the garages to the project: Their cost would be the principal element in the City's local contribution, required under the federal urban renewal financing formula; they would also be the largest revenue source from YBC facilities for repaying the bond issue required for construction. That the garages were the only sure revenue producers and the best means to pay the local share of project costs exerted some pressure on the design team to make them as expensive as possible. The two parking structures contained enough room to house nearly four thousand people in two-bedroom high-rise apartments under FHA minimum standards, or as many people as were to be displaced by the YBC project!

Selecting a Developer

Once the basic YBC urban design plan was produced, the Redevelopment Agency's task was to designate a developer for the Central Blocks. The federal urban renewal statute does not authorize local redevelopment agencies to engage in building activities directly; rather, their role is to assemble land for resale, at a marked-down price, to developers who agree to build according to agency plans. In the case of Yerba Buena Center, the private developer was to have special importance, for it was Justin Herman's decision that the financing and development of the entire twenty-one-acre Central Blocks area, public as well as private facilities, would go to a single private group. Public facilities would then be leased back to the City.

Herman's reasons for this unusual step were several. Private development of the sports arena, convention center, and other public facilities would obviate the need for public construction financing and hence the need for a public vote on a general obligation bond issue. Also, the agency could exercise direct and exclusive control over the development most effectively by having to deal with only a single partner. The development process would be speedier, Herman felt, and the "package" more attractive to the private developer if fees for construction of the public facilities were included. He made his decision despite the fact that a general obligation bond issue would be cheaper; that the South of Market Advisory Committee, headed by Supervisor Roger Boas, had recommended that type of financing; and that, based upon the information given out by the Redevelopment Agency, the Board of Supervisors presumed this would be the financing method when it approved the project in 1966. The August 25, 1965, *Chronicle*, for example, described the Redevelopment Agency's YBC plan as follows: "It would include the convention center and sports arena and parking for 3,300 cars, financed by a $42 million general obligation bond issue, supplemented by a one percent increase in the city's three percent hotel tax."[12] Herman felt that the delays and risks involved in a general obligation bond issue and public vote were to be avoided at all costs.

Herman's decision to rely on a single developer compounded the risks inherent in urban renewal projects. What is finally constructed on renewal sites tends to be more the product of subsequent negotiations between developers and agency officials, rather than procedure strictly according to the formally approved plan. A study of redevelopment in Newark in the late 1950s found that: "It is self-evident to NHA [Newark Housing Authority] officials that decisions on sites and their uses must be adapted to the demands of the investor if projects are to be successful."[13] And as one experienced corporate developer put it:

> A private redeveloper has got to have a lot of confidence in his local redevelopment authority to buy one of these programs. . . . He needs confidence that if he commits for a redevelopment which obligates him to build to a specific program over a substantial number of years, the redevelopment agency will be reasonably flexible in its insistence upon time schedules and in revisions of the program, where experience indicates the original concept to be uneconomic.[14]

Indeed, a redevelopment plan often represents little more than an open invitation to developers to engage in speculative promotions. Once a redevelopment plan is approved, the developer, not the public, becomes the single most influential client of the redevelopment agency.

Finding a single super-competent developer with diversified talents in bonding, leasing, planning, and construction willing to take on the entire Central Blocks area proved difficult. SFRA advertised for bids in June 1969. The search went slowly, and the initial deadline had to be extended. *Fortune* ads notwithstanding, only fourteen developers expressed any interest, and of those only five actually entered the competition.

Of the five, one immediately withdrew and another was unable to secure financing. The strongest of the remaining three was a joint venture of the Dillingham Corporation—a Hawaii-based land and engineering/construction giant that had developed Los Angeles's downtown Bunker Hill renewal project and San Francisco's Union Square Hyatt hotel—and Albert Schlesinger of Convention & Visitors Bureau fame, former chair of the city's Parking Authority, with an entrepreneur's talent for packaging and financing major projects. But Dillingham suddenly withdrew from the joint venture due to internal corporate disagreements about the wisdom of the project. Left were Terra California, a local consortium headed by San Francisco developer Harold Moose, who had built the Chinatown Holiday Inn,[15] and Arcon/Pacific, a partnership led by Bay Area architect/developer Lyman Jee, who had several small buildings to his credit. Schlesinger, left adrift with the collapse of the Dillingham venture, joined up with the Jee group, in a marriage reportedly arranged by Justin Herman, and in this greatly reduced competition the new partnership won handily. The group was a far cry from Justin Herman's original boast— "The development is of such proportions that I don't think there are more than three or four combines in all the world big enough to handle it"[16]— but under the circumstances it was the best that could be found. The group's proposal was conditionally adopted by the Redevelopment Agency in October 1970, and in March 1971 the decision was made final. Events, however, were to dictate that the City would jettison Justin Herman's plan and would itself take over development of the public facilities (see chapter 6).

"Protecting" the Central Blocks

One of the key planning concepts applied under Justin Herman was the "protected environment."[17] In essence, the idea was to create a *cordon sanitaire* around the renewal project's central development: peripheral construction that would provide an effective physical barrier to deter former residents from moving back into or adjacent to the area.* In San Francisco, the notion originally took shape with the Western Addition and Golden Gateway projects. As applied to Yerba Buena Center, "creating a protected environment" obviously meant large-scale demolition and people removal; it served as a code for ridding the area totally and permanently of its poor and "skid-row" populations. As the September 5, 1971, *Examiner* put it, "The late M. Justin Herman had planned to dot [the surrounding blocks] with office buildings . . . to create a powerful urban fortress." In the more graphic words of a Del Monte executive, "You certainly can't expect us to erect a 50 million dollar building in an area where dirty old men will be going around exposing themselves to our secretaries." While the gentleman's expressed concern was for female sensibilities, in reality, his concern had far more to do with the calculations of investors.

The Redevelopment Agency's plan was to surround the Central Blocks with high-rise office buildings totaling nearly 5 million square feet, classy shops, restaurants, and similar uses. This served the dual function of protecting the public facilities and providing a large number of office building sites to house the Bay Area's corporate activities.

Ridding the area of its existing population was thus a key part of the Redevelopment Agency's goals in the South of Market area and was regarded as a necessity if the downtown office area was to be successfully propelled across the Market Street divide. While forced displacement of the four thousand residents could not commence until the agency's plans were finally approved, not-so-subtle campaigns to purge the area were begun before the project's official starting date. In early 1966, the agency flooded the neighborhood with a pamphlet, illustrated by photos of napping and wine-sipping skid-row residents amidst heaps of rubbish, which stated, "They say this is good enough for you. . . . We say you deserve better." Several thousand of these pamphlets were mailed out, to all known residents of the renewal project area, although "the envelope in which the pamphlets were stuffed bore no return address."[18] Such propaganda efforts also nourished the image of South of Market as an area harboring people who were of little value to society and who might without qualm be transferred elsewhere.

*Most relocation studies, particularly of downtown area displacement projects, indicate that persons tend to relocate in a highly centripetal pattern. In a Minneapolis study, for example, 70 to 80 percent of the displacees moved within a one-mile radius, and in a New Jersey study 74 percent of the displacees moved within six blocks. See Chester W. Hartman, "The Housing of Relocated Families," *Journal of the American Institute of Planners* (November 1964), 266–86, reprinted in Chester Hartman, *Between Eminence and Notoriety: Four Decades of Radical Urban Planning* (New Brunswick, N.J.: Rutgers Center for Urban Policy Research, 2002), 74–104.

The concern expressed at the public hearings about proper relocation was handled with similar pamphleteering. Several weeks before the January 1966 Planning Commission hearings on the YBC plan, the agency distributed to area residents a brochure headed, "Of course Urban Renewal wants you out, but into safe, decent, comfortable housing you can afford." A photo was also included of Justin Herman presenting someone with a $457 check, headed "Money for the Holidays." (In a small block of tiny type, the recipient was identified as a former resident of the Golden Gateway project site. The leaflet was condemned as misleading and unethical by a group of concerned ministers working in the South of Market area.)[19]

The machinery was cranking up to cast out the old and bring in the new.

4 | The Neighborhood Fights Back

One of the greatest injustices in South of Market redevelopment has been the callous obliteration of the neighborhood's past. The name chosen by the Redevelopment Agency to dignify its project, "Yerba Buena" (Spanish for "good grass" or "good herb"), was the name of the original Spanish settlement that in 1847 became San Francisco. While preserving the old pioneering name serves public relations, in reality the project represents the destruction and eviction of a human past not regarded as worth acknowledging, much less honoring. The irony here is compounded by the fact that the original settlement was wrested from Mexican Californians by American pioneers in the Mexican-American War: The redevelopment process is but a more sophisticated wrinkle in the long American tradition of land grabbing.

Workingmen's Quarter

For nearly a century, the South of Market area, the site of Yerba Buena Center, had been a home to men and women whose lives and labors formed the rich tradition of San Francisco and the West.[1] Once also a haven for the wealthy, who moved out as the human and industrial wellsprings of their wealth closed in around them, South of Market gradually became a neighborhood populated mainly by single men: the workingmen, immigrants, transients, and hoboes who gathered to live, work, or just while away time between opportunities.

Jack London, himself born South of Market, described the division of the city's downtown area that persisted until the YBC project was devised to obliterate it. In his story "South of the Slot" (after the cable slot of the Market Street streetcars), he wrote: "Old San Francisco . . . was divided midway by the Slot. . . . North of the Slot were the theaters, hotels, and shopping district, the banks and the staid, respectable business houses. South of the Slot were the factories, slums, laundries, machine-shops, boiler works, and the abodes of the working class."[2]

There are South of Market areas in most American cities. Their primary economic function has been to shelter and maintain a reserve army of skilled and unskilled workers. Here grew up the workingmen's institutions in San Francisco: the hotels and lodging houses whose proprietors acted as bankers so that men spending their regular offseasons in the city had safekeeping for their money and could not splurge it on a single spree; saloons that furnished smorgasbord "free lunches" for ten to fifteen cents and sometimes doubled as informal employment agencies; pawnshops where a person might put up a tool or some clothing to pay for food, drink, or shelter; and, at one time, a dense network of fifty-one secondhand stores, employment agencies hiring mainly for out-of-town jobs (seven on a single block), poolrooms, movie theaters, barber colleges where apprentice barbers could practice and men got free haircuts, and the missions, varying in number with the season and the state of the economy. Until the mid-1920s, the neighborhood housed the local headquarters of the Industrial Workers of the World. Often on opposite street corners, bands, choirs, and preachers from the various missions, along with the IWW, could be heard singing different words to the same tune and making altogether different arguments. This network sheltered and supported the homeless: seamen, miners, woodcutters, men who built the railroads, agricultural and other seasonal workers, hoboes, bums, and the regular "home guard" of casual laborers who worked regularly or irregularly at unskilled jobs in the city.

The last half of the nineteenth century saw the beginning of a large-scale influx of both skilled and unskilled workers, resulting from greatly increased exploitation of western resources and the opening up of commercial activities in the Pacific region, stretching all the way to Asia. Between 1870 and 1880, the South of Market district became more congested as the city absorbed the many German, Irish, and English immigrants, families as well as single men. These same years marked a great expansion in the hotel, lodging, and boarding-house populations, continuing a tradition from the 1850s Gold Rush, when winter rains and snow drove thousands of miners to the Bay towns. Miners still returned to pass the winter pursuing the amusements of the city, joining sailors on leave and agricultural laborers from the valleys. Cyclical unemployment and the seasonal nature of many of the jobs held by South of Market residents led to great mobility; in none of the periods of 1871–76, 1880–85, and 1890–95 did more than 21 percent of the residents stay at the same address.

The 1906 earthquake and fire did heavy damage to the "made ground" over the large swamp originally covering South of Market and razed many of the area's wooden structures. Yet within three years, the city was largely rebuilt, including South of Market. Apartment and boarding houses and smaller dwellings reappeared along narrow alley streets, and hotels resumed their places along the major thoroughfares. By 1907, fifty-eight new hotels and eighty new lodging houses had been built. Small manufacturing, wholesaling, and warehousing concerns gradually rose again among these residences. The Irish and Germans who returned to their old neighborhood were joined by a large Greek community. This settlement, which occurred between 1910 and 1920, was at first largely composed of men who had worked their way across the country on railroad crews. They often opened tea or coffee houses and inexpensive restaurants, serving the Greek and other single men's communities. Other immigrants opened pawnshops and new and secondhand clothing stores. The formerly genteel South Park neighborhood just to the south became a mixed area of warehouses, machine shops, and flats housing a Japanese community. South of Market thus became a neighborhood of nearly every nationality.

Two "main stems" grew up after 1906 and remained for more than fifty years. Along Third Street, men came up to gamble in the many saloons with their special back rooms that doubled as "bookie joints," legal until 1938. On Howard Street, the men spent most of their time on the street, looking at blackboards advertising work, drinking, or pitching pennies on the sidewalk. The Howard Street area became known as the "slave market," due to the extraordinary exploitation and suffering to which migratory and unskilled workers were subjected. As most available employment was temporary and located away from the cities, the men forced into casual labor were left to the mercy of employment agencies and employers. The employers contracted with agencies to provide workers, and in turn the agencies sold the jobs for a fee, either paid in advance or out of a man's earnings. It was to the advantage of both employers and the agencies to have a large pool of unskilled and unemployed workers, who formed an industrial reserve army. Because they moved from job to job and from employer to employer, it was difficult for migratory workers and transients to organize for better pay and conditions. When they did take action, usually inspired by the IWW, it was by walking out on a temporary job, doing as little work as possible, or briefly striking. With the Depression, even the "slave market" disappeared, as there were no jobs to sell or buy, and those able to work were directed to public works projects.

In addition to fostering, sustaining, and relying on this industrial reserve army of job-hungry men, capitalist development as it occurred in California and other western states used men up in another sense. Exposure to the elements in rural jobs, the hazards of mining, logging, and construction work, lack of medical attention, insufficient diet, and arduous work made men either unable or unwilling to continue. They wore out early, with little provision by society for premature old age and premature retirement. Thus were created groups of retirees and casual workers who settled in the quarter they knew in order to pursue easier part-time or irregular work.

During World War II, heavy unemployment no longer characterized South of Market, as huge work demands provided ready jobs. In the war years, San Francisco became a dormitory metropolis housing war industry workers and military personnel. As newly arrived workers, seamen, soldiers, and sailors joined the traditional residents in the hotels, boarding houses, bars, and restaurants, South of Market temporarily revived. After the war, the cheap hotel district remained, and by 1950 single men represented 72 percent of the area's population.

Wartime brought to the South of Market one obvious change that also occurred in most northern cities, as well as in other parts of San Francisco: a substantial immigration of nonwhites. This migration of mainly black workers was followed by an influx of Asians. During the 1950s, South of Market was to become a reception area for a Filipino population of seasonal workers and, later, of family groupings.

South of Market remained a workingmen's quarter after World War II. Joining the transients and migratory workers were men who worked at the docks, warehouses, and factories surrounding the residential neighborhood, and, increasingly, those too old to work who found the network of cheap hotels and restaurants the only way of surviving on fixed pensions or welfare.

This was the character of South of Market when the redevelopment forces entered the picture in the 1950s, beginning the project that was to wipe the area clean of this past. Historian Kevin Starr's summation of the neighborhood captures its essence well:

> This district represents the most comprehensive paradigm of San Francisco. More than any other neighborhood in the city, South of Market is the part that contains the whole: the one matrix that subsumes unto

itself every successive layer of urban identity in the history of the city. Here indeed is the anchor district of San Francisco. . . . Here is the residential district of its most diverse population. . . . The other neighborhoods of the city . . . seem practically empty—or at the least mere occasions for residents—in comparison to the rich life of hotel, union hall, shipping, industrial manufacture, government office, newspaper room, church, school and orphanage, and residential life. South of Market was an urban district containing the full formula of the city.[3]

Remarkably, and only as a result of the community struggles and participatory planning chronicled in subsequent chapters, the area, although drastically transformed, has kept that character. As Starr notes, "South of Market, for all its transformations, still sustains a complex mix of residential, retail, hotel, government, small business, and light industrial uses in direct dialogue with its nineteenth-century formula."

"Skid Row" or Community?

About four thousand persons were living in the South of Market area slated for destruction to make way for Yerba Buena Center. Apart from some three hundred families, residents of South of Market were for the most part single, elderly, male, and poor, surviving on the meager proceeds of Social Security and small pensions. According to surveys undertaken for the Redevelopment Agency, 75 percent of the individual householders were more than forty-five years old, 94 percent were men, and 57 percent had incomes of less than two hundred dollars a month. Nearly 90 percent of all individual householders were white, although families living in the YBC project area were predominantly nonwhite.[4] Some were alcoholics. Most, however, were retired or disabled working men who had settled in the South of Market to spend the remaining days of their lives. The area and its forty-eight residential hotels provided them with inexpensive housing and eating places. The condition of these residential hotels varied, but a large portion was decent and sound housing, and still more was rehabilitable. That it was by no means the worst segment of the city's housing stock was indicated when the City's Public Welfare Commission in mid-1964 sent notices to 118 residential hotels warning that housing allowances to Old Age Security recipients (mainly single men and women) would be shut off in three months unless the buildings were fixed up; according to the May 22, 1964, *Examiner:* "Of the 118 buildings on the list, only five were in the South of Market district which formerly was regarded as the center of substandard housing here."

The area is sunny and flat, in a city where hills and fog abound. It is downtown, near Market Street, the city's transportation hub, and other facilities the residents needed. Most of all, it provided them with a community of other single men with common backgrounds, experience, and problems. People looked out for each other and took care of one another. Men gathered to talk, watch television, and just be with other people in the hotel lobbies, streets, restaurants, and bars. South of Market was their family and home. An *Examiner* feature from late 1965 gave some flavor of the positive aspects of life South of Market:

> William Colvin, a retired painting contractor, is typical. For years, he has lived in Room 409 of the Albany Hotel at 187 Third Street, where operator James W. Walker spent $15,000 last year for a new fire prevention sprinkler system. The rooms are clean, with a homey warmth.
>
> "Most people don't understand," Colvin said, "but let me tell you something. A man can enjoy freedom here. All of us have many friends. To us, this has been home for years. We enjoy life. . . . If you're ill, or hungry, your neighbors help. I don't think you'll find any finer people in the world. We're good citizens. . . . But most of all there is something spiritual about all this. It's something that money couldn't buy. We have something that couldn't be replaced with all the money our federal government could put in here. We like it the way it is. We want to stay. We don't want to be regimented by some agency."[5]

Throughout the hearing and planning stages for YBC, planners considered the fate of these people to be a minor matter. The area was referred to by the planners, newspapers, and City officials as "skid row," and the people who lived there were "bums," "drifters," and "transients."[6] Official agencies and the business community played on class prejudices, particularly of suburban commuters who daily passed through South of Market on their way between the Southern Pacific station and nearby office buildings and stores in the financial district and downtown shopping area. This carefully cultivated image of the residents of South of Market enabled the planners of Yerba Buena Center to present their project as a twofold public service: They were providing economic revival through construction jobs and increased tourist and convention business, and they were also helping the city clear out an "undesirable element."

But such labels were patently false. The most comprehensive social study of the area's population, prepared by a Redevelopment Agency consultant, noted that "Alcoholism, either alone or in concert with other disorders, accounted for only 15 percent [of the individuals living in the YBC area], although it stands out as the chief disorder among those enumerated."[7] The agency's attempt to dismiss the YBC area as a skid row also, of course, denied the important function the area served as a support system for those persons afflicted with alcoholism.* However, labeling of this sort permitted the power structure and the public at large to disregard or dismiss injustices being done to those who lived in the area. Property and profits were far more important than people.

But South of Market residents did not see it this way. When the Redevelopment Agency moved in and began to intimidate the residents and take away their homes, there were many who decided to resist. First acting individually, later collectively, the residents moved to oppose the destruction of their neighborhood. The heart of their struggle was a complex court battle in which they tried to secure their legal rights to decent relocation housing and to be free of the harassing tactics of the Redevelopment Agency.

Housing: The Key

Given the formidable backing for the YBC project and its lengthy preparation period, the prospects of stopping the juggernaut altogether seemed remote. What these South of Market residents were thus compelled to focus on—and what according to law was their right—was decent, safe, and sanitary relocation housing at rents they could afford. Federal law required the local renewal agency to guarantee "that there are or are being provided, in the urban renewal area or in other areas not generally less desirable in regard to public utilities and public and commercial facilities and at rents or prices within the financial means of the families and individuals displaced from the urban renewal area, decent, safe, sanitary dwellings equal in number to the number of, and available to, such displaced families and individuals and reasonably accessible to their places of employment."[8] The residents' principal issue was that the Redevelopment Agency was either unwilling or unable to properly and legally relocate the three thousand single residents and 280 families in the area.

---

*As sociologist Ronald Vander Kooi notes: "The social character of skid row, with its easy acceptance, friendship, and money for lodging, makes it a desirable place for those who have no home affiliations. . . . Since skid row is so very social, with only the most pathological of men drinking alone in their rooms or seeking isolation, demolition of skid row means that gathering places are razed and cronies separated. . . . Skid row residents . . . suffer from loneliness as old friends disperse to other parts of the city or even to other towns. . . . [W]ell over 100,000 skid rowers today face an immediate crisis in their new homelessness caused by the destruction of skid rows and their dislocation by urban renewal." From "The Main Stem: Skid Row Revisited," *Society* (September/October 1973): 67, 71.

Since these people were by and large single, mostly poor, and for the most part elderly or physically disabled, their housing was a special type: furnished residential and transient hotels at very low rents, unavailable in most other parts of the city. The agency's 1963 survey of the project population found that 37 percent of the individuals paid a monthly gross rent of less than thirty dollars, while 79 percent paid less than forty dollars.[9] In addition, it was likely that another three thousand people in the surrounding areas would be displaced from their hotel and boardinghouse residences as these were sold to take advantage of rising property values in the vicinity of YBC.[10]

The full dimensions of the problems could be seen only in the context of other concurrent public projects involving large-scale displacement. The Golden Gateway project, also in the downtown area, had destroyed the homes of two hundred single men and two dozen families living near the San Francisco waterfront. The Western Addition A-2 project, in the mostly black Fillmore district, was displacing 13,500 people. Even though neighborhood opposition to A-2 had resulted in the construction of several publicly assisted housing projects, there was a gap of many years before completed projects could provide housing for displaced residents, the number of replacement units did not come close to equaling the number torn down, and new rents were far higher than old rents. Displacement was occurring in the predominantly black Bayview–Hunters Point area, as well as from minor public projects (such as the extension of a state highway and city street that destroyed two residential hotels totaling 150 units in the vicinity of YBC), code enforcement in nearby Chinatown, and private clearance. According to a 1969 City Planning Department report, some 6,000 housing units had been destroyed in redevelopment areas, while only 662 units of publicly aided (i.e., low- or moderate-income) housing had been built in these areas.[11]

Further cause for alarm was the Redevelopment Agency's record on relocation, particularly in the late 1950s and early 1960s in the Western Addition A-1 project. There, more than four thousand households, mostly low-income African American and Asian families, were dispersed throughout the Bay Area. Many displaced families and persons had to move to other cities and communities in the East Bay or on the Peninsula; others settled in the area adjacent to Western Addition A-1—thus finding themselves in the path of Western Addition A-2 bulldozers just a few years later.

The poor housing, higher rents, and generally unsatisfactory relocation experience of the Western Addition A-1 residents had been well analyzed, after the fact, by scholars and government agencies, and the accompanying condemnation of the Redevelopment Agency served to alert others to the dangers of relocation. A U.S. Comptroller General's study of SFRA files on Western Addition A-1 relocatees listed as satisfactorily closed found that nearly half of those examined had moved to unsatisfactory housing or were forced to accept massive rent increases. About one-fourth of the dislocated A-1 residents were moved into deteriorated housing in the A-2 area and subsequently forced to undergo relocation a second time.[12] It was from Western Addition A-1 and projects like it around the country that redevelopment and urban renewal became known as "Negro removal."

SFRA's relocation plans for South of Market had been approved by the U.S. Department of Housing and Urban Development in 1966, along with federal approval of the entire YBC plan. Under the plan, only 176 units of new housing were to be built for displaced residents. These were to be in Clementina Towers, a San Francisco Housing Authority project on Fourth Street for senior citizens. This small number of replacement units for four thousand persons was supposedly justified by surveys that used a "turnover factor" to calculate the number of rooms available to displaced persons on a citywide basis.

"Turnover" was an incredible piece of statistical legerdemain. The game involved estimating the frequency with which an occupied unit is vacated and reoccupied. If it is assumed that on average all residential hotel rooms are vacated and reoccupied once every three months, a "turnover factor" of four is then applied to get the annual number of vacancies; and to project available vacancies over a five-year period, a turnover factor of twenty is applied. Based on this reasoning, the agency estimated that in a five-year period no fewer than thirty thousand vacant low-rent hotel rooms would be available for occupancy by YBC displacees.[13]

The turnover concept is obviously invalid and misleading, since it confuses mobility from one unit to another with true vacancies—those that are excess housing supply, above the amount needed to house local residents and provide for normal mobility. Only units in the excess housing supply can legitimately be counted on for relocation purposes, else relocation becomes a game of "musical chairs"—an apt metaphor, given the constant destruction of low-rent units for urban renewal and other programs, and the removal of still other units from the low-rent stock caused by rent increases, caused in turn by increased competition for the decreasing number of available units.

The federal government and most real estate experts consider a vacancy rate of 4 to 6 percent necessary to a healthy housing market, to allow for population growth, mobility, adequate housing choice, and systematic removal of substandard units. HUD regulations were subsequently amended to require one-for-one replacement of units destroyed by HUD-assisted actions when the vacancy rate drops below 3 percent. A 1969 citizen's group report, based on City Planning Department studies, found that "for units, other than studios, renting under $100 per month, the vacancy rate is zero percent."[14] And because of the obvious fallacies in this technique of "relocation planning," in 1968, two years after it had approved the YBC relocation plan, HUD barred the use of the turnover methodology by local renewal agencies.

The city's tight housing market for low-income people in 1969 was to be the precursor of a massive housing cost and availability crisis that emerged during the 1970s for moderate- and middle-income San Franciscans and exists *a fortiori* to this day.

TOOR

In all the planning and marshaling of support for Yerba Buena Center in the 1950s and 1960s, the group conspicuously absent was the area residents. Federal urban renewal statutes contained a somewhat vague "citizen participation" requirement, calling for involvement of individuals, organizations, and interest groups in the planning process. During the 1960s, when Yerba Buena planning was carried out, the group designated to fulfill the citizen participation requirement for *all* the city's renewal projects was SPUR. As the city's official Citizens Action Committee, SPUR in 1966 issued a publication entitled *Prologue for Action*, from which are taken the following statements, made at the time the Yerba Buena project was receiving its approvals from the Board of Supervisors and other City agencies:

> If San Francisco decides to compete effectively with other cities for new "clean" industries and new corporate power, its population will move closer to standard white Anglo-Saxon Protestant characteristics. As automation increases, the need of unskilled labor will decrease. Economically and socially, the population will tend to range from lower middle-class through lower upper-class. . . .
> Selection of a population's composition might be undemocratic. Influence on it, however, is legal and desirable for the health of the city. A workable though changing balance of economic levels, social types, age levels, and other factors must be maintained. Influence on these factors should be exerted in many ways—for example, changing the quality of housing, schools, and job opportunities.

Thus, the welfare of the elderly, single, poor working people of South of Market was placed in the hands of the city's corporate and financial interests. The area's residents were kept in the dark about their fate. An *Examiner* series on YBC residents quoted people as saying, "We don't know what they're going to do. . . . " "Nobody has spelled out the details. . . . " "We're all confused. . . . " "When the plans are ready—they're ready."[15] It was only when the Redevelopment Agency began to acquire buildings, evict occupants, and demolish structures, and urban renewal became a living, frightening reality, that real participation of the area's residents began, as they organized to defend themselves.

It was the Redevelopment Agency's own extreme pressure tactics on hotel occupants that provided residents with their best organizing tool. While coordinated population displacement and hotel demolition had in fact been going on in the area for several years, official displacement of YBC residents began in 1967 and accelerated in 1968–69, as the Redevelopment Agency went in and bought hotels and other buildings and cleared land wherever it could. The attempt by private investors in the 1958–61 period (after the Board of Supervisors had removed the area's "blight" designation) to undertake nonassisted redevelopment of the area had led to the demolition of ten hotels and displacement of some five hundred persons. And City housing code enforcement had the effect, if not the intent, of further reducing the population. Parking lots, the profitable "interim" use (sometimes lasting over a decade) to which urban renewal sites are often put, were studding the area as hotel after hotel came down.

By mid-1969, the agency had acquired 44 percent of the land in the project area. On taking over hotels, the agency adopted a "no vacancy" policy, designed to keep pressure on residents to move out of the area; a further consequence was to turn hotels into lonely, partially occupied, intimidating, and dangerous places, hastening the departure of remaining residents. Often displacement was carried out by private owners in anticipation of agency takeover of their properties, which meant giving residents almost no notice.[16]

For many pensioners, accustomed to forty-dollar- and fifty-dollar-per-month rents, relocation was a terrifying experience. Those who could afford it moved across Market Street into the Tenderloin District, where rents were steep, hills steeper, and the crime rate steeper still, and where development pressures were to intensify in the 1970s. Others found another hotel South of Market, keeping one step ahead of the Redevelopment Agency's bulldozers. Eviction and demolition were swift, sometimes not even allowing residents the full notice required by law. One early instance of what the

Chronicle labeled the "swift, sharp slum ax" involved the Irwin Hotel. In its rush to tear down the Irwin, the agency neglected to give residents the full ninety-day notice they were entitled to by law, which evoked a protest—but nothing more—from HUD.[17]

The Redevelopment Agency's management practices, combined with the absence of repair and code enforcement services by other City agencies, markedly hastened the deterioration of the South of Market area. Partly in order to insulate itself from public criticism, the agency contracted for outside management of hotels until the time came for relocation and demolition. Old-time hotel staff who performed important and friendly functions in the lives of the old people were replaced by often insensitive and incompetent clerks and maintenance personnel. In large part as a result of agency policy to hasten the departure of remaining guests, conditions and services at the hotels deteriorated rapidly. Heat and hot water were shut off because of "boiler problems"; lobby doors were kept locked and residents admitted only upon showing identification; linens were unavailable and maid service terminated; hall toilets were locked; comfortable lobby chairs were replaced by benches and camp chairs; mail and messages got lost; rubbish stood uncollected; desk clerks and security guards drank, slept on the job, and were insolent and on occasions physically abusive to residents.[18]

In hotel after hotel, residents signed petitions demanding better security and improved maintenance, and clergy or staff from social service agencies accompanied the protestors as advocates to negotiate with the Redevelopment Agency for better living conditions. Conditions in the hotels taken over by the agency turned dangerous. Many of the older men became afraid to leave their rooms because of increasing robberies and threats. The most violent of these attacks was the robbery and murder of James Gregory in December 1970, in the agency-owned Westchester Hotel. Ironically, the month before, Gregory had been one of the signers of a residents' petition to the Redevelopment Agency asking for improved security at the Westchester, a move that the agency rejected.[19]

A somewhat more ingratiating approach was taken by the agency in its New Start Center, an alcoholic treatment program located in a YBC hotel and run in conjunction with the City's Departments of Public Health and Social Services. The center was established in 1966, largely as a response to social workers' protests against the project voiced at the time of the public hearings. The agency held up the New Start Center as an example of its humane treatment of YBC residents and its people-oriented approach. But residents and other critics of the agency charged that the center was merely a "soft cop" approach to population displacement, facilitating the task of moving people out of the hotels and disseminating a false public image of the area as skid row. An agency publication, "Breaking the Frisco Circle: The True Story of an Innovative Approach to the Problem of Alcoholism in San Francisco's Skid Row," suggested the center had propaganda functions as well. Posing the question, "Who are the people in the Yerba Buena Center area who need New Start's medical, psychological, social and economic help?" the brochure, after responding that not all are skid-row alcoholics and that there are no "typical" residents of the area, answered: ". . . those seen most frequently on television protesting rehousing are not truly representative either." One of the more obvious questions about New Start and similar attempts by City renewal officials to stress the "human services" aspects of their work was why these services, if they were so valuable, were not made available independent of the redevelopment process.

As housing was torn down, area residents desperately began to search for a way to stop this forced removal. Many went to the South of Market office of the San Francisco Neighborhood Legal Assistance Foundation (SFNLAF), the federally funded Legal Services agency for low-income clients. They complained vehemently of the tactics employed by SFRA's relocation workers in emptying the hotels, the quality of relocation offerings made to hotel residents, and the housing to which many had already been forced to move.

The first real step toward resistance came in 1968, when the Legal Services attorneys filed a petition with HUD asking for an administrative hearing on the Redevelopment Agency's relocation plan. HUD denied the residents' petition on the remarkable reasoning that little actual displacement had yet occurred. But residents were being displaced, and the HUD response, together with city hall indifference, made them even angrier and more determined to fight it out. In the spring of 1969, South of Market residents and their SFNLAF attorneys tried once again to get HUD to reexamine the feasibility of the Yerba Buena relocation plan. Several letters were sent to HUD over a four-month period; the responses were uniformly evasive and unreasonable, contending that since HUD had no mechanism for hearing residents' complaints about relocation it was impossible to entertain these objections.

In the summer of 1969, residents began meeting in the lobby of the Milner Hotel, one of the area's better maintained and more prestigious hotels. Milner residents were to become the backbone of the struggle against the agency and for the rights and welfare of area residents. As one Milner resident put it after the first meeting, "Nobody invited me down here, and nobody is going to invite me out." Out of these meetings came the decision to establish a formal organization, Tenants and Owners in Opposition to Redevelopment (TOOR).

TOOR's organizing efforts took the usual forms, distributing leaflets and literature in the area's hotels to inform people of their rights and urge them to come to meetings. Some of the more active residents, along with a few young VISTA volunteers working and living in the area, went around the neighborhood to talk with people in hotels and with families living in flats located on the side streets. The poor health and advanced age of many of the area's residents left them incapable of engaging in militant activity and precluded TOOR's becoming a true membership organization. Solidarity was achieved through bulletins and leaflets sent regularly to residents and through mobilizing actions around Redevelopment Agency and supervisors' hearings and carefully planned protests and demonstrations. Monthly informational meetings were held, attended on the average by sixty to eighty persons, and the group also sponsored free Friday night films and provided members referrals for health and welfare problems. The TOOR office became a dropping-in spot for area residents who wanted to discuss their problems. TOOR was not an angry mass of people disrupting meetings and sitting in; it was a relatively small organization whose leaders represented the residents' interests, and its organizational strategies were adapted to the particular conditions and limitations of its constituency.

For the many retired trade unionists living in the area, organizing their fellow residents against the bulldozer harked back to organizing efforts in building the labor movement three and four decades earlier. TOOR's elected chair was eighty-year-old George Woolf, an organizer and first president of the San Francisco–based Alaska Cannery Workers' Union and earlier president of the Ship Scalers Union (later an affiliate of the ILWU). Woolf was intimately involved in the San Francisco progressive labor movement in the late 1920s and early 1930s and had his front teeth knocked out during the city's 1934 General Strike. After his retirement in 1954, he organized his fellow ILWU retirees into the Pensioners' Club, a "union within the union."[20] * He described himself by saying, "I've lived my life so that I can look any man in the eye and tell him to go to hell" (see fig. 1a). His attitude

---

*Woolf's historic and close ties to the ILWU were of no avail in seeking help from his union. He wrote ILWU international president Harry Bridges asking for support and got this 26 November 1969, reply: "Dear George: I want to tell you frankly

toward the Redevelopment Agency was uncompromising. A newspaper interview with George Woolf noted that "it was a casual remark by Redevelopment director M. Justin Herman which started him in battle."[21] Herman had reportedly called the residents of the South of Market area "nothing but a bunch of skid row bums." Woolf was indignant—"I'm not a bum and I resent being discredited and discounted." He responded by helping to create TOOR.

Co-chair of TOOR was Peter Mendelsohn, for forty years a merchant seaman who lived on the same South of Market block when he returned from the sea. Although sixty-five years old, Mendelsohn had more energy than most people thirty years younger. Like George Woolf, Mendelsohn was a union organizer and also organized for the Communist Party in the 1930s.* When Mendelsohn returned from his final voyage in the summer of 1970, he discovered that the Redevelopment Agency had taken over his hotel. He briefly visited relatives and on his return found that his room had been broken into and robbed of all his valuables, which were quite substantial, as he had been a coin collector for years. Referring to the agency's plans to move him to another neighborhood, Mendelsohn said: "I've lived on this block for 40 years. I know everyone here and they know me. To move me even five blocks away would be the same as moving me to another city. It'll take years for me to build up new relationships, and years off my life in the process." When George Woolf died in June 1972, Pete Mendelsohn became TOOR's chair.

With a staff consisting of Sandra Marks, a community organizer from Canon Kip Community House, and Stephen Dutton, a former San Fran-

---

that I don't feel sympathetic to the position outlined; and the enclosed fact sheet from Redevelopment truly does set forth the facts as far as I have been able to check. Harry."

*Mendelsohn's attempts to secure union support were no more successful than Woolf's. John Elberling, later to become head of TOOR's housing development group, provided this vignette: "Before he died in 1988, Peter Mendelsohn showed me TOOR's letter to Harry Bridges appealing for help to stop Redevelopment's demolition. . . . 'We are your Brothers,' they wrote. 'We fought the bosses together. We stood with you against the police and strikebreakers on the Embarcadero during the General Strike. We sailed with you in the Merchant Marine during the War. The Redevelopment Agency is taking our homes. It's all we have. We need your help.' Bridges had returned the original letter, with a handwritten answer in the margin, 'Sorry, but I'm on the other side [in] this, Harry.' Peter cried. I asked him the next week for a copy, but he said he burned it because he was too ashamed." (See Elberling's essay in Ira Nowinski's forthcoming photography book, *No Vacancy*, updated edition.)

cisco State urban studies graduate student, office space at the Milner Hotel, and a few contributions to cover postage, phones, and mimeographing, TOOR moved into action.

"We Won't Move"

TOOR centered its organizing activities around one goal: decent rehousing for South of Market residents. The residents were under no illusions that housing conditions in the area were uniformly adequate, and they conceded that some of the neighborhood's hotels needed to be torn down—although they pointed out that the advanced state of deterioration of many hotels was due to the Redevelopment Agency's neglect, intentionally brought about by its failure to maintain the buildings. While the problem was seen as part of an overall citywide shortage of decent low-rent housing, TOOR put forth explicit demands to be rehoused in the same neighborhood. The desirability of the area in terms of older residents' needs; their familiarity with the surroundings; the obvious defects of alternative nearby areas with residential hotels; and their adamancy not to be bulldozed out of San Francisco altogether, all meant that the residents took their stand in and for the South of Market neighborhood they knew and inhabited. These demands obviously clashed with Justin Herman's concept of a "protected environment" for Yerba Buena Center. They also were completely contrary to Herman's sentiments about YBC, expressed at a lawyers' conference in the mayor's office: "This land is too valuable to permit poor people to park on it."

TOOR's slogan was "We Won't Move," but it had a less than literal interpretation. Clearly, many persons would have to move, since some of the existing hotels were unsalvageable, and remaining on the Central Blocks slated for the convention and sports facilities did not appear feasible. "We Won't Move" therefore meant: "We won't move from the blocks needed for the public facilities unless and until we are given decent relocation housing, in the same general neighborhood." The organization was convinced that the Redevelopment Agency and the City would meet its demands only if they had no other choice. TOOR's central tactic therefore became holding onto its turf as long as possible. Its goal was to force the City to build or rehabilitate, in or immediately adjacent to the project area, relocation housing that would be permanently reserved for South of Market displacees and other low-income persons.

The corporate community's plans to make South of Market part of the city's central office district were obvious to anyone with even a minimal understanding of the economic and political forces at work in the Bay Area.

As an SFRA brochure trumpeted: "Yerba Buena Center is only the beginning. Much of the remaining area south of Market is seriously blighted. Hopefully, Yerba Buena Center will stimulate private rebuilding on this land to provide the best in urban living."

TOOR's fears of a complete transformation of South of Market were not based on speculation; there was good evidence of other development projects in the works or shortly forthcoming: office development east of YBC, reconstruction of the Transbay Transit Terminal at First and Mission, gentrification of the small black residential enclave in South Park, and other projects. The further transformation of the South of Market area in the 1970s, 1980s, and 1990s shows these fears to have been well grounded.

Out of Site, Out of Mind

TOOR's insistence that South of Market residents not be moved out of the area was based on evidence and impressions that forced relocation was causing and would continue to cause economic, emotional, and health problems. These conclusions were borne out by the results of several surveys undertaken in conjunction with the legal battles around Yerba Buena Center.

A HUD report "found that one-third of these [remaining] South of Market single residents were incapable of paying more than $40 per month rent. Another 47 percent can pay no more than $60," at a time when units renting for under $60 were "acutely tight" in San Francisco.[22] A study undertaken by the National Housing Law Project showed parallel results.[23] Among the seventy-one relocatees found and interviewed, almost all had relocated into other downtown hotels, mainly in the Tenderloin and just west of the project area. It was clear that South of Market residents were moving a very short distance from their old neighborhood because the only alternative quarters were located in these areas and because they wanted to remain in a central location.

As for housing costs, the Law Project survey showed that the median monthly rent in the YBC area prior to relocation was forty-five dollars; after relocation, it was sixty-four dollars, an increase of more than 40 percent. Almost everyone had experienced a rent increase—some as high as fifty dollars or more per month. An Arthur D. Little, Inc./URS Research Company study of Redevelopment Agency records on persons displaced from the YBC area between December 1969 and December 1972 showed that of the 250 displacees for whom such information was available, 87 percent had experienced a rent increase, 8 percent a rent decrease. The median monthly rent increase was thirty-six dollars.[24] And with the city's general shortage of low-rent residential hotels, which YBC was exacerbating, upward spiraling rents in the coming years were an inevitability. One-fourth of the persons interviewed in the National Housing Law Project survey had already received a rent increase within a few months after moving to their new quarters. For persons living on low fixed incomes of around two hundred dollars, often less, per month, an added rent burden of even a few dollars could be catastrophic, forcing corresponding cuts in their budgets for food, medical care, transportation, and other necessities of life.

Even those former residents receiving "relocation adjustment payments"—less than a third of those for whom adequate agency records were available, and doubtless a considerably lower proportion of the total displaced population—faced serious difficulties. (The Arthur D. Little/URS study reported that only 31.5 percent of the displacees for whom agency records were available received rental assistance payments. Since it can safely be assumed that no one who was not on the official caseload was receiving these government payments, which were administered by the Redevelopment Agency, the percentage of total displacees aided by these subsidies was substantially lower.) Under the 1970 Uniform Relocation Act, tenants relocated by urban renewal projects were entitled to up to one thousand dollars per year for four years (eighty-three dollars per month) to make up the difference between 25 percent of income and the cost of decent replacement housing. (For those relocated prior to 1971, the maximum annual amount was five hundred dollars, and the grants lasted only two years.) Not everyone of course received the maximum amount. One-fifth of those interviewed reported that the payment did not cover the actual amount of the rent increase. And all recipients had to face the problem that after a few years the subsidy would end and they would be forced either to absorb the full rental cost or to move to less expensive locations, likely also to be less adequate. Problems like these did not seem to bother the Redevelopment Agency. Addressing a class at San Francisco State University, a key agency official, in response to a question of what happens to people in the YBC area after relocation payments run out, answered, "Life is short."

But life would not be short enough to avoid other financial difficulties revealed in the survey interviews. Many persons reported that landlords were requiring security deposits to move into relocation housing, sums that displacees either could not afford at all or that proved very burdensome to persons with few savings. And most relocatees indicated that their expenses for food had increased since moving from South of Market, which was known for its cheap restaurants.

One of the most disturbing survey findings was the high proportion of relocatees who were not traceable within a short time after having supposedly been satisfactorily relocated by the Redevelopment Agency. More than one-fourth of the people on the agency's official list of persons relocated since December 1969 were not living at the address indicated by the agency and were untraceable at the time of the National Housing Law Project summer 1971 survey. And 18 percent of the persons on the official 1969–72 agency caseload whose records were examined for the Arthur D. Little/URS study were listed as being in an "unknown location." Once officially "relocated," the agency's legal responsibility for and interest in the fate of the South of Market residents was at an end—as one of TOOR's attorneys later put it, the agency's "out of site, out of mind" policy.

The interviews also revealed the disruption of social networks caused by displacement. For older people in particular, personal friendships are perhaps the most important aspect of day-to-day life. Loss of familiar faces in the streets and in the hotel lobbies, of people to talk to, eat, drink, and play cards with is a severe shock. Similarly, the loss of stores, restaurants, and other commercial institutions can rob people of an important basis of stability, a place to obtain credit, to meet friends. According to an account in the November 19, 1969, *San Francisco Progress:*

> These [1900 remaining] people are finding it tougher to get along South of Market. The grocery stores and saloons they went to are being closed and ripped down. The cleaning establishment they took their clothes to is closed up—the place boarded up—the little hotel next door is a sandy depression behind the high Redevelopment Agency fence.
>
> This isn't the same place it was, two years ago before demolition began in earnest.
>
> The balance is being tipped in favor of Yerba Buena Center. It is frightening, bewildering and angering to the people who remain. They don't want to leave.[25]

The popular image of South of Market put forth by the Redevelopment Agency and its booster club—extremely transient and therefore easily dismissible—was flatly contradicted by data from the National Housing Law Project survey: More than half the persons interviewed had lived in the same hotel for at least six years, and one-third had lived in the same hotel for ten years or more. Roots in the South of Market neighborhood as a whole were doubtless even deeper, given the frequent movement from one hotel to another within the area. Leaving South of Market was not merely a matter of locating a new room or apartment; for many residents, it represented a complete disruption of their lives.

But mere complaints about poor treatment, coming from low-income South of Market residents whom the City wanted out quickly, cut little ice at city hall or the Redevelopment Agency. It became clear very soon after the initial TOOR organizing meeting in early 1969 that the only way to make the redevelopment power structure listen was to take the matter to the courts.

Into the Courts

HUD's unwillingness to provide administrative relief to Yerba Buena relocatees gave the South of Market residents no choice but to turn to litigation. On November 5, 1969, represented by a half-dozen named individuals and TOOR, they filed a complaint in federal district court against both HUD and the Redevelopment Agency, contending that the agency had not located decent, safe, and sanitary housing for displacees according to rights set forth in the 1949 Housing Act.

The WACO Case

The decision to bring suit against the YBC project was inspired by a partly successful action the year before, which the San Francisco Neighborhood Legal Assistance Foundation filed against the Western Addition A-2 project. The Western Addition Community Organization (WACO) had begun a drive in the mid-1960s to exact from the Redevelopment Agency guarantees of decent housing for all displacees. Failing these guarantees and having experienced the havoc wrought by the Western Addition A-1 project, WACO enlisted SFNLAF's aid and filed for an injunction against relocation, demolition, and federal funding in Western Addition A-2 pending a valid relocation plan. SFRA and HUD responded by claiming that residents of renewal areas lacked standing (i.e., had no legal right) to challenge inadequacies in relocation plans, and that HUD's decision on the adequacy of such plans was at the sole and unreviewable discretion of the HUD Secretary. The court rejected these patently unjust claims. There was no cogent agency explanation as to why residents of HUD-assisted renewal areas were not allowed to defend their own interests, nor was there any reasonable argument why the Secretary of HUD should be protected from judicial review (which didn't stop the agency from advancing the same two arguments in its response to TOOR's subsequent Yerba Buena relocation suit).

WACO's case was aided by strong evidence of inequities. HUD's own records revealed that its approval of relocation in Western Addition A-2 hinged upon satisfying several stipulations. Finding that these conditions had not been satisfied, Federal Judge William T. Sweigert held in December 1968 that HUD's approval was arbitrary, capricious, and therefore invalid. Under these circumstances, the judge found it necessary, in order to avoid irreparable injury to residents, to halt the project until a plan could be lawfully and unconditionally approved by HUD.[1] Judge Sweigert dissolved his preliminary injunction less than four months later, when the agency filed and HUD unconditionally approved a slightly revised relocation plan.

The court's Western Addition decision, while a useful precedent for the Yerba Buena litigation, was by no means a far-reaching protection of people's rights. The court did not rule on the substance of the agency's relocation plan, nor did it agree that the courts should preempt the HUD Secretary's judgment on these matters. It merely ruled that HUD must comply with its own regulations and with federal statutes.[2]

Nonetheless, for the first time in the twenty-year history of urban renewal, a court had actually enjoined an urban renewal project[3]—and that was more than enough to inspire TOOR and its attorneys.

A Quest for Compromise

The November 1969 lawsuit seeking adequate relocation housing for the South of Market residents was accompanied by a motion for immediate injunctive relief. The residents had obtained as counsel two lawyers from the SFNLAF central office—Sidney Wolinsky (who had brought the WACO suit) and Amanda Hawes—and as co-counsel J. Anthony Kline of the National Housing Law Project, one of the specialized government-funded "back-up" centers for local Legal Services offices, then part of the law school at the University of California, Berkeley. At the core of the residents' plea were flaws in the turnover formula underlying the YBC relocation plan. More than three years had passed since HUD's original approval of the plan, and since 1966, the city's low-rent housing supply had actually decreased, contrary to the turnover formula's projections.

TOOR filed some compelling exhibits: agency building inspectors' records showed that many "approved" relocation resources were in poor physical condition, had illegal wiring, an absence of dual means of egress and fire exit signs, locked doors preventing access to fire escapes, and other serious infractions. Most of this evidence had been available to HUD in 1966; it evidently chose to look the other way.

TOOR shored up its evidence by commissioning the Bureau of Social Science Research to conduct a vacancy survey of the hotels the agency was using for relocation. After eliminating vacant units renting for more than a hundred dollars per month (a level well above then-prevailing rents in the hotels) and those for which agency inspection sheets showed gross physical deficiencies, the survey team counted only some two hundred vacancies citywide. This survey exposed the extraordinarily small number of decent low-rent units in San Francisco, at a time when "turnover theory" predicted just the opposite.[4] TOOR also submitted official police statistics showing the high incidence of crimes against persons in the areas to which most YBC displacees were being relocated—Sixth Street and the Tenderloin. These data were particularly important, since older persons are especially vulnerable to muggings and street crime. Impersonal statistics were accompanied by some sixty affidavits from present and former residents of the YBC area describing personal experiences as displacees and their fears of being displaced.

Street crime and harassment took on new meaning once TOOR filed its suit. Eddie Heider, one of the named plaintiffs, was viciously attacked on the day the suit was filed. The incident took place as he was returning to his Tenderloin hotel following a conversation with an attorney in the SFNLAF office. Witnesses to the attack, including several federal employees, stated under oath that Heider, who weighed scarcely 120 pounds and was nearly 65, was jumped by a large man. The man made no attempt to rob him and warned a young VISTA employee who tried to intercede, "I'll get you next."[5] Another named plaintiff, Joseph Padron, came to the SFNLAF office with a paper a relocation worker had asked him to sign. Padron recounted a bizarre tale of several night visits to his hotel room by an agency relocation worker, who wanted Padron's signature on a slip of paper saying:

> I, Joseph Padron, under penalty of perjury, hereby state that I have secured a place of my own that is convenient to my plan [sic] of employment and where I have friends.
>
> I have no objection to the agency Personnel and Service in helping me to move from the Colorado Hotel.
>
> Since I have been able to move to a better place, I have no further wish to be assisted with the lawsuit by the San Francisco Neighborhood

Legal Assistance Foundation on behalf of the Engineered Group known as the Tenants and Owners in Opposition to Redevelopment (TOOR).[6]

According to the April 29, 1970, *Daily Commercial News,* Justin Herman denounced reports of such incidents against YBC displacees as a "complete hoax" (following an investigation by three high-ranking agency employees) and even charged SFNLAF attorneys with "deliberately and scandalously" staging a series of phony incidents designed to discredit the agency. But the federal court in December 1969 was to issue the first of several restraining orders against interference with the residents' First Amendment and statutory rights. And in 1972, Frank Hagan, an elderly resident who had sought damages after being beaten in his own hotel by a drunken security guard hired by the Redevelopment Agency, was awarded twelve hundred dollars by a court.

Action on the TOOR suit got under way in December 1969 when Federal Judge Stanley A. Weigel conducted the first of three hearings on TOOR's contentions. Influential in these court hearings were SFRA data showing that among the first group moved out of the area, two-thirds of whom had moved via agency referrals, 44 percent were forced to pay at least one-third of their income for rent. At the conclusion of the first day, the court, expressing its concern that YBC residents were not receiving fair treatment, issued a temporary restraining order halting involuntary relocation and demolition inside YBC pending an opportunity to rule on the motion for an injunction.

In hotels where relocation efforts had not started, the court order was greeted with great relief, but in those hotels where relocation workers were already making their rounds, the order afforded little protection. The agency still posted notices in hotel lobbies, informing residents they had to move, and agency workers were visiting site residents in some cases four, five, and six times a day, trying to persuade them to move voluntarily. The Redevelopment Agency viewed the order as merely stopping state court eviction proceedings against tenants failing to move within the ninety-day period set by the relocation plan.[7]

The week before the third and last full court hearing in March 1970, TOOR's counsel appealed to Judge Weigel for a protective order preserving the residents' status pending a decision on the basic relocation and housing issues. At this hearing, the court dictated an order prohibiting all relocation activities except in instances where residents signed a notarized statement attesting to the voluntary nature of the action.

Still, SFRA relocation workers zealously pursued their quarry. One of the last residents of the Daton Hotel was visited in the hospital by two relocation workers and a notary. The relocation workers had already placed the woman's possessions in storage "for safekeeping" when she was hospitalized, making her forcible relocation an accomplished fact.

Although the Redevelopment Agency demonstrated outright resistance to preliminary court orders, Judge Weigel continued to urge the parties to reach a relocation settlement in order to avert judicial decision. Shortly after the March hearing, the court convened a settlement discussion at which SFRA, to avoid the possibility of a favorable court ruling on TOOR's request for an injunction, agreed to produce fifteen hundred units of low-cost housing. The court required SFRA to submit regular reports on the promised units, reserving the right to release the parties from the agreement at any time and rule on the original motion.

Almost immediately, it became clear that the agency had no intention of fulfilling the spirit of the agreement. TOOR learned the agency was planning to discharge its promise of fifteen hundred units by counting public housing already scheduled for construction, not through housing it would provide specially for YBC displacees. This meant TOOR would be taking low-rent housing away from others equally in need. Because of this and because intimidation of YBC residents was intensifying, the residents returned to court and renewed their request for an injunction. Supporting their motion was evidence of further harassment and violence directed against remaining residents by SFRA and its agents. Receiving this evidence, the court made a final request for the parties to settle their differences and report back in a week. The effort at compromise was futile. Judge Weigel accepted the parties' representation that no settlement could be reached and took the motion for an injunction under submission.

Two weeks later, on April 30, 1970, Weigel ordered the most sweeping injunction against an urban renewal project ever issued, immediately halting all demolition and relocation and setting July 1, 1970, as the date for cutting off federal funds if the YBC relocation plan was not satisfactorily revised.

The Injunction: Maneuvers and Politics

In his opinion accompanying the YBC injunction, Judge Weigel concluded that the Secretary of HUD "had not been provided with any credible evidence at all" in regard to the agency's YBC relocation plan and that "the record shows that at this very moment there is not adequate relocation housing in San Francisco which meets the requirements of the [1949 Housing] Act and is available for persons yet to be displaced from the Project Area." "The statute make[s] it abundantly clear," wrote Judge Weigel, "that

Congress intended residents of blighted areas to be beneficiaries, not victims, of . . . urban renewal."[8]

The next move was up to the Redevelopment Agency. On May 3, the agency filed an appeal of Judge Weigel's decision to the Ninth Circuit. To reinforce its legal maneuvers, the agency even brought in special counsel—none other than Mayor Joseph Alioto.* This was an extraordinary and blatantly political move, particularly since the City was not a named defendant and the agency already had hired special counsel to handle the litigation. During the same week, the mayor convened a bargaining session with TOOR's legal counsel, Justin Herman, and other City officials. Alioto was furious at TOOR's unwillingness to bargain away gains won in court and berated the TOOR attorneys with such statements as: "You can't have everything, you know. You're not dealing with children." "There's no feeling of weakness on our side, you know. No federal judge in the country is going to stop the Yerba Buena project. I won't permit it. I've known Stan Weigel for 20 years and he is not about to do that."[9]

But sensing Judge Weigel might just do that, the City's next move was to attempt a maneuver around him. Immediately after issuing his YBC decision, Judge Weigel had left for a six-week vacation. On May 8, Attorney Alioto moved to have the injunction "modified," in order to permit relocation and demolition to proceed on all sites in which commercial developers had expressed an interest. The City claimed it was fearful that developers who had agreed to build on parcels outside the Central Blocks, such as Del Monte, Crocker-Citizens Bank, and Taylor-Woodrow, would back out if the sites were not delivered on schedule. The Redevelopment Agency asked for an immediate hearing on its motion to modify the injunction. Presiding Judge George Harris, well known in Democratic circles and a close friend of Ben Swig, got the case. Judge Harris ordered a hearing for the following Monday.

---

*Although Alioto did not receive compensation for these legal services, he did do extensive private lawyering during his mayoral tenure, a practice which, combined with his other simultaneous business dealings, later led to a Charter amendment, passed overwhelmingly by the voters in 1977, forbidding a mayor from actively participating in any other occupation or business activity. According to Supervisor Quentin Kopp, who sponsored the measure (referring to Alioto), "I know of at least a couple of lawyers who were called into Room 200 [the mayor's city hall suite] to discuss settlement of law suits by the predecessors of the present mayor [Moscone]." And Supervisor John Molinari "also said he doesn't want the mayor taking 60 days off to go up to Washington [state] to defend a case, referring to time Alioto spent successfully defending against allegations of wrongdoing in a huge antitrust case he won for a number of Washington public power districts" (Robert Bartlett, "Supes Aim One at Ex-mayor Alioto," *San Francisco Chronicle*, 6 July 1977).

TOOR felt its back was against the wall, that it was about to see the victory it had just won go down the drain. Its attorneys were understandably fearful that Judge Harris would grant the agency's request to modify the injunction, an action sure to unleash a furious rash of eviction and demolition activity within a matter of days, thereby, for all practical purposes, ending the relocation issue. As a legal matter, TOOR's attorneys argued that Judge Harris's district court had no jurisdiction over the injunction, since the agency had already filed its appeal to the Ninth Circuit; attorney Anthony Kline even took the bold, desperate step of serving a writ of prohibition on Judge Harris in his chambers to dissuade him from going ahead with the hearing. TOOR's attorneys protested the proceedings and asked for a continuance, on the grounds that papers filed by the SFRA did not show any different circumstances from the time Judge Weigel made his decision. However, Judge Harris was convinced by Attorney/Mayor Alioto that the new hearings should be held, and TOOR's request for a delay was denied.

During the noon recess of the hearing on the SFRA's motion, TOOR's attorneys decided to try a long shot, by raising the issue of Judge Harris's personal friendship with Ben Swig and others with a financial stake in the YBC project, and asking that he recuse himself from the case. Among other things, a photograph in the judge's chamber showing him arm-in-arm with the senior Swig, combined with the judge's membership in the Bohemian Club, the preeminent men's social club in the state of California,[10] gave South of Market residents concern over Harris's ability to be impartial when the interests of Del Monte, Crocker-Citizens Bank, and Pacific Telephone and Telegraph were pitted against people whom Justin Herman had called "skid row bums."

Judge Harris granted TOOR's request to meet in chambers and reacted positively to the suggestion that the litigation issues might be resolved by means other than the federal judiciary. TOOR's counsel, Anthony Kline, then suggested appointment of a Special Master (an officer appointed to take testimony and report to the court) to devise a way for the Yerba Buena project to move ahead while ensuring adequate housing for displacees. Kline proposed the Democratic ex-governor of California, Edmund "Pat" Brown,[11] a choice immediately acceptable both to Judge Harris and Alioto, a large contributor to the recent successful campaign of Brown's son, Jerry, for Secretary of State. (The elder Brown was also very close to Ben Swig, as Brown himself indicated in the following anecdote regarding his loss in the 1966 gubernatorial race: "Ben was with us that night, having dinner. It was a real low point, but I remember he said, 'Pat, you'll be a much happier man now.' Then and there, he made me his legal counsel and put me on retainer. I was down that night, all right. But Ben's gesture was the difference between being down and completely out.")[12]

During May and June 1970, Brown conducted several conferences, took a walking tour of the area, and called in many officials to obtain a complete view of the problem. TOOR took advantage of the opportunity presented by appointment of a Special Master and, with the help of a team of architects and planners assembled by the University of California's Community Design Center, prepared a rehousing plan, which they submitted to Brown. The TOOR plan called for two thousand units of new and rehabilitated low-rent housing in the YBC project area but outside the Central Blocks. A working model of the proposal, together with lengthy documentation of financial feasibility and a schedule for phased on-site relocation, was included in the plan. By leaving the Central Blocks development intact and concentrating on the fringe area, it avoided engendering staunch opposition on the part of those interests pushing the convention and sports facilities. The plan was technically sound, consonant with TOOR's basic objectives, and one Brown could support.

TOOR's initiative caught SFRA off guard. The agency presumed an alliance with Brown and was not prepared for presentation of a serious alternative plan or a contest for Brown's mind. In late June, with Judge Weigel back from his vacation, Brown issued his report, essentially supporting a modified version of the residents' proposal to require SFRA to produce two thousand new units of low-rent housing. This report limited residents' relocation to new or permanently rehabilitated units, thus recognizing the inability of the existing San Francisco housing market to absorb more YBC displacees. The Special Master gave the agency the option of selecting sites inside or outside the project area, but it could take the latter option only if units could be produced as quickly and cheaply. Further, no one could be forced to move away from the area except into a newly completed unit.

The TOOR plan was an important turning point in the battle. Brown's virtual endorsement of it served to shift attention from relocation to replacement housing. The plan was reasonable and feasible; it was clear that the real obstacles were the agency's lack of will and Justin Herman's personal intransigence.

To no one's surprise, the Redevelopment Agency promptly and emphatically rejected Brown's report, claiming that its own vacancy survey (which Brown had seen before issuing his report) indicated sufficient relocation housing; the report was simply filed by the court. The agency also believed Judge Weigel would dissolve the April 30 injunction when it submitted the revised relocation plan Weigel had called for. The key element of the "revised" plan was a detailing of how the existing public housing supply was to be captured for Yerba Buena displacees. This feature was the result of pressure both from Alioto and Herman on the commissioners of the San

Francisco Housing Authority (all of whom are mayoral appointees) to admit Yerba Buena displacees into public housing on a "super-priority" basis in exchange for granting the Authority some additional urban renewal land on which to build more public housing.

Federal statutes require that families and individuals displaced by public action receive priority status for admission to public housing; this means that displacees get housing over others on the waiting lists, no matter how long the latter have been waiting. The effect of this super-priority plan was to turn the victims of redevelopment projects against each other and against other poor people in their desperate search for replacement housing. The Housing Authority waiting list at the time numbered thirty-nine hundred households, six hundred to eight hundred of which were Redevelopment Agency displacees from the Western Addition A-2 project. Elderly South of Market residents might wind up "bumping" African American families displaced from the Western Addition and Hunters Point. The relocation plan also ignored the fact that most South of Market residents, like urban renewal displacees all over the country, did not want to relocate into public housing.[13] Three-fourths of the residents interviewed in the National Housing Law Project survey in the summer of 1971 (see chapter 4) stated they did not wish to move to the new Clementina Towers public housing project right in the South of Market area. Yet the super-priority plan was accepted by the Housing Authority in June 1970 and used by the Redevelopment Agency to challenge Judge Weigel's April 30 court order. The sentiment underlying "super-priority" was well articulated by Housing Authority chairman William Jack Chow, who stated in the June 30, 1970, *Chronicle*, regarding people on the public housing waiting lists, "The economic importance [of Yerba Buena] to the city is more important than some inconveniences."

Throughout this period, the agency continued to evade the spirit of Judge Weigel's protective orders, which led TOOR's attorneys in late July to file a civil contempt action against the agency. "Advice" and "informational" notices to hotel residents had the effect, if not the intention, of intimidating persons protected by the court order. According to an *Examiner* report: "He [Weigel] noted that the agency, composed of 'sophisticated people' was dealing with 'unsophisticated people who would be sensitive and frightened by such a notice.' Weigel said residents would interpret the notice as one of probable eviction. . . . Weigel said he believed . . . the agency . . . had pursued a policy of moving people out willy-nilly, regardless of the injunction, and as close to the line as possible without violating the injunction. Weigel said he was 'not at all sure but what the notice constituted a deliberate, outright violation of the injunction.' "[14]

In September, the Redevelopment Agency in fact moved to have the injunction lifted, on the grounds that HUD had approved its new relocation plan. As the September 7, 1970, *Chronicle* noted: "Agency officials are obviously hoping that other factors, more political than legal in implication, will count for something in the court's consideration of the bid to have the injunction dissolved." TOOR immediately challenged the validity of HUD's approval for this revised relocation plan. A hearing was set for late October, but it was never held—by this time attorneys for both sides were meeting to work out a settlement and avoid prolonged litigation. The attorneys did arrive at a settlement by the date set for the hearing, with final acceptance contingent on TOOR's approval.

The Consent Decree

SFRA and SFNLAF attorneys presented their proposal to Judge Weigel in lieu of arguments on the revised relocation plan; the court, after receiving a promise from TOOR's attorneys that they would recommend acceptance of the settlement package, lifted its injunction—reserving the right to reimpose it if TOOR's members rejected the settlement. Three days later, TOOR held a meeting at the Milner Hotel to vote on the proposal: The tally was 9 votes for, 135 against. In George Woolf's words, "It was a lousy deal."

Hopeful that the parties could still work out their differences, Judge Weigel ordered another settlement discussion. When it failed, he drafted a consent decree, based on the proposed settlement package but with more safeguards for the residents. Its basic features were the following:

- The Redevelopment Agency was to produce within three years (i.e., by November 1973) fifteen hundred to eighteen hundred new or rehabilitated units of low-rent housing anywhere in the city, in addition to those units the City already had programmed when the YBC injunction was imposed. The figure fifteen hundred was to apply if YBC residents had priority to three hundred of those units, eighteen hundred if they did not;

- pending construction or rehabilitation of these units, the agency was to house relocatees in decent, safe, and sanitary housing within their means (this was a restatement of existing federal law);

- with the above guarantee, the agency was allowed to proceed with relocation and demolition (a three-person arbitration board was established to hear and decide any claims brought by relocatees that the housing offered them failed to meet statutory standards);

- four project area hotels, outside the Central Blocks, were to be retained as "hostages" until the replacement units were completed, with $150,000 to be spent by the agency in the interim to refurbish the hotels;

- the agency was required to fulfill all promises made in its revised relocation plan; and

- the agency was to maintain a rent-free office for TOOR and permit the organization to hold meetings in one of the hotels.

Judge Weigel urged the Redevelopment Agency to agree to the decree, thereby avoiding the necessity of ruling on the adequacy of the revised relocation plan. On November 9, 1970, Justin Herman signed the document. In return, Judge Weigel dissolved his injunction but retained jurisdiction over the case to ensure production of the fifteen hundred to eighteen hundred units by November 1973. By contrast, the proposed settlement package the residents had rejected called for TOOR to drop its lawsuit entirely, included no deadline for agency performance, and contained no arbitration procedure; all TOOR would have gotten was the agency's promise to provide fifteen hundred additional units. As George Woolf put it, according to the October 24, 1970, *Chronicle,* the original agreement would have "allow[ed] clearance of the Central Blocks 'and [would have] shove[d] half of us into some of the worst hotels in the project and [left] the rest of us to be forced into Sixth Street and the Tenderloin.' "

In the context of the history of urban renewal litigation, Judge Weigel's disposition of the TOOR suit was a landmark victory. For the first time, a court had thoroughly scrutinized the record underlying HUD's approval of a relocation plan. Examining the claim that federal relocation standards were not being met, Weigel found that the agency's plan failed to provide housing within the financial means of the relocatees and contained no assurance that the relocation housing would be decent, safe, and sanitary. In requiring that replacement housing be built concurrent with demolition and displacement, the court explicitly recognized the effects of residential displacement on the city's housing market as a whole. Weigel not only was intervening in the renewal process further than had been done to date anyplace in the United States, he was also to an extent assuming a planning function in specifying the type of housing to be built.

But progressive as it was in the context of previous urban renewal litigation, the court's action still gave higher priority to completion of Yerba Buena Center than to firm guarantees that the residents' rights would be protected; therefore, it was not a settlement TOOR fully approved. While an improvement over the original proposed settlement package, the final consent decree was not regarded by TOOR as guaranteeing protection of their rights. Given that nearly four thousand units were being removed by the project, TOOR regarded the two thousand units recommended by ex-governor Brown as a minimum replacement figure; the fifteen hundred to eighteen hundred units the agency had consented to produce were a disappointment. (The 1969 Housing Act went much further in dealing realistically with the displacement/relocation issue, by requiring replacement of occupied low- or moderate-income residential units removed by a renewal project with an equivalent number of units constructed or rehabilitated for low- or moderate-income families. This stipulation applied only to projects approved after passage of the 1969 Act and to family, not individual, units; hence, it was inapplicable to Yerba Buena. But it did indicate congressional thinking about the direction and responsibilities of the renewal program.) TOOR also felt that only by constructing replacement units in or adjacent to the YBC site would this housing be satisfactory with respect to maintaining social ties. And to minimize dislocation and ensure the agency would keep its construction promise, they also wanted guarantees that no one would be forced to move until new or rehabilitated housing was available.

Under the consent decree, the agency was allowed to proceed with its project essentially as before, although the price exacted for this permission was its commitment to provide replacement units, which obligation the court stood ready to review. True relief for the residents would have required their satisfactory relocation *prior* to continuing work on YBC. This would have delayed the project, but it would have been the only real way to guarantee the rights of displacees to decent low-rent housing. Lifting the injunction took pressure off the Redevelopment Agency and raised the possibility that its promises might never be fulfilled. Judge Weigel had proven unwilling to go much beyond the settlement negotiated by the lawyers to protect the rights of the community. In the settlement discussions urged by the court, the attorneys had spoken for the community, and even when the South of Market residents rejected the settlement, the judge was responsive to what the attorneys had thought reasonable, implying that the residents' demands were unreasonable and extreme.

People vs. Professionals

TOOR's rejection of the settlement highlighted the substantial differences not only between it and the Redevelopment Agency but also between those who are victims of urban redevelopment and those who are their outside professional advocates.

Underlying the schism between TOOR and its attorneys, brought to light by the group's overwhelming rejection of the settlement proposal its lawyers had negotiated and tentatively agreed to, are some important questions regarding community organization and struggle, particularly in lower-income neighborhoods, and the role played by outside, usually middle-class advocates.[15] TOOR was not a mass-based organization; while it was able to communicate well and regularly with its constituency, bring them out for selected hearings and events, and convince large numbers of them to take the politically most important step of all—staying put—its real muscle was the court injunction. But the organization's reliance on the courts and attorneys had its drawbacks as well. Its tangible victories and publicity were won by and associated with the lawyers. And it was the lawyers who, during 1969 and 1970, provided the spark for the organization. The inherent difficulties in building a strong, mass-based organization among elderly, often alienated and disabled persons were exacerbated by the powerful role the attorneys assumed and TOOR allowed them to assume.

By playing out its struggle in the courtroom, TOOR found itself caught up willy-nilly in the style of the game as it is played there and involved with the kinds of persons who are the key actors in that arena. Thus, Judge Weigel was assiduously pushing both sides to reach a compromise solution, and he sought to avoid making a definitive ruling on the agency's relocation plan or enjoining the project longer than was necessary to extract a substantial concession from the agency. TOOR's attorneys also sought middle-ground solutions that would advance their clients' interests to the maximum extent then thought possible, given their view of the political and legal realities of the situation, while at the same time permitting the project to go ahead. TOOR was in the position of having allowed its attorneys to take over the negotiations (a role they did not at all mind playing) but then rebelling against the attorneys when the settlement they had tentatively agreed to was revealed. In TOOR's view, by agreeing to drop the lawsuit in exchange for the Redevelopment Agency's promise to build fifteen hundred to eighteen hundred housing units, the attorneys had left the community defenseless. Based on past experience with the agency, the community group felt that SFRA promises were useless and that without the lawsuit, TOOR no longer would have its only real weapon—the ability to hold YBC land hostage—which only the injunction and continued court supervision offered. Thus, TOOR decisively rejected the proposed settlement—which the October 28, 1970, *San Francisco Progress* characterized as "obviously a bad deal for the . . . elderly South of Market residents"—and regarded it as a "sell-out"; at one point, they even discussed dismissing their attorneys.

Responsibility for this situation was attributable to both sides and may be regarded as an inevitable product of community struggle in which by mutual assent the tail is allowed to wag the dog. TOOR by and large adopted the principle that "lawyer knows best" and placed its fate in the hands of its professional advocates, regarding their judgment and skills as superior to those of the community. The lawyers by and large seemed to share this assessment. They neither sought nor were given adequate guidance by the community and were in the position of making the political decisions that, under a strong community organization, they would not have been permitted to make. In this situation, the style, predilections, and values of the attorneys came to dominate the outcome.

The attorneys were in uncharted waters in carrying out their suit. They did not know how far the court would go in protecting TOOR's interests. Courts in the past had not been notably solicitous of the rights of displacees, and the attorneys to a large extent were seeking to make new law. There was a possibility that Judge Weigel might accept HUD's approval of the agency's revised plan, although since the court had rejected the previous plan and the revised one was not much different, this was unlikely. In terms of a settlement, as opposed to a court order, the proposed agreement was probably the most that could have been gotten voluntarily from Justin Herman. He staked his reputation on the YBC project; he was incensed at the roadblocks being thrown up by the residents; and he had a particular dislike for advocate planners and legal services attorneys. Sidney Wolinsky, SFNLAF's director of litigation and chief attorney for the TOOR suit, was a special target of Herman's wrath. When Wolinsky et al. filed the TOOR suit, Herman, referring to the Neighborhood Legal Assistance Foundation's previous suit on the Western Addition project, retorted: "This is the last straw. This time we are going to beat this bunch and we are going to beat them good."[16] Herman was quoted calling Wolinsky "a clever, well-financed, able, ambulance-chasing lawyer who has no respect for poor people, is wrong and is intellectually dishonest. There is a benefit of being in redevelopment. You can go to bed each night knowing you have helped the people in the slums. Wolinsky can't do that. That man has contributed nothing. Nothing."[17] The *Chronicle* article containing this quotation notes, "The mere mention of Wolinsky's name enrages . . . Herman."

The attorneys' acceptance of the settlement agreement may also have stemmed from an understandable desire on the part of some of them to consolidate a victory and go on to other things. The litigation had lasted for more than a year and was very time-consuming; given Judge Weigel's obvious preference for a settlement rather than a clear judicial finding, a settlement that represented an advanced instance of judicial protection of displacees' rights was a significant legal victory, one for which the attorneys could take a great deal of justifiable credit. There was probably also some real concern about the strength and durability of the community organization they were representing. A further consideration might have had to do with the broader consequences of pursuing the Yerba Buena suit. If delay continued, the developers might drop out and the whole project fall through. If this happened, TOOR and its attorneys would be blamed, and perhaps neither wanted to push matters that far. As it turned out, those legal protections offered no firm guarantees, because, as the next three years were to show, the Redevelopment Agency and the City were determined to avoid and undermine the November 9 decree.

Back into Court

A surprise development came in May 1971, when the Housing Authority suddenly dropped its super-priority policy for YBC displacees. For the year the policy had been in effect, the Authority had been under constant criticism from neighborhood groups all over the city, because it threatened to rob them of sorely needed housing. TOOR itself did not want to see its housing problem solved by harming other people and had even attempted to enjoin the Housing Authority from implementing the super-priority policy in a motion denied by Judge Weigel in May 1971. The Housing Authority staff also resented the policy because it put them in the position of keeping housing from those already on its waiting lists and thus becoming the target for anger and frustration that properly belonged in the lap of the Redevelopment Agency. As one Housing Authority commissioner put it, "We're not the tail on anybody else's kite."[18] There had been long-standing ill will between the housing and redevelopment agencies, and the last straw was the SFRA's failure to produce the public housing sites promised at the time the super-priority deal was arranged. The Housing Authority had twice requested a site for 250 units of family-sized public housing in the YBC area, but the Redevelopment Agency each time turned down the request. This failure was due to Justin Herman's hostility to TOOR and its demands, and to Mayor Alioto's unwillingness to expend any political muscle pressuring Herman and the Redevelopment Agency into assisting the Housing Authority. With the Redevelopment Agency already facing serious trouble over YBC, the Housing Authority took the opportunity to get even.

The withdrawal of super-priority completely undercut SFRA's revised relocation plan. Immediately, TOOR and its attorneys went back to Judge Weigel, claiming violation of the November 9 decree. In addition, they submitted evidence that the agency had shown no significant progress in producing the fifteen hundred to eighteen hundred housing units. Rather than risk waiting until 1973, only to learn that the agency had failed to produce the required housing, TOOR moved at once for renewed protective relief against further destruction of housing and dispersal of the South of Market community. In June 1971, TOOR's lawyers filed for a second preliminary injunction. (By this time two of TOOR's attorneys, Sidney Wolinsky and Anthony Kline, had left SFNLAF and the National Housing Law Project, respectively, to form a nonprofit public interest law firm, Public Advocates, Inc., located in San Francisco. Amanda Hawes left SFNLAF in 1972 to work with a legal services group in Alameda County. All three, for different lengths of time, remained active in the case despite changing their bases of operations.)* Capitalizing on the Housing Authority's feud with the Redevelopment Agency, TOOR included an affidavit from Housing Authority executive director Eneas Kane refuting the agency's contention that it could meet the November 1973 deadline for production of the fifteen hundred to eighteen hundred units. Kane asserted that most public housing units the agency claimed eligible to meet their quota had been programmed for construction prior to April 30, 1970—contrary to the clear wording of the consent decree that units under commitment prior to that date could not be counted.

The collapse of the Redevelopment Agency's revised relocation plan served to bring the HUD's San Francisco Area Office into the fray as well. Up to this point, HUD had been a virtual rubber stamp for the agency, particularly with respect to relocation matters. Its principal interest was in the reuse of the land, not in the people being displaced. According to an assistant to the area office director, "Our main concern is for the city to get a developer and redevelop so that we can unload the land."[19] The YBC litigation was causing HUD some embarrassment, however. In mid-June, during the hearings on TOOR's motion for a new injunction, HUD advised the court that it wanted to review once again the relocation plans and practices for YBC. Area office director James Price submitted an affidavit stating his

---

*In 1975, Kline was appointed legal affairs secretary to his long-time friend, Governor Edmund G. (Jerry) Brown, who in 1980 then appointed him to the San Francisco Superior Court and in 1982 appointed him Presiding Justice of the Division Two, First Appellate District of the California Court of Appeal, his position as of mid-2001.

staff did not have sufficient information to say whether the Redevelopment Agency was obeying the relocation statutes. "We question whether agency relocation plans are adequate or whether any plan is being carried out adequately," said Price,[20] although these doubts did not lead HUD to withdraw its certification of the YBC relocation plan. Angered by this admission, Judge Weigel ordered HUD to report back to the court in sixty days the results of its relocation study and in the interim reimposed restraints against all relocation and demolition. As the June 23, 1971, *Chronicle* noted, "The allegations [Price's acknowledgment of possible law violations requiring further investigation] upset Judge Weigel, who viewed them as an effort to shift full responsibility for enforcement of housing law from the Department of Housing and Urban Development to himself." HUD's sudden involvement was probably in part attributable to political factors. Mayor Alioto, a Democrat, had some national visibility and gubernatorial aspirations, and the Republican administration in Washington was probably not averse to making him look bad. Another factor was the Nixon administration's move to cut back on urban renewal expenditures nationally, as part of general budget-pruning; any delays on the expensive YBC project would save money, at least for a time.

HUD's intervention proved not to be a one-shot affair. After extensively interviewing displacees and surveying relocation resources, HUD in August filed with the court a startling report, which concluded: "There are not now nor will there be, sufficient rehousing resources to allow the relocation of Yerba Buena Center residents to continue unabated."[21] The department thereupon ordered the SFRA to file within 120 days a refined relocation plan, updated to include developments since filing its previous plan. During this four-month period, no relocation or demolition activity was to be permitted unless specifically approved by HUD. An agency request filed soon thereafter for permission to demolish two hotels was turned down by HUD pending submission of an acceptable relocation plan.

The Redevelopment Agency was typically unmoved by HUD's findings, adhering adamantly to its stance that there was no relocation problem and people ought to leave the agency alone so that it could get on with the job of building Yerba Buena Center. The agency's deputy executive director said that the previous sixty days had been wasted and that the next 120 days would also be wasted as the agency prepared a new relocation plan: "The report sets up more paperwork, more hurdles, more obstacles to the project which will continue to slow down the project to a point in time where it simply cannot move."[22]

Thus, prompted by Judge Weigel, HUD substituted for the court injunction what in effect was a continuing administrative injunction. When the agency in December 1971 submitted its revised relocation plan, HUD rejected it outright. In a letter to Mayor Alioto dated February 23, 1972, area office director James Price stated that the agency's new relocation plan "does not meet the test of Federal law, nor in our opinion will it pass the scrutiny of Judge Weigel's Court since it does not include any commitment on the part of the City to provide *permanent* replacement housing for YBC displacees." In the same month, HUD advised the agency that the four-year relocation payments provided for under the new Uniform Relocation Act did not qualify as permanent housing subsidies. In July, the agency once again attempted to get a relocation plan through HUD, only to have it returned as "lacking clarity."[23] Finally, in September 1972, the Redevelopment Agency submitted a relocation plan that met with HUD's approval (and TOOR's disapproval; the plan was immediately challenged in court by TOOR and subsequently remanded to HUD for further documentation supporting its approval).

Housing Progress (?)

Although Justin Herman in November 1970 voluntarily signed a consent decree committing his agency to produce fifteen hundred to eighteen hundred low-rent units within three years, it is unlikely he regarded this as a serious commitment, as is illustrated by the agency's lethargic response to this promise in the two years following its issuance. In the words of a high City official who knew Herman well, "He was damned if he was going to build those units. He never believed the feds would make him."[24] As of August 1972, by the agency's own records, only eleven units were actually completed. Commenting on a TOOR motion to require SFRA to allocate a new $4.3 million YBC grant from HUD to its replacement housing commitment, Judge Weigel noted:

> [A] large body of . . . evidence is both uncontroverted and impressive in supporting plaintiffs' claim that defendant San Francisco Redevelopment Agency is failing in its obligations for provision of low-cost housing. . . . The evidence presently before the court raises serious questions as to whether defendant San Francisco Redevelopment Agency will be able to meet its legal obligations by its own voluntary deadline date of November 9, 1973.[25]

One of the agency's strategies with respect to the November 1970 decree was to allow and encourage depopulation of the YBC area. It could then maintain that providing units for people no longer there was absurd, and therefore it should be released from its full replacement housing commitment. With virtually no one moving into the neighborhood, the combination of "voluntary" moveouts, sickness, and death was reducing the area's population rapidly. (The agency was reliably reported to have included a "mortality factor" in its relocation planning, and the Arthur D. Little study of agency relocation files for the 1972 period suggests the reality of such calculations.[26] Of the 654 relocated persons for whom records were available, fifty-three, or 8 percent, were listed as "deceased," and another thirty-eight, or 6 percent, were listed as in a hospital or convalescent home; more than one-sixth of the official relocatees were listed as "location unknown," and it may be assumed that a proportion of these also died or were institutionalized.) Exact interim population figures are not available, but through a combination of all factors the original population of four thousand had dropped to about thirteen hundred by late 1970, and to about seven hundred (120 of whom were in the Central Blocks) by late 1972. In the lonely, hostile surroundings created by the agency's clearance and hotel management activities, TOOR found it increasingly difficult to convince people to stay.

The agency was constantly reminding the court and the public of how few people remained in the area, a stance designed to pressure the residents, TOOR, their attorneys, and the court. The tactic was to try to convince the general public that a handful of persons selfishly stood in the way of a major redevelopment project of benefit to the entire city. But Judge Weigel was not to be diverted by this ploy. In his July 11, 1972, ruling with respect to HUD's supplementary YBC grant, he noted:

> Defendant Agency urges that there has been a reduction in the number of families and individuals who continue to reside in the Yerba Buena area. That is true. But it is immaterial. The commitment was made to comply with the law in the light of an over-all shortage of such housing throughout the city of San Francisco. Defendant cannot get rid of its obligation to provide a minimum of fifteen hundred units of new or rehabilitated low-cost housing by getting rid of some of those who need it.

The court also took due note of the somewhat disingenuous use of these figures by the agency. A footnote to the above statement read: "The evidence also shows that defendant San Francisco Redevelopment Agency has not been unwilling to contribute to the rate of attrition."

Providing low-rent housing had always been regarded as the Housing Authority's job, and it was not until YBC that the Redevelopment Agency had to deal with the effects of its people-removal activities. Since by law, local redevelopment agencies cannot themselves be developers, SFRA's task was to "cause" the fifteen hundred to eighteen hundred units to be constructed, through either the Housing Authority or private developers. The Housing Authority's unwillingness to redirect its entire effort to bail out SFRA and its Yerba Buena Center project, combined with HUD's sudden November 1971 announcement that it was cutting off funds previously committed to San Francisco public housing construction, meant that SFRA would have to rely on private developers to provide the bulk of the needed units.

Unable to count on the Housing Authority for its fifteen hundred to eighteen hundred units, the agency had to find its own sites and subsidization funds, neither of which was in abundant supply. And the agency could not plead lack of support from the Housing Authority or HUD, since the November 9, 1970, agreement explicitly stated that failure of other agencies to assist in the production of the requisite units would in no way relieve the agency of its responsibility. HUD solved part of the money problem in 1972 by making available long-term federal rent supplement funds sufficient to subsidize 1,175 units.

The more difficult problem was finding sites for the units. Given the high cost of land for new construction, the length of time required to construct new housing, and problems of locational suitability and acceptance by the surrounding neighborhood, the agency opted to meet its commitment primarily through rehabilitation. But the defects inherent in the rehab approach were cogently pointed out by TOOR attorney Amanda Hawes when the Redevelopment Agency, following receipt of its second federal rent supplement grant, announced it was looking for 463 transient hotel rooms suitable for conversion to permanent housing:

> [Attorney Hawes] accused the city and the Redevelopment Agency of waiting to "continue to play musical chairs."
> Old hotels would be rehabilitated, she said, and their permanent guests forced to move elsewhere to make way for Yerba Buena residents. No one, however, would look after the interests of the set of guests forced to move to make way for rehabilitation.
> "It is really a crime to displace these people," she said, "because they are often as old and poor as the people in the Yerba Buena area."[27]

The problem of obtaining suitable sites related, of course, to which part of the city the YBC relocatees were moved. The only substantial supply of residential hotels suitable for rehabilitation was in the YBC area itself or in the Tenderloin, across Market Street. When TOOR proposed to rehabilitate several South of Market hotels for permanent low-rent use, the reaction of the agency and its supporters was vitriolic. The Tenderloin was opposed not only by TOOR—because of its high crime rate and difficult hills—but by many YBC supporters as well, who did not want such persons in the downtown area at all. Werner Lewin, vice president and general manager of the Hilton Hotel Corporation, made strenuous attempts to keep the YBC relocatees away from his Hilton Hotel by trying to block SFRA from using the nearby Ramona Hotel as a replacement housing resource, even threatening the agency with legal action over the matter. In an August 10, 1972, letter to Mayor Alioto, Lewin stated: "We believe that the relocation of Yerba Buena residents in the Ramona would have a very adverse effect on our guests, a great many of whom will pass the Ramona a number of times daily to catch cable cars, to shop in Union Square, and to visit other parts of our fine city. . . . The neighborhood and our hotel cannot afford any additional adverse influences." A "blight" South of Market and an "adverse influence" North of Market, the old people living on the Yerba Buena Center site would be eliminated from the downtown, and possibly from the city altogether, if the city's economic leaders were to have their way.

Pressed by TOOR, HUD, and the federal court, the Redevelopment Agency began to realize that it would indeed have to produce the promised units. The changes within the agency and in its relationship with city hall after Justin Herman's death in late 1971 (see chapter 6) doubtless were additional factors in lessening its resistance on the housing issue. But so much time had been lost in the interim that the agency clearly could not meet its three-year deadline. The February 8, 1972, *Examiner* concluded, "As things stand now, the fifteen hundred housing units will never be provided within the three-year limit set by the court."

If the agency was ever to meet its legal commitment, it would need more subsidy money than the federal government had offered, and so in August 1972, the City introduced the idea of using local funds, raised via the hotel tax, to subsidize the units. This just notion—requiring hotel users and owners to bear some of the financial burdens caused by a project designed to benefit them—eventually became the core of the plan that was finally to break the TOOR litigation stalemate.

Blaming the Victims and the Legal System

The Redevelopment Agency's attempts throughout the YBC battle to create the image that the project was being held up by malcontents and publicity-seeking lawyers served to mask the truth: The agency itself was causing the delays by ignoring federal relocation requirements at the outset—then stalling and reneging on its promise to rectify the housing short-age and the relocation inequities it had created.

The agency and its supporters waged a constant campaign to discredit TOOR, its attorneys, and even the court. One example was the November 1971 fire at the St. James Hotel on Third Street in the YBC area, which killed one resident and injured six others. The hotel was owned by Benjamin Blu-menthal, a man with heavy political connections in San Francisco. (Just months before the fire, a major controversy arose over Mayor Alioto's ap-pointment of Blumenthal to the Housing Authority board, due to the lat-ter's alleged ownership of slum properties. Angry protests followed from the Public Housing Tenants Association, the NAACP, and the Family Ser-vice Agency, including a sit-in at Alioto's office and a threatened citywide public housing rent strike. These protests moved neither the mayor nor the supervisors, who confirmed the appointment unanimously. The protests continued, however, and three weeks after the supervisors' approval, Blu-menthal decided to decline the position.)

A rash of Redevelopment Agency charges against TOOR followed the St. James Hotel fire. The agency issued press releases blaming TOOR for the loss of life because it had initiated litigation that kept the agency from moving families out of "slum firetraps." TOOR responded that it had urged rehabilitation of the St. James, but the agency instead had given Blumen-thal special treatment and allowed him to retain ownership while other ho-tels in the area were purchased and either managed or demolished by the agency.

In 1969, the St. James had been cited for no fewer than eighteen housing code violations, including an absence of sprinklers in the halls and stairways and illegal cooking in rooms. According to the chief of the City's Bureau of Building Inspection, "If they had taken care of the cooking facilities, the fire ought not to have started. If they had installed sprinklers, the fire would never have gotten out of the room."[28] The agency had let the "firetrap" re-main in order to accommodate a local political influential, who kept chang-ing his plans for the building's future but never made any improvements.

The St. James was not the only fatal hotel fire in the nearby area. In Feb-ruary 1972, a fire at the Sherman Hotel on Eleventh Street killed two per-sons, and in May 1972 a woman burned to death in the Jefferson Hotel in the Tenderloin. Unlike the St. James fire, no agency press releases came from these incidents. Both hotels had been on relocation lists for displacees from YBC.

Other instances of "blaming the victim" abounded. Project delays and resulting expenses were all attributed to TOOR. These sums ranged from seven thousand dollars a month to keep hotels open for remaining residents (who were protected by court orders), to seven thousand dollars a day for increased interest and administrative costs, to \$1 million per month due to construction cost inflation. Blame inevitably was assigned to TOOR's persistence in pressing its claims, not to the agency's adamancy in resisting the court's, and HUD's, findings and orders. As noted in a letter published in the *Chronicle*, rather than blaming citizens protecting their rights for wasting public funds,

> The commissioners of the Redevelopment Agency owe the people of San Francisco an explanation for the squandering of this great amount of money, for their non-compliance with the Court's order and their own agreement over a period of more than 14 months, and from a legal standpoint, owe the city an accounting for the waste and losses and frustrations involved.[29]

Another situation arose during the summer of 1972 over the agency's alleged inability to give former YBC residents relocation payments available under the 1970 Uniform Relocation Act. In July, the agency issued a public statement that termed "criminal" and "sickening" its inability to make these payments because of the court's injunction.[30] TOOR responded by pointing out that the agency was trying to use relocation payments as bribes to force residents to relocate into substandard housing outside the project area; TOOR also noted that such payments were no permanent solution, since subsidies would end after four years and people would still be left without decent places to live. TOOR further observed that persons leaving voluntarily during the injunction period would be eligible to receive these payments at a later date.

Pressures and personal attacks were mounted against the attorneys, and even against Judge Weigel. Attorney J. Anthony Kline later reminisced,

> Rarely has an American judge outside the South been subjected to such virulent public obloquy for courageously enforcing the legal rights of an unpopular group. . . . As a result of his ruling . . . Stanley Weigel became the subject of an intense campaign of vilification. During the many years in which Judge Weigel refused to lift his injunction . . . he was repeatedly condemned by the newspapers, the Chamber of Commerce, the building trade unions and an array of local officials.[31]

Judge Weigel later recalled that "all kinds of pressures were brought to bear. . . . I cannot tell you the number of telephone calls to me generated by civic leaders and real estate developers which I had to refuse." He also recalled the peripheral exclusion and disapproval he experienced from social acquaintances in the city.[32]* TOOR's attorneys were repeatedly attacked as "ideologues" and "outside Berkeley agitators." All three attorneys lived across the bay in Berkeley, and the National Housing Law Project was located there. The particular ideology they held and agitated for was the right of displaced residents to decent housing and the obligation of the Redevelopment Agency to obey the laws of the United States of America.

An especially strong attack on attorney Wolinsky and Judge Weigel came from the San Francisco Building and Construction Trades Council, whose primary interest was securing construction jobs for its members. In March 1972, the BCTC passed a resolution saying that Wolinsky "lives high in the Berkeley Hills by night and is a radical chic poverty lawyer by day," responsible for "an endless stream of obstructionist lawsuits." The same resolution characterized Judge Weigel as "an accommodating federal judge . . .

---

*An extraordinary letter, dated 8 December 1972, from YBC project director for the Redevelopment Agency John Dykstra to San Francisco Chamber of Commerce executive director William Dauer, sharing ideas on how to respond to Judge Weigel's continuing oversight of the project, suggests the ways in which the power structure considers influencing the judiciary:

> The matter really is in Judge Weigel's hands . . . the problem becomes one of getting the message through to Weigel that the community is becoming extremely impatient about the delay (and the cost of the delay) and that a settlement should be worked out forthwith. In this regard three avenues seem to exist: 1) Approach Judge Weigel directly and ask that he be reasonable and responsible. 2) Set up some sort of mechanism (perhaps through the Mayor's office) for the negotiation of a settlement. 3) Mount a massive public information campaign emphasizing the need to get the project moving and thereby establish a climate of urgency.
>
> All of the attorneys involved (City, Redevelopment Agency, and bond counsel) and the agency itself are opposed to approaches one and two above, which leaves number three as the only noncontroversial approach.

The issue and impact of subtle and overt pressure on judges from their social peers in their private lives receives far too little attention. Federal Judge William Wayne Justice, who in the 1970s issued decisions integrating the public schools and affirming the right of children of undocumented workers to a free public education, noted: "One day people are smiling and laughing with you and greet you on the street and the next day it doesn't happen. Sure, you're affected by it. But on the other hand, you've got to keep your self-respect. If you know to yourself that you deliberately decided against what the law was just to affect your own personal comfort, you're not much of a judge." A civil rights attorney familiar with the scene noted about Justice: "Here in Tyler [Texas], which is a very conservative town, he and his wife were completely shunned socially by the elite of the city, the people he normally would have been hanging around with, because of his decision." Quotations from "Profiles in Judicial Courage," a 1996 video produced by the Washington, D.C.–based public interest group, The Alliance for Justice.

who lives in one of the most luxurious high-rise Russian Hill penthouses and has never had to stand in an unemployment line."[33]

What was undoubtedly the most bizarre attempt to intimidate the court came in January 1972, when the Redevelopment Agency filed a motion in U.S. District Court, asking that Judge Weigel remove himself from the Yerba Buena case on the grounds of bias and prejudice and being "over-wrought and extremely emotional" in his rulings. According to the January 21, 1972, *Chronicle*, "Court observers could recall no other such accusation filed in U.S. District Court here over the last 15 years." The action clearly was a coordinated attempt on the part of elements in the city's power structure to eliminate the principal hurdle to continuation of the project. It was reminiscent of the agency's earlier attempt to bring what it hoped would be a friendly judge into the case during Judge Weigel's absence from the country.

Members of the redevelopment booster club had prepared the ground for the agency's legal maneuver over the previous two weeks. The *Examiner*'s contribution was a January 6, 1972, editorial that fairly whined:

> HOW MUCH LONGER must the city of San Francisco put up with the dictatorial decisions on community affairs of U.S. District Court Judge Stanley Weigel? . . .
>
> Weigel long has been a central figure in the semi-disastrous delays suffered by the $350 million Yerba Buena redevelopment project. This week he imposed costly new restraints.
>
> What now? How long, oh lord? . . .
>
> Weigel and the foundation [SFNLAF] refuse to give proper recognition to the Redevelopment Agency's humane and efficient program to relocate residents displaced by Yerba Buena. . . . Is there no way to get this crucial issue out of Weigel's court?

(The same newspaper just a few months earlier—in a July 11, 1971, feature—had concluded about Weigel: "Regarded as firm, fair, concerned with the individual rights of criminals, he seems the personification of the idealized federal judge.")[34]

On January 11, 1972, radio station KCBS chimed in editorially: "Judge Weigel's continued resistance regarding a removal of the injunction strikes us as poor judgment." And the same day, Redevelopment Agency board member Stanley Jensen, president of the Machinists Union local, charged that Weigel was biased and accused him of "taking a righteous attitude of doing all right and nothing wrong."[35]

The charges against Weigel, a liberal Republican corporate lawyer appointed to the court by President Kennedy, were also tied to his recent ruling, ordering the integration of San Francisco's schools by busing. Supervisor Peter Tamaras, whose family-owned hotel supply business (as noted in chapter 3) serviced most of the downtown hotels, accused Judge Weigel of being "dictatorial and biased" and of "doing a great disservice to the city . . . by the harmful political decisions he has made. . . . Except for Judge Weigel and a handful of dissidents, most people approve of the Yerba Buena Project."[36] (Tamaras was immediately criticized by the Bar Association of San Francisco for his remarks.) Noting that Weigel's children attended all-white private schools, Tamaras offered the following analysis: "Quite an irony. Maybe he feels guilty about it, but he shouldn't get his therapy by halting the Yerba Buena Center and ordering cross-town busing."

Judge Weigel responded by asking the chief judge of the Northern District of California to review the case. In February 1972, Chief Judge Oliver J. Carter rejected the agency's charges and returned the case to Judge Weigel. He noted that in November 1970 the agency had voluntarily signed a consent decree and even had expressed appreciation to Judge Weigel. "Clearly, when they thought the cards were with them they enjoyed the game," noted Carter's opinion. Commenting on the fact that remarks made by Judge Weigel in September 1970 were cited by the agency as proof of prejudice, Judge Carter noted: "For the defendants to have sat back for this long and now attempt to pick through the record and allege that prejudice was evidenced 15 months ago strikes this court as incredible." Discarding another claim that there was prejudice in Judge Weigel's remark that the agency wanted to "throw out tenants, using federal funds to do it," Judge Carter said, "It appears to me that is merely a colorful way of describing the agency's actual function."[37] The agency appealed Judge Carter's ruling, but the appeal was denied by the Ninth Circuit without a hearing. (The *Examiner* pressed the issue nonetheless; in a March 2, 1972, editorial, it urged "self-disqualification" on Judge Weigel, Judge Carter's ruling notwithstanding, out of "concern for the judicial system's all-important image in the eyes of the public.")

The blatant attempt by the agency and its constituency to intimidate the federal court did arouse considerable resentment in the legal community. Among many criticisms of the "get Weigel" drive was the following perceptive letter by two Legal Services attorneys:

> By his outrageous attack on Federal Judge Stanley Weigel, Supervisor Tamaras has dramatically revealed—perhaps unwittingly—a fundamental assumption of the San Francisco power elite. That assumption, simply stated, is that the judiciary itself is so integral a part of the Establishment that its primary duty is to rule in favor of the dominant business and political interests.

Under this view, judges are not to treat elderly hotel residents the same way they do real estate developers. . . . And whatever happens, judges are not actually to give judgment to the poor—even if such a decision is legally correct—if that decision would create "tremendous suffering to the city's tourist and convention industry." . . .

But now for the real irony. People like Tamaras—outspoken "law and order" types—would surely admonish black parents or the elderly poor not to "take the law into their own hands" but rather to proceed "within the system," i.e., through the courts. (They'll *lose* in the courts, get it?) But when they do go to court and then actually WIN, all hell breaks loose and the cat is out of the bag at last. For what judges in San Francisco are REALLY supposed to be faithful to—in the Tamaras view—is not the Constitution of the United States but rather financial interests like "the city's tourist and convention industries."[38]

6 | The Redevelopment Agency Flounders

Delays caused by TOOR's successful lawsuit and Justin Herman's obvious intransigence in the face of this legal obstacle began to implant grave doubts at city hall about the Redevelopment Agency's handling of the YBC project, doubts furthered by Thomas Mellon, the City's chief administrative officer (CAO). In early 1971, Mellon suddenly announced possible illegalities and conflicts of interest in the agency's proposed public facilities financing plan and serious defects in the convention center design. What ensued was a struggle that in a few months removed power over the YBC public facilities development from the agency and placed it in the hands of city hall and its convention industry supporters.

A Palace Revolt

Thomas Mellon's job as chief administrative officer, as well as his personal stature among local business and political figures, put him right at the heart of the growing YBC controversy. (According to the March 23, 1973, *San Francisco Progress,* his "mandatory retirement was waived . . . to allow him to see the Yerba Buena Convention Center through.") The CAO's role was to serve as grand coordinator for the City's administrative and bureaucratic apparatus. It was an extremely powerful, politically independent post, which until 1978 in effect carried life tenure. (Voters in 1977 changed the term to ten years; a 1996 voter-approved City Charter change abolished the position and recreated it as city administrator, part of the mayor's office.) Mellon, appointed by Mayor Shelley in 1963, was a successful businessman and former head of the Chamber of Commerce and the Police Commission. He was known as an extremely hard worker, served on innumerable civic and governmental bodies, knew everyone of influence in the city, and had well-honed abilities to wheel and deal. He also was responsible for annually allocating the half of the hotel tax receipts (then amounting to more than $2 million) assigned to the City's Publicity and Advertising Fund, a fund termed "the last pot of sugar in San Francisco politics." In short, he was in many ways more influential than the mayor. Allan Jacobs, who as city planning director (1967–74) experienced Mellon closely, described him as "day in, day out, the most powerful person in San Francisco government."[1]

Mellon's intervention in YBC began shortly after the agency announced its developer for the Central Blocks, and was triggered by the Hotel Employers Association (HEA) and the Convention & Visitors Bureau. Both groups were worried about possible delays in building the convention facility, given the overbuilding of new luxury hotels in the city and the resulting excess of vacant rooms. They were also eager to have a superior design better able to compete with other new centers around the country. Richard Swig had himself appointed head of a joint committee formed by the HEA and CVB to review plans for the center. When the agency showed them the detailed plans for the convention hall, Swig's group raised a great hue and cry over the design, objecting to the idea of an underground facility and to many specific design features, including inadequate ceiling heights, insufficient distance between supporting pillars, and too few meeting rooms. Swig and the hotelmen took their complaints directly to Mayor Alioto, who agreed there were real design problems. Alioto realized his powerful hotel and convention supporters had to be pacified and assigned Mellon to arbitrate the dispute. After a series of discussions convened by Mellon, the Swig group agreed to accept an underground facility (since moving it aboveground would cause serious additional delays) in exchange for an agreement to meet their other design objections. This was all done through city hall, completely bypassing Justin Herman and his developers, a move that antagonized Herman considerably. The Swigs' role in financing Alioto's 1967 election, to be repeated in his successful 1971 reelection campaign, gave Richard Swig more leverage at city hall than he could have had with Herman and the Redevelopment Agency.

More serious intervention on Mellon's part was his publicly voiced criticism of the agency's original plan for financing the YBC public facilities. The agency plan was an amalgam of political and economic considerations. The goal was to put together a scheme that would provide the most rapid, flexible, and politically acceptable method of raising funds and exercising control over their use. Albert Schlesinger's plan, developed originally for the Dillingham Corporation and later transferred to the successful bidder,

Arcon-Pacific, called for nonprofit corporations (established by Schlesinger and his partners) to issue tax-exempt bonds backed by the City's hotel tax. Schlesinger/Arcon-Pacific would then receive substantial developer's fees—more than $5 million—to build the public facilities and would negotiate a fee with a general contractor, rather than submit the project to competitive bidding. Mellon's criticisms, supported by the city attorney, concerned the legality and propriety of the arrangements. His financial cautiousness derived in part from experience with expansion of Candlestick Park stadium, where costs had ballooned to such an extent that the City was forced to impose an admissions tax of fifty cents per ticket and add a half percent to the hotel tax to guarantee the construction bonds.

Mellon accompanied his criticisms with a suggestion that the YBC project's public and private segments be split and that the City build the public facilities and fund them through a general obligation bond issue. Mellon moved ahead and won the approval of the City's Capital Improvements Advisory Committee (which he chaired) for a $118 million bond issue to appear on the coming November 1971 municipal ballot.

Mellon's motives in denouncing the original financing plan went beyond those proclaimed publicly. At issue was a fundamental power struggle between himself and Justin Herman. The Redevelopment Agency's entire operation and the economic and political control being amassed by this quasi-independent "government within a government"[2] were a distinct threat to Mellon's own empire. In making this fight, Mellon was undertaking what the April 29, 1971, *Examiner* termed a "political power play" as the leader of a group within the City administration seeking to clip Herman's wings. "Empire-building" charges against Herman had begun almost as soon as he took his job. In early 1961, he was involved in well publicized, and successful, battles with the city attorney and controller over whether the agency's support staff—attorneys, accountants, and others—were to be employed by and responsible to the agency or to city hall. Herman even went so far as to sue the city attorney to gain possession of some land acquisition files related to the agency's eminent domain activities.

Herman's initial reaction to the CAO's attack was to label it Mellon's "vendetta."[3] As the April 28, 1971, *Examiner* noted, "Mellon is reported to be upset over the fact that such vital parts of his city hall empire like the Department of Public Works and the City Architect's office would be bypassed entirely in the Yerba Buena deal."

Mellon's intervention brought mixed reactions from Mayor Alioto. On the one hand, he did not want to tangle with Mellon and thereby create political waves among his administration's backers. The mayor probably agreed with Mellon that there were numerous problems surrounding Herman's handling of YBC and that the agency's stubbornness on the housing issue might keep the project stalled in litigation for years. Alioto was primarily concerned with getting YBC built as fast as possible. On the other hand, the last thing in the world he wanted was a general obligation bond issue on the ballot, and in this he sided with the Redevelopment Agency. The mayor averted a confrontation between the chief administrative officer and the Redevelopment Agency through a series of meetings involving both Mellon and Herman. In these, the hotel owners' mild rebellion was useful as a tool to manipulate both men. According to the April 28, 1971, *Examiner* account of Alioto's strategy:

> [H]e's determined to defeat any move that might endanger or even delay the construction of the convention complex.
>
> That became clear yesterday as the Mayor summoned the pick of the City's hotelmen and businessmen to his office for a meeting to mobilize the business community to battle, if necessary, for the Yerba Buena Center. Mellon was out of town as the Mayor called the closed meeting . . .
>
> [S]ome of the top hotelmen attending the session appeared not entirely to grasp the full impact of the big City Hall intrigue in which they were called to participate. . . . Trying at all cost to avert a showdown with Mellon, et al., the Mayor was obviously laying the groundwork for assuring support for rapid construction of the Convention Center—with whatever financing method brings fastest results.

Mellon was brought to realize that a general obligation bond issue would be defeated, probably spelling an end to the entire project. In order to pacify him and still his objections to the Central Blocks financing and development plan, he himself was put in charge of developing the public facilities, and his office was authorized to devise, with the Redevelopment Agency, a new financing plan. The hotel owners for their part got a new design for the exhibition hall. The designs were redrawn to provide for more widely spaced columns and other improvements, following a nationwide tour of convention facilities in August 1971 by representatives of the Redevelopment Agency, the Chamber of Commerce, the Downtown Association, labor unions, and the hotel industry, organized and led by Richard Swig.

When the dust cleared from this internal squabble, the City, under Mellon and Mayor Alioto, emerged as the developer of the YBC public facilities; the Redevelopment Agency had been pushed to the background, with the developer it had chosen—Schlesinger/Arcon-Pacific—holding only a part of the project, the private sites in the Central Blocks. Schlesinger/Arcon-Pacific was reimbursed to the tune of $516,000, supposedly for studies and plans undertaken up to that time. Since it is unlikely that in the few months between their formal designation as developer and the City's decision to take over public facilities development the partnership could have incurred actual expenses of such a magnitude, this payment probably represented a "buy-off" as well.

Shortly after this palace revolt, Justin Herman died. And with his death, the role and power of the San Francisco Redevelopment Agency were further diminished.

End of an Era

Justin Herman suffered a heart attack and died on August 30, 1971, at the age of sixty-two. Many ascribed his demise in large part to stresses and disappointments caused by the undermining of his authority and control. At the time of his death, he and his agency had been under constant pressure from city hall to make concessions on relocation housing so that the project could get under way. Herman was adamant in his opposition to such concessions, as well as to the design changes demanded by the hotel owners and convention-tourist industry. Reportedly, his heart attack came while he was at work in his Golden Gateway apartment drafting a memorandum to the mayor explaining why he would never agree to a change in the YBC plan. "Hours before," the August 31, 1971, *Examiner* reported, "he'd mapped strategy against efforts aimed at radically changing the design of his latest monument-to-be, the convention center in the Yerba Buena complex South of Market. With a showdown scheduled in the mayor's office this morning, Herman told his colleagues: 'One more design change and I'll quit.' " *Examiner* urban affairs writer Donald Canter later observed: "One of the greatest weaknesses of M. Justin Herman was that he used to brag that he always won every battle." The stalled YBC project and the continuing successful opposition from South of Market residents threatened to present Herman with his first major defeat as head of San Francisco's redevelopment efforts. Indeed, YBC had become so problematic that the City was moving to take the whole matter out of Herman's hands and place the responsibility elsewhere.

During his dozen years in San Francisco, Herman shaped the Redevelopment Agency into a powerful force to carry out the City's redevelopment master plan. His successes earned him and the agency almost a free hand in pursuing their work. The *National Journal* probably best summarized Herman's career, characterizing him as:

> [O]ne of the great urban renewal grantsmen of the 1950's and 1960's. . . .
> In pushing through his program, Herman brusquely overrode opposition

from minority groups and small merchants in areas to be redeveloped. He was one of the men responsible for getting urban renewal named "the federal bulldozer" and "Negro removal." . . . [A HUD official said] "Herman could move rapidly on renewal—demolition or construction— because he was absolutely confident that he was doing what the power structure wanted insofar as the poor the minorities were concerned. . . . That's why San Francisco has mostly luxury housing and business district projects—that's what white, middle-class planners and businessmen envision as ideal urban renewal. . . . Also, with Herman in control, San Francisco renewal never got slowed down by all this citizen participation business that tormented other cities.[4]

In choosing a successor to Herman, Mayor Alioto was determined to further the transfer of control over the YBC Central Blocks development from the agency to city hall in order to move the project ahead. A supercompetent, inflexible director was no longer what the City administration wanted. Following the brief interim reign of an acting executive director, Mayor Alioto in December 1971 announced the appointment of Robert Rumsey, an assistant director of SFRA and a longtime Herman associate. Rumsey presented a sharp contrast to Herman's energy and charisma. Appointed at the same time were three assistant directors to serve as a "new management team," one of whom had been Mayor Alioto's former campaign manager.

The March 1972 Financing Plan

The new financing plan for Yerba Buena Center divided the eighty-seven-acre site into public and private portions. The former—on the three Central Blocks—was to consist of a convention center, sports arena, pedestrian mall, garage, and heating plant; the latter, on the remaining acreage and portions of the Central Blocks, was to be office and commercial space.

Until 1972, the project was able to proceed relying solely on federal grants and loans—over $40 million by that time—for planning, land acquisition and clearance, relocation of residents, and administration. No local money was required, and only routine local approvals were needed. While under the urban renewal program localities had to contribute one-third of these project costs, expenditures for public facilities related to a project could satisfy that requirement. Skillful renewal administrators like Justin Herman were able to manipulate what was sometimes referred to as the "credits shell game" so that a city, by counting local expenditures it would have made anyway, never had to put any cash of its own into its renewal program. For example, a portion of BART expenditures was credited as a local YBC project cost because the transit system would serve the YBC area.

When the March 1972 financing plan came before the supervisors, their lack of involvement in the project and the complexity of the plan documents overwhelmed them. What was proposed was a $219 million capital expenditure for the public facilities, to be funded via a $225 million Redevelopment Agency bond issue. The supervisors held perfunctory hearings and passed the plan unanimously. One supervisor explained, "When the financing plan came up before the Board, I asked for a two-week delay because we had no time to study the proposal. But I voted 'yes' on the plan finally because of the recommendation of the Finance Committee. But I really had no idea what was in the plan. . . . Once a project reaches the financial stage it becomes almost unstoppable." Another supervisor said, "If you really want me to tell you, we have very little control over the Redevelopment Agency." Nor had the Redevelopment Agency board earlier provided a forum for discussing the wisdom and implications of this financing plan. According to the March 15, 1972, *Chronicle:* "The Redevelopment Agency's decision to go $219 million into debt was without public discussion or question. The matter appeared as 19th on a routine and uncontroversial agenda. . . . Agency executive director Robert Rumsey explained with a few sentences the outline of the agreement and asked if there were any questions. There were none and the proposal was moved, seconded and passed unanimously in a minute or less."

Under the financing arrangement, the public facilities would be leased to the City for an estimated $14.5 million annually, enough to amortize the bonds and "cover any additional expenses which may be incurred by the Agency."[5] These payments would be made for thirty years, at which time title to the facilities would be transferred to the City. The financing agreement obligated the City to pay SFRA the stipulated "rent" and other costs, whether or not the projected revenue from the facilities and other sources covered the debt. The cost of building these public facilities was estimated to be $142 million at the time. The total cost—funded interest (a special fund to pay debt service during the construction period, prior to the opening of revenue-producing facilities), land costs, architectural and engineering fees, consultants, administration, and other miscellaneous items—would be $219 million. Taking into account interest payments on the bonds over thirty years, the total long-term cost of the public facilities, assuming then-existing interest rates, would have been around $500 million—well over twice their announced cost. The magnitude of this venture is illustrated by the fact that San Francisco's entire municipal budget for fiscal year 1973–74 was $648 million.

The supervisors did not question the plan's assumption that the bonds could be sold at a 6 percent interest rate, although a memorandum from the City's budget analyst suggested that a 7 to 7.5 percent interest rate would be more likely. And no account was taken of cost increases due to possible delays in project execution from the then very much alive TOOR suit or possible future litigation. At the time, construction costs were estimated to inflate by 8 to 10 percent, or as much as $14 million, annually.

The plan's revenue projections were perhaps most questionable. Four sources were itemized:

1. private land rents: the amount the private developer was to pay annually for the right to develop and sublease the private sites on the Central Blocks;

2. income from the public facilities: about half this amount was expected to come from the sports arena, one-fourth from a ticket tax on all public events at the arena;

3. hotel tax allocation: 36 percent of the revenue from the then 5.5 percent citywide hotel tax assigned by ordinance to Yerba Buena Center development;

4. property tax increment: all property tax revenue from privately owned land in the project area, beyond what the City received in 1965 (before passage of the YBC plan), was to be placed in a special fund to pay off the YBC bonds.

While cost figures were shaky, revenue projections were even more so. Although the exhibition hall–convention center was scheduled to produce no net income, based on convention center experience in other large cities, it would likely show a substantial operating loss. The City's existing public convention facilities in the Civic Auditorium and Brooks Hall were losing $200,000 a year, and the state-owned Cow Palace, used for both conventions and sports events, was losing $300,000 a year. The proposed sports arena was to bring in an annual revenue some $800,000 above operating costs, but the assumptions underlying this figure were wholly unrealistic, as outlined below.

Any shortfalls in the projected use of the arena and convention center would have had multiplier effects. Thus, the arena was scheduled to produce $800,000 in ticket taxes, and these City revenues were also earmarked for debt financing. If the arena was not used according to projections, the amount of ticket tax revenue would also be lower. The parking garage was supposed to bring in $1.9 million annually in net revenues, all earmarked to pay off the bonds. If the arena was not used to the extent projected, these revenues too would fall. And finally, revenues from the 1,850-stall public garage were based on an intensity of usage equal to that of a nearby 2,000-stall public garage, even though the proposed hourly rates for the YBC garage were twice as high as that of the neighboring garage (which was not then operating at full capacity).

The $2 million projected in hotel tax revenue was fairly certain, although labeling it "income" from YBC, as the Redevelopment Agency did, was somewhat disingenuous. This $2 million was already being collected from hotels all over the city.

The central component of the 1972 financing plan—accounting for three-fifths of all projected revenue—was the property tax increment. The agency's fiscal projections assumed an 840 percent increase in assessments between 1965 and 1978, a figure backed by little hard evidence, and one that struck many knowledgeable observers as highly optimistic. In addition, there likely would be a tendency to "go easy" in setting assessment values on these properties and granting abatements, in order to encourage development and owing to developers' political connections. The tax increment projections assumed that all eighteen private sites would be developed on schedule, even though at the time only three had been sold.

Perhaps the most blatant fallacy in the YBC financing plan was this use of tax increment financing as the principal source of revenue to pay for the public facilities bonds. This destroyed one of the basic economic justifications given for the project: that it would increase the city's tax base and provide more revenue for the City. If increased tax revenues from YBC were fed back into paying off its bonds, then nothing would be available to the City to pay for improved municipal services or to reduce the general tax rate.

Use of tax increment financing to pay off the Yerba Buena Center bonds would have been even more damaging to the City's treasury than was apparent at first glance, for a great deal of the economic activity that would locate in the project would have occurred elsewhere in the city, had there been no project. The 1973 environmental impact report for the project calculated that office space to be provided in Yerba Buena Center "is expected to absorb 80 percent of estimated annual demand over the next decade, [but] these developments will represent a shift in location from the Financial District and other areas rather than a net increase in economic activity and building." Thus, the renewal project's original financing plan would have siphoned off from the City's general fund tax revenues that otherwise would accrue from future development.

Rather than deriving any benefits from the Yerba Buena Center development, the general fund, under the original financing plan, would have lost substantial sums of money. For thirty years (until the bonds were retired), it would have lost the annual property tax revenue that would have been received from the land in the Yerba Buena area above the 1965 level, which would have increased annually as both assessed values and the tax rate climbed. And the tax roll for property in the area, hence tax revenue, decreased markedly after 1965, when the Redevelopment Agency began acquiring and clearing the land. This "fallow" period between clearance of the project area and completion of construction, which was to have lasted at least until 1976, and actually has already lasted three and a half decades longer, has cost the City millions of dollars in foregone tax revenues. Just through 1983, the difference between actual property tax revenues received from land in the Yerba Buena area and the estimated property tax revenue the City would have received from this land had there been no Yerba Buena project, compounded conservatively at 6.5 percent annually, was about $12 million.[6]

In the two years after the financing plan was approved, the announced annual cost of the YBC public facilities rose from $14.5 million to $18.6 million, and the total thirty-year bond principal and interest payments, plus "additional costs," rose from $507 million to $651 million. Inflation in both construction costs and interest rates was partially responsible, plus a more realistic and expanded concept of what these "additional costs" would be. The size of these commitments, their rapid rise, the lack of certainty that they would not rise even further once approvals were given, and the open-ended nature of the "additional costs" category raised public controversy in many quarters and eventually led to a series of lawsuits against the project (see below).

The Settlement Pact

Although Justin Herman's death and city hall's takeover of the YBC public facilities laid the groundwork for a final solution to the TOOR lawsuit, there was little noticeable movement on the replacement housing issue until fall 1972. The supervisors' March 1972 approval of the public facilities financing plan devised by Mellon and the agency, and the new difficulties that HUD and other lawsuits (triggered by the financing plan and environmental concerns) were creating for the project, made it obvious that new moves were necessary to meet the consent decree's November 1973 deadline. It now seemed possible for the agency to locate enough hotels suitable and available for renovation as permanent low-income housing. The problem of subsidy funds, however, was to prove more difficult, given a forthcoming federal government moratorium on housing programs and the extensive rent supplements already given by HUD to help rehouse YBC residents. In August 1972, the City proposed subsidizing the additional units needed to fill its quota by increasing the hotel tax. This tax, then a 5.5 percent surcharge added to hotel rates (excluding rooms occupied by permanent residents), had already been raised in 1967 to 5 percent from 3 percent in order to create a special fund to help pay YBC development costs. The City proposed an additional half percent increase, which it estimated would subsidize some seven hundred units.

Although another increase in the tax was politically sensitive, eliciting great anguish from the hotel industry (which, in a grandstand play, even threatened to challenge the legality of the hotel tax itself), the supervisors approved it in late 1972. However, the opposition of the hotel owners and other convention industry representatives was effective to the extent that the supervisors, in an effort to mollify these powerful interests, gave in to their "demand" that a portion of any new hotel tax revenues (approximately $100,000) go to the Convention & Visitors Bureau, increasing its annual allocation from the City to nearly $1 million.[7]

But even this new infusion of funds for housing did not solve the problem. TOOR continued to challenge before Judge Weigel the validity of the agency's rercvised, HUD-approved relocation plan and the eligibility of replacement housing units the agency listed for the federal court in its mandatory quarterly reports. Substantial numbers of these units, TOOR claimed (with evidence), either were programmed prior to April 30, 1970, or were already occupied by nontransient low-income residents, contrary to Judge Weigel's guidelines. The City's urgent need was to get on with the actual construction of YBC, as inflation kept pushing development costs higher and hotel owners and other convention industry figures kept pressing for the new exhibition facility; it was possible that continued delays could endanger the project altogether. A further consideration was that three privately sponsored housing developments outside the YBC area containing 422 units were almost ready for occupancy. About a third of these were reserved for YBC displacees, but if they were not occupied within a certain time they would be filled by other applicants. The loss of these units could jeopardize the agency's YBC relocation plan and cause HUD to withdraw its approval.

In January 1973, William Coblentz, a local attorney influential in state Democratic circles, University of California regent, and political advisor to Mayor Alioto, undertook to bring the parties together and arrange a settlement that would induce TOOR to abandon its lawsuit. This course was prompted by the calculation that TOOR, even if it lost every step of the way, could, through further legal actions and appeals, delay the project nearly two years past the November 1973 consent decree deadline—which the agency could not meet in any case.

After several weeks of behind-the-scenes negotiations, TOOR, its attorneys, and the Redevelopment Agency staff fashioned a tentative agreement:

in essence, it called for the agency and City to construct some four hundred units of new housing (over and above the previous fifteen hundred- to eighteen hundred-unit commitment) on four sites in or adjacent to the project area, in return for which TOOR would dismiss its lawsuit.

The proposed settlement not only contained a major concession, in allowing replacement housing to be built in the project area, but also called for still another increase in the city's hotel tax, to 6.5 percent from 6 percent, to pay for this housing. Mayor Alioto, wanting the Board of Supervisors to take some of the political heat for the proposal, asked that it hold hearings on the plan. In a novel proceeding, the full board held a hearing in April 1973 on a tentative agreement not yet approved by the parties involved and therefore not calling for any action by the board.

Hotel owners were livid at the prospect of a second increase within the span of a few months. Irving Baldwin, testifying for the Hotel Employers Association, decried the proposed tax increase as "immoral." "Why should visitors be forced to solve the problems of indigents in San Francisco?" he reasoned to the board, regarding a project designed to demolish thousands of low-rent housing units and displace thousands of low-income people in order to create a convention center. Baldwin's ethical sensibilities had also been offended the previous October when the hotel tax was increased to 6 percent. The October 6, 1972, *Progress* had quoted him: "It's a moral issue. The City shouldn't ask its guests to pay for indigents to be relocated. Underwriting the Convention Center is another story." But it was not morality that decided the issue; rather, it was the raw political and financial muscle the hotel owners and the convention industry exerted in the political arena. The April 24, 1973, *Examiner* observed:

> When it became known that another half cent increase in the hotel tax was proposed to help finance this housing, the hotel industry revolted. With five Supervisors up for re-election in November, the reaction to the hotel industry's stand was predictable. Feverish behind-the-scenes dickering then resulted in a complicated financial counter offer that excluded any hotel tax increase. . . . In what observers considered a show of allegiance to the Mayor, labor leaders joined the hotel industry in demanding that Yerba Buena be built but without any additional burden on the hotel tax.

What emerged was a compromise settlement, under which, by manipulating various pots of City money, a second hotel tax increase was avoided, and TOOR was guaranteed funds sufficient to subsidize several hundred housing units in and adjacent to the YBC project.

On May 15, 1973, in the lobby of the Milner Hotel, TOOR and the Redevelopment Agency put their signatures to an agreement, the essence of which was an additional four hundred permanent, subsidized low-rent units built by TOOR South of Market in exchange for TOOR dropping its lawsuit. The agreement outlined an elaborate step-by-step process, involving actions by the Board of Supervisors, Planning Commission, and Redevelopment Agency, and gave interim protection to remaining residents. (The agency nonetheless hounded its victims. An account from the July 13, 1974, *Chronicle* revealed that the SFRA had turned over to an Oakland collection agency several hundred cases of back rent owed by residents of YBC hotels. "In some instances . . . redevelopment officials conceded, poor and ailing senior citizens have been sent threatening letters that warned of legal action unless back rent was paid within 48 hours. Some of the hapless wanderers who received the ominous warnings actually qualified as 'hardship cases,' eligible for complete dispensation from back payments, redevelopment spokesmen confirmed.")

An important element in the agreement was continuation of TOOR in a new incarnation as the nonprofit, community-based housing sponsor/owner for the four hundred units (one of the provisions to which Mayor Alioto and the Redevelopment Agency originally had the strongest objections). The Tenants and Owners Development Corporation (TODCO) was assigned responsibility for architect selection, architectural program and designs, financing and subsidization plans, construction supervision, ownership, and eventually management of the units (see chapter 10). It also was given a budget sufficient to do its work properly, and Stephen Dutton, TOOR's executive director, was chosen to direct the new housing development corporation.

With respect to the fifteen hundred units of replacement housing the agency had committed to in its November 1970 consent decree, the agreement allowed the agency an extra year to complete these units and provided that in the interim TOOR would waive any objections to the agency's program for producing them. The agency did finally come up with 1,661 replacement units—mostly rehabilitated rooms and apartments in the Tenderloin, Mission, and South of Market areas. A few hundred of these were of dubious eligibility for inclusion in the count, as they had been planned before the consent decree was signed; but by this time TOOR/TODCO had turned its attention to constructing new housing.

TOOR's half of the bargain was, of course, what the City had sought for nearly four years: dismissal of its lawsuit with prejudice (i.e., without possibility of reinstituting it). The agreement required TOOR's attorneys to move immediately for dismissal in federal court, although complaints about alleged breaches could still be brought to the court.

At the agency's insistence, the agreement included an important "fail-safe" clause: The agency was not required to issue its replacement housing bonds until its public facilities bonds were sold. Thus, anything interfering with the financing of the Central Blocks facilities would also prevent construction of the replacement housing that comprised TOOR's victory in the final settlement. TOOR was even required "to use its best efforts to assist in settling all legal actions which currently or in the future interfere with execution of activities leading to the prompt completion of the public facilities, low-income housing, and private development scheduled for construction in the YBC Project Area." This provision clearly addressed the various lawsuits by then pending (discussed below) on financing and environmental aspects of the project.

The agreement thus ensured that from that point on TOOR would be as pro-YBC as the agency. To prove this loyalty, TOOR attorney Anthony Kline publicly denounced as "sheer insanity"[8] a lawsuit by conservationist-businessman Alvin Duskin to stop the YBC project entirely and his announced signature drive to place the issue on the November 1973 ballot. And the *Examiner*'s May 15, 1973, account of the press conference at which the final agreement was signed noted:

> [TOOR chairman Peter] Mendelsohn also vowed TOOR will do everything to make sure that the agreement is carried out and vowed to oppose anyone who might try to sabotage the deal. Asked to clarify this statement Mendelsohn said he was referring to Alvin Duskin's newly formed Friends of Yerba Buena organization which has announced it will start an initiative campaign to place on the ballot a measure that would veto construction of the convention complex. "They're not the friends of Yerba Buena," Mendelsohn said, adding that "no TOOR member will sign the initiative."

The newspapers gave heavy play to TOOR and effusively praised its gains in this agreement—in striking contrast to previous editorial attitudes toward the organization. The May 1, 1973, *Examiner* spoke of TOOR's "stunning victory over City Hall"; the May 16, 1973, *Chronicle* wrote of TOOR's "highly effective young legal team"; and the May 15, 1973, *Examiner* noted "the fact that the ceremony [signing of the agreement] was held in a Skid Row hotel rather than in the offices of the Redevelopment Agency left no doubt as to who emerged as the victor."

As a fitting cap to TOOR's legal victory, the court awarded Public Advocates $233,000 in legal fees—although, in keeping with the City's dilatory response throughout the litigation, nearly four years elapsed before the City paid up.

The Financing Lawsuits

Final settlement of TOOR's relocation suit by no means meant an end to litigation over the Yerba Buena project. That action dealt only with damages caused by the Redevelopment Agency's land clearance activities. The subsequent phase of public action—building on the cleared site—triggered a whole new set of concerns, actors, and lawsuits.

Immediately following the supervisors' approval of the YBC financing plan, two nearly identical taxpayers' suits were filed in state court, challenging the financing scheme as an unconstitutional attempt to encumber San Franciscans with massive long-term debt obligations without seeking voter approval.[9] At about the same time, six conservation groups, including the Sierra Club and San Francisco Tomorrow, filed suit in federal court, claiming that YBC and two other Bay Area projects violated the National Environmental Policy Act of 1969 (NEPA) in not having prepared environmental impact statements. (The environmental impact suits, which hinged on the applicability of NEPA to projects under way at the time the act was passed, led to HUD's agreement to produce an environmental impact statement for YBC, in exchange for the plaintiffs' agreement not to appeal adverse district court and appeals court decisions, which would have delayed the project for an indefinite period of time.)

The suits challenging the YBC financing plan were brought by Alvin Duskin and his attorney, William Brinton, and by attorney Gerald Wright on behalf of a small group of taxpayer clients. Duskin, who in the 1960s started a fashionable and highly successful dressmaking concern, had just led a victorious popular protest against a Texas developer's plan to turn Alcatraz Island in San Francisco Bay into a monumentally crass tourist attraction featuring a replica of the Apollo 8 moon rocket and a recreation of Victorian San Francisco. In 1971, and again in 1972, he had launched ballot initiatives drastically limiting the height of new office buildings. Although both lost, their imaginative publicity devices and campaign efforts provided the foundation for the city's antihigh-rise movements of the late 1970s and beyond (see chapter 12).

Duskin's lawyer, William Brinton, was a former planning commissioner whose bitter and public feud with Joseph Alioto over the forty-eight-story, pyramid-shaped Transamerica Building, in which Brinton alleged that the mayor exerted undue pressure on the commission to support the building, led Alioto to remove him from the commission. Both men were well known, controversial public figures (Brinton also had run for the Board of Supervisors in 1955 and for the State Assembly in 1958). By contrast, Gerald Wright, the central figure in the parallel financing suit, was relatively unknown and quiet, steadfastly refusing to reveal any information about his clients.

For reasons impossible to fathom, the City and the Redevelopment Agency, defendants in the two financing suits, for two years did not even bother to answer the complaints. In November 1973, the Redevelopment Agency did file a "validation suit"—a general action seeking to have a court validate its financing plan against any future claims of illegality and requiring any potential litigants to come forward or lose their future rights to challenge the plan.[10] When Gerald Wright did not answer the summons notifying him of the validation suit, the agency trumpeted that his suit was disposed of, a claim dutifully retrumpeted by the *Examiner* in its January 7, 1974, headline, "Yerba Buena Foes Dwindle to 1—Duskin." The quite competent and confident Wright informed the agency, when they later contacted him, that the summons he received was illegal, since it gave only twenty-seven days' notice, whereas the law stipulated a thirty-day notice requirement, and the agency thereupon quietly renewed its summons. Wright maintained—correctly, as it turned out—that the agency in any case could not dispose of his and Duskin's suits in this manner but had to respond as defendants to the actions the two already had filed. The City's tack seemed to be to try to force Duskin, Brinton, and Wright to drop their suits through public pressure depicting them as loners and cranks. In his remarks to the supervisors opening the 1974 legislative session, Mayor Alioto, according to the January 9, 1974, *Examiner*, "also managed to slam attorney William Brinton . . . by referring to Brinton as Alvin Duskin's free lawyer, who seems to be doing it [suing to halt the Yerba Buena project] on a malicious basis."

The delay in answering the two citizens' lawsuits might partly be attributed to the distraction and problems created by the TOOR suit—the fact that the project in any case could not move ahead until Judge Weigel was satisfied the agency was obeying federal relocation statutes. But the agency's and City's failure to pay sufficient attention to the Duskin and Wright suits meant that by the time they really wanted to move on construction of the public facilities—the convention center, sports arena, garage, etc.—they had to deal urgently and expeditiously with the substantial barriers these legal moves presented. The planned schedule was to complete design and construction specifications by the fall of 1974; send the project out to bid toward the end of that year; award the contract in February 1975; sell the bonds as soon thereafter as possible; and begin construction by the summer of 1975. With that timetable in mind, the City and Redevelopment Agency sought out settlement discussions with the new plaintiffs in mid-1974.

Settlement talks proceeded over the summer of 1974, principally through the mediation efforts of Supervisor Dianne Feinstein and John Dykstra, the Redevelopment Agency's former YBC project director, who had left the agency earlier that year to work for a private real estate development and investment firm. (Feinstein's involvement related to Brinton's having been finance chair for her unsuccessful 1971 mayoral run against Alioto. Brinton also, according to the September 9, 1974, *Examiner,* had contributed five thousand dollars to her campaign and loaned her another forty-five thousand dollars—figures he claims are exaggerated.)

In September 1974, all parties tentatively agreed to the following as a quid pro quo for abandonment of the two suits: (1) a reduction in the maximum bond issue from $225 million to $210 million;[11] (2) deletion of the sports arena from the public facilities portion of the bond issue (although there was a provision that it could be built with other financing); and (3) attorneys' fees were to be paid to Brinton and Wright for their work on the suits, ninety-two thousand dollars and seventy-five hundred dollars, respectively.

Since elements of the proposed settlement required Board of Supervisors' action, hearings were held, at which the central issue was the law fees for Brinton, which amounted to less than 1/2500 of the bond issue. In part, this may have been a conscious device to divert public attention from major to minor issues, but it also reflected widespread hostility to Duskin and Brinton on the part of the political establishment, most notably Joseph Alioto (with memories of Brinton's opposition to the Transamerica Pyramid and his activities on behalf of Dianne Feinstein in the 1971 mayoral race). Alioto announced he would veto such a payment if the supervisors approved it. (In fact, he allowed it to pass without his signature.) Amazingly, the supervisors in their hearings felt no need to review the financing plan they had approved for YBC, even though the sports arena—a facility projected to furnish close to $3 million of the amount needed annually to repay the bond issue—had by then been dropped. Accompanied by loud blasts at Brinton (including Supervisor Robert Gonzales's eloquent declamation that "Mr. Brinton's fees of $92,000 make me puke"),[12] they approved the settlement terms.

But in late February 1975, one point in the settlement agreement proved fatal to it. The low bid for constructing the convention center, garage, and pedestrian walkways, by the Chicago firm Gust K. Newberg, was $17 million higher than a $210 million bond issue would support. Since the type of bonds being issued, known as lease-revenue bonds, require substantial set-asides for reserves and funded interest, the amount actually available for construction, once other costs such as insurance, architectural and legal fees, and land purchase are paid, is only about two-thirds of the entire amount raised by the bonds.

How this underestimation of the needed bond issue happened is one of the mysteries of the YBC story. Duskin and Brinton maintain they knew, based on their own consultants, that the City could not finance the public facilities with a bond issue of $210 million, which is why they agreed to the settlement.

The City and agency were in a real fix. They had two upcoming deadlines: Newberg's bid would expire June 16, 1975, and the settlement agreement with Duskin et al. stipulated that the bonds had to be sold by June 30, 1975. Scrambling to come up with a solution, they proposed to squeeze the project within the $210 million limit by postponing for five years the $14 million land payment to HUD (which HUD agreed to, in order to facilitate the project) and by tinkering with the design to shave another $3 million. When asked how the City would eventually repay the $14 million to HUD, Mayor Alioto said it would come from the project's increased property tax revenues; this, even though the financing plan already assigned every penny of these revenues to bond retirement payments. Based on this premise, the Redevelopment Agency accepted the Newberg bid—the largest City contract in the preceding thirty-four years, according to Mayor Alioto[13]—conditional on selling the bonds. (" 'We'll send the pen to Mr. Duskin,' sneered Mayor Alioto," reported the March 7, 1975, *Examiner.*) And in March 1975, the supervisors passed the final financing documents—the bond repayment agreement and the lease by which the City would rent the convention center built with money raised by Redevelopment Agency bonds.

The lease agreement that actually passed was somewhat different from what had been earlier stated. Up to passage, it was assumed the City would be obligated to make an annual lease payment of $18.6 million to the Redevelopment Agency for use of the convention center—the amount needed to make annual principal and interest payments to the bondholders. But the actual lease stipulated that any and all costs beyond the $18.6 million—construction cost overruns, insurance, payments to bond trustees, *and* the Redevelopment Agency's own administrative costs connected with the Yerba Buena project—also were the City's obligation. This made the lease an open-ended commitment of City tax funds beyond the $560 million total payments over thirty years—and triggered more outrage among various YBC opponents.

The City-agency "quick fix" approach to the dilemma caused by the $210 million bond issue limit brought an immediate demand from Alvin Duskin et al. for arbitration. Under the settlement agreement, any claimed breach of its provisions had first to be submitted to arbitration, and Duskin and Wright claimed that the postponed land payment in essence violated the bond issue limit. This put them back in the driver's seat, although with a relatively narrow issue to negotiate on.

On reentering the negotiating arena, Duskin, Brinton, and Wright now found themselves with a set of newly acquired collaborators. Previously they had operated largely in a political vacuum, neither seeking allies nor being sought by others who opposed the project or had an interest in its outcome. According to one analysis:

> Brinton, Duskin and Wright had struggled against YBC without actively organizing support from the San Francisco residents on whose behalf they professed to be fighting, and their lengthy out-of-court negotiations had of course been conducted out of public view. The settlement apparently took people who were concerned with the fate of YBC, but not intimately involved with the litigation, by surprise. Calvin Welch, an organizer in San Francisco's Haight neighborhood . . . recalls that the plaintiffs settled "without explaining why they were doing it, what the strategy was."[14]

Now that the two lawsuits had emerged as significant and well publicized barriers to the project, and the City and agency were seeking to make a deal, additional players appeared on the scene, focusing mainly around Alvin Duskin, the most visible and accessible of the litigants, and the one most concerned about the political ramifications of the suits.

Duskin was disturbed about the political turn his opposition to YBC was taking. What had happened was that the City and Redevelopment Agency succeeded in framing the litigation, to the public and to various interest groups, as "lawyers vs. jobs." Believing that it was time to take the political initiative and reformulate the issue, and counseled by several urban planners and organizers in close touch with community needs and concerns, Duskin held a press conference on March 6, 1975, to issue a "Call for Citywide Decision-Making on Yerba Buena," in which he stated:

> I have felt from the beginning that Yerba Buena's financing was . . . a matter for the people of San Francisco to decide. . . . I shall use what leverage I have to open up the decision-making process, not to dictate its result. I will yield to an open decision-making process. In this City, such a process must begin with the neighborhoods. . . .
>
> The City has asked us to let them break their own settlement agreement. I ask for the possibility of a special referendum on Yerba Buena in return. . . . If a special election is called. . . . I will withdraw [the lawsuit] if a program of discussion and involvement with neighborhood and civic groups precedes any election. . . . The City must commit itself to presenting its case before the organizations and people of San Francisco, and giving opponents the same opportunity. . . . I am prepared to undertake any reasonable alternate method of determining if, in fact, the people want an election or a less expensive way of determining their wishes.

In contrast to earlier, go-it-alone moves, Duskin and his new counselors had organized an array of community support for his March 6 "Call," including San Francisco Tomorrow (the city's leading environmental group), the Victorian Alliance, and individuals identified with various neighborhood groups.

In early April, Duskin was asked to meet with the San Francisco Coalition (an umbrella group set up by the Redevelopment Agency and Human Rights Commission in 1973, consisting of some thirty organizations concerned with securing minority jobs from the YBC project), TOOR, and one wing of the city's neighborhood movement, to consider a proposal that he give up his legal fight in favor of guarantees relating to minority employment and TOOR's housing. This appealed to Duskin, in light of his concerns about the politics being generated around his suit and the pressures developing on him and his supporters; it seemed like a principled and graceful way to terminate his opposition. The result was another press conference, held April 14, at which three new demands were put forth as the basis for ending the arbitration claim, accompanied by an extensive list of organizational and individual endorsers.

> First . . . all construction and permanent jobs in the project area, both public and private, must go, wherever possible, to qualified residents of San Francisco—and half of these jobs must go to minority residents of San Francisco through an affirmative action program. All parties must agree that the San Francisco Coalition, backed by an adequate budget, will set up and monitor the affirmative action program for the jobs and contracts in the public and private blocks of YBC. . . .
>
> Second, the City must guarantee that the 400 or more units of low-income housing struggled for and won by the people of South of Market will be built. . . . All housing agreements made with TOOR must be amended to provide the housing regardless of whether the rest of YBC goes ahead or not. . . .
>
> Third, the City must guarantee that a committee of residents of the South of Market be given all necessary authority to insure that the present YBC plan permits the continued existence of the South of Market community and develop a plan for the future growth and rehabilitation of the South of Market community.[15]

Realistically, the demands, in particular the first and third, were a little mushy—the "wherever possible" clause in the jobs demand undercut it enormously, and the replanning proposal was very vague. But given the circumscribed maneuvering room the settlement agreement had left the plaintiffs and the multiple, sometimes competing pressures on Duskin from his newly found coworkers, perhaps this was the best that could be devised, particularly given the press of time and lack of any established forum or process in which to work out a coordinated strategy. Their major tactical function was to show that Duskin et al. were on the side of jobs; and they were designed to reveal that the demands of the construction trade unions, whose membership was largely white and lived in the suburbs, were not necessarily identical to those of minority workers in the city. (According to a later account, 60–70 percent of the members of the local building trade unions lived outside San Francisco.)[16]

It is important to understand the context in which this new constellation of forces and demands was developing, namely the torrent of pressure being heaped on the Duskin-Brinton crowd from the construction trade unions, egged on and sometimes orchestrated by the City and Redevelopment Agency. Quite simply, they hoped to bully the key lawsuit figures into submission. The most open form of pressure came in a mass rally and march on Brinton's office on April 17, 1975, held fittingly at Justin Herman Park in the Golden Gateway renewal project and sponsored by the San Francisco Building and Construction Trades Council, the San Francisco Labor Council, the International Longshoremen's and Warehousemen's Union, and the Teamsters Joint Council. The downtown establishment—the Chamber of Commerce, Downtown Association, Market Street Development Project, and the city's two major hotel associations—all pledged support for the event and encouraged their members to suggest that their employees attend the noontime rally. The April 9, 1975, editorial in the *Chronicle*, a paper not noted for its support of labor militancy, said: "While we do not often cheer a picket line, the one that labor unions in the construction industry are proposing to set up to convey their disgust with the Yerba Buena Center dead-end kids draws our admiration and our hope that it will work."

The atmosphere of "hard hat" intimidation was pretty clear, not only in the rally and march on Brinton's office but also in widely reported personal threats made to Alvin Duskin and William Brinton, which Duskin referred to at the end of his April 14 statement: "If anyone with an interest in the outcome of Yerba Buena attempts to threaten any other interested party or his representative by means outside the judicial process, then I will break off negotiations." The *Examiner*'s Dick Nolan, in two back-to-back columns, had this description:

> The Big Labor members of the In Bunch . . . have been called upon to mass and march the troops. Obediently, they have laid on a heavy demonstration for Thursday, with overtones just this side of inciting to riot.[17]

Negotiations [between Duskin et al. and the City] were carried on in a somewhat hectic atmosphere. I was told last Thursday that the murk around them even included urgent promises of broken legs and whatnot.[18]

A later Nolan column (April 30, 1975) went on: "It's not clear yet just what Alvin Duskin, private citizen, got out of dropping his lawsuit which had halted the big project, except possibly peace and quiet. At least one neighborhood leader who had supported Duskin's efforts had been threatened with firebombs and such, this presumably from the more muscular wing of this concerted civic effort." Attorney Gerald Wright also received threats, although of a less physical nature: "When the construction bids came in and the truth dawned, Dianne Feinstein and others entreated me to relent, extend the dates, and increase the monetary limits. I declined, although a Redevelopment Agency representative threatened to have labor goons picket my home, and Dianne threatened to torpedo a neighborhood private school for which one of my clients was seeking City approval."[19]

The *Chronicle*'s account of this carefully timed demonstration, whose size was estimated at fifteen hundred participants, noted that "City officials said they hoped the rally . . . will strengthen their hand in negotiations that resume today with Yerba Buena opponents."[20] The City's advance work to produce this scenario was noted in the April 16, 1975, *Chronicle*, which reported that "Redevelopment Agency officials confirmed that they have been deeply involved in planning the rally, an effort to pressure Yerba Buena opponents." The *Bay Guardian* reported Agency Director Arthur Evans's admission that phone calls inviting labor leaders to the April 8 breakfast to plan and announce the April 17 demonstration went out from Redevelopment Agency offices.[21]

Over the next week, the City, Redevelopment Agency, and Duskin and his allies negotiated over the precise terms of the three demands. The most concrete issue—regarding TOOR's housing—was whittled down to a commitment to release only one hundred of the four hundred units from the tie-in to construction of the convention center. The affirmative action hiring demand rapidly boiled down to how much money the San Francisco Coalition would get to undertake recruitment and monitoring activities. The squeeze the City and agency faced was that the construction trade unions were not wild about affirmative action demands to begin with; as the April 17, 1975, *Chronicle* noted, "Labor unions have resisted giving the group [the S.F. Coalition] that much power over jobs. . . . " A buy-off of the coalition seemed the easiest way out, and, according to the April 21, 1975, *Chronicle*, "The proposed agreement would give the coalition the money it had been seeking, but would not otherwise change the programs the unions have agreed to for minority workers on the project." The coalition's original demand for an annual budget of $369,000 dropped to $251,000, and they finally settled for $180,000 annually for five years—$40,000 in cash and fourteen CETA positions worth $140,000.

(Up through the time the agency ended its contract with the San Francisco Coalition, in January 1981, payments totaled $459,469. The actual number of placements was minuscule;[22] few community organizations participated in coalition activities, and the more important ones—Chinese for Affirmative Action, the Mission Hiring Hall, Women in Apprenticeship—had resigned; board membership was constantly changing, and there was no board control of staff;[23] funds were egregiously mishandled; and some of the key figures had been convicted of various crimes.[24] It was a sad story: In its eagerness to build support for and remove obstacles to the YBC project, the agency, where African Americans and other minorities had played a major role as commissioners and staff, set up a sham response to a legitimate community demand for minority jobs.)

In the end not much was left of the three Duskin demands. As a case history of this period concluded:

> When the resolution achieved by the negotiations was announced on April 20, it was clear that the City and the Redevelopment Agency had emerged the victors. The officials' concrete commitment to insuring that San Franciscans and third world people got the bulk of YBC construction jobs went no further than an agreement to pay the San Francisco Coalition $180,000 a year to monitor the affirmative action practices of the YBC contractors . . . and they have only vague promises that South of Market residents would have an effective voice in the future planning of their area. . . . Even Alvin Duskin was moved to publicly state his dissatisfaction with the pact. "I was asking the city to take a giant moral step," Duskin told a *Bay Guardian* reporter. "By refusing to accept the proposal, by nickel and diming everyone, they've destroyed the moral position I was asking for. I gave the city a chance to avoid another lawsuit. They haven't taken steps to avoid that possibility."[25]

The entire process surrounding the Wright and Duskin-Brinton lawsuits and the fallout therefrom left much to be desired. As noted, the suits and the strategies pertaining to them lacked a consistent philosophy or purpose. Although lip service was paid throughout to the principle that the bonds needed to finance YBC had to be approved by the voters, that position was abandoned in favor of a series of moves that seemed equally uninformed by a consistent or well-articulated strategy. The groups that finally congealed around the lawsuits had different purposes, not all of them openly acknowledged. Clear voices were missing from both sides. The mayor, supervisors, Redevelopment Agency, and chief administrative officer lacked a coherent strategy and negotiating position, as did Duskin, Brinton, and Wright.* And so the public negotiations were messy. All the while the clock was steadily ticking toward the two June deadlines. And a new set of oppositional forces and actors was emerging.

The *Starr* Suit

The settlement of the Duskin-Brinton and Wright suits disappointed many in the San Francisco community. The attorneys and their clients had gained some concessions from the City in the September 1974 agreement but had abandoned the principles that led them to bring their actions in the first place: opposing the waste of large chunks of public money to build YBC and the lack of meaningful public participation in key planning and financing decisions—in particular, the absence of a public vote on the huge bond issue. Duskin and Brinton, however, felt chances of actually prevailing in court were slim and regarded the settlement as the best they could hope for.

One of those convinced of the need to continue the struggle around the original principles was the author of this book, who recently had left the staff of the National Housing Law Project in order to concentrate on community-based work. (His book on the Yerba Buena project had just been published.)[26] In March 1975, with Duskin's blessing, he sent a letter to some

---

*The *Examiner*'s Dick Nolan noted that Duskin's terms "took his attorney, William Brinton, by surprise" (15 April 1975). The *Chronicle*'s story of the same day on the new demands for ending arbitration noted: "Brinton said he was surprised that Duskin's group dropped initial plans to demand a citywide election in June on Yerba Buena. Wright said he had not known the election demand was dropped until a *Chronicle* reporter informed him of the change." And the 2 May 1975 *Examiner* stated: "To make sure his forces would stick to their part of the bargain, Duskin yesterday sent to one of his lawyers, William Brinton, a letter 'instructing' him to sign Duskin's recent peace pact with the city. Brinton had been dragging his feet on the issue and was quoted as saying this week he wouldn't sign the agreement."

forty persons associated with anti-YBC activities or with neighborhood groups whose needs were in competition with the priorities represented by the project, inviting them to a meeting to discuss formation of a coalition to stop the project or change it.

The March 20 meeting, held at the Goodman Building, a symbolic center of resistance to Redevelopment Agency bulldozing efforts (see chapter 13), drew a surprisingly large and diverse turnout. Strains existed within the group, however, impeding a unified anti-YBC position. One source of tension was TOOR's housing settlement; the other was recent attempts by progressive elements in the city to put together the San Francisco Community Congress, an alliance of neighborhood activists, environmentalists, minority, and other working-class groups. The congress was the project of a tight and effective group of political activists whose immediate goal was to use it as a prime organizing step in altering the city's system of electing supervisors from an at-large to a district-based system (see chapter 11). TOOR's opposition to creating an anti-YBC coalition had been anticipated and indeed was referred to in the invitation to the March 20 meeting:

> As most of you know, the Redevelopment Agency forced on TOOR a settlement agreement tying their housing to completion of the YBC project itself: no project, no housing. This creates a real bind. In reality, there's no reason whatsoever why TOOR should not and cannot have its housing regardless of what happens to the rest of the YBC project. The funds have already been allocated by the Supervisors through the hotel tax, and the Redevelopment Agency and City could simply change the terms of their agreement with TOOR. TOOR is legitimately concerned that its chances of building housing will be reduced if any attempt is made at this point to interfere in the YBC project. But in my view any political struggle to dump or change the project would also be strong enough to force the City to honor its commitment to TOOR and its obligations to the city's low-income people.

The strong opposition to a new anti-YBC coalition on the part of those preparing the Community Congress and district elections initiative was not so clearly anticipated. They feared a new anti-YBC effort would alienate their allies in the labor movement, who were pro-YBC, and thus cost them labor support for both the congress and the initiative.

Amid considerable tensions, the March 20 meeting and a subsequent April 3 meeting of roughly the same group produced a decision to move ahead immediately with plans to file a new lawsuit, challenging the YBC bonds and lease agreement as requiring two-thirds voter approval.[27] The group also agreed to place an initiative on the November 1975 ballot, covering disposition of the YBC Central Blocks, ensuring that TOOR would get its four hundred housing units regardless of the future of the convention center, and establishing a more democratic planning process for the future of San Francisco.

As the scenario around negotiations between Duskin and his supporters and the city hall–Redevelopment Agency forces developed, it was clear that nothing but a new lawsuit could deal with the basic issues originally raised by Duskin and Wright. Ideally, YBC opponents should have allowed the City's concession to Duskin's demands to play itself out before taking further steps to implement the decisions of the Goodman Building meetings. Filing a new lawsuit would make it pointless for the City to yield in any form to Duskin's three demands, since however the settlement might be modified, a new lawsuit would still keep the project from moving ahead.

But while sound tactics called for the Goodman Building meeting participants to lie low for a while, that was not how things turned out. Within the group that voted for a new lawsuit was a contingent determined to proceed as rapidly as possible, independent of other events. Led by Jim Flack, a private economic consultant concerned with economy and sound procedure in government and with environmental issues, this contingent proceeded to assemble a large coterie of plaintiffs. On May 2, 1975, they filed their suit: *C. Starr et al. v. the City and County of San Francisco et al.* The timing was supremely foolish. The Board of Supervisors had just approved the weakened settlement of the Duskin-Wright arbitration demand—revising the housing demand to allow TOOR to build on its first site and making available needed subsidies regardless of the future of the convention center. The second and final reading of the ordinance was scheduled for the first week of May. Had the *Starr* plaintiffs waited just a few days to file their suit, the gains from the supervisors' action would have been secured, with no loss to the issues the new suit was raising.

As could have been predicted, once the *Starr* suit was filed the City had no interest in consummating the settlement. It had been willing to take a chance by allowing at least some of TOOR's housing to be built in order to placate Duskin et al., even though others might subsequently file other suits, but once another suit was a reality, TOOR was fully back in its hostage role.

The *Starr* suit focused squarely on the alleged illegality of the YBC financing arrangement. Flack and his colleagues had taken from the experience of Duskin and Wright the need to avoid compromising principle and to avoid falling into a negotiating stance or into a position where they might be sandbagged by other actors: They wanted a court once and for all to decide the basic constitutional issue of whether voter approval was or was not required for this type of financing scheme. The massive number of plaintiffs, sixty-four in all,[28] protected them against deal making, change of heart, or threats. As reported in the May 2, 1975, *Examiner*, "The filing of the new suit is almost certain to trigger violent reactions from those who now have a major stake in Yerba Buena construction. One member of the San Francisco Coalition, the group that will get the $900,000 [sic] to recruit minority workers, said last week his organization has 'ways of dealing' with any further obstructions to the project." Flack et al. selected their principled legal issue and chose to file their suit as soon as preparation of legal papers was completed. The filing of the *Starr* suit was sufficient to end this first attempt to build the convention center and its related facilities, as the Newberg construction bid expired and no bonds could be sold as long as the litigation was pending.

The City and agency prevailed at the trial court level in April 1976, but in July 1977 the California Court of Appeal unanimously reversed the lower court's *Starr* decision with respect to the City's repayment contract with the Redevelopment Agency. The appellate court held that the contract clause requiring the $14 million land payment to HUD five years after the bond issue violated Article XVI, Section 18, of the State Constitution. In the court's words:

> It [the repayment contract] creates aggregate indebtedness in 1975 (the execution date of the repayment contract) to be paid out of the City's general funds in 1980, regardless of the expenditures allotted for the year and regardless of the revenue generated by the special fund which is to finance the project. California cases make it clear that the purpose of the constitutional provision is to ensure that the legislative body of a municipality not be allowed to impose upon the general revenue of the city a long-term indebtedness without approval by two-thirds of the electorate. It is precisely such an indebtedness which is created by the repayment clause.[29]

The court also awarded $25,000 in legal fees to the *Starr* suit lawyer.

Another Sports Arena Try by Another Swig

Although the larger future of YBC and the litigation it spawned awaited arrival of a new regime at city hall, in the waning days of his administration Joseph Alioto made one last push to get a sports arena built for and by his allies, the Swigs. The favor likely was not unrelated to Ben Swig's generosity in guaranteeing a $5.4 million loan from Wells Fargo Bank secured by Alioto for one of his several family business enterprises, Pacific Far East Lines; since PFEL was at the time the largest tenant of the Port of San Francisco and Alioto appointed the Port Commissioners, the Superior Court had ruled this a violation of the City Charter. Alioto thereupon turned over his stake in PFEL to his sons, and Swig took over the mayor's loan guarantee—a rather transparent "divestiture" that hardly met the court's ruling but that the friendly district attorney, John Ferndon, allowed as the solution. The denouement was not a happy one for relations between the Alioto and Swig clans: PFEL went bankrupt in 1977, and when Wells Fargo several years later called in its loan, the Swig family—Ben having died in 1980—sued and won judgment against the Alioto group for $3.7 million. The suit was filed in Marin County because, according to Herb Caen's January 17, 1979, *Chronicle* column, "There isn't a judge in San Francisco who wouldn't have disqualified himself in anything to do with Joe or Ben." The mess did not end there, as Alioto's cousin and uncle thereupon accused the ex-mayor and his sons of having misled them as to their liability for the loan, with the jury finding partially against Joseph Alioto.[30]

The September 1974 settlement of the Duskin-Brinton and Wright lawsuits left open the possibility of producing a sports arena under a different financing scheme. And so the Redevelopment Agency and Alioto, hoping to keep some YBC momentum alive and to put at least one of the originally planned public facilities in place quickly, reintroduced a proposal to build this indoor multipurpose arena for basketball, hockey, and other events. A familiar name led the charge: In May 1975, Melvin Swig, Benjamin's older son and about-to-be owner of the National Hockey League Golden Seals team, proposed a deal to a very receptive mayor. It called for the City to form a nonprofit corporation to sell $20 million in tax-exempt bonds to construct the YBC arena. Once built, it would be leased to Swig at no charge, and Swig would run it, paying all costs, including bond retirement. The arena would be exempt from property taxes but would pay a possessory interest tax amounting to about 15–20 percent of what the property tax would be. Land for the arena would be sold to Swig for eight dollars a square foot. After twenty-five years, when the bonds had been repaid, Swig would turn the arena over to the City.[31]

As Alioto and the agency tried to sell the project to the public, it looked terrific: no City money would be required,[32] and the City would get substantial revenue and eventually own a sports arena free of charge. But in fact it was a boondoggle, intended to do a favor to the politically powerful and generous Swig family and to keep the YBC ballgame moving.

- The tax exemption feature was a $22.5 million gift to Swig (the difference between the normal property tax and the possessory interest tax payment, over twenty-five years);

- the eight-dollar-a-square-foot suggested land price was about one-third its real worth; just a few weeks earlier, SFRA executive director Arthur Evans had expressed pleasure when Taylor-Woodrow and Continental Development Corporation dropped out of their commitment to build on YBC sites; Evans stated the city could get twenty-five dollars per square foot for the land rather than the twenty dollars per square foot Taylor-Woodrow and Continental had agreed to;

- some $2 million in public improvements in the area immediately surrounding the arena would be provided by the City;

- the value of a twenty-five-year-old sports arena probably approaches zero; based on experience with Candlestick Park and other cities' arenas and stadiums, it is more likely that substantial public investment would be required before the twenty-five years were up to modernize or repair the facility, and demands to build a "new, modern" arena doubtless would be heard well before that time.

Not to be outdone by Swig, Lyman Jee, the originally designated but now largely replaced developer of the Central Blocks, entered on the bidding stage in July with his own proposal for a larger and better $30 million to $40 million arena, to be privately owned and financed and not exempt from property taxes. After a certain amount of back and forth, with the agency expressing some concern about the design quality of Swig's cut-rate proposal ("San Francisco is not Schlock City and we shouldn't start now, just to get something built," said SFRA's Evans),[33] Mayor Alioto used some muscle to produce a joint Swig-Jee arena proposal, somewhere between the two in design quality but with the original Swig financing plan. Angered that the agency was not moving fast enough and that some of its commissioners were away on summer vacation, Alioto demanded that it hold a meeting and accept the arena proposal, "whether they liked it or not."[34] Approval was given in July 1975. Swig did no little bullying of his own, saying he would not go ahead with his planned purchase of the Seals and retention of the team in San Francisco without immediate approval of his proposal.

For reasons not immediately apparent, the Swig-Jee arena scheme simply languished. None of the necessary follow-up steps was taken by the Board of Supervisors. This may have resulted in part from opposition by several groups in the city to the financing features; in part from the slowdown in board business as the supervisors approached the November election in which six of the eleven members were up for reelection; and from the imminent change of guard at city hall, as Joseph Alioto came into the final few months of his second, and, by law, last, four-year term. YBC business was so slow, in fact, that in September Chief Administrative Officer Thomas Mellon announced that he was temporarily transferring $2 million from the YBC-designated portion of the hotel tax to the City's general fund, to relieve the city's growing fiscal difficulties.[35]

Once the November elections were past, the supervisors resumed work to advance the arena. But they were none too open about it. Labeling the item on the committee hearing agenda a "recreation center" and using the name Swig and Jee had selected for their nonprofit corporation—"The City of San Francisco Entertainment Center, Inc."—they obviously hoped to minimize attention. On November 12, a joint Planning and Finance Committee hearing gave initial approval to the "recreation center," but the full board postponed consideration until mid-December, largely because the results of the mayoral race would not be decided until a December 11 runoff.

Asked by board president Dianne Feinstein to submit its comments and questions on the arena proposal in preparation for these hearings, the Citizens Committee on Yerba Buena Center—a group formed out of the April Goodman Building meetings by those who did not join in the *Starr* suit (see chapter 7)—made the following additional points.[36] The "numbers" submitted by Swig and Jee regarding projected use of the arena were thoroughly unrealistic. They projected 275 use-days annually, when the three arena consultants the City retained in 1972 had projected 185–209. A detailing of how the figure 275 was derived revealed that it was to include: eight roller-derby performances, even though the franchise had recently gone bankrupt; four professional volleyball performances, even though the sport did not exist at the time in Northern California; sixteen performances by a "children's show," with no clue to what that referred to; and fifty iceshow and circus performances, events at the time playing in the Oakland Arena and likely to continue to play at least a portion of their dates there, for East Bay audiences.

Annual revenue was projected at $3.6 million, when the entire Oakland Coliseum complex (stadium for the A's baseball team and Raiders football team, exhibition hall, and indoor sports arena) had grossed only $3.25 million the previous year. Predicted per-event attendance figures were two to four times current expectations. And a rental income based on 12 percent of gross revenues was assumed, whereas the Oakland Arena, San Francisco Civic Center, and Cow Palace were charging 10 percent, down to 8 percent for major tenants like the Seals hockey team and Warriors basketball team, and even lower rates likely with competition from a new YBC arena. (No one from the Redevelopment Agency nor any of the half-dozen supervisors at the November 12 joint committee hearing raised a single question about the numbers Swig and Jee offered.) Swig and Jee were being given a "free ride," without requiring any performance bond, earnest money payment, or option purchase on the land.

The City would suffer considerable costs if the project failed or lost money; if Swig and Jee then decided to walk away, the City would likely be stuck with operating it or selling it. If there were a default on the arena bonds, the Citizens Committee pointed out, the City would likely be compelled to bail out the bondholders in order to protect its bond rating. Jee and Swig would profit from the developer's fee and tax breaks even if the arena failed. In the later words of ex-Mayor George Christopher, "It is easy for a special interest group to make every conceivable promise in order to secure a project—and when the payments are due, they can just as easily walk away leaving the taxpayers in a dilemma."[37]

By the time the supervisors held their postponed meeting on the arena proposal, the city had a new mayor (George Moscone), with his own ideas on how to proceed with the Yerba Buena mess, and he was successful in holding off action until his own replanning mechanism was in place. Eventually thwarted via this route as well, Mel Swig took his Seals to Cleveland.[38]

Resolving the Convention Center Deadlock

The year 1975 marked a major transition in San Francisco politics. As noted previously, Joseph Alioto was legally unable to run for a third term. The stirrings of a movement to challenge downtown's dominance of the city were clearly being felt. And the Redevelopment Agency's Yerba Buena Center project was in deep trouble as a result of the various lawsuits challenging its financing.

The 1975 mayoral election featured three principal candidates, who covered the range of the city's dominant politics: on the right, realtor John Barbagelata, a six-year veteran of the Board of Supervisors, who represented the older white neighborhoods and the city's more conservative politics; at the center, Board of Supervisors president Dianne Feinstein, who had run against Alioto unsuccessfully in 1971 and represented moderate politics and downtown development interests; and on the left, state senator (and former supervisor) George Moscone, closely allied with "the [Congressman Phillip] Burton machine" and its supporters among working-class and minority people, the city's gay population, and liberal trade union elements.*

---

*"[Burton] came to control the closest thing to an old style political machine that is possible in fluid California. His was a remarkable semi-organization that reached from the old Irish parishes to the ghettos, from Chinatown to Hunters Point, from the drawing rooms of the wealthy liberals to the union halls. It remained potent, even after the power of the unions and the old Democratic clubs dissipated in the seventies" (Rian Malan, "Boss," *California Magazine* [November 1981]: 89–97, 164–65).

Moscone was the hope of the city's burgeoning neighborhood movement—those who wanted to end downtown's virtual hegemony over city hall and redirect City policies to affordable housing, preservation of neighborhood communities, blue- as well as white-collar employment, and greater access to and participation in city politics by all of the city's subpopulations and interest groups. As described by the late journalist Randy Shilts:

> Moscone was part of a new breed of ethnic politicians who had been emerging in San Francisco since the late 1960s, more concerned with abortion and marijuana reform than with getting a cardinal's cap [an acerbic reference to one of Joseph Alioto's goals for the city]. They eschewed the Catholic conservatism of old-line ethnic politicos like Joseph Alioto and were among the first figures to reach effectively to black, Chinese, Latino, and gay voters. Once considered something of a radical, Moscone had worked his way from the Board of Supervisors [where he had served from 1963 to 1966, and where he had cast one of the two votes in 1966 against the Yerba Buena plan] to the California senate, where, after one year, he became senate majority leader. Moscone entered the campaign as the strident proponent of neighborhood power, decrying the "Manhattanization" developers had wrought with their skyscrapers and corporate headquarters. He turned his back on well-heeled campaign contributors by refusing to accept any campaign gift of more than one hundred dollars.[1]

In the November 1975 general election, Moscone got 45 percent of the vote, Barbagelata 28 percent, and Feinstein 27 percent. In the required December runoff (instituted by a 1973 voter-approved charter amendment), Moscone edged Barbagelata by forty-four hundred votes. Combined with liberal victories in the district attorney and sheriff races, this ending of the Alioto era and beginning of the George Moscone administration—even by so small a margin—produced a mild euphoria among liberals and neighborhood activists and not least among those desiring basic changes in the plans for Yerba Buena Center. It was the beginning of a short-lived period of changed politics in San Francisco, although less changed than many expected, hoped for, or feared. The forces that elected George Moscone were to bring into being a housing movement in San Francisco, continue and strengthen the fight against uncontrolled high-rise development, and, for a brief period, change the structure of City government. With respect to Yerba Buena Center and its continuing controversies, it was clear that the opposition to the project was in resonance with the evolving dynamics that brought Moscone to the fore.

The Citizens Committee on Yerba Buena Center

Following the disintegration of the Redevelopment Agency's YBC plan, it was time to regroup. In June 1975, six of the people active in the Goodman Building meetings (David Fulton, a staff planner with the City Planning Department; David Gast, an architect; Victor Honig, a businessman and activist; William Shapiro, an urban planner who had been an advisor to Alvin Duskin and helped put together the Goodman Building meetings; Charles Turner, director of the University of California Community Design Center in San Francisco; and the author of this book) met to evaluate the situation and decided to form a new organization in order to create a new plan for Yerba Buena Center. They sent out letters inviting a wide variety of organizations and individuals to a replanning-oriented meeting, and, based on the lessons learned over previous months in trying to form an anti-YBC coalition, they suggested that a new YBC plan might include

- housing for a wide range of income groups;
- an "alternate budget" outlining the needs of San Francisco's neighborhoods that might be met with the tax revenues generated by private development in the YBC area;
- assurances that the rest of the existing South of Market community would be protected;
- creation of construction jobs for minority and other San Franciscans;
- fiscal feasibility plans, including an exploration of the possibility that revenues from commercial and high-income residential rentals might be used to subsidize housing for low- and moderate-income people in the area.

At their first meeting, the group adopted the name Citizens Committee on Yerba Buena Center (CCYBC) and approved a participatory planning process for YBC, to include: hearings in different parts of the city sponsored by a consortium of neighborhood groups; balloting to choose among widely different approaches represented in schematic drawings; and preparation of a preliminary plan, to be reviewed by neighborhood groups, revised, and released sometime in the fall. Chosen chair was Victor Honig, who, in a highly publicized 1970 controversy with Mayor Alioto, had quit the City's Human Rights Commission because of Alioto's disregard of the commission's concerns about City relocation policies in YBC.

In the vacuum created by the events of the spring, with little leadership coming from a lame-duck administration and a disheartened Redevelopment Agency, the Citizens Committee hoped to take the initiative. While some bad feelings and mistrust caused by tensions among the Goodman Building meeting participants and the ill-timed *Starr* suit still existed, the Citizens Committee's weekly meetings drew a group of fifteen to twenty regulars. The Community Congress held a successful gathering in June around district election of supervisors, diminishing tension from that source as well.

Delays caused by the need to oppose the hastily resuscitated Alioto-Swig-Jee YBC sports arena took up most of the summer, and it was not until October that CCYBC held a press conference announcing initiation of its participatory planning process for YBC. By that time, however, the dynamics of the 1975 mayoral race, which had been building over the summer, came to dominate the YBC story and many of the concerns related to it. But the total replanning approach that CCYBC was pushing for was to be adopted, in form at least, by the new Moscone administration.

Anti-YBC activists for the most part had close ties to the new mayor, and many were his most active campaign workers. A key Moscone staff member attended meetings of CCYBC in the months prior to the election, and Moscone asked CCYBC to provide him with a proposal for how to move on the issue once he took office. The committee's first concern was to make sure all activities on the existing plan were halted and that a total reexamination of the project be undertaken as soon as the new administration was in place. The "restudy" position in fact was shared by both candidates in the December 11 runoff. In interviews published in the December 3, 1977, *Chronicle*, John Barbagelata stated, "I think before we develop the Yerba Buena Center there should be a re-analysis as to its use. It should be made public, not like the last time, where people were misled in . . . what Yerba Buena might bring to San Francisco. . . . Before we touch Yerba Buena we'd better know exactly what we're doing." And George Moscone, picking up on the more specific CCYBC proposal, said: "What we will do in Yerba Buena is dependent on the people of San Francisco. Community hearings on it ought to start no later than January of this coming year." At the urging of CCYBC, Moscone went even further, and, using his anticipated political muscle, sent letters on November 14, 1975, to Board of Supervisors president Dianne Feinstein and Redevelopment Agency executive director Arthur Evans, urging their respective bodies "to take no further action on YBC until the new Mayor is in office."

The Mayor's Select Committee on Yerba Buena Center

Upon taking office in January 1976, Mayor Moscone chose the route the Citizens Committee on Yerba Buena Center had urged: a broadly based restudy committee to look at the entire project anew. His appointment of seventeen members to the Mayor's Select Committee on Yerba Buena Center in March 1976, however, showed the political shrewdness that had led to his meteoric rise to leadership in the state senate. It is now generally agreed that Moscone was willing to reconsider the YBC plan in toto, with the exception of the convention center: That element was nonnegotiable. It is unclear when Moscone arrived at this position: whether he all along, despite his preelection assurances to CCYBC, favored the center, or whether sometime after the election he succumbed to pressures from the downtown establishment. But it is clear, from his appointments to the Select Committee and his subsequent actions, that he intended to effect a compromise among the various competing interests along any of several dimensions, so long as the convention center remained in the plan. His choices for the Select Committee were

- John Blayney, a city planner whose firm, Livingston and Blayney, did much of the original planning for YBC under contract to the Redevelopment Agency, but who also was active in the American Institute of Planners (subsequently renamed the American Planning Association) and therefore was seen partly as a representative of his profession;
- Eugene Coleman, director of Canon Kip Community House, the principal social-service center for the residential population in the South of Market area;
- Michael Davis, a neighborhood activist representing CCYBC;
- Flora Douglass, representing the San Francisco Labor Council;
- Stephen Dutton, representing TOOR/TODCO;
- Douglas Engmann, representing the Coalition for San Francisco Neighborhoods, one of the new liberal formations in the city;
- Morris Evenson, representing the San Francisco Building Trades Council;
- Dianne Feinstein, president of the Board of Supervisors;
- Tony Grafilo, director of the Filipino Organizing Committee and a member of the City's Human Rights Commission;
- John Jacobs, executive director of the San Francisco Planning and Urban Renewal/Research Association (SPUR);
- Doris Kahn, staff member of the City's Department of Social Services and an activist in local Democratic Party politics;
- Gordon Lau, president of the City Planning Commission;

- Henri Lewin, executive vice president of the Hilton Hotel Corporation and a representative of the Chamber of Commerce;
- Thomas Mellon, the City's chief administrative officer;
- Jack Morrison, representative of San Francisco Tomorrow, the city's principal environmentalist lobby and a former supervisor, who was the second anti-YBC vote on the board in 1966;
- Rick Sorro, representing the San Francisco Coalition (the Redevelopment Agency–funded affirmative action group for YBC employment) and an organizer for the International Longshoremen's and Warehousemen's Union.

Moscone selected retired Superior Court Judge Leland Lazarus to chair the committee.

While the Select Committee certainly represented a broad number of interest groups, it had its clear "sides" from the outset.[2] On the basis of either past positions taken with regard to the project or organizational self-interest, even an outsider to the situation could have concluded that Coleman, Davis, Engmann, and Morrison would be opposed to simply reintroducing the major elements of the discarded project, while Douglass, Dutton (because of the TOOR–Redevelopment Agency agreement), Evenson, Feinstein, Jacobs, Lewin, Mellon, and Sorro would be pro-YBC in something at least akin to its original form. Blayney might be expected to join the latter camp, while Kahn, who had been attending CCYBC meetings, might be expected to join the opponents. Grafilo was described as follows in a review of the committee's work:

> As leader of the Filipino Community south of Market, Grafilo worked out an affirmative action agreement with the hotel industry to guarantee Filipinos a larger percentage of jobs in return for support of their position on Yerba Buena. Grafilo's friend George Moscone knew this and appointed him to the Select Committee for precisely that reason. It enabled Moscone to appear to be appointing a leading minority group, neighborhood-oriented figure to the committee, whereas in Grafilo he was actually appointing what amounted to another representative of the hotel industry lobby that was after a convention-center-based YBC for profit reasons.[3]

At the outset, the committee decided its final recommendations had to secure two-thirds of the members' approval (i.e., twelve votes). Judge Lazarus, the chair, announced early in the proceedings that he would vote with the majority, whatever their position turned out to be. The mayor's charge to his Select Committee stipulated that the plan it was to produce had to meet three tests: (1) It must be developed quickly in order to get a project under way—the committee would have five months to complete its work; (2) it "must result from genuine reconsideration of what is best for San Francisco"; and (3) it must have public support.

The hard-working committee and its small staff (headed by Dan Gardner and Greg Oliver of the mayor's economic development staff, with Haight-Ashbury activist Calvin Welch hired to do community outreach as a concession to the neighborhood organizations that had backed Moscone) held a series of neighborhood public hearings and formed subcommittees (on such issues as housing, economic development, and transportation). Following these hearings, the committee produced a set of six alternative plans, each stressing a specific type of land use or combination of uses: housing, light industry, open space, and others. All but two of the alternative plans retained the convention center, albeit with variations as to size and whether it was to be aboveground or underground.

Making sure the convention center was underground was an issue of central concern to those on the Select Committee who cared about urban design. As *New York Times* architecture critic Ada Louise Huxtable wrote regarding New York City's four-block-long aboveground convention center, then under construction:

> A convention center is not in itself a vitalizing force. . . . It is, essentially, an enormous box, often of heavy concrete, stretching for hundreds of feet and many blocks, offering blank vistas of endless solid walls. It lays a dead hand on everything around it. It breeds empty streets, except at show or meeting time, when it brings streams of traffic. . . .
>
> Such a blockbuster creates not life but parking garages. . . . Convention center territory . . . turns into a featureless no-man's land. Contrary to . . . redevelopment promises, its warehouse character does not bring attractive construction at human scale or revitalize in an appropriate human context.[4]

Tivoli Gardens

Of central importance in the Select Committee's considerations of future YBC developments was the Tivoli Gardens proposal of architect Richard Gryziec, former president of San Francisco Tomorrow, who took the opportunity of the committee's public hearings to lobby for his idea, which he had originally developed for the Citizen's Waterfront Committee in order to forestall an Alioto-backed proposal for a high-rise in the Ferry Building area. He now sought to locate the gardens South of Market. Gryziec, one of the more persistent and forceful advocates of a single idea to be found anywhere, proposed a close copy of Copenhagen's twenty-acre pleasure park, to be built atop two of the YBC Central Blocks, partly sitting above an underground convention center.[5]

As *Chronicle* architecture critic Allan Temko later described it:

> This is a wonderful source of both broad fun and higher kinds of cultural enjoyment for people of all backgrounds and ages. Most activities, but not all, are available to those with small purses, and some are free. There are exciting rides, concerts, shows, restaurants, and quiet areas of repose, enriched by fountains, art, and beautiful plantings, exquisitely illuminated at night. The atmosphere is festive, non-puritanical, with a general old-fashioned grace.[6]

Gryziec's proposal was accompanied by careful and attractive design presentations, detailed attention to the economics of the project, and a bevy of supporters. Gryziec and others pushed the Tivoli Gardens idea throughout the Select Committee's hearings and deliberations; and in the end, as will be seen, the proposal took on a lasting role, as symbol and potential reality, in subsequent conflicts and proposals having to do with YBC.

The Revised YBC Plan

Despite the care with which George Moscone chose the members of his Select Committee, it was necessary to do a little head-banging to get the progress he wanted. Near the end of its deliberations, when the committee seemed bogged down in internal controversy, Moscone intervened directly. Apprised of a possible serious rupture between the two sides, Moscone requested that the committee call a special meeting at which he would appear. According to one account of the meeting, "Moscone came down hard. He said he 'feels strongly' about the convention center—stating this after directing the committee to investigate 'a full range of possible uses' three months previously."[7]

The Select Committee approved its final plan in September 1976 by a twelve-to-five vote (Coleman, Davis, Engmann, Kahn, and Morrison dissenting). Judge Lazarus, voting for the first time in the committee's deliberations, provided the last vote necessary to achieve the two-thirds majority. In essence, the plan was as follows:

- The convention center would be built on Central Block 3 (bounded by Third, Fourth, Howard, and Folsom Streets), underground if financially feasible, with some version of Richard Gryziec's Tivoli Gardens covering both that block and Central Block 2 (bounded by Third, Fourth, Howard, and Mission Streets).

- Financing for the convention center would come entirely from the hotel tax, to be raised for this purpose to 8 percent from 6 percent, with half the total hotel tax revenue (the new 2 percent plus the 2 percent of the existing levy already assigned to YBC) going into a special YBC fund to repay lease revenue bonds. (The property tax increment district, created in 1973 for the original plan, was retained, with actual allocations requiring Board of Supervisors' approval.)

- A nonbinding voter opinion statement on YBC would be placed on the upcoming November ballot. (According to the August 6, 1976, *San Francisco Progress,* "Committeewoman Doris Kahn . . . futilely tried to pass a resolution that would put the committee's full YBC plan and financing on the November 1977 ballot. Kahn's appeals met resistance from Supervisor Dianne Feinstein, who said the issue should be placed on the November 1976 ballot as a policy statement.")

- Several structures in the YBC area that historical preservationists were particularly concerned with—notably, St. Patrick's Church and the Jessie Street Substation (the latter designed by famed San Francisco architect Willis Polk)—would be retained.

- Additional market-rate and subsidized housing would be provided (although the specifics were vague).

The bottom line was that Moscone and the convention center backers had their principal concern satisfied, albeit in somewhat altered form, and his neighborhood and environmentalist supporters got significant concessions. The public hearing process and the alternative plans were, to some, a charade for public consumption. John Sanger, a City Planning Department consultant working with the Mayor's Select Committee, reported, "[N]one of the members with fairly strong viewpoints tended to change their basic attitudes (or apparent attitudes) toward project goals as a result of discussion and argument with other members." Doris Kahn stated, "After four months we arrived at the old Redevelopment Agency plan with only a little more housing and open space."[8]

Calvin Welch, however, felt that, beyond the important shift in financing, keeping the convention center underground and pushing it southward from Central Block 2 to Central Block 3, with open space recommended for both blocks, was a significant gain, reducing overall development density for the Central Blocks. And the strategic thinking of the neighborhood and environmental representatives on the Select Committee—apart from differences on the convention center issue—made it possible for them to develop some common positions and use the two-thirds approval requirement they pushed through to ensure concessions on everything but the convention center.

The Citizens Committee on Yerba Buena Center on balance was disappointed with the results of the process. To its dismay, the mayor never regarded as part of the replanning process whether or not there would be a convention center. Further, CCYBC objected to the notion that the hotel tax was a special property of the hotel owners, to be used only in their interests and not for City services needed by all San Franciscans.

CCYBC also criticized the Select Committee's continued reliance on lease revenue rather than general obligation bonds, which would have been far cheaper. (In its answers to the plaintiffs' interrogatories in the *Starr* suit, the City acknowledged that, compared with the cost of a general obligation bond issue for that plan, using lease revenue bonds would result in additional interest charges over the life of the bonds of approximately $108 million.)[9] Once again, the voters were being circumvented, at a huge financial cost to the voter-taxpayers, because the decision makers feared they could not get the required two-thirds approval. And in place of a binding vote on a specific plan and bond issue, the voters would be fed a vaguely worded, nonbinding opinion statement.

The shift in convention center financing, from the property tax to the hotel tax, marked a major concession on the part of the hotel owners, who had long regarded this tax (which their guests, not they, pay) as something they have a right to control and which they must be cajoled into paying—a stance the City seems to share. (This is a far cry from the governing principles editorially enunciated by the *Chronicle* when the tax was introduced in the early 1960s: "The first principle, we should say, is that this revenue belongs to all the people of San Francisco, to be disposed of in the broad general interest and not in the limited interest of the proprietors of the 1158 [probably a misprint] hotels and motels who collect it from their customers and pay it over to the city.")[10] In fiscal terms, the hotel tax in fact is no different from any other source of City revenue, and any hotel tax money sequestered to aid the convention industry is money unavailable for social and health services, public transit, libraries, and other programs.

The actual hotel tax rate increase did not have to be imposed for two years, until new designs were prepared and the project was ready to go out to bid. In preparation for this move, the City's new chief administrative officer, Roger Boas, sent a memo addressed to "Members of the S.F. Hotel and Motel Industry," which ended, "I would be grateful if the members of the

San Francisco Hotel Industry would give me their approval for this tax increase."[11] And the hotel owners would agree to the hotel tax hike only if the funds thereby raised, beyond what was needed for bond repayments, would not go into the general fund. A memo by the CAO's office, reporting a meeting with hotel industry heavies, noted:

> It appears that the hotel industry representatives are most concerned that the potential additional surplus over and above that required for debt service not be directed by the Board of Supervisors to other purposes or in fact to even go into the general fund. Further, it would appear that this would be an opportunity for marketing money within the budget of the [convention] hall that would be an additional marketing factor for convention business for the city in addition to that which is provided by Bob Sullivan's [then–executive director of the Convention & Visitors Bureau] organization.[12]

For their part, the citizenry of San Francisco felt little reluctance to raise the hotel tax. A post–Proposition 13 "revenue package" went on the ballot in June 1980, seeking new revenue sources beyond the property tax (which that statewide proposition had severely limited); of the six new revenue measures the voters were asked to approve, increasing the hotel tax from 8 to 9.75 percent received the greatest margin of approval, winning 73 percent to 27 percent.

The seemingly voluntary nature of the hotel tax reveals itself in other ways, too. A memorandum dated March 28, 1978, from Richard Sklar, then in charge of the YBC project for the chief administrative officer, to CAO Roger Boas, noted:

> As I have expressed verbally on a number of occasions, it is my belief with no proof that the hotel tax revenues that go to finance YBC are probably less than they could be and ought to be. My guess is that the tax collection operation involves no auditing of the submitting hotels. My guess would be that each hotel fills out a return as it sees fit and remits what it thinks it can get away with. In all likelihood the larger businesses probably remit accurately, but I guess the great number of the operators do not pay all that they should.

While Sklar pressed this issue on Boas, noting that his office now had a professional audit staff, apparently no action was taken.

Proposition S

The Moscone administration, having secured a recommended plan from the Select Committee, immediately placed the voter opinion statement on the

November 1976 ballot. Proposition S read simply: "Shall the City construct a convention exhibit hall at Yerba Buena Center, using a 4 percent hotel room tax to finance lease revenue bonds, underground if financially feasible, otherwise above ground?"

The city's power structure moved solidly behind the measure, with Mayor Moscone listed as Honorary Chair of Citizens for Proposition S and, as sponsors, ten of the eleven supervisors, Congressman Phillip Burton, State Assembly Speaker Leo McCarthy, Assemblyman Willie Brown, the major downtown organizations, and most unions. Their campaign literature stressed the themes of "No Cost to Taxpayers, Homeowners or Renters"—perpetuating the myth that using hotel tax revenues entailed no opportunity costs—and "S Means Jobs." Editorials in the print and electronic media solidly backed Proposition S, as exemplified by the following cloying, sexist ode, "Yerba Buena: San Francisco's Siren," aired by KPIX-TV on September 16 and 17, 1976:

> Her shops, restaurants and hotels, her museums, parks, and theaters create an atmosphere of charm that few can resist. But as in any relationship, she must constantly prune and preen to remain attractive . . . and to keep ahead of the other girls.
> The lovely seductress I'm referring to is the City of San Francisco. Her lovers are the throngs of visitors who travel here to enjoy her favors. . . .
> About half of San Francisco's visitors come here on conventions. . . .
> This city may resemble a lovely lady, but she'll have to offer more than cable car rides if she's going to keep her admirers happy. KPIX urges you to vote in favor of the convention center. To put it plainly, our lovely lady needs more room in which to operate.

The No on S Committee was chaired by Victor Honig of CCYBC and four of the five dissenting Select Committee members—Coleman, Davis, Engmann, and Kahn. Sponsors included a raft of neighborhood and environmental groups and figures. For the most part, however, the energies of progressive elements in the city were focused on the initiative to change the at-large method of electing supervisors to a district-based system (see chapter 11), and neither the money nor volunteers were available to mount a winning campaign against S.

Proposition S won, 58 percent to 42 percent. Faced with no alternative to the YBC plan, voters may have taken the gloomy position later expressed by longtime YBC opponent Dick Nolan of the *Examiner:* "I don't know how the rest of the rotten opposition feels, but for my own part I am beginning to wish we had all kept our traps shut. So they've gone ahead, as programmed, with the Great Yerba Buena Convention Center Complex and

Hockey Puck Palace. Anything, to anybody's profit and whatever profligate cost, would be better than those devastated acres we're living with."[13] Or as the *Guardian's* Robert Levering put it, "The sad truth is that most people would probably vote for a replica of the Taj Mahal to be built in Yerba Buena under those terms—no tax expenditure to put a huge monument on what now looks like a bombed out moonscape."[14] Because the vote was not on a specific bond-issue authorization, little in the way of detailed, hard financial data had to be offered to justify construction of the convention center, and the campaign was largely slogan oriented.

Proposition P

Another interesting and relevant item on the November 1976 ballot was Proposition P, initiated by the fiscally conservative and mayorally ambitious Supervisor Quentin Kopp. This proposed City Charter amendment banned issuance of most revenue and lease revenue bonds without approval by a majority of voters, thus eliminating, as Kopp's Voter Information Pamphlet argument put it, "this kind of tricky financing plan which led to the lengthy lawsuits over Yerba Buena, pushing up costs until the project had to be scrapped and redesigned from scratch." At the time, the City's bonded indebtedness on issues that had not required voter approval—such as Candlestick Park, the Social Services Building, and numerous garages—totaled $275 million, an amount half again as large as the $179 million in outstanding general obligation bonds issued with voter approval.[15] Additionally, the corporations formed to carry out projects funded by these revenue bonds ("a nice, neat, closed clique," as Supervisor John Molinari described them)[16] were barely accountable to the public.

Doubtless disturbed by New York City's well publicized experience with runaway indebtedness, San Francisco's voters approved Proposition P, three to one. Supervisor Kopp's concern for voter approval of indebtedness, however, did not extend to the large and controversial financing scheme he used to illustrate the evils of the system Proposition P was designed to end: His wording of the ballot measure specifically exempted from its provisions bonds approved by the Board of Supervisors prior to January 1, 1977.

One Last Lawsuit

The mandate provided by voter approval of Proposition S cleared the way for the massive work of redesigning the somewhat smaller, underground convention center, a task that was to take a year and a half. (The magnitude of design work for a project of this size is suggested by the weight of the bidders' packet of plans and specifications for the first design—195 pounds.) Of equal importance was redesigning the financing plan, now based entirely on the hotel tax. And various City bodies—most notably, the Redevelopment Agency and Board of Supervisors—had to approve a raft of official actions, including amendments to the YBC plan, revision of the hotel tax ordinance, and new financing documents.

Shortly after the Moscone administration took office, a new set of actors was put in place. Chief Administrative Officer Thomas Mellon, whose office was responsible for constructing the convention center, named a YBC project manager, John Igoe. Mellon in 1972 had been allowed to extend his retirement five years to see YBC through, but with no end yet in sight, he announced his retirement in the summer of 1976. In January 1977, a new CAO, Roger Boas, replaced him. (Moscone at first attempted to name as Mellon's replacement Rudy Nothenberg, his former chief of staff on the state senate Ways and Means Committee. But the supervisors refused to confirm Nothenberg, "in part because the supervisors felt he did not have the business experience and in part because they felt he would be too politically aligned with Moscone.")[17]*

Roger Boas had been a member of the Board of Supervisors from 1962–73 and was a former state Democratic Party chair. During his years on the board, he was not known for his backbone or hard work. As political reporter Larry Hatfield described him, "[H]e hated to commit himself in advance because he couldn't be sure how the other supervisors would vote, and he didn't want to be on the wrong side of the close ones and the tough ones and the controversial ones. He also hated committee meetings and rarely bothered to attend them."[18] Another account of his supervisorial days noted that "long term colleagues recall . . . a . . . tendency to doze off at meetings of the city legislature. Boas himself tends to shrug off his own supervisorial achievements ('I can't recall anything in particular'). . . ."[19] But Boas, owner

---

*A sartorial theory also was bruited about: "Rudy wore a pony-tail," Roger Boas said upon leaving the post ten years later. "If it hadn't been for that, he'd be the CAO going out of office now instead of me." Nothenberg, however, cleaned up his image after the failed first appointment to the post: "Early in his career, Nothenberg wore his hair in a pony-tail. After he became deputy mayor, however, he started wearing expensive suits, white shirts and an expression of elegant disdain" (see Carl Nolte, "Rudy Nothenberg's Rise inside City Hall," *San Francisco Chronicle*, 7 October 1986). Nothenberg thereupon remained with Moscone as deputy mayor, a post he retained with the subsequent mayor, Dianne Feinstein, until appointed general manager of the City's Public Utilities Commission in 1983. He finally made it as CAO, when Feinstein, who as supervisor had led the opposition to his appointment to that post by Moscone, appointed him upon Boas's retirement in 1986. (See Dave Farrell, "Mayor Picks Nothenberg for No. 2 S.F. Job," *San Francisco Chronicle*, 7 October 1986.)

of one of the city's largest auto dealerships, was close to and trusted by the business community, and that was the sine qua non for the position, described by SPUR's director of research as "that Chamber of Commerce sinecure known as the Chief Administrative Officer."[20] A later profile of Boas observed: "One charge leveled against him is that his office is more accessible to downtown interests, to business, than it is to the general public. That's probably true. In Boas's eyes, the business of the CAO *is* business."[21] (According to *Bay Guardian* publisher Bruce Brugmann, Boas's appointment also was attributable to his willingness to drop out of the race to replace Congressman William Mailliard in favor of John Burton, younger brother of the late congressional powerhouse Phillip Burton.)[22]

As Boas tells it, when George Moscone nominated him for the CAO position, he said, "I'm going to put you in charge of getting that blankety-blank convention center built. I'll back you all the way, I'll help you in any way I can. But if you don't do anything else as CAO, you damn well better get that convention center built. The City needs it; it's got to have it."[23] The *Examiner* noted in early 1978 that "Mayor Moscone has made construction of Yerba Buena his Panama Canal Treaty, placing all the prestige of his office behind sweeping away bureaucratic barriers."[24] Moving quickly, Boas announced plans to begin site excavation in January 1978 and sell the bonds that July, with an October deadline for receipt of bids.

Several delays in this plan occurred, one due to the discovery that an additional $10 million of foundation and construction work was necessary, a second because HUD decided it had to do a new environmental impact statement, as the changes the City planned made the original 1974 statement obsolete. Also, under California's Environmental Quality Act, the newly redesigned YBC plan required a new state environmental impact report. With these unexpected impediments, Boas revised his schedule, calling for the bond sale in January 1979, construction beginning a month later, and a completed center by July 1981. Joint City Planning Commission/Redevelopment Agency hearings were held in February and March 1978 on the draft report. The hearings dragged on, as several commissioners were truly troubled by unanswered questions in the report and criticisms brought forward by CCYBC and others. But in the end only one member, Charles Starbuck of the Planning Commission, voted against it, although, as the April 26, 1978, *Examiner* reported, "Two [other] commissioners expressed uneasiness. Charlotte Berk of the agency board [later to become its chair] said, 'I feel thoroughly incompetent to judge such questions (as those) about projections for financing.' And planning commissioner Ina Dearman said, 'I'm sure I'll be paying for it if I can still afford to live in the City.' She has expressed doubts in the past about the hotel tax's ability to pay development costs."

The report process complete, the Redevelopment Agency and supervisors moved immediately to act on the new financing agreements, specifically the bond issuance documents and the leasing agreement between the City and the agency for the convention center, which was to be financed with agency bond money and owned by the agency, but built by the CAO's office and operated by the City. The City-agency lease called for the City to make lease payments to the agency in an amount sufficient to allow the agency to repay the bondholders.

The new documents, the escalating cost estimates, and above all the reliance once again on a bond issue structured to circumvent the need for voter approval continued to strike many in San Francisco as unacceptable. It was clear that the mayor, the supervisors, and the agency could not be persuaded to put the actual financing plan before the voters, and so, in April 1978, the Citizens Committee on Yerba Buena Center and its allies started meeting once again to explore other avenues for stopping the revised YBC financing plan.

Once the various public bodies formally approved the necessary documents, however, and everything was in place to move rapidly, the Redevelopment Agency took the initiative. On July 11, 1978, it filed another "all persons" suit, to have a court validate its new YBC financing plan and smoke out all potential litigants. The CCYBC principals took up the challenge and responded to the agency suit, in addition to filing their own separate action to bring the City in as a party and raise other legal issues. Respondents to the agency's "all persons" action were Michael Davis (CCYBC's representative on the Mayor's Select Committee on YBC), Victor Honig, and the author of this book. In their own separate but parallel action, the CCYBC plaintiffs were Davis and four other CCYBC activists.[25]

On August 1, 1978, two weeks before the deadline for responding to its validation suit, the agency and City signed a right-of-entry agreement, permitting the City to begin site work on the convention center land. The agency received HUD's permission to take this extraordinary step—commencing excavation while its own validation action was still pending in court—only on the condition that the City assume full risks of that move: that if the agency was not able to prevail against the new legal challenge, the site would have to be restored to its previous condition. It was an $8.8 million gamble—the costs of the excavation, shoring, and dewatering work, and of later undoing that work if need be vs. the psychological and political momentum to be gained in beginning actual construction of the convention center. A premature start on construction could influence a court's decision on whether to stop the project, temporarily or permanently. A December 16, 1981, *Examiner* profile of Roger Boas at the time the convention center finally opened contained this recollection by the CAO about James

Brosnahan, chief of the legal team hired by the agency to handle the suit: "Brosnahan," Boas recalls, "suggested one more tactic to enhance chances of winning the lawsuit. Aware that a judge would be less likely to rule against the City if construction were under way, the lawyer advised Boas to take a $6 million gamble with city money by starting excavation for the center in March 1978, months before the bonds could legally be sold." (Boas, not known for his mastery of details, was incorrect on the amount and month.)

The principal legal point of the new challenge was the by now traditional one: that the financing plan violated Article XVI, Section 18 of the California Constitution by not securing two-thirds voter approval for what in fact was a long-term financing commitment by the City and a conditional sale of land. The "original sin that refuses to stay submerged . . . that denied the public a chance to vote on the bond issue for the project"[26] once again was holding up Yerba Buena Center and threatening to sink it. As the *Examiner* had stated back in 1971, "Winning voter approval for the project would be a near miracle."[27] Each of the financing plans therefore involved an end-run around the voters/taxpayers. The *Examiner*'s Dick Nolan explained it: "At no time did the promoters ever intend to subject this project to the kind of scrutiny that occurs in an honest municipal bond election. That's what all the hokey-pokey has been about—doing privately and expensively what might have been done more cheaply and honestly if the promoters thought for a minute that the voters would buy this turkey. . . . The people who have been doing the Yerba Buena thing do know what they want, they have been asked, and they know how to get their wishes. Moreover, they know how to get us to pay for what they want and we don't. It is why they are rich."[28] Nolan adds a nice historical perspective to the scam:

> What's additionally funny about the situation is a curious role reversal as between the power bunch and the general public. The power bunch used to distrust the people for a different reason entirely.
>
> In times past, when the people were in need of such things as schools, drinking water, street cars, sewer systems and such, the big brokers feared the spendthrift propensities of the unmoneyed masses. Hell, if left unbridled, the people might vote themselves all kinds of gewgaws.
>
> So the bunch hedged the public borrowing power about with restrictions. Instead of a simple majority vote, it was decreed that two-thirds of those voting had to approve a bond issue before the bonds could be sold. And there was a limit put on the amount of such bonds, just in case.
>
> Now the power bunch has become the spendthrift element, for sound reasons of profit. And they wear the chains they forged, and the chains are chafing.[29]

William Brinton, Alvin Duskin, and Gerald Wright had promised to drop their suits if the Yerba Buena convention center was placed on the November 1974 ballot, but "officials at city hall . . . resolutely opposed the policy vote as inappropriate 'grandstanding.' "[30] When, following filing of the *Starr* suit in mid-1975, some supervisors considered placing the issue on that November's ballot, Mayor Alioto came to a board meeting to say, "I would hope that you would not put the statement on the ballot. Instead of a great divisive debate, let's just go ahead."[31] City officials and newspaper editorial writers blithely continued to insist, nonetheless, that the project had overwhelming popular support. In response to one such *Chronicle* editorial, attorney Gerald Wright dryly observed, in a letter published in the March 10, 1975, *Chronicle:*

> I see that Richard Nixon's "vast majority" is with us again. That group springs from the minds of those who obtain public support merely by announcing that it exists. We are told, by your editorial of March 3, that the v.m. has enthusiastically approved the Yerba Buena Center project.
>
> Interestingly, the only request ever made by the taxpayers who opposed the project is that the public be allowed to express its opinion. The lawsuits sought to establish that the California Constitution requires voter approval for Yerba Buena. The constitutional provision at issue requires the affirmative vote of two-thirds of the electorate. For the sake of settlement, the taxpayers are willing to accept a simple majority vote. City hall has steadfastly refused to place the matter on the ballot under any conditions. Who knows what the v.m. wants?

The new case went to trial in October 1978. The power structure and their newspaper editorial-writer allies waxed self-righteously indignant. The August 13, 1978, *Sunday Examiner & Chronicle*—not yet having seen the papers in the suit, which was to be filed the next day—pontificated: "It seems to us that any new lawsuit can and should be promptly dismissed on the grounds of undiluted obstructionism." A few days later (August 16, 1978), the *Chronicle* chimed in: "Time and time again, legal obstructionists have been turned down by public body after public body"—ignoring the fact that the public body known as the San Francisco Redevelopment Agency had been forced to provide more than two thousand low-rent housing units and made major changes in its original YBC plans in response to three of these suits and that another public body known as the California Court of Appeal had upheld one of these actions by legal obstructionists.

Lawyers for the plaintiffs in the new suit were Fred Altshuler and Stephen Berzon, two former public interest attorneys (Berzon had been on the staff of the National Housing Law Project in the early seventies), while the City and Redevelopment Agency, as in the past, turned to one of the largest and most expensive law firms in town, in this case Morrison & Foerster. (Although the City refused to release exact figures on how much they paid Morrison & Foerster for this suit, various newspaper accounts put the figure at between $700,000 and $840,000.) Sparing no expense, Boas also hired the public relations firm of Arnold, Palmer and Noble to generate publicity favorable to the convention center, at a cost of at least $125,000.[32]

Apart from legal arguments, the principal strategy of the defendants was to cite to the court the millions of dollars already spent on the project. At least $10.5 million had been spent between July 1, 1971, and December 31, 1976, and in excess of $12 million spent or committed between January 1, 1977, and September 30, 1978—according to their trial brief, which added: "If a court were to stop the current project, the City would be required to fill in the hole that already has been dug . . . which would cost several million dollars." Also cited was the cost of delays, which the City/Redevelopment Agency asserted was $500,000 a month.

An argument developed by the plaintiffs' lawyers during the trial centered around the City's obligation during the construction phase (1979–81, according to plans) to contribute to the cost of construction some $34 million from accumulated hotel tax revenues, beyond the $66 million in construction funds the planned $97 million bond issue would yield, and the City's contractual obligation to complete construction of the convention center, if necessary.

There had been a series of cases—leading to what is known in legal circles as the "Offner-Dean rule"—in which the California Supreme Court tried to delineate just what specific types of "creative financing" by public bodies fall within and outside of the strictures of Article XVI, Section 18. One general rule is that if under a lease revenue bond a government agency each year gets use of a specific service or facility for its annual lease payment, then the arrangement is regarded as annually renewable and thus not subject to the provisions of the article. Altshuler and Berzon argued that no such fiction could be fashioned around the two-year construction period: The City was obligating itself to supply some $34 million in tax revenues but would receive no use or occupancy of the facility in return during that time. Practically speaking, the City could not simply abandon a nearly completed center if the projected hotel tax funds were insufficient; moreover, under the lease agreement it had an obligation to complete the construction. Investors would not buy the YBC bonds without that assurance, else they might themselves wind up owning an unfinished convention center.

While CCYBC attorneys maintained this overstepped the "Offner-Dean rule," Superior Court Judge John Benson saw things differently, and on November 30, 1978, filed his Memorandum of Intended Decision in favor of the City and Redevelopment Agency. Their attorneys, backed by solemn statements from City officials, stoutly maintained that no obligation to complete construction existed on the City's part, that there was no pledge of City money beyond one year, and that the Board of Supervisors was free to appropriate or not appropriate City funds for the YBC convention center in 1979, 1980, and 1981. "For the purpose of defending the lack of any public vote on YBC," *Examiner* columnist Dick Nolan had earlier written, "the guarantee is seen as no guarantee. For the purpose of assuring the bondholders they'll get their investment back, plus tax free interest, the guarantee is described as ironclad."[33] The City maintained that it was no more than a "construction manager" for the project, a representation the trial court accepted, and that any potential economic or practical necessity to complete the project was not the same as an indebtedness or liability, which is what Article XVI, Section 18 speaks to. Altshuler and Berzon argued that the "just a construction manager" theory was disingenuous, since the City a year and a half earlier had hired the Turner Construction Company at a cost of several million dollars to perform exactly that function. They further argued that the issue was not one of implied promises, but an express obligation on the City's part to complete construction, as contained in both the bond resolution and project lease. Nonetheless, the court held against them.

The next step was the California Court of Appeal. Both sides agreed to an expedited appeal schedule, and the hearing was held in February 1979. The City and Redevelopment Agency pressed their claims that the project was too far along, with too much money already spent, for a court reasonably to stop it. On March 6, 1979, the Court of Appeal handed down its unanimous decision upholding the trial court ruling. The decision placed great weight on the documents produced and representations made by the City and Redevelopment Agency. "In such a case," the appeal court decision stated, "where the interpretation of the writing turns upon the credibility of extrinsic evidence and inferences reasonably to be drawn therefrom, we as a reviewing court are bound by the trial court's determination, if supported by substantial evidence. . . . Questions of credibility must be resolved in favor of the fact-finder's [trial judge's] determinations, and when two or more inferences can reasonably be drawn from the evidence, a reviewing court may not substitute its deductions for those of the trier of fact."[34]

The plaintiffs made one last effort, asking the California Supreme Court to review the "Offner-Dean rule" in its entirety. The petition for rehearing stated,

> It takes very little perspicacity to see that this transaction bears almost every mark of an installment contract [which the California Supreme Court has ruled is an illegal evasion of the constitutional requirement to obtain voter approval]. The length of the "rental" obligation is specifically tied to the repayment of the bonds which finance construction; the amount of the "rent" varies so as to cover the agency's project expenses; all insurance premiums covering risk of loss are assumed by the City; the agency's insured interest decreases as the bonds are paid off, rather than remaining at the full replacement cost of the building. Most important, title vests in the City at the conclusion of the "lease" without any further payment; since the "lease" ends when the bonds are retired, this means simply that, as with any conditional land sale contract, title vests in the buyer as soon as the debt is paid off.

As a more general law review critique of the "Offner-Dean rule" observed:

> Such judicial interpretations have thwarted the [Article XVI, Section 18] drafters' clearly indicated intent to curb excessive tax levies and to restrict growth of public debt. Capital borrowing has not been significantly impeded. It has simply been diverted into less secure and more costly modes of financing, using techniques that require either no approval of the electorate or a simple majority vote. Furthermore, these sophisticated financing devices are exceedingly difficult for the general public to fathom and thereby undermine the drafters' foremost aim of popular control of the creation of local government debt.[35]

But the Supreme Court declined, under these circumstances at least, to rescrutinize its line of reasoning regarding the "Offner-Dean rule," and within days of that last decision, all legal barriers having been removed, the Redevelopment Agency sold its $97 million YBC bond issue. Postexcavation construction work began in June 1979, and the YBC convention center opened its doors in December 1981 to a meeting of two thousand dermatologists.

South of Market Conquered

While opening the Moscone Convention Center (named after the city's assassinated mayor—see chapter 11) marked a monumental step in the transformation of the South of Market area, development forces had not dallied in incorporating this part of the city into the financial district. Particularly to the east of Yerba Buena Center, directly across Market Street from the financial district, office construction had been proceeding at a furious rate since the 1970s. Nearly three-fifths of the total office space constructed in downtown San Francisco in the 1972–82 period was built South of Market.[1] And despite massive delays in developing the core of the project area and similar difficulties on many of the sites in the sixty-six acres outside the Central Blocks, the Redevelopment Agency had managed to spur development on some project area parcels: a downtown community college branch, several new and rehabilitated office structures, and a data processing and telephone long-lines center.

Thus, while the YBC project was introduced in the early 1960s as a wedge to expand the office district across Market Street—and to an extent performed that function by clearing the area of its former uses and users, promising a major public-private project in its place, and eventually coming through with some of those promises—the imperative to provide land to meet the city's administrative headquarters functions had a compelling momentum of its own.

Developing the Central Blocks

The forces George Moscone set in motion to get the Yerba Buena Center project off dead center had served to build the convention center. Far more problematic was progress on the three YBC Central Blocks, which included the surface area covering the underground convention center. The Redevelopment Agency was in charge of these twenty-one acres, but, as happened in the early 1970s, destructive conflict again arose between the agency and the City's chief administrative officer.

After Moscone's Select Committee on Yerba Buena Center finished its work in 1976, capped by passage of Proposition S that November and parallel with planning and constructing the Moscone Convention Center, the Redevelopment Agency turned to replanning the Central Blocks. The divided responsibility between the agency and CAO Roger Boas—Boas in charge of building Moscone Center; the agency and Boas jointly responsible for what was to go atop the Center; the agency in charge of the total surface acreage, but Boas panicking at the possibility of the center becoming a "white elephant"[2] if the surrounding acreage was improperly developed—was an important contributing element to the extensive delays in making any real progress. Another was the incompetence and extreme cautiousness of the Redevelopment Agency, which had been taking a beating for quite a number of years.

Much of the Boas–Redevelopment Agency conflict centered around Richard Gryziec's Tivoli Gardens plan for Central Blocks 2 and 3, which the Mayor's Select Committee had embraced. In mid-1977, Gryziec was hired as an agency consultant to develop the design and economics of the huge pleasure garden. But before long he was complaining about lack of agency staff support for his plan, a complaint exacerbated by the agency's decision to bring in the Skidmore, Owings & Merrill (SOM) architecture firm to prepare a new Central Blocks master plan and by the firm's strong opposition to the Tivoli Gardens proposal, out of fears that it would, despite Gryziec's clear intentions to the contrary, become a mini-Disneyland and further the "boutiquing" of San Francisco. (The competing egos of architects, never known for their minuscularity, may have played a role as well in the acrimony that rapidly developed between the agency's principal design consultants.)

Beyond design questions, Boas felt strongly that Gryziec's facility might endanger the success of the convention center if it was underused or used by people convention-goers regarded as threats or nuisances. The CAO's strong preference was for a smaller, more orthodox green space atop Moscone Center, and office, hotel, and commercial development on the two adjacent Central Blocks, which he felt would be more in keeping with the needs and style of the convention trade. He therefore backed the design guidelines SOM produced in 1979, which were more supportive of his ideas on how development should proceed, and turned thumbs down on Gryziec's gardens. From the outset, "the hiring of Gryziec nettled Boas, who wished to build the convention hall expeditiously with only himself in charge,"[3] and so it was not surprising that conflict between Boas and Gryziec became open and heated. (Gryziec on the CAO: "It appears to me that Boas has a severe personality or ego problem. Boas must be the all-powerful final voice to be heard, the only voice to be obeyed.")[4] Boas, for his part, was openly threatening the Redevelopment Agency, which he regarded as incompetent. In late 1980, he wrote the commissioners: "As I am responsible for the economic well being of the convention center, I want to make certain that whatever plan is adopted is compatible with the needs of the convention center and does not damage it. . . . If the plan is not a sound one and in fact endangers the economic viability of the convention center, then I will regard it as my duty to oppose it and to block it," thus reminding the agency commissioners of his veto power over development on top of the underground facility. He pointed to difficulties in Los Angeles, Memphis, and Norfolk, where convention goers were shunning new convention centers because of "not secure . . . unpleasant or incompatible surroundings."[5] In urban design terms, he wanted the Central Blocks surface development to create a gateway on Market Street that would lead people directly through Central Blocks 1 (bordering Market) and 2 to the convention center and to build on these two blocks market-rate housing and "strong commercial activity, along with an appropriate amount of open space." In other words, Boas was seeking to ensure that YBC was developed as a major extension of the existing downtown center, rather than chancing isolation of the new convention center with an untested, unorthodox open space development.

George Moscone's death in 1978 had removed a powerful Gryziec supporter and the architect's important access to the mayor's office. Although a member of the Mayor's Select Committee on YBC, which strongly backed the Tivoli Gardens idea, Dianne Feinstein, who succeeded Moscone as mayor (see chapter 11), did not feel completely bound by Moscone's commitments to the committee's recommendations, and she was less willing than he had been to take risks with an unconventional plan. By the end of 1979, with Feinstein and her administration feeling more confident as a result of winning the mayoral election (her 1978 appointment as acting mayor to succeed the assassinated Moscone was mandated by the City Charter), the Tivoli Gardens concept in its original conception had lost much of its momentum. As the agency finally moved to seek a Central Blocks developer in 1979–80, the Tivoli Gardens concept had been—depending on who was asked—either jettisoned or modified considerably.

Gryziec continued to fight a losing battle with Boas and with key parts of the agency bureaucracy and its consultants until May 1981, when he quit, in a highly publicized manner, charging the agency staff with "amateurism," insufficient commitment to the Tivoli Gardens concept, freezing the public out of any meaningful participation in the process of negotiations with the developer, and lack of strength and leadership in its negotiating posture with the Central Blocks developer it had chosen in the interim.[6]

A key agency decision was its unusual and highly criticized step of issuing not an RFP (Request for Proposals), but an RFQ (Request for Qualifications). Rather than providing a detailed plan for the Central Blocks and inviting developers to submit proposals for fulfilling that plan, including the price to be paid for the land, the Redevelopment Agency and City chose to prepare only a rough, very general description of what was desired for the area, then ask developers to compete, based on their qualifications as evidenced by past work, financial capability, and the strength of their "team." As the *Examiner*'s Gerald Adams observed: "It [the RFQ process] is unusual in that the bidders for the right to build the $300 million–plus Yerba Buena Center central blocks are not competing with money. They need not say what they intend to build. They don't have to vie in an architectural competition, or even draw a scheme. They don't have to say what ideas they might have for the blocks, nor do they have to offer pot-sweeteners such as a downtown museum or subsidized housing. They only have to document the ways in which they are qualified for the job."[7] The developer the agency regarded as most qualified would then be given exclusive negotiating rights to come up with a detailed development plan, which would form the basis for a subsequent land disposition agreement and land price.

The thinking behind this somewhat unusual strategy likely was born of the cumulative fears and frustrations of the previous decade and a half: The Redevelopment Agency and City administration were extremely worried that, given the rocky history of the project and the high costs of preparing a full-scale proposal of this magnitude (estimated at $500,000–$1 million per bidder), no one would bid, especially in a time of general economic recession. The cheaper route of simply asking developers to enter what some disparagingly referred to as a "beauty contest" would at least increase the likelihood that lots of contestants would show up.

At the first stage at least, the strategy seemed to pay off. In April 1980, the RFQ went out, and by the June 4 deadline, ten developers had responded, eight of whom were regarded as serious candidates. The following six-month process of selecting from among the contest entrants indeed had all the earmarks of a beauty contest, with elaborate exhibits and films of each firm's past projects, documentation of financial strength and health, and a range of superstars from the design field, backed by a slew of "consultants" from the local political arena. In addition to the local showings, agency staff and commissioners visited nine cities across the U.S. and Canada to view first-hand the results of the past projects the bidders were touting so mightily.

By July, four of the hopefuls had been dropped. According to SFRA executive director Wilbur Hamilton, the decisions were based on weaknesses in these areas: "experience with creating 'significant open space and cultural-recreation uses in an urban setting; architecture, planning and design capabilities; financial ability; clear lines of coordination between the agency and developer; affirmative action requirements; and deal-making talents of the key individuals.' "[8] While Hamilton doubtless intended the broadest possible business-related construction of that last phrase, it did highlight one of the more telling aspects of the selection process: the rush of every team to find one or more local political "heavies" to go to bat for it.

The lineup is described by Larry Liebert in his October 2, 1980, *Chronicle* article, "Getting By on Juice":

> San Francisco is a small and incestuous town, as those who know its politics will tell you. Perhaps that's explanation enough for all those familiar faces lined up for a piece of the action at Yerba Buena Center. . . .
>
> The six developers still under consideration all are basically out-of-town operators, with several of them based in Canada.
>
> But most have signed up prominent San Franciscans as "consultants"—and that's often a euphemism for citizens with clout, with juice, with connections. With an inside track at city hall.
>
> Williams Realty Corp. of Tulsa had the savvy to hire the omnipresent Bill Coblentz, the well-known lawyer, city airports commissioner, raconteur and friend of mayors and governors. Coblentz is a city commissioner who makes a lucrative habit out of appearing before other city commissioners on behalf of his clients.
>
> Olympia and York of Toronto, working in tandem with the Marriott Hotel people, signed up Assemblyman Willie Brown Jr., the attorney, legislator and snappy dresser. Brown seems not at all embarrassed by his increasingly rewarding sideline of representing clients before one level of government while serving as an elected official at another level. . . .
>
> The developer team of Campeau and Rouse has enlisted such well-connected citizens as Tom Mellon, the city's former chief administrative officer; Sim Van der Ryn, former state architect; lawyer Charles Clifford and black attorneys Cliff Jeffers and Ben James. Richard Swig of the influential family that owns the Fairmont Hotel would manage this developer's hotel.

Portman Properties, which developed the Redevelopment Agency's Embarcadero Center, has brought into partnership its Embarcadero manager, James Bronkema, who also happens to be a close friend of one of the Redevelopment commissioners.

What do these developers get for their investment in well-connected San Franciscans? These hired hands would surely insist that they offer solid advice about the way the city works. . . . At the very least, the men with connections provide "access"—the ability to get a phone call returned, to arrange a meeting with the mayor, to drop in a word or two at all the right cocktail parties, to suggest which candidates should be given contributions in the November election.

With $300 million at stake, those services are quite enough to make these high-class functionaries very valuable to the developers who hired them.

Each team also had its architectural superstars: Yerba Buena Associates hired I. M. Pei to do its master plan; Trammel Crow hired Skidmore, Owings & Merrill; Forest City Enterprises hired John Carl Warnecke; John Portman imaginatively hired the president of Tivoli Gardens (the real one, in Copenhagen) as a consultant.

Finally, the list was narrowed down to two Canadian firms, Olympia & York (teamed with the Marriott Corporation as hotel developer) and Cadillac-Fairview, each of whom was encouraged to strengthen its team by cannibalizing the most attractive features from those teams dropped from the competition.[9] Olympia & York/Marriott picked up Bill Coblentz from the Williams team, and, as both partner and participant, James Rouse (developer of the new town of Columbia, Maryland, Boston's Faneuil Hall, and Baltimore's Harborplace) from the Campeau team.

In October 1980, the O&Y/Marriott team, coupled with San Francisco architect Beverly Willis as a 2 percent partner, was chosen. (As the November 21, 1980, *Chronicle* put it, "Willis, who runs her own architecture and design firm, is seemingly out of place alongside the other two mammoth international firms." Willis, however, had taken the project to Olympia & York originally, and, as the story continued, "among architects, Willis is regarded as quite politically adept. She is well acquainted with Mayor Dianne Feinstein, and once headed an architects group supporting former Mayor Joseph Alioto when he was running for mayor. Willis's support for Feinstein goes back to her initial, 1969, run for Supervisor, for which Willis hosted a fundraising party; and in 1971 she co-chaired the group that successfully fought Alvin Duskin's first antihigh-rise initiative and her office served as campaign headquarters for that fight.") Olympia & York's zest for "juice" did not end with its eventual selection in the RFQ contest. As the

September 11, 1981, *Chronicle* noted, "The developers are apparently touching every political base to assure a smooth future for their plans. O&Y has hired veteran labor lobbyist and campaign advisor Dave Jenkins as an advisor. . . . [Willie] Brown's able fundraiser Wendy Links has been hired as a public relations advisor, along with Jim Augustino, a well known leader of San Francisco neighborhood organizations."

Given widespread concern that the Tivoli Gardens proposal might become a minor league Disneyland, the choice of Marriott as Olympia & York's partner seemed somewhat quixotic. As the *Chronicle*'s architecture critic Allan Temko noted, "Rouse and Olympia & York . . . have built some authentic dogs. But their architectural standards have been incomparably higher than those of the Marriott Corporation, builders of those giant theme parks paradoxically called 'Great America,' as well as some of the ugliest hotel architecture in the world."[10] The Marriott chain's blatant anti-union record (only one of its 130 hotels at the time was unionized—and that only because it was unionized when Marriott purchased it)[11] became an issue, particularly with Redevelopment Agency commissioner Leroy King from the International Longshoremen's and Warehousemen's Union. In this union-conscious town, Marriott prudently changed its stance and agreed not to oppose unionization in its new Central Blocks hotel. But once the hotel opened in 1989, Marriott went back on its word, putting roadblocks into the union organizing drive. (See below for the denouement of this issue.)

An added bit of political juiciness was the revelation that Marriott's chief financial officer, Gary L. Wilson, was a social and business associate of the mayor's new husband, Richard Blum. Wilson, it turned out, was a 15 percent investor (a share worth sixty-five thousand dollars) in URS Corporation, an architecture/engineering firm of which Blum was vice president[12] (the firm also had prepared the 1973 environmental impact report on YBC for the Redevelopment Agency). In addition, Wilson had donated $300 to Feinstein's 1979 election campaign and the Marriott Corporation $750, then the legal maximum.[13] Alone among the Yerba Buena bidders, Olympia & York president Albert Reichmann had been given a private meeting with Mayor Feinstein prior to the agency's final selection, a meeting arranged by Willie Brown. Although Feinstein characterized it as merely "a courtesy call . . . possibly five minutes,"[14] that entree is a textbook example of *Chronicle* writer Larry Liebert's "juice" mechanism at work. An additional Blum-Marriott financial connection emerged in early 1982, when it was reported that an investment group led by Richard Blum had purchased the 107-restaurant Farrells' Ice Cream Parlour chain from the Marriott Corporation for $15 million. Blum, as noted in chapter 11, also shared office space with

Rubin Glickman, an attorney who was a Redevelopment Agency commissioner from 1977 to 1981. (See chapter 11 for discussion of Blum's role as Feinstein's money man.)

Olympia & York/Marriott emerged victorious, and with their selection, entered into a period of exclusive negotiations, after which a final design, development, and land disposition agreement would be completed. As those who criticized the process from the outset predicted, this procedure left the City somewhat at the mercy of the developer—in this case the world's largest of the breed, with, conservatively estimated, $3.5 billion in real estate assets and multitudinous other investments in oil and gas, newsprint, asbestos, copper, and forest products. O&Y had major development projects in New York City (the $1.5 billion, six-million-square-foot Battery Park City), Boston, Los Angeles, Portland, Hartford, Toronto, and Calgary. It made its big splash on the U.S. scene in 1976, at the nadir of New York City's financial crisis, when it bought eight blue-ribbon office buildings controlled by the National Kinney Corporation for $350 million, an investment whose value increased sixfold in six years. The deal was described as "the coup of the century beyond a shadow of a doubt" and "the best deal since the Louisiana Purchase" by the *New York Times,* which also characterized O&Y as "perhaps the most prominent force in the topsy-turvy world of New York City real estate."[15] Olympia & York was a privately held family company, owned by the Reichmann clan, described in a 1982 book as follows: "In the real estate world there are the Reichmanns, and then there is everybody else. . . . They are the deans of the real estate development world, unparalleled chess players in making deals, possessed of infinite patience and down-to-earth common sense and practicality."[16]

Dealing with Olympia & York/Marriott

Against so skilled and powerful a developer as Olympia & York/Marriott, the Redevelopment Agency was at a disadvantage, for its staff lacked the corresponding talents and experience. The type of selection process used by the agency put O&Y in the driver's seat: They could always explicitly or implicitly threaten to pick up their marbles and go back to Toronto, leaving the City in a terrible spot politically. Abandonment of the project by the developer might mean years of additional delay, with other developers possibly even more reluctant to get involved if Olympia & York couldn't succeed with it. O&Y's financial investment in the negotiation process was not that large, and they had plenty of work to keep them busy elsewhere, so they truly had the upper hand in the negotiations as to what would be developed on the acreage and the price they would have to pay for the land. The non-results for three-and-a-half years following their designation in October 1980 illustrate how little control the City really had and continued to have in these negotiations. According to the Request for Qualifications, the period of exclusive negotiation was to have culminated in January 1981 with execution of a land disposition agreement between the agency and the developer. Eleven times the agency staff requested, and the commission routinely approved, extensions of that deadline. According to one commissioner, "the other commissioners read little, care less. They let the lawyers do it. Nobody on the commission even follows the Olympia & York negotiations."

Skidmore, Owings & Merrill's 1977 report for the Redevelopment Agency, "New Directions for Yerba Buena Center," had as its central theme the need to avoid repetition of the "grand plan" fallacy:

> Earlier plans for YBC have been flawed by an over-dependence upon a single major developer and by large scale development concepts. Previous plans have depended upon one massive integrated development covering a number of city blocks. In each case, the planning idea, however exciting in concept, has been based on the precise fiscal and physical integration of public and private uses. . . . When one aspect of these arrangements became problematical, the whole plan proved fragile. . . . The larger the project, the more it became vulnerable to any single weakness. The plan strategy might be likened to a house of cards.

Then–city planning director Rai Okamoto commented, "It may be easier for the [redevelopment] agency to deal with one developer, but I think that is too much power to hand to a single developer."[17] Okamoto also would have required the three or four finalists to submit competitive proposals—converting the Request for Qualifications into a Request for Proposals once the field was narrowed and the remaining developers felt more willing to invest funds in generating a concrete proposal. In addition to the competitive juices this would have stirred among the most talented and powerful of the bidders, the City and agency would then have had a solid commitment from the developer they selected. It was clear from the response to the RFQ that there was considerable developer interest in Yerba Buena, but the agency did not tap and manipulate it to the City's best advantage.

As noted above, the agency's April 1980 Request for Qualifications document contained only the most general description of what the agency wished to see on the Central Blocks, which they somewhat confusingly renamed Yerba Buena Gardens, possibly in an attempt to capture whatever support for Tivoli Gardens still existed. Their listed "requirements" in the

RFQ did no more than state the approximate number of square feet to be devoted to office, retail, entertainment, open space, and cultural uses, and the approximate number of housing units and hotel rooms. It was wide open to the winning developer, during the negotiating period, to make any proposal it wished within these parameters or to operate around them.

In September 1981, O&Y at last submitted three remarkably similar "alternative plans," dubbed "The Esplanade," "The Square," and "The Terraces." A formal proposal was submitted to the agency in November 1981 but was returned because it lacked sufficient information to permit evaluation. It was clear that once they had won the beauty contest, Olympia & York/Marriott was moving slowly to put its team together, many of whom were busy on other projects, and work was merely limping along.

Detailed information on offers and counter-offers between the City/Redevelopment Agency and Olympia & York/Marriott was kept in the "superclassified" category. O&Y/Marriott made its first concrete financial offer in January 1982, and the City rejected it. The developer was steadily upping the ante—a major concession was the City's agreement to add two and a half acres to the development parcel on the east side of Third, between Mission and Howard Streets (known as East Block 2), raising the total development site to twenty-four acres. "The additional site promises to be a lucrative one," noted the September 2, 1981, *Examiner*, "since it includes 128,000 square feet in a South-of-Market area where quoted prices have been running $200 a square foot and up." This addition raised the total amount of development on the parcel from 2.5 million to 4–4.5 million square feet. It was also rumored by insiders that because of City pressures on the developers to include and maintain various nonrevenue producing areas (the cultural facilities and open space), O&Y was offering to purchase the land for a vastly lower sum than originally had been bruited about— according to knowledgeable sources, one dollar for the whole site!

The bind the agency and City were in was that they could not accept too low a price, for that would look to the public as if they were giving away the store completely; but neither could they accept a cutback on the various public benefits, the open space, and the cultural facilities, which had considerable public support and were part of the social and aesthetic rationale for the entire venture. And yet if they pressed too hard, they risked a "take it or leave it" posture from O&Y/Marriott, who could walk away from the project without the loss of great amounts of money or face.

Through this entire process of plan preparation and negotiation, the public was shut out. The agency maintained it would be at a negotiating disadvantage if it had to reveal everything taking place. Public interest groups regarded this stance as simply self-protective: to insulate a not very competent or experienced negotiating partner from public scrutiny. Consumer Action even brought a lawsuit against the agency in 1981 to compel disclosure of the various documents the agency and O&Y/Marriott were using. In a letter to the agency, the group stated, "We believe we, the public, as sellers need to be told by our broker, the Redevelopment Agency, what would be a fair return to us. This is the normal practice when real estate is being put on the market."[18] But neither the agency nor the courts were having any part of this concept of "public agency," and no documents were let out.

Even the Board of Supervisors would not act to secure and review these documents, although it eventually had to approve the land disposition agreement. When the YBC issue came before them in November 1981, in the form of a technical supplement to the environmental impact report, Supervisor Nancy Walker introduced a resolution asking for the negotiating documents, but could not get majority support for it. "If the past is any indication," she stated in a press release, "the Board will be presented a cumbersome document a day or two before the vote, and will be asked to approve a project that it knows nothing about. We cannot be coerced into approving a project whose benefits to the City and County are unclear," she optimistically and unrealistically concluded. The board in fact received the 163-page environmental impact report just three days before it was calendared, and even board president John Molinari acknowledged he had not read it all. Nonetheless, it was approved, seven to two. As the *Bay Guardian* concluded, "The Redevelopment Agency, accountable to no one save the developers with which it deals, has proceeded to develop a project that suits the needs of no one save those same developers. The Board of Supervisors, overworked, understaffed and heavily lobbied, has once again folded and given the agency blanket approval."[19]

Instead of an open process, SFRA executive director Wilbur Hamilton promised to make everything public once the two parties reached a tentative agreement but before consummation of the agreement, giving the public an opportunity to intervene only at that point. By that time, however, the chances of significantly influencing the results would be minimal. Involving the public throughout the negotiations probably would have strengthened the Redevelopment Agency's hand, in that more could be demanded from the developers, and resistance could be organized to the developer's demand for concessions. But the agency has never trusted the public and never seen its participation as anything other than a source of trouble; instead, it assumed the "drawing up the bridges" stance of a weak and beleaguered body.

The Redevelopment Agency functioned poorly as a public broker and ne-
gotiator during the developer selection process and afterward. It did not develop a specific set of public expectations or demands in terms of public revenues or public benefits from use of this valuable land. No asking price was
developed or put forth. No clearly articulated "public benefits package" was
demanded with respect to subsidized housing, open space, cultural facilities,
and financial support for social services. In such a situation, any smart developer will make as few concessions as possible.

In April 1984, the agency and Olympia & York/Marriott finally announced a tentative agreement on the Central Blocks.

The General Services Administration/Marriott Site

The Marriott interests had partnered with O&Y in order to secure for themselves a good hotel site near the convention center, and they chose 49 Fourth
Street as their spot. According to an O&Y representative, without the site
the deal was off and "there will not be a project."[20]

On the east side of Fourth between Market and Mission, 49 Fourth was
the site of a Veterans Administration building, closed in 1973 because of
failure to meet San Francisco's earthquake standards and since vacant. At
various times, the federal government talked of building a new federal office complex on the site or trading it for another site on which to construct
offices. At other times and in other quarters, it was discussed as a possible
addition to the YBC project area, a prime location for a privately developed
office building or hotel. But nothing happened, despite unanimous opinion
by agency consultants that the site should be acquired immediately.

There then ensued one of the more farcical political minuets of the entire YBC story, involving the General Services Administration (GSA), the
Congress, the Marriott Corporation, and city hall.

The GSA can at times rival the San Francisco Redevelopment Agency in
ineptness and lethargy. Having held the property vacant for a decade (at an
opportunity cost calculated by GSA at $13 million to $19 million, plus the
loss of $1.9 million to $2.5 million in property taxes to San Francisco were
it privately developed),[21] GSA still was unsure what it wanted to do. The
new GSA administrator under the Reagan administration, Gerald Carmen,
a former tire dealer who directed Ronald Reagan's successful 1980 campaign
in the key New Hampshire primary, was committed to privatizing much of
the federal government's unused real estate. He therefore responded fa-
vorably to the Marriott request—solicited by Mayor Feinstein when it became obvious the Redevelopment Agency wasn't moving effectively on the

matter—that GSA sell the site to the agency, which in turn would sell or lease it to Marriott. This favorable response may or may not have had anything to do with:

- the Marriott Corporation's prominent place on the Republican campaign donation rolls (Marriott officials, members of the Marriott family, and the concern's political action committees contributed $107,000 to Republican committees and candidates in the 1979–80 election campaign, $40,000 more in the first half of 1982);[22]
- the fact that Carmen had met with Marriott's lawyer to discuss the proposed sale;
- a "Dear Gerry" letter to Carmen from Marriott executive vice president Fred Malek (White House director of personnel during the Nixon administration), pointing out that the sale would benefit "not only the city of San Francisco, but also President Reagan."[23]

The Malek-to-Carmen epistle, it turns out, was written at the suggestion of Mayor Feinstein and SFRA executive director Wilbur Hamilton, although they were not necessarily responsible for the crass wording. These new revelations generated charges of political favoritism, intensified by the unorthodox way in which the proposed sale had made its way through the GSA hierarchy. Administrator Carmen had simply, as the *New York Times* put it, "overturned the recommendations of five levels of professionals in the GSA."[24] Carmen "denied political motivations in his decision" and through a spokesperson replied, "Absolutely not," when asked if he had imposed any shortcuts to speed up the sale, but "it was learned through the files that Mr. Carmen waived a GSA procedure under which other Federal agencies are screened for 30 days to see if they have a need for excess federal space."[25]

Regional GSA officials and those in the GSA Washington bureaucracy, more concerned with its mission of providing needed federal office space, regarded selling the building as unwise, given the need for more federal office space in San Francisco and the difficulty of leasing space or obtaining alternative sites. Finding a new site would be far easier with a valuable site to trade. The less politically inclined among the GSA senior staff were angry at Carmen's virtually unheard of act of overriding the unified regional and central staff recommendation that the building not be sold. The GSA had even allotted funds in its proposed budget to construct a new federal office building in San Francisco and had submitted a prospectus for the building to the House Public Buildings and Grounds Subcommittee.

The issue rapidly became politicized along partisan lines in Washington, where Democratic Congressman Elliott Levitas of Georgia held a hearing on August 4, 1982, before the joint Public Buildings and Grounds and Investigations and Oversight Subcommittees of the House Committee on Public Works and Transportation. The GSA's inspector general undertook his own investigation and found that, "While there was no evidence to prove or disprove that the Administrator's decision was influenced by political considerations," his "decision to sell the 49 Fourth Street property was made without sufficient comparative cost data necessary to decide whether to sell or exchange the property."[26] The inspector general recommended that the administrator request an analysis of the exchange vs. sale option in order to aid in making a decision in the government's best interest. The inspector general's report also concluded that the appraisal of 49 Fourth Street obtained by the GSA may have understated the property's value, at $17.4 million, as it did not take into account "assemblage" or "plotage" value to the Redevelopment Agency, which owned land on three sides of the site.

Gerald Carmen, by this time annoyed and publicly embarrassed by his exposure on this land deal, decided to wash his hands of it by putting the property up for public sale to the highest bidder—although without following the inspector general's recommendation that he obtain a new and better appraisal. He did offer, however, to sell the site to the Redevelopment Agency if Congress would affirm that the GSA had done nothing "illegal or improper" in connection with the proposed $17.4 million sale.[27] But Rep. Levitas was having no part of this demand for (Democratic) congressional absolution.

Alarmed at the possibility of losing this valuable hotel site in an open bidding process, the City decided to scare away any potential competitors by threatening them with eminent domain action to take the site, should anyone dare to enter into a bidding war with the Redevelopment Agency.[28] Letters transmitting this threat went out to all 258 persons who picked up the bid package, and the tactic worked.[29] "Before publication of the Redevelopment Agency's warning of eminent domain procedures," the Examiner noted, "a number of influential developers and real estate firms had applied for bid packages."[30] But in the end, only one bid was entered besides the agency's $17.4 million minimum upset price bid—$27,297 offered by one Ben M. Lee of Guam ("My bidding was a mistake. I thought the minimum bid was $17,000.")[31] In April 1983, GSA accepted the agency's $17.4 million bid for the 47,000-square-foot site, "well below the going rate in prime Financial District blocks."[32] "In my judgment," according to John Gaillardia, the retired acting commissioner of the GSA's Public Building Service, in testimony before Congress, "I think we had aces up in our hand and gave it away."[33]

Not one person at GSA or in the Congress seemed bothered by the likely drubbing the taxpayers took in all this: The $17.4 million appraisal was, as noted above, probably well below the site's value to the agency and its client, Marriott, and the bullying tactics the agency used to scare away other bidders meant that the real value of the site—which probably would have been realized had any number of those 258 potential bidders gotten into the fray—was not obtained by the public.

In mid-1983, the Redevelopment Agency issued $28 million in bonds, a portion of which was used to pay the federal government for the 49 Fourth Street site (the remainder to pay off the balance of the HUD loan and grant contract for YBC, thereby closing out the project for federal fiscal purposes). And in 1989 the Marriott opened its massive fifteen hundred–room hotel, a hugely successful operation but unfortunately one of the town's more comic pieces of architecture—termed by *Chronicle* architecture critic Allan Temko "the biggest jukebox in the world."[34] San Francisco subsequently sought to offer an alternative site to GSA, and Mayor Feinstein got embroiled in some nasty public disputes over the issue with Oakland Mayor Lionel Wilson, but Oakland wound up with the region's new federal building and its two thousand jobs. (However, in the end, San Francisco will after all be getting a new federal office building, at Seventh and Mission Streets—an eighteen-story concrete tower with glass walls and a stainless steel screen draped over one side that has drawn heavy criticism for its design and "disregard of context . . . totally inappropriate," in the words of the city's former planning director Lu Blazej, "[It's] the kind of building you have in Houston or Los Angeles."[35] Construction is scheduled to begin in the summer of 2002.)

Once built, the Marriott perfidiously challenged labor and unionization agreements that presumably had been settled nine years earlier when the hotel officials signed a letter, assenting to demands by Local 2 of the Hotel and Restaurant Employees and Bartenders Union regarding organizing rights, in exchange for the union dropping opposition to the Marriott/O&Y bid to develop a hotel on this valuable site. The notoriously antiunion hotel chain began to renege on earlier commitments to allow union recognition based on employees' signed union cards rather than a formal voting procedure;* to give first consideration in its hires to members of Local 2; and to remain neutral in the organizing process. This reversal of commitment led to litigation, in which the hotel's challenge to its earlier agreement (based

---

*This is "a strategy that the nation's labor movement is increasingly embracing. Labor leaders are pressing employers to recognize unions based on card signings, instead of elections, asserting that during election campaigns, employers often intimidate workers, fire union supporters and hire consultants to propagandize against the union" (Steven Greenhouse, "Union Hopes to Gain Support by Shaming Met's Opera Fans," *New York Times,* 27 September 1999).

on its claim that the agreement violated federal labor laws) was at first up-held in the federal trial court, but overturned unanimously by the Ninth Circuit Court of Appeals, which remanded the case to the trial judge ("It should be beyond cavil that a party cannot reap the benefits of a bargain and then exercise its right [nine years later] to rescind," wrote Federal Judge Marilyn Hall Patel, who appointed a special master, a process that resulted in a 1994 consent decree favorable to the union).[36] In early 1996, Local 2 began its organizing drive, the union was certified as the employees' bar-gaining agent for three-quarters of the hotel's eleven hundred employees, and contract negotiations got under way.[37] Marriott then began to sweeten wage and benefit levels in an effort to turn workers against unionization, so as to produce a decertification vote.

The issue has become a very big deal. In July 2000, following a thirty-three-month investigation, the National Labor Relations Board issued a complaint, charging Marriott with more than eighty violations of federal labor law, including repeatedly refusing to bargain in good faith, firing union supporters, threatening employees with reprisals for engaging in union ac-tivities, engaging in surveillance of union activities, and withholding regu-lar wage and benefit increases from union-represented employees. Local 2 wants a fair contract with those basic rights that are the norm for other unionized hotels in San Francisco: regular days off, overtime pay (employ-ees often are required to work six and seven days in a row), retirement ben-efits, and seniority rights. As of early 2002, hotel-union negotiations were looking promising; the Marriott had agreed to several major union demands. There had been regular picketing of the hotel, plus more dramatic actions as well, such as a hotel lobby sit-in, in which Supervisor Tom Ammiano and fifty-one others were arrested, and a November 1998 1,250-person demon-stration, during which AFL-CIO president John Sweeney and 149 others were arrested for blocking traffic. A Labor Day, 2000,[38] boycott of the Mar-riott, announced by Mayor Willie Brown, was also effective.

The Fall of Olympia & York

Starting in the early eighties, O&Y got into serious financial trouble, leading to bankruptcy filings in the early nineties, events so powerful in their finan-cial community ramifications that they made the front page of the *New York Times* on several occasions.[39] Illustrating the worldwide importance of the bankruptcy filing, the mediator named by the federal bankruptcy judge was former Secretary of State Cyrus Vance, who had just ended a nineteen-month stint trying to negotiate a settlement of the fighting in the former Yugoslavia.

In San Francisco, the impact of Olympia & York's downfall was to eliminate them as developer of the building sites they had won in the RFQ competition, including the planned forty-story office tower on Market Street between Third and Fourth Streets (originally with a promised May 1986 starting date but until very recently, with construction on the new Four Seasons Hotel/condominium structure, an embarrassing gaping hole with a temporary fence that has been defacing the Market Street sidewalk for nearly three decades), for which O&Y had originally paid $68 million in development rights—negotiated down to $37 million in the late eighties when O&Y's troubles started getting serious. A combination of forfeited earnest money and letters of credit that the Redevelopment Agency was able to collect on yielded some $25 million that has been used to partially fund the cultural and recreational uses atop Moscone Center that make up Yerba Buena Gardens (see chapter 10); but, as the July 17, 1992, *Examiner* noted, "The agency ended up using $40 million in public money to cover what should have been on the developer's tab."*

The New Downtown Baseball Stadium

The new downtown stadium once threatened to be as long-running and controversial an act as Yerba Buena Center. Where to build a new baseball-football stadium to replace much-maligned Candlestick Park preoccupied the city for a decade and a half, during which a variety of plans and locations were produced and discarded.

Candlestick Park was completed in 1960 as a home for the New York Giants baseball team, which San Francisco had lured to the West Coast. Development of the stadium created something of a scandal, involving contractor Charles Harney, who had purchased sixty-five acres in Hunters Point from the City for twenty-one hundred dollars an acre and then (with the assistance of Mayor George Christopher) formed a nonprofit corporation, Stadium, Inc., to float City-backed bonds, with himself and two employees as the board of directors. Harney then sold forty-one acres of the land he had purchased from the City back to Stadium, Inc., for $2.7 million ($65,853 per

---

*While, ironically, O&Y thus proved of great indirect assistance in the eventual creation of the Yerba Buena Gardens cultural and open space, it was not quite the scenario Mayor Feinstein had in mind in this flowery statement from the 1982 Redevelopment Agency Annual Report: "The agency has selected a world-renowned developer team for the proposed $750 million Yerba Buena Gardens which, I assure, will be carried out with such quality, imagination and dignity that one day all of the world will attend, admire and applaud."

acre, a 3,000 percent profit); Stadium, Inc., without public bidding, awarded Harney's construction company the $7 million stadium construction contract.[40] In 1969–70, major expansion and renovations, funded by a $24 million City bond issue, were made to Candlestick, to accommodate the 49ers football team, and in 1972 the City tacked on a fifty-cent admission tax to Candlestick Park tickets and diverted additional hotel tax money in order to meet these bond payments. General funds have also been used to pay maintenance costs. The City's expenditures to build and run the stadium have always been far more than has been openly acknowledged to the taxpayers.

Fiscal shenanigans aside, Candlestick Park (since 1995, technically and officially 3Com Park, when the City sold "naming rights" to the 3Com computer networking company—although virtually no self-respecting San Franciscan employed the new name in speech, any more than he or she would say "Frisco")* had for a long time been heavily criticized by fans and players: It is on a cold and windy site that is somewhat hard to reach, public transportation is poor and parking inadequate, and a certain amount of crime against spectators and their vehicles was alleged to emanate from teenagers living in the surrounding Bayview–Hunters Point neighborhood.

The Giants' owner until recently, Robert Lurie (characterized as "one of the 400 richest men in the U.S. . . . a formidable figure who apparently has Mayor Dianne Feinstein and most of the mayor's top officials in his corner,"[41] a position abetted by the very substantial campaign contributions he made to Feinstein), long claimed he was losing money—although, like almost all professional sports teams, which are privately owned, the books are not open to public scrutiny, and claims of distress and suffering should be regarded with skepticism as largely self-serving tales.[42] Lurie had purchased the team in 1976 in order to keep it in San Francisco. His threat was that he would move the team from the city in 1994, when the Candlestick lease ran out, unless there was action to create a better playing facility.[43] "Owning a

---

*Naming rights are all the rage these days, covering everything from museums to hospitals to streets and highways, even state parks. The city's public transit system is considering selling naming rights to its stations. (See Edward Epstein, "Muni May Sell Naming Rights to Metro Stations," *San Francisco Chronicle*, 28 January 2001.) For a good review of the landscape and issues, see Julie Edelson Halpert, "Dr. Pepper Hospital? Perhaps, for a Price," *New York Times*, 19 February 2001. And the pitfalls of the naming game were vividly illustrated in early 2002, when the Houston Astros paid $2.1 million to Enron Corp. for the right to remove that disgraced company's name from what had been called Enron Field. (See Frank Ahrens, "For Enron Field, Whole New Ball Name," *Washington Post*, 28 February 2002.)

baseball team is the closest thing America has to royalty," sagely observed San Francisco Tomorrow's February 1993 newsletter.[44]

In March 1982, the team released a study it had commissioned, ostensibly exploring two options: building a new domed stadium in a downtown location or doming Candlestick Park.[45] According to Corey Busch, the Giants' administrative vice president (and former press secretary to Mayor Moscone), the cost of a new domed stadium (exclusive of land and interest but paying off the Candlestick Park bonds and utilizing revenues from selling off the Candlestick Park land for private development) would be $95 million; the cost of doming Candlestick and making other improvements to the concession facilities, restrooms, scoreboards, sound system, etc. (exclusive of interest), $60 million.

A City task force, a SPUR task force, and later a $300,000 feasibility study funded by the Board of Supervisors all went to work on the issue. While the consultant's feasibility study was supposed to be ready in March 1983, there were lots of delays, secrecy, premature leaks, and doubtless a bit of manipulation of the findings, which were: the cost of doming and renovating Candlestick Park would actually be as much as $135 million, not the $60 million put forth in the Giants' study; a brand-new seventy thousand-seat retractable dome stadium could be built on a state-owned site South of Market for somewhere around the same price; and Candlestick Park was falling apart at the seams.[46] As to the "numbers" in the study containing this recommendation, Supervisor Richard Hongisto observed, "Put it this way for now—if your accountant had done the figures in the task force report, he'd be serving five years."[47] Board of Supervisors budget analyst Harvey Rose issued a blistering sixty-three-page report in early 1984, criticizing the report of the mayor's stadium task force for a number of key omissions and methodological shortcomings, including hiring some of the same consultants the Giants used for their March 1982 study to verify the Giants' study.[48]

The stadium game then began in earnest, with many echoes of Moscone Center, starting with mayoral (Feinstein) promises that work could begin in early 1985, with a 1987–88 opening date. The original desired site was state-owned land bounded by Second, Berry, and Third Streets and China Basin, originally intended to be part of the uncompleted Interstate 280 freeway, although it was uncertain whether the state would make the site available and whether the federal government then would demand reimbursement of the 90 percent of the acquisition funds it had furnished.[49] Within a short time, attention was refocused on another site identified by a task force appointed by Mayor Feinstein: 7th and Townsend, at the base of Potrero Hill. Proposition W, placed on the November 1987 ballot by Feinstein and the Board of

Supervisors, asked, somewhere between disingenuously and dishonestly: "Shall a baseball park be built at 7th and Townsend on land at no cost to the city with no increases in taxes and all debt repaid with nontax money?" Despite the sugary wording, it lost 53 percent to 47 percent. Potrero Hill neighborhood opposition—derived from concerns about traffic congestion—and opposition by the leading mayoral candidate in the 1987 race (Art Agnos) and voters skeptical of the false promises of politicians—joined those who supported renovation

Art Agnos, once mayor (1988), pushed for a China Basin spot, five blocks from the site identified in Proposition W, and in July 1989 he and Giants owner Lurie announced that a deal had been struck: a 45,000-seat, $95 million stadium (to be developed by the Philadelphia-based Spectacor Management Group), with the City donating 12.5 acres for the site, $2 million a year for ten years to defray operating costs, plus a $1 million annual loan for ten years, not to be repaid for twenty-five years (the funds to come largely from hotel tax revenues). The City also would be obligated to build a fifteen hundred-car garage, and Lurie's Giants, who would lease the facility from Spectacor (with no requirement to fully disclose the terms), would be exempt from property taxes. Again, widespread opposition: traffic ("Gridlock Park" was suggested as the name for the new facility); raiding the hotel tax to pay for it; interference with long-standing plans to develop China Basin for housing and light industry; secret negotiations. Two more propositions were placed on the November 1989 ballot: P, ratifying the City's agreement with Lurie, lost by two thousand votes (a critical factor was the Loma Prieta earthquake just three weeks before election day, which distracted and scared voters, slowed down the proponents' campaign, and also led to nostalgia and support for old Candlestick Park, which weathered the quake well in the midst of game three of the nationally televised Giants–Oakland A's World Series); and V, a citizen-initiated policy declaration supporting renovation of Candlestick Park, won with 51.4 percent of the vote.*

---

*For those acquainted with it, the Yankee Stadium saga was a cautionary tale: When the Yankees threatened to leave the Bronx in the 1970s, cash-strapped New York City bought Yankee Stadium and renovated it—with the construction bill rising from the original $24 million estimate to $100 million; to save money, the neighborhood improvement component of the project was cut out. (See Malcolm Gladwell, "Built by Ruth, Threatened by George," *Washington Post*, 29 July 1993.) George (Steinbrenner) subsequently became embroiled in a well-publicized threat once again to take his team out of Yankee Stadium, with city and state officials scrambling mightily to offer whatever inducements it might take to keep the team in New York, including $275 million worth of renovations and building a new stadium elsewhere, while New Jersey offered competitive bids to induce the team to cross the Hudson.

Bob Lurie didn't follow through on his threat to move the Giants out of San Francisco (not that he didn't try: He negotiated to sell the team to a group of Florida investors, who would move it to Tampa–St. Petersburg, but the league's team owners' organization vetoed the plan). However, in 1993 he sold the team for $100 million (some accounts put it at $110 million—in any case a nifty profit, since his 1976 purchase price was a reported $8 million–$10 million)* to a group of local investors headed by Safeway board chair Peter Magowan (another key member of the owner group was real estate mogul Walter Shorenstein). And by 1994 the China Basin site was back in serious contention, although with a revised plan that largely shifted direct costs from the City to the private sector—a change substantial enough to convince voters to give their approval in a March 1996 special election. The new forty-one thousand-seat stadium—naming rights went to Pacific Bell Telephone for a cool $50 million—was now on track to open for the year 2000 season, which it did.

Opponents—and there still are many—stress that there are lots of (mostly hidden) public costs and financial risks:[50] the need for increased City services; monumental traffic jams; totally inadequate parking facilities; no nearby BART service; likely sewer back-up problems; vastly exaggerated employment and economic development benefits;[51] interference with the area's burgeoning multimedia industry; potential earthquake vulnerability of the landfill site; blockage of waterfront views; weather conditions no better than Candlestick; and no guarantees that the Giants will remain in San Francisco.†

---

*Lurie's megaprofit pales in comparison with National Football League franchises. "An NFL team cost about $600,000 in the early 1960s, compared to $140 million paid for the Carolina and Jacksonville franchises in 1993 and $700 million paid for Houston in 1999" (Alan Abramson and Sam Farmer, "NFL Ledgers Reveal Profits Depend on New Stadium," *Los Angeles Times*, 13 May 2001).

†No matter what agreement is signed, a "commitment" to play in a given stadium for a number of years, even if in the form of a signed lease, provides little guarantee that the team actually will keep its word; if it becomes more profitable to break a lease and move, a team will go. Ex-mayor George Christopher, father of Candlestick Park, phrased the issue perfectly: "Will the Giants and the 49ers agree in an ironclad contract to remain in San Francisco for a period of years sufficient to amortize the cost of a new stadium? It would be foolhardy for the City to encumber itself for over $160 million and then be deserted as is happening in Oakland" (George Christopher memoir, "Review of the Acquisition of the San Francisco Giants Baseball Team," unpublished document, September 1992). The Oakland Raiders, as sports fans well know, abandoned the Oakland Coliseum in 1982—built for the team by Alameda County in 1966—for the more lucrative Los Angeles Coliseum (after the Rams moved to a new stadium in Anaheim), thereby leaving Alameda County taxpayers with $20 million in unpaid bonds. Among the many lawsuits that ensued was the fascinating one brought by the City of Oakland, which instituted an eminent domain action against the team to force its return, a legal move which, had it been successful, could have allowed a municipality to use these powers to prevent the de-

The entire issue of moving sports teams around, building their stadiums and arenas, and use of public moneys arises in city after city and raises important questions about public priorities.[52] And there is hype to spare. Sports columnist Allan Barra, in an op-ed in the October 21, 1993, *New York Times*, observed: "One disingenuous way [big league owners argue] is ... that spending money on a professional team eventually pays for itself by boosting the economy. Almost no legitimate economists believe that the millions spent on sports stadiums are really a good investment." Raymond Keating of the Cato Institute in an April 5, 1999, *Washington Post* op-ed wrote:

> During the 20th century, more than $20 billion (in 1997 dollars) has been spent on major league stadiums and arenas, including at least $14.7 billion in taxpayer subsidies. This does not include billions in subsidies through the use of tax-free municipal bonds and interest paid on debt. Looking at the rest of 1999 and the next several years, another conservative estimate points to more than 13.5 billion additional dollars being spent on new major league facilities, including more than $9 billion from taxpayers. . . . [R]eports from hired-gun consultants . . . amount to the worst kind of economic guesswork. More realistic analyses examine actual changes in the economy resulting from the presence of stadiums. These studies have found no positive impact from professional sports; some even have found a negative effect. . . . [M]any economists who have studied the issue have concluded that cities and states almost never gain by giving in to teams' demands for new stadiums.

A 1996 article from the *New York Times* business pages noted that municipal bonds issued in the 1991–96 period for sports complexes and stadiums exceeded those issued for libraries and museums, and that "most troubling to critics is the evidence that the money spent on sports stadiums provides few economic benefits to the surrounding community. Indeed, several studies indicate that communities could benefit more if these investments, which

---

parture of any business or industry important to the local economy. But the action, filed in early 1980, was dismissed in July 1983, and an appeal to the California Supreme Court was denied in June 1986 (the Raiders' lead lawyer: former San Francisco mayor Joseph Alioto). The Raiders have since moved back to Oakland, where lawsuits involving the team, the National Football League, and the Oakland Coliseum Authority abound: In May 2001, a jury rejected the Raiders' breach of contract claim (for which, represented by Joe Alioto *fils*, they were asking $1.2 billion in damages) that the NFL had forced the team to leave Los Angeles by sabotaging a deal for a new stadium. (See Leonard Shapiro, "NFL Prevails in Raiders' Suit," *Washington Post*, 22 May 2001.) For some of this history, as well as additional information on the Raiders' quirky owner, see Ira Simmons, *Black Knight: Al Davis and His Raiders* (Rocklin, Calif.: Prima Publishers, 1990), chap. 11; and Mark Ribowsky, *Slick: The Silver and Black Life of Al Davis* (New York: Macmillan, 1990).

cost taxpayers hundreds of millions of dollars a year, were spent on other forms of economic development."[53] Similarly, Lake Forest College economist Robert Baade notes, "When you take into account that the money spent on a stadium could be invested in roads or bridges or industrial parks or schools, all of which have much greater return, it may well be that stadium-building actually has a negative impact."[54] In a related observation, Princeton political scientist Michael Danielson notes, "In an era of less government, professional sports is the glaring exception; cities with decrepit schools and crumbling infrastructure compete to build glittering new arenas and stadiums; governors who slash taxes and cut welfare rolls commit millions of public dollars to sports ventures."[55] Increasingly, these sports franchises are owned by big corporations and financial figures, such as Rupert Murdoch, H. Wayne Huizenga, ITT, Cablevision, and Time Warner. And like most corporations, these owners are turning to local, state, and national governments for financial assistance, so it is not surprising to find them in the ranks of the big campaign contributors.[56]

To its credit—albeit only as a result of the persistent opposition of community groups and the voters—San Francisco has managed to be the exception, the first for decades: a new ballpark paid for, at least in terms of direct costs,* by the private owners who stand to benefit handsomely from the new facility (among other goodies, the value/selling price of a team inflates considerably and immediately as a result of the new arena). Seattle, Houston, Milwaukee, and many other cities likely wish they could say the same thing.†
Opening day, April 11, 2000, was a huge success (marred only by a 6–5 loss to the hated Dodgers).[57] And, with sellout crowds throughout, the team managed to turn a profit for the first time since 1993, nearly doubling the revenue it took in at Candlestick Park the year before.[58] Parking problems are monumental, for stadium neighbors as well as fans.[59] The stadium has had and will continue to have a powerful impact on its surroundings ("a formerly forlorn backwater of warehouses and factories . . . [where the] stadium's location . . .

---

*The financial package for the $319 million stadium does have a couple of relatively minor public components: a $1.2 million annual land lease from the City and $15 million in financing from the team's future sales tax revenues. And there are costs for increased Muni service, police, traffic control, new sidewalks, and sewers.
†Seattle's new Safeco Field is proving to be a true disaster. Originally supposed to cost $250 million, it wound up costing $517 million (the most costly single-sport stadium in North America); a lawsuit is brewing between the team's owners (who include Microsoft billionaires) and King County; seat sales for the Mariners are far below projections; cost-cutting owners have allowed popular but expensive players to sign up with other teams; fans are picketing the facility. See C. W. Nevis, "Seattle Ballpark Fiasco," *San Francisco Chronicle*, 15 July 1999; Timothy Egan, "What Price the Most Expensive Diamond of All?" *New York Times*, 17 July 1999.

had an immediate gentrifying effect even before the foundation for the park was laid, driving up both commercial and residential rents and marking every vacant patch of land for development.")[60] And time will tell whether the predictions of other doomsayers—regarding the need for increased City services, interference with the multimedia industry, minimal employment and economic development benefits, no guarantee of long-term retention of the team in San Francisco—have validity. It also will be interesting to see whether San Francisco's financing scheme will impact other cities. Giants' vice president and CEO Larry Baer noted that other teams were none too happy with his team's deal, "fearing it might be proof that professional teams don't need taxpayer help. 'The reaction wasn't all that warm. For a while, we wore the scarlet letter.' "[61] Relatedly, the Minnesota attorney general's office began a probe in 1997 to see whether the Minnesota Twins conspired with other baseball teams to boycott cities that don't provide taxpayer-financed stadiums—a probe that was disallowed by the Supreme Court due to major league baseball's extraordinary exemption from antitrust laws.[62]

In mid-2001, the South of Market sports arena idea was resuscitated with reports that the Giants were preparing a proposal for a twenty-thousand-seat sports/entertainment center across China Basin from Pac Bell Park. Learning from their ballpark experience, the Giants were thinking of carrying this out with private financing.[63]

The 49ers's Football Stadium

No sooner was there an apparent victory for the Giants in their quest for a new playing facility than the 49ers got into the act with a grand plan for a new $525 million, 75,000-seat football stadium/1.4 million-square-foot entertainment–shopping complex on the Candlestick Park site (along with open space preservation on the bay shoreline). Like most sports moguls, 49ers owner Edward DeBartolo Jr. has been a political heavy in the city,[64] and elsewhere, and moved quickly, following the Giants' success, to get a proposition (D) onto the June 1997 ballot, calling for a $100 million bond issue to build the stadium, along with a companion proposition (F), amending zoning ordinances and height limits to allow construction of the new stadium and waiving competitive bidding requirements. The propositions were strongly backed by Mayor Willie Brown and a host of lesser endorsers (more than two dozen paid arguments favoring the technical amendments proposition alone appeared in the Voter Information Pamphlet, nominally "representing" constituencies ranging from 49ers fans, Giants fans, some unions, the Chamber of Commerce, restaurateurs, San Francisco's Irish community,

lesbians and gays, women business leaders, Republicans, and city planners—
virtually all listed as paid for by the 49ers' snappily named front group, A
Committee to Develop and Build a New Stadium for the 49ers and Create
Jobs and Economic Opportunity for Bayview–Hunters Point. Arguments
stressed both the issue of retaining the 49ers—in time to host the 2002 Superbowl—as well as economic development/job generation potential (at least
$300 million in economic benefits during Superbowl week alone, as well as
more than ten thousand jobs—if supporters' claims in the ballot arguments
for D and F were to be believed) for the Bayview–Hunters Point community.
The extremely vague economic plan and projections promised revenues from
increased City taxes of various types to assist virtually every pressing social
need: job training, affordable housing development, health services, schools,
and transit. Further, these revenues would be in excess of the funds the City
would need to pay off the bonds—payments that, with interest, would
amount to $224 million over the thirty-year life of the bonds.

Opponents raised a plethora of issues:

- wildly unrealistic projections of economic benefits, which, if unreal-
  ized, leave the city's taxpayers holding the bag (a scenario predicted by
  the City's venerable budget analyst Harvey Rose and consistent with
  recent history of stadium projects in St. Louis, Cleveland, Houston,
  and Toronto);
- lack of public input or hearings, hence absence of relevant details as to
  the City's relationship to the project;
- wholesale exemption from citywide land use and other regulations
  (the Proposition M development limits described in chapter 12, the
  City's Waterfront Plan, Transit First Policy, Board of Permit Appeals
  design review, and competitive bidding rules);
- neglect of, or actual harm to, the Third Street Corridor, Bayview–
  Hunters Point's existing neighborhood commercial area;
- shifting of commercial activity away from other areas of the city;
- deleterious impact on the Candlestick Park State Recreation Area, the
  city's only state park;
- and no mechanisms to guarantee fulfillment of the extravagant job
  benefit claims, designed to enable people to get off public assistance,
  relieve the high unemployment rate in Bayview–Hunters Point, and
  provide construction job training.

In addition, there was real resentment that this "megamall" (Candlestick
Pork, as some labeled it) was being done for the megamillionaire DeBartolo

(identified by *Forbes Magazine* as one of the richest men in America, worth an estimated $650 million), who not only owned a team worth $200 million (the value of which would increase enormously with this development)[65] but also had a major ownership interest in the Ohio-based real estate investment trust that was poised to develop the site.

In a very close vote, preceded by an extraordinary publicity blitz by the 49ers (the most expensive ballot campaign in the city's history, costing proponents $2.5 million to $3 million—$33 per vote),[66] as well as by DeBartolo's repeated threat to take his team elsewhere if the vote went the wrong way, both propositions narrowly passed, D by 50.2 percent to 49.7 percent, F by 50.1 percent to 49.8 percent.[67] There were widespread charges of fraud, and a lawsuit was brought to throw out the election results, but the suit was dismissed for lack of proof that such shenanigans affected the outcome.

However, the story did not end there. In late 1997, DeBartolo resigned as chairman of the 49ers when it was disclosed that a federal grand jury might indict him and former Louisiana governor Edwin Edwards after a long investigation of riverboat casino licensing and other business deals. Edwards was accused of attempting to extort $400,000 from DeBartolo so the State Gaming Board would award a consortium that includes DeBartolo the license for the state's fifteenth and last riverboat casino. DeBartolo (who admitted handing over $400,000 in one hundred dollar bills to Edwards during a San Francisco meeting) struck a deal to provide evidence against his friend Edwards (who claimed the payment was not extortion but a voluntarily given "consultant" expense), in exchange for pleading guilty to concealment of the alleged extortion plot. He agreed to pay up to $1 million in fines and was placed on two years' probation.[68] In May 2000, Edwards was convicted of racketeering, conspiracy, and extortion and the following January was sentenced to ten years in federal prison.[69]

DeBartolo's resignation in turn triggered some difficult and damaging intrafamily tensions with his sister, who took over as team president, as well as with other senior team officials, and these developments, plus the inherent weaknesses of the new stadium plan, make it unlikely it will move ahead, at least in its present incarnation.[70]*

---

*The *Examiner's* 21 March 2000 editorial, "Eddie D. Departs," attempted a balanced assessment of DeBartolo's twenty-two-year tenure as owner of the 49ers: His record-breaking five Superbowl titles and nostalgia for the likes of Joe Montana, Terrill Davis, Deion Sanders, Fred Dean, and Steve Young were cited, but also included was the description of DeBartolo as "rude and crude. A mostly absentee landlord. A spoiled, temperamental man with a penchant for acting the bully. A spendthrift and a gambler. . . . [T]he time had come for Eddie to go. He was stinkin' up the place."

A site near the football stadium project warrants mention as well. The 550-acre ex–Navy Hunters Point shipyard, decommissioned in 1974, has great development potential but possibly greater problems. Used for decades (including years after the Navy close-down, when it was leased to a private ship repair firm, but eventually closed down for good in 1991) to build ships, repair them, and service submarines, it is a huge toxic waste repository— the city's only Superfund site. Carcinogenic soil, gases, solvents, oil products, radioactive materials, benzene, cyanide, PCBs, heavy metals, petroleum byproducts, pesticides—you name it—have been leeching into ground and pouring into the bay. The Navy, sad to say, has been truly derelict in its efforts and promises to detoxify the site[71] and in mid-2001 actually was fined by the Environmental Protection Agency for failure to notify the agency and the surrounding community of a smoldering fire that was releasing toxins into the air.[72] Nor is the toxicity that endangers Hunters Point confined to the ex–Navy Yard. Near the Superfund site is the former Bay Area Drum Factory, which reconditioned fifty-five gallon industrial drums, containing all manner of toxics, for a wide range of clients, including General Motors, the University of California, Chevron, Delta Airlines, Lockheed Martin, BART, and even a federal agency, the U.S. Defense Reutilization Marketing Service. When Bay Area Drum declared bankruptcy in 1987, its customers, who under state law are legally responsible, agreed to foot part of the cost of the cleanup with the state. But work has been slow, and toxic pollutants continue to plague the surrounding neighborhood.[73] And the Navy's irresponsibility has possibly even more ominous ramifications for the Bay Area, beyond Hunters Point. Massive amounts of radioactive waste—the same kinds of fifty-five gallon drums (an estimated 47,500 of them), carcasses of animals used in experiments at the Naval Radiological Defense Laboratory at Hunters Point, and even an entire 10,000-ton radiation-contaminated aircraft carrier—were dumped, over a twenty-five-year period, at the Farallon Islands Nuclear Waste Dump Site, just thirty miles west of San Francisco. The waste site encompasses most of the Gulf of the Farallones National Marine Sanctuary that includes some of the Pacific Ocean's most fertile fishing waters.[74]

There are some exciting development proposals for the Hunters Point area, much of which could help the surrounding, largely black community greatly, and there is clear public support for serious clean-up efforts (a November 2000 nonbinding voter opinion statement demanding that the Navy allocate sufficient funds to make the ex-shipyard safe for housing got 87 percent approval). But it likely will take a long time and need more money than will be forthcoming to turn any of these development plans into reality.

Mission Bay

As profound as Yerba Buena Center's impact has been on South of Market, and on downtown San Francisco generally, it will be dwarfed by the Mission Bay project. Originally a 195-acre development, to be built over a fifteen- to twenty-year period, it has since—following four discarded plans—been expanded to 303 acres (well over three times the land area of the Yerba Buena project), to be developed over a twenty- to thirty-year period, at a total cost of $4 billion. The changing plans, conflicts, and controversies surrounding this mega-megaproject may turn out, retrospectively, to make the YBC saga look like a piece of cake.

At the outset of the plan, all of the land was under the ownership of Southern Pacific (SP), the city's and state's largest private landowner.[75]* As originally announced in mid-1982, the project, designed by I. M. Pei, was to contain up to seven thousand market-rate housing units; possibly 18.4 million square feet of office space (attempting to take advantage of the early eighties office boom); fifty-eight thousand jobs; two thousand hotel rooms; canals, lagoons, and islands; and eighteen thousand enclosed parking spaces.[76]

Various elements in San Francisco are, of course, deeply concerned about the impact of this development, including

- those who fear their magnificent views will be blocked, particularly residents of neighboring Potrero Hill (a Southern Pacific representative at one community meeting assured: "We're not ruining your view, we're just bringing it closer");

- housing activists angry that the plan showed no intention of helping to meet the city's need for lower-income housing, although the railroad originally received most of its California land, including large parts of the Mission Bay site, from the state as a grant or at bargain-basement prices;

- planners and others wary of the impact of creating what in effect would be a second downtown on a site 50 percent larger than the current downtown district; and

- blue-collar workers concerned with loss of the area's existing industrial and warehousing jobs.

---

*At first, Southern Pacific transferred title to a subsidiary, Southern Pacific Land Development Company; in 1984, when Southern Pacific and Santa Fe Industries merged, becoming Santa Fe Southern Pacific Corporation, the Mission Bay land was transferred to the Santa Fe Pacific Land Development Corporation, an entity renamed Catellus in 1990. In this text, until the time of the transfer to the Catellus name, "Southern Pacific" is used for convenience.

Since City approval is required for the necessary rezoning of the area from industrial to commercial use, an action that by itself inflates land values enormously, City officials have considerable leverage over the giant transportation conglomerate. However, Southern Pacific has immense economic and political power and at the outset hired Assembly Speaker and skid-greaser Willie Brown as its legal and political advisor, as well as retired liberal Congressman John Burton (Phillip's brother, and as of mid-2001 president pro tem of the California State Senate).

One early example of comparative strength in the railroad vs. the City contest was the City's location choice for the proposed new baseball stadium. The choice rated best overall by the mayor's stadium task force—weighing the criteria of acquisition costs, access, public acceptance, technical considerations, size and fit, assembly time, and policy conflict—was the SP land that is one of the more valuable subareas of their Mission Bay development plan.[77] But Mayor Feinstein selected a site tied for fourth best according to the task force's criteria, a decision that would have added $8 million–$9 million to development costs because of poorer soil conditions alone. "Southern Pacific," according to the mayor's task force report, "to this date has rejected suggestions for redesigning Mission Bay plans to include a new stadium on Site 14 [the SP-owned site]." Apparently, the City was willing to accept the railroad's rejection without a whimper, and at the time no thought was given to taking the preferred site by eminent domain—using public powers to regain land the public originally gave away.

Relatedly, Assembly Speaker Brown's muscle paid off for SP when, in early 1984, he introduced legislation requiring the state Department of Transportation to enter into negotiations with the City to sell the China Basin land the department originally bought for Interstate 280, which was part of the City's preferred stadium site. City acquisition of the China Basin site would clearly benefit SP, by eliminating from stadium competition the SP-owned site that, according to the mayor's task force report, was the best location for the stadium, but which SP did not want to give up. How large a fee Brown received from SP is not known (he refused to reveal information about his private law work), but, according to the economic interest statement all state legislators must file, in 1982 Brown had at least twelve clients who paid him ten thousand dollars or more and in 1983 at least thirteen clients in this category, including Southern Pacific, YBC developer Olympia & York, office builder Gerald Hines, and condominium converter Richard Traweek, whose malodorous activities are described in chapter 13.[78]

In early 1984, Southern Pacific received from the City's Assessment Appeals Board the largest reduction in that body's seventeen-year history, when 122 acres of the proposed Mission Bay project were reassessed from $113 million to $60 million, lowering SP's 1983–84 tax bill on the site from $1.3 million to $693,000. The City's original upward reassessment action was triggered, under terms of Proposition 13, the state's 1978 property tax reform measure, when land title was shifted from the conglomerate's railroad subsidiary to its land-development subsidiary. The city assessor's office, using comparable sales in the South of Market area and the eastern foot of nearby Potrero Hill, arrived at the $113 million value, a figure that, under prevailing practices, ignored potential value increases due to SP's planned future development of the site. SP, using comparable sales based on the Bayview–Hunters Point area several miles south, put forth a vastly lower figure—and, according to SP's attorney, the board "just accepted every number we gave them."[79] The assessor's office official who prepared the City's documents commented, "I've appraised thousands of properties downtown, and I can't be that far off. . . . I can never remember a case where the figures approved by the [Assessment Appeals] board were the same [as those submitted by the appellant] right down to the penny."[80]

The board's action was issued without publicity and was not picked up by the newspapers for several days. Among the more bizarre and disturbing revelations was that Southern Pacific's attorney had taken the highly unusual step of suggesting that Assessment Appeals Board member John Zante, a CPA, disqualify himself, something Zante did "as a matter of courtesy" after SP threatened legal action. Southern Pacific alleged no conflict of interest on Zante's part—the usual grounds for requesting disqualification; they merely wanted a "more balanced" appeals board, suggesting as Zante's replacement board alternate (and real estate agent) Gertrude Turner. The actual replacement was a different real estate agent, giving SP the balance it wanted: one real estate agent, one title company officer, one accountant. The senior board member, Thomas Brady, called the SP letter asking for Zante's removal an "extraordinarily unusual procedure . . . we were amazed." But apparently amazement gave way to pressure tactics, which included a letter of complaint to Mayor Feinstein about the new assessment, sent by SP president Alan Furth.

San Francisco assessor Sam Duca was incensed by the appeals board ruling, terming it "incompetent and without merit."[81] He noted that the per-square-foot valuation of the SP land was reduced to less than the value of the nearby Todd Shipyards, half of which is under water, and that some Mission Bay neighbors recently bought their properties for up to ten times what SP's land was revalued at by the appeals board. Duca then took the extraordinary step of filing a court action challenging the appeals board action, and in November 1984 Judge Ira Brown ruled that the board's decision was not supported by sufficient evidence and that it had failed to follow prescribed appraisal methods and standards, a decision affirmed by the state Court of Appeals in early 1989, which sent the case back to the board. The board thereupon redid its calculations and issued a new figure of $90 million, lower than the $100 million figure arrived at by an independent appraiser hired by the City and still a victory for SP.[82] Southern Pacific is not alone it its successful efforts to lower its tax payments to the City through reassessment petitions. A survey of ten major downtown commercial properties showed that reduced assessments cost the City somewhere between $9.5 million and $23.6 million in potential property tax revenues just in the six-year period 1993–98.[83]

At around the same time this brouhaha was unfolding, Supervisor Bill Maher proposed turning Mission Bay into a development with up to fifteen thousand to twenty thousand new dwelling units, more than twice what SP planned, and that the City buy the land and lease it out to developers in order to control costs. He even began thinking eminent domain thoughts, and asked the city attorney to begin drafting the necessary legal documents to allow the City to take the 122 acres aided by the reassessment action. Said Maher, "They [Southern Pacific] have established a worth. . . . If that's what they say it's worth, we should take them at their word."[84]

The eminent domain threat served to push SP to produce a new, compromise plan, reducing office/commercial/hotel space to 10.6 million square feet, reducing somewhat the height of three high-rises, and increasing the number of housing units to ninety-two hundred, one thousand of which would be affordable to lower-income tenants, with SP donating seven and a half acres of land to the city for this purpose—revisions still inadequate to quiet critics, including Mayor Feinstein.[85] So the supervisors' finance committee in May 1984 unanimously voted to send an eminent domain resolution to the full board, offering SP the $60 million it said the land was worth as the first step in a taking proceeding. Individual members then began getting cold feet, and the board voted to delay consideration.[86] A number of supervisors noted that their decision followed intense lobbying; Supervisors Bill Maher, John Molinari, and Richard Hongisto acknowledged pressure from Willie Brown and John Burton. Despite the delay, however, SP announced in June that it would again propose a redesign, and in August, the City and SP said they had reached agreement on a Mission Bay project: Building heights were limited to eight stories (the earlier revision had brought the high-rises down to thirty-five and thirty stories); 30 percent of the 7,577 residential units were to be at below-market rents, with costs shared by SP and the City; office space was reduced to 4.1 million square feet, along with 2.6 million square feet of commercial space and 200,000 square feet of retail.[87] Two weeks after the agreement was announced, the board's finance committee voted to table Maher's eminent domain proposal and ended any threat of wielding that club.[88]

But this step represented only the broad dimensions of a plan for Mission Bay. In January 1985, Planning Director Dean Macris announced that the City and SP would jointly create a "community plan" for the actual development process, to be financed by SP but controlled by the Planning Department—a somewhat path-breaking step for a purely private development. *Chronicle* architecture critic Allan Temko observed, "No other U.S. city has forced developers to accept such an arrangement in a project of this magnitude, the largest in the history of San Francisco."[89] But Supervisor Nancy Walker correctly criticized Macris's approach, which she characterized as "back assward. . . . We should determine what the city's housing and job needs are and then see what Mission Bay can do about them."[90]

Into the breach stepped a new forty-member coalition of neighborhood, housing, and environmental groups, the Mission Bay Clearinghouse, which put forth an alternative plan for the area: Mission Bay Gardens—possibly to echo Yerba Buena Gardens. (The clearinghouse was designated as the official citizens advisory body and by 1990 had doubled its organizational membership.) Developed by architect Tom Jones, the plan stressed public open space and amenities, included substantial amounts of affordable housing, avoided large-scale structures, and incorporated variety—all in the tradition of San Francisco neighborhoods and contrary to Southern Pacific's emphasis on private open space, monumental scale, upper-income housing, lack of diversity, and segregation from the rest of the city. The following September, Macris announced that the company's real estate subsidiary would fund a $600,000 planning budget. But there were limits to SP's generosity. In February 1986, it was revealed that SP was resisting paying for studies proposed by a group of low-income housing organizations and endorsed by the San Francisco Coalition of Neighborhood Groups—an alternative plan to construct ten thousand housing units and limit office space to 1 million square feet.[91] By that time, a second citizens group, the Mission Bay Consortium, representing the city's active neighborhood nonprofit housing development corporations and their umbrella group, the Council of Community Housing Organizations, had become a force as well, pushing for an affordable housing and economic development project. In June of that year, the Planning Department and SP came up with four alternative plans for the site, one of which was the ten thousand-unit option.[92] By the fall of 1986, SP submitted its proposal, which was not too different from what they and the City had agreed to in 1984.[93]

Debate over the project continued through 1987. Community groups kept pressing for more housing and a greater percentage of affordable units (half, rather than one-third), as well as lowering the "affordable" definition, from the forty-three thousand–dollar annual income maximum set forth in the City plan to twenty-nine thousand dollars.[94] And the election of Art Agnos as mayor in 1987 added pressure for more housing, more affordable housing, and less office space (positions Agnos put forward forcefully in his campaign—although he was to back away from this later in his term).

The draft environmental impact report for Mission Bay was released in August 1988, and—pursuant to the settlement of an earlier lawsuit filed by San Franciscans for Reasonable Growth challenging the adequacy of the City's Downtown Plan EIR—it was required to address the cumulative impacts for all current development projects and to ensure as well that its form was comprehensible to laypersons with no technical background. (The report, with its mandated new dimensions, was so impressive that it won an award from the American Planning Association.) This cumulative impact analysis revealed that, in conjunction with other development, Mission Bay would produce massive traffic congestion over the coming decade.[95] Even more significant would be the housing market impact. Office and commercial development would create an estimated demand for at least twelve thousand units of subsidized affordable housing, while under the SP proposal only some twenty-three hundred such units would be produced. The Mission Bay Clearinghouse, San Francisco Tomorrow, the Mission Creek Conservancy, and the Potrero League of Active Neighbors continued to press for more affordable housing. But, echoing Supervisor Nancy Walker's lament, the *San Francisco Bay Guardian* editorialized: "Progressive city planning starts with a simple premise. Planners should determine what the city needs, what the public wants, and then look for ways to provide it. San Francisco starts with the opposite premise: The Planning Department determines what a real estate developer wants, how that developer can best get rich, and then looks for ways to make it happen. Mission Bay is a classic, tragic case in point."[96]

In the fall of 1989, SP and the City were near agreement on yet another plan for Mission Bay: eight thousand housing units, three thousand of which would be subsidized, and 5.7 million square feet of commercial and office space. The October 17, 1989, Loma Prieta earthquake raised a new issue: like the Marina District (which took the brunt of the quake), the Mission Bay site had been built primarily on landfill. In addition, the site contains toxic materials that could present leakage problems under earthquake conditions.[97] SP, after much arm-twisting, agreed to pay for cleanup of hazardous wastes.[98] And for the first time, the project's financial details were spelled out: SP would agree to spend $231 million on infrastructure, hazardous waste testing and cleanup conforming to state and federal environmental regulations, community facilities, transit fees, and parks. The City would receive an estimated $4 million annually in net revenues, with an additional $2 million a year going to the port; the City would be obligated to spend $100 million on housing subsidies in the first thirty years of the project (although the source of these funds was unclear).[99] Criticism of the plan centered on the persistent jobs/housing imbalance and insufficient amounts of truly affordable units, traffic congestion and air pollution, the dangers of hazardous wastes, the need for more open space and protection of wetlands, and the lack of any firm guarantees or enforcement mechanisms regarding SP's (since renamed Catellus) commitment to give 75 percent of the twenty-three thousand projected jobs to San Franciscans and to run effective training and affirmative action hiring programs.[100] The wetlands issue was not trivial: Mission Creek, which runs through the Mission Bay site, is the last of the city's wetlands—85 percent of the tidal marshes in San Francisco Bay had been destroyed since 1950, leading to degradation of air and water quality, since marshes act to clean pollutants from both air and water. The City's plan, supported by Mayor Agnos, omitted wetlands in favor of playing fields.[101]

In August 1990, the Planning Commission unanimously approved the Mission Bay plan, amending the original version to deepen the subsidies for the one-third affordable housing and requiring Catellus to pay for construction of 250 residential hotel rooms near the development.[102] Catellus agreed to contribute $2.5 million for job training and other economic development and another $2 million for affordable housing within six months of breaking ground for the first office portion of the project; they also agreed to hand over an additional two acres for affordable housing every four years. Additionally, they promised to begin construction of five hundred units of housing within two years of receiving all government approvals for the project.

Strangely, the various debates over the content of the development seemed to ignore the development control ordinance passed in November 1986 (Proposition M—see chapter 12), limiting office construction to 475,000 square feet per year. The Mission Bay plan of course could not be implemented unless an exception from Proposition M was granted. And so Proposition I on the November 1990 ballot sought to do just that. But an alliance of neighborhood groups (backed principally by a substantial financial contribution from real estate mogul Walter Shorenstein, who wanted to eliminate potential competition with the nine million square feet of downtown office space he owned),[103] defeated the measure by fewer than six hundred votes.[104] Catellus, responding to the vote, announced it would revise its plan in time for consideration by the Board of Supervisors, which in February 1991 approved a revised development agreement, containing, among other things, 250 more units of moderately priced housing and raising the proportion of subsidized housing to 40 percent.[105] Despite Catellus's constant refrain that the amount of office space they sought was essential to the project's economic viability, they announced in October 1991 that the first phase of development would include six hundred housing units (ranging in price from $100,000–$350,000) and a single 400,000-square-foot office building.[106]

But little happened after that. Catellus began to experience financial problems (shades of Olympia & York) and in 1995, responding to a changed real estate market, proposed building a 275,000-square-foot megastore for Home Depot, with an eleven-hundred-space garage and possibly a sports-entertainment complex, including a golf driving range (permission promptly denied), and began to renege on the agreement to clean up the toxic hot spots, proposing also to relocate the planned housing developments to less attractive parts of the site. The city's real estate downturn starting in the early nineties essentially put a hold on the project, and the development agreement—such as it was—expired in 1996.

At that point, and propelled by incoming Mayor Willie Brown's new ideas, the Redevelopment Agency entered the picture—primarily to create the opportunity for tax-increment financing (sequestering future increased property tax revenues from the development, in order to support the development), and the result has been creation of an urban renewal project covering a far larger area, broken into Mission Bay North (sixty-five acres, bounded by Third Street, Townsend Street, Mission Creek, and Seventh Street, adjacent to the new Pac Bell Ballpark and Caltrain Terminal) and Mission Bay South (238 acres, bounded by the 280 Freeway, Terry Francois Boulevard—named for the ex-supervisor—and Mariposa Street).

Projected for Mission Bay North: three thousand housing units, 20 percent at below-market levels; 350,000 square feet of "urban entertainment retail space," concentrated on the blocks adjacent to the Giants's new stadium; 155,000 square feet of retail space; and six acres of public open space.

Maximum projected development for Mission Bay South includes: 3,090 housing units, 36 percent below market; a five-hundred-room hotel; approximately 6 million square feet of commercial/industrial space; 210,000 square feet of retail space; forty-three acres of public open space; a new public school; and an expanded fire and police station—the centerpiece of all to be a new forty-three-acre, $800 million University of California–San Francisco research campus/biomedical center, containing 2,650,000 square feet of instructional, research, administrative, and support space, and some eight thousand jobs (groundbreaking for which took place in October 1999). Mission Bay North has a planned seven-year build-out period; the anticipated build-out period for Mission Bay South is somewhere in the twenty- to thirty-year range originally projected for the project.[107] As of early 2002, the only housing construction that has begun is one hundred units of below-market apartments being developed by the nonprofit Mission Housing Development Corporation and one market-rate project.

It's a big, big deal, now involving lots of City agencies and Catellus, which owns virtually all of the privately held land in the area—some of which it is scheduled to donate for public facilities and affordable housing. Thirty-one thousand new permanent jobs are projected, along with a $145 million City investment in new public infrastructure. If it all works out as planned, that's a terrific employment generator—but with only a little over six thousand added housing units, the project will vastly exacerbate the city's notorious jobs/housing imbalance.

Given the close-to-two-decade "planning process," the number of powerful actors involved, the city's shifting economics and politics, and vicissitudes in the larger economy, it clearly ain't over till it's over. Pamela Duffy of the blue-ribbon Coblentz, Cahen, McCabe & Bryer law firm, lead counsel for both Mission Bay and Olympia & York clients, was quoted more than a decade ago saying, "I specialize in large, never-ending projects."[108] Not the least of the megaworries and imponderables is the toxic soil/liquefaction danger: Mission Bay is not built on granite—just as the name says, it's a bay. The worst case scenario is historian Gray Brechin's: "Mission Bay is a toxic landfill site that in an earthquake will liquefy, spilling biogoop everywhere."[109] The 1989 Loma Prieta Earthquake apparently wasn't enough of a wake-up call. Watch that space! In December 2001, Catellus announced it was suspending construction work on its massive 275,000-square-foot office building due to the bankruptcy filing of its key tenant, the Internet consulting company Marchfirst.

Moscone Center Doings

When Moscone Center opened in December 1981, it got rave architectural reviews. An exuberant Allan Temko, the *Chronicle*'s highly respected urban design critic, announced: "In the unprecedented exhibition hall of Moscone Center—a column-free underground space nearly 880 feet long, nearly 300 feet wide, and 37 feet high—San Francisco has another structural wonder of the world. . . . Moscone Center is not only a technological feat, worthy of a place in the empyrean of engineering with the great bridges spanning the Bay, but also a work of art."[1]

But convention centers must be judged in more functional terms as well, and early evidence showed Moscone Center to be a highly troublesome work of art—most likely the result of political pressure to open the facility "on time," even if it was not quite finished. A bare six months after its opening, serious water leaks were discovered in the foundation of the underground facility, whose floor is twenty feet below the water table. Despite $3 million worth of waterproofing in the original construction, leaks penetrated through the ten-foot-thick poured concrete slab floor and thirty-inch-thick concrete walls. The most serious dangers were to the electrical system and the concrete floor's reinforcing steel, which could corrode and expand, causing the concrete to crack. In one case, water burst through a foundation crack in one of the underground utility tunnels and, according to a project engineer, "just shot right across to the opposite wall (five feet away) in a real hard stream."[2] And during a heavy rainstorm, "There was so much flooding that officials called the Fire Department, which manned the pumps for six hours."[3] The various contractors, subcontractors, construction managers, and public agencies naturally pointed the finger at one another. City officials were extremely unhappy ("We paid for a dry building. We're not happy with a wet building," commented the City's on-site project manager);[4] the supervisors called for an investigation; Mayor Feinstein threatened a lawsuit and was openly critical of CAO Roger Boas,[5] who had boasted right before the center opened, "The building is waterproof as a bathtub."[6] Later, taking a somewhat different tack—that the leak problem "is something we've known about. . . . We expected a certain amount of water to get in . . . "—the CAO's office pooh-poohed the problem.[7]

While the issue pretty much disappeared from the front pages and the political arena, an *Examiner* report following up on the original story noted that "while city officials said contractors had remedied '99%' of the leaks, the *Examiner* this week found unrepaired leaks and water pouring into the tunnels through pipes designed to alleviate pressure on the foundation. During Tuesday's rain storm, the tunnel gutters were rushing with water. One of the building's four major sump pumps failed, flooding the pump room and the fire services room."[8]

Other construction and design flaws appeared. A review of these in the December 3, 1982, *Examiner* noted: "The entire building was painted a flat white that isn't washable. The unsealed granite floors and light blue rugs are impossible to keep clean. Utility tunnels continue to leak. The computer system isn't fully installed. . . . The City still [one year later] hasn't accepted the work of 10 of the 26 prime contractors, including those who did concrete, mechanical and electrical work, as well as installing the security system. . . . " These problems "already have cost taxpayers more than $1 million—and will cost even more." The City's Bureau of Building Inspection did not give the center a certificate of occupancy until December 1983, two years after its opening, and there are suggestions that the permit was granted only under great pressure.

Water was leaking into the center, and equipment was leaking out. In October 1982, it was reported that more than five hundred chrome custom-upholstered chairs, worth fifty thousand dollars, had disappeared. The loss was not reported to the police or insurance carrier for two months (and apparently wasn't made public for five months thereafter).[9] Several days later, the papers reported a ten-thousand-dollar baby grand piano had been stolen from the center.[10]

In the same month, it was revealed that the head of the City's new Department of Convention Facilities—overseer for Moscone Center, Brooks Hall, and the Civic Auditorium—had falsified his resume and had been closely involved with a number of organized crime figures.[11] It was subsequently revealed that the official had also steered an audit contract to the firm that had helped select him for the fifty-seven-thousand-dollar-a-year post, overruling the views of Facilities Management, Inc., operators of Moscone Center under contract to the City.[12] The incident once again caused Mayor Feinstein to publicly castigate CAO Boas, who, according to Feinstein, showed "cloudy judgment" and had ignored her suggestion, made two months earlier, that the man be dismissed ("I am disappointed, absolutely, in how Mr. Boas dealt with this particular incident.")[13] And again, as the facts subsequently revealed, Boas seems to have misspoken when he maintained that his new department head did not have the power to make or influence contract awards.[14]

The center's $1.4 million computer system and sophisticated automated energy conservation system were glitching away. The computer brought overhead doors banging down unexpectedly and turned lights off mysteriously, and back-up computers twice failed to activate when the main computer failed. The computer system monitors and controls safety equipment such as rolldown smoke partitions, smoke detectors, door alarms, and water flow switches that activate fire sprinklers. Using the Honeywell energy conservation system, the center racked up a $940,000 power bill during fiscal year 1982–83, whereas a Pacific Gas and Electric expert had estimated, just prior to the center's opening, that basic annual power charges would come to $316,000, perhaps as much as double that figure with miscellaneous other charges.[15]

Art and Politics

True to its history, Moscone Center's opening was marked by controversy, in this instance over some of its commissioned works of art. One brouhaha surrounded a skit by the San Francisco Mime Troupe at a public "open house" featuring many local cultural groups. The highly political street theater group presented their short play, titled "Ghosts," that centered on the former residents of the convention center site, in an attempt to exhume and remind the public of that history. In their usual irreverent manner, the troupe portrayed such current political figures as Mayor Feinstein and Redevelopment Agency executive director Wilbur Hamilton in less than flattering terms. City officials were offended, and Roger Boas, when asked about the skit, responded with the incredible comment, "We may have displaced some parking lots, but people—no way."[16]

Contretemps of greater duration sprang from two artworks commissioned for the new center. Both, in different ways, contained political elements disturbing to the city fathers and mothers and led to considerable public controversy. The lesser row involved a ceramic mural by Katherine Porter, an artist-in-residence at Stanford University. When City officials told Porter they had slightly enlarged the space for the mural, she added a border, titled "Winds of the People," after a song by the Chilean poet Victor Jara. On that border, she placed "George Jackson," "Martin Luther King," "Dorothy Day," "Wounded Knee," "Emma Goldman," "Paul Robeson," "I. F. Stone," and "Cesar Chavez," names she felt were in keeping with the human rights spirit of the Jara song. The City's Arts Commission demanded she remove the names before they would accept the work, a demand she refused. "It makes a political statement," stated Arts Commission chair Dimitry Vedensky, "and I don't think any kind of political statement is appropriate. It's a very bizarre and personal list of people." Responded Porter: "There's a tremendous irony in all this because George Moscone was a progressive mayor who cared about the rights of all people—that's the reason I was attracted to this project. . . . The names are there to represent blacks, women, Chicanos and other individuals important in American history and in the struggle for human rights."[17] The Arts Commission maintained Porter had made the changes without their approval; the December 1, 1983, *Chronicle* noted, "Although [the commission] conceded that other artists had made similar alterations without consent from the commission, they objected to the aesthetics of Porter's new frame." The mural was never placed, and at the Arts Commission's insistence, a thoroughly disgusted Porter returned her nineteen-thousand-dollar advance.[18]

The most vitriolic arts controversy involved the memorial bust of George Moscone, commissioned from Robert Arneson, a noted sculptor on the University of California, Davis, faculty. It was not Arneson's portrayal of the late mayor's head that caused the furor, but the pedestal on which the head rested. On the base of the eight-foot-high sculpture, titled "Portrait of George," Arneson had inscribed some two dozen phrases and several images, which together attempted to give a flavor of the late mayor's richly varied life and symbolically violent death. Among the phrases were simple biographical reference points ("Santa Rosa Junior College," "Mayor 76–78," "Born Nov. 24, 1929, St. Luke's Hospital," the names of his children enclosed within a heart, "S.F. Board of Supervisors," "Class of 47, St. Ignatius H.S.," a facsimile of his signature, "Outstanding Freshman Senator," "All City Basketball," and so forth); and some cryptic phrases ("What did the pelican say?" "Don't call it 'Frisco,' " "Shrimpers and Rice, Everything's Nice," "Duck Soup"), which, according to Arneson, were supplied him by Moscone's widow, apparently personal language within their family. (See fig. 4.)

The primary cause of the controversy, however, was the appearance of many explicit references to the November 1978 city hall assassination of Moscone and Supervisor Harvey Milk by ex-supervisor Dan White (see chapter 11): "Harvey Milk too!" "Bang Bang Bang Bang Bang," "Oh, Danny Boy," "Monday Nov. 27, 1978, shortly before 11 am, snub-nosed .38," "Tolerance for deviants," "Feinstein Becomes the Mayor," and "Twinkies" (a reference to the so-called "Twinkies defense" used by White's lawyer at the trial—the "diminished capacity" argument, in which an element was that White's heavy consumption of such sugary "junk food" triggered chemical-psychological reactions that helped cause mental disorder). In addition to these explicit words, the pedestal was riddled with what appeared as blood-stained bullet holes and an imprint of a revolver. When the sculpture in its final form was unveiled, Mayor Feinstein, at least some members of her Arts Commission, and a goodly segment of the public were in an uproar, although the issue was partially played out around whether what Arneson had delivered was what was ordered. (Beth Coffelt, in an article in the August 8, 1982, issue of *California Living*, reported that two weeks before the opening, Arneson invited the Arts Commission to view his work, that only one commissioner came, "and he reported back that it was magnificent.") Clearly, some heavy questions about what constitutes public art, as well as more specific political concerns, were involved.

On opening day, the issue was handled by draping the pedestal with a red silken shroud, providing the late mayor with a toga-like garb. Arneson defended his work mightily, as did much of the arts community. "It's a piece for the people. It's a realist work. It's about George. It's about truth. What else could an artist do?" said Arneson.[19] In her article "Un-American Graffiti" in the April 1982 issue of *San Francisco* magazine, Katharyn Regan offered this judgment of the art work as a whole: "The bust and pedestal make an extraordinarily lively portrait of a decent, essentially ordinary man, the most startling fact of whose life was his death at the hands of another rather ordinary man." The January 23, 1982, issue of *Art Week* spoke of the bust itself as a "caricature of a smiling pol—close to parody but with a radiant vitality, a large benign dignity." And as noted by Frederic Stout of the Stanford University Urban Studies faculty,

> Arneson's bust of Moscone was terrific, and its removal by an embarrassed ruling class was an art event of real importance. Arneson's mistake was in presenting the city mothers/fathers with something honest, engaging, and provoking . . . that is to say, with a work of art. What the rulers wanted, of course, was not a work of art at all. They wanted an object of ritual magic: the smiling head of a dead politician. What they

got was art—reality, history, meaning, humanity—and that was just too much for them to bear.[20]

But George Moscone's successor was determined not to leave Arneson's bust at the new convention center. The understandably agitated sculptor charged "that Feinstein had a personal reason for objecting to the sculpture: 'It might recall how someone became mayor. . . . Am I being paranoid?' "[21] Whatever her real reasons, Feinstein had a letter hand delivered to each Arts Commissioner just before their vote on whether to accept the bust, asking them to reject it, and by a seven-to-three vote, reject it they did. At the City's request, Arneson returned the thirty-seven thousand dollars he had been paid to do the work. It was removed from Moscone Center several days after its unveiling and purchased by San Francisco gallery owner Foster Goldstrom for fifty thousand dollars, was on exhibit for a few weeks in early 1982 at the San Francisco Museum of Modern Art, and now is in a private collection. In December 1994, a new, more acceptable bust of George Moscone, by San Francisco sculptor Spero Anargyros, was unveiled: a statesman-like portrayal of the mayor (which, to this observer at least, doesn't look much like him), smiling, pen poised to sign some weighty document, below which are these words of his, painfully inappropriate in view of his ending: "San Francisco is an extraordinary city, because its people have learned to live together with one another, to respect each other, and to work with each other for the future of their community. That's the strength and beauty of this city—it's the reason why the citizens who live here are the luckiest people in the world."

What It Cost(s)

The original Moscone Center was completed at an announced construction cost of $126.5 million. The money came principally from the proceeds of a $97 million tax-exempt bond issue, supplemented by some $34 million in accumulated hotel tax revenues.[22] In a November 21, 1977, letter to the mayor and supervisors, CAO Roger Boas had announced that the projected construction cost for the center had risen from $85 million to $100 million, amending his March 10, 1977, press release, which had set the cost at $85 million and had quoted him as saying, "That was the mandate of the people—that the center be built and that it conform to rigid environmental and cost standards. Those standards will be met." The $100 million figure, when approved by the supervisors in May 1978, was described by Boas as one that included "projected inflation increases in cost over the period of construction" and "an allowance . . . for contingencies, and for increased costs due to unforeseen circumstances."[23] Five months later, at the time the final financing lawsuit went to trial (see chapter 7), the cost had risen to $104.5 million, and when construction bids were received right after the trial, the cost was publicly reported as $110 million.[24] That the actual cost turned out to be $126.5 million—a figure that does not take into account $13.2 million subsequently sought by contractors via litigation against the City or the $20 million announced as the cost of adding meeting rooms—and did not deter Boas from boasting that "we did it within four percent of our budget."[25]

Capital costs for construction represent only one type of public cost for the convention center. The first year's operating deficit for Moscone Center was $2.6 million.[26] By comparison, the 1978 environmental impact report on YBC had predicted an annual operating loss for the first five years of $1 million (the report was silent about operating losses after that time), and CAO Roger Boas, in his "Report on Yerba Buena Convention and Exhibit Center" (May 9, 1978) noted, "It is likely, however, that annual net operating deficits would be smaller [than the $1 million a year]."

Boas's announcement of the deficit led to a public row with Mayor Feinstein, who (unaccountably, since as president of the Board of Supervisors she had voted to approve the 1978 environmental impact report) responded, "I am shocked and dismayed. . . . They should at least break even."[27] The mayor later conceded she should have expected the deficit: "When my mind was refreshed I do remember it being discussed."[28] Equally disingenuous was her statement, "I am going to suggest to Mr. Boas that it [Moscone Center] be organized so the facility is at the break even point from now on."[29] In fact, in early 1982 the City reduced rental rates at its meeting halls by about 25 percent in order to try to attract more conventions in a period of weak economic conditions.[30] In 1985, Moscone Center ran a $2.6 million deficit,[31] and by 1987, the center was losing $2 million annually.[32] By 1999, Moscone Center officials indicated that annual operating losses were approaching $4 million.

Given the constant, rapid rise of labor, utilities, and other operating costs and the imperative to keep rental charges low, there is reason to believe the operating deficit will continue to remain high, and the cumulative operating loss over the thirty-year life of the bonds likely will approach, possibly exceed, $100 million. Not included in these operating cost figures are the tens of millions of tax dollars spent by the Convention & Visitors Bureau in promoting Moscone Center.

Bookings at Moscone Center also reflected a shift of business away from other City facilities. Shortly after the new convention center opened, the City-owned Brooks Hall/Civic Auditorium complex, for example, saw its occupancy rate drop from 80 percent to 60 percent in fiscal year 1984–85, yielding a related one-third increase in its operating loss to $658,000.[33] Once again, these pathetic words from the City's administrative head: " 'We felt when Moscone opened, Brooks and Civic would continue to do well,' said Roger Boas . . . , the official overseer of the three convention facilities. 'We thought the only meetings Brooks and Civic would lose would be the big shows that went to Moscone. It hasn't happened that way.' "[34]

Competition from other convention centers in the region, particularly for smaller shows, of course exerted downward pressure on Moscone Center rents as well. Oakland opened its new downtown convention center in mid-1983, with a sixty-one-thousand-square-foot exhibition hall, attached to a new twenty-story Hyatt Regency Hotel, and immediately began to talk of expanding it. Both Santa Clara and San Jose have opened new convention centers. According to Robert Eaton of Lavanthol and Horwath, hotel industry consultants, " '[Moscone Center] will have to offer every possible inducement' to keep bookings as soon as new convention centers are built in the Bay Area. . . . The most common lure to attract conventions will be free rent at the new convention center. . . . Surrounding cities, such as Oakland and San Mateo, are starting to attract more state and regional groups that are balking at San Francisco's high prices."[35]

To be sure, there has been constant pressure from the convention industry itself to keep rents low and correspondingly to increase the City's operating subsidy for the new center. A CAO office report of a December 1977 meeting with hotel owners regarding use of the hotel tax to subsidize the center notes: "It appears that it is of primary interest to the hotel industry and Bob Sullivan [executive director of the Convention & Visitors Bureau] that they be able to project to their market a reasonable rate for the use of the hall, but not one which is constantly being pressured upwards by a Board of Supervisors trying to establish a break even position for the operation of the hall."[36] (The hotel owners' influence over operations of Moscone Center apparently extended to selection of who would get to use the space. The May 14, 1980, *Examiner* recorded complaints by Bert Tonkin, representing the semi-annual gift show, regarding allocation of space in Moscone Center: "Tonkin claims that because his show's tenants, many of them owners of little shops in small towns, don't stay at the grand hotels, big hotel managers are 'dictating policy' in favor of greater priority for shows whose delegates do bed down at the major ones.")

Is It Worth the Price?

So heavy a public capital expenditure and annual operating deficit might be considered a socially useful investment of public funds if the benefits to the city's population were overpowering in terms of jobs, added tax revenues, or quality of urban life. But it is hard to assert such a claim indisputably. Past claims put forth by the convention industry, the Redevelopment Agency, and their newspaper editorial-writer allies have been lavish: Yerba Buena Center meant hundreds of millions of dollars in business and tax revenues, thirty-six thousand jobs.[37] And in an era when the economy is slow, cities are revenue-starved, and unemployment is a serious problem (as was true in the eighties), people want to believe such promises, especially when no alternative plans are being put forth by those who control public and private investment. The new convention center, and YBC generally, were held out as the instrument of growth for the city's "number one industry." An early economic consultant to the Redevelopment Agency even projected— simply through the "methodology" of continuing a straight-line rate of growth from what the industry had experienced in the 1960s—that, with the new facility, San Francisco's convention business would grow by 6 percent annually: 1,250 conventions by 1980; 1,550 by 1985 (some two-and-a-half times what the real figure turned out to be).[38]

The real issue of course was not whether a new facility would be used, but how many *new* conventions it would bring and how many existing conventions it would retain that might not return unless a new and better facility was provided. Such information is hard to come by, and the sources are clearly biased. The trade groups, the hotels, and the Convention & Visitors Bureau naturally preferred a new facility, especially if it were costless to them—what the managing director of New York City's Coliseum referred to as the "playground syndrome": "Every manager in the world when asked by questionnaire whether he would like to have a convention center in New York will respond in the affirmative. It simply gives him another playground, another place for bargaining . . . and after all a new playground costs him nothing."[39]

It was not until the 1978 state-mandated environmental impact report and federally mandated environmental impact statement that more sober and realistic assessments of the economic potential of a new convention center were disseminated. These pointed to the lack of data and studies on which to base firm predictions, and the best the EIS could muster were these at least honest words: "At this time, there are only opinions and speculations over the long term results [of building the convention center]. The numbers of convention delegates and other visitors to the YBC facility will not be a net decrease to San Francisco."[40]

The total number of conventions coming to San Francisco fluctuates considerably from year to year, and the opening of Moscone Center appears to have had little influence on those numbers. In 1969, there were 679 conventions; in 1978, 914; in 1980, 702. In the year after Moscone Center opened—1982—the total fell to 631.[41] The number rose steadily later in the 1980s, but by 1987 the total—887—was still less than a decade earlier. However, conventions were larger, as reflected in the increase in convention participants, from 734,000 in 1978, to 991,000 in 1987. Convention and related expenditures rose in the 1978–87 period, from $305 million to $595 million—a substantial portion of which was a function of inflation. Since 1988, "The number of groups [conventions] is not calculated any longer since a single group may be included in the totals submitted by many different hotels."[42] And from that year on, the method of calculating attendance was also changed in a way that yielded considerably higher figures. Using this new system, the Convention & Visitors Bureau reported an increase in convention, meeting, and trade show attendees from 1,093,000 in 1988 to 1,450,000 in 1995, with a corresponding increase in convention and trade show–related expenditures over this same period, from $494 million to $896 million—again, in part a function of inflation. One disquieting contextual thought about the economics of conventioneering, from David Owen in 1983, used New York as his example: "While it may be true that out-of-town conventioneers spend a great deal of money in New York, it is also true that New Yorkers spend a great deal of money at conventions in other cities—money they might have spent in New York if they'd stayed at home." Tax revenue losses were involved as well: "When a New Yorker goes to Pittsburgh for a convention, Pittsburgh, Pennsylvania, and the federal government all earn tax revenues—but New York City, New York State, and the federal government *lose* revenues, because the attendee writes off every penny he spends on his trip."[43]

The Jobs Issue

The first honest public discussion of the jobs issue appeared with publication of the first and second rounds of YBC environmental impact reports and statements (1973–74 and 1978, respectively). These analyses made clear, for those who bothered to read them, what any honest assessment of the value of the project would have earlier revealed: that the "36,000 jobs" figure was chimerical; that the vast majority of whatever jobs YBC would create were office sector jobs; and that many, if not most, of these jobs would be created in other parts of downtown San Francisco if the development sites did not exist in the YBC area. As the 1978 EIR phrased it: "Net employment is defined as that which would not be generated elsewhere if Yerba Buena Center were not developed. . . . It is assumed . . . that office development could occur elsewhere in the City. . . . This assumption would mean that, in the absence of YBC development, market forces would lead to the development of equivalent amounts of employment-generating office space elsewhere in San Francisco."[44] Thus, office jobs, some 90 percent of projected employment in the YBC project area, can hardly be said to have been "created" by the project.

A key fact relating to the jobs issue is that the convention hall—the centerpiece of public investment—is itself a most unintensive source of direct permanent employment. This massive facility, taking up two large city blocks and costing hundreds of millions of dollars in public funds (counting bond repayment and operating losses), employs fewer than two hundred persons full time.

A substantial amount of construction employment of course was produced in building this massive project, and, as has been noted above, this was an important element in generating union support for the center. But, again, such jobs are created whether the public uses its tax funds to build socially useful or socially wasteful projects. Job-hungry construction workers were not given the alternative of going to work on public transit improvements, affordable housing, community centers, street repairs, schools, and clinics vs. building a convention center. The public and private movers and shakers in effect gave them the option of building YBC as presented or not having jobs.

When the Redevelopment Agency submitted its first financing plan to the supervisors in 1972, and it looked as if TOOR's relocation suit might delay the project, the San Francisco Central Labor Council, Building and Construction Trades Council, and International Longshoremen's and Warehousemen's Union jointly distributed a pamphlet headed, "What Ever Happened to Yerba Buena Center? And Those 30,000 Jobs!" According to a labor spokesperson, "The pamphlet had been written and distributed to union officials by the Redevelopment Agency."[45] And, cynically appealing to the concerns of minority construction workers, that not very pro-labor paper, the *San Francisco Examiner*, at the time the power structure was trying to get Federal Judge Stanley Weigel off the TOOR case, ran a front-page editorial (a gambit the paper almost never used in its weekday editions), crassly headlined, "Attention Minorities," which began: "Tell them enough is enough. Tell them you want those minority jobs filled. Tell them you want Yerba Buena on track."[46] (See chapter 6 regarding the irresponsible way the Redevelopment Agency actually handled the minority jobs issue in YBC, setting up an ineffectual and corrupt front group and allowing it to operate for eight years, virtually unsupervised.)*

One virtually forgotten fact is that the project displaced seventy-six hundred mostly blue-collar jobs in 723 small businesses; and these were stable businesses—their average age was twenty years, and in a prerelocation agency survey, fully 90 percent stated they planned to remain at their location.[47] By the time most had been displaced—mid-1974—40 percent had either discontinued operations or relocated outside San Francisco. (Job loss due to urban renewal was one of the program's rarely publicized costs: According to SFRA data, its various projects have displaced more than twenty-five hundred businesses, with no overall figure available on how many people these businesses employed.) The more general shift in San Francisco from a blue- to white-collar job structure was markedly hastened by the YBC project, not only via direct public agency activities but via private market ripple effects as well. A notable example was Emporium Capwell's sale of its 345,000-square-foot warehouse, a block from Moscone Center, to Hong Kong investors, involving a shift of the store's warehousing operations to a private, nonunion contractor located down the peninsula (ironically, in Union City). Some 240 unionized blue-collar jobs were lost as a result.[48]

---

*It is also relevant to note that there is enormous discrimination and racial hierarchy in convention industry jobs. A 1974 survey of forty hotels by the San Francisco Human Rights Commission showed that, while minorities held 54 percent of hotel jobs, they were poorly represented in such areas as administrative services, front office, engineering and maintenance, and security personnel (S. F. Human Rights Commission, *FYI: Affirmative Action News,* summer 1974). A 1983 Human Rights Commission survey of nine Fisherman's Wharf restaurants on leased Port Commission property showed similar discrimination: 61 percent of the workers at these restaurants were minority, but only 25 percent had "visible" jobs—hostess, captain, waiter, waitress, bartender, and so on. (Human Rights Commission raw data, tabulated by Jim DuPont). And in the early 1970s the Federal Equal Employment Opportunity Commission and the Employment Law Center each brought actions against various hotels, restaurants, and waiters and bartenders locals, alleging racial discrimination in hiring and assignments *(James Gay et al.* v. *Waiters' and Dairy Lunchmen's Union Local No. 30 et al.,* Civil Action No. C-73–0489 Superior Court, City and County of San Francisco; *San Francisco Chronicle,* 30 March 1973). Although remedial consent decrees were signed and some progress made, these practices have by no means been eliminated, according to Employment Law Center attorneys.

Until YBC is completed, no calculus is possible on the project's net impact on jobs. When such a figure finally is derived, its calculation must take
into account not only the number of people employed at YBC but also the
types of jobs and how this relates to the amount and nature of pre-YBC employment on that site. An honest assessment also will have to take into account the costs, to the City and its residents, of the fallow period between
job displacement and job creation—which for some parts of the project will
exceed thirty years.

The New York State Comptroller, commenting on his state's direct and
indirect involvement in subsidizing convention centers in New York's larger
cities, noted: "Various statements have been released in support of these
centers, citing the creation of new jobs and additional tax revenues, which
would be generated. However, the accompanying data, on occasion, may un-
derestimate costs and overstate the jobs and taxes without adequate supporting data. . . . No followup studies are made," he also observed, "nor data
released evaluating the initial claims."[49] Would that such honest words ever
emanated from San Francisco's public officials.

Tourist City?

The "Is it worth the price?" question must be asked along other dimensions
as well. One big question is what kind of city San Francisco has become as
a result of such prodigious effort to promote conventioneering and tourism,
which results in a somewhat unstable economic base, due to a number of
factors. The instability and unpredictability of convention business was illustrated in a 1982 *Wall Street Journal* article:

> The American business convention is losing a lot of its hoopla this year.
> Suffering from the weak economy, companies are sending fewer people
> than usual to the gatherings—and allowing them to spend less money.
>   In San Francisco, a printers' convention that was expected to fill 4,300
> rooms filled only 1,700.
>   To make matters worse, much of the loss of business involves disrup-
> tive no-shows. . . . The Hyatt Regency Hotel in San Francisco's Embar-
> cadero Center says its washout rate for convention groups has risen to
> between 8% and 20% lately from the normal 5% to 12%.[50]

Those who have to pay their own way to conventions think twice about
incurring the high costs of fare, lodgings, meals, and registration fees. High
prices result in shorter stays, and conventioneers are less likely to bring
their families. Teleconferences replace face-to-face meetings. As one of the

most expensive North American cities, San Francisco may find it increasingly harder to lure (especially) dollar-conscious tourists (who, unlike conventioneers, bear the full costs of their visits themselves). Nor are conventioneers indifferent to the high hotel and restaurant costs. The late Herb Caen, in his August 8, 1982, *Sunday Examiner & Chronicle* column, noted that "About 10,000 lawyers [are] . . . here for the national convention of the American Bar Association. . . . [T]he original projection was for 15,000 delegates, but a few canceled out upon finding out about our hotel rates." Doctors as well as lawyers seem to be sensitive to this phenomenon. The California Medical Association, which traditionally alternated its annual spring conference between Los Angeles and San Francisco, decided to switch its 1980 meeting from the Fairmont Hotel to San Diego's Town and Country Hotel, because rates were 55 percent lower.[51]

"Every meeting planner contacted by the *S.F. Business Journal*," concluded that publication in 1983, "says the city's hotels, restaurants and services are too expensive. Jeanne Hayes, meetings director for the National Solid Waste Management Association, says one of the delegates attending the group's convention in San Francisco earlier this month remarked, 'At least Jesse James had the courtesy to hold a gun in his hand when he held people up.' . . . High prices are prompting other groups to consider moving their meetings out of San Francisco."[52] "The City is rapidly becoming a place where only the wealthy can afford to meet," started off another local feature article, which in 1981 quoted a member of the National Rural Electric Co-ops as saying, "We're not coming back. Rural people aren't used to these prices. Our people have to go to their co-ops and report these prices. People back home think they're off on a lark rather than a business trip."[53] Even the Convention & Visitors Bureau acknowledged this to be a problem. In a 1981 interview with the bureau's then–executive director, George Kirkland, the *Examiner*'s Jeff Jarvis observed, "Kirkland won't say so outright, but he implies that San Francisco's skyrocketing hotel rates tend to discourage a number of groups."[54] Clearly, CAO Roger Boas's boast that "conventions are a solid undertaking. . . . There's darn little of recession or inflation that can wash the convention side of it away" was more than a little fatuous.[55]

Another instability factor is the strength of the dollar against foreign currencies: A strong dollar makes it more attractive for Americans to vacation abroad and less attractive for foreigners—who account for more than a third of all visitors to the city—to come to the United States. This was the case in 1982 when foreign tourism dropped.[56] American cities that attract foreign visitors thus find themselves rather oddly welcoming times when U.S. currency is weak. A 1982 report by Security Pacific Bank on the region's tourist trade noted, "a weak dollar on international foreign exchange markets was . . . one bright area in the tourist business."[57]

A visitor-based economy is also vulnerable to all manner of unexpected occurrences that keep tourists and conventioneers away from San Francisco. Some examples that have occurred in the past are:

- The shutdown of the city's cable car system—a major-league attraction for San Francisco's visitors—for nearly two years beginning September 1982 to allow for its total reconstruction was predicted to reduce tourism revenues by $30 million to $40 million a year;[58]

- strikes by hotel and restaurant workers (in 1980, hotel workers struck for twenty-nine days, during which time hotel tax receipts fell 22 percent), transportation system workers, and others;

- a ten-to-zero vote by the Board of Supervisors in 1979 supporting the United Farm Workers' Chiquita Banana boycott led the American Farm Bureau Federation to shift its fifteen-thousand-person January 1982 convention from San Francisco.[59] In the highly politicized city of San Francisco, the left-leaning Board of Supervisors frequently, under pressure from constituents, passes resolutions on foreign and domestic policy issues that wind up offending less liberal parts of the nation. In 1981, the Convention & Visitors Bureau published a list of seventeen organizations that allegedly had vowed not to come to San Francisco because of actions by the Board of Supervisors (the extent to which this may have been an exaggeration and scare tactic by these organizations and their CVB colleagues is unknown). Boycotts and counterboycotts of specific locales can take a real toll. The convention boycott of states that did not ratify the Equal Rights Amendment, organized by the National Organization for Women, cost Chicago, Kansas City, New Orleans, St. Louis, and other cities an estimated $100 million;[60]

- earthquake fears and realities.

Finally, there is the question of what this visitor-related economic base is doing to the quality of the city itself. A Convention & Visitors Bureau vice president once rhapsodized about this "smokeless industry [that] does not dissipate our natural resources, nor . . . desecrate our natural environment."[61] Yet there is real concern that the very qualities that have made San Francisco "everyone's favorite city" are being destroyed by the growth of tourism/conventioneers. The late Charles McCabe of the *Chronicle* penned frequent and eloquent jeremiads on the problem. The following comments are drawn from columns of 1974, 1979, 1981:

Our notions of what is wrong and what is right in urban life are so mis-directed that a reasonable man could not be faulted for believing the Devil himself has been called in as planning director. . . . Tourists, who are supposed to be our greatest economic asset, are becoming an environmental abomination. . . . I've only been a resident since 1955; but I've watched a real city turn plastic in that time. The new downtown hotels are structures precisely designed to debauch a metropolis. They are ugly, and they are wasteful of both space and amenity. . . .

The city itself becomes more and more a huge hotel. . . . This tarting to the tourist has dehumanized and alienated our city. The fact that I live in a city whose largest industry consists of turning the city, and especially its many and considerable amenities, over to strangers is the biggest beef I have against tourism. . . . San Francisco mortgages its soul to the tourists.

The sad truth about tourism is that it first debases and then destroys the reason for its existence.[62]

Los Angeles Times columnist Robert Jones was quoted in the July 30, 1989, *Examiner* as having said, "San Francisco turned prettiness into a profession" in the 1970s. "It began a sordid game of wooing outsiders to pay its keep."

The environmental degradation that comes from raising tourism to the city's "number one industry" is of course linked with the development of San Francisco as a corporate headquarters town: the same kinds of massive buildings, with their negative environmental impacts, house office workers and out-of-towners. Again, Charles McCabe in 1979: "We are running a government for strangers, the temporary ones who despoil us a couple of days at a time from their cells in the various Hiltons and Hyatts, and the types who wiggle into and out of our office buildings to their aeries in the suburbs."[63]

While there was a good deal of self-deceptive nostalgia and narcissism in the way old-time San Franciscans spoke about their city's past and changes taking place, it is hard to dismiss the realities described by McCabe.

Too Small

Within a year of the new convention center's opening, convention officials began to clamor about the shortage of meeting rooms. One result of the long process of cutting back the scale of the planned center and putting it underground had been to reduce the amount of small meeting spaces. According to a former Redevelopment Agency commissioner, the plan all along had been to consciously underbuild the center, in order to circumvent some of the opposition, then to add elements later as the need for them was "discovered."

Once again, the Convention & Visitors Bureau trotted out the horror stories: loss of $324 million in major convention business, seventeen professional societies and trade associations that had already "offered significant resistance to the Moscone Center due to an inadequate number of meeting rooms," expected cancellations unless there was firm assurance that meeting space would be added, and so on.[64] James Bronkema, head of the Chamber of Commerce's committee on convention business (and director of the Embarcadero Center in the Golden Gateway urban renewal project), announced in 1985 that eleven major associations had canceled and that fifty-eight more had threatened cancellation, due to the center's "cramped facilities."[65] The papers chimed in with their standard lamentations, dutifully transmitting the unsubstantiated claims of the Convention & Visitors Bureau, as in this editorial statement from the November 3, 1986, *Chronicle:* "Without the new additions, San Francisco faces the loss of more than 150,000 convention delegates each year, with a corresponding loss of more than $150 million a year in business revenue." (But the impetus more likely was coming, again, from the needy hotel industry: The July 11, 1986, *Chronicle* noted that, "According to Chief Administrative Officer Roger Boas, local hotels are in the midst of a building boom and will badly need large conventions to fill their rooms.")[66]

Convention officials and the CAO's office maintained they had been aware of the facility's shortcomings all along. A spokesperson for the architectural firm that designed the center, Hellmuth, Obata & Kassebaum, said the problem was apparent during the early design phase: "We found there was not enough room in the hole to get enough meeting rooms. What San Francisco knew is that [Moscone Center] was not targeted toward housing the largest conventions." (Yet Boas's office in 1979 had prepared a fact sheet describing Moscone Center as "a complex of exhibition halls and meeting rooms of a size to accommodate the largest conventions and trade shows.") And so in early 1986 Mayor Feinstein formed a committee of City and business officials, headed by none other than CAO Roger Boas, to study expansion of the center.[67] And just two months after that, the committee released its none too surprising proposal to double the size of the center, at an estimated cost of $73 million.[68] Over the months that followed, cost estimates for the expansion varied wildly, reliving the original scenario. Three months after the committee's report, Boas announced a price tag of $140 million; one day later, it went down to $125 million.[69] Despite real concerns as to what the expansion would do to promises to cover the underground center with the recreation-cultural complex now named Yerba Buena Gardens, the Board of Supervisors placed on the November 1986 ballot a voter opinion statement (Proposition

B) on issuing $140 million in lease revenue bonds, with "no cost to the voters" (that is, by increasing the hotel tax from 9.75 to 11 percent—as usual, ignoring the question of opportunity costs: using this tax for other purposes, such as affordable housing, as had earlier been done to assist TODCO).

It was déjà vu all over again. The *Chronicle*'s Allan Temko wrote,

> Opened five years ago as a $127 million gift to the convention industry, Moscone Center was heralded by city officials as a "state of the art" facility that would serve for a quarter of a century. . . . The cost of Moscone Center, which actually will top out at closer to $200 million when bond interest and other unpublicized expenses are counted, will zoom toward $400 million in November if the voters approve a scheme to double the size from 310,000 to 650,000 square feet. . . . All [that] the Supervisors will have to go on today [when deciding whether to place the proposition on the ballot], will be vague, hurriedly prepared drawings and wildly fluctuating cost estimates. . . . [70]

Not so, according to Supervisor John Molinari, who at least acknowledged the board's past derelictions: "The government was jerked around when it approved the first convention center. We want it done right this time."[71] Temko continued,

> The whole future of Yerba Buena Gardens may be jeopardized, simply because city officials, from the mayor on down, have swallowed hook and sinker the tourist industry's line that unless we build Moscone II, Moscone Center I will no longer attract high-spending types such as lawyers and surgeons. They will opt instead for Dallas or Anaheim, and our poor provincial town will be doomed to chase gatherings of impecunious dental hygienists. Even if we build Moscone II, Boas admits, the bloated hotel industry—with 8,000 rooms either recently built or planned within easy distance of Moscone Center—may come back with a demand for Moscone III after the year 2000.

Temko's warning of course came true, many years earlier than his prediction.

But the hype worked, and in November 1986 voters approved Proposition B by a 62 to 38 percent margin, abetted by the standard support from the dailies. In May 1992, Moscone North, the expanded facility, adding 330,000 square feet of exhibition space under Central Block 2 and 110,000 square feet of meeting rooms, opened to its first convention—fittingly, the American Society of Association Executives. A little over a year earlier, the Esplanade Ballroom, an aboveground facility, opened, as part of the same expansion project.

After that, it was a piece of cake to carry out yet further expansion. The same routine: Convention & Visitor Bureau laments inadequate space, compared to other cities, and how much convention business the city is losing; more bond issues; more construction. Once the facility was there, the additive logic was compelling, with no reason not to keep rolling along. "Moscone Center West" (working title), funded by a $157.5 million lease revenue bond issue, along with a further increase in the hotel tax, from 12 percent to the current 14 percent, was approved by the voters in March 1996, 66 to 34 percent, increasing the facility's capacity by about half. It's scheduled to open in 2003.

The 1984 Democratic Convention

The major event in Moscone Center's early life was the July 1984 Democratic National Convention, giving the new facility and San Francisco a national focus possibly unparalleled in the city's recent history.

Bringing the convention to San Francisco was a major coup for the city's political and business community. One determining factor was that Democratic national chairman Charles Manatt hailed from California. "For Los Angeles lawyer Manatt, 46, getting the convention for California has been a goal since he became chairman in 1981," reported the *San Jose Mercury News*.[72] With Los Angeles preparing for the 1984 Olympics, beginning just a week after the July 16–20 convention, San Francisco was the obvious California location. It was also felt that this decision might help the Democrats take California, Ronald Reagan's home state, which they had not done since 1964. The fact that there were no statewide races in California in 1984 meant the party could put all its energy and resources into the convention and its aftermath. Also, the Democrats had not held a convention in California since 1960 (the Los Angeles convention that nominated John F. Kennedy) and had not held one in San Francisco since 1920.

San Francisco wooed the party's bigwigs with a whirlwind tour of the city's facilities and delights, plus promises of substantial local cash inputs to subsidize the event. Nearly $200,000 in air travel, hotel rooms, and restaurant meals were donated to wine and dine the sixty members of the party's Site Selection and Site Advisory Committees during their March 1983 visit. Over a quarter of a million dollars in an upfront cash donation to the Democratic National Committee was raised at a "Salute to San Francisco" dinner organized by and honoring real estate magnate and Democratic Party financier Walter Shorenstein; more than a thousand people attended at $250/per, and "about 35 percent of the attendees were Republican business leaders or their representatives who realize an undertaking like a political convention can be good business for the city."*

Ironically, one of San Francisco's principal shortcomings in the competition with other cities—notably, Chicago and Detroit[73]—was its new convention center, in particular the low ceilings, which create problems with sight lines and television coverage; relatedly, "The convention selection committee is worried that its low ceilings will create a hazy, smoke-filled room effect."[74] Roger Boas, in a 1978 report, boasting of the column-free design of the exhibition hall, had noted, "This design allows a 37-foot ceiling, which is high enough to accommodate everything from tall boats to bleachers for especially large conventions."[75]

The City responded to these concerns by agreeing to some $4 million in renovations for the two-year-old center: building skyboxes, camera platforms, and suspended booths and cabling for television coverage, podium construction, seating platforms, carpeting, lighting and power, security improvements, VIP boxes, and new restrooms. Beyond these renovation costs, the City also announced it would spend $2.5 million–$4 million, largely for

---

*The selection of San Francisco inevitably caused bad feelings among the other contenders. Chicago was eager to erase memories of the zoo-like 1968 Democratic Convention, and, with Harold Washington's April 1983 mayoral victory, the idea of firming up minority support in the 1984 election by holding the convention there had its attractions. But the intraparty fragmentation caused by Washington's primary victory over the Democratic machine and the narrow margin by which he beat his Republican opponent ruled Chicago out. Detroit was attractive largely in symbolic terms—the on-the-ropes Midwest industrial city that had sunk even deeper into despondency during the Republican administration. As one veteran Democrat captured the image: "A growing number of people are wondering whether the party should pass up the chance to stand on the spot where Ronald Reagan was nominated and say to the voters, 'Are you better off than you were four years ago?' " (John Fogarty, "S.F. Said to Have the Votes in Race for Demo Convention," *San Francisco Chronicle*, 19 April 1983). Detroit tried hard in the final few weeks of the selection process and was mighty annoyed at losing. Mayor Coleman Young was incensed after the decision was announced. "He charged that Manatt . . . had rigged the selection of San Francisco from the start. In a comment he apparently thought would not be overheard, Young told Manatt, 'You f—— us and I'm not going to forget it. This is not the place to talk. I'll talk to you later. I don't like a stacked deck and I know goddam well this was a stacked deck. This kind of b—— the Democratic Party does not deserve' " (John Fogarty and Marshall Kilduff, "The Demos Are Coming," *San Francisco Chronicle*, 22 April 1983; delicate use of dashes is in original). The intercity rivalry at times focused on the comparative worth of the two cities' police forces, leading to some of the more childish exchanges in the row. Mayor Young had complained that the San Francisco police force was the worst among the competing cities, to which Mayor Feinstein retorted, "I'll take three of his cops to one of ours" (ibid.).

security.[76] By contrast, Dallas hosted the 1984 Republican Convention without use of public funds, raising from private sources the $4 million it needed for policing, rental of the Dallas Convention Center, and other services.[77]

Despite CAO Roger Boas's vow that the City's construction costs to host the convention would not exceed $4 million, by March of 1984, $1.8 million in additional expenditures were announced, $1.5 million of which was for such Moscone Center improvements as lighting, the sound system, and the seating platform. Although the contract between the City and the Democratic Party capped the City's construction expenditures at $4 million and recorded, comically, that "The City has carefully examined the technical and financial requirements of the convention, [and] has received competent professional advice as to the feasibility and expense of fulfilling its obligations under this agreement," the additional City money was appropriated. City Public Works director Jeffrey Lee, in charge of the improvements, and Convention Facilities director John Mullane a year earlier had told Boas the $4 million figure was inadequate. In a round of finger pointing, Mayor Feinstein said she had relied on Roger Boas, Boas said he had relied on the Convention & Visitors Bureau, and CVB executive director George Kirkland "said the early budget was adopted with 'every expectation that there would be changes and refinements.' " "I can't say for sure that this will be the final amount," added Boas.[78] (For the record, Mayor Feinstein, in mid-1982, stated: "Because of pressures on the general fund for transit, libraries, and hospitals and other essentials, I do not believe tax money should be used to stage a convention.")[79]

On the other side of the financial ledger was the increased convention business that party delegates, alternates, guests, and media personnel could bring in. Published estimates of attendance and expenditures at this "combination of the World Series and Super Bowl for political junkies"[80] ranged up to thirty-five thousand people and $60 million.[81] Offsetting this was the convention business lost by bumping shows that had been scheduled during the six weeks prior to the Democratic convention (time needed to carry out renovation work on Moscone Center) and the two weeks afterward (takedown time); some were rescheduled in San Francisco, but at least one—the seventy-five-hundred-person Winetech Exhibit—moved its four-day event to the Los Angeles Convention Center. The City received no rent from the Democrats for the nearly two months they needed to use Moscone Center.[82]

The convention's political benefits to the city were many; not the least of the beneficiaries was Dianne Feinstein, who, ironically, had to be convinced that the city ought to make a pitch for the convention. "Let me tell you a secret," Charles Manatt said after the decision was announced: "The mayor of San Francisco was not particularly enthused. . . . She wasn't sure she wanted us."[83] "All else aside," *Examiner* columnist Dick Nolan observed, "a convention staged here offers a remarkable showcase for the political talents of Mayor Dianne Feinstein. If, as one presidential candidate has suggested, it's time for the party to nominate a woman to be vice president, well, here she is, winsome and willing, and also demonstrably able."[84] In fact, the July convention did push Feinstein into serious consideration as Walter Mondale's running mate. Mondale's national cochair, Duane Garrett, confided, "We were looking for a bold way to change the stereotype of Mondale as a fifty-five-year-old white male button-down Norwegian,"[85] and both Feinstein and New York Congresswoman Geraldine Ferraro were featured on the cover of *Time* magazine in a story titled, "Why Not a Woman?"—a competition Ferraro won. But, as was noted at the time, "The mayor's newfound prominence from being a close contender for the vice presidential spot on the Democratic ticket will be invaluable should she seek higher office . . . "[86] (as of course she successfully did; subsequent developments along these lines are described in chapter 11).

Figure 1a. [top] "I've lived my life so that I can look any man in the eye and tell him to go to hell." George Woolf (1898–1972), first president, Tenants and Owners in Opposition to Redevelopment. Photo, Ira Nowinski.

Figure 1b. [bottom] Eviction of International Hotel residents, midnight, August 4, 1977. Four hundred police and sheriff's deputies confronted two thousand defenders of the tenants. Photo, Rachelle Resnick.

Figure 2. Mr. Bream, Joyce Hotel (torn down for Yerba Buena Center), 1971. Photo, Ira Nowinski.

Figure 3. Mendelsohn House (Robert Herman, architect), TODCO's 189-unit low-income housing development for seniors, across from Moscone Center and adjacent to Museum Parc, luxury apartments; named for TOOR's second president, Peter Mendelsohn. Photo, ©Richard Barnes.

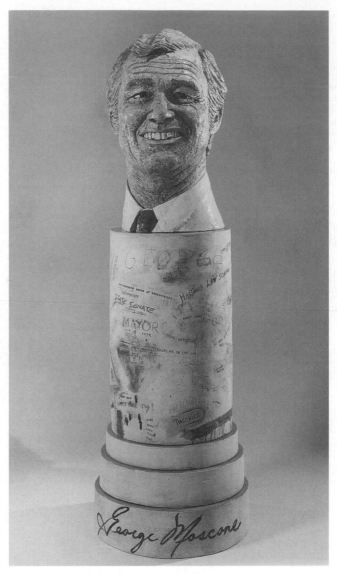

Figure 4. Bust of Mayor George Moscone (in office 1976–78);
artist Robert Arneson. Photo, M. Lee Fatheree, courtesy of
Foster and Monique Goldstrom, Oakland, California.

Figure 5. San Francisco's diversity: homeless man in front of Moscone Center. Photo, Gary Fong, courtesy of the *San Francisco Chronicle*.

Figure 6. "San Francisco Mayor Dianne Feinstein put on a convention hat and said 'Whoopee!' this morning after the announcement by Democratic National Committee officials that San Francisco had been selected as the site of the Democratic National Convention in 1984" (*Peninsula Times-Tribune,* April 21, 1983). Photo, Joe Melena, courtesy of the *Peninsula Times-Tribune.*

Figure 7a. [top] Yerba Buena Gardens: carousel center, Moscone Convention Center behind it, Sony Metreon on left, Marriott Hotel looming above it. Photo, Perretti & Park Pictures, courtesy of the San Francisco Redevelopment Agency.

Figure 7b. [bottom] "We're not blocking traffic—we *are* traffic" (Critical Mass biker). San Francisco's monthly Critical Mass bike ride; Howard Street, passing Moscone Convention Center. Photo, Chris Carlsson.

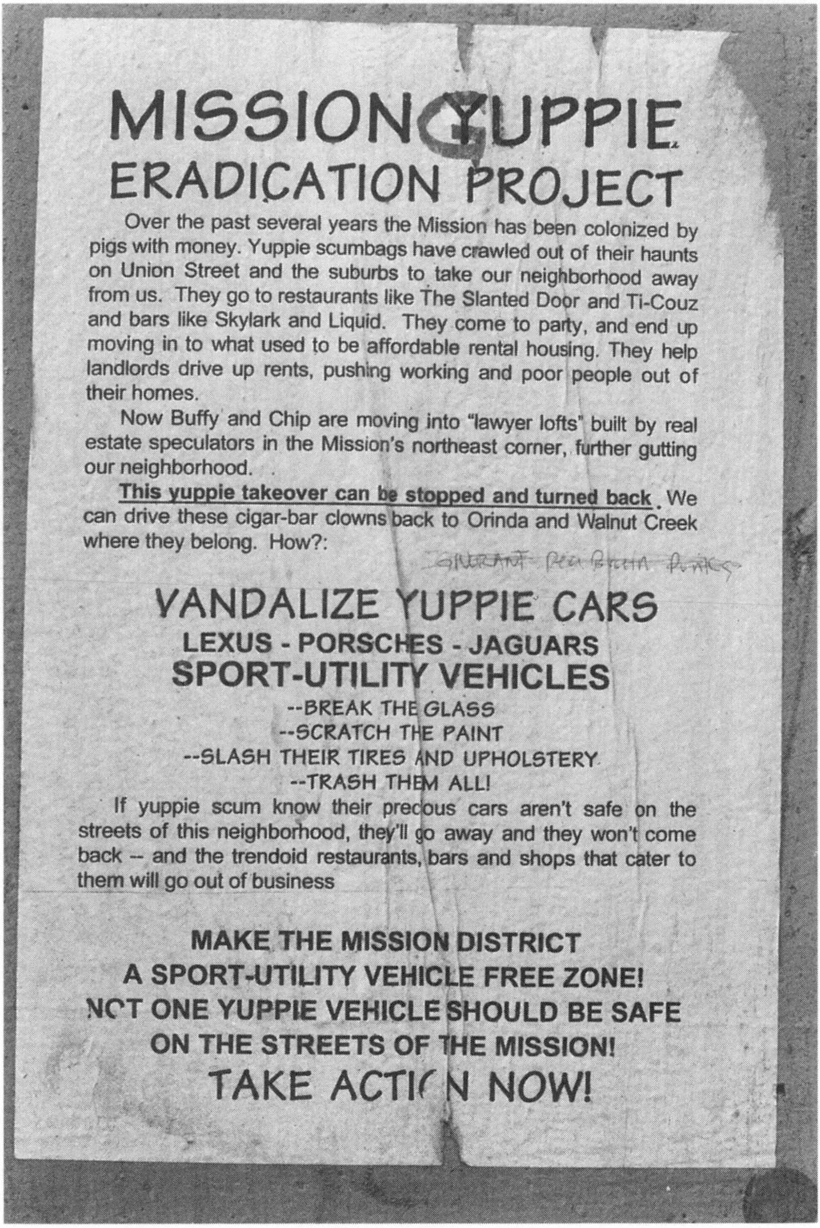

Figure 8. Response to gentrification in the Mission District. Photo, Frederic Stout, stoutfoto.

"THEY BUILT SO MANY HIGHRISES THE WHOLE CITY SANK IN THE BAY"

Figure 9a. [top] Cartoon by Ken Alexander, ©*San Francisco Examiner;* used with permission.

Figure 9b. [left] Official seal, San Francisco Redevelopment Agency ("Everyone wants to live in the city of San Francisco.")

Figure 10. San Francisco mayor Willie Brown (1996–2004). "Willie Brown's life is about a black man being smarter, harder working and better skilled, and rising to tremendous power in an entirely white world" (John Jacobs, McClatchy Newspapers). Photo, Dennis DeSilva, courtesy of the mayor's press office.

Yerba Buena Gardens, TODCO's Housing, and the South of Market Neighborhood

Yerba Buena Gardens

Building the underground convention center was one piece of work. What was to go on top of it was a whole other story. The first significant step toward developing the Central Blocks atop Moscone Center was taken in April 1984, at a splashy luncheon presentation for seven hundred people, to announce tentative agreement on a land disposition plan for the aboveground development, now named Yerba Buena Gardens. The process of creating a multicultural space on these two dozen acres was not an easy one, either in concept or execution. And the fall of Olympia & York as developers of this complex that began around this same time slowed the process, but, ironically, also wound up creating opportunities, as a combination of forfeited earnest money and letters of credit that the Redevelopment Agency consequently was able to collect on yielded some $26 million that has been used to fund many cultural and recreational activities on Central Blocks 2 and 3 that make up Yerba Buena Gardens. O&Y's option on this acreage formally terminated in February 1993, allowing the Redevelopment Agency and City to bring in another developer, Millennium Partners/WDG Cos.

The Yerba Buena Gardens cultural amenities plan is firmly rooted in Richard Gryziec's original Tivoli Gardens scheme and the work of Mayor Moscone's Select Committee on Yerba Buena Center. It hasn't been anywhere near a straight line from then until now nor a trouble-free process, but the cultural-recreational complex—almost fully developed as of early 2002—is an impressive public works project and piece of urban design, one that owes its existence to the persistence of a range of community activists, many from the arts and cultural community, who, for two decades, pressed to see that this central downtown space would be creatively and imaginatively used—by San Franciscans as well as outside visitors.

Among the key features are:

- the Center for the Arts, a two-building complex containing a 750-seat theater, multipurpose forum, galleries, media room, and gardens.
- the Children's Center, a complex containing the wonderful carousel formerly located at Playland-at-the-Beach, a twelve-lane bowling center, a thirty-two-thousand-square-foot ice skating rink, a child care center (for residents of the area and employees working nearby), a studio for technology and the arts, and a learning garden.
- a five-and-a-half-acre esplanade with an outdoor theater and a moving Martin Luther King Jr. memorial, approached via a twenty-two-foot-high, fifty-five-foot-wide waterfall.
- the 350,000-square-foot Metreon super high-tech entertainment center (a "swank, city-wise mini-Disneyland," as the *New York Times* characterized it),[1] courtesy of the Sony Corporation: fifteen movie screens, an IMAX theater, Microsoft's first store, a Discovery Channel store, a Moebius shop, "Where the Wild Things Are" fantasyland, food court—the works, marrying technology to business and entertainment. "A more obsequious monument to global capitalism would be hard to find," as Rebecca Solnit aptly characterizes it.[2]

On sites adjacent to and surrounding Yerba Buena Gardens are, or soon will be, the new Museum of Modern Art, the Ansel Adams Center for Photography, the California Historical Society's new offices and museum, and lots of new hotel rooms, offices, apartments and condos, and even a new 259-unit single-room-occupancy (SRO) hotel. A Jewish Museum is forthcoming in the historic Jesse Street Substation, and the Mexican Museum may eventually relocate from Fort Mason.

In 1999, Yerba Buena Gardens received the prestigious biannual Rudy Bruner Award for Urban Excellence (which carried with it a fifty-thousand-dollar prize). What seemed most to impress the selection committee in this national competition, which focused on "the complex process of urban place-making," was the process that led to creation of the gardens, as well as its inclusiveness in terms of the population it serves and the neighborhood of which it is now a part. "The mixed-use development," asserted the news release announcing the award, "enables cultural, social justice, and economic development agendas to coexist within a network of collaborative management practices," and it noted that the judges "applauded the evolution of the project's development process to an inclusive model involving multiple constituencies." (See fig. 7a.)

The Bruner Award also (albeit with more than a little overstatement and a total failure to appreciate how community pressures forced such changes) acknowledged changes wrought over three decades, not only in the project but also in the responsible agency: "The Selection Committee believes Yerba Buena Gardens represents the successful transformation of an urban Redevelopment Agency from a powerhouse committed to the 'bulldozer' federal planning of the 50s to a sophisticated development co-ordinator attending carefully to the complex balance of interests important in a 1990s setting. In its newfound commitment to inclusiveness over 'highest and best use,' the Agency has demonstrated a way to translate the vision of large-scale urban revitalization into the process of neighborhood empowerment."*

---

*Letter to the author, dated 6 April 1999, from Simeon Bruner. As noted in the text, the results were achieved despite considerable resistance. TODCO's John Elberling, a major force in fighting to make Yerba Buena meet the needs of the city's nonrich, recounts this experience in saving the Garden's bowling center, which was on the verge of being dropped from the project:

> "That's *your* fun," I sermonized to the Commissioners and Agency staff [testifying at a Redevelopment Agency hearing], "to go to gala openings at MOMA [Museum of Modern Art] and the galleries, dress up in black tie and evening gowns, enjoy the boutique wines and rub shoulders with the City's social elite. But what about the kids of the central city? What fun will there be in Yerba Buena for them, what alternatives to hanging out on the streets . . . ? The gangs beat them up when they go across town to other bowling alleys. The Market Street pimps and dealers hustle them at the so-called Fun Center arcade. A Filipino boy disappeared there three years ago and was never found. That's all the commercial recreation they have downtown. . . . A Redevelopment Agency that hands out free land for art museums for the wealthy in Yerba Buena but can't find funding for a Bowling Center too has no moral values, and if the Agency has no moral values, then it's time to shut it down."
>
> Cliff Graves, the new [SFRA] Executive Director, looked pained, several Commissioners glared. They hated this reminder about the class warfare that runs through the postwar history of Yerba Buena and San Francisco, even though it is now disguised so discreetly with planners' jargon about "revitalization" and endless "visioning" sessions on the City's future. But they backed off; there will be bowling on top of Moscone Center. The arts crowd and the Central City kids may even rub shoulders some day. That's unique, what I really like about the ultimate Yerba Buena Gardens that has resulted from all the plans, the maneuvers, the politics, the deals.

The letter appears in Elberling's essay in Ira Nowinski's updated edition of *No Vacancy,* a compelling collection of South of Market photographs.

TODCO's Replacement Housing

As described in chapter 6, the 1973 settlement agreement that finally led to a resolution of the displacees' lawsuit against the Redevelopment Agency provided for TOOR—which had incorporated the Tenants and Owners Development Corporation (TODCO) in 1971 to be its nonprofit housing development arm—to build some four hundred permanently subsidized low-rent units on four sites within the YBC project area. After Stephen Dutton left as TOOR/TODCO's director in 1977 to pursue other activities, he chose as his successor John Elberling, an environmental and transit activist with little previous housing experience, but who learned fast and well. Under Elberling's direction, TODCO's production activities over the subsequent two-and-a-half decades have progressed extraordinarily well and have become a true model for community-based housing and economic development, as well as cultural life.

Even though the YBC bonds had not yet been sold, the City in early 1977 decided to release sufficient hotel tax funds to TODCO for preliminary designs and administrative expenses. The motivation for abandoning their previous "hard-line" stance was primarily financial: The federal government was about to make available additional subsidy funds for low-rent senior housing, and moving on TODCO's initial project right away could save the City much money, since the federal funds would reduce the amount of City hotel tax funds needed, and in 1976 TODCO had secured a preliminary financing commitment from the newly established California Housing Finance Agency that would enable their use. TODCO and its architect, Robert Herman, moved quickly to develop plans for their first building site, the southwest corner of Fourth and Howard Streets, directly opposite the convention center site. (Somewhat ironically, Robert Herman, TOOR learned later, was Justin Herman's second cousin, although a person of very different sensibilities and loyalties.) Dutton chose Herman largely on the basis of his design of a development for the elderly in Chinatown (done for the San Francisco Housing Authority)—and, as Dutton put it, "because he was the only architect I talked to who didn't offer to pay for my lunch."[3]

Begun in January 1978, Woolf House I—named to honor TOOR's founder, George Woolf—opened in June 1979, a nine-story, 112-unit building, with street-level storefront space leased by TODCO for a neighborhood convenience store. Woolf House II, an attached seventy-unit expansion, opened in late 1982. (Thirty additional units of assisted-living housing for disabled seniors—Woolf House III—were built over its parking lot in

1996.) Financing has been a complex package—mortgage bond financing from the California Housing Finance Agency, state bonds, federal Section 8 rent subsidies, hotel tax funds, and a deferred loan from the state Department of Housing and Community Development. A full-scale on-site meals and activities program is provided there. On the roof sits a spectacular thirty-five-hundred-square-foot garden with twenty-eight small growing plots and four greenhouses. Woolf Houses' three sidewalk storefronts were rented to neighborhood convenience stores.

Woolf House I, which was featured in the August 1981 *Progressive Architecture,* is remarkable in its dignity and sensitivity.[4] Steve Dutton recollected: "It had to be very good. Woolf House was TODCO's first building and if it wasn't very very good it would no doubt be the last. I mean, who the hell are we? Three people with no experience, sitting around in a dingy office. We had to build the finest building possible with the money available. I think we did."[5] According to one description:

> Woolf House lifts itself from the general desolation south of Market
> Street with a calm elegance and simple pride of being that delights the eye
> and heart while seriously disarranging expectations. A small, impeccably
> tasteful and deftly modeled residential highrise with broad bay windows,
> neatly recessed balconies, solarium and protected garden, the building
> ornaments a neighborhood that has suffered "redevelopment" and, conse-
> quently, now resembles and has for the past ten years resembled the main
> exterior set for a film about the rebuilding of Berlin after World War II. In
> such a venue, Woolf House seems as abruptly incongruous as Gucci
> footwear on a warthog—seems as if it ought to be on Russian Hill com-
> muning with the $600,000-a-pop condominium conversions, or in Pacific
> Heights nestled amongst the consulates and former embassies.[6]

TODCO's second development, Ceatrice Polite Apartments—named for an active TOOR member, a mother of eight children who lived in one of the hundred wood frame family flats located on alleyways that were demolished for YBC—is a ninety-one-unit building, also designed by Robert Herman, on the same block as Woolf House and across the street from Clementina Towers, the San Francisco Housing Authority development for the elderly that was the sole replacement housing planned as part of the original YBC project. It opened in late 1985, financed by hotel tax funds and a low-interest loan under HUD's Section 202 program. Its two sidewalk storefronts are "rented" for free to important local senior services: a YBC senior drop-in health clinic run by the community-based South of Market Health Center, and the office of "Senior Power," a longtime senior-run advocacy group.

TODCO's third development—the 189-unit Mendelsohn House, named after George Woolf's successor, Peter Mendelsohn, who died in 1988—is just south of Moscone Center and opened in 1988, another Robert Herman design. (See fig. 3.) Adjacent to Mendelsohn House is an eighteen-thousand-square-foot plot of land (Alice Street Gardens) TODCO has leased from the Redevelopment Agency as a permanent community garden, containing some three hundred twenty-five-square-foot growing plots. This replaced the slightly smaller site on which Ceatrice Polite Apartments was built, which had earlier become one of the city's lesser known marvels. The elderly Chinese residents of Clementina Towers many years ago simply took over this vacant site and began planting, on tiny plots, a dazzling array of vegetables. Fencing and watering facilities were provided by the City and some private groups, and the sunny spot was alive with people all day. TODCO, sensitive to the "turf rights" that had built up around this land, and to the psychological and financial importance of gardening, made replacing the old garden site a condition of moving ahead with Mendelsohn House. The garden plots are available to residents of all South of Market senior housing. Mendelsohn House—adjacent to and almost indistinguishable (in terms of design as an outward reflection of social class) from an adjacent luxury rental/condo development, Museum Parc—in 1990 deservedly received an American Institute of Architects Honor Award for design excellence and a People in Architecture award from the AIA's California Council. Describing Robert Herman's sensitivity to his clients' needs, the August 1991 *Architectural Record* noted: "The lobby, Herman says, was intended to be 'reminiscent of a comfortable residential hotel. . . . ' There is seating at the front door for 'inconspicuous people-watching.' Extra space was given to the area around the mailboxes—a major social center." A nonprofit senior-wellness program was secured as a commercial tenant, paying a below-market rent. Opened in 1990, this sixty-five-hundred-square-foot facility, funded with federal community development block grant money, foundation grants, and a $125,000 Redevelopment Agency grant, provides nutrition, therapy, and health monitoring to frail seniors living in YBC, South of Market, and the Tenderloin every day.

In 1977, as a condition of its initial administrative funding, the City required TODCO to relinquish the fourth replacement housing site (directly opposite Mendelsohn House) to a Filipino organization, which then built the 147-unit Dimasalang House, also utilizing HUD's Section 202 senior housing program. This project opened in 1980 and is now named the San Lorenzo Ruiz Center. TODCO is not involved in its ownership or management.

These four developments—built as a result of TOOR's successful fight against the original relocation scheme—contain more than six hundred permanently affordable low-rent units, with 850 residents, almost all of whom are elders or persons with disabilities, typically living on Social Security or SSI assistance of $680 per month for a single person, $1,185 for a couple. Most pay only 30 percent of their income—$250–$300 per month—as rent for housing that is next door to market-rate housing that charges $1,500 per month and up for the same size apartment. About three-quarters of the occupants are Asian Americans (mainly persons moving from overcrowded Chinatown and Filipino housing in other South of Market areas and the former Manilatown), with a more recent influx of Russian immigrants. Only five were relocatees from the former YBC renewal site hotels (although they have admissions priority), due to the length of time between their displacement some three decades ago and creation of replacement housing and to the advanced age of most of the former site residents.

All of TODCO's housing is managed by a contracted property management agent. Over the years, TODCO has built up a resident services/activities program for its tenants, providing a range of social services: nighttime patrols, community clinic, case management, creative arts and writing workshops, exercise and recreation therapy, field trips and shopping transportation, the community gardens, two daily lunch dining rooms and nutrition programs, counseling, wellness programs, and parties.

To further expand this substantial Yerba Buena senior/disabled housing resource, in the 1990s TODCO undertook a twenty-four-unit development of family-sized two-bedroom apartments for people with disabilities of all ages (The Leland Apartments, on Howard, between Fifth and Sixth Streets), completed in 1998, utilizing City hotel tax funds and HUD's more recent Section 811 program for housing for persons with disabilities. And TODCO also plans to develop an eighty-five-unit senior residence adjacent to the Clementina Towers public housing project, on Howard Street, directly across from the latest of two expansions of Moscone Center (see chapter 9), for which another HUD Section 202 funding commitment was secured in 1998. Completion, including extensive relandscaping of Clementina Towers, is planned for 2003.

This continued development of new senior housing by TODCO and others during the 1990s was made possible by the organization's successful effort in 1988 to amend the City's hotel tax ordinance so as to extend and make permanent use of this revenue, formerly designated for development of the four YBC sites TOOR won, in order to fund new nonprofit senior housing development citywide. By 1999, this hotel tax assistance had reached some $5 million per year.

With completion of the four YBC housing sites, TODCO in the late 1980s determined to turn its attention to the broader South of Market neighborhood, especially the Sixth Street area, the neighborhood's other large concentration of residential hotels, to which many former YBC residents, along with pawnshops and other businesses, had relocated. During the 1980s, Sixth Street became the city's acknowledged skid row. Aided by City community development block grant funding, Redevelopment Agency grants, and private foundation funds, TODCO proceeded to purchase and renovate both family housing and rundown South of Market hotels for single occupants and build new SRO replacement housing to compensate for any reduction in total supply.

The 1989 Loma Prieta earthquake did substantial damage to the South of Market area, especially around Sixth Street, due to its foundation of filled-in marshland (some five hundred households and eighty to one hundred businesses were displaced, along with considerable impact on the infrastructure).[7] This brought TODCO—now a "conglomerate" of seven corporate entities—into a major role with respect to planning for the larger South of Market area and providing a range of social services as well as expanding its housing work.

The organization's first role in post-earthquake planning was to lead community efforts to establish in 1990 an emergency South of Market earthquake recovery redevelopment project, focused on the Sixth Street area, and then prepare "An Alternative Future for the South of Market" (1992) to identify positive community development alternatives for the Redevelopment Agency's work. TODCO also is renovating several earthquake-damaged hotels into assisted and independent living facilities for physically disabled persons. TODCO then used state disaster relief funds, along with Redevelopment Agency grants, to build San Francisco's first new SRO (a Robert Herman design again). This 140-unit project is on the site of the Anglo Hotel, which had to be demolished due to earthquake damage, and is named the Knox, after Walter Knox, another former TOOR member, who once lived at the Anglo and who was the former "mayor" of the Clementina Street community gardens. Opened at the end of 1994, it is a "state-of-the-art" SRO: Each unit has a kitchenette with a small refrigerator, cooktop, and microwave, and is furnished with carpeting, a fold-down bed-mattress unit cum sofa, dresser, and wardrobe; there is a twenty-four-hour desk staff, power-opened doors, a community kitchen, laundry room (with subsidized machine prices), a five-thousand-square-foot roof deck and garden, a playroom for residents' preschool-aged children, a lobby with big-screen video, and five small lounges. Sheets and towels are available for sale at wholesale prices; there are food vending machines with very low prices; and an on-site social worker. Rents are kept at low-income levels through financing via a subsidization package that involves Redevelopment Agency grants, a deferred state Department of Housing and Community Development mortgage, and substantial equity investment by Fannie Mae, utilizing the federal Low Income Housing Tax Credit program. This leaves no debt service for tenants to repay, only operating expenses: $334 per month in 2001. The Knox SRO's tenants reflect the general downtown hotel population, with approximately 40 percent African-Americans, 40 percent whites, and the remaining 20 percent Asian Americans (especially Filipino Americans), and includes elders and mothers with children as well as many single men and women.

TODCO then also utilized Redevelopment Agency funds to purchase and rehabilitate the Grand Southern Hotel, at Seventh and Mission, located atop hazardous soil conditions. This brick building was structurally retrofitted and fully renovated, using a grant from the Federal Emergency Management Agency, below-market deferred mortgage financing by the City's Seismic Retrofit Program, and federal Low Income Housing Tax Credit equity investment by the California Equity Fund (a national pooled corporate investment trust), combined with federal Section 8 rent subsidies for most of the units, supplied through the federal McKinney Homeless Assistance Program, administered by the San Francisco Housing Authority. Renamed the Hotel Isabel (after Isabel Ugat, a longtime South of Market neighborhood activist and TODCO's president, despite becoming wheelchair-bound after a 1990 stroke), this seventy-two-room SRO reopened in 1999 with a tenant population similar to the Knox SRO, but with most rents set at 30 percent of income (the Section 8 standard) and therefore affordable even to recipients of General Assistance (the principal income source for most homeless persons).

TODCO's continued strategy is to purchase and rehabilitate other South of Market hotels on a steady basis, especially those standing vacant or damaged by the 1989 earthquake or by fires. Next on TODCO's agenda is the Delta Hotel on Sixth Street at its key Mission Street intersection, severely damaged by a 1997 fire that took two lives. It will also be fully reinforced structurally and renovated as a 140-room SRO, to be renamed Bayanihan House, to respect its former Filipino ownership and predominantly Filipino tenants. (*Bayanihan* is the very important Tagalog word for mutual support and assistance.) The hotel's entire ground floor will be converted into a new community center to serve the central city's large Filipino population around issues such as immigration and employment. The center will be operated by the new community-based Filipino-American Development Foundation, to which TODCO is providing start-up technical assistance. As an interim step, TODCO also relocated the Filipino Veterans of World War II Equity Center, located at the Delta Hotel before the fire, to a storefront in its new Hotel Isabel a block away. (For a half century, the U.S. government refused to honor wartime promises to Filipino veterans for citizenship [finally granted in 1989], veterans' benefits, and family unification. As a result, about one thousand veterans, who are seventy or more years old, live in slum hotels in San Francisco, many frail and isolated.) Using a Redevelopment Agency grant, TODCO purchased the derelict Delta Hotel in 1999, with completion planned for 2003.[8]

All in all, as of early 2002, TODCO has 728 units in operation, 235 more in process. A product of the resistance and litigation that began in the late 1960s, this exemplary neighborhood nonprofit housing development corporation is bringing into being nearly one thousand finely designed, permanently affordable housing units, with a full range of needed services, creating/restoring a neighborhood that was never meant to be—quite an extraordinary feat for what began as "three people with no experience, sitting around in a dingy office."

Much as the Redevelopment Agency's YBC project aimed to obliterate the neighborhood's history, TOOR/TODCO's long struggle has achieved success in memorializing that history via the naming process. In Robert Herman's words: "So, we have George Woolf, Ceatrice Polite, Peter Mendelsohn and Walter Knox honored for their independent actions. Who would ever have dreamed such 'ordinary' people might one day be so honored by the community?"[9] As John Elberling notes, "Yerba Buena's a very, very good place to grow old."[10]

TODCO's considerable success is in part attributable to the more cooperative stance on the part of the Redevelopment Agency and city hall over the last twenty years; in part due to a very supportive state housing bureaucracy during Governor Jerry Brown's administration and to the not inconsiderable talents of TODCO's own staff and consultants.* In its expanded

---

*TODCO's staff director, John Elberling, an enormously persistent and dedicated person, while now blessed with a good working relationship with the City, has had his occasional run-ins with city hall, and in mid-1982 was subjected to what seems to have been a personal vendetta on the part of a few City officials. The district attorney brought charges against him and a recent TODCO employee for alleged mishandling of funds in connection with TODCO's rehabilitation work. Elberling was

South of Market role, TODCO has worked collaboratively with other community groups, such as the South of Market Business Association, the grassroots Sixth Street Merchants and Residents Association, and the South of Market Problem Solving Council coalition. It also has evolved from the role it first needed to play as antagonist to a major, implementation-oriented stakeholder in physical and social development of a larger area than was its original focus.

But while TODCO has been able to secure substantial assistance from the Redevelopment Agency, this has been accomplished only with great struggle (illustrating how hyped was the outsider's view of the agency propounded in the Bruner Award). As John Elberling notes, "Damn near everything is still an uphill fight with them." As examples: The agency had to be pressured (TODCO even threatened a lawsuit) to comply with state law requiring replacement of the SRO units removed in the hotel rehabilitation projects, as well as completing replacement of the units lost in the 1989 earthquake, as called for in the redevelopment plan. Another illustrative instance: The agency initially opposed the planned Filipino community center at Bayanihan House and turned around only when Filipino community leaders and supporters showed up in force at commission hearings, which led the agency board to overrule the staff.

TODCO's role and ambitions in the broader South of Market area are no less than to recapture the Yerba Buena Center project and its enormous resources to benefit low-income residents of the area. This involves creating permanent employment opportunities for South of Market people at Moscone Center, the area's luxury hotels, restaurants, service businesses,

---

charged with violations of the state's bookkeeping laws for allegedly transferring rehabilitation funds from one account to another, practices which, even if true, are fairly common in the world of housing development; it was not claimed that Elberling in any way personally benefited from these transactions. The move against Elberling was also generally considered an attempt to give a black eye to the city's nascent community housing development movement by bringing down the director of what was the most successful effort of this type in the city. The liberal political community reacted to this "get Elberling" move forcefully and effectively. His past leadership work in the city's antihigh-rise movement helped bring him many supporters. A June 1982 benefit for the John Elberling Defense Fund included as sponsors State Assemblyman Art Agnos, Supervisors Harry Britt, John Molinari, Nancy Walker, and Wendy Nelder, several City commissioners, SFRA assistant director Wes Willoughby, and the associate director of SPUR. In July 1982, after a preliminary hearing, charges against Elberling were dropped for lack of evidence. (See "Judge Drops Fund Charges against Housing Activist," *San Francisco Chronicle*, 8 July 1982.)

and retail establishments, as well as with property management firms; ensuring the full range of health and assisted-living services needed by a population largely of elders and persons with disabilities; providing addiction services; developing a site for a childcare facility; creating appropriate neighborhood-serving retail outlets, such as a small supermarket; increasing amenities for pedestrians, via signalized crosswalks, sidewalk improvements, and bus shelters; abating nuisances by regulating truck and bus access to Moscone Center; arranging senior discounts at local businesses; advocating for community-serving elements in the Yerba Buena Gardens development atop Moscone Center, such as the bowling center, childcare center, and mini-park. One of TODCO's imaginative community economic development strategies is to take advantage of the large potential rental revenue from street-level commercial spaces in these affordable housing developments—bountiful rent streams made possible by the patronage generated by Moscone Center and other elements of the Yerba Buena Center project—to permanently support extensive services for low-income elderly and disabled residents of these developments.

TODCO has also sought to strengthen the mixed-income character of the neighborhood by encouraging market-rate housing with portions set aside at below-market rents. Counting its own housing developments, other low-income projects, and market-rate housing, Yerba Buena now is also a neighborhood with some eighteen hundred seniors and two thousand others who did not live there prior to redevelopment—a population about equal to that displaced, in a new and successfully mixed (by class and land use) residential neighborhood that never was supposed to be. Using its half of the fifty-thousand-dollar Rudy Bruner Award, TODCO is updating the neighborhood plan it prepared in 1981 by producing *YBN* [Yerba Buena Neighborhood] *Plan 2004*. That target year reflects the fact that, under "sunset" provisions of California's redevelopment laws, it is the official termination date for the Yerba Buena Redevelopment Project—forty years after designation of the Yerba Buena Center Project Area—engendering a need for a successor body to ensure continuation of community benefits. As TODCO's planning process document asserts, "The achievement of Social/Economic Justice for the people of the Central City must at last become *integral* to the YBN and to YBC, and commensurate in scope with the extraordinary scale of the potential resources of YBC." In a remarkable reversal of roles, TODCO seeks to take the lead as guardian and creator of the Yerba Buena Neighborhood once the Redevelopment Agency bows out of the picture.

In the supporting documents accompanying application for the Bruner Award, John Elberling, on behalf of the Yerba Buena Consortium (a council of the area's housing, health, and social service providers), summed up the advice he would give to other community groups, based on TODCO's experience:

1.   First, master the technical process of redevelopment—the applicable redevelopment laws and regulations, the environmental review procedures, and local civic review procedures in order to understand how to exert maximum pressure and leverage at just the right time to achieve community goals;

2.   develop an understanding of real estate development economics to realistically evaluate what can and cannot be expected in community benefits from for-profit development;

3.   define a holistic vision for how the project becomes part of their community to a meaningful degree and turn that into specific proposals that can be addressed one at a time and also pursued on independent tracks;

4.   use every procedural and civic opportunity to relentlessly assert the community's goals, and to build a broad base of civic support for them;

5.   identify the real senior decision makers and their key advisors, especially in the private sector, and negotiate directly with them;

6.   network with larger politically active community coalitions that can support the community's goals;

7.   assume that the effort will require ten to twenty years of consistent effort by successions of community representatives and plan accordingly; and

8.   be committed and bold—reject token or symbolic accommodations and pursue community benefits at the largest scale that appears practicable, which will have a genuine positive impact for real people in the community.

The South of Market Neighborhood

The larger South of Market area has of course been changing rapidly, triggered in part by the YBC project, as well as by larger market forces. For some two decades, the area has been indisputably "chic." An April 1982 *Sunset* magazine article, titled "South of Market: No-Nonsense San Francisco," noted that visitors to the area are "discovering art galleries, historic buildings, no-frills stores with considerable bargains, and unusual little restaurants often tucked behind inconspicuous facades." The article mapped out a driving/looking tour of the South of Market area and ended cheerfully, "There's a bustle and excitement to the street scene here, and a sense that the whole area will be radically different five or ten years from now."[11] A June 1981 SPUR report was insensitively titled "South of Market: A Plan for San Francisco's Last Frontier." Trendy new restaurants have popped up all over the area. In the western portion of the neighborhood, a regional center for wholesalers of commercial and interior furnishings (the Galleria Design Center, Showplace Square, a gift mart, and a "data mart") has developed in the 1900s-vintage factories and warehouses.[12] Software, multimedia, and Internet companies—now a major force in the city's economy—have turned part of the area into "Multimedia Gulch." Pricey "lawyer loft" housing units are going up by the hundreds (see chapter 13). The traditional gay community is being impacted by these developments.[13] East of YBC, between Fourth Street and the Bay, a half dozen luxury high-rise apartment and condominium complexes are under construction, with more doubtless coming.[14]* And massive projects like the new baseball stadium and Mission Bay alter the area entirely.

Without question, South of Market has been transformed.

---

*Nicely bookending the events chronicled in this history is the fact that the largest of the developments going up, a fifty-one-story mixed condominium-apartment tower—the tallest residential tower west of the Mississippi—is being built by Swig-Burris Equities, one of whose partners, Kent Swig, is Ben's grandson.

City Hall

The Board of Supervisors and District Elections

As has been demonstrated on many occasions, the city's governing Board of Supervisors gave virtually reflexive approval to the various steps in the Yerba Buena project whenever required. More generally, the board reflected its members' economic and social ties to downtown interests, through their business dealings, campaign finances, social relationships, and class alliances.

Starting in 1900, the eleven-person board was elected on a citywide, or "at-large," basis, a system requiring in recent years enormous financial support to mount election campaigns—as much as $250,000 to run successfully for an office that until the early 1980s paid an annual salary of $9,600, a sum virtually guaranteeing that everyone in the position except the wealthy must hold another job. (In November 1982, voters approved a charter amendment raising the salary to $23,924, and a June 1998 voter-approved charter amendment raised it to $37,585.) In addition, supervisors who are attorneys, insurance brokers, real estate operators, and the like can derive substantial business benefits from the position, a part-time one. Beyond campaign financing issues, the at-large system reduces the possibility that smaller, identifiable population groups and areas of the city will be directly represented in the governing process.

As early as 1970, neighborhood activists in San Francisco and others striving to reduce the influence of downtown business saw the need for changing the method of electing supervisors. Creating districts and allowing the residents of each to elect a candidate who lived in the same district would increase the probability of being represented by supervisors with closer ties to the neighborhoods and their problems, reducing as well the dominance of downtown power and money.

The key movers of this plan organized as Citizens for Representative Government (CRG), a small, hard-working group of activists with strong roots in the Haight-Ashbury district. In 1970 and 1971, they held community meetings around the city to discuss their ideas and created an eleven-district city map. In August 1972, they presented their plan to the supervisors, who responded by placing on the November ballot a complex, unwieldy advisory measure that presented voters with five alternative plans for restructuring the board election. Not surprisingly, with so many options, none received an overwhelming mandate; but two-thirds of the voters did favor a change from the at-large system, and among the alternatives, CRG's eleven-district plan received the most votes. Encouraged, CRG placed its plan on the November 1973 city election ballot through an initiative. In a low turnout vote, however, the measure lost, two to one.

Analyzing the loss, CRG saw the need to move out more widely into the community in order to expand their activist base and relate the district election plan to more substantive neighborhood concerns. In 1974, they began an elaborate organizing and educational process, which led to the formation in August 1975 of the San Francisco Community Congress, a series of district-based and citywide meetings. The congress galvanized reform energies around a wide range of substantive reforms and carried out the sensitive task of drawing the district boundaries, both to facilitate the organizing process and to discourage an at-large board from doing it.

Nine issue conventions were held around the city (on health, women, housing, jobs and economic development, governmental changes, criminal justice, environment, the arts, and energy). These culminated in a citywide convention, attended by nearly a thousand people, at which "A Community Program for Change in San Francisco" was adopted. The movement for structural change was closely tied to the mayoral change of that year, as (winning) candidate George Moscone actively supported this reform. CRG then midwifed creation of a broader grouping, San Franciscans for District Elections (SFDE), a coalition of nearly four dozen neighborhood and city-wide groups. They decided to wait until November 1976 before placing an initiative on the ballot again, reasoning that turnout would be higher in a presidential election year and that high turnouts generally favor progressive measures; they would also thereby avoid repeating the 1973 situation, when five incumbent supervisors used their reelection campaigns as a platform against district elections. (Supervisorial elections were later changed from odd-numbered to even-numbered years in 1980, via a voter-approved change in the City Charter.)

An important additional factor in 1976 was the growing dissatisfaction of organized labor, particularly City workers, with the policies and actions of the supervisors, sentiments that led most major unions actively to support the district elections move. More generally, there was dissatisfaction with the apparent stagnancy of the board and the difficulty newcomers had replacing incumbents: In the preceding seven supervisorial elections, only five incumbents were defeated out of thirty-six seeking reelection.[1] There was a real desire for change in local politics in San Francisco in the mid-1970s, of which the election of George Moscone as mayor was one expression. Restructuring supervisorial elections offered another promise of hope and change in the uneven distribution of power in the city. It was, in effect, a recall of the entire Board of Supervisors.

The campaign for SFDE's eleven-district proposal, Proposition T, was well orchestrated. It raised twenty-five thousand dollars (about one-fifth coming from organized labor) and was run by a paid staff of seven, with an army of volunteers numbering several thousand. It emphasized the composition of the at-large Board of Supervisors—in particular, that nine of the eleven members lived in either St. Francis Wood or Pacific Heights, two of the city's poshest residential areas. (Five of the proposed new districts had no resident board member.) While the "No on T" forces spent more than twice as much (fifty-three thousand dollars), and the measure was, as expected, opposed editorially by the *Examiner* and *Chronicle*, their campaign lacked real verve, a result in part of underestimating voter dissatisfaction with the city government. (The arrival of increased property tax bills just before election day did little to assuage that alienation.)

Proposition T won, 52 to 48 percent, carrying eight of the city's eleven new districts, the exceptions being Pacific Heights, Parkside/Lake Merced, and the Sunset. According to its terms, the first district-based election, for the entire board, would be November 1977—with a coin toss determining whether the odd- or even-numbered districts would serve only a two-year term at first and with subsequent elections to be for four-year terms. The Community Congress planned to hold further issue and nominating conventions in most of the city's districts, carving out a political identity for each one. The Proposition T campaign was run by assuming the districts already existed, and the district election strategists hoped to build on that process to create strong district organizations to which candidates would be accountable, sharing a common program and bound to the overall citywide organization.[2]

But the luxury of following their long-range plan was not possible. Within weeks of the victory, a group met at the home of San Francisco Chamber of Commerce staff member Ed Lawson to plan a repeal election.[3] Five of the existing at-large supervisors—John Barbagelata, Al Nelder, Peter Tamaras, Dorothy von Beroldingen, and Terry Francois—then announced they would not run under the district system, a combination of pique, scare tactics, and, for some, self-preservation in the face of possibly having to run against an incumbent. Although Francois reputedly was organizer of the meeting, he had been quoted as saying, the day after Proposition T passed, "The people have spoken: we must abide by it. Any effort on the part of this lame duck board to put something else on the ballot to repeal it, I would oppose vigorously."[4]

The downtown forces—taking the name Citizens for Total Representation—quickly rounded up enough signatures to put the repeal measure (Proposition A) on the ballot, in a special August 1977 election. Their timing was tactical: A low turnout summertime election would favor the conservatives. Their arguments stressed the themes that ward politics and "bossism" would take hold, and that the move was part of a "radical takeover" of San Francisco.[5] *Chronicle* columnist Herb Caen had perhaps the best retort to that canard: "We've had 'ward' politics for years—one ward—run by a powerful politico-economic coalition, pronounced 'Downtown.' "[6] And it was hard to make a case that this structural reform was by itself radical. It is the system by which Congress, state legislatures, and most county boards of supervisors in California are elected (San Francisco is by itself a county as well as a city); and among the country's large cities, only one-sixth have solely at-large representation in their local legislative bodies. One-third have ward-only systems, and half have mixed at-large/ward systems.[7]

The repeal effort brought out big financial support from downtown, which had been caught napping the previous November: $3,500 each from the Bank of America, Chamber of Commerce, and Southern Pacific; $2,500 each from Standard Oil of California and Wells Fargo; $2,150 from Crown Zellerbach; $2,000 each from Crocker National Bank, Macy's, and Emporium-Capwell; $1,000 each from United Airlines, I. Magnin, and Citizens Savings and Loan; $750 from the Transamerica Corporation. Beyond money, some of these organizations also sent memos to their employees, urging them to sign and circulate petitions for the August repeal vote. The potential meaning of district election of supervisors had finally sunk in. As the *Examiner*'s Dick Nolan observed:

We're dealing here with something rather historic. It's a transfer of power. So far we've talked about it in a kind of shorthand, saying that when district elections won, the downtown interests lost, which is true enough but not nearly full enough. The clearest indication of who's backing Proposition A is, of course, the tabulated campaign contributions. All the money power is there: the real estate interests, the banks, the insurance companies, the airlines, the heavy contractors, the mercantile firms, friendly Southern Pacific, and so forth and so on.[8]

In a crassly worded editorial, the Chamber of Commerce magazine *San Francisco Business* exhorted: "Most business leaders, unfortunately, don't reside or vote in San Francisco and must, therefore, rely upon their persuasive powers and their money to influence the course of local politics."[9]

But what the downtown conservatives did not count on was being outflanked from the right, in the form of Supervisor John Barbagelata, loser by a narrow margin to George Moscone in the 1975 mayoral runoff election. Barbagelata hit upon his own plan to subvert the Proposition T vote: a Machiavellian complex charter amendment (Proposition B) that

- effectively recalled the mayor, the district attorney, the sheriff, the city attorney, the treasurer, and the entire Board of Supervisors, requiring all to run again in the November 1977 election Proposition T called for, and to be elected by a majority rather than plurality vote, with a runoff election if necessary;
- retained all eleven supervisorial districts of Proposition T and the requirement that supervisors elected from each district be resident in that district, but provided for all seats to be chosen by the electorate at large; and
- removed all appointed commissioners and the chief administrative officer (whose term would be reduced to six years), allowing the new mayor to make fresh appointments to all the posts, and required all commissions to have at least one woman appointee.

Barbagelata's scheme, facetiously labeled the "fire everybody petition," was cynical and none too principled. For example, he had previously opposed a successful charter amendment requiring at least one woman on the police, fire, and civil service commissions. Including what he had previously opposed was designed to confuse voters and perhaps pick up feminist support. Many viewed the measure simply as Barbagelata's attempt to get back at George Moscone, who, he felt, had stolen the 1975 mayoral election from him.[10] Certainly Mayor Moscone saw it that way—"There's only one goal in his mind and that's to dump me. I just know this plan of his has nothing to do with reform, and if John tries to sell that to anybody, it's a loser."[11]

It was more than just revenge, however. The Chronicle's crusty Charles McCabe—writing about himself as well—put it this way:

> [Barbagelata] represents the San Francisco that is no more, a coalition of the dying. . . . John Barbagelata represents what is left of what used to be San Francisco, the San Francisco that Herb Caen writes about as if it still exists, the San Francisco that in a generation has gone down the tube, largely because of the minority groups that have come in since 1940 and sent scurrying to the suburbs the Irish and the Germans and the Italians that were the traditional power base around here.[12]

Barbagelata's move angered the downtown power structure. The conservative neighborhood (West Portal) realtor was not part of the downtown establishment, did not have their sophistication, and his plan was too wild, too disruptive. Both dailies inveighed against it editorially. Downtown leaders in fact urged people not to sign the petition, realizing correctly that it would divert attention from the "pure" district election repeal, and that, with it on the ballot, the entire city hall structure would mobilize for the August special election.[13] As one district election supporter put it, the Barbagelata initiative "will force the mayor and all the others to crank up their political machines and . . . bring all the factions together again to wage political war. We'll have the help of political organizations which might have stayed home if the repeal measure was alone on the ballot."[14]

And they did crank up their machines, fearful that the quixotic Barbagelata and his forces might just pull it off. Democratic County Central Committee chair Agar Jaicks later acknowledged that "the 1977 situation generated so much concern that Moscone allies from as far away as Los Angeles flew planeloads of volunteers here to walk precincts."[15] As the Chronicle's Herb Caen put it, "Barbagelata's brainstorm . . . will give the ultras a chance to come out of the bushes. They can stand up and be counted in the anonymity of the voting booth—the lawnorder types, the gay-haters, the anti-blacks, those who blame all the ills of the city on the bleeding hearts."[16]

The Proposition T campaigners mounted a combined "No on A and B" campaign; the Moscone forces ran a separate "No on B" campaign. Barbagelata, unable to raise much money, was outspent, five to one.[17] While the district elections folks couldn't match the downtown in money, their well-oiled campaign machine was able to overcome this disadvantage. On August 2, 1977, the repeal initiative (Proposition A) lost, 58 to 42 percent, an even better showing for district elections than its victory the previous November. Barbagelata's Proposition B lost, 64 to 36 percent. Charles McCabe, with his customary lack of subtlety, put it this way:

> We are going to have to get used to an entirely new kind of Supervisor. . . . They may not even speak very good English. Their manners are likely to smell of the street. Their dealing will be naked, probably done in the middle of pool halls rather than in the pleasant obscurity of a downtown club. They are going to irritate the hell out of some of us; but they are the future, and we had better get used to it.[18]

In November 1977, the first district-based elections were held under the new system. The need to immediately defend their November 1976 victory had undercut the district-building process and the Community Congress organizers' hopes of having district nominating conventions (although district platforms were developed and approved at a second citywide Community Congress in September 1977). In all likelihood, such a plan would not have worked in any case, political factions and personal ambitions being what they were. A total of 113 candidates ran for the eleven district slots.

On the surface there were big changes. As noted above, five supervisors from the old board chose not to play in the new arena at all, in itself a rather amazing fallout of the structural reform. The remaining six—after two, Ron Pelosi and John Molinari, moved to safer districts, leaving no incumbent in a position of having to compete with another incumbent—were reelected: Pelosi in the Sunset (District 11), Quentin Kopp in Parkside/Lake Merced (District 10), Robert Gonzales in Potrero Hill/Bayview–Hunters Point (District 7), John Molinari in North Beach (District 3), Dianne Feinstein in Pacific Heights (District 2), and Gordon Lau in the Richmond (District 1).

The newcomers, a diverse lot, several of whom likely could only have been elected on a district basis, included Ella Hill Hutch, from the largely African American Western Addition (District 4); gay activist Harvey Milk, from Haight-Ashbury/Castro/Noe Valley (District 5); Dan White, from Visitacion Valley/Crocker-Amazon (District 8); and Lee Dolson, a conservative who won in the liberal Potrero Hill/Outer Mission (District 9) when neither of the two liberal candidates, Bob Covington or Michael Nolan (representing different and competing formations within the city's progressive movement), would yield to the other. "The new members," concluded a study coauthored by the director of the University of California's Institute of Governmental Studies, "generally paralleled the demographic and political characteristics of the districts from which they were elected. . . . The sources of power which had previously drawn strength from a citywide base—downtown business, organized labor, and the two major papers—found their influence sharply reduced, while neighborhood groups grew in power. The role of campaign financing was downgraded."[19]

As supporters predicted, campaign expenditures were considerably lower with a smaller territory to cover and mass media of limited use. Campaigns stressed district mailings, canvassing voters on foot, and personal appearances. The average expenditure per winning candidate was $31,000, compared with $69,000 in the 1971 at-large supervisorial election (an even greater difference when expressed in constant dollar amounts). The lowest expenditure by a winning candidate was $8,000, the highest $66,000; in 1971, the range for winning candidates was $46,000–$99,000. Nonincumbent winners spent on average less than half what incumbent winners spent, $19,000 vs. $41,000.[20]

But, for all these surface changes, the first district-elected Board of Supervisors of this century represented little change from the older at-large board. As Calvin Welch, one of the campaign's principal strategists, pointed out, the board elected in 1977 contained only one clear supporter of the new system, Harvey Milk. In District 6, the principal district elections-oriented candidate, Al Borvice, was defeated. In District 9, the infighting among progressives elected conservative Lee Dolson, who was not favorable to district elections. And District 8's Dan White had also opposed district elections. The system changed, but the players (the incumbent majority and all but one newcomer) did not, at least regarding belief in the new system. Moreover, once in office, the newcomers were by and large frozen out or outmaneuvered by the incumbents, and little in the way of conversion to the new system took place.

The City Hall Assassinations

The Moscone era ended dramatically and tragically on November 27, 1978, in one of the most bizarre tales in the history of American politics, when District 8's Dan White went to city hall and shot to death Mayor George Moscone and Supervisor Harvey Milk.[21] Although the idiosyncrasies of personalities and the sickness of the assassin were necessary ingredients, it was an event with profound political causes and political impacts, intimately related to the issues that gave rise to the district-based elections system and to citywide tensions that system exposed and exacerbated.

The background to the assassinations lay in White's sudden decision in early November to resign his seat, just eleven months after taking office.

White, a native of the city, former star high school athlete, Vietnam War paratrooper, former city policeman, and a San Francisco firefighter, was elected at age thirty-one. He represented the older values and way of life of the city's white, largely Catholic, working- and lower-middle-class population. He detested the changes taking place in the city: the increasing number of minorities, the pervasive presence of gay people and their culture, the political radicalism and alternative life styles that characterized the city in the 1960s and 1970s. The neighborhoods he represented (Portola, Excelsior, Visitacion Valley, Crocker-Amazon) were among those "forgotten" parts of the city that by and large had not been directly affected by the various economic, political, and social forces that had shaped San Francisco since World War II. District elections gave these neighborhoods a chance to have one of their own at city hall, and Dan White fit the bill perfectly, defeating twelve other District 8 candidates.

White's decision to resign took everyone by surprise. He gave family finances as his reason: The law required him to give up his fire department position in order to take the ninety-six-hundred-dollar-a-year supervisorial seat, and his wife had recently left her schoolteacher position to have their first baby. The family had just bought a "Hot Potato" fast-food franchise at the new tourist-oriented Pier 39 development, but it had not yet proven able to support the family. True as these economic facts of life were, White's decision probably was also largely shaped by his frustrating experiences as a supervisor. He found his colleagues and the city hall world distasteful, and he was ineffective in his role. Angry, humiliated, and deeply disappointed, he announced his resignation without consulting anyone.

His supporters immediately besieged him to change his mind—not so much his district supporters but the Police Officers Association, which had helped greatly in his victory, and downtown forces such as realty interests. (This included Pier 39 developer Warren Simmons, whose connection with White raised questions about a possible illegal payoff involving the fast-food shop, questions the FBI had begun to investigate.)[22] These supporters did not want to see White replaced via an appointment by the liberal Moscone. "White had started as an angry blue-collar populist," writes Harvey Milk's biographer, "but he quickly turned into the great white hope of downtown interests—a politician with a future."[23] After a few days of being criticized for being a quitter, White just as suddenly changed his mind and asked for his seat back. George Moscone, who genuinely felt sorry for White, at first agreed to disregard his letter of resignation.

By this time, however, Moscone's liberal supporters, in particular Harvey Milk, had seen the opportunity this sudden resignation offered and were placing powerful counterpressures on Moscone. The mayor had been losing on several issues before the Board of Supervisors by six to five votes; replacing White with a Moscone ally would provide a generally supportive board for Moscone's policies. Before White reversed his decision to resign, Harvey Milk had extracted from Moscone a commitment that whoever he appointed would vote to support establishment of a gay community center, for which Milk had five votes lined up. (Milk in April 1978 had sponsored the city's gay rights ordinance; Dan White was the only supervisor to vote against it.) Voices from White's own district also were being heard urging Moscone to replace White, as the new supervisor was delivering few benefits for his neighborhoods. Poor communication and vacillation characterized relations between Moscone and White during the third and fourth weeks of November, and in the end Moscone finally decided to replace White with Don Horanzy, a real estate appraiser employed by the HUD Area Office and former president of the major District 8 neighborhood group, the All People's Coalition. White learned of this decision not from Moscone, but from a television reporter who called to get White's reaction.

The next morning, November 27, 1978, feeling betrayed and publicly humiliated, this man of weak character and huge temper strapped on his old police service revolver, sneaked into city hall to avoid encountering a security metal detector, and asked to see Moscone. The mayor, just about to leave for his press conference to announce the appointment of Horanzy as White's replacement, agreed to see him, in order to explain the matter to him and console him. Several minutes later, the mayor lay dead, with four bullets in him, the last one a coup de grace. Dan White then reloaded his gun and walked to the other side of the city hall rotunda to the supervisors' bank of offices and asked Harvey Milk if they could have a talk. Milk agreed, and a few minutes later he too was dead, with five bullets in him, the last one another coup de grace. Later White claimed Milk had "smirked" at him—a climactic moment between two men who represented opposite poles of San Francisco's life and history.

White turned himself in to the police immediately thereafter, and his May 1979 trial mirrored the conflicts and controversy surrounding the killings themselves. The district attorney's office was highly criticized for its handling of the prosecution. It was charged that the prosecutor, Deputy DA Thomas Norman, was reluctant to raise the political overtones and issues that a first-degree murder conviction, requiring a premeditated motive, necessitated and that he instead allowed a temporary derangement defense to prevail. (White's campaign brochure, which he wrote himself, had stated: "You must realize there are thousands upon thousands of frustrated *angry* people waiting to unleash a fury that can and will eradicate the malignancies which blight our beautiful city. . . . I am not going to be forced out of San Francisco by splinter groups of radicals, social deviants, incorrigibles.")[24] The jury—no open gays, only one nonwhite, five Catholic women old enough to be White's mother—found him guilty of voluntary manslaughter, by reason of "diminished capacity," the minimum possible finding. In July 1979, he was sentenced to seven years and eight months in jail. With time off for good behavior and the six months he served between his arrest and the trial, he was released on parole in January 1984, having served less than six years. In mid-February, he was reported to be living in a Bel-Air mansion, with a fifty-thousand-dollar advance on a book-movie deal.[25] The next year he quietly returned to San Francisco, where he committed suicide in his garage on October 21, 1985.[26]

The night of the verdict, gays and others, shouting "We want justice" and "Kill Dan White," rioted at city hall, and the police rioted back. "Sara Jane Moore got life for *missing* Gerald Ford," observed one of the demonstrators.[27] The long-standing hostility between San Francisco's gays and the police erupted that night, during which seven police cars were burned. Mike Weiss concluded:

> The killings of Moscone and Milk and White's ensuing trial stirred deep fears and passions in San Francisco, because they brought to the surface wounds and divisions that the politicians and the image mongers preferred to keep hidden. Nobody wanted to talk about the graffiti on school walls that said DEATH TO ALL FAGS or FREE DAN WHITE. Police and firemen contributed substantial amounts of money to White's defense fund, which apparently raised over $100,000. To a lot of people, White was a hero for taking justice into his own hands.[28]

Whether anything more sinister than the acts of a single man lay behind the murders of George Moscone and Harvey Milk is still debated. But it is incontrovertible that those nine bullets Dan White fired on November 27, 1978, changed San Francisco's politics in ways that White and his political supporters fervently desired.

The slain mayor was immediately memorialized by naming the still-to-be-built convention center after him. Perhaps born of honorable intentions, the move was cynically interpreted by some as motivated at least in part by a desire to influence the appeals court, which was to decide on the legal challenge to the financing plan for building the new facility (as described in chapter 7).

Dianne Feinstein, Acting Mayor

As provided for under the City Charter, the president of the Board of Supervisors, Dianne Feinstein, immediately became acting mayor upon George Moscone's death. The city was in a state of collective trauma. The city hall shootings had occurred less than two weeks after the Jonestown, Guyana, mass suicides and murders, in which 913 members of the People's Temple took their own lives and five people were murdered (San Mateo Congressman Leo Ryan, three media personnel, and a fleeing cult member).[29]* Before moving en masse from San Francisco to Guyana, the sect had in a few years become a potent force among the city's black and politically progressive populations, and its charismatic leader, the Reverend Jim Jones, had been a political figure of no little weight, capable of delivering his thousands of members virtually as a voting bloc.† Moscone had appointed Jones first to the City's Human Rights Commission, then as Housing Authority chair.

In the chaotic and frightening aftermath of these events, Dianne Feinstein, with her Pacific Heights, Junior League bearing and sensibilities, and "her inoffensive brand of moderate politics,"[30] provided a welcome, calming, normalizing force.‡ When the time came for her former colleagues to choose a mayor to fill out the remaining year of Moscone's term, she was the ordained choice.

Neither George Moscone nor Dianne Feinstein represented any extreme along the political spectrum, but the differences in personality, background, ideology, and backing were sufficient to tip the city's balance of power markedly. Feinstein, a supervisor since 1969 (the first woman in the city's

---

*In early 2000, Jonestown lost first place in the record books for the worst modern cult-related mass killing, when Ugandan authorities raised the death toll for the Movement for the Restoration of the Ten Commandments doomsday sect to 924. See "Uganda Cult Toll, at 924, Passes Jonestown," *New York Times,* 1 April 2000.

†"[Jones] exercised fierce political power in San Francisco, with that city's establishment eating from his hand." James Reston Jr., *Our Father Who Art in Hell* (New York: Times Books, 1981), 57. Deborah Layton reported: "During these times, then-California State Assembly Speaker Willie Brown presided over a dinner in honor of Jim. In his flamboyant introduction of the now powerful and influential church leader, Brown proclaimed, 'Let me present to you a combination of Martin Luther King, Angela Davis, Albert Einstein and Chairman Mao' " (Deborah Layton, *Seductive Poison: A Jonestown Survivor's Story of Life and Death in the People's Temple* [New York: Anchor Books, 1998]).

‡A 1983 laudatory feature on Feinstein in a popular women's magazine described that earlier image as "Goody Two Shoes: The Straight-Laced, Upper Middle Class Lady in Frilly-Necked Blouses with No Ideology Deeper or More Original Than the Protestant Work Ethic" (Moira Johnston, "The Political Odyssey of Dianne Feinstein," *Savvy* [September 1983]: 38–42).

history to win without having first been appointed) and a two-time aspirant for mayor, from the first was a politician with whom downtown interests could live comfortably. While she was somewhat presumptuous and ill-advised in challenging Joseph Alioto in 1971, and strong pro-neighborhood sentiment among voters worked against her in 1975, by 1979, when her interim term as Moscone's replacement ended, she was just what the business community and many in the neighborhoods wanted. The huge $864,000 war chest she raised for her campaign that year came primarily from downtown corporations and big business.[31] (It is fascinating to note how rapid was the rise in mayoral campaign spending levels—and the corresponding dependence on the business community for contributions—in just four years: In 1975, George Moscone spent $127,000 to win the mayoralty.)[32] Feinstein's election in her own right in 1979 was, however, less automatic than most people had predicted: In November, she squeaked by Supervisor Quentin Kopp by only three thousand votes, and with gay realtor David Scott making a good showing, could not get the majority necessary to avoid a runoff, in which she did, however, beat Kopp, 54 to 46 percent.

The Second District-Elected Board Supervisors

With the second district-based election of supervisors in 1979, some significant political changes began to appear in the board, mainly through the election of progressive candidate Nancy Walker in District 9, who beat incumbent Lee Dolson, and Inner Sunset neighborhood activist John Bardis in District 11, who, in a surprise victory, unseated twelve-year incumbent Ron Pelosi. Together with Harry Britt, whom Feinstein, under pressure, had appointed to Milk's seat (Britt was on a list of preferred successors in Milk's last will and testament), progressives for the first time had substantial representation on the board, which was beginning to mirror the city's actual political complexion. Among other things, the 1979 elections made it clear that incumbency was no longer a guarantee of reelection, as four of the six incumbents running were defeated.

But even with the addition of Walker and Bardis, the basic political character and actions of the Board of Supervisors changed far less than district election supporters had hoped and predicted. An important explanatory factor here is the role of the mayor in appointing supervisors when vacancies occur—a long-term feature of the San Francisco political system. When Dianne Feinstein took over as mayor in November 1978, she immediately had three of the eleven seats to fill—her own, Harvey Milk's, and Dan White's.

Subsequently, she peopled the board with other direct appointments: In 1981, Willie Kennedy replaced Ella Hill Hutch (who had died of a heart attack); in 1986, Thomas Hsieh replaced Louise Renne, whom Feinstein had appointed city attorney following the death of George Agnost; and later that year, her aide James Gonzalez replaced Quentin Kopp, who was elected to the state senate. While such appointments don't always produce effective political control over the appointees—in particular, as with Britt and Horanzy, when exogenous factors either determined the choice or reduced options markedly—their role, aided by the subsequent advantages of incumbency, which usually results in these persons being elected to continue service on the board, gives a mayor strong and continuing political power over the independently elected Board of Supervisors.

Nevertheless, the threatening appearance of genuine progressives on the board and the rightward shift in the city's political climate, fostered by the Moscone-Milk assassinations and the accession of Feinstein, led downtown to mount yet another, successful attack on the district system. Once again employing the device of an August special election, when turnout would be low, the downtown forces—this time under the name Citizens for Better Government, chaired by ex-supervisor Terry Francois—placed a repeal measure on the August 1980 ballot, where, as the sole item on the ballot, it won by just sixteen hundred votes. Several factors contributed to the loss:

- a 35 percent voter turnout;
- the lack of strong district elections support from the board itself (only Walker, Bardis, and Britt were openly for it, and Britt, by then a nationally known figure in the gay community, had a citywide constituency as well);
- divisions between labor and community-based progressives as a result of simultaneously running a housing-reform initiative and an antihighrise initiative the previous November (see chapters 12 and 13);
- the financial and energy drain on the city's housing activists in the course of their successful turnback of the statewide antirent-control initiative just two months before (see chapter 13);
- the deflection of energies caused by a 1978–80 effort to reform the City Charter; and
- the long-term emotional fallout of the Moscone-Milk assassinations—associated by many moderates with district elections (an irony, considering assassin Dan White's opposition to that reform).

District elections supporters revved up for one further try—a heroic effort that gathered thirty-five thousand signatures in three weeks—to place the matter on the ballot once again in November 1980. But they were beaten there, too, 51.6 percent to 48.4 percent, in a highly confusing election in which all sixty-five candidates had to run citywide, whether they supported or opposed district elections. Two contradictory items were on the ballot: the district elections restoration measure and the actual election of supervisors under the at-large system. Candidates supporting district elections running successfully in the at-large election would have that victory nullified if the restoration measure they also supported won.

The next attempt to restore district elections came in 1987 (Proposition P), spurred by the victory of the antihigh-rise forces that passed the dramatic 1986 slow-growth initiative, Proposition M (see chapter 12); the growth issue and its activists overlapped with the concerns and aims of district election supporters. Proposition P established eleven districts generally resembling the boundaries of the earlier version but, unlike its predecessor, had a runoff provision similar to the city's mayoral elections, requiring the winner to secure a majority vote. Although it was endorsed by both major mayoral candidates, Assemblyman Art Agnos and Supervisor John Molinari (but opposed by outgoing Mayor Dianne Feinstein and Assemblyman Willie Brown), it lost 56 to 44 percent. Interestingly, black supervisors Doris Ward and Willie Kennedy did not support the measure, fearing they might lose their seats, given the city's declining African-American population.[33] (The black population in the city has continued this decline, in both absolute and relative terms: Blacks made up 13 percent of the city's inhabitants in 1970; by 1998 the proportion had dropped to 11 percent; the city's Asian population—36 percent—and Latino population—15 percent—have passed African Americans as larger racial groups.)[34] Heavy spending by downtown interests (Bechtel, Embarcadero Center, Bank America, Golden Gateway Center, Potlatch, St. Francis Hotel, and Wells Fargo were among the big contributors) and the continuing legacy of the 1978 city hall assassinations (typical was a "No on P" flyer with this not so subtle allusion: "We had district elections in 1978 and 1979. They turned into a nightmare.") determined the result.

The way supervisors are elected emerged again in the mid-1990s. In November 1994, voters passed Proposition L (initiated by Supervisor Terence Hallinan),* establishing a nine-member Elections Task Force (members

*Terence Hallinan, son of the legendary Vincent Hallinan, radical lawyer and 1952 Progressive Party presidential candidate, was elected supervisor in 1988, fol-

nominated by the mayor, Board of Supervisors, and registrar of voters) to study alternatives to the at-large system. The task force issued a report in April 1995 recommending that the supervisors place on the ballot a two-part referendum. One would ask whether to maintain the at-large system in its current form; the other would ask voters to choose among four alternatives, including cumulative (each voter getting as many votes as there are open seats, with votes to be cast in any way, including giving all votes to a single candidate) and preferential (allowing voters to rank candidates according to preference) voting systems—which could achieve similar representational aims as district elections without the need for the messy and conflict-filled process of drawing and establishing geographic districts. The task force was also mindful of recent U.S. Supreme Court decisions outlawing race as the principal basis for drawing legislative districts.

The supervisors rejected the task force recommendation and refused to put the issue on the March 1996 ballot. Instead, they placed their own two items on the November 1996 ballot: Proposition G (1970s district elections redux) and Proposition H (citywide elections, using the preference voting system studied by the task force). But although there was little overt opposition to Proposition H (it was the only ballot proposition not to have an argument against it submitted to the Voter Information Pamphlet), and it received widespread official endorsements (ranging from the Harvey Milk Democratic Club to the S.F. Police Officers Association to the Mexican American Legal Defense & Education Fund), it lost 56 to 44 percent. The consensus is that it was too complex, that voters did not understand it, and that in such situations people either vote against it or pass it over (nearly one-fifth of those voting in the November 1996 election didn't cast a vote for Proposition H).

---

lowing unsuccessful runs in 1975, 1977, and 1980. A typical colorful San Francisco political figure (nicknamed "Kayo" for his amateur boxing skills—which almost got him a berth on the 1960 U.S. Olympics team—as well as from his occasional extra-ring fisticuffs), Hallinan was elected district attorney in 1995, at the same time that Willie Brown was elected mayor, bucking the trend in criminal justice circles favoring hard-liners, and was narrowly reelected in 1999. A career defense lawyer (the State Bar earlier ruled him ineligible to meet its "good moral character" admission standards, based on numerous sixties civil rights and anti–Vietnam War arrests, plus a few apolitical brawls, but Hallinan challenged the ruling in court and won) elected to a prosecutor's role, Hallinan "believes prostitutes and minor drug offenders should not be jailed, . . . opposes the death penalty, . . . advocates greater gun control and . . . says he will work around California's '3 strikes' law by using it only against 'vicious, violent criminals.' " See Kenneth B. Noble, "Soft Steps in Agenda on Crime," *New York Times*, 18 January 1996; Thomas G. Keane, " 'Kayo' Hallinan Will Do His Fighting in City Hall Now," *San Francisco Chronicle*, 9 January 1989.

Proposition G—the return to the 1970s version of district elections, with eleven districts (but with quite different boundary lines) and a runoff provision—did pass, however, 57 to 43 percent, mandating the first election under the new system for November 2000.[35]

Feinstein's Reelection Campaigns

Although the Feinstein administration's policies regarding downtown development and its impacts on housing, transportation, and the urban environment generated substantial hostility in the neighborhoods, no strong opposition to her 1983 reelection bid had emerged. Then an unexpected event arose early that year, which made her reelection a foregone conclusion and in effect moved the election up from November to April.

In June 1982, Feinstein, long a foe of handguns, had introduced an ordinance, which the supervisors narrowly passed, banning unauthorized ownership of handguns in the city, a move not a little influenced by popular revulsion over the 1978 city hall assassinations. (San Francisco voters had approved, 60 to 40 percent, a 1982 statewide initiative requiring handgun registration, which was defeated by the state's voters, 63 percent to 37 percent.) Passage of the ordinance, the first such legislation by a major U.S. city, drew considerable opposition from the gun lobby all across California and the nation (plus positive publicity for the city from other quarters), and the California Court of Appeals later that year struck down the city ordinance, holding that regulation of firearms was an area preempted by the state.

Among the most vociferous opponents of the law was the White Panther Party, a small and not-easy-to-pigeonhole left/counterculture collective in the Haight-Ashbury whose various run-ins with the San Francisco Police Department had made news throughout the 1970s. At one point, their group house was burned down, an action the party attributed to the police. A long legal battle was fought over their occupancy of a forty-room house in the Haight, abandoned at the time they moved into it. The group's most notorious confrontation with the law came in 1975, when the police, who had been hassling them on a regular basis, picking up members no fewer than fifty-three times in the previous eighteen months, raided their commune without a warrant; warning shots were fired by some Panthers, and two members, leader Tom Stevens and Terry Phillips, spent three years in San Quentin as a result.

The group believed passionately in the right to bear arms and in self-defense. The original White Panther formation was established in the Detroit–Ann Arbor area in the late 1960s, as a white counterpart to the Black

Panthers, and was active in civil rights and Vietnam War protests. The San Francisco group organized free rock concerts in Golden Gate Park and ran a successful five-thousand-member alternative food distribution system, The Food Conspiracy. Their occasionally disruptive tactics, emphasis on publicity, and reluctance to participate in coalition politics or establish unified neighborhood positions on Haight-Ashbury issues led to a history of poor relations with other progressive formations in the neighborhood and city. An April 20, 1983, *Examiner* feature described them as a "difficult, principled group, avowedly communist and dedicated to working in the interests of poor people, as they see them."[36] (The two members convicted in the 1975 shoot-out incident could have avoided jail, had they agreed to probation, but refused to do so.)

The Feinstein handgun control ordinance, even though declared invalid by the state courts, spurred the Panthers in a totally unanticipated direction: They undertook to gather signatures on a mayoral recall petition, a move requiring voter signatures equal in number to 10 percent of those voting in the previous mayoral election. They chose to collect their signatures primarily in the city's gay neighborhoods, reasoning that gays, furious over Feinstein's recent veto of an ordinance passed by the supervisors granting fringe benefits to nonspousal domestic partners of City employees regardless of sex, would eagerly sign the petitions, irrespective of who the circulators were or their motives. And they were right. In a few months, twenty people gathered thirty-five thousand signatures, and the matter was on the ballot, a loose political cannon if ever there was one.

The recall election was set for April 26, 1983, and the dilemmas and ironies the situation created were monumental. Here was a group few in the city knew about or liked, motivated by an issue on which most progressive forces would take a different stand, and a recall effort with which many ultraconservative forces might agree, albeit for different reasons. Feinstein and her backers moved well and quickly to line up virtually every elected official and public figure against the recall, based not necessarily on support of her but on a combination of anti-Panther red-baiting, the city's stability and reputation, and "fairness." Those who opposed Feinstein politically had to choose between aligning themselves, implicitly or explicitly, with the White Panthers or with the mayor. That the recall could not prevail at the polls was pretty clear from the outset, so Feinstein opponents also had to decide whether they wanted to back a sure loser. In the end, as the April 6, 1983, *Bay Guardian* noted, "Most of the city's liberal establishment . . . rallied around a mayor many of them opposed on nearly every issue."[37] For progressives, it was a trap: They could either line up against the recall, hoping such a stance would not be interpreted as support for Feinstein, or they could back a losing horse, trying to create their own message to explain why the Panthers' recall move should be supported. The question really was not whether Feinstein would be recalled but what her margin of victory would be: Getting less than 55 to 60 percent of the vote would be seen as a clear signal she was weak and would encourage strong opposition the coming November; a walkaway victory would scare opponents off.

Feinstein's antirecall campaign was helped enormously by a friendly ruling on the part of the city attorney: that since this was not a candidate election, statutory limits on campaign contributions were inapplicable. And did the money then flow! Nearly half a million dollars came in within a few weeks, almost all from large corporate contributions garnered at a February fundraising dinner: $14,500 from the Shaklee Corporation's Good Government Fund; $10,000 each from Standard Oil of California, Bechtel Power Corporation, Bank of America, Southern Pacific, Pacific Telephone, Pacific Gas and Electric, Foremost McKesson; $9,250 from Transamerica Corporation; $5,000 each from Shearson–American Express, Dean Witter–Reynolds, Host International, and Duty Free Shoppers Ltd.; $4,000 from the Campeau Corporation of California; $3,000 each from Am Fac and the First Interstate Bank of California; $2,500 from Citicorp; and others as well.[38]

Based on analysis of the first $345,000 of the $600,000 Feinstein raised, 63 percent was accounted for by forty-eight contributions exceeding $1,000. ("The companies want stability in government. They want to make sure that there isn't a bad business climate in the city," said a Feinstein spokesperson.)[39] "No contributions on that scale have ever been made public in a campaign for a S.F. city office," observed the March 18, 1983, *Chronicle*. "Downtown officials seem genuinely angered and embarrassed for the city's image by the recall. But some also have confided privately that it makes sense to put money on the mayor during the recall that she is expected to win, rather than playing favorites among competing candidates in a regular mayoral election," the story went on to explain.

Credit for this phenomenal and immediate outpouring of cash was attributable to Feinstein's financier husband, Richard Blum; as the April 3, 1983, *Examiner* noted, "When Mayor Feinstein married Richard Blum three years ago, she gained a husband and political partner who is emerging as her ambassador to the City's corporate community, raising thousands of dollars in contributions for the mayor's recall campaign." (Interestingly, the City Charter allows a mayor to bill the City for expenses incurred in a recall campaign—although there appear to be no guidelines as to how much can be spent and reimbursed. Blum, in explaining Feinstein's reliance on big contributors, generously noted, "We could have billed the city. We decided we would just pass the hat and not ask the city to reimburse us.")[40]

The Feinstein campaign aimed at convincing voters that "the recall is a low blow, a sleazy move respectable citizens would do best not to be associated with."[41] The explicit and subliminal theme of her literature, billboards, and statements was that approval of the recall would be a victory for anarchy and chaos, that the forces of darkness (echoes of Jim Jones and Dan White) would prevail, that the city would be leaderless. Feinstein chose as her recall election campaign manager Clint Reilly, who had managed Quentin Kopp's 1979 mayoral race against her and was media advisor in the 1977 district elections victory ("Reilly said that he is a passionate partisan for his clients but he also is a flexible professional.")[42] As described in the *Bay Guardian*, "Reilly is subtly, deftly and cynically playing on a profound sense of unease that has its roots in this city's recent political history."[43] Feinstein labeled the recall, in doubtless carefully chosen words, "a guerilla attack on our system."[44] Feinstein's official statement on the recall, as printed in the Voter Information Pamphlet, focused on the Panthers as "radicals who have a history of confrontation with police and other authorities. Theirs seems to be a persistent battle against established authority." She noted that the two signers of the notice of recall petition had spent time in jail and stressed that "the pattern of White Panther activity is designed to undermine our institutions."

The *Sunday Examiner & Chronicle* editorial of April 2, 1983, intoned this theme:

> They [the nation and world] will be watching to see whether this community has lost its balance, its sense of responsibility, so that it drifts toward the status of a radical clown show rather than standing as a world-class city to which people everywhere may look for inspiration and example.

More to the point, the editorial continued:

> [If Feinstein is not returned], then a great reappraisal of San Francisco [will] begin all across this broad land. Potential investors in housing and everything else will have serious second thoughts. Employers, present and potential, will hesitate and wonder if this city is going over the deep end, into eventual rule by a gaggle of assorted radicalisms supported by countless voices of single-issue disaffection.

Other of the dailies' antirecall editorials stressed the impropriety of using the recall process so close to the time of a regular election and when no claims of corruption, malfeasance, or incompetence were involved. But San Francisco Tomorrow president Tony Kilroy, in a letter in the April 15, 1983, *Examiner*, pointed out the situational ethics of the newspaper's editorial writers: The *Examiner* had supported the unsuccessful August 1977 special election called by supporters of an initiative to repeal district elections just ten months after passage of the initiative that created the new system and four months before a regularly scheduled election at which the same issue could have been placed on the ballot without the need to spend $450,000 on a special election. And in August 1980, the *Examiner* editorially supported the initiative again placed on the ballot by district election opponents, also in a special election just four months before a regularly scheduled election, which initiative in effect recalled all eleven supervisors (by requiring them to run again if the initiative passed), six of whom had taken office just seven months before, and none of whom was accused of corruption, malfeasance, or incompetence. Cost or disruption in the city's operations were not important issues to the *Examiner*'s editorial writers when the question was getting rid of progressive measures.

The theme of civic embarrassment was brought home forcefully the Sunday before the election when CBS's *60 Minutes* did a segment on the recall, which stressed the city's kookier aspects, said little about most of the city's real problems, and managed to offend almost everyone in San Francisco officialdom. The *Chronicle*'s Larry Liebert noted, "One top city official said it was lucky the feature on the city's unconventional politics didn't air a week earlier—before last week's decision by the Democratic National Committee to hold the party's 1984 presidential convention there"[45] (see chapter 9). The show paid considerable attention to one Jack Fertig (aka Sister Boom Boom), part of a group of men who dress in full make-up and nun's habit and call themselves the "Sisters of Perpetual Indulgence." Running under his *nom de campagne* and accompanied by the slogan "Nun of the Above," he finished ninth in the 1982 supervisorial race, racking up twenty-three thousand votes in the process. (City election laws were subsequently amended to require persons running for local office to run under their legal names or names they have used for at least one year.) San Francisco voters seem to enjoy voting for colorful candidates: In the 1979 mayoral election, Jello Biafra, lead vocalist for the Dead Kennedys punk rock group, came in fourth out of ten candidates, garnering sixty-six hundred votes.[46]

Feinstein's game plan, as noted, was to get people to vote on the issue of the propriety of a recall election, rather than having to defend her four-and-a-half years in office. Even the Republican Central Committee backed the antirecall campaign. Real and current political issues were avoided. "She has steered clear of debates that the struggling pro-recall coalition has wanted on such issues as her downtown development policies and her moderate stance on rent control and condo conversions," as an *Examiner* story a week before election day summed it up.[47] She refused to debate opponents face to face, instead sending political allies to meetings to represent her.[48] The April 6, 1983, *Bay Guardian* reported, "Rarely does Feinstein's name appear on her campaign posters; nowhere is there any mention of specific policies or achievements. The focus is conservative, the tone sweet reasonableness, the appeal to the loyalty and good judgement of responsible citizens."[49]

The strategy was phenomenally successful. On April 26, she won, 82 to 18 percent, taking every voting precinct in the city save the Panthers' home precinct (which she lost by a single vote). Voter turnout was 45 percent. The pro-recall campaign hardly got off the ground. A small coalition of Feinstein opponents, formed as Citizens for a New Mayor—some housing activists, high-rise foes, and neighborhood groups (the San Francisco Tenants Union, San Francisco Tomorrow, the Victorian Alliance, Citizens for Representative Government, the Haight-Ashbury Neighborhood Council), gay groups (Harvey Milk Gay Democratic Club and the Stonewall Gay Democratic Club—the Alice B. Toklas Memorial Democratic Club was pro-Feinstein), San Franciscans for Public Power, Citizens to Stop the Sewer Tax, the San Francisco Libertarian Party—mounted a brave, vastly underfunded, and quite ineffectual "damage control" campaign, which stressed their various complaints against the administration, staying away totally from the handgun control issue, on which they disagreed with the White Panther position. The Panthers ran their own, rarely visible campaign, stressing their single issue. Together, the pro-recall groups spent $6,000, 1 percent of the nearly $600,000 spent by the mayor.[50]

The non-Panther pro-recall coalition felt that although Feinstein was going to prevail in any case, a substantial (say, 30–35 percent) pro-recall vote might encourage others to run against her in November and embarrass her on issues of substance like housing and downtown growth. While it seemed possible at the outset to pull off such a campaign, the conservative neighborhood forces, led by ex-supervisor John Barbagelata, could not stomach anything having to do with the White Panthers; the antihigh-risers were busy organizing for a November ballot initiative; the gay community cooled off a bit, realizing that Feinstein on balance was reasonably supportive of gay rights; and neither the housing groups nor anyone else could raise much money for a campaign.

A key element of the Feinstein campaign was her use of volunteers and the absentee ballot. Early on, she and her campaign strategists saw that even a big victory in a very low turnout election might be discounted. Her problem was how to secure a reasonably respectable turnout in a special, single-item election, particularly when polls showing her easy victory might lead supporters to stay at home. The August 1980 single-item election repealing district election of supervisors had drawn barely one-third of the city's registered voters.

The campaign therefore was divided into two elements: the traditional money-raising, money-spending professional job of getting out literature, putting up billboard signs, radio and TV ads, and so on, that Clint Reilly would run, and a parallel get-out-the-vote grassroots effort. For this latter strategy, Feinstein turned to Fred Ross, senior and junior. Fred Ross Jr., a former organizer for the United Farm Workers union, was itching to get back to organizing work. His father, the legendary Fred Ross Sr., had been one of the UFW's central organizers, using techniques he learned in his close relationship with the granddaddy of modern community organizing in the United States, Saul Alinsky. What the Rosses did was organize volunteers—brought together through the old UFW technique of house parties, to which volunteers invited their friends, and at which further house parties were organized, in chain fashion—who were assigned to distribute absentee ballots.[51] Under San Francisco law, any registered voter can vote via absentee ballot without having to give a reason. It was a technique used successfully by the Republicans at the state level in securing the surprise victory of State Attorney General George Deukmejian against Los Angeles Mayor Tom Bradley in the November 1982 gubernatorial race.

Feinstein's campaign workers, numbering seventeen hundred according to Ross's claims, fanned out all over the city, setting up at shopping centers and street corners, using ironing boards as stands from which to distribute campaign literature and absentee ballot forms (a colorful touch that gave rise to the image and esprit of "ironing board brigades"). In addition, nearly seventy thousand absentee ballots were mailed to every registered Republican in the city.[52] In the final election, just under one-third of the total votes came from absentee ballots; 89 percent of the absentee votes were against the recall. The 45 percent voter turnout was good for a special, single-item election. The figures were sufficient to amount to a tremendous, undisputed coup for the mayor. Looking to November and anyone brazen enough to oppose her, a cocky Feinstein boasted, "We'll cream 'em."[53] And in fact, Feinstein coasted to an easy, almost unopposed victory that November with nearly 70 percent of the vote.

It is amusing to compare Feinstein's reliance on absentee voting with the views she had expressed a mere half year earlier in the City's official Voter

Information Pamphlet opposing a June 1982 election measure pushed by Supervisor Harry Britt to allow local elections to be carried out entirely by mail ballots. Feinstein urged a "no" vote on the proposition (which lost, 70 to 30 percent) because it would "lessen individual responsibility for exercising, in private, behind the drawn curtains of a voting booth, the right to vote. Instead, mail-in ballots can give inordinate advantage to well organized special interests. The disciplined political action groups can line up their followers to vote in unison. . . . Voting is a personal matter, to be exercised freely in the privacy of the voting booth." Running an entire election via mail ballot likely increases total turnout, which is why the progressive Britt attempted to institute the change. Encouragement of absentee mailed ballots among selected constituencies, on the other hand, like Feinstein's, is a form of voter manipulation that can be used for any political purpose and requires only sufficient funds to use the fairly expensive computerized mailing lists now very much in vogue among campaign professionals.

While Feinstein's campaign stayed away from issues, in true politician style her post-victory claims trumpeted the overwhelming mandate her policies had received. Earlier, *Chronicle* political analyst Larry Liebert noted that "The only flaw in this masterful campaign strategy [limiting campaign debate to the propriety of using the recall process] . . . is that she can't honestly interpret a big victory over the recall as a vote of confidence in her policies."[54] But whether she could do so honestly or not, do so she did. As reported in the April 29, 1983, *San Francisco Progress:* "What the vote proved," [Feinstein] said, "was that people want hands-on management of this City, by a mayor who works seven days a week. It reflects success in turning a budget deficit into a surplus, in bringing down crime. I consider it a tribute to the fact that human services, and even our streets, are better than they were five years ago when I took this job."[55]

Claims aside, the recall election was an enormous and unanticipated political boon to Feinstein's career. The *Examiner's* Bill Mandel—presumably tongue-in-cheek—began his January 17, 1983, column, titled "Mayor's Little Helpers," just after the recall signatures were filed: "What clever political mind in Dianne Feinstein's office invented the White Panther Party? Who at the committee to reelect the mayor dreamed up the party's campaign to recall Feinstein?" Locally, it cleared the way for the November 1983 shoo-in. The national visibility it gave her was a factor in boosting her name as a serious Democratic vice presidential candidate the next year (see chapter 9).

The recall election also gave Feinstein what she never had before—a large and heterogeneous cadre of local volunteers. The *Chronicle*'s Larry Liebert noted, "The recall proved a political blessing because the mayor—a moderate who seldom inspired zealous admirers—came away with a winner's reputation and a long list of new downtown financial backers and neighborhood volunteers."[56] It also gave her new independent political power, as the *Chronicle*'s Guy Wright analyzed the post-recall political situation in San Francisco: "Before the recall, Feinstein was mayor by grace of the power brokers. Now she is a power broker herself. Before the recall, there was no Feinstein political machine. . . . Now she has a machine of her own."[57] Up to that point something of a political loner, Feinstein, by virtue of her recall campaign, was for the first time in close touch with the rest of the city's Democratic Party powers. Right after her election, Feinstein even offered to make her volunteers available to help Sala Burton in the special congressional election being held to replace her husband Phillip Burton, who had died suddenly two weeks before the recall.[58]

Not so happy was the recall story's ending for the White Panthers. Three months after the election, in another legal action against the Panther leader, Tom Stevens received an incredible eighteen-month jail sentence on two misdemeanor counts. Three other Panthers received sentences of three to twelve months. Eighteen months in jail for misdemeanor convictions is virtually unheard of. "The worst abuse of the judicial system I've ever seen in this town," said a former police inspector. "A year and a half for two misdemeanors? Dan White got only five years for killing the mayor and Harvey Milk," said a senior law enforcement official.[59] In the late 1980s, the White Panthers left the city.

One further fallout from the Feinstein recall campaign was voter passage of a charter amendment the following November, making recall elections far more difficult to hold, by raising the necessary number of valid signatures from 10 percent of those voting for mayor in the last election to 10 percent of all registered voters (the prevailing formula in all other California cities and counties). In this instance, the Panthers would have needed 37,707 rather than 19,357 valid signatures.

It is difficult to summarize the nearly ten years Dianne Feinstein ruled city hall, from 1978 to 1988. She clearly was a calming influence at a time when the city, virtually traumatized by the city hall assassinations and the Peoples Temple mass suicides, needed that touch. In terms of the transformation of San Francisco, her biographer, *San Francisco Chronicle* city editor Jerry Roberts, writes: "Feinstein . . . oversaw the greatest downtown building boom in city history" and quotes her saying, "San Francisco was never going to be an Italian fishing village. It was a corporate and service headquarters city. That remains its destiny." Between 1978 and 1987, office space in the city, virtually all in downtown high-rises, grew from 59 million square feet to 74 million square feet (see chapter 12). "When Feinstein left office," Roberts continued, "the *Chronicle* poll showed that citizens believed her greatest shortcoming had been the high-rise development issue. Frustrated by their inability to park, shop, or find affordable housing in the neighborhoods, more than 50 percent said she had ignored neighborhood problems at the expense of promoting downtown development."[60] However, Roberts concludes: "Immersing herself in detail and working long days, she established herself as one of the most popular mayors in the city's history, by paying passionate attention to day-to-day issues of providing government services."[61]* But a far less complimentary view of her performance is provided by Richard Sklar, at various times head of the Yerba Buena Center project in the CAO's office, general manager of the Public Utilities Commission, and chief of the City's mammoth wastewater treatment program: "She responds to whatever appears to be the crisis of the moment and makes cosmetic changes. Fussing over details is not the same as management."[62] One undisputed legacy is the $172 million budget deficit she left for her successor—in part attributable to increased spending requirements to deal with AIDS and homelessness, to expenditures related to voter-backed legislation increasing the salaries of City employees and eliminating some utility taxes, and to the downturn in the city's economy.[63]

Feinstein's Post-mayoral Career

Unable by law to run for a third term, Feinstein began searching for a different elected office. Her initial, highly ambivalent, focus was on the special April 1987 congressional election for the seat that unexpectedly came open with the death of Sala Burton, who had been anointed to take her husband, Phillip's, seat. At first, Feinstein indicated she would leave office early to run for this opening—an election most thought she could win easily—

---

*In a poll of experts (urban historians and other academic social scientists), rating more than seven hundred mayors who had served in the country's fifteen largest cities, Feinstein ranked thirty-first, putting her in the top 5 percent. See Melvin G. Holli, *The American Mayor: The Best and Worst Big City Leaders* (University Park: Penn State Press, 1999), 178.

but then she vacillated and finally issued a statement "end[ing] 48 hours of intrigue and maneuvering."[64] Her withdrawal opened the way for a mad rush of supervisors to enter the race—Harry Britt, Carol Ruth Silver, Bill Maher, Doris Ward—none of whom won when the remnants of the "Burton machine" decided to back Democratic Party fundraiser Nancy Pelosi, whom Feinstein (and Sala Burton, on her deathbed) endorsed.[65] It was a disappointing decision for the city's progressive forces (strong backers of Britt, who had become a highly visible figure on the national scene and, with nomination for this sure-thing Democratic seat, would have become the first openly gay person to be elected to Congress), especially since Pelosi, who had never held elected office, was at odds with much of the city's liberal politics: She had voted against the antihigh-rise initiative Proposition M in 1986 (see chapter 12); opposed adding vacancy controls to the city's rent control ordinance (see chapter 13); and as chair of the 1984 Democratic Convention Host Committee had censored several convention guide articles for mentioning controversial subjects like gay activism.[66]*

After leaving office in early 1988, Feinstein turned her attention to California's 1990 governorship race. She overcame an early and substantial lead by Attorney General John Van de Kamp to win the Democratic primary, but lost in the general election, 49 to 46 percent, to Pete Wilson, who returned to his state just two years after winning his second term in the U.S. Senate (a move dictated largely by the Republicans' desire to protect party interests in the 1992 reapportionment process).

During the 1990 race, husband Richard Blum's role as money man and campaign fundraiser from the business community took on even greater prominence in a statewide context. While Blum's personal contribution to the gubernatorial race was limited by law, there was no limit on the amount the couple was allowed to spend from their jointly held assets, and, according to a *San Francisco Examiner* account, "The couple will probably contribute between $1 million and $1.5 million. . . . That would be in addition

---

*In the subsequent decade and a half, Pelosi has moved considerably to the left, in the process becoming a congressional powerhouse. She appeared on the cover of the 6/13 August 2001 *Nation* magazine, and the accompanying article noted that she is "poised to become the most powerful woman in Congress [Democratic whip] . . . with one of the most progressive voting records in the House . . . with a very real possibility, perhaps in the not too distant future, of becoming Speaker of the House, and the certainty of inclusion on vice-presidential short lists for 2004" (John Nichols, "Is This the New Face of the Democratic Party?" *Nation* [6/13 August 2001]: 13–14). The following October, one was elected minority whip.

to the more than $300,000 that Feinstein and Blum already have contributed and to the $125,000 that Blum raised through June 30 via his wide network of business contacts."[67] A later report on that campaign indicated that "during 1989 . . . Blum raised $190,000, or nearly one-fifth of the cash collected by his wife. By lending her $1.3 million, Blum was responsible for nearly two-thirds of the money in Feinstein's campaign treasury. Much of Feinstein's outside money comes from executives and businesses with ties to the candidate or her husband."[68]* But there was also criticism that Blum—with an estimated net worth between $50 million and $100 million—had not dug deeply enough into his own pockets. (His close friend, San Francisco Airports Commission President Morris Bernstein, commented, "If I were in the business he's in [investment banking], I'd want my wife to be mayor or governor or senator. What I wouldn't give for that.")

Also during the 1990 gubernatorial campaign, Feinstein, the most visible female candidate in the nation, warmly embraced feminism, a notable departure from her earlier actions and expressed views.† As mayor, Feinstein's inner circle of top advisors was exclusively male; she rarely accepted invitations to speak to women's groups; refused to sign a Board of Supervisors' resolution commemorating the tenth anniversary of the *Roe* v. *Wade* abortion rights decision; slashed the budget of the City's Commission on the Status of Women; and thrice vetoed "comparable worth" pay equity legislation for City workers passed by the supervisors. Feinstein had publicly praised a 1984 federal court decision overturning a California statute—coauthored by then–Los Angeles Assemblywoman (now Congresswoman) Maxine Waters—requiring employers with five or more employees to give female employees up to four months' unpaid maternity

---

*A report by Robert B. Gunnison cites as an example of this connection Feinstein's strong support of the new Marriott hotel in Yerba Buena Center, the two thousand dollars this traditionally Republican firm gave to Feinstein in 1989, and the one thousand dollars she received from former Marriott executive Frederic Malek (no traditional Democrat either: Malek was a former Nixon administration official), at the time president of Northwest Airlines, for whom Blum helped raise $400 million in a buyout of the airline ("The Money Is Flowing to State's Gubernatorial Candidates," *San Francisco Chronicle*, 23 March 1990). See also chapter 8.

†In his article, "Some Feminists Question Feinstein's Commitment to the Cause" (*San Francisco Chronicle*, 26 May 1990), Jerry Roberts observed that most knowledgeable people regarded Attorney General John Van de Kamp as far more genuinely committed to feminist issues, quoting Congresswoman Barbara Boxer as saying "Van de Kamp is the best feminist in this race," and Feinstein's friend City Attorney Louise Renne as saying, "Frankly, John has always been more supportive of women's issues."

leave and reinstate them to the same or a comparable job. Feinstein's position: "I believe that women have the choice. If they make the choice for career and children, there is no question there are problems. But I don't think the work market has to accommodate itself to women having children."[69]

Pete Wilson's victory indirectly led to Feinstein's next, and successful, electoral bid for higher office. After becoming governor, Wilson appointed state senator (and former president of the California Association of Realtors) John Seymour as his senate successor, to fill his seat until the next general election. With the 1992 election featuring two open seats—the other to replace retiring Alan Cranston—Feinstein opted to run for the two remaining years of Seymour's senate term, leaving the six-year term race to be fought by Lieutenant Governor Leo McCarthy, Santa Monica Congressman Mel Levine, and S.F./Marin County Congresswoman Barbara Boxer (the eventual winner). Feinstein's opponents in the primary were Controller Gray Davis (subsequently governor) and, briefly, San Francisco attorney Joseph M. Alioto, son of the city's former mayor. When both Feinstein and Boxer won, the country's most populous state wound up with two women U.S. senators ("two Democratic Jewish mothers from the liberal San Francisco Bay Area," as Jerry Roberts characterized it)[70]—an occurrence then unparalleled in U.S. history, with Feinstein once again capitalizing on being a "born again feminist."[71] In 1994, she was reelected to a full six-year term, in a race against Republican Michael Huffington that set an all-time record for spending in a Senate campaign, with Huffington spending close to $30 million of his family fortune, Feinstein raising and spending $13 million.[72]* In 1998, despite the entreaties of President Clinton—related to California's importance to the year 2000 presidential race and the reapportionment fights following the 2000 Census—Feinstein chose not to run for governor, even though polls showed she would easily win both the primary and general election.[73] She overwhelmingly won reelection to the Senate, 56 to 44 percent, in November 2000 against liberal Silicon Valley Congressman Tom Campbell (and the Green Party candidacy of Medea Benjamin).

*Huffington's record was short-lived. In 1998, Democrat Al Checchi spent $39 million of his own money in a losing bid for his party's gubernatorial nomination in California. In 2000, Wall Street banker Jon Corzine spent $62 million of his own money in his successful Democratic Party race to succeed Frank Lautenberg as U.S. senator from New Jersey. In 2001, Michael Bloomberg spent $76 million of his own money to become mayor of New York.

The Post-Feinstein Mayors

As noted above, limited by law to two terms (not including the remaining years of George Moscone's term that she served), Dianne Feinstein was unable to run again for mayor in 1987. The lineup to succeed her included—from left to right, politically—State Assemblyman Art Agnos, City Attorney Louise Renne, Chief Administrative Officer Roger Boas (whose term expired at the end of 1986), and Board of Supervisors President John Molinari (who had Feinstein's endorsement). Renne dropped out early, and in the November election Agnos got 48 percent of the vote, Molinari 25 percent, Boas 22 percent.* Agnos then easily won the December runoff against Molinari, with 70 percent of the vote.

Art Agnos was a quite liberal politician (the only candidate of the four to endorse the antihigh-rise Proposition M in 1986) who put forth, in an eighty-two-page campaign booklet, "Getting Things Done: Visions & Goals for San Francisco," distributed to 200,000 households, a detailed presentation of his ideas, organized as forty-one goals, covering everything from "The Library," to "Fighting AIDS," "Transit First," "Encourage Small Business," "Preserve Public Housing," "Remove Abandoned Cars," "The Waterfront," "The Arts," and "Honor Labor." But, as noted above, he inherited from Dianne Feinstein a $172 million projected budget shortfall (the largest in the city's history); was surrounded, at the state and national level, by conservative/reactionary administrations; and during his administration stylistically changed from the participatory, grassroots way his campaign was run, to a secretive, wheeler-dealer mode, particularly around big projects like the new downtown stadium and Mission Bay. He came off as weak, indecisive, and confused and wound up sorely disappointing and angering his followers, even though his appointments—particularly to the Redevelopment Agency and Planning Commission—were excellent.[74] As San Francisco State political scientist Richard DeLeon harshly concluded about Agnos's term: "Progressive critics viewed Agnos as a bait-and-switch political con artist who got himself elected as a slow-growth progressive but

---

*Following his defeat, Boas dropped out of public life, save for the ignominious publicity he received less than a year later when he was indicted for and pleaded guilty to seven felony charges of statutory rape for patronizing a teenage prostitution ring (which scandal led to the indictment of thirteen others, including a San Francisco police officer). The sixty-seven-year-old Boas was fined $100,000 and ordered to do a year of community service work (picking up trash and cleaning graffiti under a sheriff's manual-labor program), as well as undergo psychiatric treatment. See David Dietz and Dave Farrell, "Boas Fined $100,000—Gets a Year of Work," *San Francisco Chronicle,* 19 November 1988.

then governed the city as a pro-growth liberal. They saw him as secretive in his deal making with business elites; inaccessible and nonconsultative in his relations with progressive constituencies; and mediocre at best in fulfilling his campaign promises. . . . Once elected, he gravitated instantly to the larger clumps of power that still survived in the city's fragmented polity. Faced repeatedly with budgetary crises, he made deals with the big corporations, local millionaires, and outside investors to bring fresh capital to the city."[75]

While Agnos was a true disappointment to his original supporters, he was a victim of bad luck as well, in terms of the deteriorating overall economic climate that gave him four straight years of revenue shortfalls and declining federal and state support, as well as a general sourness in the city's zeitgeist during the late 1980s. The *Examiner's* Bill Mandel labeled him "the Velcro mayor. . . . Everything sticks to him. People hold him accountable for the rotten weather this summer," and observed, "Most problems for which Agnos is blamed have their roots in the Dianne Feinstein administration."[76] After being defeated for reelection in 1991 (the first time since the early 1940s that voters dumped an incumbent mayor), Agnos was appointed to head the Region IX office of the U.S. Department of Housing and Urban Development, a position (with slightly altered title and duties) he held until the advent of the George W. Bush administration.

When Agnos ran for reelection in 1991, his opponents were another liberal, Supervisor Angela Alioto (the former mayor's daughter and Agnos's closest board ally); his police chief, political amateur Frank Jordan; former supervisor and former sheriff/assessor (to which post he had been elected in a special election just five months before) Richard Hongisto; and conservative Supervisor Tom Hsieh. The November election again gave no one a majority: Jordan got 32 percent (a surprise showing, as polls had placed him a distant third), Agnos 28 percent, Alioto 19 percent, Hongisto 10 percent, Hsieh 9 percent. In the December runoff, Agnos—whom neither Alioto nor Hongisto endorsed, and who by that time had been written off by most progressives—lost to Jordan (who received Hsieh's endorsement), 52 to 48 percent, largely via a record number of absentee ballots and the Asian-American vote.[77] In his campaign, Police Chief Jordan had stressed quality-of-life issues—homelessness, crime, and dirty streets in particular—squeaking in as a result largely of progressives' divisiveness, and aided to no small degree by heavy contributions from the business community. The conservative mood of voters was reflected as well in simultaneous November passage of a referendum rejecting the rent control ordinance the supervisors had recently passed (see chapter 13).

Rarely has a chief executive gotten off to a worse start than did Frank Jordan. Looking back over his first three months, a *New York Times* account had this to report: "After 100 days of Frank Jordan as Mayor, San Francis-cans are still debating whether his amiable but inexperienced governing style is refreshing or inept, and whether he is his own man or the pawn of his handlers. The early months of the Jordan administration have included some quirky appointments, botched dismissals and assorted blunders. The new Mayor concedes he has had a 'shaky' start. . . . So far the conventional wisdom, even among Jordan aides in private conversation, is that he is in-experienced, although well meaning. . . . "[78] The *Examiner*'s Bill Mandel quoted a City department head: "[Jordan's] like Reagan without the staff. He doesn't have a clue," and went on, "Judging by word from inside Jor-dan's office . . . the appearance of clueless paralysis isn't a crafty facade."[79] Political scientist Stephen McGovern noted, "Jordan quickly developed an image as a well-meaning neophyte, even a bumbler"—an image he was never able to shake off.[80] *SF Weekly* dubbed him "Mr. Magoo."

A bizarre but illustrative set of incidents from the early part of his term showed Jordan (as well as Richard Hongisto) at his worst. Jordan had as-tounded everyone by appointing Hongisto to his own former post as chief of police. Hongisto was widely known as someone whose views and record on social issues and law enforcement contrasted sharply with Jordan's: While sheriff, Hongisto had sported a peace sign on his badge, allowed his deputies to wear long hair and beards, and, as noted in chapter 13, even served time in jail for initially refusing to evict elderly Filipino residents from the In-ternational Hotel.* In the April 1992 street demonstrations that followed the Los Angeles verdict exonerating the police who beat Rodney King, Hongisto's police at first made some three hundred arrests, mainly for loot-ing. But at subsequent demonstrations, the police arrested some two thou-sand persons, half of whom were peacefully marching.† *The Bay Times,* a

---

*Hongisto's career had been quite colorful and mercurial: As a *Chronicle* account put it, "Hongisto never avoided controversy. He feuded with Mayor Joseph Alioto, inviting him to 'kiss my ass' when Alioto gave the Sheriff's Department a budget cut" (L. A. Chung, "Hongisto Challenged 2 Mayors," *San Francisco Chronicle,* 20 September 1991). Hongisto left San Francisco in 1978, shortly after the Interna-tional Hotel evictions, to become Cleveland's police chief under that city's new young, progressive mayor, Dennis Kucinich, but departed three months later, ac-cusing Kucinich of committing unethical acts that he refused to describe and label-ing Kucinich "fascistic." He returned to San Francisco for a brief period, but then left to become New York State Prisons Commissioner, a post he also left within a year to return once again to San Francisco, where he was elected supervisor in 1980. In 1990, he ran for city assessor and won, and had been on the job a mere three months when he accepted Jordan's appointment.

†A group of those arrested brought a class action suit against the City, and in January 1999 were awarded $1 million.

paper for the gay community, then ran a front-page doctored photo of Hongisto wielding his nightstick "in a lewd manner" (as the *New York Times* delicately put it; "a nightstick in his groin" was the *Washington Post*'s more precise description), and Hongisto apparently instructed several of his officers to remove the papers from various street racks.[81] A huge flap ensued, and the Police Commission summarily fired Hongisto, following which Jordan hinted he might rehire him.[82] "This prompted a city official who spoke under the condition of anonymity to say the mayor looked like a 'ditherer.' . . . Even allies have said the Hongisto episode revealed Jordan as a mayor who does not seem to be in charge."[83]*

Jordan, as had been expected, was thoroughly aligned with pro-development interests, and his appointments to key agencies—mainly Planning and Redevelopment—were polar opposites to those of his predecessor.[84] His four years were essentially a historical accident in the city's politics, a strange interlude "occasioned by intense anti-Agnos sentiments and factionalism on the left. . . . [P]opular disenchantment with Mayor Agnos' abrasive personality and progrowth initiatives fractured the progressive coalition, sabotaged his reelections campaign, and ushered Frank Jordan into office. . . . Plagued by lingering economic recession, declining federal and state assistance, repeated revenue shortfalls, ill-chosen staff appointments, and opposition from a liberal-progressive Board of Supervisors, the politically inexperienced Jordan had little to show for his four years as 'citizen mayor.' . . . Rather shy and reserved as a public figure, Jordan failed to develop a dynamic leadership style or an inspiring vision for the city's future."[85]

Jordan's successor—in many (but not all) respects, his diametric opposite—is a legendary figure, Willie Lewis Brown Jr., term-limited out of his powerful post as speaker of the California Assembly (a position he held for a record-breaking fourteen years), where he represented a San Francisco district for thirty-one years and built one of the country's more fabulous political careers, all the more notable given Brown's origin as a poor black from a small town in Texas.[86] Brown was one of the main targets of California's successful 1990 pro–term limits initiative campaign, mandating a maximum of three two-year terms for assembly members, two four-year terms for senators and other statewide elected officials: "Just think, when

---

*In a civil suit against Hongisto, *The Bay Times* was awarded fifty-six hundred dollars and its editor thirty-five thousand, and the City had to pay legal fees to the paper's lawyer.

term limits pass it will be, 'So long, Willie Brown,' " read one fund-raising letter.[87]*

Brown's competitors in the 1995 mayoral race included ex-supervisor Roberta Achtenberg, who had gone to Washington to be assistant secretary for Fair Housing & Equal Opportunity at the U.S. Department of Housing and Urban Development—the nation's highest openly gay appointed official;† once again, Supervisor Angela Alioto; and Frank Jordan, seeking re-election. The anti-Jordan candidates represented a choice among three quite different progressives, leading many observers to predict that the inevitable runoff election (since no one in this field would receive a majority on election day) would pit Brown against Achtenberg, splitting the progressive community along two of the city's principal fault lines: race and sexual orientation.[88] The predictions proved wrong, however; Jordan came in a very close second to Brown (the two getting 34.7 percent and 33.7 percent of the vote, respectively), Achtenberg third with 26.9 percent‡ (Alioto dropped out

---

*In April 1997, a federal district court overturned California's term-limit initiative (in the process, also overturning a 1991 California Supreme Court ruling that upheld the term-limits proposition), holding that while the new law's limit on consecutive terms was constitutional, the lifetime limit on the number of years a state-elected official can serve was impermissibly broad, depriving voters of the right to vote for candidates of their choice. By then, however, the assembly had been fully transformed, with every member elected since 1992 forced to retire by 1998—a metamorphosis that substantially increased the state's legislative representation by women, Hispanics, and Asian Americans. See B. Drummond Ayres Jr., "Term Limit Laws Are Transforming More Legislatures," *New York Times,* 28 April 1997. A three-judge Ninth Circuit U.S. Court of Appeals ruling later in 1997 upheld the district court decision, but the circuit, sitting *en banc,* then ruled otherwise, and in early 1998 the U.S. Supreme Court allowed that decision to stand. See Todd S. Purdum, "California State Term Limits Overturned by Federal Judge," *New York Times,* 24 April 1997; William Booth, "Court Voids California Term Limits," *Washington Post,* 8 October 1997, which observed, "One of the most famous targets of the initiative was flamboyant Assembly Speaker Willie Brown."

†Achtenberg's confirmation hearings brought out the expected condemnation from the Right, including Senator Jesse Helms's notable characterization of her as a "damn lesbian" (Anna Quindlen, "A Political Correction," *New York Times,* 13 June 1993). A fund-raising letter from the Rev. Jerry Falwell of the Liberty Alliance (successor organization to Falwell's Moral Majority) began: "President Clinton's nomination of Roberta Achtenberg, a lesbian, to the Department of Housing and Urban Development is a threat to the American family" (John Batteiger, "Bigotry for Bucks: The Right Is Pulling in Big Money by Targeting Roberta Achtenberg," *San Francisco Bay Guardian,* 7 April 1993).

‡Following her defeat, Achtenberg joined the staff of the San Francisco Chamber of Commerce as senior vice president of public policy, a post she still held as of early 2002.

prior to election day and backed Achtenberg), setting up a far neater choice for the December runoff, in which Brown beat Jordan handily, 57 to 43 percent, becoming the city's first mayor of color. And it was an exciting election: As the *Washington Post* reported it, "In an age of media politics, the San Francisco race is a glorious throwback. It is an intensely local exercise battled out not on the airwaves but at bus stops and train stations at peak commuting hours, in precinct walks and tea parties, at endless high school candidates' forums and late-night bar crawls. Residents expect to see their candidates in the flesh."[89] Brown's style was well captured in this *New York Times* account: "Mr. Brown was at his insouciant one-of-a-kind self as he made his announcement [of his mayoral candidacy] today at noon on the Peace Plaza in Japantown, one of the most politically important of San Francisco's many ethnic enclaves. He worked the crowd much as he has worked the assembly for the past three decades, glad handing, back slapping, sweet talking, quipping here, whispering there, and flashing his 1000-watt smile."[90]

Brown's long career in state government, where he demonstrated extraordinary legislative skills, was characterized by a mixture of quite progressive positions and actions on a range of social issues (racial justice, gay rights, safety net programs for the poor, social services, environmental protection, rent control, labor rights), offset by at least an equivalent amount of tawdry deal-making and distinctly unprogressive representation of corporate and development interests. "A *California Journal* poll released this month [February 1996] ranked him the smartest member of the assembly but 76th out of 79 members on integrity."[91] Stylistically flashy in all respects, from his ostentatiously expensive wardrobe to his fleet of top-of-the-line cars ("My body would reject a Plymouth"),[92] Brown was depicted as follows in a *New Yorker* profile: "A dapper and jaunty cricket of a man, Brown has long had about him a sportive, Cyrano-esque panache not unlike the raffish flair of the Bay City itself. . . . A San Francisco boulevardier of semilegendary swank, arraying himself in sleek three-thousand-dollar Brioni and Kiton suits and four-hundred-dollar Borsalino beaver fedoras, and collecting a fleet of, at times, nine cars, ranging from Jaguars to Porsches and Ferraris. . . ."[93]

Brown's name and career have been synonymous with money: He has been a genius at raising political contributions and doling out funds and other perks so as to maximize his power and influence.[94] "He has made perhaps his greatest mark by soliciting tens of millions of campaign dollars from oil, tobacco and other corporate interests. . . . It is how Brown has wielded . . . power and for whom—the wealthy as well as the poor, corporations as well as traditional liberal causes, and most of all, for Brown himself—that has made him a legend. . . . By 1994 Brown had become the nation's leading beneficiary of campaign money from the tobacco industry—$600,000 all told—five times more than Sen. Jesse Helms."[95] *

"Conflict of interest" simply is not in Brown's vocabulary: "Brown Paid as Southern Pacific Advisor While Handling Bills Benefitting Railroad" was a not atypical headline (this from 1984).[96] Brown's law practice while in the assembly consisted largely of lobbying for development interests before public agencies, with virtually no disclosure reports on these activities ("That's the way I make my living. I certainly don't make my living here in Sacramento.")[97]† As the *Examiner* understated it, "Some believe the most valuable commodity Brown has to offer clients is not his legal expertise but political power. He acknowledges some might hire him because of his position."[98] In the more direct phrasing of one San Francisco supervisor, "When the Speaker of the Assembly testifies on behalf of a huge corporation before the Board of Supervisors or the Planning Commission, it's pretty hard to say no."[99] "You are a sum total of who you are and you have to accept that," the speaker philosophized,[100] and "I need to work, I need to generate an income. If I could do that (drop the law practice) I would, because let me tell you, law practice is not a terribly enjoyable occupation. You have to deal with clowns who are in some cases exploiters, in some cases pure criminals, in some cases despoilers of the environment, in some cases first-class assholes."[101] Beyond distributing money to and withholding it from colleagues in the legislature, Brown was astute in manipulating other

---

*Such activities did not prevent the American Cancer Society from giving Mayor Brown a Humanitarian of the Year award, honoring San Francisco for becoming the first city to sue cigarette makers; *Newsweek's* account of this award gave $750,000 as the amount he has collected from "Big Tobacco" (David A. Kapland and Patricia King, "City Slickers," *Newsweek*, 11 November 1996).

†Brown of course is not alone in performing such double duty. In mid-2001, it was reported that a New York developer was told by San Francisco's port director that he should hire state senator John Burton as consultant in order to improve his firm's chances of winning a major waterfront development project (see Chuck Finnie, Jenny Strasburg, and Lance Williams, "N.Y. Developer Says Burton Was Touted for Lobbyist Job: S.F. Port Director Allegedly Urged Hiring," *San Francisco Chronicle*, 28 June 2001). Burton's efforts (for which he was paid forty-three thousand dollars) were unsuccessful, however, when the Port Commission decided to award the development contract to another firm, reportedly due to pressure from the master lobbyist, Willie Brown. (See Chuck Finnie, Jenny Strasburg, and Lance Williams, "Supervisor Rips Decision on Pier Deal: Leno Upset over Report S.F. Mayor Swayed Vote," *San Francisco Chronicle*, 31 July 2001).

effective powers of the speaker. In the late eighties, facing a threat to his speakership from a cabal of five conservative Democrats, "the speaker stripped the dissidents of committee chairmanships, big staff and parking spots, and banished them to offices just large enough for them to change their minds."[102] He also has played a role on the national scene, serving as national chair of Jesse Jackson's 1988 presidential campaign.

Elected to the assembly in 1964, Brown became speaker in 1980 in a maneuver that captured the essence of his political style. Harold Berman, a liberal Los Angeles assemblyman and majority leader (later elected to Congress in 1982) was backed for the speakership by Governor Jerry Brown, Cesar Chavez of the United Farm Workers, and other left-of-center notables. Willie Brown, "spying a political opening, announced he would be 'fair to agricultural interests' [a code phrase meant to appease the growers] and promised to support several GOP-sponsored bills. The Republicans moved to support Brown, who won the speakership with more GOP votes, twenty-eight, than Democrats, twenty-three."[103] While the Republicans doubtless underestimated Brown, expecting him to fall on his face, he was brilliant, and largely unprincipled, in using the full powers of the office to consolidate and maintain power. ("The Speaker [in California] is the closest thing in the world to the Ayatollah," he observed.)[104] A classic Brown move in 1994 echoed this earlier ploy. The 1994 elections gave the Republicans a two-seat majority in the assembly, but Brown engineered a forty-forty tie vote for speaker (leaving him in the post), getting a disaffected Republican to vote for him by appointing the dissident to chair a key committee. Even after he stepped down as speaker in June 1995 to run for mayor, Brown maneuvered to control the choice of his successor, assembling enough votes to elect a series of renegade Republicans, who agreed to preserve the Democrats' committee assignments and staff through the 1996 elections and even had Brown elected to the previously nonexistent post of "Speaker Emeritus," with powers to be granted to this new "office-holder" by the new friendly speaker.* "In a stunning display of political power, Mr. Brown, a

---

*Brown's classic rewards scheme provided several renegade Republicans from the assembly shenanigans with payoffs after he became mayor. Brian Setencich, a Republican assemblyman from Fresno, whose political career went into a tailspin after siding with Brown during this power struggle, was hired as a special assistant in emergency communications for the city (at a salary of $80,571). Setencich was subsequently indicted by a federal grand jury for allegedly taking a bribe five years earlier while a member of Fresno's city council; although acquitted on that charge, he was convicted of tax evasion and served four months in a halfway house (during which time he collected full City salary). Similarly, Paul Horcher, a Republican assemblyman from Los Angeles County who also sided with Brown, was rewarded

Democrat, not only chose his own successor, but in so doing chose someone from the other party and the other sex and the most obscure back bench."[105] John Jacobs, the late political editor for McClatchy Newspapers, perceptively summarized a major motor force in what makes Brown tick: "Willie Brown's life is about a black man being smarter, harder-working and better skilled, and rising to tremendous power in an entirely white world."[106] (See fig. 10.)

Brown's lobbying activities on behalf of developers were particularly effective in San Francisco. "The litany of his achievements as an attorney working for major downtown firms is staggering," concluded one of the *San Francisco Bay Guardian*'s many attacks on Brown.[107] He was the attorney who: secured City permission for demolition of the City of Paris building—a major losing historic preservation fight—on behalf of Neiman-Marcus; helped developer Gerald Hines win City approval for his many projects; helped remove obstacles to the Pier 39 Underwater World development by carrying a bill in the legislature benefiting Golden Gate Park's Steinhart Aquarium, which led the aquarium to drop its opposition to the new fish tank (a move that led to a State Bar investigation of Brown, which produced no negative findings);[108] worked for Olympia & York smoothing the path for its Yerba Buena Center plans; played an influential role in defeating the first (1983) Proposition M antihigh-rise initiative; and aided the Mission Bay developer. Some of these activities involved appearing in person before local agencies, but as speaker, observed the *Bay Guardian*'s Craig McLaughlin, "[Brown] instead works by telephone, placing calls to supervisors, mayors and board members. Another specialty is setting up meetings."[109]

Brown's election to lead the city certainly made a big initial media splash: a cover story in *Newsweek* (November 11, 1996); a *New Yorker* feature (October 21–28, 1996); a fashion photo spread in *Esquire,* a *People* magazine feature ("No Mere Mayor," June 24, 1996); a long, fawning valentine in the

---

with a city hall job, first working as Brown's liaison to the Board of Supervisors, then as an executive in Parking and Traffic; after that he was placed in charge of the City's Office of Solid Waste Management (at a salary of $107,976). According to the *Chronicle* account, "Since Horcher took charge, critics have complained that the office has been plagued with mismanagement, hiring irregularities and incompetence. In 1997, the office was roiled by allegations of racial harassment. Staff member Martha Diaz filed a complaint alleging that Horcher had forced her to quit because she refused to tolerate ethnic slurs by Horcher's top assistant and former Sacramento aide, Ron Brand." See Lance Williams and Chuck Finnie, "Willie Brown, Inc.: How S.F.'s Mayor Built a City Based on 'Juice' Politics," *San Francisco Chronicle,* 29 April 2001, and "Mayor's Patronage Army: Brown Fattens Payroll with Loyalists, Colleagues, Friends," 30 April 2001.

May 15, 1996, *Washington Post* "Style" section; a phone call from President Clinton at Brown's swearing-in ceremony (held at Yerba Buena Gardens), in which the president told the mayor, "You're the real Slick Willie" ("No Mere Mayor," *People* magazine, 24 June 1996, 105). The man has style and knows how to please crowds and get publicity—for example, a mass "marriage" ceremony of 175 gay couples at which Brown officiated ("I now pronounce you domestic partners"), symbolic marriage certificates and all, marking the City's same-sex marriage law.[110] He also has a terrific sense of humor: When the list of President Clinton's White House overnight guests came out that included Brown, he told the *Washington Post* that "he passed on the Queen's Bedroom in favor of the Lincoln bed because 'although the allure for my constituents was somewhat tempting, I went with the cat that freed me.' "[111] He made some striking early appointments, including the city's first Chinese American police chief and two African American deputy chiefs and the first African American fire chief (a man who had been a leader in a decade-long legal battle challenging race and gender discrimination in the city's overwhelmingly white Fire Department).

But running a city is a very different job from being commander-in-chief of a state legislative body, as Art Agnos (and to a lesser extent, George Moscone) proved, and Brown knows this. He once dismissed the mayor's job, saying "street lights, dog-doo and parking meters are not my cup of tea."[112] San Francisco, as other chapters in this book have shown, is a city beset with the standard litany of urban problems and without sufficient resources to deal with them. *Newsweek*'s 1996 cover story concluded: "The fact remains that his tangible accomplishments so far are modest relative to the wave of good feelings his administration has generated." The *New Yorker*'s 1996 review of Brown's initial efforts noted:

> In truth, after not quite a year there seems little more to measure Brown's mayorship than simply its effervescence. San Francisco is still faced with the same obdurate maze of troubles that beset many other of the country's cities: a deteriorating infrastructure of services like public transit; decaying public housing; homelessness; a pathology of drugs and crime; an overburdened school system; and a health-care system critically strained—especially, in San Francisco's case—by a mounting weight of AIDS patients. . . . By late summer Brown had still managed only glancing moves, for the most part, against the complex of plights that San Francisco shares with other cities. . . . For the time being, Brown has found that "You don't even have to be delivering if people have just the perception that you're really trying—they'll stay with you."

This is a very iffy proposition in the long run. A particularly troubling and telling event was Brown's sudden cancellation of a planned summit on the city's egregious homelessness problem (see chapter 13), asserting that the problem was "unsolvable."

Brown himself insightfully captured the intractability of the city's problems, in comparison with politics at the state legislature level: "To make things happen in the legislature was simply to move bills. The only thing that has to be done is contact the majority of every committee, and I appointed them all. And the end effect the legislation has is never measurable. That's a walk in the park by comparison with trying to get Muni to work, or to solve the homeless problem. The variables are not controllable, cannot be influenced. . . . What effect a program for Muni has is measurable *instantly.* 'Cause either the bus moves on time or it doesn't."[113] By late 1996, housing advocates were furious with Brown for deal making that ran counter to his earlier commitments to support the end of vacancy decontrol of rents, and they held a raucous protest that led to nine arrests; as well, those concerned with police brutality were highly critical of Brown's appointed Police Commission for failing to discipline an officer involved in a highly charged case involving an African American who died while in police custody.[114]

Before long, the news accounts were headed, "For the Mayor by the Bay, the Honeymoon Is Over" (*New York Times,* March 5, 1998),* "Willie Brown Besieged" (George F. Wills's column, *Washington Post,* November 7, 1999), and "San Franciscans Tire of the Life of the Party" (*New York Times,* December 1, 1998). This last account, by reporter Evelyn Nieves, noted that only three of ten voters in a recent *Chronicle* poll said they were inclined to vote for Brown again.

> San Franciscans are upset . . . with Mr. Brown's seeming inability to make the buses and trains run on time or to get the homeless off the streets. And they are upset at downtown traffic jams, a lack of public parking, litter, mediocre schools and the Mayor's "arrogance." . . . Mr. Brown's glamour and glitz have begun to grate on a city where homelessness is so prevalent and two-thirds of the residents are renters who may never be able to afford to buy in San Francisco's exorbitant housing market. . . . Then there are those who are disenchanted with the machine-style politics Mr. Brown brought with him from the assembly, where backroom wheeling and dealing was the norm.

*Reporter James Brooke goes on to say, "After walking on air for much of his first two years as mayor, the exuberant and elegant Mr. Brown is losing altitude."

Some of these criticisms, of course, are not too different from those made of recent former mayors, such as Dianne Feinstein and Art Agnos.

Brown, needless to say, is neither self-effacing nor pessimistic. To the *New Yorker*, Brown summed up some key aspects of the city's future—possibly excessively roseate on the first, racial observation (to say nothing of the second):

> [Brown] noted, San Francisco is graced with two special differences. The first is its apparent exemption from the racial fissures that are a fundamental distress of other cities. "The rest of the country lives separate and apart, but in San Francisco you can observe around the streets people of every color living together—not just on the job sites, not just in the schools, it happens in housing, literally every aspect of life here," Brown said. . . . He didn't neglect to add that the second special grace attending San Francisco's potential for reinvigoration is Willie Brown himself.[115]*

The 1999 mayoral election was one of the most dramatic and interesting in the city's history. An embattled Willie Brown—running for his final four years (term-limited out of his municipal office as he had been from his state office)—faced, as his principal opponents in a fourteen-person field, Frank Jordan, trying to win his seat back, and Clint Reilly, the ubiquitous political consultant for campaigns of all stripes (including manager for Jordan's 1991 winning effort) now turned candidate. Both men were considerably to the right of Brown and straight white males. Then, all of twenty days before election day, Board of Supervisors president Tom Ammiano announced he was a write-in candidate. (One interpretation is that he reversed his earlier decision not to run after being disturbed by the nasty tenor of the campaign; another was that he planned this move all along, in part to avoid the need to raise lots of money and involve himself in the unpleasantries of the campaign.)† Whatever his motives and decision-making pro-

---

*Exaggerated laudatory characterizations flow easily off the lips of Brown's friends as well: this, from Reverend/about-to-be-ex-Supervisor Amos Brown, at a Grace Cathedral interfaith service celebrating the mayor's second inauguration: "Rev. Brown recalled that H. G. Wells once said there were six great figures in history, among them Jesus and Buddha. 'I'd like to add a seventh son of greatness—one Willie Lewis Brown, Jr.' " (Ilene Lelchuk and Rachel Gordon, "Inauguration: Mayor Commences His Second Term," *San Francisco Examiner*, 9 January 2001).

†*Examiner* columnist Rob Morse articulated the latter view: "But Ammiano saved money, kept his name unsullied . . . and escaped being trashed or closely examined. If you knew the wily likes of Reilly and [Jack] Davis [Brown's campaign consultant] were lying in wait for you, you wouldn't want to let them have months to shoot at you. You would take cover behind a wall of indecision as long as possible, like a good last-minuteman, then you'd let them have it" ("Milk's Gone—Got Ammiano?" *San Francisco Examiner*, 4 November 1999).

cess, Ammiano's entry was a bombshell and totally changed the dynamic of the 1999 mayoral campaign.

Tom Ammiano was a former San Francisco public school teacher, the first such to come out (1975) openly as gay (and so featured in an *Examiner* profile). He then ran twice, unsuccessfully (1980, 1988) for the School Board, eventually (1990) winning and later (1992) becoming board chair. Next stop was the Board of Supervisors and its chairmanship. And somewhere along the way he moonlighted as a stand-up comedian. Ammiano's politics are clearly to the left of Brown's on many issues—most notably development/housing/gentrification and its impact on the city. Described as "stand[ing] virtually no chance of winning" in a *Washington Post* article on the election,[116] the very popular Ammiano galvanized voters—mainly younger people on the left—and pulled off the almost unheard of feat of coming in second as a last-minute write-in, beating out both Jordan and Reilly (who spent $4 million of his own money—by one count, $140 per vote).[117] However, Reilly should not be counted out—his high-profile activities in 2000 with respect to the Hearst Corporation's purchase of the *Chronicle* (see chapter 2) and his bankrolling of the 2000 Proposition L office growth control campaign (see chapter 12) suggest he has in mind a future race.

Ammiano's successful last-minute campaign—in which he spent just twenty-five thousand dollars but amassed a large and enthusiastic army of largely young, Generation X volunteers, most of whom had earlier decided to sit out the campaign—forced a run-off with Brown. (One expression of the base he organized: According to thirty-four-year-old Kim Alexander of the California Voters Foundation, "I heard that when Ammiano announced he would run for mayor, it took about three hours for that information to travel through The City via e-mail.")[118] The November results gave Brown 39 percent of the vote, Ammiano 25 percent.

The six-week campaign between election day and the December run-off election was exciting and revealing, but Ammiano never really had a chance. Brown's money and contacts just were too much. He brought in stars like Jesse Jackson and David Dinkins, was endorsed by Governor Gray Davis and Senators Dianne Feinstein and Barbara Boxer, even drew on President Clinton (who, on his way to the World Trade Organization meeting in Seattle, held a fundraiser for the Democrats' upcoming election campaign but "us[ed] the opportunity to cheer on embattled Willie Brown," and recorded radio commercials and telephone voice messages—which went to sixty-five thousand voters—on Brown's behalf during the November general election).[119] Brown (aided mightily by his soft-money supporters) raised a record-breaking $5.5 million for both phases of his campaign, about half "independent spending by business, labor and Democratic groups . . . skirt[ing] The City's tight campaign contribution limits."[120] Among the complex, indirect, and hard-to-trace "independent" contributions to aid the Brown campaign—reporting requirements are such that much of this information does not need to be filed until months after the campaign—were $22,600 from the Building Owners and Managers Association; $400,000 from San Franciscans for Sensible Government (an independent committee formed by business lobbying interests); $300,000 from various labor organizations; $30,000 from the state Democratic Committee; $200,000 from the Alice B. Toklas Lesbian and Gay Democratic Club; $40,000 from the Golden Gate Restaurant Association; $90,000 from SKS Investments (a developer of live-work studios); and $30,000 from California Realtors PAC. Ammiano's total expenditures for the two phases of the campaign were a meager $300,000, including a measly $18,000 in soft money from independent sources.[121] Brown got scads of local political endorsements (most of which were solicited when his only opponents were Reilly and Jordan). And for the precinct-walking and get-out-the-vote drive on and preceding election day, his friends in Sacramento sent over legislative staff members—150 was the reported number—as volunteer campaign workers, who were provided with four nights at the San Francisco Hilton, meals, and a party.[122] Brown swamped Ammiano, 60 percent to 40 percent, in a hard-fought election that brought out a higher voter turnout than the November general election.

The campaign both revealed a lot about present-day San Francisco and is likely to have some nontrivial reverberations for the coming years. It was an "only in San Francisco" political event, pitting possibly the country's most adroit and successful African American politician against a colorful radical, who, if elected, would become the first openly gay mayor of a major U.S. city. And yet the principal dividing line really turned out to be generations and class.* Having a mayor of color was no big deal in multiracial, progressive San Francisco. And gays had established themselves politically in the city some time ago. (In fact, the major gay political groups were divided: The Alice B. Toklas Lesbian/Gay Democratic Club endorsed Brown, who had a long and distinguished record supporting gay rights; one-upping

---

*"Polls taken just before the Nov. 2 election showed that 56 percent of voters under age 30 supported Ammiano. One-fourth of that group said they support Brown. Among voters 65 and older, just 6 percent supported Ammiano while 45 percent supported Brown" (Ilene Lelchuk, "Generation Gap in SF Mayor Race," *San Francisco Examiner*, 9 December 1999).

them in the naming category, the Harvey Milk Lesbian, Gay, Bisexual, Transgender Democratic Club endorsed Ammiano.)

Mayor Brown moved to the right during the runoff in order to capture the one-third of the city's electorate who had supported Jordan and Reilly (although Reilly endorsed Ammiano). He sought and received support from the local Republican Party* as well as from landlord groups such as the San Francisco Apartment Association—the latter related to his support of a controversial proposal, introduced by the rental property owners, to study the City's rent control law, a move seen by tenant advocates as the first step to weakening or abolishing this safeguard. Ammiano constantly stressed the downsides of gentrification, holding himself out as the champion of neighborhoods, inveighing against chain stores and big box stores. He also introduced and worked hard to pass a "living wage" ordinance that would guarantee every worker employed by a City contractor or by businesses that lease property from the City at least eleven dollars an hour, plus benefits (subsequently enacted, but at a lower level—see chapter 13). Ammiano also pushed the image of Brown as a deal maker, beholden to development interests, a machine politician, antagonistic to citizen participation.† A related charge was Brown's undermining of neighborhoods and neighborhood-

---

*"In one of the most amazing twists yet to San Francisco's crazy mayoral election, the county Republican Central Committee voted last night to endorse the reelection of its longtime archenemy, Mayor Willie Brown . . . the man whom California Republicans have long reviled as the very symbol of errant Democratic liberalism" (Edward Epstein, "Republicans Grit Teeth, Back Brown," *San Francisco Chronicle,* 9 November 1999).

†In mid-2001, the *Chronicle* published an extraordinary five-part series detailing, in what some regarded as overkill fashion, Brown's brand of public sector/private sector politics as mayor. The titles *(seriatim)* of the five articles (published on 29, 30 April, and 1, 2, 3 May 2001, and written by reporters Lance Williams and Chuck Finnie) give a flavor of the bombardment: "Willie Brown, Inc.: How S.F.'s Mayor Built a City Based on 'Juice' Politics"; "Mayor's Patronage Army: Brown Fattens Payroll with Loyalists, Colleagues, Friends"; "Time and Again, Brown's Allies Win the Bid: Many Contractors Have 'Juice' with Mayor—Critics Say It's No Coincidence"; "Gusher of 'Soft Money' a Bonanza for S.F. Mayor"; "Brown's City Hall Is Politics As Usual Despite Election [of new anti-Brown district-based Board of Supervisors]: New Board Has Little Effect, So Far." Among other accusations, the articles noted the creation of some 350 new mayoral "special assistant" jobs with an annual payroll topping $45 million, and hundreds of millions of dollars in City contracts, development deals, subsidies, and grants going to bidders who are Brown's associates or have retained Brown's associates as lobbyists or consultants. Publication of the series led to a protest demonstration outside the *Chronicle* building, charging the paper with bias against African Americans. See Dan Evans, "Crowd Protests Chronicle's Expose on Mayor," *San Francisco Examiner,* 31 May 2001.

serving small enterprises—what George Will referred to as the "Starbuck-ization, Blockbusterization and Rite Aidization of the city . . . "[123] Brown for his part pressed the image of Ammiano as too divisive, too radical, some-one unable to get his proposals through the Board of Supervisors. (Ammi-ano in fact presided over a board, six of whose eleven members had been appointed by Brown; in several instances, when thwarted by his colleagues, Ammiano succeeded in bringing the matter to the voters in the form of an initiative, which passed.)[124] "Mr. Brown hammered Mr. Ammiano with a conservative-sounding barrage of complaints. Mr. Ammiano, he said, was an inexperienced free spender who would not forge a consensus among the city's competing interests and would send developers running scared."[125]

Although Ammiano lost, his last-minute campaign produced "a new po-litical machine in town, composed of tenant activists, gays and lesbians, en-vironmentalists and the more progressive elements in labor."[126] As *Exam-iner* columnist Rob Morse put it, "There's a feeling of crusade to Ammiano's campaign that's invigorating in a city where bohemians are being pushed out by newcomers in cars from Bavaria, and the demand for social change has been replaced by a demand for spare change."[127] To an extent, the 1999 mayoral runoff embodied class warfare, San Francisco style: "The divide be-tween haves and have-nots is pulling the city apart," as a *Washington Post* feature on the election summed it up; "Ammiano is plugging into these feelings. Asked his three main issues, Ammiano replies, 'housing, housing, and housing.' "[128] Again Rob Morse, commenting perhaps a bit over-optimistically on Ammiano's post-election party: "There was that high feel-ing of fellowship in a high cause we used to have at demonstrations. These folks actually thought they were going to win. . . . Ideals are back. The neighborhoods have been put out front. The Internet generation got wired on politics, not just caffeine."[129]

A year later, the November 2000 second-time election of supervisors by districts—a reform championed by Tom Ammiano—clearly manifested his longer-term impact and undercut Brown enormously. What Willie Brown's politics and political legacy will be, as played out during the remainder of his second and last term, remains to be seen. And what role he will play, come 2004 when he no longer is mayor (he will be sixty-nine years old then), also is up for grabs. (A December 2000 *Chronicle* story was headed, "Willie Brown Scouts Out Job as State Democratic Chair." In mid-2001, Brown hinted that he would try to return to the state legislature—this time as a state senator. And a new round of late fatherhood also is upon him— "Da Mayor, 66, Says He'll Be a Dad Again," headlined a January 19, 2001, *Chronicle* story—although Brown said he has no plans either to divorce his current wife, from whom he's been separated for twenty years, or to marry the baby's mother, his chief fund-raising coordinator.)

One thing is certain: Come January 2004, Willie Brown will not go quietly into the night.

District Elections Redux

Election of a new district-based Board of Supervisors in 2000, mandated by Proposition G of 1996, turned into something of a rerun of the Brown-Ammiano mayoral race of the year before, only this time with Ammiano the clear winner. As with the first round of district elections, it started off as a free-for-all: eighty-seven candidates running for the eleven seats, seventeen in (the new) District 6 alone (part of the Mission and Potrero Hill, South of Market, Hayes Valley, the Civic Center, and downtown). Three of the sitting supervisors were out of the game entirely: Sue Bierman and Barbara Kaufman term-limited out, Leslie Katz a voluntary dropout due essentially to the interplay of housing costs with strategic planning (she lived in Bernal Heights, the same district as Tom Ammiano, who was sure to beat her, but "I couldn't afford to move [to District 6, her announced plan] . . . I'm living on debt").[130] For several others, the expected strategic relocation did occur, the most egregious instance of which involved Amos Brown, who moved from his Ingleside Terrace residence (owned by the Third Baptist Church, where he is the minister) to a house he owns in the Oceanview neighborhood, where he felt he had a better shot, but in the process evicting a sixty-four-year-old woman, her disabled son, and two-year-old grandson—an event that housing activists loudly decried, especially given Brown's past antitenant positions. The evicted family has sued Brown (who, after failing to win reelection apparently did not move back to his house; as of mid-2001 the civil suit still is pending).[131] In only one district did someone run unopposed: incumbent Gavin Newsom in District 2 (essentially, Pacific Heights). While Tom Ammiano had some token opposition in District 9 (Bernal Heights and parts of the Mission), he was a clear shoo-in. Several previously significant figures in the city's political life—notably, ex-Sheriff/Police Chief/Assessor/mayoral candidate/Supervisor Richard Hongisto and ex-Supervisor Carol Ruth Silver—did especially poorly.

As could easily have been predicted, December runoff elections were required in nine of the eleven districts, as no one there received more than 50 percent of the first-round vote. In virtually every case, there was a Brown-backed candidate and an Ammiano-backed candidate, so the supervisorial election became a replay, by proxy, of the previous year's political war. Money again entered the picture in a big way, largely through "independent" soft money contributions. A campaign reform measure passed overwhelmingly by the voters in 1998 established a voluntary limit of seventy-five thousand dollars in direct candidate expenditures for the general election, twenty thousand dollars for the runoff, but all candidates had to agree to abide by it; in fact, in most districts, at least one candidate chose to ignore the limit, thus freeing all of his/her opponents to spend more as well. The Brown-backed candidates, as to be expected, were the principal beneficiaries of the soft-money funnel (a provision of the campaign reform measure abolished the spending cap if soft money expenditures—which have no upper limit under the law—exceed 25 percent of the seventy-five-thousand-dollar limit). Such "outside" funds, intended to support "party-building" activities, are used for everything: signs and billboards, mailings, field operations, opposition research. As one account summed it up, "For candidates struggling to stay within the voluntary cap, the soft money can be a godsend. For their opponents, it can cause a lot of damage, because the soft money often pays for attack pieces."[132] San Franciscans for Sensible Government (the business lobbying group) once again was a key funder, using dollars supplied by corporations such as the Gap (fifty thousand dollars), Chevron (fifty thousand dollars), and Bechtel (ten thousand dollars).[133] Other contributors included the Building Owners Association (twenty-five thousand dollars), Forest City Development—the folks seeking to place Bloomingdales, a hotel, and shopping mall on the old Market Street Emporium site (fifty thousand dollars). And Joe O'Donoghue's Residential Builders Association (see chapter 13) raised $235,000 before the general election, with an additional $1.5 million pledged for the run-offs.[134] As should be obvious, almost of all this soft money—as well as much of the money for the candidates' direct expenditures—came from outside the supervisor's own district. Among the eighteen persons in the December runoff, only two (Aaron Peskin in District 3 and John Shanley in District 4) reported that the majority of their money came from within their districts. The soft-money system is about as antithetical to accountability as can be: Such contributions are usually organized outside the city, the candidates are not required to report activities promptly to the City's Ethics Commission, and funds are routinely transferred through a series of committees that disguise their original source.[135] These financial facts of political life of course severely undercut one major argument for the district system: that it will make representatives more beholden to their neighborhood constituencies, less so to outside interests.*

But—welcome surprise—in the end, and revealingly, this time money wasn't the kingmaker. "Low-budget campaigns that focused on grass-roots organizing thumped traditional—and often negative—approaches that focused on direct mail and phone banks."[136] In a series of upsets, the Ammiano-backed candidates—Jake McGoldrick (District 1), Aaron Peskin (District 3), Matt Gonzalez (District 5), Chris Daly (District 6), Sophie Maxwell (District 10), and Gerardo Sandoval (District 11)—all won. Along with Leland Yee, a Brown critic (District 4), and Ammiano himself, who of course was reelected and in January 2001 was reelected board president, there was a strong, veto-proof anti-Brown majority on the board. "I think everyone ran with one thing in common," said Supervisor Gavin Newsom about the December run-off. "He or she who hated Willie Brown the most won." It produced a totally different scenario from what Willie Brown dealt with during his first term (six of whose members Brown had originally appointed: Alicia Becerril, Amos Brown, Leslie Katz, Mark Leno, Gavin Newsom, and Michael Yaki). The board elected in 2000 has seven "rookies" and some relative youngsters (Chris Daly at twenty-eight, Gavin Newsom at thirty-three, Matt Gonzalez at thirty-five); just before the December runoff election, Gonzalez publicly dropped out of the Democratic Party and registered as a Green Party member, a move newly elected school board member Mark Sanchez also announced a month later.[137] By lot, Ammiano as board president and the five members from odd-numbered districts (Matt Gonzalez, Tony Hall, Jake McGoldrick, Aaron Peskin, and Gerardo Sandoval) drew four-year terms. Chris Daly, Mark Leno, Sophie Maxwell, Gavin Newsom, and Leland Yee have two-year terms. And for the 2003 election there likely will be a need to redraw district boundaries as a result of Census-mandated redistricting, given the city's 7.3 percent population increase in the 1990s.[138]

It is beyond doubt that Brown was the main issue in the runoffs. How this plays out in the remaining portion of Brown's second term will be fascinating to watch. In early April 2001, things were looking a little dicey, as

*Daniel Evans's article, "Follow the Candidates' Money . . . Everywhere" (*San Francisco Examiner*, 4 December 2000) contains this rather perverse, self-justifying view from losing District 11 candidate Amos Brown (who raised just 1 percent of his campaign war chest from the district he had newly moved to: "When you have a lot of money coming in from within your district, you have a tendency to have people who are going to expect things. Having less contributions from the districts gives me more independence."

Brown and new supervisor Chris Daly got into a heated argument about homelessness issues "that started with cursing and, witnesses said, almost led to a fistfight."[139] While Daly took the first step to apologize and smooth things over, the incident unfortunately raised echoes of the violence that accompanied the city's first experience with district elections.[140]

The Redevelopment Agency/The Planning Commission: Connections

Two key City agencies presiding over the transformation of San Francisco have been the Planning Commission and the Redevelopment Agency. Both agencies are run by commissions whose members are appointed by the mayor (until a 1996 City Charter change, the Planning Commission had two ex-officio members: the chief administrative officer and the general manager of the Public Utilities Commission). Both agencies have relatively large staffs and key formal, legal roles in approving and shaping the decisions and activities of the private development sector. And both agencies for the most part—particularly in the Alioto, Feinstein, Jordan, and Brown years—abdicated any serious planning function or concept of themselves as stewards of the public interest. Instead, they have basically functioned to assist and abet the profit-oriented development decisions of the real estate community; only sporadically, weakly, and when forcefully prodded have they moved to limit development and interject more public-regarding concerns into their deliberations and decisions. In playing this role, they have reflected the values and allegiances of individual agency officials, and of the person who appointed them, who has the power to reappoint and remove them, and to whom they feel accountable.

The San Francisco Redevelopment Agency has suffered a comedown since the halcyon days of Justin Herman and his staff of 450 full timers: By 1975, the agency was down to 320 staff members; by 1983, staff numbered 138; and the early 2002 figure is 115. Despite this decline, the agency has proved itself far more tenacious and adaptive than predicted in the mid-1970s after the new federal Community Development Block Grant (CDBG) program replaced "categorical" programs like urban renewal—a change eliminating the agency's direct financial pipelines to Washington and requiring dependence on a local political process of allocating block grants from city hall for a range of agencies and functions.

Competition for funds has been coming from a variety of sources—in the housing area most notably from community-based housing development corporations that have been active in the Mission, Bernal Heights,

Potrero Hill, Bayview–Hunters Point, Chinatown, and other neighborhoods, entities that showed they could develop housing faster, less expensively, and in a manner more responsive to neighborhood needs and conditions than could the Redevelopment Agency (see further discussion in chapter 13). These groups, under the umbrella Council of Community Housing Organizations (led by some former district election activists), have been successful in redirecting substantial amounts of CDBG moneys to affordable housing activities.

The agency has, however, found other sources of income and other ways of operating. For a while, increased income from land sales and leasing— the result of not being able to move projects along, as inflation increased land values—gave the agency new cash, beyond what it needed to repay federal loans (by 1984, more than half of the agency's estimated budget derived from land sales). And increased use of agency bond financing for its various projects allowed it to generate much of its operating income from expense budgets included in such bond issues.

The agency underwent a shift in leadership beginning in 1976 following the election of George Moscone as mayor. Moscone rapidly gained control of the agency board, via replacement of existing members (including appointment of the agency's first female commissioner, Dian Blomquist, since its establishment twenty-eight years earlier) and expansion of the board from five to seven members.

The new board acted fairly soon to oust the agency's executive director, Arthur Evans, who had taken over in late 1974, upon the retirement of Justin Herman's successor, Robert Rumsey. Evans received "kiss-off" money from the agency in the form of a six-month, twenty-five-thousand-dollar consultancy, and became a San Francisco–based housing developer and packager in the private sector.[141]

Wilbur Hamilton, the agency's deputy director since 1974, former Western Addition project director, and in the late 1960s an agency commissioner, was immediately named acting executive director by the new board and, following a nationwide search, was named executive director in early 1977. The several-month search period was characterized by severe acrimony between Commissioner Hannibal Williams, Hamilton's in-law—who resented the other commissioners' insistence on a nationwide search just when an African American was poised to take over the agency—and the other members—who wanted "the best" and did not want the appearance of nepotism.[142] Williams continued sniping at other commissioners, whom he denounced as "white liberal zoo-keepers," and openly criticized Mayor Moscone for not doing enough to defend African American interests in the city; he "resigned" in late 1978 and was replaced by Parree Porter, pastor of the First AME Zion Church in the Western Addition.[143]

The *Examiner's* Donald Canter observed that "the statement by some board members that they wanted an executive director 'who felt as they did' raised considerable doubt whether Hamilton, who's been part of the agency's establishment for eight years, would fit the bill."[144] The correct observation would have been that the new post-Alioto redevelopment commissioners for the most part were only superficially and marginally different from their predecessors, as was made clear in the choice of a new executive director and the board's actions over the years to come. "New breed" and "end of an era" images notwithstanding, the Moscone-appointed redevelopment board did little immediately or in the long run to alter the city's basic redevelopment activities. To its credit, however, the new board worked hard, to an extent opened up its deliberations and listened to the public, cut back on the agency's traditional bulldozer operations, preserved some important and useful older buildings, and on occasions showed a real concern for urban design and open space.

Dianne Feinstein, upon assuming the mayor's post following Moscone's 1978 assassination, replaced virtually all of Moscone's appointees to the agency board. Its direction, allegiances, operating style—none of which had markedly shifted during the brief Moscone years—didn't deviate very far from its role in the Alioto administration. Community groups continued to decry, with justification, their exclusion from the decision-making process, and the agency continued to approve projects despite opposition from residents and neighbors in its development areas. One example was its approval of construction of a twelve-story senior citizen apartment building in Japantown in the fall of 1986, despite objections by the surrounding community as to the building's height and its high rents (eighteen hundred dollars a month), unaffordable to most of the neighborhood and a force for driving up rents in the area generally.[145]* In relations with potential developers, the agency's system has been to grant sites to those who presented a good-looking plan, in an effort to get something built, and then hope for the best. In essence, the agency gave developers a fishing license and then prayed something good would be reeled in. Accommodations to what developers

---

*There's not much left of Japantown: The World War II internments, urban renewal, and, most recently, gentrification have pretty much reduced the neighborhood to a few symbolic features and not a whole lot of Japanese Americans. A bill before the California legislature would establish an official cultural designation for the country's three remaining Japantowns: in Los Angeles, San Jose, and San Francisco (Zoë Mezin, "Japantown Time Crisis," *San Francisco Examiner*, 14 June 2001).

wanted and wanted to change were virtually always granted. As the *Examiner*'s Gerald Adams put it: "Redevelopment Agency commissioners . . . to be fair, are in the business of selling city real estate rather than upholding concerns for city sociology and urban design."[146]

Wilbur Hamilton, an ordained minister with a large congregation in Seaside, near Monterey (where he worked while in the agency post), in late 1986 announced his intention to retire and devote himself full time to ministry. In mid-1987, the commissioners hired as his replacement Edward Helfeld, former director of the Los Angeles Community Redevelopment Agency.[147]

The election of Art Agnos as mayor in December 1987 brought about some immediate dramatic changes in the Redevelopment Agency, although their long-term impact is debatable. Most striking was his appointment of a new chair and vice chair in 1988. As head of the commission, Agnos appointed Gilbert "Buck" Bagot, a radical neighborhood (Bernal Heights) affordable housing activist and head of the Non-Profit Housing Association of Northern California, and under him, Vivian Fei Tsen, a progressive housing consultant who had worked closely with the Chinese Community Housing Corporation.[148] (Also appointed was tenant attorney Paul Wartelle, who resigned in early 1991 to avoid possible conflicts of interest.) The agency's emphasis on provision of affordable housing—a sharp departure from YBC priorities—was reflected in a revised 1989 agency mission statement, promulgated following discussion with community groups and housing organizations:

> This new period marks a break with the past role of the SFRA in which it engaged in redevelopment programs as a semi-independent agency, concerned mainly with the completion of plans it devised in only part of the city.
>
> The agency's mission has evolved toward a comprehensive view of the City as a whole and cooperation with other City agencies and community and neighborhood groups aimed at solving citywide housing and development problems defined by elected officials and citizens of San Francisco. . . .
>
> The SFRA will assist ongoing efforts of other City agencies and community-based and other non-profit affordable housing producers in increasing the supply of housing targeted for lower-income households. Using its financial powers and funding sources available only to the SFRA, the agency will, in consultation with affordable housing producers, *both* non-profit and profit motivated, develop funding mechanisms for the increased production of permanently affordable housing.[149]

Additionally, the mission statement outlined the agency's economic development policy, designed to "support and enhance community initiatives for new neighborhood serving economic opportunities."

The statement was remarkable, not only for the changed goals it set forth, but also for the stated intention to assist and consult with other agencies, community groups, and housing organizations. But the results of this dramatic new direction were mixed. There are limits to how quickly a major public agency can change course: Commitments to former projects cannot be simply abandoned, nor were they; realistically, it is hard for a board to dictate to a staff; the agency's long-term "corporate culture" was hard to change, even with the best efforts of the part-time commissioners. Helfeld, although appointed by Feinstein's commission, remained in his job throughout the Agnos term (and beyond). A considerable boost was given to affordable housing production, particularly by community-based nonprofits, but the city's budgetary problems limited the financial support that could be given, and the actual results fell far short of the ambitious goals the Agnos administration agency set for itself. In terms of operating style, the agency was far more accessible. TODCO's John Elberling observed at the time, "There has been a real opening up. Commissioners are talking to us to see what we want instead of waiting until the eleventh hour and acting in secret." Council of Community Housing Organizations activist Rene Cazenave stated that his ability to work with the agency on its affordable housing program was "a 180-degree change from the past."[150] His colleague Calvin Welch, however, in 1991, viewed the agency's retrospective self-congratulations for its effort to build housing as "absurd" in light of its actual record.[151]

The ascension of Frank Jordan as Art Agnos's replacement in the mayor's chair after the 1991 election signaled yet another shift in the Redevelopment Agency, back to the Alioto-Feinstein mold. Most of Agnos's appointees were replaced with more pro-growth, downtown development-oriented folks, and some of the former bad habits returned. Commissioner Ben Hom, chair of a loan origination company, was accused of financial improprieties—steering business to an associate and requesting donations for Mayor Jordan's office account from a developer seeking Redevelopment Agency permission to build on a YBC site.[152]*

---

*In 1999, Hom once again involved himself in an unsavory financial transaction, in apparent conflict with his official position. Mayor Willie Brown had appointed Hom to the Public Utilities Commission in March 1999. (Hom, a prominent Republican in city politics, had run for mayor in 1995 "and was thought to have helped

With respect to Willie Brown's appointments, there is little to say but the obvious: He has "shuffled rubber stampers into every commission."[153] Wes Willoughby, the agency's (recently retired) spokesperson for thirty years, observed, "In effect the Redevelopment Agency now is being run out of City Hall."[154] Of real concern is the degree to which Brown relies on the agency's increasingly shaky borrowing powers to finance his favorite projects—Mission Bay (his former law client) and development of the Navy's abandoned Hunters Point shipyard (see discussion in chapter 8). As an important February 1998 *SF Weekly* feature emphasized, the agency "is rapidly approaching the governmental equivalent of maxing out on its credit cards."[155] To carry out its projects, it floats bonds that are to be repaid via the increased property tax revenues these projects will generate. But, in fact, few of its projects wind up providing sufficient revenue (Golden Gateway being the notable exception to date); much of the new development is tax-exempt (Moscone Center, Yerba Buena Gardens, and the Museum of Modern Art being prime examples); and projections of revenue and other benefits are routinely, often wildly, exaggerated. A significant portion of the bond proceeds also is siphoned off to pay the agency's operating expenses, and so Tax Allocation Revenue Bonds (which, unlike the agency's long-term debt—now in the $700 million range—do not require voter approval) are sold to make up the difference between revenues and expenditures—a shortfall that has occurred for at least the last decade. A further problem for the agency is that tax increment dollars do not go directly into the agency's coffers, but into the City's general fund, to be allocated by the Board of Supervisors, which must take care of all of the city's needs (a task that the statewide 1978 Proposition 13 property tax relief initiative has made all the more difficult). The agency has a troublesome near future, to say the least.

As for the Planning Commission, it too underwent transformation with the election of George Moscone in 1975. During the Alioto years (1968–75), the commission was blatantly supportive of virtually any downtown de-

---

then-assemblyman Willie Brown win by pulling conservative Chinese-American voters away from [Mayor Frank] Jordan [who was running for a second term]. This year, he has campaigned enthusiastically for Brown" (Lance Williams and Chuck Finnie, "PUC Vote on Lease Could Be Conflict for Hom," *San Francisco Examiner,* 23 November 1999.) The following August, the commission voted (with Hom neither recusing himself nor revealing his connection) to negotiate a lease on a Chinatown building on which Hom was cosigner of the $1.7 million mortgage. His fellow PUC commissioner Dennis Normandy said he offered the proposal at the commission meeting at Hom's request. Following the publicity on this breach of ethics, Hom resigned from the commission.

velopment that came along. In the city's redevelopment areas, the commission has a limited role, compared to the Redevelopment Agency, of devising preliminary plans and approving the agency's plans, planning changes, and organizing environmental impact reports. And on redevelopment projects, it has chosen to do little but go along. As Allan Jacobs, Alioto's planning director, put it in his 1978 memoir, "Our involvement with urban redevelopment projects would be minimal. . . . The agency had all the marbles. It had a large highly qualified staff; it had money; it had political and media support; and its staffers knew their way around city hall. Unfortunately, there was no way of becoming a colleague of the agency's director [M. Justin Herman] without also becoming his servant. We would, therefore, try to stand apart from the city's redevelopment efforts."[156]

George Moscone's Planning Commission looked different on the surface, and some of its members, notably Sue Bierman and Charles Starbuck, spoke out repeatedly against unlimited downtown expansion and on occasion even voted against projects they thought were detrimental to the city. But they were a minority, and as Moscone himself acknowledged in a 1978 letter to *Chronicle* publisher Richard Thieriot, defending himself against the latter's charge that he was "anti-growth": "Since 1976, when my Planning Commission took over, not a single *major* project has been turned down. Indeed, eleven have been approved."[157]*

But as Dianne Feinstein took control in 1979–80, there were signs that the Moscone Planning Commission might be on the verge of threatening serious interference with the downtown growth machine, in large part due to the quasi defection of Public Utilities General Manager Richard Sklar, who, as the person responsible for the city's public transit system, was seeing the disastrous effects of unlimited growth on people's ability to get downtown and back home. With the prospects that Bierman, Starbuck, and Sklar might win over a fourth member and constitute a Planning Commission majority, and with some individual projects being hotly contested at commission hearings, Feinstein moved to replace Moscone's troublesome and potentially troublesome appointees when their terms ended.

---

*Moscone's ties to the business community appeared to strengthen during the course of his tenure. In late 1978, just before his death, Moscone reportedly was even the target of investigations by the FBI, the state attorney general's office, and the state Fair Political Practices Commission, in connection with alleged payoffs by Howard Hughes and his Hughes Airwest and their attempts to secure expanded space at San Francisco International Airport. See David Johnston, "Was the Alleged $10,000 Hughes Bribe Merely a Downpayment to Influence Moscone on Airport Expansion?" *San Francisco Bay Guardian*, 5 October 1978.

Starbuck and Ina Dearman (the latter an opponent of condominium conversions and an occasional but inconsistent defender of neighborhood interests against downtown) were replaced by C. Mackey "Butch" Salazar, a Mission District attorney and builder, and Jerome Klein, a business representative of Local 250 Hospital and Institutional Workers Union and close ally of the construction trades unions, in what the *Examiner*'s Gerald Adams labeled "A move that portends an historic pro-development shift of the San Francisco Planning Commission."[158] (Salazar and Klein later resigned at Feinstein's request when it was reported that they, through a firm both were associated with, Lanaco Insurance and Financial Services, were soliciting business—selling savings and retirement plans to employees of nonprofits—from groups that lobby the commission for project approvals.* Feinstein did this at a time when the Board of Supervisors was debating a ballot measure—eventually abandoned—designed to restrict City commissioners from representing clients before other City commissions.)[159]

Neighborhood groups and environmentalists certainly saw the change of personnel as the actions of a mayor who perceived that progressives, environmentalists, and neighborhood organizations had nowhere else to go politically, leaving her free to carry out this purge. The change in commissioners was accompanied by a change in the Planning Department's staff leadership in March 1981, when Moscone's planning director, Rai Okamoto, was forced out and replaced by Dean Macris, a close Feinstein ally and an extremely adept practitioner of the art of planning politics (skills sharpened as assistant planning director and community development director in the Alioto administration). Part of this same purge was Feinstein's removal of the more troublesome members of the City's Landmarks Preservation Advisory Board, as described in chapter 12. Feinstein also reappointed three of Moscone's planning commissioners—chairman Toby Rosenblatt, a business consultant, and Yoshio Nakashima, a dentist, both of whom had voted consistently in favor of downtown development, and Sue Bierman, whom Feinstein kept on partially out of personal loyalty (Bierman actively supported Feinstein's reelection campaigns and was an important member of the Democratic Party Central Committee), and partially not to completely antagonize neighborhood groups.

*Klein's later career found him as an "expediter," paid by developer clients to win quick approval for building permits through contacts and insider knowledge at the Planning Department and Building Department. See Diana Walsh, "Well-Paid Insiders Slash Red Tape for Builders," *San Francisco Examiner*, 20 November 2000.

It clearly was Feinstein's commission. At the time she appointed Klein and reappointed Bierman, she stated her expectations pretty bluntly: "You are part of an administration. There will be times when I call you and want a vote but that will be a minority of the time. If you can't give me that vote, please resign."[160] Klein got the message: "She appointed me. She has my vote."[161] When a tough issue came up in Chinatown around development by the powerful Chinese Six Companies of a nine-story condominium that would put the neighborhood's only playground in shadows, and the Planning Commission seriously objected to this loss of open space, Feinstein told chairman Rosenblatt, "Toby, this one has to go. . . . I am committed to this. . . . If commissioners have problems with the administration, I don't mind them resigning. There are a lot of people wanting to serve in commission posts."[162] (Until voters approved a City Charter change in 2002, planning commissioners could be summarily removed by the mayor. See material below.) The commission voted four to three to uphold the Chinese Six Companies development. In a 1982 KQED-TV documentary, Richard Sklar concluded about the Planning Commission: "It certainly hasn't turned down any projects during my lifetime in the city and I don't think it will. All it does is tinker with the facades on the buildings, occasional changes with the outline and shadow patterns and get a few amenities here and there, but development continues at the developer's pace, limited only by the economics of building highrises."[163] Commission chair Toby Rosenblatt echoed Sklar's observation: "If one looks back at the last five years, which is the time I've been on the Commission, ultimately we have not denied permits for any office building presented."[164]

No real *planning* characterized the commission's deliberations and overall work in this period, nor at any time in San Francisco's history. One review of the commission's role concluded:

> Today, as the city undergoes what [Planning Director Dean] Macris agrees is one of the heaviest periods of development since the Gold Rush, this key administrative panel is mired beneath a huge, all but unworkable case load. Its approach to this plethora of projects is essentially mechanical, rubber-stamping virtually every new development and permit. Decisions are made not in the service of an articulated master plan, but rather in a gray haze of disparate controls: "building bonuses," "special-use districts," "floor-area ratios," and vague architectural and environmental strictures.
>
> Since there are no bottom-line definitions, even such basic concepts as "affordable housing" and "transit capacity" become political bargaining chips—when they are not ignored altogether.[165]

"In the absence of Planning Commission policies," concluded the *Examiner's* Gerald Adams in 1981, "that vacuum is starting to be filled by such groups as the San Francisco Planning and Urban Research Association and the Chamber of Commerce"[166]—an apt observation, except with respect to time frame: A review of the commission's history would suggest that SPUR, the chamber, and kindred development interests had been the city's planners for quite a long time.

When Art Agnos took office in January 1988, the entire Planning Commission resigned. His appointees (among whom was a reappointed Sue Bierman) were expected to adhere to his campaign promise to carry out "the planning guidelines contained in Proposition M [the dramatic slow-growth measure passed by the voters in 1986—see chapter 12], including housing and historic preservation, and small business development."[167] The strictures contained in that new law narrowed the commission's discretion greatly, the initiative process having to a large extent transferred the overall planning parameters to the voters.

Frank Jordan, when he took office in 1992, then replaced all of Agnos's planning commissioners with a far more business-oriented group, including two developers, a property manager, and, to cement things for the highrise crowd, a representative of the International Union of Elevator Constructors. Three of the new commissioners had publicly opposed Proposition M in 1986, two of whom even signed Voter Information Pamphlet ballot arguments against it. In early 1992, Dean Macris, described by *Chronicle* reporter Marshall Kilduff as "probably the most powerful figure in the San Francisco development game,"[168] resigned, taking advantage, after eleven years as planning director, of an early retirement package, but also knowing that the new mayor wanted to have someone new in that position.

As for Willie Brown's planning commissioners, ditto what was said above about his Redevelopment Agency appointments: He has, not surprisingly, "shuffled rubber-stampers into every commission."[169] Again, former planning director Allan Jacobs, writing in 2000, and using the identical (and accurate) expression in characterizing the City's official planning functions and activities of recent years: "Today the [City Planning Department of San Francisco] is considered largely a rubber stamp agency, a costly hurdle to be bypassed whenever possible by special legislation and an elite group of pragmatic doers in the mayor's office."[170] Brown's actions in 2000 were typical: In September, he fired planning commissioner Dennis Antenore when Antenore refused to back the deceptive and weak "slow growth" initiative Brown had placed on the November ballot in order to undercut the more radical Proposition L (see chapter 12).[171]* And both for Antenore's replacement and a second appointment he made earlier, Brown chose persons with connections to the real estate industry. One was real estate professional Roslyn Baltimore, the other, William Fay, is the son-in-law of San Francisco real estate magnate Robert Lurie (a connection that went unmentioned in the mayor's official announcement of Fay's appointment to replace Antenore).[172] Another planning commissioner appointed by Brown is Hector Chinchilla, "a lawyer whose clients have included a property owner using the Ellis Act to try to evict three families" (see chapter 13).[173]

Both Redevelopment Agency and City Planning commissioners as well as their staffs, of course, have close working relations with the business community they are supposed to regulate. The Redevelopment Agency is in essence a real estate operation, and so it should come as no surprise that the links between the development community and the agency, at both board and staff levels, get pretty thick, as people traverse the thin public-private line in this lucrative area of enterprise. As illustrated earlier with respect to agency chair Walter Kaplan (see chapter 3), SFRA board members, drawn largely from the business community, often make less than sharp distinctions between their public and private hats, and once they have left agency service these connections can be of great service to their clients. For example, Howard Wexler, Redevelopment Agency chair from 1977 though 1980, was a partner in the law firm of Feldman, Waldman, and Kline. Several of the firm's clients did business with the agency, an issue raised at the time of Wexler's confirmation hearings before the supervisors' Rules Committee.[174] On matters having to do with the firm's clients, Wexler abstained from voting and turned the chair over to another commissioner; however, such formal, open acts of distancing are inadequate to offset the effects of these known relationships on fellow commissioners and agency staff. A client of Wexler's firm, the Gift Mart, obtained an option on a YBC property through private negotiations rather than open bidding.[175] When

---

*According to one observer, Brown's action may have backfired in terms of the November 2000 election of supervisors under the new district system: "But it was Willie Brown's firing of Planning Commissioner Dennis Antenore that some think may be what propelled the most vehement anti-Brown candidates into office, claiming he was too friendly with developers. Antenore was widely seen as a proponent of neighborhood interests, [who] opposed chain stores and, in what proved a fatal move, split from other planning commissioners and refused to endorse Brown's ostensible slow-growth measure, Proposition K" (Christopher Merrill, "New Supes Work to Hamstring Mayor," *San Francisco Examiner*, 24 January 2001).

Wexler left the agency board, he began appearing before his ex-colleagues himself on behalf of clients.[176] (A key official of that same client, Grosvenor Properties, was Nat Taylor, a former City Planning Department staff member.) SFRA general counsel Leo Borregard had been a partner in Wexler's law firm.[177] Wexler also has appeared before the Planning Commission on behalf of developer clients.[178] Mayor Feinstein dropped Wexler from the Redevelopment Agency when his term expired, reportedly because of the number of development projects he represented.

Another agency commissioner, Rubin Glickman, resigned in 1981 to devote more time to his real estate business. "Glickman also indicated that he was sensitive to the suggestions of conflict of interest, although he denied any improprieties. . . . Among Glickman's recent business ventures were several condominium conversions that brought him before other city agencies such as the Planning Commission."[179] Glickman also shared offices with Richard C. Blum Associates (Mayor Feinstein's husband) and Blum's Farrell's Ice Cream Parlours, purchased from the Marriott Corporation, the YBC Central Blocks developer. Several years after resigning from the commission, attorney Glickman appeared before his former body to argue for a height-limit exemption for his client, American Lifecare, developer of the luxury Japantown apartment building noted above—a perfectly legal action under agency regulations.[180] Redevelopment Agency chair (during the Feinstein administration) Melvin Lee appeared before the Planning Commission regularly on behalf of clients.[181]

Nor is this simply a historical pattern: In early 2001, Mayor Brown (who knows a thing or two about such matters) criticized Redevelopment Agency commissioners (other City commissioners as well) for their dual public-private roles and asked them to adopt antifavoritism and full disclosure rules.[182]

Redevelopment Agency staff also have done double duty. The agency's former YBC project director, John Dykstra, left public employ in 1973 and a year later was representing developers seeking agency contracts for YBC high-rises, under the firm name Pacific Rim Associates. "Dykstra said he has . . . met with agency staff members about the enterprise."[183] Ex–SFRA executive director Arthur Evans appeared before the agency on behalf of the developer of a Tenderloin project being financed with agency bonds.[184] William Rosso, the agency's former director of architecture, represented developer Alexander Maisin in negotiations regarding an option to build on an agency-owned site at Geary and Van Ness. Redmond Kernan, former deputy director of SFRA, was codeveloper of a YBC site.[185] Former agency official Morris Phillips was employed by Fillmore Center developer Donald Tishman in the Western Addition project area (this, despite Phillips's earlier conviction for attempted extortion in connection with agency business).[186]

The list of those appearing before the Redevelopment Agency board (either formally or simply showing up to be seen on behalf of their clients) has been a veritable "Who's Who" of current and former public officials: David Cincotta, formerly of the mayor's Office of Housing and Community Development; former supervisor Terry Francois; John Igoe, former YBC project coordinator for the chief administrative officer; former Planning Commission President and Supervisor Gordon Lau; and the ubiquitous Willie Brown.[187]

Over at the Planning Commission and Planning Department, a similar litany of borderline (and crossing-the-border) conflicts of interest can be catalogued. During a Planning Commission debate on a proposed thirty-eight-story Campeau Corporation building on Bush Street, attorney/lobbyist Tim Tosta (who "makes no secret of his hope to carve out a place for himself as San Francisco's premier attorney for big developers, a position currently shared by Assemblyman Willie Brown and William Coblentz. . . . ")[188] scrawled a note and passed it to Planning Director Dean Macris, "Do we have four votes?" to which Macris wrote back, "Not at this time."[189] Tosta and Macris eventually got their votes.

A *Chronicle* feature from late 1982 on a Planning Commission meeting reported:

> A seemingly never-ending stream of rented politicos, past and present, crop up before the San Francisco Planning Commission. Take last Thursday: a half-dozen of these bigshots-for-hire were bumping into each other in the city hall corridor outside the planning meeting.
>
> "You remember me," Woo [George Woo had retired from the Department of Public Works to become executive secretary of the Chinese Six Companies, which was seeking Planning Commission approval for a twelve-story condominium project in Chinatown] said cheerily, addressing staff members by their first names. "I guess I'm now on the other side."
>
> Next Howard Wexler, former Redevelopment Agency president, with a six-story office building in North Beach.
>
> Then came Airports Commissioner William Coblentz, one of the heaviest hitters around. He won a routine delay for a 26-story highrise at 388 Market Street, property owned by Hong Kong investors. Coblentz was co-chair of Barbara Boxer's successful run for Congress and his lawfirm was one of the major contributors to the winning candidates for Board of Supervisors.

Coblentz is always well-briefed, pleasant and humorous, but sometimes his breezy confidence can be a little embarrassing. Several weeks
ago he and his associates sent Planning Director Dean Macris a batch of
birthday balloons with the messenger dressed up like a clown who arrived in the middle of the weekly planning meeting. The chummy birthday note was inscribed to "Dean" and signed by "Bill" and several others
from his firm who also used just their first names.

At the end of the long agenda were former supervisor [and Planning
Commission president] Gordon Lau, who regularly shows up on behalf
of Chinese clients, and former appellate judge John Molinari, whose son
is the supervisor. Both lawyers were involved with small development
projects that were put off to a future meeting.[190]

To be fair, one must point out that such "connections" are not confined
to the planning and redevelopment bodies. From *Chronicle* reporter Marshall Kilduff's August 17, 1985, account:

> Airports commissioner Bill Coblentz represents highrise builders before
> the Planning Commission. His law partner, Lou Giraudo, who sits on the
> city Public Utilities Commission, represents clients before other city
> agencies. Giraudo earlier left a post on the Board of Permit Appeals be-
> cause a number of Coblentz's clients came before him. This tail-chasing
> got even more complicated last week. During a bitter vote over a China-
> town housing and office complex known as Orangeland, public utilities
> commissioners Nancy Lenvin and John Sanger showed up as lobbyists
> for the developer before the Board of Supervisors.

In early 1986, Lenvin and Sanger resigned from the PUC, Coblentz resigned from the Airports Commission, former supervisor Gordon Lau resigned from the Ports Commission, and Piero Patri resigned from the Arts
Commission, all in response to a letter Mayor Feinstein sent to two hundred appointees "telling them [but not their associates or business partners]
to cease lobbying on behalf of clients before city boards, commissions and
departments."[191] But as a January 29, 1986, *Chronicle* story headlined, "Feinstein Ban Unlikely to Affect Lobbying," accurately noted, "No one thinks
the mayor's action will lessen the role of influential advocates, who often
play a role in steering campaign funds to elected officials. . . . 'The lobbying
that goes on by influential people will continue with one-on-one lobbying,'
" said a person in a position to know about such things, Board of Supervisors president John Molinari.

The boundaries between the public and private sectors over at the Planning
Commission and Redevelopment Agency clearly are far more permeable
than is healthy for the people of San Francisco.

12 | High-Rises and the Antihigh-Rise Movement

The transformation of San Francisco over the past four decades finds its concrete expression in the height and bulk of the new buildings that have replaced the old. One sometimes forgets how recent this change has been: From 1930 to 1958, only one major office building was constructed in San Francisco, and the city's first modern high-rise, the Crown Zellerbach building on Market Street, was built in 1959. But as a *California Magazine* article puts it, "This city, once mythologized as Baghdad by the Bay, might now be better christened Houston by the Pacific."[1]

Arguments and data regarding the impact of high-rise development— on the city's tax base; on job generation and who benefits from these jobs; on job displacement; on the direct and indirect costs of municipal services to serve high-rises; on the various environmental impacts; on housing availability and cost; on traffic, transit, and congestion—have flown thick and fast over the years. The *San Francisco Bay Guardian* in 1971 published *The Ultimate Highrise: San Francisco's Mad Rush toward the Sky*, a piece of advocacy journalism/scholarship that did much to increase public consciousness of the issue, provide some facts, and raise the questions that have been asked for three decades since.[2] A series of "definitive" studies of the fiscal effects of downtown development was produced in the 1970s and early 1980s, each reaching somewhat different conclusions and coming under criticism for its methodology or sponsorship.[3] The San Francisco Planning and Urban Renewal Association in 1974–75 received funds from HUD and two private foundations to study the issue, but the consultants it chose were not regarded as impartial, and the fact that the corporate community's Blyth-Zellerbach Committee (see chapter 1) was reconsidering its subsidy to SPUR during the study period didn't help to create the desired impression of distance and objectivity.[4] The Sedway-Cooke planning firm in 1979 was commissioned to analyze the fiscal effects of downtown development, in response to the threat posed by an antihigh-rise initiative, and concluded that after passage of anti–property tax Proposition 13 in 1978, "Costs may exceed revenues in the downtown by as much as 25 percent" and that "New downtown development will not solve the city's growing fiscal problems; without new revenue sources, development will make it worse in the long run."[5] The San Francisco Chamber of Commerce in 1980 commissioned Arthur Andersen and Company to calculate revenues and costs of the downtown high-rise district. The conclusions were that in 1976–77 revenues exceeded costs by 61 percent (a $56 million gain) and that in 1978–79, with the impact of Proposition 13, the benefit dropped to 48 percent (a $53 million gain). But the firm's methodology was roundly criticized for excluding costs not directly in the City budget (such as BART, whose deficits are covered by a half percent sales tax) and for treating the downtown essentially as a Vatican-like separate city, with no maintenance responsibility for facilities and services not used or used only minimally in and by the financial district (health care, parks, libraries, schools, jails and courts, social services, general government, etc.).[6] Employing the Andersen data but applying different assumptions regarding externalities, San Franciscans for Reasonable Growth (SFRG) concluded that the post-Proposition 13 downtown area actually incurred a more than $50 million deficit.

Not surprisingly, these various studies have done little to convince San Franciscans one way or another about the issue. The assumptions and "models" used, what data were considered relevant, and how to interpret the data, all have reflected the values and positions of those who undertook and sponsored the studies. The more narrowly one defines the issue, the better the case to be made for the economic advantages of high-rise development; the more one takes into account citywide economics and other dimensions of the growth issue, the more frightening appear the impacts of "Manhattanization."

Economic impacts aside, unrestrained high-rise development has disturbing environmental effects. Box-shaped, poorly angled skyscrapers create powerful street-level winds that can become gales—up to sixty-five miles per hour—overturning newspaper racks, potted trees, and other objects, and even breaking store windows.[7] Less extreme wind currents can make walking or merely being downtown highly uncomfortable. Relatedly, tall, bulky buildings can reduce or completely block out sunshine: "In San Francisco," wrote *Chronicle* architecture critic Allan Temko, "when the breeze comes in from the sea, sunlight is the difference between comfort and chill for most of the year. The sun is the key to the half-Mediterranean mood . . . that the mammoth new buildings have partly destroyed. When we lose the sun the joy goes out of a place."[8] An early eighties study by the University of California's Environmental Simulation Laboratory concluded that "The next 38 to 50 skyscrapers in San Francisco . . . could darken the downtown sky . . . reducing visible sky to slivers of light and creating a partial-eclipse-like darkness along sidewalks."[9]

Concerned over loss of sunshine in public parks and playgrounds from adjacent high-rises, the supervisors placed on the June 1984 ballot a measure (Proposition K) designed to protect this important amenity—although as a sop to the development community, several unbuilt but already approved towers were exempted. Demonstrating their concern on this issue, the voters approved the measure, 61 percent to 39 percent.

A related environmental issue is transit and traffic, the impacts of which caused by downtown high-rise development are staggering. Already by 1982, the load factor for the city's public transit system at peak hours was 91 percent of recommended seating and standing capacity. (Capacity is defined as standees equal to 50 percent of seating capacity for surface motor and trolley coaches, 121 percent of seating capacity for light rail vehicles.) Completion of the 17.3 million net square feet of downtown office space then under construction, approved, or under formal review was projected to raise Muni's load factor to 136 percent—over one-third more than the recommended seating and standing capacity; the transbay BART lines' load factor was projected to rise to 128 percent; the East Bay and Peninsula commuter buses' (AC Transit and Samtrans) load factors were projected to rise to 101 percent and 104 percent of capacity, respectively; and the load factor on the Southern Pacific/Caltrain commuter railroad to the Peninsula would rise to 112 percent.[10]

Those cumulative impact data were based only on office space and did not take into account new hotel projects, most of the construction to come in the Yerba Buena Center and Rincon Point–South Beach projects, the mammoth Mission Bay project, and other known developments coming down the pike. The current sad state of Muni (the City public transit agency whose name is invariably preceded in news accounts by some version of "chronically troubled") is a reflection of failure to heed those earlier projections and warnings. BART is not free from serious problems and heavy criticism either. A three-part *Chronicle* series in early 2001 documented severe deterioration in the system's equipment, leading to frequent breakdowns.[11] As one environmental impact report noted, using the technical language of transit planners that spells grief for tens of thousands of commuters: "As cumulative demand increases, the length of time of peak loadings would increase, spreading the peak-of-the-peak conditions over time."[12]

With respect to auto traffic, peak-hour congestion at two of nine downtown intersections rated in early 1980s environmental reports for downtown office buildings would, with the projected 17.3 million net square feet of office construction, reach a 100 percent volume. This level "represents a jammed condition. Back-ups from locations downstream or on the cross street may restrict or prevent movement of vehicles. . . . "[13] (This restricted movement impedes the same Muni buses and streetcars that planners hope people will turn to, in order to relieve auto congestion.) The bridge and freeway system serving the city was already near capacity in peak hours during the early eighties and is currently a horror. A 1999 nationwide study of mobility by the Texas Transportation Institute ranked the San Francisco–Oakland area as the third most congested, behind L.A. and Seattle.[14]*

Pedestrians are not much better off than drivers. Projections of pedestrian volumes for a nineteen-story building planned at 222 Kearny Street showed that at noontime in 1990 at the two nearest corners, one would be "crowded" ("restricted choice, high probability of conflict"), the other "constrained" ("some choice restriction, multiple conflicts"), and that in the afternoon both would be "constrained."[15]

Other environmental impacts of high-rise office construction include deteriorating air quality, in particular from increased vehicular emissions of carbon monoxide. Demolition, excavation, and construction noise can occur over periods averaging two years per building, which, with so many buildings being constructed over a small area, can turn into a constant feature of the environment. Environmental impact reports described interference with speech, concentration, and telephone conversations, disturbance to daytime sleepers at nearby residential hotels, and general distraction for office and retail employees. Noise can be so severe as to require raising voices and even shouting in order to be heard at a distance of two to three feet.[16]

---

*The Texas study ranked cities on several variables, leading to differences in the way the results were reported. The *Washington Post* account noted: "Washington slipped yesterday from second to third in its ranking among the nation's traffic-clogged urban areas, according to a closely watched report that periodically examines the misery of driving. But the slightly improved ranking indicates only that the San Francisco–Oakland area, which tied Washington for second last year, got even worse—not that Washington got better" (Katherine Shaver, "Traffic Misery Slips—on Paper: San Francisco Overtakes D.C. for Commuter Pain," *Washington Post*, 8 May 2001).

The Antihigh-Rise Movement

While few people bother to read the lengthy and dense environmental impact reports or otherwise acquaint themselves with the data, concepts, and language of these studies, there nonetheless has been a long and successful history of protest and active opposition to the transformation of downtown San Francisco. Environmentalists worry about such issues as traffic, air quality, sunlight, and noise. Historic preservationists are concerned about the heritage of the city's built environment. Neighborhood residents have witnessed the transformation and destruction of their communities, either directly due to private or public redevelopment or indirectly via its ripple effects. Many individuals and groups are concerned about fiscal integrity and equity, about whose dollars are paying for the transformation and to whom the financial benefits are accruing. And some are deeply concerned for the city's residential character, employment structure, politics, and culture; they do not want to see lower-income and minority people pushed around by development or forced to leave the city, and do not want to see San Francisco as a city where primarily white middle- and upper-class people can live, with a job structure rigidly hierarchical by race and class.[17] Over the past three decades, these overlapping constituencies often have put aside their occasional differences or antagonisms and come together to fight the onslaught of high-rises. And while it cannot be said that they have held high-rise development at bay, they have had some notable successes.

The progenitors of the antihigh-rise movement were the successful campaigns by residents of the Marina, Telegraph Hill, and Haight-Ashbury neighborhoods to stop the planned eight-lane freeway system designed to run through the city and connect the Bay Bridge to the Golden Gate Bridge. The freeway would have desecrated Golden Gate Park and demolished nearly six hundred homes. Its opponents also managed to halt the Embarcadero Freeway in mid-air, and the stubs of uncompleted elevated highway along the Embarcadero and near Van Ness Avenue in the Western Addition remained for many years (in the case of the Embarcadero, until the 1989 Loma Prieta earthquake obliterated that "monument") as dramatic visual reminders of the success of their struggles.

During the late 1960s and early 1970s, architectural preservationists and environmentalists focused their attention on particularly ugly, ponderous, and poorly located buildings. The fight against a planned 550-foot U.S. Steel tower on the waterfront was successful.[18] Those against the Bank of America World Headquarters building and the Transamerica Pyramid were not. (Some observers believe, however, that the Transamerica campaign did stop what threatened to be a movement of downtown development up Columbus Avenue toward the city's fabled Chinatown and North Beach districts.)

At the time, a modicum of order regarding disorderly high-rise development was proposed via three elements: the City's 1968 downtown zoning study; Planning Director Allan Jacobs's 1971 urban design plan, which established guidelines for building height, bulk, shape, orientation, color, and views; and the City's 1972 establishment of height-limit districts. It remained clear, however, that more forceful, outside intervention was needed to prevent the city from becoming another Manhattan.

Two early, dramatic attempts to control downtown growth were the 1971 and 1972 ballot initiatives organized by Alvin Duskin, which called for severe height limits of 72 and 160 feet, respectively, for new buildings in San Francisco, with provisions for granting exceptions under certain conditions. While both were defeated, they dramatized the issue effectively and founded a high-rise growth control movement that has remained a powerful force in the city.[19]

Antihigh-rise energies next turned to electing a new mayor to replace downtown favorite Joseph Alioto. George Moscone promised much and delivered on some of those promises. "There will be no highrise development approved by my Planning Commission. It desecrates the city, it causes your tax rates to zoom. When I'm the mayor there will be no new highrises in San Francisco."[20] This was music to the ears of his neighborhood supporters, and to back this promise, once in office Moscone changed the composition of the Planning Commission (noted in chapter 11). As former planning director Allan Jacobs wrote, "Before 1975 . . . most of the [planning] commissioners [came] from San Francisco's white, male establishment."[21] Moscone appointed people who were close to the antihigh-rise movement, most notably Sue Bierman and Charles Starbuck, the latter the executive director of the San Francisco Ecology Center and one of the plaintiffs in the 1975 *Starr* suit challenging the YBC financing plan (see chapter 7).

But changing faces was not enough to stop the high-rises. Moscone himself, in the manner of politicians everywhere, in key areas performed differently from his promises. "I've seen six mayors pretty closely and have yet to see one who can stand up under the pressures of the real estate developers," sagely commented the late Jack Morrison, former supervisor, mayoral candidate, and close confidant of George Moscone.[22] The new mayor lacked any clear vision for the future of his city. He pushed to ensure construction of the new convention center and, beyond his Planning Commission appointments, did little to halt the high-rises. By and large, his appointees also responded to pressures from the real estate developers. During the 1975–79 period, 8.2 million square feet of downtown office space went up, just a shade less than the 8.6 million of the previous five (Alioto) years.[23]

During the later part of the 1970s, the campaign for the district election of supervisors, the subsequent supervisorial elections, and defenses of that structural reform against repeal attempts absorbed much of the energy of pro-neighborhood forces. By 1979, with the downtown-oriented Dianne Feinstein as mayor and likely to be reelected, electing officials to change City policies toward high-rise growth seemed an unlikely path. The pressures to which Feinstein responded, as well as the arrogance and sexism of the business community, are illustrated in the following excerpt from a February 5, 1979, feature by *Chronicle* political reporter Larry Liebert:

> Sixteen urban gentlemen met the mayor . . . in a private dining suite at the Bankers Club, on the 51st floor of the Bank of America tower.
>
> The guest list of corporate chairmen and senior vice-presidents represented such prestigious corporate names as Southern Pacific, Bank of America, Foremost-McKesson, Wells Fargo, Crocker, Macy's and Transamerica.
>
> Eventually, the conversation turned to highrises and to the city's continued economic development as a West Coast center for corporate headquarters.
>
> "If it's going to be a headquarters city," one of the corporate chairmen lectured Feinstein sternly, "some consideration must be given to the headquarters companies—to not let groups that are contributing little or nothing to the headquarters concept have the final say."
>
> "Nobody's anti-business in this city," Feinstein said.
>
> "Crocker is about to think you're anti-business if you don't let them build their extra stories," retorted a corporate official [referring to a proposed 49-story building the bank wanted to build at Post and Kearny, 200 feet beyond the existing height limit; the compromise solution was to let them exceed the height limit to a lesser degree, by constructing a 38-story building].

Deciding it was time to again go to the voters directly, the antihigh-rise San Franciscans for Reasonable Growth drafted a series of amendments to the Planning Code and placed them on the November 1979 ballot as Proposition O. The measure reduced downtown height and bulk limits (as expressed in "floor-area ratios," which relate a building's total square footage to the square footage of its site) and established an alternative set of "bonuses," allowing for somewhat greater height and bulk in exchange for certain designated socially desirable features. Under Proposition O, the maximum height would have been 260 feet in the most intensively developed down-town zone, 150 feet and 130 feet in the other three downtown zones. (Roughly speaking, ten vertical feet equal one story.) The then-existing bonus system, based on building design modifications and amenities such as open space and malls, would have been revised to offer incentives instead to developers who provide housing and energy conservation measures, en-courage mass transit use, and improve pedestrian environments.

Proposition O was strongly opposed by a coalition of labor and downtown interests called San Francisco Forward, which claimed jobs and taxes would be lost and fiscal burdens shifted from downtown to homeowners if the ini-tiative passed. Other arguments—captured in the slogan, "Don't Los Ange-lecize San Francisco"—claimed that the proposed height and bulk limits would in the long run backfire by forcing growth to spread out to areas adja-cent to downtown, without lessening its rate.[24] SFRG raised $35,000. San Francisco Forward raised $500,000. The measure lost, 54 to 46 percent. SFRG's inability to garner labor support, particularly in the building trades, was one factor. And the dilution of energies between Proposition O and Proposition R, the comprehensive housing reform initiative on the same ballot (see chapter 13), was another. While many of the campaign organizers were committed to both issues, the large role played by organized labor in supporting the hous-ing initiative effectively prevented any coordination of the two campaigns.

Although Proposition O lost, the margin was narrow enough to convince the City and downtown interests that something had to be done to pacify those who wanted to control the impact of high-rises. As the first step, SPUR, the Chamber of Commerce, and other business interests assembled $460,000, funneled through the City Planning Department, to pay consultants to pro-duce an environmental impact report (EIR), analyzing the various growth control proposals. After two-and-a-half years of studies and preliminary re-ports, the EIR effort was suddenly scuttled by Planning Director Dean Macris in favor of producing a "Downtown Plan." According to critics, Macris was concerned that the EIR studies fueled support for growth controls and that the mandatory public hearings and required publication of advocates' argu-ments in the City's final document would add to that support. Others claimed that the studies provided an excuse for the two-and-a-half years of inaction, and, whether they came to fruition or not, were a bargain well worth the half-million dollars downtown interests contributed to fund the EIR.

The Downtown Plan

Macris's Downtown Plan was unveiled in August 1983 amid some of the more orchestrated publicity in memory. The August 28 *Sunday Examiner*

& Chronicle hailed it as "undoubtedly the most famous urban design document in this nation right now." It made the front page of the daily *New York Times* and was featured in that paper's Sunday edition as well.[25]

The proposal called for:

- reduction in permitted building heights;
- reduction in floor-area ratios (building bulk);
- preservation of 266 architecturally significant buildings and lesser protection for 222 others (allowing owners, however, to avoid economic loss by transferring their development rights to the South of Market area);
- mandatory preparation of shadow studies, to preserve sunlight;
- consideration of various mass transit projects; and
- promotion of architectural treatment of tops of new buildings, to produce a more attractive skyline and avoid the "refrigerator row" look.[26]

The City Planning Department, with release of its proposed Downtown Plan, recommended a one-year moratorium on permit approvals for all financial district buildings greater than fifty thousand square feet in size, in order to avoid a developers' gold rush while the plan was being considered by the Planning Commission and Board of Supervisors.

Reactions to the Downtown Plan were interesting. Some analyzed it primarily as an architectural, rather than an economic or political, document. (The writer of both *New York Times* articles was the paper's architectural editor, and his description stressed such features as the rejection of the "international style" in office building design.) Others saw, correctly, that the plan really did not limit office growth in San Francisco, but merely shifted it from the financial district to the South of Market area, along with strong steps to protect remaining urban design amenities in the financial district, and discouraged office development in the Tenderloin and Chinatown areas. The *Chronicle*'s architecture writer, Allan Temko, in a talk before the Commonwealth Club, offered a far more sophisticated analysis than appeared in the *New York Times*:

> Maybe architecture is the least important. It certainly is to me less important than the enormous volume of speculative development that the Plan still permits. . . . [These issues] should be understood because they have been hidden under a kind of post-modern razzle-dazzle that is really cosmetic.[27]

And with regard to the architectural elements in the plan, Temko added these biting words:

> Nor would I trust [Planning Director Dean] Macris' chief assistant on
> design matters. . . . His contributions to the Plan would not require ar-
> chitects but milliners. So we'd put these party hats on buildings, as if we
> didn't have the most colossal dunce cap in the world on the Transamerica
> Building.

While Macris's publicity strongly pushed the notion that the plan was a
growth limitation measure, the reality was otherwise.[28] The plan merely
limited growth "potential"—what theoretically could be, but in actuality
would not be, built, were all sites to be developed to their maximum potential, which would involve demolishing and replacing all old buildings.
Under the plan, by the year 2000 there would have been 24 million square
feet of new office space built (primarily in the South of Market area), housing 100,000 additional workers, a rate of growth 83 percent as great as the
1965–81 growth rate. Not included in these figures was Southern Pacific's
$4 billion planned Mission Bay project (see chapter 8), which lies outside
the area treated in the plan; with Mission Bay added, the total growth rate
would exceed the 1965–81 total. (It is also fascinating to note that the
Downtown Plan's "restricted growth" proposals yielded the same 24 million square feet as that proposed in the Chamber of Commerce's high-
growth scenario analyzed in the Planning Department's downtown environmental impact report.)

In addition to allowing growth to proceed at nearly the same rate it had
for the prior fifteen years, the plan did far too little to provide for the housing and transportation needs such growth would generate. It recommended
that one thousand to fifteen hundred units of housing be built annually to
accommodate the new workforce, but offered no answer to who would build
the housing, where it would be built, how it would be financed, or who
would be able to afford it. It went no further than the clearly inadequate
Office Housing Production Program (discussed below). In the absence of
housing subsidy programs, such developments could only mean luxury condominium or rental units. Nor did the plan address how needed transit improvements would be paid for. By allowing more office growth without first
ensuring the housing and transportation to accompany it, the plan put the
cart before the horse.

Major transit improvements take ten to twenty-five years from conception to completion, and their public funding sources are uncertain, as are
housing subsidization funds; privately financed office buildings take three
to four years. What the Planning Commission approves are buildings to be
soon built, whose impacts are soon felt; mitigation measures are more in
the nature of a wish list.

The Downtown Plan ignored the rest of the city and its relation to downtown, issues of quality of life, neighborhood preservation, and class relations. And of course it ignored the "Big One":

> The certainty that such a quake will occur, the probability of heavy damage and thousands of casualties in the crowded downtown area, the disruption of supplies, communications and transportation essential to the functioning of a complex urban region—all throw doubt on the wisdom of adding another 100,000 people to the dangerous and vulnerable downtown area. . . . Any city plan that ignores the earthquake hazard is itself a hazard.[29]

Another, more graphic, though no less realistic critique:

> THE FIRST CONSIDERATION IN ANY RATIONAL PLANNING IN SAN FRANCISCO SHOULD BE THAT TWO CONTINENTAL PLATES MEET TEN MILES FROM DOWNTOWN. Not even Willie Brown nor Walter Shorenstein can stop them from eventually moving in a great quake.
>
> When the Big One comes, predictable things will happen. People will be thrown across flexible steel frame structures and crushed by moving office furniture. Unreinforced brick buildings and some highrises are likely to collapse on their own, while others that have been built flush to one another will likely demolish each other as they begin oscillating at different frequencies. Tons of glass and facing veneers will rain into the streets which may themselves subside.
>
> What happens next is even scarier. In those streets will be not only people, but thousands of automobiles, each with a gas tank. Crushed, there will be free gasoline all over downtown. Then there will be a fire, as in 1906. But unlike 1906, there will be no way for people to get out through blocked streets. Nor will it be possible for the Fire Department to get in, even if they were capable of fighting simultaneous fires in highrises.[30]

The 1989 Loma Prieta earthquake, almost the Big One, gave good warning, one hopes.

The First Proposition M

As happens frequently in the planning world, the underlying motive for developing and releasing the Downtown Plan was as political as it was professional. Earlier in 1983, high-rise foes had put together another coalition and another initiative for the city's November election. The San Francisco Plan Initiative was designed to be less subject to interpretation by voters as antigrowth than was the 1979 Proposition O, and more likely to win labor support, or at least to avoid active labor opposition. The initiative (Proposition M, the San Francisco Plan Initiative) did not call for specific height and bulk limits, nor did it embody a concrete ordinance. Rather, it required the Planning Commission and Board of Supervisors to take several actions dealing with growth problems, all before the November 1984 supervisorial elections (thereby creating a built-in issue around which to focus those elections). It stipulated that the Planning Commission had to adopt a master plan that, unlike the existing master plan, was internally consistent with respect to its several elements—housing, commerce and industry, transportation, energy conservation, etc.—and had as its priorities such goals as maximizing employment opportunities for San Franciscans, economic diversity, protecting small businesses from displacement, conservation and expansion of affordable housing, an adequate transportation system to meet development needs, and maintenance of the cultural and ethnic diversity of the city's neighborhoods. It also required the Planning Commission and Board of Supervisors to conform the city's zoning ordinances to the new master plan and further mandated the supervisors to pass ordinances requiring new office developers to provide affordable housing for the workforce their developments generated and to pay for the costs of additional public transit capacity needed to service their workers. Finally, the relevant City agencies—most notably, the Redevelopment Agency, which for all intents and purposes is exempt from Planning Commission controls and the requirements of ordinances applicable outside redevelopment areas—were required, prior to approving any office development, to certify that a project was meeting its public transit and housing obligations and conformed to the city's master plan.

The content and timing of the Downtown Plan must be seen against the background of this far-reaching initiative, the strong coalition pushing it—which included small businesses from Fisherman's Wharf, the Cannery, and Ghiradelli Square—and their easy success in getting enough signatures to qualify it for the ballot. As happened several years later in the case of rent control (see chapter 13), the City was trying to head off a popular revolt by proposing or enacting something in the direction of change demanded but far less stringent. According to *Examiner* political analyst Bruce Pettit, "Planning Commission President Toby Rosenblatt believes that the downtown plan can deflect votes that would have gone for the [San Francisco] Plan Initiative."[31] The *Chronicle*, in an October 9, 1983, editorial, urged "promptness by the Board of Supervisors in acting on the Planning Commission's [accompanying] permit-freeze recommendation," as it "could be important to the fate of the Downtown Plan. Voters will be deciding November 8 on the more extreme antihigh-rise implications of Proposition M. With the moratorium in place as the overall plan is under review, the issue could be decided in a relatively reasonable atmosphere, with highrise policy under the careful official and public consideration it deserves." Mayor Dianne Feinstein of course supported the plan and moratorium proposed by her Planning Commission and came out against Proposition M (as did Assemblyman Willie Brown).

While downtown interests did not embrace the one-year moratorium, they by and large appeared to accept the Downtown Plan. As described above, the plan was a way of permitting virtually unabated growth while giving the appearance of satisfying the growth controllers. By shifting growth (and growth problems) to the South of Market area, in the pithy words of the lobbyist for San Francisco Forward, the Chamber of Commerce front group organized in 1979 to defeat Proposition O, "It's the way to go. Downtown has been done."[32] (An interesting tidbit was that the president of San Francisco Forward, Zane Gresham, of Morrison & Foerster, was lead attorney for the Redevelopment Agency and City when his firm was retained to defend against the 1978 legal challenge to the agency's YBC financing plan described in chapter 7.) Property owners in the financial district would lose nothing, as they could transfer their development rights across Market Street, the locus of future action. This appeared to be a decision by the power structure to move toward "a veritable second downtown of 25 or 30 slender, tapering, neo-historical office buildings and tourist hotels, concentrated mostly South of Market Street and scattered toward the Civic Center."[33]

The November 1983 growth control initiative came very close to passing—losing by fewer than two thousand votes. With Dianne Feinstein virtually unopposed as a result of her overwhelming victory in the April recall election (see chapter 11), no significant opposition in the sheriff's and DA's races, and no supervisorial race, voter turnout was low. Some who supported high-rise limitations found the measure complicated, vague, and ambiguous. And the downtown forces once again vastly outspent neighborhood groups—some $700,000 to $60,000. With contributions to ballot proposition measures not subject to any legal limitation, the developers poured it on. Frightened by polls showing that Proposition M was comfortably ahead, the downtown interests mounted a furious last-minute campaign, with saturation mailings and several full-page newspaper ads. The campaign raised jumbo contributions: forty-two thousand dollars from Norland Associates, thirty thousand dollars from Lincoln Properties, twenty-five thousand dollars from Gerald D. Hines, ten thousand dollars each from Marathon US Realties, Standard Oil of California, Embarcadero Center's Rockefeller interests, General Atlantic, Dover Park Investments, Tai Associates Architects, and Cahill Construction Company, and additional large contributions from Southern Pacific, Bank of America, Skidmore, Owings & Merrill, and others—huge amounts by local campaign standards but minuscule compared to development profits.

The supervisors passed a financial district building permit moratorium several weeks after the November 1983 election. But, in response to developers' political pressures, they grandfathered in seven office projects (including developments by Walter Shorenstein, the Rockefeller group, and Lincoln Properties, totaling 2.4 million square feet). Mayor Feinstein vetoed the legislation as virtually meaningless—the ordinance was to expire in August 1984, and the exempted space amounted to considerably more than the annual average additional space built in downtown San Francisco, besides exempting Port Commission and Redevelopment Agency activities altogether. An amended ordinance was then passed and signed by the mayor in February 1984; it allowed the seven projects to go ahead, providing they met the new zoning guidelines in the draft Downtown Plan.

Right after the November elections, the supervisors also unanimously approved what in effect was an eighteen-month moratorium on development in a forty-block area South of Market, excluding the Yerba Buena Center project and located west and south of it. During the moratorium period, the Planning Department was to produce a rezoning plan for the area, and in the interim the moratorium was to protect the neighborhood's remaining six thousand to eight thousand blue-collar jobs and one thousand small businesses—printing, warehousing, building supplies, tool and machine shops, laundries—from the pressures of sharply rising land prices characterizing the South of Market area, which would be exacerbated by the shifts in development concentration the Downtown Plan mandated. No exemptions were allowed in the South of Market moratorium, and there was little developer opposition to the move, since at the time virtually no one had a project under way in these blocks.

During this period, San Franciscans for Reasonable Growth, mainly via the persistent litigation and negotiating of its indefatigable attorney Sue Hestor, was challenging individual building projects and winning concessions from developers in the settlement process. Needless to say, this created consternation, not only in the development community, but also among City officials, embarrassed that the group's interventions were extracting far better deals than those negotiated by Mayor Feinstein's supine Planning Commission.[34] An example was Hestor's negotiations around Norland Properties' planned forty-seven-story high-rise at 345 California, which produced nearly $1 million for affordable housing, public libraries, and Chinatown open space. As the July 6, 1986, *Examiner* noted: "The settlement illuminates . . . [h]ow Hestor was able to use the threat of a lawsuit to extract more valuable concessions from a downtown developer than Planning Director Dean Macris or the City Planning Commission were able to secure in the permit process." (While these concessions are valuable, the building of course gets built.) Chagrin reached its peak in mid-1985 when Feinstein ordered District Attorney Arlo Smith to investigate SFRG for criminal wrongdoing in its activities. Nothing damaging emerged from this investigation. The ever-pugnacious Hestor responded: "If there is any accusation of a shakedown to be made, it should properly be laid at the feet of the mayor," referring to her heavy financial support from downtown interests.[35] Planning Director Dean Macris acknowledged the obvious—that the City's planning powers were being undercut by SFRG's work: " 'If an outside group could force the developer to shrink his project,' Macris reportedly said [at a meeting of prominent development attorneys] 'citizens might begin to believe the [Planning] Commission had been derelict in not negotiating the same deal.' "[36]

The Second Proposition M

The second Proposition M,[37] the "Accountable Planning Initiative," placed on the November 1986 ballot by the reinvigorated slow-growthers, was, as San Francisco State University political scientist Richard DeLeon characterized it, "the most restrictive growth control measure of any large U.S. city. . . . It allowed expanded citizen participation in the city's development policy arena. It set new rules for the land-use game and altered the terms of the city's public-private partnership with business."[38] The move built on the near-victory of the 1983 Proposition M and the overwhelming 1984 approval of the "sunlight preservation" initiative (Proposition K).* Proposition M embodied the following:

- an annual limit of 950,000 square feet of permits for new office construction—875,000 in large projects, 75,000 in small (less than 50,000 square feet) projects (practically speaking, this amounted to only

---

*A slight detour in this progression was the 1985 Proposition F, a surprise venture by maverick activist Joel Ventresca and some other neighborhood activists impatient with SFRG's legal challenge/developer concessions tactics. The initiative measure called for a three-year ban on office buildings and hotels exceeding fifty thousand square feet. Openly opposed by Sue Hestor and Calvin Welch of SFRG in Voter Information Pamphlet arguments and editorially by the *Bay Guardian*, it both illustrated and temporarily exacerbated splits between the no-growth and slow-growth wings of the antihigh-rise movement. Proposition F lost, 59 to 41 percent.

475,000 square feet for several years, until the then-existing pipeline of already approved permits was emptied—although provision was made for voter-approved exemption of individual buildings exceeding that limit);

- reservation of a portion of this allocation for small buildings;
- eight priority policies for amending the City's Master Plan (dealing with preservation of neighborhood character, affordable housing, transit, a diverse economic base, earthquake protection, historic preservation, sunlight, preservation of neighborhood-serving retail uses, and enhanced opportunities for resident employment and ownership);
- a requirement that no permits be issued unless they are consistent with those priorities;
- a job-training program for city residents.

It was a significant advance over the Downtown Plan—a permanent, citywide ordinance covering small as well as large buildings that also dealt with the "pipeline" issue.

The result was a slim (5,311 votes) but definitive victory, carried out by a coalition of neighborhood activists, small-businesspersons, environmentalists, tenant advocates, gay and lesbian organizations, and some labor support. It was a reunion of the Moscone coalition. The fifteen-year trajectory of such efforts was clear and steady: The win:loss gap for Alvin Duskin's 1971 losing growth control initiative was 24 percent; for his 1972 initiative, 14 percent; for the 1979 Proposition O, 8 percent; for the 1983 Proposition M, 1 percent; and victory in 1986.[39] Opposition to the second Proposition M was surprisingly weak: Only a little over half the amount spent to oppose the 1983 effort was raised (although it was still a not trivial $361,000).[40] With the city's increasing office vacancy rate, a split in the realty community also emerged, between those owning existing buildings with empty space and those developing new projects.

Richard DeLeon's eloquent summation of the history that led to passage of the second Proposition M captures the overarching forces at work:

> A plausible case can be made that the progrowth regime over a long period of time created the instrument of its own destruction. By overbuilding office space, it produced a surplus that divided the interests of the business community. By inducing formation of a service economy, it encouraged a new middle class of slow-growth postmaterialists while displacing blue-collar workers who supported progrowth materialist goals. By Manhattanizing the downtown financial district, menacing nearby neighborhoods, obliterating sunlight, accelerating housing costs,

burdening the infrastructure, and snarling traffic, the progrowth coalition assaulted the environmental sensibilities and communal identities of the new populations it had brought forth. By displacing the poor, creating high-end jobs for commuters, and building housing for the rich, the progrowth promises of "small opportunities" for low-income minorities and resident workers could not be kept. In effect, the progrowth regime's social production performance significantly altered the physical and social environment that had originally given rise to the progrowth regime. The collective goals first set for the progrowth regime had begun to change dramatically. To many residents, that regime had become vestigial and even dysfunctional. A fundamental shift took place in the struggle over urban meaning—a struggle that took concrete form in the battle over Proposition M.[41]

The years following passage of Proposition M were characterized by a general slowdown in growth pressures, in large part related to the region's and country's larger economic picture: tighter credit markets and a general economic downturn. Views regarding its value and impact vary, of course, but it is interesting to note the conclusion of a 1992 backward look from Thom Calandra's "Money Talks" financial column in the March 8, 1992, *Sunday Examiner & Chronicle* ("Separating Prop. M Fiction from Fact"): "[Proposition M] is a policy statement that benefits all San Franciscans. It is not a mere square-footage quota for office towers."

In the last years of the century, office construction activity came to the fore again with a vengeance, triggered largely by the dot-com revolution, which helped eat up the 3.5 million square feet of unused, banked allowable development that built up between the late 1980s and mid-1990s period, when the savings and loan crisis, the state's real estate recession, and resultant high financial district vacancy rates stopped the city's building boom.

The invasion of the "dot-comies" hit San Francisco in the late 1990s with earthquake-like force. Somewhere between five hundred and seven hundred Internet-related companies (the speed and nature of these start-ups makes counting them difficult), created an estimated fifty-five thousand jobs, located mainly South of Market and in the Mission. These excerpts, from mid-2000 news accounts, give the flavor:

> In a land grab reminiscent of the Gold Rush, dot-com companies are snapping up every available foot of office space here. . . . Landlords have seized the moment, evicting longtime tenants and even demanding stock in startups along with million-dollar deposits. . . . [The dot-coms] crave the cachet of The City, its potential for networking and its proximity to the high-tech mother ship of Silicon Valley and clients of the wired

world. . . . "The whole world is watching what we're doing here," [said a spokesman for Digital Think]: "If you're ambitious, and you're building a company, you move to San Francisco." . . . The Midas-rich venture capitalists, sleepless entrepreneurs, and trendy-hipster-brainy kids who populate the new digital-network industries have decided among themselves that San Francisco, and especially San Francisco's old, southeastern industrial region, is the only place to be.[42]

The impact on space has been profound, beyond shortage and staggering rent inflation. "It's an interesting situation when you feel lucky to spend $2.5 million to renovate a building you don't own," said the same Digital Think spokesman. And the shift in the city's economy was nicely captured in the move of NBC Internet, with its 750 employees, into eight floors of the Chevron Building on Bush Street (north of Market, in the financial district), formerly used by the oil company and the old-line law firm of Pillsbury, Madison & Sutro. Architectural style follows—"industrial chic" or "Internet funk" is the order of the day: "white walls, lots of light and chrome, exposed pipes and wires. Employees will sit on ergonomically correct chairs made of fiberglass mesh to maximize air circulation and will be able to relax in a 'Zen room.' "[43] The overwhelming demand has led to many illegal conversions of industrial buildings to office space, something the flabby, development-oriented Planning Commission either ignores or approves after the fact: "Over the past few years, illegal conversions of industrial buildings—often old warehouses or factories in the Mission and SoMa districts—into offices for use by dot-com or other high-tech companies have become a rampant problem largely unchecked by the city."[44] Aside from the many other problems the "new media" industry is creating, the vagueness of legal definition of these activities means that most of the new start-ups do not pay the affordable housing and child care fees that are important to balanced growth in the city. The quirkiness of the situation is captured in the following observation from the February 2000 issue of San Francisco Tomorrow's newsletter: "Literally the same business is being called an office use if it is in the Chevron building in the C-3 [zoning designation], but is called non-office at 19th & Harrison [Bryant Square]. The term keeps changing—research and development, business service, light industrial. Anything but 'office.' "

The most recent attempts to control growth via ballot measures occurred in mid-2000, when a revived coalition of growth controllers easily secured signatures sufficient to place Proposition L on the upcoming November ballot, with 1999 mayoral candidate Clint Reilly picking up a good portion of the tab.[45] Not to be outmaneuvered, Mayor Willie Brown and four supervisors, minutes before the November ballot submission deadline, placed a competing and confusing measure (Proposition K) on the same ballot.

The key features of the two measures were as follows: Proposition L retained the 950,000 square foot annual limit of 1986's Proposition M, but allowed additional space in future years and exempted large projects already in the works (such as the proposed George Lucas film studio at the Presidio (see chapter 13) and a new federal building at Seventh and Mission (see chapter 8). It also banned office construction in parts of the Mission, Potrero Hill, and South of Market, and temporarily halted it in Bayview–Hunters Point until a community planning process is completed. And it reclassified live-work lofts (see chapter 13) as housing, requiring developers to pay more in fees, also reclassifying dot-coms as offices (rather than as "business services," which allowed this enormous development tsunami to evade the Proposition M limitations).

Proposition K contained a series of loopholes that together would allow an estimated seven million square feet of new office space before April 2001, via higher limits and a great-grandfather clause clearly designed to aid Mayor Brown's political supporters in the development community.[46] A principal beneficiary would be real estate lawyer James Reuben, who assisted in drafting Proposition K and was active in a failed litigation effort to rule Proposition L off the ballot: "In the hours just before the mayor submitted his measure, city planning records show, Reuben & Alter [his law firm] hand delivered letters to city zoning administrator Larry Badiner requesting rulings on seven projects. . . . [U]nder the grandfather clause, Prop. K regulations won't apply to developers who, by 5 p.m. on August 9, when Brown submitted his ballot measure, got requests into The City's zoning administrator. . . ."[47] Up to eleven million square feet of new office space would be allowed over the succeeding four years.[48] Live-work lofts would be exempted from coverage and controls by the new law, continuing the scam by which they are converted to straight office use after construction. It also exempted all federal, state, and local offices as well as all port land (Proposition L contained only one waterside exemption, Pier 70 on the central waterfront). While interim protection was given to the Mission, Potrero Hill, and South of Market, these neighborhoods would be open to commercial office development if the Planning Department failed to produce protective plans within two years—a highly worrisome feature in light of the fact that the department had failed after three years to finish planned industrial protection zoning controls for much of the same area, as well as the clear pro-development orientation of the Planning Commission under Mayor Brown (see chapter 11)—labeled "The Builders and Developers'

Rubber Stamp Agency" by one *Examiner* columnist, with another referring to "the mayor's dictatorial insistence on appointing pro-development
planning commissioners."[49] Finally, Proposition K called for creation of a
new "Growth Management Coordinator" position—a ten-year appointment, to be made, of course, by the developers' good friend, Willie Brown.

In the November election, Proposition K lost badly, winning just 39 percent of the vote, and L also lost, but by a tiny margin (it got 49.8 percent).
Campaign expenditures were, as usual, lopsided: $2.3 million was spent by
developers and business interests on K, while the L folks raised just
$132,000.[50] So it's up to the new (2000) district-elected Board of Supervisors
(see chapter 11) to try to deal with this issue vital to the city's future. Larger
economic trends in the region and nationally will play a major role, and no
one has a crystal ball on that scenario. Ken Rosen, chairman of the Fisher
Center for Real Estate and Urban Economics at the University of California,
Berkeley, estimated in October 2000 that "80 percent of the local dot-coms
will go out of business in the next three years. That would ease the space
crunch and drive down rents."[51] But that of course is just a prediction, and
demand for San Francisco office space comes from many sources other than
the dot-coms. In the same month Rosen offered his views, San Francisco was
named the country's top commercial real estate market for the fifth year running, according to a study by Lend Lease Real Estate Investments and Price-
waterhouseCoopers—beating out Los Angeles, New York, Boston, Washington, D.C., and all the other hot spots. Prime office space in downtown San
Francisco at the end of 2000 averaged $85 per square foot, almost double the
previous year's average of $49.50. And even the Proposition L growth con-
trol measure, backed by the same folks who got Proposition M passed in
1986, would have allowed up to 8.3 million square feet of new office space
in the subsequent four years, compared with 5.4 million that Proposition M
allows. So continued downtown growth is inevitable.[52]

Preserving the City's Architectural Heritage

An important and interesting component of San Francisco's antihigh-rise
movement has been the historical preservationists—those with a deep concern for the city's cultural and architectural heritage, as expressed in individual structures and groups of buildings. The city is a treasure trove of important and invigorating buildings, not only downtown but also in many
of its neighborhoods. A 1968 publication sponsored by the Junior League
of San Francisco, *Here Today: San Francisco's Architectural Heritage*—a
well illustrated citywide survey carried out by league members under the

supervision of a group of architectural historians—provided an important step in creating public consciousness of the need to protect older buildings.[53] The year before its publication (but related to the survey process, which had begun several years earlier), the Board of Supervisors passed legislation creating the Landmarks Preservation Advisory Board. The nine-member mayorally appointed board is an advisory body to the Planning Department and Commission and to the supervisors. It works closely with the National Trust for Historic Preservation (whose western regional office is in San Francisco), the Foundation for San Francisco's Architectural Heritage (commonly referred to as "Heritage"), established in 1971, and various other private groups such as San Francisco Tomorrow, the Victorian Alliance, and neighborhood groups in Pacific Heights, Telegraph Hill, the Mission, the Richmond, and other areas.

The Landmarks Board has taken its role seriously, and for the most part the Planning Commission and supervisors have followed its advice. Apart from publicizing threats to historic buildings and referrals to the technical and financial services that various preservation groups in the city offer, in order to encourage owners to save their buildings and adapt them to more viable uses, the board's designation of a building as a landmark can trigger Planning Commission and Board of Supervisors actions requiring a delay in the permit-issuing process, during which time attempts can be made to persuade an owner to alter plans that threaten the building. In addition to acting on individual structures, the Landmarks Board and others, including property owners, have midwifed creation of eleven historic districts, in order to maintain each area's architectural integrity. Heritage also succeeded in persuading the Redevelopment Agency to save some Victorian houses in the Western Addition renewal area, by moving them from one renewal site to another (on which the agency had just demolished similar Victorians). And later preservationist pressure on the agency led to saving several key buildings in the Yerba Buena Center project area.

As might be expected, preserving valued architectural history may not always be consonant with maximizing real estate returns, and some of the city's stormier conflicts have arisen around such issues as saving the City of Paris department store and the Fitzhugh office building on Union Square against the desires of Neiman-Marcus and Saks, respectively, to construct their edifices there. The developers brought in their heavies—Assembly Speaker Willie Brown, lawyer-influential William Coblentz, and their crew—and despite enormous and anguished protests on the part of a unified preservation community, the Planning Commission and Board of Supervisors for the first time overruled the Landmarks Board, and down came the old (although as a sop to the protestors, Neiman-Marcus's architects incorporated a truncated version of the elegant City of Paris rotunda into the new store's entrance).

Growing "obstructionism" by the Landmarks Board and its allies led to the "Friday the 13th massacre" of June 1980, when Mayor Dianne Feinstein summarily fired five of the board's nine members, including its president and vice president. In some quarters, the move was interpreted as a way to divert attention from a more pinpointed desire to remove board president G. Bland Platt. Platt was taking her role far too seriously for the mayor and the development community and, as one of the board's most knowledgeable and experienced members (she was an appointee to the original 1967 board, had been a key figure in putting together the Junior League's 1968 book, and was board chair since 1973), was looked to for leadership by other members. According to some accounts, the mayor—caught in a tight runoff in 1979 with conservative Supervisor Quentin Kopp—agreed to dump Platt as part of a deal for downtown support in the runoff election. At a minimum, the style with which the removal took place—no prior personal notice to Platt, with whom the mayor had worked closely on several past projects—was less than gracious. (The changes in Planning Commission membership described in chapter 11 were another element in this move to oust dissidents from City boards and commissions that regulate growth.)

Battles of this type have provided the preservation community with an education in how San Francisco politics works and have created some interesting and useful tensions between people of the same economic and social class. By and large, those appointed to the Landmarks Preservation Advisory Board and activists in Heritage are upper-middle-class whites; those responsible for the high-rise development that threatens the city's architectural heritage are their neighbors, friends, acquaintances, and, sometimes, relatives.

Issues of social class also are relevant to the way in which the preservationist community relates to other forces in the city seeking to control growth and its impacts. Organizational support from the preservationists was not forthcoming for the various high-rise control initiatives—Alvin Duskin's 1971 and 1972 efforts, Proposition O of 1979, and Proposition M of 1983. The fifteen-hundred-member Foundation for San Francisco's Architectural Heritage in fact opposed Proposition M in November 1983, partly out of concern that in the long run the proposed controls might have a negative impact on building preservation, in part because of the very substantial pro-preservation features in the Downtown Plan, which, as noted above, in effect was the alternative to Proposition M.

Nor has there been much overlap between the organized preservationists and the city's housing reform movement or the movement to elect supervisors by district, although individuals connected with the preservation movement have supported these related efforts. In part, this lack of mutual support has been due to differences in style and tactics—with the preservationists stressing "professional" critiques, development of alternative plans, and a less confrontational style than has been true of the housing and antihigh-rise activists; more recently, these differences have been narrowing, as the mode of well documented critiques and preparation of counterplans has come to be more widely adopted.

Heritage has focused much of its concern on the financial district, through its detailed 1979 compendium, *Splendid Survivors: San Francisco's Downtown Architectural Heritage.* But it also provided considerable technical assistance in the Tenderloin (a connection helped by the fact that then–executive director of the North of Market Planning Coalition, Brad Paul, formerly was on the western regional staff of the National Trust for Historic Preservation).* Heritage helped rehabilitate the Cadillac Hotel in the Tenderloin and organized a politically important exhibit on the city's residential hotels, their rehabilitation, and potential for rehabilitation, held in the Cadillac.[54]

Transit Remedies

As noted above, the city's surface and underground public transit system is notoriously overcrowded, and new high-rises severely exacerbate the critical peak-load problem. Several fare hikes in past years have done little to increase user satisfaction with service. These have been triggered primarily as a result of state legislation designed to force Muni to raise its fares by granting operating subsidies from the one-half percent BART sales tax only to local transit systems within the BART district that generate at least one-third of their operating costs from fare-box revenues. At the same time, Muni's operating losses have been increasing rapidly, from $86 million in 1979 to $184 million in 1990 to $245 million in 1998.

---

*Paul was later named deputy mayor for housing by Mayor Agnos, a remarkably imaginative and successful appointment. One of the first acts of Agnos's successor, Frank Jordan, was to fire Paul and replace him with Ted Dienstfrey, a real estate development consultant to mega-developer Gerson Bakar and others, "best known for his strident opposition to rent control" (Jim Balderston, "Jordan Fires City Housing Boss Brad Paul," *San Francisco Independent,* 4 February 1992); see also George Raine, "Jordan Ousts Housing Director, Names His Own," *San Francisco Examiner,* 29 January 1992.

Two basic reform proposals have been put forward by antihigh-rise activists and labor groups. Both are designed to make downtown developers and property owners pay more to support the transit system, which delivers the concentrated aggregates of workers whose labor creates corporate profits. The proposals are a one-time, per-square-foot transit fee upon construction of new downtown office space and creation of a permanent special downtown transit assessment district, an area in which a special assessment would annually be levied to cover part of the costs of providing this service. (An earlier variation of the transit assessment district proposal was an annual fee, which would have permitted classification of buildings by their transit impact and adjustments in the fee schedule to reflect differential impacts.)

The reasoning behind a special assessment of this type is simple: The increased land values in downtown San Francisco, the ability to charge among the highest per-square-foot office rents in the nation for buildings whose basic construction and ongoing operating costs vary little by regional location, are in large part created by Muni's ability to assemble a workforce and customers efficiently. Muni in effect provides a massive subsidy for downtown businesses; an assessment district or fee is the neatest way of recovering that subsidy and requiring downtown businesses to pay their rightful costs.

In May 1981, following a good deal of pressure from neighborhood activists, antihigh-rise groups, the San Francisco Labor Council, Service Employees International Union Local 400 (the City workers' union), the Gray Panthers, and others—supported by City transit chief Richard Sklar and Public Utilities commissioner John Sanger—the Board of Supervisors and mayor reluctantly acted. They instituted the one-time development fee and approved enabling legislation for the special transit assessment district, giving themselves additional time to enact detailed legislation regarding the district's boundaries, actual fees, and mechanics.

The victory had its roots in the 1979 Proposition O high-rise control campaign, with its focus on downtown's transit needs. Attempting to respond partially to this pressure, as well as to undercut support for Proposition O, the Planning Commission, in the summer of 1979, for the first time added to its approval of a high-rise application (specifically, the Federal Reserve and the Crocker Bank buildings) transit mitigation requirements, in the form of a commitment to "participate in a downtown assessment district or similar fair and appropriate mechanism, to provide funds for mass transit, should such a mechanism be established." All subsequent environmental impact reports from 1979 to 1981 contained these commitments.

The coalition pushing the transit aid, known as the San Francisco Budget Task Force, had worked diligently on the technical and political level in putting together and lobbying for this needed assistance. Among their headline-grabbing tactics in 1981 was chartering a Muni bus, decking it out with a red cellophane bow on the roof, and driving it to the Chamber of Commerce office, where they attempted to present it, along with a mock ignition key and pink registration slip, to the chamber, representing the "free transit service" the chamber's members were getting.[55] On the other side, the developers worked in vain to head the legislation off, although reports noted, "It . . . has been stalled in committee because of lobbying efforts by Assembly Speaker Willie Brown and others."[56]

The annual assessment measure was regarded as the more effective and remunerative approach. Unlike the one-time development fee, it would require existing as well as new buildings to pay and, as a regular assessment, would provide a predictable source of annual income. Under the proposed formula (thirty cents per square foot, less than 1 percent of the thirty-five-dollar-per-square-foot average annual rent at the time for downtown office space), it was estimated that revenues would begin at $21 million a year and rise steadily thereafter as new office buildings were added. (An earlier attempt by the Chamber of Commerce to form a voluntary transit assessment district, requiring assent of property owners representing at least 50 percent of the assessed property values downtown, failed, "reportedly because developer Walter Shorenstein and the owners of Embarcadero Center balked.")[57] Although not as lucrative as the assessment district, the one-time fee did represent a substantial source of help: A major office structure, such as the then-proposed thirty-three-story Campeau Corporation building on the Sutter/Montgomery/Bush/Kearny block, containing 522,000 gross square feet, would yield a payment of over $2.6 million for Muni.[58] But while the City had calculated that the share of additional Muni costs attributable to new downtown office buildings should be $9.82 per square foot (and excluded from that figure the capital cost of new transit vehicles), the one-time fee passed in 1981 was set at only $5.00 per square foot, as a concession Mayor Feinstein made to the Chamber of Commerce.

Downtown nevertheless reacted angrily, and apparently perfidiously, to this attempt to make big business pay for the transit services necessary to its effective operation—"one of the most outstanding examples of municipal avarice I've ever seen," in the words of one corporate vice president.[59] Mayor Feinstein had earlier negotiated with the Chamber of Commerce the issue of increasing City revenues following passage of Proposition 13 and thought she had chamber support for the transit fee and the rest of the "revenue package" she placed on the June 1980 ballot: increases in parking, hotel, payroll, and business taxes; taxing the City's nonprofit garages and airport concession revenues; and changing the system by which the City's retirement system is amortized. But whether the chamber changed its mind, as some charged ("their bad habit of reversing themselves," in the words of one downtown leader), whether Feinstein attempted to impose more than the agreement called for, or whether the chamber simply was unable to control all its members is impossible to unravel. While Feinstein attempted to dismiss downtown's negative reaction, business leaders were being quoted (anonymously) as saying: "They're mad as hell at her. Just furious." "They're not like the activists who march into her office. Businessmen don't act this way. But they're getting together a big legal fund to fight these things."[60] "Who the hell does the Chamber think it is to impose that on building owners?"[61] Related to the city hall–Chamber of Commerce tension was the removal of the chamber's long-term executive director, William Dauer, who had been something of a hard-liner against downtown concessions on transit subsidies and new taxes, and his replacement by the more sophisticated and urbane John Jacobs, SPUR's long-term executive director.

Feinstein at first tried to hold fast: "Two-thirds of Muni routes go downtown. The Muni is saturated at peak hours, people packed like cattle. The Muni riders did their fair share with a doubling of the Muni fare [in March 1980]. The tourists did their bit with the hotel tax increase."[62] But, she insisted, "my hand is out to downtown"[63] —a remark that doubtless must be interpreted in its conciliatory sense. The mayor's lack of backbone on this issue—which enraged labor and community groups—was described by Richard Sklar, the wealthy businessman and Democratic Party activist George Moscone brought into City government to head the mammoth wastewater treatment program and, for a time, the YBC project (under the chief administrative officer), and the man Dianne Feinstein later confirmed as general manager of the City's Public Utilities Commission:*

*Sklar has had a quite varied career, both within and outside of San Francisco. His most recent incarnation, rooted in work on Bill Clinton's 1992 presidential campaign, was reported in a 5 July 1996 *Washington Post* story, headlined "Mr. Fix-It Goes to Bosnia," which began: "After building 11 airports, digging sewage systems, renovating San Francisco's cable cars, constructing a basketball arena in Cleveland and making himself and those around him fabulously rich, Sklar, 61, accepted perhaps the most challenging assignment of his varied career as salesman, engineer and Democratic Party operative." That assignment: President Clinton's special representative in Bosnia, "to try to resuscitate the flagging fortunes of the Dayton peace deal." Needless to say, it was not one of his more successful ventures.

We had an agreement with the Chamber of Commerce that in exchange for the fare increase a one-time downtown development fee would be paid at $5 a square foot. The chamber endorsed it in their own editorial. It was a commitment they made, and they backed away from it. Then the mayor backed away too. . . . Dianne Feinstein is not the world's most courageous person. She doesn't like a lot of heat. She is much more comfortable with downtown, with large business executives, than she is with the labor community for example, or the people in the neighborhoods.[64]

The business leaders did indeed react as predicted. The most prominent action was taken by Walter Shorenstein, the city's number-one real estate mogul ("He is said to have played a part in the construction of some 12 million square feet of office space, and his firm [Milton Meyer and Company] is the leasing agent for millions more")[65]* and a key figure in Democratic Party fund raising.† Shorenstein and his lawyer, William Coblentz, led a

---

*A not atypical account of Shorenstein's larger political role, from the 14 June 1987 *New York Times* ("Democratic Fete Highlights Power of a Top Fundraiser," by E. J. Dionne Jr.), reads: ". . . when Walter Shorenstein decided that the nation's top Democrats should come here [San Francisco] for a party, they came. . . . [F]ive of the seven Democratic Presidential candidates [Richard Gephardt, Albert Gore Jr., Jesse Jackson, Bruce Babbitt, Paul Simon; the two who were not present, Michael Dukakis and Joseph Biden, sent their wives] appeared Friday night to pay homage to Mr. Shorenstein." Governor Babbitt was quoted as saying, "The candidates are all here on bended knee, that's what it's all about." "At the news conference," the account went on, "Mr. Shorenstein sat in the middle of a long table, surrounded by important Democrats. . . . One by one, they spoke in praise of Mr. Shorenstein. Shorenstein announced at the dinner in his honor that the event would raise at least $800,000." Limits on individual campaign contributions put a premium on getting friends and associates to contribute, and Shorenstein has enormous power and influence with respect to friends and associates. A 2 March 1997 *Washington Post* story by Bob Woodward on the fund-raising flap over Vice President Gore's activities ("Gore Was 'Solicitor-In-Chief' in '96 Elections Campaign") featured a photo of Shorenstein and noted, "In California, the Vice-President's chief money man is Walter Shorenstein . . . who is reportedly worth $500 million and is considered the Democrats' key monied patron in the West." A chart in the 9 January 1999, *Washington Post* showing the nation's major individual "soft money" contributors (for which there were no limits) lists Shorenstein as number five, having given $463,000 in 1997.

†Shorenstein wields stick and carrot masterfully in San Francisco development politics. And he knows how to use his civic beneficence to advance his business interests as well. When the Planning Commission reversed earlier disapproval of his planned twenty-seven-story office tower at Mission and Main Streets as too bulky and blocking too many views, the 12 August 1983, *Examiner* noted, "Privately, commissioners had expressed apprehensions about demanding more rigid standards from a developer who had assumed a leading role in raising funds so the city could accommodate the Democratic National Convention next summer." *Chronicle* columnist Herb Caen commented (15 August 1983), "There's only one way to read this: give Walter his latest toy, or he'll turn off the spigot that is pouring millions into the convention."

group that challenged the legality of the transit fee, which therefore was put on ice until a court ruled on the matter. Shorenstein et al. claimed that the one-time fee violated Proposition 13, which requires approval by two-thirds of the voters to introduce a new tax; the City claimed it was not a tax but a fee, and therefore excluded from the provisions of Proposition 13. A fundraising luncheon hosted by Shorenstein was rumored to have yielded $300,000 to pay for this litigation, $100,000 of which came from Southern Pacific, which would have had to cough up millions in connection with its massive proposed Mission Bay project.[66] The case went to trial in early 1984, but not until May 1987 did the state Supreme Court rule on the matter (a unanimous decision, confirming earlier Court of Appeals and trial court rulings), upholding the fee, by which time $28.5 million had accrued in an escrow fund.[67]

A 1991 Planning Department report stated that 144 office projects had contributed $58.7 million to the fund.[68] However, many builders who should be paying these fees nonetheless manage to escape the requirement. One instance, reported in early 2001, involved the developers of 650 Townsend Street, South of Market, a huge wholesale apparel showroom renovated primarily as office space for high-tech companies that has evaded paying at least $3.2 million in transit fees for its 640,000-square-foot project. The "complex shell games the city allows developers to play to avoid paying such fees" in this case involves the law's wording that the money is to be paid before a "certificate of final completion and occupancy" is issued. Such a certificate is issued by the Building Inspection Department, stipulating that the City has given the project a final okay and occupants can move in. Zoro, LLC, developer of 650 Townsend, maintains that under building code rules, no such certificate is required because the building code classification did not change: no certificate issued, no fee due. While obviously a strained, self-serving reading of the law (which clearly is intended to generate transit funds when new office space is created, as certainly happened here), the Planning Commission (before whom Zoro appeared in order to gain permission for the project—and as a result of which Zoro did pay the required affordable housing and childcare fees associated with such developments, but not the transit fee) has been less than forceful in pursuing the City's claim. Unfortunately, this is not an isolated case: "City officials and planning watchdogs suspect that the building . . . is just one among maybe a dozen, or more, that owe the city millions of dollars meant to improve the transit system."[69] Assuming a dozen such projects at the same required fee, that would amount to a hefty $38 million to assist long-suffering Muni riders.

The May 1981 transit assessment district proposal never led to an actual ordinance. By mid-1982, "as a result of an agreement worked out in a private meeting with Chamber of Commerce executive director John Jacobs, the mayor no longer supports the assessment district."[70] At the public hearings required pursuant to creation of a special assessment district, downtown business representatives raised a fearful row, and the message got through to city hall. The idea was shelved (by a ten-to-one vote of the supervisors in July 1983), and Feinstein proposed in its place a small increase in the City's payroll/gross receipts tax, to be allocated to Muni, a tax producing far less revenue (under $3 million a year) and relatively less burden for downtown, as it applied to businesses throughout the city.

In 1994, a coalition representing environmentalists, the elderly, the disabled, neighborhood activists, transport workers unions, and others collected enough signatures to place a proposition on the November ballot, supporting creation of a transit assessment district and allocating up to $300,000 for preparatory work, including updating the 1981 studies. Proponents cited City budget analyst estimates that the annual cost of servicing the downtown area—to and from which 78 percent of Muni service is devoted during commuting hours—had risen to $54 million. Although supported by seven supervisors, a Chamber of Commerce–led campaign resulted in a 55 to 45 percent defeat for the measure.

The most recent move to improve the city's public transit system appeared on the November 1999 ballot, a widely backed initiative (Proposition E) labeled the Muni Reform Charter Amendment. The progenitor was Rescue Muni, "A Transit Riders' Association," formed in 1996 as a result of constant consumer complaints—mainly about late and unreliable service. ("In mass transit, beauty is being on-time, and being on-time is beauty. And that is all you need to know to understand why San Franciscans hate the Municipal Railway.")[71] Extraordinary failures, such as the August 1998 "Muni meltdown," when all the light rail vehicles in the Market Street tunnel broke down, trapping panicked riders under the streets, helped trigger the revolt of the masses. The measure—product of a dizzying political process involving SPUR, Mayor Willie Brown, elements of the business community, and organized riders[72]—passed, creating a unified, more or less politically independent transportation agency out of the former Public Transportation Commission and the Department of Parking and Traffic. It is designed to protect public transit from budget cuts; strengthen the City's Transit First policy; impose strong standards for service, backed by merit pay; and reform union work rules. This last feature, even in a town as union-conscious as San Francisco, had widespread support: Existing work rules permitted a situation whereby on any given day some one-third of all workers were absent from all or part of their shift, without a requirement to call in and without effective disciplinary measures. Poor management practices, faulty equipment, and insufficient support for mass transit doubtless create a depressing and inefficient work environment that in turn leads to poor morale and absenteeism. The business community favored the measure in large part because it deflected attention from creation of a downtown transit assessment district, stressing instead increased financing from the City's general fund (a move that could well mean shortchanging other needed City services). After Proposition E passed, Mayor Brown appointed, and the Board of Supervisors approved, the seven members of the new Municipal Transportation Agency. By law, at least four had to be regular Muni riders, and the others must ride an average of once a week. Brown's choices were a disappointment to many Muni critics and reform advocates: "Mayor Willie Brown's new board to run Muni has no pedestrian advocates. No bicycle advocates. No well-known Muni reformers," began the *Examiner* account. No member of Rescue Muni—the key advocacy organization that produced the reform—was appointed (although they did get token representation on the agency's fifteen-member citizens advisory committee).[73]

Housing Remedies

With respect to housing mitigation measures—requiring developers to provide housing to meet the demand created by the office workers employed in their buildings—results have been slightly better, but far from adequate. The principal tool has been the Office Housing Production Program (OHPP), subsequently renamed the Office Affordable Housing Production Program, a somewhat loose set of requirements imposed on developers by the City Planning Commission as part of its plan approval process. This measure had its origins not only in recognition of the housing burdens created for the city by office development but also in the necessity to devise alternatives to traditional federal housing subsidies that all but dried up with the advent of the Reagan administration. In principle, such exactions are by no means new. Local governments often require suburban housing developers to dedicate streets, sewer lines, recreation areas, schools, and other facilities, the need for which arises from the housing construction. San Francisco, New York, Santa Monica, Boston, Denver, and Washington, D.C., are among the many cities that have been using this device most creatively or considering its adoption.[74]

San Francisco has been imposing such requirements on downtown developers for many years. When the Ramada, Holiday Inn, and Hilton Hotels came to the Planning Commission in 1980 for permission to build a total of twenty-four hundred new luxury hotel rooms, the commission, concerned about the impact of the development on the adjacent Tenderloin neighborhood, and pushed hard by well-organized residents of the area, extracted an agreement from the Ramada and Holiday Inn to create a housing subsidy fund for the neighborhood, by adding fifty cents per room per night onto the room rate for 80 percent of the new hotel rooms (the assumed average occupancy rate for the hotels) for twenty years, producing $5.4 million over the life of the agreement; the two hotels also agreed to pay $400,000 over four years to fund neighborhood-designated social services and to give priority in 50 percent of the jobs at the new hotels to Tenderloin residents. (The Hilton, after initially balking at giving in to such demands, later acceded to those same conditions.) OHPP converted an ad hoc bargaining process, responsive largely to neighborhood pressures, into a more structured, codified system.

San Francisco's exactions from developers originally were based on the California Environmental Quality Act (CEQA), under which housing market impact is regarded as an environmental effect, around which mitigation measures can be demanded. A complex formula developed by the City Planning Department, originally applicable to all new commercial buildings larger than fifty thousand square feet (subsequently amended to include projects larger than twenty-five thousand square feet), combined an assumed number of square feet per worker and the percentage of such workers assumed to live in San Francisco, yielding a requirement to provide housing for a certain number of workers (applying then a figure representing how many workers are in the average San Francisco household).[75]

This seemingly scientific formula (which has been criticized for underestimating the proportion of the downtown workforce that winds up living in the city,[76] and for using an average household size that includes only workers, not the total household, all of whose members need living space) then, under the original program, was diluted with a variety of somewhat arbitrarily conceived incentives and escape routes to make things less onerous for developers. Substituting "credits" for "dwellings" as the currency with which deals were made, the formula permitted multiple credits for units provided for low- and moderate-income households and for extra bedrooms beyond one. (This formulaic sleight of hand meant that if all the OHPP units produced were standard two-bedroom units, the city would get only about half the housing units it needs, according to its own inadequate calculations; in the unlikely event that all the units built were two-bedroom apartments for low-income households, for which triple bonus credit was given, the city would wind up with about one-sixth of the units it needs.) For a time, the formula also allowed developers the option of paying six thousand dollars per unit into the City's Home Mortgage Assistance Trust Fund, a pool used to reduce mortgage payments for first-time homebuyers taking advantage of the already lower-interest mortgages made available under the City's mortgage revenue bond program.

When OHPP was revised and renamed in 1985, a per square foot fee was established ($7.05 up to 2001, when the formula was changed—see below), giving office developers the option of producing housing directly or paying the fee. Most have chosen to do the latter. Such fees then are deposited into the Citywide Affordable Housing Fund, administered by the Director of Planning, in cooperation with the Mayor's Office of Housing.

In the OHPP period (1981–85), thirty-eight office developers assisted in the creation (via rehabilitation as well as new construction) of 5,690 housing units, 3,841 of them "affordable"—using a somewhat capacious definition. Between 1985 and 1994, ten office projects kicked in slightly over $8 million in "in-lieu" fees to the Citywide Affordable Housing Fund (which money is used as deferred payment loans), in addition to direct construction of 255 residential units and 47 affordable to low- and moderate-income households.[77] But shockingly, as is the case with transit subsidy fees (see above), many millions of dollars ($12 million to $22 million is the estimate) in these housing fees, as well as related fees for child care, schools, and open space, have either been uncollected or "lost" in the system during the late nineties construction boom. Some admixture of incompetence and lack of political will to burden developers led to this situation. Communications failures between the Planning Department, responsible for collecting most of these fees, and the mayor's Office of Housing, which is the beneficiary of the largest portion of these moneys, is one problem. "[City Planning] Department staffers this week could not produce a list of all the office projects required to contribute to affordable housing and how much each developer owed. Nor could they say exactly how much money was currently in the fund. According to planning staff . . . [t]here is no system for monitoring compliance with the agreed-upon conditions, including fees for affordable housing, child care and public transportation." Related communications/coordination problems between the other City collection agencies and the receiving entities are at work as well. The Planning Department also has not adjusted the fees for inflation, as the City codes require.[78]

In February 2001, the Board of Supervisors enacted the Jobs Housing Linkage Program (JHLP), an expansion and improvement of the Office Affordable Housing Production Program. Under the new ordinance, developers of commercial office, entertainment, hotel, retail, and research and development projects larger than twenty-five thousand square feet now have an increased set of mitigation requirements to offset the impact on housing demand created by their workforce. A detailed formula dealing with numbers of housing units by affordability level governs the program's requirements for linkage fees (or alternative benefits) to be paid to the City-wide Affordable Housing Fund. Not only are the fees higher than under the former ordinance (and are adjusted annually, in addition to a requirement that the entire formula must be updated via new studies every five years), but the scope of coverage is far broader. Under the old ordinance, only office buildings in the downtown area were covered; now the full range of development projects listed above are covered, and the offset benefits are mandated for projects anywhere in the city. (Fees vary by type of development, with office, entertainment, and retail projects paying the highest fees, hotels and research and development projects the lowest.) And to ensure enforcement and accountability—a weak element in the earlier effort—the City Planning Department is charged with public notice responsibilities; occupancy permits will not be issued unless the requirements are met. Either payment of an in-lieu fee into the City fund or contribution of money or land to a housing developer (for construction or acquisition—developers also are permitted to self-develop, although none has chosen to do so to date) will satisfy the requirement; also, 60 percent of rental housing developed with such contributions (100 percent of ownership developments) must remain affordable to households earning no more than 60 percent of median income.[79]

In some cases, lower-income households clearly have benefited from these programs, such as through the $3.5 million payment by the Marathon Corporation to help the City finish a three-hundred-unit project in the Hunters Point renewal area that had exhausted its funds, and the $2.5 million payment to the Housing Authority by Cahill Construction Company to help renovate the notorious "Pink Palace" housing project in the Western Addition.[80] In the process, developers and large corporations create an image for themselves as socially conscious public benefactors, whose officials are featured in the newspapers and on television handing over checks to the mayor and planning director. Many of the contributions to rehabilitate low-rent units also turned out to be a lot cheaper for the developers—twenty-two hundred to five thousand dollars per unit, compared to the six thousand dollars per unit in-lieu cash payment.[81]

It is clear, however, that whatever their benefits for the public and the developers, these programs compensate for only a small portion of the city's housing needs created by these developers' projects, let alone the needs that exist apart from their new projects. Only a small portion of the units produced under the program are affordable by low- and moderate-income households. The tool, while clearly of some help, doesn't even begin to resemble a housing plan, an attempt to match known housing demand with units of the necessary size, type, and income level; it is simply an attempt to squeeze some housing, any housing, out of a development community eager to build offices, with the hope that somehow this will help ameliorate the city's housing crisis.

Significantly, the program has met little resistance from the development community. "Call it extortion or blackmail, depending on your judgment," commented an official of Canada's Marathon Corporation, "but we're pragmatic. We've come to San Francisco to build quality projects and when you come to a community, you observe the rules."[82] And a law review evaluation of the program noted, "Although developers consider OHPP to be an annoyance, they do not find the price of participation prohibitive. OHPP will increase costs to office developers, and office tenants, by less than three percent. . . . Office developers have adjusted to OHPP by treating it as a nonprofitmaking investment of resources."[83] Significantly, passage of a state law in 1982, undercutting the City's reliance on the state's Environmental Quality Act for imposing mitigation measures and requiring cities to pass their own ordinances to establish a legal basis for such exaction—a bill that, according to one Planning Department official "had San Francisco written all over it"—caused almost no disruption in the actual workings of the OHPP program. Although the City's process of drafting such an ordinance took an unaccountably long time, during which there technically was no legal basis for the OHPP exactions, the Planning Commission met with no refusals by developers to undertake these commitments (likely because developers, fearing more stringent growth control measures, were eager to get their projects through the commission as expeditiously as possible).

The second prong of the high-rise opponents' earlier efforts with respect to the housing obligations of office developers has been litigation to prevent Planning Commission approval of new buildings. This was based on the City's failure to have an approved housing element in its master plan, as required under CEQA, and on the failure of the City's environmental impact reports to assess the cumulative impacts of individual developments, including likely but at that time as yet unapproved projects such as the Yerba Buena Center Central Blocks and Southern Pacific's Mission Bay. On these grounds, a string of nearly a dozen lawsuits was filed in 1981 and 1982 by San Franciscans for Reasonable Growth's Sue Hestor, challenging virtually every building and environmental impact report that went before the Planning Commission for approval. The claim was that no mere violation of a technicality of law was involved, but that traditional practice illustrated a fundamental point the group had made all along: that allowing virtually unlimited office growth without a corresponding plan to provide housing for the city's old and new residents guarantees the kinds of shortages and market pressures that drive older and poorer residents out, thereby converting the city into a middle- and upper-class enclave. The City's efforts to produce a housing element acceptable to state officials had been an embarrassment. Twice in less than a year (1982) the state Department of Housing and Community Development rejected what the City submitted, declaring the second time "that the housing plan was so deficient it was unable to determine if the City was 'making good faith, diligent effort' to produce affordable housing."[84]

The City's response to the housing element challenge was classic: The developers and city hall teamed up to do an end run around these protests and lawsuits by sneaking into a bill pending before the state legislature an amendment stipulating that, in San Francisco only, office development permits issued before May 1, 1983, cannot be invalidated because of the City's failure to comply with the CEQA housing element requirements, providing the permits are conditioned upon developers meeting the City's Office Housing Production Program requirements. According to the *San Francisco Progress*, "The amendment was introduced by . . . Jim Costa (Dem. -Fresno), reportedly at the request of Assembly Speaker Willie Brown. . . . Some of the key projects involved in the SFRG suits are represented by Attorney William Coblentz, who allegedly instigated the legislative move to protect high-rise permits."[85] According to the *Chronicle*, Mayor Feinstein had urged this devious maneuver, and "San Francisco attorney Bill McCabe, who, with his partner William Coblentz, represents a number of downtown buildings, acknowledged that he had helped draft the language of the controversial amendment."[86] And the *Bay Guardian* reported, "Sources have also confirmed that Mayor Dianne Feinstein called Costa to argue in support of the amended bill,"[87] which passed easily, effectively undercutting this entire set of SFRG lawsuits.

In early 1984, a state Court of Appeals panel unanimously ruled in favor of Hestor's suit on the adequacy of the City's environmental impact reports. "We remind those agencies directly responsible for compliance with the law . . . that they do a great injustice to both the developers and members of the general public by an insufficient evaluation of the potential severe impacts upon the environment of San Francisco which results from construction of these types of projects (for example, the impact caused by transporting more live bodies in and out of an already highly congested and geographically confined area)." The opinion went on: "The only reason we can infer for the [planning] commission's failure to consider and analyze this group of projects was that it was more expedient to ignore them."[88] The court refused, however, to halt already approved projects, on the grounds this would create "economic havoc," but told the Planning Commission to prepare fuller environmental impact reports, in order to provide the public with adequate information. The City decided not to appeal the ruling.

A more recent litigation struggle revolves around rebuilding the old Emporium department store site—on Market Street between Fourth and Fifth, down to Mission Street. Planned reuse (as of mid-2001) is a Bloomingdales, a 465-room hotel, a nine-screen movie theater, a couple of dozen units of housing, offices, and a shopping mall—the works. By incorporating the proposed development into the Yerba Buena urban renewal project area, it's exempted from various planning controls. One issue is unionization: After some struggle, a compromise was reached, whereby the developers (Forest City Development Corp.) agreed to allow the card check system rather than formal election procedures to determine if employees want union representation, as well as other steps to make unionization easier—concessions that exclude the Federated Stores' Bloomies, as there was less leverage on that parcel compared with the rest of the development site, for which the City is scheduled to lend Forest City $27 million. The issue on which litigation was brought in December 2000 by environmentalists, preservationists, and neighborhood activists has to do with destruction of the Emporium building itself (vintage 1908, a category one historical structure with an architecturally important facade and dome), as well as perhaps a dozen other historic structures, which might violate state environmental protection laws, plus violation of the City's Downtown Plan, related to the transfer of the project to the Redevelopment Agency's YBC project: Although the plaintiffs received an adverse ruling in May 2001, they have appealed the decision.[89]

The Housing Crisis and the Housing Movement

San Francisco's housing costs are among the highest, if not the highest, of any of the nation's large cities. The Planning Department's annual report indicated that the median monthly rent in 1999 for a two-bedroom apartment was $2,500.[1] An early 2001 *Chronicle* feature reports that the average rent for an apartment of this size is $2,752.[2] What is astounding is not only the high rents—in a city where some two-thirds of the residents are tenants—but also the staggering rapidity with which rents have risen in just the past couple of years. The 1997 median figure for a two-bedroom unit was $1,600; in 1996, it was $1,350; in 1995, $1,100.[3] To be able to pay even twenty-five hundred dollars a month as rent, using the federal guidelines (for subsidized housing) of 30 percent of income, a tenant needs an annual income along the order of $100,000.

Looked at from the another angle, HUD's 2000 annual State of the Cities report concluded: "A person earning the minimum wage in San Francisco would have to work the equivalent of 174 hours a week [six more hours than there are in a week] just to pay the median rent."[4] A September 2000 study by the National Low Income Housing Coalition reported that a renter in San Francisco would need to earn an hourly wage of $28.06 to afford a modest two-bedroom apartment—the highest figure in the nation in this report on nationwide housing problems.[5] The gap between salaries, at least at the lower end, and housing costs is staggering. In mid-2000, the City finally (after two years of hard-core lobbying and delicate negotiating) enacted a "living wage" law of the type more than eighty cities and counties now have, mandating an hourly wage of nine dollars, plus benefits, for employees of City contractors and leaseholders, nonprofit agencies with City contracts, and businesses at San Francisco International Airport—affecting an estimated twenty-one thousand workers in all. In 2001, the living wage rose to ten dollars, to be followed by 2.5 percent raises in the three following years. (By contrast, California's minimum hourly wage is just $5.75; the San Francisco law is a watered-down version of the original proposal by Supervisor Tom Ammiano, which called for an $11.00 hourly wage.) But Ammiano pointed out this San Francisco reality: "Everyone knows it's not a living wage. It's still a minimum wage."[6] A far more realistic take on the city's income problem is provided in the "Self-Sufficiency Standard" developed by Diana Pearce of the University of Washington: "how much money is needed, for a family of a given composition in a given place, to adequately meet its basic needs—without public or private assistance." For San Francisco, using just one example of household type, a single parent with a preschooler and one child in school would require an hourly wage of $24.64, yielding an annual income of $52,040—three-and-a-half times the federal poverty standard for a family of three, more than two-and-a-half times the new City "living wage."[7] Add to this the fact that Money Magazine in 2000 rated San Francisco as "the best place to live" among all U.S. cities.

The result is pathetic absurdities like this: fifty-seven hundred applicants for fifty-five affordable housing units (three-bedrooms for $693 a month, courtesy of City, state, and federal subsidies) at the new Bernal Gateway development at the corner of Cesar Chavez and Mission; more than sixteen hundred applicants for the fifty-five low-income units that opened in December 2000 at SOMA Residences at Sixth and Minna.[8] Another sad tale, as headlined in an April 4, 2000, Examiner story, "Hot S.F. Rent Market Is Cool to Vouchers: Hundreds of Section 8 Families Can't Find Housing": This federal-local program, run by the Housing Authority, covers the gap between the market rent (with a federally set local cap) and 30 percent of the tenant's income, but a shortage of available units (plus occasional landlord discrimination against certificate holders) turns the program into a cruel joke for all too many families. The New York Times ran a feature on the plight of would-be San Francisco renters as "supplicants," describing situations in which as many as a hundred applicants showed up for an open house and people offered more than the already sky-high asking rent. "Rental agents are suggesting that prospective tenants come armed with renters' resumes detailing their credit and job history, credit reports and references. They also suggest that renters wear professional attire and show enthusiasm for the apartment, as though the $1,800-a-month junior one-bedroom walk-up overlooking the freeway were their dream pad, the place they wanted to make a home for life. 'Renting a place in San Francisco, peo-ple have to treat it as if they are applying to an Ivy League college,' said . . . [the] president of . . . an apartment-listing service. 'You have to kiss up to the landlords. The landlords can pick the crème de la crème of tenants, the absolute perfect person for their space.' "[9]

Home ownership is an increasingly wild financial stretch for most fami-lies. The median price as of February 2001 for new and existing homes and condos was \$512,500.[10] The so-called "affordability index" published by the California Association of Realtors—the percentage of households that can afford to purchase a median-priced home in their area—was a staggeringly low 10 percent for San Francisco in December 2000, the lowest of any county in the state (as noted, San Francisco is a county as well as a city; the index is created for counties). By comparison, the figure was 32 percent for the state as a whole,[11] 55 percent for the entire United States.[12] A similar type of index published by the National Association of Home Builders—the Housing Op-portunity Index, which measures the percentage of homes sold that a fam-ily earning the median income can afford to buy—showed the San Francisco metropolitan area as the least affordable in the nation: Only 11.9 percent of homes were affordable in the third quarter of 1999 (a steep drop in just three months, from the 15.7 percent second quarter figure).[13]

Not surprisingly, as a 2001 *Examiner* report on a Chamber of Commerce survey headlined, "Housing Tops S.F. Voters' Worries": 38 percent of those polled cited tight and unaffordable housing as the city's worst problem, up from 14 percent in 1997.[14] Similar results came from a late 2000 *Chronicle* poll, which asked, "Thinking of all the issues affecting your part of the Bay Area, what do you think is the biggest problem today?" Forty-three per-cent of San Francisco respondents said housing prices/availability, more than twice the 19 percent figure for the next most frequently cited problem, traf-fic/transportation.[15]

This enormously popular and attractive city has seen much of its lower-income housing lost to wrecking balls, both in redevelopment areas like Yerba Buena Center and Western Addition A-1 and A-2 (over ten thou-sand units in these three areas alone were demolished—a portion was re-placed, but mostly for different income groups and after passage of many years) and via private market redevelopment activities, as well as to gen-trification and conversion of rental units into condominiums. Planning De-partment data show that in the 1975–85 decade alone, more than seven-teen thousand affordable rental units were demolished, converted to condominiums, or converted to commercial use.[16] New housing is being built, although at a rate far below what is needed (and offset by losses to the stock, due to demolitions, conversions, code enforcement, mergers, and fires); for the most part, however, these additions are at prices and rents affordable only by the upper-middle class. Mayor Dianne Feinstein's planning commissioner, Jerome Klein, stated it well as far back as the early eighties: "It appears very difficult to get any housing built where it is needed."[17]

Pressures on the city's housing stock come from many sources. Demographic changes such as marital breakups, a more independent elderly population, and children leaving home earlier all lead to an increased number of small households. Foreign immigration, particularly from Central America and various parts of Asia, adds to demand, as does the city's role as the "gay capital of the world"—another source of immigration, by small, relatively affluent households. But the principal pressures stem from expansion of the downtown office-based economy, which brings new workers to the city, increasing the effective demand for existing housing by corporate employees who can outbid older residents, and in recent times from the "Silicon implants" (in the *Bay Guardian*'s felicitous phrase): young affluent professionals from the new industrial sector who prefer San Francisco to living on the Peninsula (even if there were enough housing for them there). A November 28, 1998, *Washington Post* account of these developments observed:

> The massive growth of the computer industry in Silicon Valley an hour's drive south of here has created a extreme new housing crunch in the city in the past two years. Wealthy young computer programmers are stampeding into poor neighborhoods here [San Francisco], snatching any apartment they can find and pressuring city officials to clean up the blight. Rents are soaring and evictions are rising as property owners rush to profit from the migration. . . . In the Mission district, where many residents are poor, there is so much tension over the influx of affluent newcomers that some long-time residents have plastered the neighborhood with fliers calling for a "Yuppie Eradication Project" and encouraging vandalism of sports-utility vehicles parked there. [See fig. 8.]

The result is not only soaring rents and house prices, but also (relatedly) an overall shortage: The city's true vacancy rate (above and beyond what is needed for normal mobility) hovers around zero.

People have been forced out of the city in vast numbers or have doubled up as the only way to stay in San Francisco. Eviction data are not systematically collected (a major issue is how to define evictions—whether to count only those who leave after formal legal processes have been initiated or to include as well those who "voluntarily" depart under the threat of eviction or because rent increases make their unit unaffordable). Formal evictions rose from slightly more than two thousand in 1971 to nearly six thousand in 1983.[18] The San Francisco Tenants Union, which monitors this issue most closely, states: "We have maintained a periodic watch over court records and our most recent informal count has showed Municipal Court evictions in the 6,000–8,000 [annual] range since 1986. A 1992 survey of three months of court data, however, projected 1992 evictions at about 9,500."[19] While the very "cleansing" process that gentrification causes has already cleared out the easiest to expel tenants, eviction rates are still high. The San Francisco Tenants Union reported in late 2000 that there are 7.5 evictions a day, or more than twenty-seven hundred annually.

The virtual disappearance of direct federal subsidy programs for new housing has of course exacerbated the problem. The head of the University of California's Center for Real Estate and Urban Economics, Kenneth Rosen, concluded in the early eighties, "At this rate we could become a place only the elite can afford."[20] Entire neighborhoods of San Francisco, a city known for its diversity and pluralism, have become largely enclaves for households known as "DINKS" in planners' jargon—double incomes, no kids.

Perhaps the saddest, and most dramatic, neighborhood transformation is taking place in the Mission, as captured in this 1999 *New York Times* account:

> The entire Mission District, port of entry for San Francisco's Hispanic immigrants for more than 50 years, is changing by the day. New people, people who have money, are moving in, altering life for everyone. Sagging Victorian houses that landlords had chopped into two or three rental units are sold for a half million dollars, and warehouses are becoming loft condominiums in the $300,000 to $400,000 range. . . . In the last three years, rents here have jumped from $600 a month for a two-bedroom apartment to $1800; a house that cost $150,000 is now $450,000. More tenants have been evicted in the last three years than at any other time by landlords using a city ordinance that allows eviction if the owner or a relative plans to move in for at least a year. Last year, 1400 apartments in the city were emptied for this reason, most of them in the Mission District. Tenant advocates say the real numbers are much higher because scores of families simply moved out when asked by their landlords. . . . "Evictions are all we do these days," says Matt Brown, a lawyer who directs the St. Peter's Housing Committee in the Mission, a tenants' advocacy group. "We'd like to do other things, like community organizing, but the housing situation has made it almost impossible." . . . So Mission residents are increasingly moving out of the city. Those who stay often rent space in friends' or relatives' apartments, miserable single-room-occupancy hotels, garages, storage barns or even vans.[21]

The reporter then quotes a Mission displacee—sounding for all the world like the folks moved out for the Yerba Buena Center project:

"I've been displaced from everything I knew. I had a plot in a community garden. I had my doctors, my grocery stores, my restaurants. I used to go to the stores and buy things on credit, or cash checks with the storekeepers. I also miss the transportation." She stopped, caught her breath and wiped away a sudden flow of tears. "It's not that the Mission was any utopia," she said, "but it was my home."

Current changes in the Mission are in sad contrast to the neighborhood's antigentrification efforts in the late sixties and early seventies. As community organizer Mike Miller, staff director of the Mission Coalition Organization from 1968 to 1971, describes it in his unpublished November 1999 paper, "Creating an Atmosphere Inhospitable to Investment": "Since the late 1950s, when the Bay Area Rapid Transit system was on the drawing boards, [the] Mission District has been targeted for speculative investment as well as being an attractive place for gentrification; it was threatened with urban renewal and red-lined by lenders." During the 1966–71 period, two community organizing efforts—first the Mission Council on Redevelopment (MCOR), later the Mission Coalition Organization (MCO)—were able to forestall speculators, urban renewal, and invasion by yuppies, and preserve the affordable housing stock for the neighborhood's multiethnic, multiracial residents—at the time, large numbers of Irish and Italian families in addition to the predominant Latino population. MCOR was able to defeat before the Board of Supervisors a bulldozer urban renewal project, and, later, MCO was able to control Mayor Joseph Alioto's Model Cities project by becoming the official "citizen participation" component required under federal law. Contrary to what Alioto envisioned, the Model Cities program pumped millions of dollars into the neighborhood for community-preserving activities and helped spawn such organizations as the Mission Housing Development Corporation and the Mission Hiring Hall. In both cases, victory was possible because the organizations represented a coalition—formed by good community organizing—that included conservative white ethnic and Anglo homeowner and small merchant associations, Catholic and Protestant churches, and a variety of Latino and other nationality, social action, and civic associations. MCO came to encompass more than one hundred churches and block clubs and homeowner, tenant, senior citizen, youth, community social agency, small merchant, and other groups. Their tactics embraced militant marches and demonstrations—rent strikes, sit-ins, and other disruptive actions—mixed with lobbying based on careful research. Miller wrote,

> MCO was able to mix breadth of representation with militancy in tactics because it took seriously the obligation of being a multi-constituency,

multi-issue organization. The organizing staff worked with homeowners and merchants as well as with tenants and employment-seeking youth. From this work came action on issues important to the various constituencies. When one member organization couldn't win a battle alone, it came to MCO for assistance from other member organizations. Youth got to know seniors; homeowners got to know tenants; merchants got to know the unemployed. Relationships were forged among them as they supported each other. Preserving the family-oriented, affordable housing and store-front character of the neighborhood was an overarching value connecting everyone.

Miller, who participated in the Civil Rights movement in Mississippi in 1964, emphasizes the important role of disruptive direct action with a broad base of organizational support—the history of the labor movement in the 1930s provides the same lesson. "People power" must accompany efforts to achieve results through legislation, regulation, and the administration of housing and economic development programs if gentrification and speculative buying in affordable housing neighborhoods are to be stopped. San Francisco's current political climate, however, makes this impossible: The economic and political power behind gentrification of the Mission is just too great.

There has been some community organizing against gentrification, but it likely is too little, too late. The Mission Anti-Displacement Coalition, an association of more than a dozen local organizations, formed in mid-2000, held community meetings, testified before public bodies, and otherwise sought to create a force to stop the financial bulldozer. One such event, a Planning Commission hearing on a plan to convert the National Guard Mission Armory, at Fourteenth/Fifteenth and Mission, into offices, got citywide publicity when it turned pretty raucous, with dozens of sheriff's deputies and police and a wrestling match that ensued when a Mission activist was ordered to stop speaking after exceeding his allotted testimony time (by less than ten seconds).[22] Other forms of protest have emanated from the Mission Yuppie Eradication Project (mentioned in the *Washington Post* excerpt above), which puts posters advocating vandalism against upscale vehicles and restaurants on mail boxes, telephone polls, and utility boxes.[23] (See fig. 8.) While the armory issue remained unsettled as of early 2001, other major Mission neighborhood projects are done deals. Bryant Square, a five-story, six-building, square-block complex (bounded by York, Bryant, Nineteenth, and Twentieth Streets) will provide 150,000 square feet of office space. Opposed strongly by area residents, it was a slam dunk before Mayor Brown's Planning Commission; the $100,000 contribution to Brown's 1999 reelection campaign by the developer, Dan Kingsley of SKS Investments, is a not irrelevant tidbit.[24] Perhaps saddest, and most telling, of all is the tale of the

Bay View Federal Savings & Loan building, at Twenty-Second and Mission Streets, the neighborhood's sole high-rise. In late 1999, its two dozen tenants—community newspapers and radio stations, small business associations, child care referral agencies, social service groups, health agencies, family and immigration lawyers, and bilingual accountants serving the neighborhood's Latino community—were given six-month vacate notices so the building can be converted to more upscale commercial office use. (The redeveloper, the Robert J. Cort Trust, caused a recent uproar when it whitewashed a five-thousand-square-foot mural—the kind of neighborhood art characteristic of the Mission—from a nearby Harrison Street building.) A similar tale involved the Redstone Building at Sixteenth and Capp, home to forty-five arts and grassroots political groups. Among the groups evicted: the gay Theater Rhinoceros, the feminist theater Luna Sea, the Latino El Teatro de la Esperanza, the Mission Area Federal Credit Union, the Filipino-American Employment and Training Center, the Industrial Workers of the World, the Homeless Children's Network, the Coalition on Homelessness, *Hard Hat Magazine,* the Eviction Defense Network, California Prison Focus, and others.[25] When groups like this are disrupted or forced to go out of business because no affordable alternative space is available, the collective resources to fight the very gentrification forcing them out are eliminated. (The Housing Rights Committee of San Francisco, which teaches tenants about their legal rights, was forced out of its building in 2000.)[26] And of course to the extent that nonprofit social service groups no longer are around, either needed services will not be available or the City will have to absorb the costs of providing them. The impact of losing nonprofits affects a wide network: For example, the San Francisco Bicycle Coalition, facing a rent increase from five hundred dollars to three thousand dollars a month, might have to cut staff or terminate operations, causing serious impacts not only on the city's huge bicycle commuting population but also on traffic congestion and safety more generally.

The threat to arts and other nonprofit groups of all sorts is not confined to the Mission. A September 2000 survey by the City's Arts Commission, funded by the William and Flora Hewlett Foundation, found that about two-thirds of the organizations surveyed were either leaseholders or subtenants subject to market forces (and commercial rent control is illegal in California). Thirty-five percent of the groups surveyed were threatened in the short term: They either had already lost their lease, were month-to-month renters, or were scheduled to lose their lease by the end of 2001. Average square foot rents for arts groups at the time were $12.75, compared with $55.00 for new arts space being leased.[27] Victims include cutting-edge dance groups, indie rock, rehearsal and performance space of all sorts, avant-garde galleries, and theater groups. Many organizations have been and are steadily being displaced; those that can remain report massive rent increases, some along the order of 400 percent. "In some cases, the sale of whole buildings has thrown many artists onto the street. Five hundred bands were evicted earlier this month [October 2000] from the funky Downtown Rehearsal complex near Hunters Point when the owner sold it to Cupertino-based JMA Properties for $14 million. Since then, two other rehearsal spaces, Rocker Guitar and Secret studios, have begun raising their rents," as shortage begets market-induced rent inflation.[28] It's a double whammy for young artists of all stripes: They can't afford housing, and the places where they ply their trade are also being priced out of existence. Some have already moved to Los Angeles or New York and other locales. At the same time, and in keeping with trends in other aspects of the city's life, the "high culture" institutions, such as the San Francisco Opera, San Francisco Symphony, San Francisco Ballet, Museum of Modern Art, and the American Conservatory Theater report robust contributions and attendance figures.[29]

While Mayor Brown has termed the situation a "major crisis," and said "the city will do more in coming years to help arts organizations cope with soaring rents and disappearing rehearsal venues," obviously "in coming years" is a bit on the late side.[30] Plans to create new space at Hunters Point, the new Octavia Boulevard, or Pier 70, east of Potrero Hill, are years off, if they ever happen. In October 2000, the Board of Supervisors took a minor step to stanch the bleeding: It passed a proposal, introduced by board president Tom Ammiano, to create a $1.5 million, one-year emergency rental assistance fund in the form of grants, administered by California Lawyers for the Arts, for arts groups with an annual budget of $1.2 million or less that have been in the city at least two years and have seen their rents at least doubled recently.[31] Not long afterward, the board added to the pot by allocating another $3 million: a $500,000 rent subsidy fund to assist nonprofit service providers and a $2.5 million capital fund to help nonprofits, arts organizations included, buy or fix up buildings or secure long-term leases.[32]

Nor is the City itself immune to the rent wars. The City government rents 3.7 million square feet of privately owned office space for its many agencies. As a late 2000 account noted, "The cost of two recent lease renewals for prime Civic Center properties reached stratospheric heights, when property owners raised the city's rents in one case by 180 percent, in another by 212 percent."[33] This has spurred thoughts, if not plans, to purchase buildings and/or renovate old and obsolete buildings it already owns, such as vacant schools.

A somewhat recent phenomenon in the city has been the "loft" issue, the creation of so-called live-work spaces, both in renovated old warehouses and industrial structures as well as newly created units. A 1988 City Planning Code change, which exempted such development from various zoning restrictions, intended to provide inexpensive and fitting spaces for San Francisco artists to do their work (along the order of the Goodman Building model, noted below), but it has been manipulated and transformed into very expensive, gentrifying "lawyer lofts" that are at the same time generating destructive tensions with existing uses and users. Typically, these consist of one large room, almost always with a loft and separate bathroom. Unlike other housing developments, they are exempted from the requirement to set aside a portion of the units at below-market rents, they do not have to meet requirements for disabled access and open space, and they pay a lower, one-time fee for schools. Located largely in the South of Market area, North Mission, and Potrero Hill, many of these "artists lofts" (in the case of the newly constructed buildings, often very ugly, as well as large, with as many as forty units) are going for $300,000–$700,000; median sales price in 1998 was $270,000 and heading upward. This new "industrial chic" appeals to the (overwhelmingly white) "DINKS" crowd, and some three thousand such units have already gone up, about a third in the South of Market alone (thirty-three hundred more in the pipeline), with, until recently, little attempt by the City to control the phenomenon or see to it that the original purposes and kinds of users are benefiting.* In September 2000, the Planning Commission approved the largest live-work project in the city's history: 172 units (plus 480 parking spaces) on Fourth Street South of Market, with no requirement for even a single below-market affordable unit.[34]

---

*A major political force on the loft development scene has been the Residential Builders Association, headed by the powerful and aggressive Joe O'Donoghue; see the massive feature article on him by Susan Sward: "The Housing That Joe Built: How Belligerent Construction Giant Has Reshaped S.F.," *San Francisco Chronicle*, 17 July 2000. " 'Jobs, jobs, jobs is our simple motto,' O'Donoghue says." Among his reshaping activities is "influenc[ing] key personnel moves [at the Department of Building Inspections] enabling those who see matters his way to advance and sidetracking those who don't. . . . His reach doesn't end there: It extends to other government entities [Board of Appeals, Planning Commission] that affect building in San Francisco." A 2001 audit of the Department of Building Inspections by the city controller documented clear patterns of favoritism given to permit expediters, some given by inspectors under pressure from their supervisors. (David R. Baker, "Audit Finds S.F. Office May Show Favoritism to Building Experts: Permit Expediters Get Preference, Workers Say," *San Francisco Chronicle*, 12 June 2001.) The association makes heavy campaign contributions at the state as well as local level. The (pre-2000) Board of Supervisors even voted to declare a "Joe O'Donoghue Day."

The loft phenomenon has "prompted a mass exodus of both artists and blue-collar employment. . . . [T]he history of these projects shows far too many instances of direct and indirect displacement."[35] Invading loft-dwellers have been pushing out surrounding nightclubs, residents, and businesses—not only via direct land-use replacement, but because "the residents . . . find their desires for a quiet night of sleep in conflict with the needs of local industrial businesses and clubs that continue conducting business late into the night."[36] And: "On the down side . . . the potential for incompatibilities between adjacent activities, whether next door, across the street, or the floor above or below, is greatly increased. These diverse environments necessitate a degree of tolerance on the part of all users, yet we're finding that some of the newcomers are less accommodating of such an eclectic environment than they thought they would be, or were led to believe they needed to be by their real estate agents."[37] In the Mission District, loft-ism has displaced blue-collar jobs. An October 2000 study by the Mission Anti-Displacement Coalition reported that since 1991, the 540 lofts built there have been a major factor in the loss of 1.7 million square feet of industrial space, a 57 percent decrease. Although interim zoning controls enacted in August 1999 prohibited new loft construction, the group charged that the Planning Department and Commission have been lax in enforcing these restrictions. Since, as defined by law, lofts are not required to pay the school impact fees that are obligations of traditional residential developers, the study estimated that in the Mission the City has lost an estimated $22.6 million in such fees, and that citywide the loss probably exceeds $100 million.[38]

In February 2001, the Board of Supervisors, by a nine-to-one, veto-proof vote, approved a six-month citywide ban on construction of new live-work lofts (introduced by board president Tom Ammiano; it became law when Mayor Brown neither signed nor vetoed it). During this period, the supervisors are to work with community activists to draft new plans to create more affordable housing for low-income and middle-class residents.[39] (A less legalistic approach to the loft phenomenon—in the vein of the Mission Yuppie Eradication Project—occurred in late October 2000, when investigators from the U.S. Bureau of Alcohol, Tobacco and Firearms ruled that a fire at a twelve-unit live-work loft under construction at Ninth and Mission had been deliberately set. One of the partners in the firm developing the building "said he fears that the building may have been singled out because of anger over the live-work boom in the area.")[40] But moving in the opposite direction was a May 2001 ruling by the City's Board of Appeals that in essence gave official permission for the widespread practice of using loft space primarily for office functions, with minimal actual residential living taking place.[41] In August 2001, the Live Work Task Force, established earlier in the year, recommended an outright ban on additional live-work lofts.

The longer-term impact of the recent dot-com meltdown (by April 2001 it was reported that thirty-eight dot-coms had folded since the previous January in the city alone, beyond those failing elsewhere in the region)[42] on San Francisco's housing costs (as well as on the city's office demand and overall economy) is not clear. There has been, during the latter half of 2000 and the first half of 2001, some relief from the city's staggering rental and ownership costs, as various headlines in the dailies note ("Now Is the Time to Buy a House," "Rent Rocket Recedes"). But these same stories contain contradictory information: The story under the former headline notes, "Here in San Francisco, as usual, the market is tighter than in other Bay Area counties, as the housing supply is limited but the demand is not. The median price of a home here has risen from $486,000 last year to $589,000, according to . . . [the] president of the San Francisco Real Estate Association."[43] Other headlines indicate the crisis isn't going to go away any time soon: for example, "[S.F. Chamber of Commerce] Survey Says City's Rents Drives [sic] Many to Look Elsewhere." And as a May 2001 *Examiner* story noted, the city's downtown is increasingly becoming a massive pied-à-terre for the superrich: Featured were Bill and Linda Klipp, retired Charles Schwab executives (forty-three and forty-two years old, respectively), who closed on a $1 million condo, their second home, where they spend on average one week a month. "While a great many buyers [of downtown luxury condos, in the $500,000–$3 million range] are wealthy Silicon Valley executives looking for a second home," the story continues, "some are young professionals who want to live in the city. Others are retirees who like the idea of living in a full-concierge service condo right across from the baseball park. . . . The housing market is as tight as it has ever been."[44] One should not have excessive faith that the business turndown of 2000–2001 will spell much relief for San Francisco's overburdened housing consumers.

But these same forces creating a housing crisis in San Francisco have also produced probably the strongest local housing movement in the nation.

San Francisco's Housing Movement

TOOR's fight against displacement from the South of Market area and related struggles in the Western Addition were the 1960s forerunners of San Francisco's housing movement. Starting in the early 1970s, the Tenants Action Group and later the San Francisco Tenants Union[45] organized individual buildings around maintenance and repair issues and provided tenants' rights counseling, mainly in the Haight-Ashbury and Fillmore neighborhoods, via a "hotline" and publication of tenants' rights handbooks. Their members also contributed importantly to later initiatives and struggles as they arose. Although low-budget, volunteer efforts, these groups not only provided important services, but also created an ongoing tenant consciousness and public awareness of the city's housing problems.

Among the important manifestations of increased consciousness of and militancy around the city's housing problems was community protection of specific buildings, such as the International Hotel and the Goodman Building. The former, a 150-room residential hotel for elderly Chinese and Filipinos, located at Kearny and Jackson Streets, at the edge between Chinatown and the financial district, was the symbolic and real remnant of the Manilatown community ("The I-Hotel was the life of the *manongs* [elder brothers], the life of Filipinos. It was their heart, it was their poetry, it was their song," in the words of poet Al Robles),[46] and the threat to destroy it epitomized perfectly the conflict between downtown profit interests and people's needs. The attack on the I-Hotel produced some of the most dramatic protests and confrontations in the city's history (see fig. 1b). Attempts by realty tycoon Walter Shorenstein in the late 1960s to turn the hotel into a parking facility were vigorously opposed by the neighborhood, and Shorenstein thereupon sold the hotel to the Hong Kong–based Four Seas Development Corporation, which over the next few years aggressively sought to evict the tenants. Neighborhood, ethnic, and church groups (including massive contingents from Reverend Jim Jones's People's Temple) rallied to prevent the evictions, with demonstrations as large as five thousand people. The political pressure was so intense that Sheriff Richard Hongisto, elected in 1975 by a liberal-gay coalition, at first refused to carry out a court-ordered eviction, for which he served five days in jail. Additional community pressure forced a reluctant Board of Supervisors to allocate $1.3 million in Community Development funds so the Housing Authority could take the hotel via eminent domain for resale to the tenants. But a court ruled unconstitutional this attempted use of eminent domain powers, on grounds that the Housing Authority was not authorized to convey land to private parties—a mindblowing contrast to Yerba Buena, where the Redevelopment Agency was able to use eminent domain to throw four thousand low-income people out of their homes so their land could be conveyed to private developers.

The eviction was carried out in August 1977 in a midnight scene of high drama, with two thousand I-Hotel defenders surrounding the building and four hundred police and sheriff's deputies (led this time by a somewhat metamorphosed, sledgehammer-swinging Sheriff Hongisto) battering their way through to empty the building of its few dozen remaining tenants. (See fig. 1b.)* Following the evictions, community pressure and litigation held up demolition of the hotel for nearly two years.[47]

A Citizens Advisory Committee was appointed by Mayor Feinstein to review Four Seas' plans for the site. When by early 1984 no agreement had been reached regarding a development plan—Four Seas proposed to maximize commercial use and income, while the Citizens Advisory Committee was pushing to maximize provision of affordable housing—the City threatened to take the land by eminent domain. In July of that year, a deal was finally announced: two twelve-story towers, one mixed commercial-residential (140 studio apartments, renting for $225–$325 a month, with these low rents to be maintained for only five years, after which they would be subject to limited increases over the next forty years then converted to unregulated market rates), the other entirely commercial.[48] Two years later, with no progress made, the agreement disintegrated, Four Seas claiming the project was economically infeasible due to increasing vacancy rates for downtown office space. In early 1987, another development agreement was announced, this time for an eight-story tower with three levels of underground parking, three levels of retail space, and 126 units of affordable senior housing (rent levels per the previous agreement). The proposal was contingent, however, on receiving Planning Commission approval for a nine-story office building on a neighboring site.[49] The City agreed to provide $3 million in housing subsidies, with the building to be operated by a

---

*A decade later, reflecting back on that night, Hongisto attempted to justify his actions, which were captured in a sledgehammer-wielding photo widely reproduced on political posters. His explanation: He was showing his deputies, who were destroying the room doors, how to break down the doors in the least destructive way, smashing in just the door panels, so as to do minimal damage, in order to let tenants nail a piece of plywood and have a working door, should they be able to return. (See "Lest We Forget," *San Francisco Bay Guardian*, 29 July 1987.) For his initial failure to carry out the court-ordered eviction, Four Seas sued Hongisto, who said he spent thirty-five thousand dollars in legal fees before settling the suit in 1984. (See Tim Redmond, "The I-Hotel: The Deal Falls Apart," *San Francisco Bay Guardian*, 16 July 1986.) In a later reminiscence, Hongisto had this to say: "In the case of court-ordered evictions, the sheriff has the responsibility of carrying it out. . . . I opposed it as long as I could . . . I did the evictions because I was one of the foremost jail reformers at the time. We were doing exciting things at the county jail and I didn't want to lose all of that . . . I was pleased that I had done it without anyone getting shot, and the tenants weren't hurt. But I was disgusted that I had to do it" (Bernice Yeung, "The 'I' Is for Irony," *SF Weekly*, 6 June 2001).

nonprofit partnership of Chinatown community leaders. Neither was that plan ever consummated. In December 1991, yet another development plan was announced, similar to the previous one, but with a new developer: A Taiwanese company had taken over the project from Four Seas.[50] The current project calls for construction of 105 units for low-income seniors and disabled people, with a community room and gardening areas for the residents, plus a new K–8 private school for St. Mary's School and Parish (their Stockton Street location had been badly damaged by the Loma Prieta earthquake), as well as a small Filipino American Museum and Cultural Center (and, happily, with Robert Herman, architect of TODCO's marvelous housing, as part of the design team)—all on top of a three-and-a-half-level underground garage. As of early 2002, ground had been broken for the garage; assuming (fingers crossed) no delays or unforeseen future snafus, the housing should be ready for occupancy in 2004 or 2005. Like the Yerba Buena Center displacees, however, few if any of those evicted from the I-Hotel will be around to occupy the new development—as of 1987, only twelve to sixteen of the evicted tenants were still alive.[51] If and when the new apartments eventually get built, close to three decades will have elapsed between the eviction/demolition and the replacement housing, and in the intervening decades there was nothing but a big hole in the ground (save for its symbolically appropriate use as an occasional residence for a few homeless persons).

Another rallying point was the Goodman building, a communal living and working space for artists (a genuine one) in a wonderful 1869 building on Geary, just west of Van Ness, at the edge of the Western Addition A-2 renewal area, which held out against the Redevelopment Agency for ten years, with a wide range of community support and alternative plans, including having the structure placed on the National Register of Historic Places. The agency finally succeeded in evicting the residents in July 1983— at least, as a result of the struggle and publicity, for remodeling into subsidized low-income housing and not for replacement with a high-rise office tower, as was the agency's original plan.[52] A spin-off from the struggle has been creation of the new Goodman 2 Artists' Live/Work Studio Building and Art Center on Potrero Hill, a nonprofit (part of a larger market-rate housing development) containing thirty live-work artists lofts (real ones), a shared atrium, amphitheater, multimedia work space, and theater, completed in 1995 with substantial City subsidies.[53]

There were other less protracted and dramatic struggles: demonstrations against Japantown evictions in the Western Addition A-2 project area, organized by the Committee Against Nihonmachi Evictions; the campaign to oppose expansion of the University of California Medical Center in the Inner Sunset; the effort to prevent eviction of elderly tenants from a planned office conversion project at 1000 Montgomery Street in the North Beach area; the fight to save the Straight Theater in the Haight-Ashbury district— to name a few. These building support campaigns were key elements in creating a citywide housing movement and consciousness that has been fighting both to regulate the overheated San Francisco housing market and ensure provision of new and rehabilitated below-market-rate housing for lower-income households.

In 1977, largely growing out of the International Hotel controversy, a coalition of neighborhood groups sought to have the supervisors pass an ordinance controlling building demolitions by stipulating that a demolition permit could be granted only if adequate relocation housing was available. Early the next year, another coalition attempted to get the supervisors to pass an "anti-speculation tax"—in effect, a steep capital gains tax (in form tied to the City's existing real estate transfer tax) that would discourage the rapid buying and selling of properties for big profits, by taxing away large portions of the increased sales price on buildings bought and sold within a year or two. Although a few supervisors voted for each of these ordinances, neither passed. (The supervisors did, unanimously, enact a demolition ban a decade later, temporarily prohibiting demolition or major alteration of all single-family homes and most duplexes.)[54]

In late 1978, the citywide housing movement tried a ballot initiative to force landlords to pass on to tenants the windfall savings from state Proposition 13, passed in June of that year. The state measure rolled back property tax assessments to 1975–76 levels, limiting local tax rates to 1 percent of full cash value and annual assessment increases to 2 percent (but allows assessments to be updated when property title changes). Although Proposition 13 was sold to voters as home owners' relief, the principal beneficiaries were owners of commercial properties, who reaped well over half of the total $7 billion in property tax savings the first year the new system was in effect. Proposition 13 granted nothing to San Francisco's tenants. Even though tenants in effect paid their landlords' property tax bills—a fact traditionally and routinely demonstrated when landlords raised rents to offset increases in their property tax bills—the benefits of the voter-mandated assessment rollback went to the "middle man" between the tax collector and true taxpayer: the landlord.

Housing activists quickly drew up an ordinance requiring landlords to pass on to tenants their first-year Proposition 13 windfall, and without difficulty got enough signatures to place it on the November 1978 ballot as

Proposition U. But the hastily organized campaign was able to raise only ten thousand dollars. Real estate interests raised ten times that amount, to portray the "Renters Rebate Initiative" as a thinly disguised form of the dreaded rent control. (The proposed ordinance limited rent increases so as to prevent landlords from circumventing the law's intent via the obvious ploy of raising rents to offset the required rebate to tenants.) Using sophisticated polling and publicity techniques that were to blossom in later elections, the real estate group was able to defeat the Renters Rebate Initiative, 53 to 47 percent. A landlord leaflet quoted Supervisor Dan White to the effect that rent control "will clog the courts, put more criminals on the streets, and lead to less respect for the law."

Winning Rent Control

Although failing to pass an ordinance clearly beneficial to tenants in a dominantly tenant city was discouraging, the organizers drew valuable lessons: start earlier, organize better and more widely, aim higher. And so, right after the November 1978 elections, the Proposition U campaign group, along with organizers from Catholic Social Services, began an outreach process to pull together a wide range of supporters for a comprehensive housing reform ordinance, to be placed on the November 1979 city ballot. The fifty-member San Franciscans for Affordable Housing coalition consisted of church, neighborhood, labor, gay, and women's groups. An elaborate four-month process of community meetings and plenary drafting sessions, held between January and May of 1979, determined what would go into the ordinance. Signatures were gathered in May and June, and the initiative was placed on the ballot as Proposition R.

Of great help in the organizing process were the actions of one particularly avaricious landlord, Angelo Sangiacomo, who in March 1979 announced across-the-board 25–65 percent rent increases in his seventeen hundred apartments, inhabited mostly by middle-income tenants, a move universally denounced, even by other landlords.[55] Sangiacomo's announcement led the supervisors to pass a sixty-day rent freeze, while they tried to fashion a solution. A five-member special committee of the board was then appointed to draft a law giving tenants some protections; it was chaired by Supervisor Ron Pelosi (who had been quoted as saying, "What's a tenant's rights anyway? They have the right to decent, safe, sanitary structures. Beyond that they have no rights").[56] Sangiacomo's actions also brought many middle-income tenants into the Proposition R campaign, and this has become an important feature of the city's housing movement.

Proposition R contained several elements: rent control; evictions limited to "just causes"; a seven-hundred-unit annual limit on conversion of rental units to condominiums, with protection for occupants not wishing to purchase their units; housing speculation and demolition controls; and mechanisms for increasing the overall supply of housing, primarily via community-based housing development corporations, using hotel tax funds, municipal bonds, Community Development Block Grant monies, and surplus City land and buildings. The momentum seemed there for an all-out push to control the city's housing market in the interests of moderate- and lower-income residents.

But the supervisors, seeing the handwriting on the wall, undertook their own preemptive strike. In June 1979, they unanimously passed their own, weak rent control ordinance and acted to limit condominium conversions as well.

There were substantial differences in what Proposition R and the supervisors' rent control ordinance called for. Proposition R limited rent increases to a percentage equal to the Rental Housing Component of the Consumer Price Index (CPI), a rate at that time about half the CPI (reflecting that mortgage repayment costs, typically half of a landlord's costs, generally are fixed and do not rise with inflation), and also required landlords to appeal to an elected rent control board in order to justify a greater increase. It controlled apartment rents (owner-occupied two- and three-unit buildings excepted) regardless of change of tenancy. And it was to remain in force as long as a housing crisis existed in San Francisco. By contrast, the law the supervisors passed set a 7 percent annual limit on rent increases (echoing then-President Carter's "inflation guidelines," but somewhat higher than the CPI Rental Housing Component at the time), over and above any increases to cover improvements and repairs. It placed the burden to challenge any increase above that figure on the tenant and stipulated that if the tenant did not make such a challenge within thirty days, he or she lost the right to appeal the increase; it also required tenants to appeal to a mayorally appointed (rather than elected) rent stabilization board. It exempted owner-occupied buildings with four units or fewer. Most significantly, it embodied vacancy decontrol, meaning that in between tenancies landlords were free to raise rents as high as they wanted.

The supervisors' move fulfilled its intended purpose. Whereas San Franciscans for Affordable Housing raised $54,000, the city's real estate interests waged a $700,000 campaign decrying the evils of strict rent control (sure to produce the kind of building abandonment that would turn San Francisco into the South Bronx), and playing on the theme of "let's give the new law a chance." Proposition R lost, 59 to 41 percent. Comparatively low registration rates and low voter turnout in lower-income, minority, and renter precincts were big factors.[57] Another was the extremely sophisticated use of targeted mailings by the real estate groups. These were possible through highly accurate polling techniques and computer adaptation to demographic analysis, in order to produce specially tailored brochures stressing the concerns and views of targeted subgroups.[58] As used in the anti-Proposition R campaign, "Renters and homeowners alike received more individually targeted pieces of mail than some unpopular people would have received in a lifetime."[59] The "No on R" forces fashioned fourteen separate campaign brochures for use with different groups: small landlords, home-owners, blacks, affluent renters, gays, and others.

The well-honed techniques of Don Solem and Associates, the campaign consultant who handled the anti-Proposition R and anti-Proposition U campaigns (as well as the developers' campaign that beat the November 1983 growth control initiative described in chapter 12) are described as follows:

> Solem & Associates utilize a set formula, which varies little from cam-
> paign to campaign. Extensive phone-polling occurs two to three months
> prior to the election, which gives Solem and his staff a preliminary grasp
> of general voter trends, concerns, anxieties, and gaps in issue awareness.
> This furnishes a blueprint for what "lines" can be profitably exploited,
> ignored or co-opted. . . . His strategy is to lie low until the last three
> weeks of the campaign, and then unleash a barrage of TV and radio com-
> mercials, billboards, newspaper advertisements, and targeted leaflets
> speaking to specific demographic groups. Underfinanced opponents are
> unable at this stage to counter misrepresentations and distortions.[60]

The Proposition R campaign was still a real victory for the housing re-form forces—the notion that even the most reactionary supervisors would vote to control rents and condo conversions was inconceivable a year earlier. And the campaign and formation of so broad a coalition marked a watershed in development of the city's housing movement, one that has set the agenda and parameters for the movement's future activities. But the law the supervisors enacted was weak, and its passage had the intended effect of undercutting voter pressure to act decisively on the city's housing crisis.

The actual working of the city's new rent control ordinance has proved to be of limited aid to the renters it was ostensibly designed to serve. Some egregious attempts to impose rent increases greater than 7 percent were foiled by appeal to the newly established Residential Rent Stabilization and Arbitration Board; but in most cases, the appeals process served only to somewhat lower excessive increases, not keep them within the 7 percent limit. One major form of evasion was routine, unaudited pass-through of rent increases for alleged capital improvements.[61] Relying on tenant complaints to trigger effective implementation of the law was of course a major weakness in the ordinance: The reality is that tenants—particularly lower-income, minority, and recent immigrant tenants—often are not aware of their legal rights and not likely to use a bureaucratic mechanism they perceive as inaccessible or unresponsive. This is particularly true in San Francisco, where tens of thousands of residents do not have legal immigration status or facility with the English language. A review of the geographic origin of petitions and complaints filed with the rent board during its first two years showed that a distressingly small number came from the city's minority or working-class neighborhoods.[62] Of 5,034 such items, only sixteen came from Bayview–Hunters Point, the city's principal black neighborhood, forty-one from Potrero Hill, and forty-one from Parkside—the latter two areas with large white working-class populations.

The composition of the mayorally appointed rent board gave further grounds for cynicism on the part of the city's tenants: By law, the five-person body has to consist of two landlords, two tenants, and one who is neither; yet until early 1984, almost five years into the new law, no activist tenant leader was appointed to the board, although several openly antirent-control landlords were. (The lack of "tenant consciousness" among the tenant appointees was well illustrated in the fact that both tenant members voted against a recommendation to end the ordinance's vacancy decontrol feature.) Board president from 1981–84 and an original landlord appointee was Russell Flynn, president of TRI Realtors and himself owner or co-owner of ten apartment houses, with 460 units, worth $6.2 million. One of the city's principal condo converters, Flynn was a leader in the fight against Proposition R and a five-hundred-dollar contributor to Dianne Feinstein's 1979 mayoral campaign, the maximum allowable contribution at the time.[63] (TRI's role in shaping city housing policy was not confined to the rent board: Preston Cook, in the early eighties chair of the San Francisco Housing Authority, was a partner of the same firm. A less public-serving member of the firm was TRI board chair William Rosetti, against whom the district attorney filed a series of civil suits in November 1983 on charges of selling condominiums for illegally high prices. The suits were settled in 1984 for approximately $150,000.)[64]

The first tenant activist appointee to the board, Polly Marshall, was named as an alternate rather than regular member. Her candidacy to fill a board opening was pushed by the city's major housing reform organizations, and the housing movement's success in getting the Board of Supervisors to enact strengthening amendments to the rent control ordinance in early 1984 provided the political impetus to convince the mayor to appoint Marshall, who, as of early 2002, has served for eighteen years, under four mayors.

Compounding the inherent weaknesses and biases of the rent board was the failure of City Attorney George Agnost to prosecute those few cases the board referred to his office for legal action, a form of inaction that sent a clear message to landlords. In early 1984, tenants brought suit against Agnost to compel him to seek injunctions against landlords in such cases, to establish written procedures for handling these referrals, and to require written explanations when no action was taken.[65] More generally, there was increasing recognition of the essentially political role the city attorney was playing in San Francisco housing and development issues via his rulings and opinions. Agnost's rulings played an important role in weakening Supervisor Harry Britt's 1984 proposed amendments to the City's rent control ordinance; by bringing about a weakened ordinance regulating conversion of residential hotel rooms to tourist accommodations; by delaying a Board of Supervisors' moratorium on South of Market high-rise development; by making it more difficult for neighborhood residents to secure interim protective zoning; by weakening a proposed charter amendment protecting sunlight in city parks and playgrounds from shadows cast by adjacent high-rises; and by other actions evincing a pro-development bias on the part of his office. In early 1984, the supervisors' increasing dissatisfaction with Agnost led to a proposal, subsequently dropped, that the board hire its own outside counsel, because they believed the city attorney was not merely advising them but also attempting to influence their policies.[66] Also in early 1984, controversy arose over a deputy city attorney going to work, with Agnost's permission, for a developer whose project she had earlier handled for the City.[67]

Vacancy Decontrol

Vacancy decontrol was the principal flaw in the supervisors' rent control law. The 1979 law was rooted in an analysis of the city's housing problem that acknowledged a need to protect not the housing stock as a whole, but only individual sitting tenants, in a view that the city's housing problem was a temporary aberration rather than a relatively permanent structural feature. Landlords' profit motivations were to be interfered with as minimally as possible. But vacancy decontrol led to increased evictions because it put a big-time money premium on tenant turnover—and rents on vacant

units, raised as high as landlords desired, zoomed beyond the reach of growing numbers of San Franciscans.

With vacancy decontrol, landlords are less willing to give tenants any
slack—late rent payments or keeping a pet in violation of lease terms may
trigger an eviction action instead of being excused with a warning or over-
looked. Whereas landlords formerly put a premium on a stable tenancy,
they began to value and foster mobility among their tenants. The number
of unlawful detainer (eviction) actions brought in San Francisco Municipal
Court rose immediately as soon as this flawed ordinance was enacted: from
3,975 in 1977 to 4,519 in 1979; 5,241 in 1980; 5,801 in 1983.[68] (A small number of additional evictions are brought in Superior and Small Claims Court.)
As noted above, formal eviction actions of course do not represent the full
picture of forced moves: "Voluntary" moves upon receiving a rent increase
and landlord lockouts of tenants are another way in which displacement effectively takes place. And City Planning Department data contained in the
1981 report of Mayor Feinstein's Citizens Housing Task Force showed that
in the two years after passage of the supervisors' version of rent control,
rent levels for vacated units went up on average 29 percent and 30 percent.
(Vacancies also increase the selling price of buildings. The spring 2000
Zephyr News, a single-sheet newsletter put out by a local realty company,
contained this candid item, headed "The Value of Vacancy": "[I]t is no surprise that buildings which are delivered vacant sell for considerably more
than those which are partially or wholly tenant occupied. . . . A concrete example of price differential is provided by a duplex on Masonic Avenue which
Zephyr listed early in 1999. The upper unit, which had been owner occupied, was vacant at the time the building was first marketed; the lower unit
was occupied by a couple who had lived there for several years but were not
'protected' tenants. The building went into escrow at $569,000 but after the
inspections the buyer backed out (possibly due to tenant related anxieties).
Shortly after the deal fell out of escrow the tenants notified the owner that
they had purchased a home and would be moving in 30 days. The owner
took the building off the market and once the unit had been vacated had the
floors refinished and the unit painted [the cost of these improvements was
approximately $10,000]. The building immediately sold for $670,000, a
whopping $101,000 over the tenant occupied price! Knowing this difference
in price, is it any surprise that owners will seek extreme measures to de-
liver a building vacant?")

Although the City's ordinance has "just cause" eviction protections, such
restrictions are relatively easy to circumvent if motivation is high. A law
that retains rent control regardless of tenancy change provides little in-

centive to circumvent eviction protections. The City's ordinance, however, provided every incentive to do so, and landlords behaved in a predictable manner.

The City's rent board, while it has handled fairly well those complaints of wrongful rent increases that were brought to it, was of little help in protecting tenants complaining of wrongful eviction.[69] (At first, the board was issuing highly misleading reports on its work: "Statistics were altered on outcomes before the board, so that a landlord who successfully raised the rent on 100 tenants was counted as one pro-landlord decision, but 100 tenants who received even a partial remission of the landlord's requested increase were tabulated as 100 pro-tenant decisions.")[70] Through voluntary move-outs and evictions, a substantial portion of the city's rental units becomes vacant each year. A rent control law with vacancy decontrol likely does not reduce the rate of rent increases over the long run; rather, it merely changes the pace and rhythm at which rents are increased. It may even be that in some cases vacancy decontrol causes more rapid escalation of rents, as landlords raise rents in between tenancies more than they otherwise would, as a hedge against the possibility of limited increases during a long-term tenancy. A 1983 study released by Supervisor Harry Britt concluded sadly: "Today the ordinance is, if anything a stimulus to tenant displacement and rent increases."[71]

In 1980, under pressure from the city's housing movement, the supervisors narrowly (six to five) passed an ordinance extending the life of rent control and amending it to add a limited form of vacancy control—between tenancies, rent increases would be limited to the allowable 7 percent annual figure, plus an additional 5 percent for each year over two the departing tenant had lived there. Mayor Feinstein—as noted below, herself a landlord—vetoed the ordinance. A fifteen-month extension then was unanimously passed, retaining vacancy decontrol but tightening up somewhat on eviction protections and providing increased penalties for wrongful rent increases.

By the time the City's rent control ordinance next came up for extension, in 1982, the housing movement was in a better position to strengthen it. Led by a new organization, the Affordable Housing Alliance (AHA), it brought about a considerable tightening of the law. While vacancy control was not included, the major revision was to turn around responsibility for exceeding the 7 percent annual limit: Under the amended law, landlords had to seek permission from the rent stabilization board in order to exceed that figure, rather than requiring tenants to challenge an excessive rent increase. And the law was extended indefinitely, rather than having a short-term life. Mayor Feinstein reluctantly signed the bill.

The Affordable Housing Alliance also worked to develop organized tenant voting power as a lever on supervisorial candidates. In the November 1982 elections, it endorsed a "tenant slate," sending out its slate card to thirty-five thousand voters and at the same time urging them not to vote for Lee Dolson or Richard Hongisto, who had consistent antitenant voting records. Their efforts played a not insignificant role in incumbent Dolson's defeat and in the victories of slate members Doris Ward, Nancy Walker, and Wendy Nelder (who, by getting the most votes, became board president).

In late 1983, Supervisor Harry Britt introduced separate pieces of legislation to lower the automatic annual allowable rent increase for occupied units from 7 percent to a figure equal to 60 percent of the Consumer Price Index, but in no case higher than 7 percent or lower than 4 percent, and institute vacancy control. A report Britt released accompanying this legislation forcefully stated the case for the latter provision:

> Most San Franciscans . . . decry [the] homogenization of the city's neighborhoods. Preserving the city's diversity will require more than nostalgia, however. It will require that the city recognize rental inflation as the engine of displacement and take steps to halt that inflation. It is not enough to assist embattled long term tenants to cling to their rent controlled apartments. In a living city people must be able to move, to start families, to begin new lives. Vacant units must be affordable.[72]

The lobbying on both sides was fierce.[73] The landlords' oppositional campaign, run by Clint Reilly (also manager of Mayor Dianne Feinstein's antirecall victory in 1983—see chapter 11), was on the heavy side. Among the pressure tactics was a threat, made privately to individual supervisors, that if they passed the Britt amendments, the landlords would throw their support and money behind a June 1984 City Charter amendment ballot measure to reduce the size of the Board of Supervisors from eleven to seven members, a change that, if successful, would deprive four incumbents of their jobs. The spokesperson for the landlords' Coalition for Better Housing—Russell Flynn, then-president of the city's Residential Rent Stabilization and Arbitration Board—was quoted as follows: "As far as any formal position, we are on record as not taking a position" on the charter amendment. "But it would only be fair and obvious that if the vote went contrary on vacancy control [to the landlords, the far more hateful of the two Britt amendments] there would be a lot of sentiment to change that position."[74]

The supervisors passed both amendments, the lowered formula for rent increases by nine to one, vacancy control seven to three. The victory largely was for the principle of vacancy control—the ordinance permitted a 14 percent increase each time an apartment turned over and thus had no annual cap, a feature particularly harmful to those living in residential hotels, where turnover is more frequent than for apartments. But the victory was short-lived: Mayor Feinstein vetoed the vacancy control ordinance, while accepting the lower rent increase formula, and the necessary eight votes to override her veto were not there.

The Affordable Housing Alliance subsequently filed suit, under the state's Political Reform Act of 1974, challenging Feinstein's veto, on conflict-of-interest grounds, since as the owner of rental units (the partially residential Carlton Hotel) she would personally gain by preventing this ordinance from becoming law. While, under a state Fair Political Practices Commission ruling, supervisors are disqualified from such votes if they own five or more rental units, ever-accommodating City Attorney George Agnost ruled that the mayor can act, as the only person who can exercise the veto power. The AHA suit maintained that the mayor does not have to act: She can refrain from either vetoing or signing the bill and simply allow the ordinance to become law without her signature and, in view of her conflict of interest, ought not be permitted to act. The suit also argued that since, during several days of the ten-day period a mayor is given to act on an ordinance passed by the supervisors, Feinstein was out of the city and had appointed various supervisors as acting mayor on a rotating basis, any of these persons, who did not have a conflict of interest, could have been allowed to perform this function of the office. Tenant groups brought the matter to the state Supreme Court, which in June 1986 refused to hear the appeal.[75]

Subsequent gains in strengthening the City's rent control ordinance were spearheaded by a new formation, the San Francisco Housing and Tenants Council, a thirty-member umbrella group that included the Tenants Union, AHA, the Chinatown Coalition for Better Housing, Old St. Mary's Housing Committee (a parish council that expanded to other areas of the city), and the organized tenants at several of the city's very large rental complexes—Park Merced, Stonestown, John Muir Apartments, and the Golden Gateway. This last-named group, consisting for the most part of well-to-do residents of the luxury apartments in that urban renewal area, formed itself quickly in response to the massive rent increases levied in 1983 when the Federal Housing Administration lifted its requirement that it approve such increases on apartments built with federally guaranteed mortgages. John Muir Apartments residents organized in response to the owner's attempt to circumvent a City law barring conversion of the development into condominiums. Stonestown and Park Merced tenants organized when their landlords' pass-through of utility cost increases jacked up rents 29 percent in three years. The size and organizing abilities of these largely middle-class and upper-middle-class tenants of big developments enormously strengthened San Francisco's housing movement, and at the same time created some strains between them and older groups like the Tenants Union and AHA, which for the most part represent lower-income tenants and a more populist political analysis and stance.

Rent control has been a salient and divisive issue in the city ever since, the tenant side pushing for vacancy controls and other strengthening features, the landlord side trying to gut the ordinance completely. The gutting moves have come largely at the state level. As far back as 1976, frightened by voter passage of rent control in Berkeley and growing tenant activism in other California cities, the California Housing Council, an association of the state's largest corporate landlords and housing developers, pushed a bill through the California legislature, preempting, for state action, control over rents—that is, denying local governments jurisdiction over this area. Only a last-minute veto by Governor Jerry Brown thwarted the move.[76]

Their next attempt came in the form of an initiative in the June 1980 state primary elections. This was one of the sorrier, more misguided efforts on the part of that usually savvy interest group. Quite simply, they attempted to manipulate and deceive the voters beyond what reasonable people thought fair. Calling themselves Californians for Fair Rents, the group circulated "Rent Control" petitions, a title the state's attorney general even assigned to the initiative. (According to the breezily frank wording of the newsletter of the California Association of Realtors, one of the proposition's sponsors, "This title may appear misleading to Realtors as the measure would in no way establish rent controls. However, the title is more likely to make getting signatures easier since the majority of state voters appear to favor some form of rent controls.")[77] But what the proposed constitutional amendment actually called for was the repeal of all existing local rent control ordinances (an estimated 800,000 California households were at that time protected by such ordinances in nineteen localities, including San Jose, Los Angeles County, Berkeley, and Santa Monica, in addition to San Francisco), and replacing them only if new construction was permanently exempt; if annual rent increases equal to the full Consumer Price Index were allowed (over and above increases to recover improvement and repair costs); if the voters themselves passed the ordinance via the initiative process (rather than passage by the local legislature); if the ordinance provided for vacancy decontrol; and if the ordinance expired after four years. Californians for Fair Rents spent $6 million (including a $395,000 contribution from the state's mobile home park owners' organization and $240,000 from a single Los Angeles apartment management company) trying to persuade voters that no rent control was rent control—the second most costly ballot campaign in the state's history.[78] But the campaign was a bit too much to stomach for anyone concerned with the integrity of the electoral process, and even such pro-property papers as the *Los Angeles Times, Los Angeles Herald-Examiner,* and *Oakland Tribune* came out editorially against the proposition on those grounds. (Alone among the state's major papers, the San Francisco dailies supported the proposition editorially; another San Francisco supporter was Russell Flynn, the landlord chair of the City's rent board, which would have been abolished had the proposition passed.)

Housing activists in all parts of the state—including the Golden State Mobilehome Owners League—saw their best hope of beating a $6 million propaganda campaign was to seize on the issue of voter manipulation, and accordingly constituted themselves as Californians Against Initiative Fraud. While they could raise only forty-two thousand dollars, they were able to effectively use the Federal Communications Commission's (since discarded) "fairness doctrine" (a technique profitably used earlier in the Proposition U and Proposition R campaigns) to persuade television and radio stations to give them free air time, in about a 1:4 ratio to the time the realty interests had bought. The group used most of its money to produce some extremely clever and sophisticated thirty-second spots, featuring such icons of integrity as Henry Fonda, Jack Lemmon, and Ralph Nader, which hit squarely on the issue of voter fraud. The result was a 65 to 35 percent rout of the proposition.

The next state-level move by real estate interests was another attempt to have the California legislature pass a law limiting local rent control efforts, imposing restrictions similar to those the state's voters had just rejected. Introduced by Los Angeles Democratic assemblyman Richard Alatorre, a bill written by the California Council for the Environment and Economic Balance (a trade association of large corporations and building trade unions) passed the assembly in June 1983. It set standards to which all local ordinances had to conform, such as vacancy decontrol and permanent exemption from rent control of all units first occupied after February 15, 1983.[79] This latter clause meant that should a city decide, say, five years down the line to enact controls over existing housing, the controls could not apply to housing built in the previous five years. The bill didn't make it out of the Senate, due in large part to lobbying efforts by the statewide housing movement and by local governments concerned about encroachment on their own traditional powers. Following that came virtually annual attempts, almost all led by Fresno Democratic Assemblyman Jim Costa, to preempt local controls via state legislation that, in various versions, would bar cities with rent control from receiving housing assistance funds (a particularly self-defeating feature), ban vacancy controls, exempt single-family homes, new housing, and owner-occupied structures, plus other categorical exclusions. Legislative maneuvering, for the most part via State Senator President Pro Tem David Roberti of Hollywood, aided at critical moments by Assembly Speaker Willie Brown, prevented these bills from becoming law.[80] A different attempt to use the state's superior powers in order to discipline unruly local governments occurred in 1991, when former San Francisco Supervisor Quentin Kopp (by then a state senator, elected in 1986 as an Independent) introduced legislation that would require tenants subject to eviction action to put up twenty days of prospective rent in order to get a hearing on the case—something many tenants could not afford and which has no parallel in any other comparable civil action: Case law holds that constitutional due process requirements preclude payment of a fee in order to get a hearing.[81] The bill was defeated.[82] Conservative state legislators finally achieved a victory in this area against unruly localities when in July 1995, after nearly two decades of frustration, they passed legislation striking vacancy controls from the five California cities that had it, allowing incremental increases for incoming tenants over a three-year period until market rents are attained. San Francisco, never having been able to enact such controls, was at least spared the trauma of having this reform negated by a (legally) superior level of government.

The election of Art Agnos, a strong housing movement supporter, as mayor in 1987 led to renewed efforts to strengthen the system but also revealed serious political splits within the movement. Agnos had made a campaign commitment to support vacancy controls, but the splitting issue was how strict the controls would be. The competing plans were the "10:20" and the "4:7" schemes, referring to a base allowable percentage rent increase in between tenancies and to capping the amount that could be added as further increases, a function of how long the departing tenant has been in the unit. Agnos, and the less radical elements of the housing movement—notably, the Affordable Housing Alliance—were advocating higher limits, reasoning that such an ordinance was more likely to be enacted; that establishing the principle of vacancy controls was critical; and in part hoping thus to head off a likely landlord referendum to overturn a stricter ordinance, which would doubtless bring out heavy real estate contributions and the kinds of sophisticated campaign techniques that go with big money. Groups like the San Francisco Tenants Union, St. Peter's Housing Committee, the North Mission Association, and the major gay and lesbian Democratic clubs took the opposite position, holding that allowing a 10 to 20 percent increase between tenancies wasn't even worth fighting for. The Tenants Union collected enough signatures to put a 4:7 initiative (Proposition U—a different one from the 1978 Proposition U—containing other strengthening features as well) on the November 1988 ballot, but it lost, 58 to 42 percent, and did not receive support from Agnos or from such progressive supervisors as Harry Britt and Nancy Walker. True to form, real estate interests poured close to $800,000 into the campaign (the largest single contribution being the $75,000 from the owners of the thirty-five-hundred-unit Park Merced complex).[83]

That defeat notwithstanding, prospects for introducing vacancy control were enhanced by the results of the same November 1988 election, in which two new pro–rent control supervisorial candidates, Angela Alioto and Terence Hallinan, were victorious. But it turned out that Hallinan was, at least for a year, conflicted out of voting on rent control, given his recently divested ownership (a waiting period is required, however) of a family trust that owned rental property—certainly an ironic prohibition, since Hallinan was a vote against his economic self-interest as a (former) landlord.*

In mid-1989, Mayor Agnos proposed a vacancy control ordinance that was indisputably on the weak side: the 10:20 system, further diluted by "hardship" provisions for landlord appeals.[84] The supervisors didn't get to vote on the measure until February 1990, largely because of the delaying

---

*"Supervisor Hallinan Faces a Paradox on Rent Control Issue," *San Francisco Chronicle*, 1 February 1989. Supervisor Carol Ruth Silver also had (just) purchased a four-unit apartment building, which disqualified her as well from voting on the measure. Her action, likely designed to permit her to avoid a controversial vote, was particularly malodorous, as the building she bought was co-owned by William Rosetti, partner at TRI Realty, along with Russ Flynn, president of the Coalition for Better Housing, the leading landlord antirent-control group; a secondary loan of forty-thousand dollars to purchase the building was a note from Rosetti and his partner. (See Jim Balderston, "Carol Ruth Silver, Landlord," *San Francisco Bay Guardian*, 4 May 1988. Silver, a former Legal Services lawyer turned real estate broker, "who was appointed this week to head a key land-use panel of the Board of Supervisors, has been sending out letters to campaign contributors soliciting real estate business." See Evelyn Hsu, "Carol Silver Asks Backers to Buy Real Estate," *San Francisco Chronicle*, 12 January 1985.) Having alienated tenant groups, her original base of supporters, Silver lost her bid for reelection in 1988, the only incumbent supervisor to lose that year. Her metamorphosis is rather sad: A recent book describes her civil rights activities during Mississippi's 1964 Freedom Summer. See Debra L. Schultz, *Going South: Jewish Women in the Civil Rights Movement* (New York: NYU Press, 2001). And that earlier work still is important in her life, as evidenced that she is chair of the fortieth reunion of the 1961 Freedom Riders, which took place in Jackson, Mississippi, in late 2001.

tactics and fence-sitting of Supervisor Wendy Nelder (daughter of former San Francisco Police Chief and Supervisor Al Nelder). Nelder had openly supported vacancy controls, and, as noted above, was on the Affordable Housing Alliance's 1982 "tenant slate," but, now planning to run for city assessor, needed downtown support. Her tactic was to fail to show up at meetings of the three-member Land Use Committee, one of whose members, Terence Hallinan, was, as noted, not permitted to vote on the matter, thus preventing committee action to move the bill to the full board. She also asked for a ninety-day delay to consider the matter.[85] But the bill could get only five votes—Supervisor Richard Hongisto (by now a rent control supporter, and running for assessor as well, against Nelder) was a rental property owner, and thus, like Hallinan, unable to vote. Nelder, along with Willie Kennedy, reversing their former positions, were "no" votes.[86] It was reported that both Nelder and Kennedy received considerable campaign contributions from the real estate industry during the ninety-day delay period Nelder had requested. "Nelder," reported the February 14, 1990, *Chronicle*, "who had supported all rent control measures in the past, received $11,150 from realtors, property owners and real estate lobbyists between July and December 1989. The amount represented nearly one-third of her total cash intake for her 1990 reelection campaign committee. The contributions included donations from residential realtors who are staunch opponents of vacancy control and who have not contributed as generously to her campaign in previous years. . . . The bulk of the receipts poured into Nelder's reelection campaign kitty after September, when she requested a 90-day delay on sending the proposed legislation to the full board. . . . Supervisor Willie Kennedy, meanwhile, received $8,295 from realtors and apartments [sic] owners before August and September last year—almost two-thirds of her $13,611 total for that period." An indignant Nelder, to be sure, denied any relationship between her funding sources and her vote switch—"That's the most absurd thing I ever heard."[87]

But the struggle went on. In the November 1990 elections, three new, progressive supervisors came onto the board: Roberta Achtenberg, Kevin Shelley (another ex-mayor's offspring), and Carole Migden, all rent control supporters. (Another source of vengeful pleasure to the housing movement was Nelder's loss, to Richard Hongisto, in the assessor's race.) Again, rent control activists moved to take advantage of this new support. And again, political splits within the movement emerged, with the Tenants Union, St. Peter's Housing Committee, and the Harvey Milk and Alice B. Toklas Democratic Clubs pushing for the 4:7 percent cap on increases at the time of tenancy turnover, while the Affordable Housing Alliance and others argued that only a higher cap could elicit board support.[88] How rigorous an enforcement mechanism to have was a further source of conflict: While, realistically, true widespread enforcement would necessitate registering all apartments protected under the ordinance so that tenants could easily verify the legal rent, the bureaucracy and cost of such a system (wildly exaggerated by those opposing registration) constituted a persuasive argument for more lenient provisions.[89] In May 1991, legislation with a 10:14 percent cap was introduced, sponsored by board chair Doris Ward, Angela Alioto, Roberta Achtenberg, Kevin Shelley, and Carole Migden. New tenants would be allowed only 120 days to contact the rent board if they suspected overcharging, and no such rights were given to subsequent tenants.[90] It passed later that month, on the left condemned as too weak (tenant activists filed notice of intent to circulate a petition to qualify a stronger initiative measure), on the right challenged as illegal, with claims that the measure required an environmental impact report (a pretty stretched claim, which the Superior Court threw out the following August).[91] The real estate folks then collected enough signatures to put a referendum on the November 1991 ballot, sponsored by the San Francisco Board of Realtors, San Francisco Apartment Association, and the Coalition for Better Housing, to overturn vacancy control, which had the effect under City law, once the petitions were filed, of halting enforcement of the new law. The growing divisions within the housing movement, as well as the fatigue factor—many activists felt that vacancy control legislation was by then too late to preserve much affordable housing, and they wanted to move on to other pressing issues—plus a Clint Reilly–sponsored special campaign, complete with misinformation and misleading tactics,* gave the landlords a 56 to 44 percent victory, throwing out the recently passed new set of controls. For this campaign, real estate interests spent more than $1 million, but it was the last time rental property owners were to win at the ballot box.[92]

This discouraging defeat sent the tenant activists back to the drawing boards in an effort to revive their organizations, power, and credibility. A series of tenant miniconventions around the city led to a May 1992 citywide convention that agreed to work on two initiatives, one to lower the 4 percent floor on annual rent increases for sitting tenants, the other to tighten owner move-in provisions (see discussion below). While the latter effort

---

*One that stands out was an antivacancy control letter from landlord rent board commissioner Tim Carrico, designed to look as if it came from the board itself. See "Landlords Warn Tenants of Dire Prop. M Results," *San Francisco Bay Guardian*, 23 October 1991.

was dropped, the former (Proposition H) finally led to victory—the very first at the ballot box for the tenant movement and a major morale and organizing booster. It passed in 1992, 53 percent to 47 percent, despite proponents having been, as usual, badly outspent, in a campaign that successfully linked rent control to broader issues of economic justice.[93] The new law lowered the 4 percent floor on annual permissible rent increases to 60 percent of the Consumer Price Index for the Bay Area, which in actuality over recent years has limited increases generally to the 1–2 percent range (up to 2.9 and 2.8 percent in 2000–2001 and 2001–2002, respectively), thus providing real protection, at least to those tenants who do not change residence. A further victory came in November 1994, when voters passed Proposition I, extending rent control to owner-occupied two- to four-unit buildings. Interestingly, the anti-I campaign was able to raise only $100,000, as the larger landlords had little interest in contributing to this campaign. And a landlord effort to repeal Proposition I in November 1997 failed even to collect sufficient signatures to get on the ballot; the anti-I campaigners continued collecting signatures, however, and got the repeal measure on the June 1998 ballot as Proposition E, where it lost badly, 61 to 39 percent, despite a $400,000 landlord campaign.

In the past couple of years, the front burner issue for the housing movement activists has been owner move-ins (OMIs). Serious abuses have been documented, all related to the incentives that vacancy decontrol offers to evict tenants, particularly long-term tenants, disproportionately seniors, whose rents are lowest. Two 1989 San Francisco Tenants Union studies, based on a sample of their intake forms,[94] had shown that virtually no owners wanted to move into units where the tenant had been living less than seven years; that the average monthly rent for a sample of cases of eviction for landlord move-ins and related landlord conflicts was $531, compared to $665 for those in the sample without those characteristics; and that "[OMI] evictions [account for] typically one-third of all eviction problems that come into our office every month; almost universally, these involve tenants of many years." Forty-three percent of those in their sample who moved did so as a result of eviction, and 17 percent of these tenant movers left the city. An October 30, 1991, *San Francisco Bay Guardian* feature reported Residential Rent Stabilization and Arbitration Board figures showing that 473 of 1,498 eviction notices issued from May 1990 through February 1991 claimed as the reason for eviction move-in by the owner or a close relative (the law allows the owner's children, parents, grandparents, siblings, spouse, or the spouse of any of these other relatives the same eviction rights as the owner—expanding enormously the number of persons who have a legal right to evict sitting tenants). *Bay Guardian* reporters investigated forty-three OMI evictions issued in August 1990: For five, they were unable to determine who was living in the unit; of the thirty-eight others, seven (18 percent) were not owners or eligible relatives. "A city official, who asked not to be named," reported the *Guardian*, "estimates that 60 percent of OMI evictions are a ruse to raise rents." Another Tenants Union study showed that OMI evictees had lived in their unit an average of 9.5 years, almost twice as long as other movers. "According to Mary Foran, an attorney with the Eviction Defense Office of the Tenderloin Housing Clinic, 'You almost never see people in market-rate housing being evicted.' " The impact on evicted tenants is severe: Their pre-move rents averaged $592, then shot up 71 percent, to $1,016; expressed as a percentage of tenants' income, the increase was from 26 percent to 42 percent. Typically, the tenants' posteviction units were smaller and in less desirable neighborhoods.[95] A more recent Tenants Union study documented the sharp increase in OMI evictions: 831 for the statistical year ending February 28, 1997, compared to 439 in the prior statistical year.[96] It also concluded that "Tenants evicted for owner move-in generally are tenants with longer term tenancies [31 percent of OMI evictions involved seniors who had lived in their apartments for an average of twenty years] whose rents are significantly below the market rent [the average rent of tenants evicted for OMI was 25 percent lower than that of the average San Francisco tenant]."[97]

In order to halt what clearly has been massive profit-driven abuse of the owner move-in provisions, an ordinance was introduced in 1996 to tighten the law considerably: extending to thirty-six months (from twelve) the amount of time the owner or his/her relative must live in the unit from which the eviction is taking place; increasing from 10 percent to 50 percent the ownership share required to invoke this right to evict (plugging up holes in the "Tenancy-in-Common"—or TIC—device, a widely used tool to permit OMIs, whereby a group of households pool resources to purchase a multifamily building for their own occupancy, share overall ownership, with each investor having the exclusive right to a certain unit, for eventual conversion to condominium ownership);[98] prohibiting the eviction if the landlord owns a comparable unit (even in another building); requiring the move-in to occur within three months; prohibiting eviction of residents sixty-two years and older and those with ten or more years of residence; requiring relocation payments of up to five thousand dollars, depending on length of tenancy; and, where the owner or relative does not in fact move in, a requirement to offer the former tenant the unit at the old rent. This quite stiff, and likely effective, change in the eviction laws proved a bit much for the supervisors, who shelved it but then passed a temporizing eighteen-month moratorium on OMI evictions. In early 1998, however, the Superior Court ruled it an unconstitutional property taking. Shortly thereafter, the Board of Supervisors passed a modified version (drafted by tenant groups), to be in effect for a year.

Not content with the supervisors' action, housing activists—buoyed by their victory at the polls in handily turning back the ballot measure to restore owner-occupied two- to four-unit buildings to the uncontrolled stock—placed Proposition G on the November 1998 ballot, incorporating some of the features of the new strengthened (but temporary) ordinance; making permanent the provisions applying to the protected classes of tenants; and limiting OMI evictions to one per building. The latter provision was aimed at the more recent device of using the state's Ellis Act, which permits owners to evict all tenants with just sixty days' notice (plus a moving stipend) if their intention is to go out of the rental housing business; the owners then are free to market the units under tenancy-in-common deals, for later conversion to condominium form of ownership. Sixty-six buildings were emptied under the Ellis Act in 1998, 211 in 1999.[99] Proposition G passed handily, 57 to 43 percent. According to City rent board data, in 2000, 881 rental units were removed from the housing stock via Ellis Act evictions.[100] The supervisors also passed a permanent ordinance. This new law

- prevents OMIs if the tenant is sixty-two years of age or older or disabled and has lived in the unit for ten or more years (five or more years if the tenant has a catastrophic illness), and outlaws discrimination against prospective tenants who fall under the protected classes;
- increases the ownership interest required to recover possession for units acquired after February 1991;
- limits OMI evictions to one per building;
- prohibits an OMI eviction if another comparable unit (in any building owned by the landlord) is available;
- establishes a maximum period (three months) within which the landlord or his relative must move into the recovered unit and a minimum amount of time (thirty-six months) during which the owner or his relative must maintain the unit as his/her principal residence;
- places limits on move-ins by relatives;
- requires the landlord to offer a replacement unit, if available and, if the OMI occupant leaves within thirty-six months, to offer the recovered

unit back to the displaced tenant at a rent no greater than that which would have been the rent had the tenant remained in continued occupancy and the unit remained subject to the rent control ordinance;

- and provides for a one-thousand-dollar relocation payment to tenants living there for twelve or more months.

Adding force to the new laws, the supervisors then passed the so-called Bierman-Katz ordinance (named after its two sponsors, Sue Bierman and Leslie Katz), taking aim at what was becoming unbridled use of the Ellis Act escape route around the Proposition G provisions: It amended the Planning Code to require that an owner (of a building with three or more units built before the 1979 passage of the city's rent control ordinance) desiring to use the Ellis Act as a device to move into her/his own building must obtain a conditional-use permit from the Planning Department; and that the primary focus of the conditional-use determination must be the impact on the city's housing stock. This one-two punch sent the real estate industry up the wall, and they (the Greater San Francisco Association of Realtors, the San Francisco Apartment Association, the Coalition for Better Housing, and twelve individual plaintiffs) brought suit in March 1999 against the City, the Board of Supervisors, the Residential Rent Stabilization and Arbitration Board, and the Planning Commission, seeking to set aside the Bierman-Katz ordinance as well as those provisions of Proposition G that prohibit one or more owners from moving into any unit in a building they own—the legal arguments being that the state Ellis Act preempts Bierman-Katz, as do the provisions of Proposition G, plus constitutional claims of impermissible takings (which, even if upheld, would require compensation) and violation of the equal protection clause.[101] In June 1999, the court temporarily enjoined enforcement of the Bierman-Katz ordinance, and the following September granted a permanent injunction, but sustained a demurrer as to other parts of the law. In July 2001, the state Court of Appeals ordered a trial as to the constitutionality of the Proposition G provision limiting a landlord's right to evict tenants under OMI provisions. (The ruling reversed an earlier Superior Court decision that dismissed the landlords' challenge.)[102]

In December 1999, the Board of Supervisors unanimously passed legislation upping the relocation fee that must be paid to low-income tenants to forty-five hundred dollars. A state law that took effect January 1, 2000, requires landlords to wait a year (rather than sixty days) before evicting disabled tenants or tenants over sixty-two years of age (four months for other tenants); further tightening of the act may still come from Sacramento. But, in anticipation of this, the *Examiner* noted: "October [1999] was the busiest month ever for Ellis Act filings. There were 49, compared with 98 for the rest of the year. Prior to 1999, there have been only 65 petitions filed in The City since the law was passed in 1986, according to the San Francisco Rent Board. . . . [On January 1, 2000, more stringent restrictions went into effect on Ellis Act evictions.] To qualify under the old rules, the petitions had to be filed before Nov. 1."[103]

In November 2000, tenant activists placed two more initiatives on the ballot and emerged with one win, one loss. Proposition H, which won, 58 percent to 42 percent, placed severe limits on pass-through of capital costs for building improvements to tenants. Prior to passage, landlords were permitted (via a formal approval process by the Rent Stabilization and Arbitration Board requiring strict documentation) to pass on such costs—for roof repairs, furnace replacement, exterior repainting, updating plumbing and electrical service, new windows, structural work, etc.—to tenants, on an amortized basis, in the form of rent increases. Rent board data showed a substantial increase in these allowable pass-throughs: In 1997, fifteen hundred units were affected; in 1999, thirty-eight hundred units.[104] Consequent rent increases then frequently force tenants to move, giving landlords the freedom to set new and higher rents for replacement tenants. Another argument against this practice, of course, was that such improvements increased the value of the property, which increase would accrue to the owner, and making tenants bear the cost of this added profit was unfair: "making them unwilling investors in an enterprise in which they have no financial stake," as one observer neatly put it.[105] The revised law permits, with some very limited exceptions, only capital costs associated with seismic retrofitting to be passed on as rent increases (again, in amortized form over many years and with a limit of 5 percent over the standard allowable annual rent increase). But a month after the electoral win, a superior court judge temporarily enjoined enforcement of the new ordinance, responding to a suit brought by the San Francisco Apartment Association, the Coalition for Better Housing, and a group of individual property owners. While the ordinance guarantees that landlords will receive a "fair rate of return," the judge ruled that until the rent board issues regulations specifying how this rate will be calculated, enforcement must be held up. In August 2001, a superior court judge ruled Proposition H unconstitutional, as it does not provide landlords with a constitutionally guaranteed fair return on their properties.

The losing measure was Proposition N (it went down, 53 to 47 percent), which attempted to place an upper limit on the number of TICs by including them as part of the two-hundred-unit annual limit placed on condominium conversions. While several hundred rental units were being lost each year via the TIC route (more than four hundred in 1999 alone), it is a two-edged sword, and the mixed results of the two November 2000 ballot propositions are understandable: "On one hand, tenant groups want to preserve the stock of rental housing for the majority of residents who will never be able to afford to own a home in San Francisco. On the other hand, with rents skyrocketing, those who can pull together enough money for a down payment are looking for a way to buy a home and free themselves of the insecurities of renting. However, while renters may aspire to be owners, they still want to keep their rents as low as possible."[106] In mid-2001, the Board of Supervisors passed a measure that limited TICs to four hundred per year (the figure to include condominium conversions, which already had a two-hundred-unit cap), with additional restrictions (although exempting two-unit buildings from the cap, if the tenants agree to the conversion, and exempting as well conversions already in process). Mayor Brown vetoed it, but the supervisors overrode his veto—the first such defeat for Brown in the five years he had been in office.[107] Whether this will be sufficient to block the profiteers remains to be seen: "They'll find another way to evict. There are other forms of ownership, and those will be figured out by the speculators," said one who knows, Janan New, director of the San Francisco Apartment Association.[108]

Condo Conversion Controls

San Francisco housing activists also have been effective in limiting, although not banning, the loss of rental units through sale to individual purchasers, a wave of landlord profit-taking that hit many U.S. cities starting in the 1970s. Such condominium conversion reduces the supply of rental units; causes substantial displacement, particularly of the elderly; diverts capital and entrepreneurial efforts away from providing new housing and renovating substandard units; encourages speculative ownership; and leads landlords to hold units vacant in order to facilitate sales.

In mid-1979, the supervisors established an upper limit of one thousand units a year on the number of allowable conversions, and a series of protections were enacted for those living in converted units. Owners who did get permission to convert their rental units were required either to set aside a portion of the units as low- and moderate-income housing, replace the lost units, or make an "in-lieu" payment into a City replacement housing fund. They had to pay moving expenses for tenants who did not wish to purchase their units. Tenants sixty-two years of age and older and disabled persons not wishing to purchase were entitled to a lifetime lease. And in order to obtain permission to convert, at least 40 percent of current tenants had to sign forms indicating either intent to purchase their unit or intent to seek a lifetime lease from the landlord.

But even with these reforms, City records showed that three-fifths of converted units were being purchased as speculative investments by people who were not occupying them; that only 15 percent of sales were to tenants who had signed "intent to purchase" forms; that a large portion of newly built condominiums were unsold; that the average annual income required to rent preconversion units was twenty-two thousand dollars, compared with an average annual income of eighty-seven thousand dollars required to purchase those same units; and that almost no condo converters were paying "in-lieu" money into the City's housing development fund (needless to say, none was building replacement housing and almost no one was setting aside converted units at prices low- and moderate-income purchasers could afford).[109] In fact, according to the 1982–83 Civil Grand Jury report, as of May 1983, nearly four years after passage of the original condominium control ordinance establishing this fund, the city's chief administrative officer, responsible for promulgating rules and regulations governing it, had done no more than produce draft rules and regulations, and the mayor had appointed no one to the five-person Housing Development Fund Loan and Grant Committee that is supposed to administer the moneys (which totaled all of $192,000 as of that date).

Against this factual background, the city's housing activists in 1983 were able to secure a temporary moratorium on conversions, followed by a seven-to-two vote supporting an ordinance introduced by Supervisor Carol Ruth Silver (in her prelandlord/realtor incarnation) banning condo conversions altogether when the city's vacancy rate is less than 5 percent. But, ever eager to please her real estate supporters, Mayor Feinstein vetoed the bill, and despite the margin of supervisorial support, the eight votes needed to override the veto were not there. (Supervisors Richard Hongisto and Lee Dolson were advised by the city attorney to disqualify themselves from voting, on conflict-of-interest grounds, because of their rental property holdings. As noted above, a ruling of this nature reduces the possibility of getting the eight votes always needed to override a mayor's veto. Even if a landlord supervisor chooses to vote for stronger rental housing controls, contrary to his or her economic self-interest, but perhaps out of political self-interest— as the mayorally ambitious Richard Hongisto might have chosen to do— that supervisor is not permitted to.)

Feinstein did agree to sign a compromise bill limiting conversions to two hundred units a year for 1983, 1984, and 1985, and banning conversions altogether in buildings with twenty-five or more units. The law was renewed upon its expiration in 1985 and still is in effect.

The city's sharply reduced condo conversion limit inspired another attempted end-run around City government via the state legislature, this time not by the organized real estate industry, but by one of its more flamboyant practitioners. Southern California real estate tycoon Richard Traweek had bought the 720-unit John Muir Apartments complex in the Lake Merced area and applied to convert it to condominiums, a move that could have meant as much as $40 million in profits.[110] Traweek attracted some twenty-five hundred investors—eighteen hundred of whom invested in the John Muir deal—into his Traweek Investment Company, for which he held pep rallies featuring such guest speakers as Assembly Speaker Willie Brown, Howard Jarvis (co-originator of Proposition 13), and San Diego mayor (later U.S. senator and California governor) Pete Wilson. To protect his John Muir plan, Traweek had state senator Henry Mello introduce legislation in effect requiring San Francisco (although the legislative language was not so blatantly drafted) to process any condo conversion applications received before the City's December 1982 passage of the new limit. The bill duly passed the Senate.

Once it reached the assembly, however, reports of Traweek's generous and well placed campaign contributions began to leak out. Beyond the forty-three thousand dollars he had spent lobbying for this bill, he had contributed thirty-five thousand dollars to the campaigns of key legislators, including members of the Assembly's Housing and Development Committee, which was to hold hearings on the bill. In 1982 and through April 1983, Traweek and his various entities had donated over thirty-eight thousand dollars to Willie Brown. Since Traweek did not bother to file required state reports on these various gifts, the state's Fair Political Practices Commission began an investigation. Faced with considerable adverse publicity and the distaste of the Board of Supervisors and Mayor Feinstein for this breach of local home rule, the assembly defeated the Traweek-Mello bill. Traweek for his part (represented, somewhat bizarrely, by ex-Mayor Joseph Alioto) filed suit against the City, Mayor Feinstein, Chief Administrative Officer Roger Boas, and the eight supervisors who voted for the ordinance that prevented the John Muir conversion, alleging actions in restraint of trade. In April 1984, Traweek's case against the individual City officials was dismissed, but he was allowed to proceed with his $800 million suit against the City. A flap later arose over a letter from eleven state legislators, all recipients of Traweek's largesse, to the judge in the case, in support of the realtor, a move the judge criticized as "improper communication."[111] Traweek's antitrust suit was eventually dismissed.[112]

A landlord-initiated proposition on the November 1989 San Francisco ballot (Proposition R) called for raising the annual conversion limit to seven hundred units, eliminating the cap altogether after three years, and allowing conversions in buildings of any size. That one lost, 69 to 31 percent.

In 1991, Supervisors Bill Maher, Jim Gonzalez, Willie Kennedy, and Tom Hsieh (the board's right wing) placed a ballot measure (Proposition N) on the November ballot, at the behest of developer Zev Ben-Simon and his Taldan Investments, owner of a large Diamond Heights complex, eliminating altogether the annual limit on the number of units that could be converted to condos, so long as a majority of tenants approve, tenants are given a chance to buy their units at 75 percent of market value, and tenants are offered financing for at least 90 percent of the selling price. Tenants not wishing to buy could remain with lifetime leases, and units in buildings of any size could be converted. It lost heavily, 67 to 33 percent.

Much of the rent control activism described above also, directly as well as indirectly, has been a dampening force to reduce the impact of condo conversions, as part of a general movement to protect renters and the city's stock of rental housing—the largest proportionally of any major U.S. city.

Community-Based Housing Development

One of the city's most important assets has been the affordable, nonprofit housing built and operated by the several neighborhood-based housing developers, of which TODCO, TOOR's development spin-off (see chapter 10), is just one example. Other substantial producers are the Mission Housing Development Corporation; the Chinese Community Housing Corporation; Asian, Inc.; the Tenderloin Neighborhood Development Corporation; and Catholic Charities. These groups, and others—in Bernal Heights, Potrero Hill, Haight-Ashbury, and elsewhere—have been highly effective in providing and preserving low-rent housing oriented to the specific needs of the neighborhoods they work in and in which they are based. In 1978, an umbrella group, the Council of Community Housing Organizations (CCHO, or Choo-Choo, in the local parlance), was formed to work on a range of issues that have kept growing since its inception: rezoning, revision of the residence element of the City's Master Plan, capacity-building, downtown growth controls, increasing Community Development Block Grant allocations for this work, improving the City's Office Affordable Housing Production Program (see chapter 12), assisting with neighborhood planning and encouragement of neighborhood-serving retail uses, providing technical and earthquake recovery assistance, and serving as overall advocates for this housing stream. An April 1991 CCHO report indicated that by that time, more than eighty-five hundred units of affordable housing, both new and rehabilitated, had been completed or were under way, over thirty-two hundred of which are owned by these neighborhood nonprofits.[113] By early 2002, it is estimated that some twenty-two thousand affordable units in various parts of the city have been produced or assisted by these community housing corporations—about half are new construction, half acquisition followed by rehabilitation.

Numbers aside, these developments have been undertaken in troubled neighborhoods, often under difficult conditions, providing imaginative solutions and supportive social services, with substantial neighborhood participation.

Protecting Residential Hotels

Another focus of San Francisco's housing movement has been protection of the city's stock of residential hotels (SROs or single-room-occupancy hotels) of the type the Yerba Buena project massively destroyed in the late 1960s and early 1970s. With the loss of those four dozen hotels containing some thirty-two hundred rooms, the only areas with a substantial supply of this special type of remaining housing—apart from those hotels still standing in the blocks surrounding YBC, which rapidly have been falling victim to market forces in the South of Market area—are Chinatown, the Tenderloin, and parts of the Mission. In the 1975–79 period, the city lost 6,098 residential hotel rooms.[114] Some seventeen hundred housing units were lost in Chinatown alone from the mid-1970s to the mid-1980s due to immense pressures to convert buildings to office use. A huge influx of overseas Asian investment capital has driven commercial and residential rents to unheard-of heights, forcing out small businesses and residents alike. In response, Self Help for the Elderly and the Chinatown Coalition for Better Housing (consisting of representatives of the Asian Law Caucus, Asian Neighborhood Design, and the Chinatown Neighborhood Improvement Resource Center) organized to push for a temporary moratorium on hotel conversions in the Chinatown area, an ordinance the supervisors passed in April 1984, with a one-year limit.[115] Citywide, from 1997 to 1999 alone, more than twelve hundred SRO units were lost to fires and conversion to apartments.[116]

A more serious, long-term approach to the problem primarily focused on the fifty-square-block Tenderloin area, on the north side of Market Street, an amalgam of many uses and forces. To its east is the retail and luxury hotel district, to the west the Civic Center complex, and the somewhat vaguer northern boundary moves up into Nob Hill. Residentially, the Tenderloin is a very mixed area, containing about fifteen thousand small rental apartments and residential hotel rooms (the latter make up 40 percent of its entire housing stock), which house a population of twenty-five thousand: the independent elderly, transients, mentally and physically disabled persons, and recent refugees—including a large portion of the city's newer Southeast Asian population (which has added markedly to the number of children in the area—estimated now at four thousand—and strengthened it as a neighborhood).[117]

As a residential community, the Tenderloin is being attacked on many sides. From the east the hotel district has been expanding. From the Civic Center/Van Ness corridor have come new, pricey condos. From within, the force eating away at the Tenderloin's housing stock is hotel conversion—change from residential to tourist status, to meet the need for "San Francisco's number one industry." (Appropriately enough, Mayor Feinstein and her husband, Richard Blum, partly converted to tourist use their North of Market hotel, on Sutter Street.) Conversion from rooms generally renting in the five-hundred- to eight-hundred-dollar-a-month range to rooms renting for $60 and up a day is obviously a real estate developer's fantasy come true, and so, much creative energy has gone into trying to empty hotels of their mainly elderly permanent residents.

Often wholesale eviction notices were sent—an illegal tactic—and the elderly, being frightened and confused, not knowing their rights, not wanting any fights, just left. *San Francisco Chronicle* columnist Warren Hinckle wrote about one Tenderloin hotel:

> What is happening at the Dalt is eviction by another name—call it forced inconvenience, terror, harassment, or simply rudely letting old people know they're now no longer welcome because the tourist can pay more. . . . [According to Dr. Denis Stone of the San Francisco Health Department], "If you subject old people to the sort of conditions they experienced at the Dalt it will increase ten to 30-fold the possibility of morbidity. The instances of death and serious illness at that hotel beat all the actuarial tables. The Dalt is a very stressful environment."[118]

Some clever landlords were able to empty their hotels by another method, called "let the City do the dirty work." As described by Hinckle: "A past or present owner allows property to become so rundown that the city steps in and condemns the building. The tenants then have to move out, which is just ducks for the landlord."[119]

A March 1983 *Tenderloin Times* feature contained these vignettes:

When Charlie Mullaney, who is 74 years old and in poor health, left his room at the Abigail Hotel on McAllister on New Year's Eve to go to the hospital about some problems he was having, it was the last time he would set foot in the building. When he called the hotel from the hospital, he found that the owner had made good on his threat to lock him out of his room. After nine years at the Abigail, Mullaney was gone. . . .

"They don't do nothing," says tenant Sarge Flanagan. "They don't sweep, they don't vacuum, they don't put out toilet paper, they don't even have a sponge. They stopped the pest control after August—the roaches loved it, the mice loved it. There's probably not a person here who has not had a mouse run across his face while sleeping. When a window breaks, it stays broke, when a bathtub backs up, it stays backed up. They don't offer no service and they don't intend to," Flanagan concludes. . . .

"They brought in these two goons," says Wayne Parkhouse, a six-year tenant. "They were pretty rough talkers, intimidating. They said I had to be out in one month and they told me they could go up to my room right away and move my things out. I was speechless. I didn't know what to say. They didn't give any notices but they said they were going to completely remodel and renovate the place. They said they had other properties and they would make up the difference between [current rent of] $166 and what [future] rent you get. But what do you do after a year? You're screwed."

The tenants say [Dr. Peter] Bullock [owner of the Glenburn Hotel] harassed them and made their lives miserable in an effort to drive them out. They say the harassment took such forms as making people change rooms, sending out streams of rent increase and eviction notices, cutting off linen service, and refusing to let residential tenants linger—much less sit—in the lobby.

Shades of Yerba Buena.

Lawyers for the tenants were at least able to succeed in damage suits against the more heinous landlords. In August 1981, the owner of the Dalt Hotel on Turk Street agreed to pay tenants $425,000 (which he finally paid in mid-1983) against their claims that the hotel manager locked out social workers taking food to bedridden residents, nailed garbage chutes shut, took away the lobby furniture, sprayed unpleasant substances, shut off the elevators and heat, even painted over front windows so tenants couldn't see out. Aided by Legal Services lawyers, tenant groups won other large awards over the years against greedy hotel owners, as high as $2.2 million and $4.5 million, and even got one put in jail.[120] But the deterrent effect of such actions was inadequate to offset the economics inherent in running an SRO versus a tourist hotel.

In the late 1970s, the Tenderloin tenants and their organization, the North of Market Planning Coalition, moved to secure conversion limitations and provide protective rezoning. Led by the Gray Panthers and Legal Assistance to the Elderly, they succeeded, in late 1979, in getting the Board of Supervisors to enact a moratorium on converting rooms to tourist use. In February 1981, the supervisors passed a fairly strong protective law to replace the moratorium, but it was immediately tied up in court by lawsuits brought by the hotel owners. In June 1981, the supervisors passed a far weaker law, requiring residential hotel owners to register their units and replace any units converted to tourist use, or make an "in-lieu" payment to the City's housing replacement fund. But it also gave owners the right to rent vacant residential units at tourist prices from May 1 to September 30 (presumably while the elderly Tenderloin residents are summering at Martha's Vineyard or in Europe) and created a system of record keeping and verification that was virtually unenforceable.[121] And so, between 1981 and 1989, more than seventeen hundred such units were lost to conversion or demolition.[122] The combination of a weak law, an overworked and unwilling bureaucracy, and wholesale circumvention by the hotel owners with strong economic incentives to do so, led to continuing conversions.[123] A March 1984 *Tenderloin Times* feature reported that twelve hotels containing more than a thousand rooms had been given permission to convert since passage of the ordinance, using a loophole in the law exempting buildings that had already begun conversion at the time the ordinance was passed. Another hotel was illegally converted, but the City declined to act against the owner because the tenant who brought the complaint had not lived there thirty consecutive days—he had missed one day in the middle and thus lost his standing to sue under the law. Other hotel owners were keeping rooms vacant seven months in order to avoid delays and hassles in renting those same rooms during the five-month tourist season. Overall, this portion of the city's housing stock dropped, between 1975 and 1988, from thirty-three thousand rooms to nineteen thousand rooms, and took a further hit from the 1989 Loma Prieta earthquake, which took out ten such hotels. Whereas in the 1960s the city had far more single-room-occupancy hotel rooms than tourist hotel rooms, the picture now is totally turned around.

In 1990, a considerably strengthened protective ordinance was passed, increasing the amount the owner had to pay into the City fund to replace converted units; limiting an owner's right to leave rooms vacant during the tourist off-season; and giving local nonprofits standing to enforce the law. The new law was at first ruled an unconstitutional taking, in a suit filed by the Golden Gate Hotel Association and a disgruntled owner, but was upheld upon appeal in March 2002 by the California Supreme Court.

In the early eighties, largely in response to learning of the three new tourist hotels planned for the area, the North of Market Planning Coalition collected five thousand signatures in support of a rezoning proposal for the neighborhood, and the Planning Commission, as City law then required, adopted these new zoning regulations on an interim basis, pending completion of a Planning Department rezoning plan. The interim controls embodied an eighty-foot height limit on new development and protection of existing residences and neighborhood businesses.[124] In 1992, the North of Market Planning Coalition issued its own plan for the neighborhood;[125] and limited but impressive work to provide affordable units, for families as well as individuals, through rehabilitation, construction, seismic upgrade, and provision of supportive services, is being undertaken by an array of locally based entities: the Tenderloin Housing Development Corporation; the Indochinese Housing Development Corporation; the St. Vincent DePaul Society; the Chinese Community Housing Corporation; Asian, Inc.; the North of Market Development Corporation; Community Housing Partnership; and Housing for Independent People.[126] The upshot of the rezoning proposal was establishment of the North of Market Residential Special Use District, providing limited protection against new development destructive to the existing neighborhood.[127] But the development pressures coming from the Van Ness corridor and the tourist industry are powerful. Mayor Feinstein's ecstatic words at a 1982 civic luncheon given for the sponsors of the new North of Market Ramada Renaissance Hotel (subsequently sold and renamed The Parc 55, then once again renamed as The Renaissance Park 55) give a chilling sense of the area's likely future. According to the May 3, 1982, *Examiner,* "She told the project sponsors . . . that the hotel is aptly named because 'you are bringing a renaissance to the area.' The mayor joyously announced she was ready to 'turn cartwheels. . . . I am so proud and grateful.' . . . Then she went on to rhapsodize about the anticipated 'ripple effect' from both the Ramada and the nearby San Francisco Hilton." There is something more than a little disconcerting about a mayor so grateful she wants to turn cartwheels in gratitude for a developer's hardly sacrificial investment in one of the most attractive real estate markets in the world—especially when such development can only add to the problems of the city's neediest citizens.

Among the more recent wrinkles in the residential hotel game is the so-called "musical rooms" gambit: not allowing residents to stay more than

twenty-eight days in the same room so as to avoid City and state laws stipulating that after a continuous stay of thirty days under state law, thirty-
two days under City law, a tenant is entitled to the same rights as an apartment dweller, including protection under San Francisco's rent control and
eviction control ordinances. Hotel residents were evicted after twenty-eight
days, then reregistered. Eviction for the purpose of preventing tenancy is a
violation of both City and state law. In mid-2000, the city attorney's office
finally acted against two of the more egregious violators, the owners of the
Hotel West and Drake Hotel in the Tenderloin. The hotel owners in May
2000 signed a consent decree terminating the practice—widespread throughout the Tenderloin, Mission, and South of Market neighborhoods. Ending
the practice throughout the city likely will take more than this, however.
Current law calls for fines up to twenty-five hundred dollars per violation
under state law, one thousand dollars a day under City law. More effective
than that, however, would be imposing criminal sanctions on violators. The
impact of residential insecurity on the vulnerable citizens who live in these
SROs—primarily poor, disabled, elderly, and mentally ill persons—can
justly be termed criminal.[128] These hotels increasingly are being used for
family living (technically illegal), especially by recent immigrants, and
there's even an official City SRO Family Working Group.[129]

In July 2001, the supervisors finally (and unanimously) passed an ordinance requiring all SRO hotels with more than twenty rooms or those that
have three or more stories to install in-room sprinkler systems. In the previous four years, eleven fires had broken out in these hotels, destroying 840
rooms and killing three residents.[130] Some three hundred hotels are affected
by the new law; enforcement may be another matter. Lax City enforcement
of health and safety laws seems to be the rule. According to a 1999 *Examiner* account:

> The City has failed to use a 2-year-old law designed to step up enforce-
> ment against unsafe residential hotels. Despite continual problems in
> many hotels—rats and roaches, missing fire extinguishers, garbage
> blocking exits, lack of heat—city officials have not taken criminal ac-
> tion against any hotel owners, which the law allows them to do. . . .
> Supervisor Gavin Newsom . . . estimated there are tens of thousands
> of violations for which building owners receive just a slap on the wrist.
> The law allows the district attorney to charge building owners with
> misdemeanors if they fail to correct violations that affect tenants'
> health and safety. Before the ordinance was passed, most violations
> could be charged only as infractions. The only exception was failure to
> provide heat.

The article then mentions several problem-plagued hotels that appear on a list used by the City and its contractors for low-income people in need of temporary housing.[131]

Public Housing

San Francisco has more than three dozen public housing projects, with some six thousand apartments (one-third of which are for seniors and disabled persons), plus about the same number of units of privately owned low-rent housing subsidized under the federal Section 8 program—housing some twenty-five thousand people in all. Many of the projects are in rough shape, reflecting the legacy of years of neglect, at both federal and local levels, and inadequate subsidies. Nearly two decades ago, the condition of many of the city's public housing projects led the San Francisco Civil Grand Jury, in its April 4, 1983, interim report, to comment: "On February 9, 1983, this Grand Jury visited the San Bruno Jail. On March 9, 1983, this Grand Jury visited some of the Public Housing Projects including Yerba Buena Plaza West [in the Western Addition]. It is our conclusion that it is far more dehumanizing to be a resident of Yerba Buena Plaza West than an inmate of the San Bruno Jail."[132]

As far back as 1985, HUD put the San Francisco Housing Authority (SFHA) on its "probation list" due to a range of serious financial and management problems. The authority was running a monthly deficit of $170,000 and had nearly $6 million in unpaid bills.[133] When, shortly thereafter, the authority's executive director, Carl Williams, resigned, he was described as "the fourth consecutive executive director to leave the agency under a cloud of controversy."[134] Williams had been appointed in 1978 to replace Walter Scott, who was demoted to deputy director during a financial crisis that strongly resembled the one Williams was criticized for. Before Scott, the Housing Authority had been run for nearly twelve years by Eneas Kane, who resigned in January 1977 and several months later was indicted for embezzling Housing Authority funds (he pleaded guilty to one count of grand theft and was placed on three years' probation). Kane's predecessor was John Beard, who, after running the authority for twenty-two years, was forced out in the midst of charges of racial discrimination by civil rights groups.

Three years after HUD's critical move, headlines of the déjà-vu sort appeared. From the September 12, 1988, *Chronicle:* "[Mayor Art] Agnos Sets Meetings on 'Crisis' at S.F. Projects." And from the September 9, 1988, *Chronicle:* "Housing Projects in San Francisco Reported 'Out of Control.' " The HUD regional management division had written Housing Authority

Chair Harry Chuck that "the authority has virtually lost control of entire developments," referring to the fact that in half of the agency's developments, repair and maintenance efforts were paralyzed and drug dealers and vandalism were rampant. In May 1989, David Gilmore, a specialist in saving troubled public housing authorities from his earlier work in Boston, was appointed to head the SFHA.[135] Gilmore was successful in reducing the authority's vacancy rate, speeding up repairs and rerenting procedures, getting additional federal funds, improving record-keeping procedures, and paying off most of the authority's long-term debt.[136] He departed in 1993, pushed out by Mayor Frank Jordan, in reaction to complaints from some tenant groups that he cared more about physical improvements to properties than about tenants and was unresponsive to their needs and demands, particularly with regard to proposals for tenant groups to assume management of their developments. ("My arrogance, for which I am well known, got in the way. Clearly, I did make mistakes in San Francisco.")[137]

In March 1996, HUD issued a report characterizing the Housing Authority as mired in mismanagement that left many of its projects with unsafe living conditions and (no doubt related) poor rent collection results. It had failed to meet the eighteen recommendations for improvement that the federal agency had issued in 1992. As the *New York Times* report put it, witheringly:

> In recent years the authority . . . has gone from bad to worse. It could not keep an executive director, running through about one a year for the last five years and sending several packing amid controversy and finger-pointing. . . . Backlogs of requests for repairs have swelled, and Mr. Marchman [HUD's assistant secretary for Public and Indian Housing] said this week that it was effectively bankrupt. . . . A HUD memorandum last year said that the authority had "little or no capacity for property management" and that its staff of about 500 had been conditioned to believe that the blight in the projects was acceptable and that change was impossible. . . . [The Housing Authority Board] seemed to bicker endlessly, wrapped up in politicking and personal agendas.[138]

HUD Secretary Henry Cisneros, visiting a San Francisco project, had the eye-opening experience of walking into a local drug deal in progress. Following the HUD blast, then–executive director Shirley Thornton resigned, and the commissioners voted to turn the authority over to HUD,[139] which, until September 1997, was in charge of the city's public housing. In June 1999, the authority was formally removed from HUD's "troubled" list.

But removal from the HUD doghouse did not mean the end of the Housing Authority's troubles. In 1999, a federal grand jury indicted the agency's relocation manager, Patricia Williams, her assistant Yolanda Jones (daughter of Hunters Point trucker and political heavy Charlie Walker—often described as "the mayor of Hunters Point—and the self-described goddaughter of Mayor Willie Brown), and more than twenty others on bribery charges. Between 1996 and 1998, when thousands of public housing residents were being displaced due to demolition of their deteriorating projects, bribes (as much as twenty-five hundred dollars) were solicited and paid in order to get Section 8 housing vouchers or placement in another Housing Authority apartment. In late 2000, Williams was found guilty of thirty counts of bribery, conspiracy, and other charges.[140] An equally disturbing story involves the Housing Authority's new executive director, Ronnie Davis, who had originally come to San Francisco from the Cleveland (Cuyahoga) Housing Authority in 1996 as part of the HUD assistance team. Davis then was named to head the Housing Authority, but in an unusual and not clearly explained arrangement that had the agency paying him not as an employee but as a corporation (Ron C. Davis Co., based in Utah). In March 2000, Davis, whose performance was deemed highly successful, became a formal Housing Authority employee, with a $188,000 salary, $12,000 signing bonus, six weeks' paid vacation, a car, and lots of other perks. But less than a month later, "Federal authorities released a scathing audit criticizing the financial practices of San Francisco Housing Authority Director Ronnie Davis . . . asking that he be punished for $11 million in questionable spending at his former job in Cleveland [where he was chief operating officer for that city's housing authority]." "The fact that Davis maintains financial responsibility as housing director in San Francisco, continues 'HUD's exposure to additional loss of funds,' the audit said. 'We believe HUD should pursue the strongest administrative action' against Davis." But this is not just a piece of elsewhere history: "The separate San Francisco audit, released Monday, charged that The City's Housing Authority wasted hundreds of thousands of dollars by handing out contracts without proper bidding and paying excessive salaries to managers. It called for the Housing Authority to repay nearly $2 million to the federal government and asked HUD to impose sanctions on Davis and his top managers."[141] In December 2000, HUD announced it was withholding $20 million in special grants to the Housing Authority, mostly for replacing rundown projects, labeling as "deficient" a federally mandated five-year plan that, according to HUD, would fuel racial segregation at the agency's three largest developments.[142] And in March 2001, Davis was indicted by a federal grand jury in Ohio, "charged with stealing hundreds of thousands of dollars in public money during his tenure at the Cleveland housing authority."[143]

HUD's HOPE VI program is providing funds to demolish and replace or rehabilitate a number of the city's older and more deteriorated projects. While in some respects a welcome step, the program has some clearly troubling aspects. HOPE VI both reduces the total number of housing units, and, by stressing mixed-income redevelopment, even further reduces the number of low-income units. For example, the Hayes Valley project had 463 units prior to demolition and will have only 195 in the redeveloped complex. Yerba Buena Plaza East, in the Western Addition, will wind up with 353 apartments, replacing nearly 500 being torn down. Given that the Housing Authority has a waiting list of 14,000 families, this reduction in the low-rent housing supply is more than a little disturbing.[144] Equally disturbing is that a substantial number of former public housing families displaced from HOPE VI projects leave the city—doubtless because they cannot find relocation housing locally. Displaced tenants are given Section 8 rent certificates, but few can find housing within the Fair Market Rent levels required to use these certificates. Thirty percent of the families displaced from Bernal Dwellings left the city, as did over a third of those displaced from the Hayes Valley project. And since about half of all families in San Francisco public housing are African American, such displacement has been a major factor in reducing the city's black population—San Francisco is one of the very few major U.S. cities with a declining black population—and in increasing neighborhood racial concentration as well.[145] Census data showed the city lost one in seven black residents during the 1990s.

One further disturbing development in the city's public housing is the conflict between African American households and the more recent Asian American arrivals to the projects. Some quite serious problems, including violence, have arisen in Alice Griffith (located near Candlestick Park in the Hunters Point section) and other projects, as Vietnamese and other Asian Americans are moved into predominantly black projects. The Asian Law Caucus in fact brought suit against the Housing Authority in 1993, claiming the agency was botching HUD-mandated project integration by not providing appropriate support services, bilingual staff, and other resources necessary to make such transitions go smoothly.[146]

Other Subsidized Housing

In addition to the low-rent public housing projects owned and operated by the Housing Authority, San Francisco has close to ten thousand privately owned, but government-subsidized, low- and moderate-rent units in more than one hundred developments, the residents of which are threatened with huge rent increases and possible eviction. These developments, known as "expiring use projects," were built under a federal program that furnished low-interest construction loans and imposed controls and provided additional subsidies to assure affordability; but in order to entice private developers to participate, the program allowed them, after twenty years, to prepay the mortgage and opt out of government controls. Many of these projects are in locations that can provide owners with far greater profit if the units are converted to condominiums or rehabilitated for a higher income group; and without controls, rents can be raised on existing tenants even if no improvements are made.[147] Statewide, some eleven thousand of these apartments have already been converted to market-rate levels.[148] The Nonprofit Housing Association of Northern California, the California Housing Partnership Corporation, the San Francisco Redevelopment Agency, and other groups have been acting to preserve this stock of affordable housing and protect the thousands of San Francisco households vulnerable to this impact.[149] Some federal legislation (the Low Income Housing Preservation and Resident Homeownership Act) earlier provided partial protection, and in 1990 the Board of Supervisors passed an ordinance requiring owners opting out of the program to give tenants reasonable advance notice, provide relocation payments, and make it easier for tenants and nonprofits to buy the developments and retain them as affordable housing.[150] A disproportionate number of the immediately threatened projects are in the Tenderloin, Western Addition, and Bayview–Hunters Point, meaning that the most vulnerable parts of the city's population are again under attack.

Homelessness: The Ultimate Housing Problem

Homelessness is a phenomenon now epidemic in cities large and small across the United States, as the housing crisis takes its most extreme toll, affecting families and individuals of all ages and races. The causes are many: loss of centrally located rooming houses and residential hotels due to public and private actions; rising rents; shrinking vacancy rates; joblessness; a shredded safety net; absence of needed social services; and deinstitutionalization of persons with mental problems, without concomitant creation of needed noninstitutional care facilities.

The size of any city's homeless population is inherently hard to establish, hence controversial. The general accepted figures for San Francisco range from ten thousand to sixteen thousand, and there's consensus that the problem is growing* and that it is possibly twice what it was ten years ago; that families are representing a higher portion of the total; that nothing effective is being done to deal with the underlying problems (as opposed to efforts to hassle and shoo away the homeless); and that the city's resources for dealing with the problem are totally inadequate. The massive and continuing loss of inexpensive single-room-occupancy hotels has left the poor with few options to the street other than the quantitatively and qualitatively deficient shelter system, and high, rising rent levels have pushed families out of conventional apartments.[151]

Homelessness begets an increase in "street people," an especially undesirable element in the eyes of those seeking to create the optimum environment for tourism (and no picnic for the homeless, 169 of whom died on the streets in 1999, the highest figure in any year since 1985, when this kind of macabre tracking began).† And so it is not surprising that for years the police have been harassing such folk, in the downtown area, the Haight-

---

*Point-of-time counts are one way of measuring the magnitude and significance of the homelessness problem. Another is to determine how many people have ever been homeless at one time or another. Researchers at the Columbia University School of Public Health came up with these staggering figures, based on a national sample: Over the five-year period 1985–90, 5.7 million people had been literally homeless at one time or another (sleeping in shelters, bus/train stations, abandoned buildings, etc.), while 8.5 million people reported some type of homelessness (staying with friends or relatives) during this period. Lifetime figures were 13.5 million (literal homelessness) and 26 million people (all types of homelessness). See Bruce Link et al., "Lifetime and Five-Year Prevalence of Homelessness in the United States," *American Journal of Public Health* (Dec. 1994): 1907–12.

†Jonathan Curiel, "Record Number of Homeless People Died on S.F. Streets in '99," *San Francisco Chronicle,* 23 December 1999. "Homeless Deaths Are Rising in San Francisco," *New York Times,* 21 December 1998. See also Steven VanderStaay, *Street Lives: An Oral History of Homeless Americans* (Philadelphia: New Society Publishers, 1992), which includes accounts from San Franciscans "Tony" (38–41), "Jaime" (74–76), "Tony" (92–94), "Sherry" (144–46), and "John" (150–52). A related threat and reality is the increasing violence homeless people experience, sometimes as they are sleeping, leading to injuries and even deaths, often carried out by young men attracted to "bum-bashing." Evelyn Nieves, in "Violence Is Become a Threat for Homeless" (*New York Times,* 23 December 1999), cites reports by the National Coalition for the Homeless that twenty-nine homeless people were killed in 1999 in eleven cities, San Francisco included. In Denver, five were pummeled to death and two beheaded; in Richmond, Virginia, one was beaten, stabbed, and beheaded, and his head was then carried nearly a mile and placed for display on a footbridge. Danger and death come to others as well, as occurred in Worcester, Massachusetts, in December 1999, when six firefighters were killed fighting a fire in an empty warehouse. The fire started when a homeless couple began arguing with each other and knocked over a lighted candle. They left the building without notifying authorities of the fire or that they were themselves safe. The six men who died believed people were still inside (www.telegram.com/fire).

Ashbury and Mission districts, and the Polk Street gay commercial district. The problem is an old one: In the two years from August 1980 through July 1982, San Francisco police made at least thirty-four hundred arrests under a section of the penal code that prohibits "willful and malicious obstruction of the sidewalks." These charges were commonly dropped at arraignment or dismissed outright. Pressure from merchants was of course a big spur (the head of the Haight-Ashbury Improvement Association was quoted as saying, "There is simply no harassment on Haight Street, and if there is, it's deserved").[152] After the state court of appeals overturned California's public drunkenness law, the City continued to push street people out, particularly from the UN Plaza area on Market Street between Seventh and Eighth Streets. According to Bernard Averbush, executive director of the Market Street Project (a City-sponsored beautification program), "Mayor Feinstein looks out on this plaza from her office window and she's irritated by the element she sees there."[153] "If all these ideas work," wrote *Examiner* columnist Bill Mandel, "Market Street's drifters will look to Yerba Buena Gardens, an enormous open space that will rise atop the Moscone Convention Center. . . . That thought scares Averbush, a derelict-hunter for 20 years. 'We have to control this element now,' he said, 'as a test of our methods in keeping Yerba Buena Gardens free of them in the future.' "[154]

In the fall of 1984, police began cracking down on people "loitering" around the Powell Street Muni station, where tourists throng at the cable car turnaround, and in Civic Center Plaza, triggering a protest by the American Civil Liberties Union (one of whose attorneys himself had been arrested when he refused to produce identification for a police officer).[155] And regular police patrols to move the homeless on were institutionalized in response to complaints from a growing number of neighborhoods around the city. Police policies are that homeless people have a right to use parks and sidewalks and cannot be ordered to "move along" because there are no valid laws against loitering or vagrancy; that police may not stop or question anyone based on "dress, unusual or disheveled or impoverished appearance" without a specific suspicion of criminal activity; that police cannot search the body or belongings of homeless people except in the case of a lawful detention or arrest. However, a 1988 poll of 284 homeless people by the Coalition on Homelessness, an organization of homeless people, lawyers, health workers, and shelter operators, nonetheless revealed that 98 percent said they had been ordered by the police to move on; 93 percent said they had been ordered to show identification when they were doing nothing wrong; and 70 percent had been threatened with arrest or actually arrested for loitering.[156]

The election of Art Agnos as mayor in 1987 gave promise of a better approach. His campaign book, "Getting Things Done: Visions & Goals for San Francisco," stated: "The homeless need more from the city than one night stands in low rent hotels. . . . A night's shelter does not bring the homeless closer to self-sufficiency. We can do better. One of my goals as mayor will be to implement a proper case management system that comprehensively addresses the problems of the homeless." But police, under orders from Mayor Agnos, began enforcing an until then ignored 1972 City ordinance forbidding sleeping in cars, an emerging phenomenon in residential neighborhoods, mainly in the Haight, on streets bordering Golden Gate Park and the park's (appropriately named) Panhandle.[157] The Vehicular Residents Association, an organization of these homeless persons, brought suit against the City, but in August 1990 the state court of appeals unanimously affirmed a trial court ruling upholding the ordinance against claims that it discriminated against the poor: In a variation of Anatole France's famous dictum, the court observed that "Motor homes are not used exclusively by the poor. Indeed, it is common knowledge that many persons inhabiting motor homes are economically advantaged and use their vehicles for recreational purposes rather than out of economic necessity."[158]

In the Civic Center Plaza area, Mayor Agnos moved from an initial stance of semitolerance (police periodically enforced clean-up of possessions and structures, but people were allowed to remain) to more hard-line tactics, giving as his reason two newly opened multiservice centers—notwithstanding the fact that these two centers together contained only four hundred beds, whereas an estimated eight hundred to one thousand people were sleeping in the Civic Center and other parks. In this more punitive stance, he employed a nineteenth-century law against "lodging" (Sec. 647(i) of the Penal Code)—lingering too long in a public place (such as sitting on a park bench with gear—as opposed to just sitting there taking in the rays). From mid-1991 to mid-1992, hundreds of people were cited or arrested for violation of the "lodging" law or for aggressive panhandling.[159] This development was in large part due to pressure from the Convention & Visitors Bureau, which in May 1990 released a study stating that 23 percent of two thousand tourists polled listed street people as the worst thing about the city. Holger Gantz, general manager of the Hilton, attributed one-third of his hotel's 20 percent decline in business the preceding year to increased panhandling in the Tenderloin.

In late 1989, Agnos had issued his master plan, "Beyond Shelter," providing a series of programs relating to prevention of homelessness, creation of affordable housing, benefits entitlements, mental health services, and emergency shelter services. His plan had set forth for the first time a coordinated, explicit set of goals—a great improvement over the ad hoc, reactive methods of operation that characterized previous efforts—but in truth "Beyond Shelter" more closely resembled a wish list than an actual plan for action and implementation.[160] The 1989 earthquake, while eliminating some five hundred residential hotel rooms, proved to be a boon of sorts.[161] Mayor Agnos was skillful in securing recovery funds from HUD, the Federal Emergency Management Agency, and the Red Cross, monies he used to open two of the multiservice centers he had promised in "Beyond Shelter."

One particular activity in the Haight (later expanded to the Mission and Civic Center)—the feeding program run by an anarchist-pacifist group, Food Not Bombs—caused considerable police overreaction. Those feeding the homeless (at a site bordering Golden Gate Park), as well as those being fed, were regularly hassled, threatened, and arrested. According to the police, the feeders needed a permit. The Food Not Bombs folks maintained they had applied more than a hundred times, without success. Ignoring an injunction against the free food distribution, some one thousand people were arrested at one time or another. One of the activists, Robert Kahn, was sentenced to sixty days in jail for giving out soup and bagels near city hall.[162] Food Not Bombs cofounder Keith McHenry, regularly arrested on misdemeanor, and occasionally on felony, charges, narrowly avoided a life sentence under the state's "three strikes and you're out" law.[163]

Agnos failed badly in trying to deal with the city's homelessness problem, which in turn constituted one of the principal reasons for his failure to gain reelection. A January 1990 *Examiner* poll found that nearly two-thirds of respondents listed homeless people on the streets as the city's worst problem and disapproved of the way Agnos was dealing with panhandlers and the homeless in general.[164] Large budget deficits—Dianne Feinstein's mayoral legacy—as well as federal and state cutbacks were major factors, forcing a tradeoff between a more holistic approach and required emergency services. But an important additional factor was the stirrings of what is sometimes genteelly referred to as "compassion fatigue": public hostility to the homeless and dismay at the failure of efforts to date to ameliorate, let alone eliminate, the problem.[165]

With ex–police chief Frank Jordan's victory over Art Agnos in the 1991 mayor's race—an event, as noted, in no small part due to public dismay over Agnos's inability to deal with the homelessness problem (it almost became a test of his ability to run the city) and Jordan's promise to make this a central concern of his administration[166]—things got tougher for the men, women, and children on the street. Jordan's scientifically labeled "Matrix Program," a wholesale police sweep against the homeless for a range of "nuisance crimes" (obstructing doorways, urinating in public, sleeping in a public park), racked up twenty-seven hundred citations or arrests in a two-and-a-half month period, and by the end of 1993 the total was four thousand.[167] The sweeps produced few convictions—but that was not their real purpose: Only thirteen people were found guilty by the end of 1993.[168] In response to the observation that the city has only fourteen hundred emergency beds on a given night, Jordan said: "If you want to call it an unresolved issue, then call it that. I'm not going to let them sleep in parks and playgrounds."[169] Assistant Public Defender Ron Albers pointed to one case in which a person spent thirty-one days in jail for sleeping in a doorway: "For $300 a night—nearly $10,000—we warehoused this guy for a little over a month, without doing anything to help him out. If that is what Matrix is supposed to accomplish, I guess the mayor is to be congratulated."[170] Interestingly, the sweeps brought condemnation not only from the homeless, their advocacy groups, and civil liberties organizations, but also from some neighborhoods: "Wealthy residents of San Francisco protested Jordan's get-tough program mostly because it shifted the homeless from the downtown to their residential neighborhoods."[171]

Public antagonism toward the homeless was shown in the results of two ballot initiatives. Mayor Jordan put Proposition J on the November 1992 ballot, outlawing (and defining) "aggressive panhandling," which passed, 55 to 45 percent. And a November 1993 ballot measure (Proposition V) was approved, 61 to 39 percent, adding a durational residency requirement for General Assistance applicants and providing for fingerprinting them—a particularly picayune but clearly symbolic put-down and expression of public anger and frustration.

This latter measure reflected a recurrent theme from city hall that any effort to provide serious aid to the homeless would cause homeless people from other areas to migrate to everyone's favorite city. San Francisco likely has the third largest homeless population in the nation, after New York and Los Angeles. In the early eighties, it was reported that "Mayor Feinstein wants to avoid turning the city into what she termed 'a magnet for the homeless of the entire Bay Area, the state and the U.S.'"[172] But it is highly unlikely that homeless folks just hanker to live on San Francisco's streets as opposed to Chicago's or Atlanta's. The problem for the most part afflicts local residents who, due to poverty, the city's housing crisis, and, for some, personal issues, are frozen out of the housing market. Sentiments such as those expressed by Feinstein are heard by city officials all over America and mask an unwillingness to provide the needed services. Paul Boden, director of the city's Coalition on Homelessness, accurately notes: "I don't know of one city in the country that doesn't say it's a magnet and that homeless people come from somewhere else. Fargo, North Dakota, was calling itself a magnet. It's kind of sad, actually."[173] What is undeniable is the massive gap between need and resources: The city's now fifteen hundred shelter beds can serve about one-tenth the number of homeless persons on and around the streets. And conditions at the city's shelters, not surprisingly, are woefully deficient. A late 2000 survey of fifty-one shelters around the city by the Coalition on Homelessness documented extensive defects. As one respondent put it: "No laundry facilities. No toilet paper. No towels. They don't clean. I guess the same sheet was on there when I got there. It was dirty. The blankets stank. And the staff are really rude." With regard to staffing, Paul Boden of the coalition observed that shelter workers need better pay, training, and support, and the chance for advancement to other jobs, such as fund-raising, case management, or bookkeeping, that could translate into careers.[174]

To be sure, these various antihomeless measures have not gone unopposed. As noted above, the San Francisco office of the American Civil Liberties Union (along with the San Francisco Neighborhood Legal Assistance Foundation) since the early eighties has regularly challenged the police actions in court, and there is a long history of complaints, suits, consent decrees, violation of consent decrees, and other actions. Mayor Jordan's Matrix Program was challenged in court for its vagueness and discriminatory application. The City was granted summary judgment at the federal district court level, and the American Civil Liberties Union for Northern California appealed to the Ninth Circuit, which dismissed the case (and vacated the district court decision) just before the case was to be argued, on the grounds that it was moot, since Mayor Willie Brown, shortly after taking office in 1996, had officially suspended the Matrix enforcement order[175] (even though in fact arrests were continuing—see below).[176] In April 1996, the municipal court, supported by the city's new district attorney, Terrence Hallinan (who on occasion handed out free food with the Food Not Bombs gang), dismissed some thirty-nine thousand citations against homeless people issued since 1993. The bad news, however, is that, in actuality, police harassment of the homeless and those feeding them hardly abated with the arrival of the Brown administration. An October 1996 *Washington Post* report noted, "Police statistics show the number of arrests for some Matrix-like offenses have continued at the same pace under Brown."[177] A subsequent account noted that in the first eleven months of the Brown administration, 1,750 more police citations were issued to homeless people than were issued in all of 1995 under Jordan's Matrix Program.[178] "[In 1999], the police here [San Francisco] issued more than 20,000 citations for violations of ordinances like trespassing, camping, carrying an open container and violating park curfews, compared with 17,500 in 1998 and 15,700 in 1997."[179]

More worrisome was Mayor Brown's sudden apparent "I give up" stance regarding this deep-seated social problem, revealed in late 1996, via his last-minute cancellation of a summit on homelessness, after seven months of preparation, due to his feeling that there was lack of common ground between advocates and the City, and his sad, but perhaps realistic, statement: "This is the most complex problem I have faced as mayor. It is not one that lends itself to readily triable, replicable solutions."[180] Further lamentations from Brown—"I can't talk with these people any more. They're not on the same page. There are some people who just don't want to live inside, and there's nothing you can do with them. They are the hoboes of the world. They just don't want help"—illustrate his frustration, impatience, and anger.[181] In November 1998, Brown got three pies thrown in his face, courtesy of the Bionic Baking Brigade, which said its purpose was to call attention to the City's lack of solutions to homelessness.[182] Other of Brown's antihomeless stances include: a proposal (later abandoned) to use California Highway Patrol helicopters with heat-seeking vision to locate homeless people living in Golden Gate Park and the confiscation of shopping carts used by homeless persons to store and transport their belongings.[183]

The mid–Market Street area (roughly from Fourth Street to the overhead Central Freeway, and including side streets) has been getting a lot of recent attention due to proliferation of narcotics sales, unauthorized street vending, public drinking, littering, and homeless encampments. Concerns emanate from tourist-oriented enterprises ("City officials say San Francisco's tourism and entertainment industry suffers from the street's scruffy image")[184] and occupants of stores and buildings, as well as passersby. Daily street sweeps by police (Operation Midway) were instituted in mid-2001. The usual lineup of competing interests presents itself. The Market Street Association (merchants) want to see a business-friendly official redevelopment zone, and lots of real estate investors are poised (in some instances, already have jumped) to make a killing. On the other side are various nonprofits and marginal business enterprises with reasonable office rents (for example, at the Grant Building at Seventh and Market), who fear gentrification, as well as those who deal with the very social ills prominent on the street, and who realize that street sweeps do nothing to solve these problems, but just add to the sufferers' woes and relocate those afflicted with drug, alcohol, mental, and housing problems to other areas.

It's clear that "compassion fatigue" had set in, as captured in headlines about San Francisco from national news accounts: "City of Tolerance Tires of Homeless,"[185] "Homelessness Tests San Francisco's Ideals."[186] And that— at least from city hall's biased and jaundiced perspective—"Willie Brown has become the third mayor of San Francisco in a row to enter office with a plan for dealing with the homeless only to discover that nothing works."[187] As Paul Boden of the city's Coalition on Homelessness observes about San Francisco's political climate: "There is an attitude that with unemployment at record lows, with the stock market at record highs, if you're poor, it's your own damn fault. This is not the same liberal mecca it used to be. Homelessness is off the radar. It's all quality-of-life issues now. All of these officials see what Mayor [Rudolph] Giuliani has done in Manhattan, how Times Square is so clean now, and they want to do the same thing. But the homeless in New York haven't disappeared, they've just been moved out of the spotlight. Here, there's no place to move them."[188] One of the ironies reflecting prevailing priorities was the offer, in early 1998, to provide overnight shelter for homeless persons in the city's super-posh new animal shelter—fitted out with doggy futons, Persian throw rugs, skylights, couches, jungle gyms, potted grasses, and fish videos (for the cats' diversion)—an offer with supposed benefits for both types of creatures, as the animals would have human buddies, the humans both a warm, dry bed and some animal company. Paul Boden observed that the new animal shelter was nicer than the recently opened six-hundred-bed China Basin shelter for the homeless: "It's condescending, it's weird and it's a little creepy. . . . The more you think about it, the more bizarre it becomes, because of the statement that the nicest shelter in town is going to be the one for the animals."[189]

The homelessness problem can only grow and is to be seen not as a discrete phenomenon but as one end of the continuum of San Francisco's housing woes described throughout this and other chapters. Unlike other housing problems, such as slum conditions, overcrowding, and excessive rents, which are localized in specific, often remote parts of the city or are privately experienced, homelessness is a very public problem—and one that is deeply annoying to many residents of and visitors to the city. Public space—the streets, playgrounds, and parks (Golden Gate Park, one of the country's outstanding urban spaces, has undoubtedly suffered from fires, littering, and loss of wildlife attributable to the presence of homeless campers)—is made dangerous and inaccessible. But criminalizing homelessness is clearly no answer,[190] and sooner or later all the nation's cities will have to face the costs of dealing with the underlying issues that cause homelessness, ranging from housing availability to jobs to providing the full range of needed social services.

The Presidio/Treasure Island

Two recent mega–land use developments and opportunities the city currently is dealing with are the Presidio and Treasure Island. Important housing issues are present in both, although other uses and considerations are prominent. Plans for both are largely tentative and fluid.

The Presidio, a 1,480-acre former army base, first established in 1776 (by the Spanish rulers of Mexico), located in the northwestern corner of the city (amounting to 5 percent of the city's land area—larger than Golden Gate Park), was formally abandoned in 1994 by the Sixth Army as part of national base-closing moves. Congressman Phillip Burton had the remarkable foresight back in the early seventies to include in legislation creating the Golden Gate National Recreation Area a provision that, should the base ever be closed down, it would become part of GGNRA. The site is magnificent, some of the most gorgeous and well located urban land anywhere in the world, overlooking the Pacific, the Golden Gate Bridge, and San Francisco Bay. It was a self-contained community, with eight hundred structures, five hundred of which have potential historical significance, more than eleven hundred homes and apartments, its own hospital, post office, airfield, water treatment plant, bowling center, pet cemetery, museum, library, churches, fire and police stations, theater, golf course, beach, and massive amounts of open space—forests, meadows, scenic headlands, long beaches, some 400,000 trees in all—and, as the *New York Times* characterized it, "long known as one of the cushiest military duties around [which] saw little combat until now."[191] While initially there were fears, expressed by Mayor Agnos, Congresswomen Barbara Boxer and Nancy Pelosi, the American Federation of Government Employees Local 1457, and the Chamber of Commerce, that closing the base would have a severe negative impact on the city's economy (the chamber predicted a 2 percent drop in the city's economic output, given that five thousand people were employed at the base, in civilian as well as military jobs, earning $138 million annually, plus $666 million in construction-related expenditures and services), as well as the burden of paying for additional City services,[192] others saw the incredible potential in reusing the site. And since the late eighties, as might be expected from San Franciscans, there have been innumerable proposals and "plans," for everything from a new University of California campus to an aviation museum, an environmental education center, a YMCA, an arts community, a conference center, luxury housing, low-rent housing, a massive golf course, an AIDS sanctuary and treatment center, and a facility for sheltering the homeless.[193]

The planning process for Presidio reuse began as early as 1990, with a series of public hearings convened by the National Park Service (and in fact some buildings were turned over to the GGNRA several years before formal base transfer).[194] In the subsequent decade, controversy was rife—beyond specific reuse plans—over such fundamental issues as finances, historic preservation, what it means to have a national park within a city, citizen participation/decision-making authority, and congressional politics.

The Presidio Trust (a public benefit corporation, in partnership with the National Park Service) was created by the Republican-controlled Congress in 1996, and in April 1997 President Clinton appointed seven persons to govern reuse of 80 percent of the former base.[195] The Trust has vast powers, including authority to borrow from the U.S. Treasury and provide loan guarantees to encourage private sector investment. Its congressional mandate—rooted in the Republicans' market orientation—is to make the project economically self-sustaining within fifteen years of the date when the Trust assumed management of its portion of the Presidio, that is, by 2013, at which time federal appropriations are to end, an arrangement that, in turn, requires some $36 million in annual net revenue. According to the Presidio Trust legislation, if the Presidio does not achieve financial self-sufficiency by that time, it will revert to the General Services Administration to be divided and sold. Needless to say, this puts severe constraints on what can and can't go on there and engenders deep controversy with the city's more public-regarding forces and actors.* (It is possible that a future

---

*For a very different approach to use of this unique resource, see "Sustainability and Community Development at the Presidio National Park: Strategies and Recommendations Presented to the Presidio Trust," a June 1997 report by the Urban Habitat Program, offering this public-regarding perspective: "In order for the Presidio to become an extraordinary urban national park serving a diverse public, park management goals must also include priorities of public ownership and stewardship, environmental conservation, protection and restoration, inclusion and accessibility, and social justice." An Urban Habitat proposal to take the entire Presidio "off the private utilities grid"—advancing self-sustainability in its environmental, rather than market economics, meaning, by creating model self-sufficient, sustainable water, sewage, and electrical technologies—was of course never seriously entertained by the Trust, and instead Pacific Gas and Electric took over. "Sustainability" has a very different meaning to the Presidio Trust, however: The September 1999 issue of the Trust's monthly publication, *Presidio Post*, defines it as "the idea that the Presidio will provide for its own operational needs and capital investments required over the long term to care for the park."

shift to Democratic control of Congress, along with federal budgetary sur-
pluses, could alter this federal mandate to make profits.) There is no precedent for a national park to become essentially privatized and a money maker
in order to avoid the need for federal subsidies.[196]

Among the Presidio's many serious problems are those in the environmental area: seismic instability, asbestos removal, toxics cleanup, lead and
plumes of petroleum under the surface—the detritus of more than two hundred years of military use, some of which possibly is still to be discovered
and uncovered.[197] (The Department of Defense has promised to provide
$100 million for environmental cleanup.) Historic preservationists have
their concerns: "Will the Directors see their prime role as curators of a splendid treasure which oddly combines a mine of military history with some of
the most unspoiled landscapes in the Bay Area? Or will the Trust put foremost the aims of the cost-cutting Congress which approves Trust legislation only if the maximum revenue is achieved?" asks the April 1997
newsletter of San Francisco Tomorrow.

As of early 2002, close to four dozen nonprofit organizations ("park partners," as they are termed)—groups such as the Tides Foundation, the
Thoreau Center for Sustainability, the Energy Foundation, Wilderness Society, Corporation for National Service, Gorbachev Foundation USA, the
Institute for Global Communications, and the Urban Habitat Program—
have moved in, along with some profit-making businesses (e.g., the Arnold
Palmer Golf Management Company).

A major upcoming development decision has to do with replacement of
the twenty-three-acre Letterman Hospital complex. In 1999 and 2000, tentative approval was given for a mega-development by Lucas Digital Ltd., an
amalgam of Industrial Light + Magic, LucasArts Entertainment Company,
Lucasfilm THX, Lucas Learning, and the George Lucas Educational Foundation—which beat out a more conventional office complex proposal from
the city's largest landlord, real estate magnate Walter Shorenstein. The
Lucas venture—essentially a corporate campus with underground parking
for fifteen hundred cars—still is in the planning process as of mid-2001,
and, needless to say, is extremely controversial. Carl Anthony of the Urban
Habitat Program warned, "The deal moves the Presidio perilously close to
being San Francisco's newest business park."* The development has also

---

*A taste of the commercialism Lucas brings to the Presidio is suggested by an
item in the 28 March 2001 *Washington Post* (Paul Fahri, "King's 'Dream' Becomes
Commercial"). The article describes a television image of Martin Luther King's 1963
"I Have a Dream" speech, only King is addressing a totally empty Washington Mall.
The image is accompanied by a voiceover: "Before you can inspire, before you can

come in for heavy criticism based on design and environmental issues: too big, too dense, too walled-off from the public. "My feeling is that this will be a gated community," commented one observer.[198] In late 2000, the National Park Service, the California Office of Historic Preservation, and the advisory council of the National Trust for Historic Preservation blasted the plan. The Park Service concluded that "the overall size, scale, materials, detailing and siting of the proposed development are incompatible" with the Presidio's landmark district status. And the National Trust observed that the Lucas complex design "creates a major adverse effect on the site, giving the appearance of a private, suburban office enclave."[199] In early 2000, fifty-six environmental organizations, including the Audubon Society, Wilderness Society, Natural Resources Defense Fund, California League of Conservation Voters, Earth Island Institute, and San Francisco Tomorrow, signed a letter to the Presidio Trust complaining it had failed to implement the letter or spirit of the Presidio's 1994 general management plan, which " 'envisioned a global center dedicated to the most critical environmental, social and cultural challenges'—not making better digital films."[200] The Trust's overall planning process has also come in for its share of criticism: "Park service officials and environmentalists say the Trust has squelched any sense of candor and openness with community groups in mapping out its development plans."[201] The $5 million in annual revenue the Lucas venture is scheduled to produce obviously is a major draw, given the need to move rapidly toward financial self-sufficiency. And that triggers concerns environmentalists have regarding the precedent the Presidio plan could embody: "The trust implies, after all, a kind of Darwinian scenario for the national parks—one where only the economically fit survive."[202]

Housing is a major part of the Presidio reuse plan. A substantial portion of the housing stock is currently occupied, and many of these units have been renovated. Residents include Park Service employees, employees of the organizations housed at the Presidio, park police and firefighters, students, some remaining military families, and the general public. Monthly rent levels, as of early 2000, ranged from $450 for a student single to $6,000 for one of the officers' mansions. Given the requirement for financial self-sufficiency, there is no reason to believe that Presidio tenants will be immune from the severe upward trend of the city's rents. A worrisome note from the April 2000 issue of the Trust's monthly publication, *Presidio Post*,

---

touch, you must first connect. And the company that connects more of the world is Alcatel, a leader in communications networks." The company that produced this monumentally tasteless ad: George Lucas's Industrial Light + Magic shop.

suggests this: "When Federal appropriations to the Trust end in 2013, housing leases are projected to provide more than half the funds needed to operate and enhance the Presidio."

The big housing controversy to date was over the 466 units of "Wherry Housing" (built under a long-ago federal government subsidy program named after its Senate sponsor), which the Park Service originally planned to tear down (and partially did). These dwellings could provide needed quarters for homeless persons (by the time the protest was organized, fifty-eight units had already been demolished, at a cost of $1.4 million). Although these apartments are seismically sound, lead- and asbestos-safe, and well maintained, their retention, especially if they might be occupied by homeless persons, was clearly not to be countenanced by those seeking upscale development of this valuable piece of San Francisco real estate. An interfaith coalition—Religious Witness with Homeless People—has held a series of demonstrations and civil disobedience actions, at which more than two hundred persons have been arrested.[203] Studies by the mayor's Office of Housing and a pro bono consultant, endorsed by Mayor Brown, indicated that the Wherry units could be brought up to code standards for $9 million (less than twenty thousand dollars per unit), in contrast to the Park Service's overblown figure of $47 million and the $12 million to $16 million estimated cost of demolishing the units.[204] Carl Anthony, also president of the Earth Island Institute, noted the irony embodied in the environmental concerns for Presidio development: "We are concerned with the moral legitimacy of demolishing $80 million of viable housing stock to make way for open space and recreation when homeless people are sleeping in city parks."[205] A voters' opinion statement placed on the June 1998 ballot (Proposition L), urging preservation of the existing Presidio housing (and open space), passed 53 to 47 percent. Although it is likely that most of the housing will be preserved, it is unlikely that any of it will be used to house the homeless.

Treasure Island is another story, again the fortuitous result of a base-closing (in this case, the Navy). It is four hundred acres, with a hundred more on the connected Yerba Buena Island (both islands are humanmade, created as a WPA project for the 1939 Golden Gate International Exposition and a Navy base since 1941), in the bay, halfway between Oakland and San Francisco, with none-too-easy access and huge earthquake and toxic problems.[206] The two islands contain some one thousand housing units. As of early 2002, these units are under stewardship of the City, which has leased them from the Navy. The Housing Authority is using Section 8 housing subsidies to make eighty units available for homeless families (of some, but limited, help for the twenty-five hundred homeless families on its list—a lottery system will be used). Two hundred and eighteen other units are being subleased to nonprofit agencies and rented to formerly homeless or drug-addicted tenants, with 157 more such units to be used for similar households five years hence. And 750 units are being subleased to the John Stewart Co. for remodeling and renting at market rates.[207] As of early 2002, monthly rents there for two-bedroom apartments ranged from $1,650 to $2000; for three-bedroom apartments, $1,870 to $2,700; and for four-bedroom apartments, $2,300 to $3,200. Mayor Brown has taken an especial interest in the Treasure Island development, attempting to maximize its income-generating potential for the City's general fund. A large Job Corps training center is functioning there, eventually to have an 850-student capacity. A consortium of nonprofits known as the Treasure Island Homeless Development Initiative ("tie-dye")—in which TODCO's John Elberling has been active—is playing a key role in ensuring that the islands' housing and economic development provides substantial benefits for homeless persons.[208] In mid-2001, Mayor Brown and other city dignitaries unveiled designs for a planned $120 million International Heritage Education Center and national monument—an amorphous, privately funded venture, described in the press handouts as the "West Coast equivalent of the Statue of Liberty." Things are still in the beginning stage, and among the unknowns are the impact that reconstruction of the Bay Bridge (severely damaged in the Loma Prieta earthquake) will have on the islands and how the area's serious seismic problems can be handled.

The Bottom Line

There's no getting around the fact that San Francisco's crisis-level housing problem is here to stay—at least for the foreseeable future. It's of course not that much of a problem for folks with money or for those fortunate enough to have bought their homes before prices took off. But it is for just about everyone else. Given the gap between housing costs and the average person's income, only massive subsidies—of a magnitude far beyond what any city government can afford—or a fundamental restructuring of the housing system to create a large nonspeculative, nonprofit sector to build, own, rehabilitate, and maintain permanently affordable housing will be up to the job.[209] Housing problems and programs go beyond narrow definitions. As long-time San Francisco housing activist Calvin Welch writes: "National and state economic policies, tax codes, and funding priorities must be changed."[210]Another long-time San Francisco housing activist, Randy Shaw, accurately observed that while

San Francisco has the most comprehensive scheme of local laws to protect socioeconomic diversity of any major American city. . . . The current
housing crisis shows how local solutions can be overwhelmed by outside
forces; it also reveals how federal cutbacks in housing subsidies over the
past two decades have left those suddenly displaced from their homes
without a safety net. Without federal assistance most victims of the
economic cleansing of San Francisco cannot obtain alternative housing in
the city. . . . Fighting for increased federal housing funds and national
policies that reduce rather than foster gentrification is essential for preserving San Francisco's economic diversity as we enter a new century.[211]

It is clear that the business community also sees housing as an important issue, deriving from its own self-interest. The Bay Area Council, representing the region's large corporations, as far back as 1980 issued a policy position, the opening statement of which was, "Many businesses are
concluding that inadequate housing is a formidable obstacle to the region's
continued job and economic growth."[212] "The Bay Area Council," the report went on to say, "believes the business community has a responsibility—based both on self-interest and on corporate citizenship—to address
the housing crisis." The BAC's thirty-member Housing Task Force, chaired
by Alan Rothenberg, senior vice president of Citizens Savings and Loan
(and a former San Francisco Redevelopment Agency commissioner),
warned: "If current trends continue, large segments of the Bay Area population will be priced out of the housing market. The results: a dwindling
labor market as low- and middle-income families leave the area in droves,
economic hardships for those who remain, and demands for higher salaries
and wages."[213] The relationship between housing costs and labor market
costs is bruited about quite openly in the BAC report. The chairman and
president of Fireman's Fund Insurance Company complained, "Recruiting
or transferring personnel from outside the Bay Area is also a critical problem that's quite costly for the company. People will naturally demand considerably higher compensation to move where homes are so much more expensive."[214] Much more recently, G. Rhea Serpan, president and CEO of the
San Francisco Chamber of Commerce, writing in the June 1999 issue of *San
Francisco Business*, warned:

> The good news is the economy is booming, unemployment is low and
> wages are high. The bad news could be phrased in the same way. The
> high cost of housing and relative lack of availability of housing units are
> fast becoming a serious challenge to businesses' ability to grow and stay
> competitive in San Francisco. . . . With high housing costs come higher
> wages for otherwise comparable labor, as housing is the single largest
> expenditure in most household budgets.

Higher labor costs are not the least of the specters stalking Bay Area corporate leadership. "Also of concern," warned the BAC report, "is the potential for disruption and violence. Recent news stories from Europe and South America describe incidences of protest and rioting touched off by severe housing shortages, and small armies of squatters occupying condemned or otherwise vacant housing. Some observers of the Bay Area situation are not so sanguine as to believe it couldn't happen here."[215] The horrible consequences that squeezing out the poor may cause are captured eloquently in this summary paragraph by the BAC: "Imagine: a society in which everyone can afford to drive a BMW or Mercedes but there's no one to pump the gas."[216]

Whether there's anyone left to pump the gas remains to be seen. As of early 2002, the dot-com tsunami has abated considerably and dramatically, giving rise to front-page headlines of the type gracing the March 26, 2001, *New York Times:* "With New Economy Chilling, San Francisco's Party Fizzles," and from the March 27, 2001, *Wall Street Journal,* "Home Prices Are Beginning to Decline in Upscale San Francisco Neighborhoods" (although the story reports the mind-boggling statistic that the median home price the month before was $512,500). Dot-com firms are folding by the dozens, relieving the office space crunch South of Market, in the Mission and elsewhere downtown. Regardless, damage has been done, people have left and will not return, housing will remain out of the reach of working-class and, increasingly, middle-class people.

14 | The Lessons of San Francisco

San Francisco's development history in the post–World War II period has been overwhelmingly dominated by business interests, by those in the position to reap the largest profits from this development. They have by and large controlled and peopled the city's government at all levels. They have established their own planning and watchdog mechanisms and agencies, and funded others, to ensure the kind of future they want. The connections between the business community and public policy run the gamut from massive plans to intimate personal ties. At one end of the scale are the strategies and manipulations of the Bay Area Council, the Blyth-Zellerbach Committee, SPUR, the Convention & Visitors Bureau, and the Chamber of Commerce to shape overall development policy for the city and region. At the other end of the scale are items like the personal "goodwill" gifts from the Moscone Center architect to the City's chief administrative officer* and special vacation arrangements the executive director of the Convention & Visitors Bureau secured for city hall's Yerba Buena Center project coordinator†—favors and symbols that express and create class and personal bonds and obligations.

---

*A letter dated 10 February 1977 from Gyo Obata to Roger Boas ends, "I have enclosed for you two small booklets by my parents that might be of interest to you," next to which is written by hand (presumably by Boas to one of his aides), "Tom—write him a short reply of thanks for the books on flower arranging and brush drawings. Put them on the gift list. R."
†A letter dated 7 July 1977 from Robert Sullivan, executive director of the Convention & Visitors Bureau, to John Igoe, YBC project coordinator for the chief administrative officer, reads: "Dear John: I believe my colleagues have done the best

Although much of this private sector planning and manipulation is done out of public view, it would be incorrect to describe the transformation of San Francisco as a large-scale secret conspiracy. Rather, it is a confluence of powerful public- and private-sector actors operating in their class and personal interests. Much of what transpires is and must be done openly, and it has been the purpose of this book to chronicle and analyze those mostly open acts in order to reveal their order and purpose.

As is to be expected, "the golden rule" usually explains the outcome—those who have the gold get to make the rules. In an economic and political system that relies centrally on private market forces to initiate investment and create economic activity, the business community and its plans appear to be the only game in town: Its decisions on whether and where to invest become the reference point, and those decisions create or destroy jobs and the city's tax base. The private investment community thus comes to be seen as performing functions in the public interest. Jobs and taxes are needed, and private profit-driven development activity can provide these things. With few or no alternatives envisioned as possible, the strong imperative is to take what is offered, try to wrest some concessions in the process, and accept the concomitant social costs. Particularly in the context of cutbacks in government programs at all levels, such "contributions" to solving housing, transportation, community facility, and social service needs as can be extracted from the private sector are regarded as almost an act of munificence. Nowhere is there the concept of a joint obligation to meet those needs as part of a social contract.

Government in this setting serves two principal roles—"capital accumulation" and "legitimation," as they have been termed by political theorists. That is, elected and appointed officials at city hall and its agencies, such as the Planning Commission and Redevelopment Agency, have as a central function assisting the private sector in carrying out its entrepreneurial activities, by establishing ground rules, and providing the necessary supports and infrastructure to facilitate the functioning of the private market. At the same time, government must manage conflict generated by such market activities and thus functions to preserve the social peace by providing benefits and compensations to those damaged by the process or who protest these developments, and more generally by stabilizing and reinforcing the existing social and economic order. Beyond these two basic economic, social, and

---

possible for you and the family. Hope you have a wonderful vacation. You certainly deserve it. Sincerely, Bob."

political roles, those in elected and appointed positions act in their immediate self-interest: to remain in office, rise within the political system, and reap the many personal benefits therefrom.

In concrete local terms, San Francisco city government overall has been extremely supportive of what the corporate community wants to do in and to the city. The individuals elected and appointed to major positions in city government—at city hall, the Board of Supervisors, the Redevelopment Agency, and the Planning Commission, to cite the principal bodies that oversee development—have come overwhelmingly from or are closely linked, economically and socially, with the business community. Exceptions exist, of course, but they are infrequent and of short duration. The oil of this electoral politics machine—cash—has flowed easily, in quantities that overwhelm what other organizations, individuals, and sectors can provide, to elect or retire individual candidates and officeholders and, most notably, to determine the results of the ballot initiative form of law-giving, which is used quite extensively and creatively in San Francisco and in California generally. Such contributions represent an infinitesimal portion of business profits, wisely invested. The business community has a collective sense of itself and its needs, initiates plans, and directly influences the plans prepared by government agencies. Individuals representing groups and interests demanding policies and programs aimed at achieving greater social justice may be elected or appointed to key positions. But should local government, pressed by popular protest movements, challenge business hegemony too greatly, threats of capital flight and abandonment, with attendant job and tax revenue loss, serve to discipline the public sector. And where necessary, the superior powers of state government countervail local government activities that threaten the private sector. It is not a contest of equals.

There is no meaningful countervailing force in the public sector. Planning by public bodies is shaped by the demands and designs of the private sector, or these bodies simply do not plan—they respond, react, muddle through. There is in fact little difference between a "public" enterprise such as the Yerba Buena Center urban renewal project and the Mission Bay project Southern Pacific originally planned as a private undertaking. "What's missing . . . ," in the words of John Elberling, TODCO's executive director and an activist in San Franciscans for Reasonable Growth, "is a vision of our city's future that is any better than 'national trends'—and the guts to make it happen."[1]

The city's basic development needs are for jobs, investment, and tax revenues to support public services and for housing resources that match economic development plans. At no point in the South of Market/Yerba Buena

Center development process or in any other project the City initiated or approved was the basic threshold question posed of how the City's resources and intervention could best be used to maximize fulfillment of those needs—clearly, what a rational process of planning for social needs would call for. Instead, opportunities were limited to those that private-sector developers initiated and would cooperate with. This is the nature of public planning in America, even in one of its most "progressive" cities.

What Is to Be Done?

The strength, persistence, and success of community-based opposition to the transformation of San Francisco, despite its relative lack of material resources, have been considerable. Those whose homes, jobs, businesses, and neighborhoods are directly threatened, and those who do not like the changed downtown, changed economy, changed society, and changed politics this corporatization or "Manhattanization" brings about have acted effectively and with great organizational sophistication. Their string of successes in recent years has included a unanimous Board of Supervisors vote for (weak) rent and condominium conversion controls; supervisors' approval of amendments to those ordinances, lowering the permissible annual rate of rent increases and lowering the maximum number of rental units that may be converted to condominiums; moratoria and controls on the conversion of residential hotels to tourist accommodations; preservation of several historically important buildings; mandatory payment of a transit subsidy fee and provision of housing by downtown office developers; protection of sunlight in public open spaces; modification of the city's most ambitious urban renewal project to provide within the project area a large number of permanently subsidized low-rent units and an inclusive multiuse cultural/recreation complex; and an annual limit on new office construction. Some of these victories have been thwarted or delayed by mayoral vetoes and lawsuits, others turned into half-victories as a result of blatant, last-minute moves to undercut more popular measures that were likely to win unless the power structure acted in some way to respond to a pressing problem. Outside observers should temper their praise for progressive actions by city hall and the business community in San Francisco with the understanding that they came into being only in response to powerful pressures from a more progressive popular movement of resistance.

Community opposition to the transformation of San Francisco has effectively employed a variety of useful strategies: direct protest actions, litigation, publicity, election of progressive people to office and defeat of less-progressive candidates and officeholders, influence of appointments to government positions, ballot initiatives to directly institute new laws and charter changes, lobbying for and against specific pieces of legislation, and creation of alternative plans. And lessons learned in one fight are applied to subsequent battles: The many concessions wrought from Southern Pacific/Catellus regarding the Mission Bay project built on strategies and negotiation victories won in Yerba Buena Center.[2]

It is important to highlight the usefulness of litigation, a tool often decried by the opinion-givers and newspapers as "harassing" and "obstructionist" (when brought by neighborhood groups and activists—such characterizations are not used when a Democratic Party influential, like realtor Walter Shorenstein, sues to stop the transit fee the City has imposed on downtown developers to cover part of the additional transit costs such developments create). In the case of Yerba Buena Center, the several lawsuits brought the following results: The TOOR suit produced many hundreds of units of first-rate permanent new and rehabilitated subsidized low-rent housing that otherwise would not exist; and the various project financing suits ended the plans for the costly (to the public) sports arena, scaled the original convention center down, reduced the public facilities bond issue from $225 million to $97 million, and shifted the source of City subsidy funds from the property tax to the more progressive hotel tax.

While TOOR's displacement/housing suit brought a victory unprecedented in U.S. urban renewal history, it is important at the same time to realize that the victory hardly mitigated the disaster visited on the four thousand residents (and seven hundred–plus businesses) displaced from the site. They lost their homes, neighborhoods, and social networks; wound up paying considerably higher rents, often for substandard housing; and in all too many cases were forced to move again due to the ripple effects of YBC and related projects. Very few were able to occupy the replacement units, which in themselves amounted to less than one-quarter of the units destroyed. And the only reason the residents gained as much as they did (or lost as little as they did) was through a combination of refusal to give up possession of the turf they occupied until maximum concessions were wrought (a function in no small part of their particular labor union backgrounds) plus an aggressive use of the courts that was characterized by a near perfect, and therefore atypical, combination of an excellent fact situation, a sympathetic, steadfast, and courageous federal judge, and exceptionally talented and tenacious (and free) attorneys.

But important as all these gains have been, it must also be realized that they have not succeeded in halting the transformation of San Francisco, most notably in the South of Market area. Gentrification has happened with a vengeance. And its more recent wrinkle, via the Internet revolution, has delivered a particularly painful blow to the San Francisco we all knew and loved. As Paulina Borsook describes the repercussion of current gentrification forces,

> The speed, libertarian ethos, irritating hipster pose and chilling finality of this invasion put it in a different light from earlier ones. . . . The result is a city whose unique history and sensibility is being swamped by twerps with 'tude. . . . [T]he Internet culture that celebrates all work all the time doesn't accord value to anything that isn't easily monetized—or corporatized. The importance of leisure time, of being able to support yourself with a day job to pursue other ends, to rehearse and canvass and organize and noodle and reflect, is totally at odds with the all-connected-all-the-time upside-potential lifestyle of the dot-com people. . . . They haven't lived here long enough to know or care about civic issues . . . and . . . there's not much reason for them to care. . . . Take politics. The in-flow of new people into the political process is what a city relies on to keep it vital. But San Francisco's newest arrivals seem utterly disengaged.[3]

A similar eloquent jeremiad is heard from Rebecca Solnit writing about "hollow city"—the corrosive effect of wealth on civic culture:

> In a way, all of San Francisco is being delivered vacant to the brave new technology economy, and altruism and idealism are two of the tenants facing homelessness. . . . This place has been one of the great laboratories for broadening and transforming our understanding of human rights, justice, economics, work, gender, sexuality, the natural world. . . . San Francisco has been not only the great refuge for the nation's pariahs and non-conformists; it has been the breeding ground for new ideas, mores and movements social, political and artistic. To see the space in which those things were incubated homogenized into just another place for overpaid-but-overworked producer-consumers is to witness a great loss, not only for the experimentalists, but for the world that has benefited from the better experiments (and been entertained by the sillier ones). Civic life and cultural life everywhere are in decline because of the acceleration of work . . . and the public sphere itself is more and more merely the space people pass through on errands and commutes. . . . The accelerated and equipped . . . carry their private space with them, and privatization becomes not just an economic issue but a social attitude (expressed in such items as car alarms, which place the right of private property in public over the auditory peace of the neighborhood). . . . The sense of the city as home is eroding as the public sphere ceases to be a place where people feel at home . . . the new arrivals seem to live in it as though it were a suburb. One has the sense that San Francisco . . . is populated by

people who just don't get urbanism or just don't value it. Urban life . . . requires a certain leisure, . . . a certain willingness to engage with the unknown and unpredictable. For those who feel impelled to accelerate, the unknown and the unpredictable are interference as the city's public space becomes not a place to *be* but a place to traverse as rapidly as possible. . . . There is a real sense in San Francisco that the social contract is being torn up by those who own it. The social contract has been steadily dismantled over the past two decades by the elimination of social services, by the creation of a two-tier economy, by the creation of a homeless population many Americans are too young or too forgetful to remember hardly existed two decades ago.[4]

It may be too late to do anything about this transformation. Some changes are not reversible, and the activists who created the San Francisco of not-so-old and fought gentrification are fast losing their offices and their homes to rampant real estate inflation. But if there is to be any hope of fighting gentrification successfully, at a minimum the following elements will be needed, some of which are part of the standard litany of democratic reforms that have been suggested locally and nationally for years and can be derived from elementary civics textbooks, but remain none the less true.

First, there must be fundamental campaign spending reforms, to limit the amount that can be contributed to or spent on local candidates and issues and/or (better) to shift to a system of full public financing of political campaigns. The fact that corporate and downtown interests regularly outspend neighborhood forces by a factor of ten to one, and spend that money in highly sophisticated, often dishonest ways, simply loads the deck too much. True democracy is a sham when one side has virtually unlimited sums to throw into a campaign.[5] Structural reforms like electing supervisors on a district basis rather than at-large can alleviate this profound inequity to an extent, but that reform has no effect on citywide offices or on ballot initiatives—and, as has been shown, the same rule by dollars can determine whether more democratic structural reforms will prevail and be retained and how they will function.

Second, people must pay more attention to what's going on in their government, to the deceit and manipulation that are rife, as issue after issue, incident after incident in San Francisco shows. Better daily press and electronic coverage—one that reported the news more carefully and analytically and offered more incisive and varied perspectives on events through editorials, columnists, and commentators—would go a long way toward creating a more informed and caring public. But in the absence of this critical force, other publications, media, and forums must be developed by neighborhood groups and other alternative sources. The enormous number of distortions and outright lies that emanate from the movers and shakers in both the public and private sectors—as extensively documented in the preceding chapters—simply must be exposed and countered. That in itself would go a long way toward producing better and more accountable public policy.

Third, community-based groups must demand to participate in the planning process at an earlier stage in order to generate and introduce their own plans as alternatives to what the business community and the official planning agencies put forth. Reactive planning is what San Francisco has seen to date; and it is because citizen groups are put in the position of being able to enter the planning process only at the last minute that so much disruption and litigation have characterized the city's recent development history. The alternative plan for Mission Bay put forward by the Mission Bay Clearinghouse, the various teach-ins on the Downtown Plan, and Richard Gryziec's Tivoli Gardens proposal to the Mayor's Select Committee on Yerba Buena Center all are examples of a more effective way of participating. Adequate technical assistance must be created for community groups to do their own planning, and the official planning process must be forced to encourage and admit this work at an early stage of developing plans and projects. Community-based planning must start by posing questions of public policy and then deciding how to answer them—the best way to produce jobs, tax revenues, economic development, affordable housing, and better public services—rather than attempting to fit into a public interest framework and rationalize plans derived elsewhere and out of other motives. San Francisco's strong tradition of community organizing has been a real progressive force, but as a Mission District legal-aid lawyer put it, when, to prevent evictions, immediate housing defense needs are pressing, there is little time or opportunity to assist communities in organizing for positive change.

Fourth, there is a clear need for the two major strands of the oppositional movement in San Francisco—the housing forces and the growth control forces—to work together. Their sources of dissatisfaction and opposition stem from a common adversary, but they have been divided largely by a distortion of the jobs issues—by being presented with an argument that jobs come only from downtown office development. A more democratic, participatory planning process would put forth plans that create jobs through projects generated via an assessment of what social needs must be met, and would ensure that housing and community facility needs are met *pari passu* with economic development. Such projects probably would have to rely more on public- than private-sector funding. The key to a unified, and probably successful, movement to oppose the corporate-led transformation of San Francisco lies in joining these two issues and not letting the other side make them into a divisive force. The alternative is not only a less effective fight against high-rise office development, but also a system of buy-offs and trade-offs, whereby in exchange for abandoning resistance to a project, protest groups are given some concessions in the form of a public benefits package of housing and social service subsidies. While such concessions are useful in slowing down the juggernaut, providing needed aid that otherwise would not be available and creating pockets of uses and users that are not part of the office-growth behemoth, in the not-so-long run the broader fight will be lost.

Finally, there is need for a regional approach to growth, one planned by community groups all over the Bay Area and not just by the Bay Area Council. Any rational overall resource allocation plan for the Bay Area would not continue to stuff high-rise office buildings into downtown San Francisco, placing an impossible burden on the city's transit system and its housing stock, and thereby causing enormous suffering among residents of the city least able to bear those costs. A sound regional growth plan would spread this development throughout San Mateo, Alameda, Contra Costa, and Marin Counties, a diffusion that prevailing communications technology facilitates.[6] (To a minor extent this is already occurring, but not nearly fast enough or to an extent sufficient enough to prevent the destructive effects of out-of-control growth on San Francisco.) Rather than allowing continued massive downtown growth in San Francisco and taking belated quarter-measures to meet the housing, transportation, and community facility needs this growth generates, rational public planning would permit office construction only to the extent that housing and transportation capacity was sufficient to meet the new demand. The key factor causing San Francisco's more recent housing crisis has been the invasion of the "Silicon implants." In the second half of the 1990s, Silicon Valley created 220,000 new jobs, but only 28,000 homes were added.[7] A regional approach is that missing vision that can both meet economic and human needs and retain what's left of San Francisco's wonderful diversity of class, ethnicity, race, age, and lifestyle. To achieve that means dealing with heavy political and cultural issues as well as creating a regional tax structure.[8]

The future of the nonrich in San Francisco, and in other U.S. cities with similar downtown growth pressures and patterns, is bleak. Many will be shoved out of the city altogether. Others will increasingly concentrate in more outlying parts of the city, in overcrowded conditions caused by a need to double up in order to afford prevailing rent and ownership costs, and will be forced to pay 40 to 50 percent or more of their income for housing. More and more they will become a permanent underclass supporting, through their labor and taxes, a predominantly upper-middle-class population and a city that exists largely to serve those who do not live there.

What has happened and is happening in San Francisco can and should serve as a guide for analyzing the forces at work elsewhere. Downtowns are rebounding all over the country: A recent Fannie Mae Foundation/Brookings Institution study, based on the 2000 Census, reported that of a sample of twenty-four cities studied, eighteen saw increases in their downtown population and that "Increases in white residents led to the resurgence in downtown living."[9] The transformation of San Francisco may well be a paradigm for other cities in the United States and around the world.

Notes

CHAPTER 1. THE LARGER FORCES

1. R. W. Apple Jr., "Even in Fog, That City on a Hill Dazzles," *New York Times,* 25 June 1999.

2. "It's the Rule in San Francisco: The Pizza Must Go Through," *New York Times,* 14 July 1996.

3. Jane Gross, "Dummy Is on the Ballot (He Isn't Seeking Office)," *New York Times,* 30 October 1993; John Boudreau, "The Short Arm of the Law," *Washington Post,* 13 December 1993.

4. Tim Golden, "Political 'Party' Goes So Far, Even San Francisco Is Aghast," *New York Times,* 10 May 1997.

5. Paul Dorn, "Pedaling to Save the City," *SFUI [San Francisco Urban Institute] Quarterly,* vol. 1, no. 4 (spring 1998): 11–13; John Boudreau, "Pedaling Meddling: The Great Bike Traffic Jam," *Washington Post,* 14 March 1994.

6. "San Francisco Workers Get Sex-Change Coverage," *New York Times,* 18 February 2001.

7. Evelyn Nieves, "Another Minority Flexes Its Muscle in San Francisco," *New York Times,* 24 February 2001.

8. Evelyn Nieves, "New San Francisco Ordinance Decrees That All Sizes Fit," *New York Times,* 9 May 2000.

9. Eric Brazil, "3-Way Compromise on Track to Retain Doggie Diner Head," *San Francisco Examiner,* 25 January 2000.

10. Evelyn Nieves, "For Patrons of Prostitutes, Remedial Instruction," *New York Times,* 18 March 1999.

11. "Pained by Quotas, Body Piercers Organize," *Washington Post,* 17 January 1998.

12. R. B. Cohen, "The New International Division of Labor, Multinational Corporations and Urban Hierarchy," in *Urbanization and Urban Planning in*

Capitalist Society, ed. Michael Dear and Allen J. Scott (New York: Methuen, 1981), 303.

13. State of California, Employment Development Department, Labor Market Information Division, "Projections—June 1998," "Occupational Employment Projections, 1995–2002, San Francisco County," table 6.

14. Susan S. Fainstein, Norman I. Fainstein, Richard Child Hill, Dennis R. Judd, and Michael Peter Smith, *Restructuring the City* (New York: Longmans, 1983), 211.

15. Memo from Larry Badiner, senior planner, to Gerald Green, director of planning, San Francisco Department of City Planning, 23 February 1999.

16. Quoted in Paul Rupert, "Corporate Feast in the Pacific," *Pacific Research and World Empire Telegram* vol. 1, no. 4 (January/March 1970): 3. For a later treatment, see Joel Kotkin and Paul Grabowicz, *California, Inc.* (New York: Rawson, Wade, 1982), 214–54.

17. Wells Fargo Bank, N.A., Branch Expansion Department, *San Francisco, Central Business District: A Growth Study,* February 1970, 22.

18. Wallace Turner, "Chinese Favor San Francisco for Renewed Trade," *New York Times,* 1 February 1983.

19. For a history of the early growth of Chinatown, see Yong Chen, *Chinese San Francisco, 1850–1943: A Trans-Pacific Community* (Stanford: Stanford University Press, 2000), and Victor Nee and Brett de Bary Nee, *Longtime Californ': A Documentary Study of an American Chinatown* (New York: Pantheon, 1973). The political schisms in present-day Chinatown, reflecting international politics and migration streams, are outlined in Nina Wu, "The City's Two-China Chinatown," *San Francisco Examiner,* 31 May 2001.

20. Sabin Russell, "Mayor, 3 Hopefuls Talk Business," *San Francisco Chronicle,* 24 April 1987; see also Moira Johnson, "In the Wake of the Takeover Wars," *California Magazine* (May 1987): 10–13.

21. John Markoff, "The City by the Bay Holds Its Collective Breath," *New York Times,* 15 April 1998.

22. Diana B. Henriques, "Bank of America to Cut up to 6.7% of Work Force, or 10,000 Jobs," *New York Times,* 29 July 2000.

23. Les Shipnuck and Dan Feshbach, "Bay Area Council: Regional Power-House," *Pacific Research and World Empire Telegram* vol. 4, no. 1 (November/December 1972), 3–11.

24. BART Impact Studies Final Report Series, vol. 4, pt. II (Berkeley: Institute of Urban and Regional Development, University of California, 29 June 1973), 27. See also Victor Jones, "Bay Area Regionalism" (Berkeley: University of California Institute of Governmental Studies, 1972).

25. The Bay Area Council's rise in relation to penetration of the Pacific region is covered in a special study of the giant Bechtel Corporation: Burton H. Wolfe, "BART—Steve Bechtel's $2 Billion Toy," *San Francisco Bay Guardian* vol. 7, no. 8 (14 February 1973).

26. J. Allen Whitt, *Urban Elites and Mass Transportation: The Dialectics of Power* (Princeton: Princeton University Press, 1982), 40–41. The book also doc-

uments the system's massive cost overruns, absence of public control, techno-logical and safety defects, managerial problems, and the way "private engineering interests (especially Bechtel) virtually captured the BART design and construction process" (78).

27. Ibid., 48.

28. R. A. Sundeen, "The San Francisco Bay Area Council: An Analysis of Non-Governmental Metropolitan Organization" (master's thesis, University of California, Berkeley, 1963).

29. Whitt, *Urban Elites and Mass Transportation,* 50.

30. Burton H. Wolfe, "Must San Francisco Choke Itself to Death?" *San Francisco Bay Guardian,* 18 June 1968.

31. *San Francisco Examiner,* 28 November 1962, quoting a committee report of the Board of Supervisors. The story continues, "The South of Market Advisory Committee thus outlined yesterday one of the biggest problems it faces in trying to restore economic life South of Market."

32. Frederick M. Wirt, *Power in the City: Decision Making in San Francisco* (Berkeley and Los Angeles: University of California Press, 1974), 190.

33. "Financiers Set on Redevelopment," *San Francisco Examiner,* 18 January 1957.

34. *San Francisco News,* 18 May 1956.

35. Aside from Blyth and Zellerbach, the original members were: Ralph Gwin Follis, former chairman of the board, Standard Oil of California; S. Clark Beise, president, Bank of America; Stephen Bechtel, president and senior director, Bechtel Corporation; Donald J. Russel, president, Southern Pacific Railroad; Ransom M. Cook, president, Levi Strauss; Mark Sullivan, former president, Pacific Telephone and Telegraph; James K. Lochead, president, American Trust Company; Emmett Solomon, vice president, Provident Security (later president, Crocker-Citizens National Bank); George Granville Montgomery, chairman of the board, Kern County Land Company, director, Wells Fargo-American Trust Company; James B. Black, president, Pacific Gas and Electric; Atholl Bean, president, Gladding-McBean and Company; Jerd F. Sullivan, chairman of the board, Crocker-Citizens National Bank. Whitt, *Urban Elites,* notes that "BART [bond vote] campaign manager Henry Alexander pointed out to me that the B-Z Committee and the Bay Area Council had overlapping membership."

36. "How Business Spurs a City Revival," *Business Week* (9 September 1961). For a lengthy account of my almost humorous and totally abortive attempt to elicit some basic information about the Blyth-Zellerbach Committee via direct mail and phone inquiries, see my article "Just How Secretive Is SF's Invisible Government?" *San Francisco Bay Guardian,* 12 October 1983.

37. Quoted in *San Francisco Chronicle,* 30 April 1959.

38. Letters to author, dated 19 July 1982 and 7 September 1983, from Michael S. McGill, San Francisco Planning and Urban Research Association.

39. A privately printed biography, produced for his seventy-fifth birthday, is the source of much information on Swig's personal and financial history. See Walter H. Blum, *Benjamin H. Swig: The Measure of a Man* (San Francisco,

1968). For a more recent but equally fawning biography of Swig, see Bernice Scharlach, *Dealing from the Heart: A Biography of Benjamin Swig* (San Francisco: Scott Wall Associates, 2000), replete with photographs of Swig with Harry Truman, Eleanor Roosevelt, Earl Warren, David Ben-Gurion, Adlai Stevenson, Ronald Reagan, John F. Kennedy, Bobby Kennedy, Golda Meir, Rev. Sun Myung Moon, Pope Paul VI. . . .

40. G. William Domhoff, *Fat Cats and Democrats* (Englewood Cliffs, N.J.: Prentice-Hall, 1972), 72.

41. Marsha Berzon, "Yerba Buena: A Case Study in How SF Development Went Wrong—Too Little Planning, Too Much Swig/SPUR/Downtown Muscle, No Community Participation, All Edifice Complex," *San Francisco Bay Guardian,* 17 April 1970.

42. *San Francisco Examiner,* 12 October 1955.

43. *San Francisco Chronicle,* 25 October 1955.

44. Dick Nolan, "Showdown Nearing on the Swig Plan," *San Francisco Examiner,* 27 November 1955.

45. *San Francisco Chronicle,* 14 March 1956.

CHAPTER 2. SUPERAGENCY AND THE REDEVELOPMENT BOOSTER CLUB

1. Frederick M. Wirt, *Power in the City: Decision Making in San Francisco* (Berkeley and Los Angeles: University of California Press, 1974), 297–98.

2. George Dorsey, *Christopher of San Francisco* (New York: Macmillan, 1962), 230.

3. Allan Temko, "San Francisco Rebuilds Again," *Harpers Magazine* (April 1960): 53.

4. *San Francisco Examiner,* 26 and 27 April 1956.

5. Thomas C. Fleming, "San Francisco's Land Development Program," *Sun-Reporter,* 27 November 1965.

6. U.S. Department of Housing and Urban Development, San Francisco Area Office, "Task Force Report on HUD Assisted Programs in San Francisco, California, 1972," 111–14. The ratio of annual administrative budget to total grant was 1:77 for Pittsburgh and 1:55 for Boston, while San Francisco had a 1:22 ratio.

7. For portraits of the few figures in the urban renewal game who rivaled Herman, see (on Robert Moses) Jeanne Lowe, *Cities in a Race with Time* (New York: Random House, 1967), 45–109, and Robert Caro, *The Power Broker: Robert Moses and the Fall of New York* (New York: Alfred A. Knopf, 1974); (on Edward Logue) Richard Schickel, "New York's Mr. Urban Renewal," *New York Times Magazine* (1 March 1970). See also Jewel Bellush and Murray Hausknecht, eds., "Entrepreneurs and Urban Renewal: The New Men of Power," in *Urban Renewal: People, Politics and Planning* (New York: Doubleday Anchor, 1967), 289–97. Further description of Herman is found in William Lilley III, "Herman Death Ends an Era," *National Journal* (18 September 1971): 1939.

8. Allan B. Jacobs, *Making City Planning Work* (Chicago: American Society of Planning Officials, 1978), 74.

9. *San Francisco Chronicle*, 18 January 1962.

10. San Francisco Convention & Visitors Bureau, "1998/99 Program of Work Highlights and Schedule of Promotional Activities."

11. Dorothea Katzenstein, "Tom Mellon's 'Trickle Down' Policy," *San Francisco Bay Guardian*, 5 July 1972.

12. Carol Kroot, "Budget Wrangle at Board Hearing," *San Francisco Progress*, 21 April 1978.

13. San Francisco Convention & Visitors Bureau, "1998–1999 Membership Directory and Reference Guide."

14. Quoted in Louis Trager, "Trouble in Touristland," *San Francisco Examiner*, 30 July 1989.

15. "San Francisco's Empty Rooms," *Business Week* (17 March 1973).

16. Interview quoted in John Emshwiller, "Yerba Buena: A New Colossus for San Francisco," paper submitted to Political Science 109 and Social Science 100BC, University of California, Berkeley, spring 1972.

17. Nathaniel Lichfield, "Relocation: The Impact on Housing Welfare," *Journal of the American Institute of Planners* (August 1961): 199–203.

18. For a description of the Western Addition protests, see John H. Mollenkopf, *The Contested City* (Princeton: Princeton University Press, 1983), 186–89.

19. "Shelley Not Happy with RA Dynasty," *San Francisco Examiner*, 15 September 1966.

20. For a history of Embarcadero City, see Richard Reinhardt, "On the Waterfront: The Great Wall of Magnin," in *The Ultimate Highrise: San Francisco's Mad Rush toward the Sky*, ed. Bruce B. Brugmann and Greggar Sletteland (San Francisco: San Francisco Bay Guardian Books, 1971), 92–137; and Wirt, *Power in the City*, 197–204.

21. The source for this is an unpublished but widely circulated study by Francis Fury and Andrew Moss, "Moving out the People" (San Francisco, 1970).

22. Quoted in *San Francisco Examiner*, 8 September 1967.

23. Quoted in *San Francisco Examiner*, 12 September 1967.

24. Quoted in *San Francisco Examiner*, 9 September 1967.

25. Walter H. Blum, *Benjamin H. Swig: The Measure of a Man* (San Francisco, 1968), 50; see also *San Francisco Examiner*, 13 September 1967; *San Francisco Chronicle*, 17 September 1967.

26. Dick Nolan, "Showdown Nearing on the Swig Plan," *San Francisco Examiner*, 27 November 1955.

27. Norman Melnick, "Alioto—Key Figure in the Arena," *San Francisco Examiner*, 8 September 1967.

28. Quoted in *San Francisco Examiner*, 10 September 1967.

29. Wirt, *Power in the City*, 175.

30. Quoted in Peter Wiley and Robert Gottlieb, *Empires in the Sun: The Rise of the New American West* (New York: G. P. Putnam, 1982), 99.

31. Dick Meister, "Labor Power," *San Francisco Bay Guardian*, 23 December 1970.

32. Letter to author, dated 14 October 1982, from Helen Sause, San Francisco Redevelopment Agency.

33. Donald Canter and Tom Hall, "Redevelopment Officials Indicted for Extortion," *San Francisco Examiner*, 8 October 1976; Donald Canter, "A Year for Redevelop Ex-Aide," *San Francisco Examiner*, 23 February 1977; Guy Wright, "An Easier Out for Joe Mosley," *San Francisco Examiner*, 9 January 1977.

34. Quoted in *San Francisco Chronicle*, 4 January 1968.

35. Quoted in *Wall Street Journal*, 27 May 1970.

36. See Dick Meister's lengthy and informative essay, "Labor Power," *San Francisco Bay Guardian*, 23 December 1970.

37. Wirt, *Power in the City*, 168. For an earlier critique of both papers and the Bay Area press generally, see William L. Rivers and David M. Rubin, *A Region's Press: Anatomy of Newspapers in the San Francisco Bay Area* (Berkeley: University of California Institute of Governmental Studies, 1971). *Chronicle* editor (and former *Examiner* editor) Phil Bronstein, certainly a man who ought to know, was quoted in 2001 as saying, "I don't think San Francisco newspapers have ever been taken seriously in the world of journalism, or in the larger world." See Howard Kurtz, "Phil Bronstein's San Francisco Beat," *Washington Post*, 21 May 2001.

38. Dick Walker and the Bay Area Study Group, "The Playground of U.S. Capitalism? The Political Economy of the San Francisco Bay Area in the 1980s," in *Fire in the Hearth: The Radical Politics of Place*, ed. Mike Davis, Steven Hiatt, Marie Kennedy, Susan Ruddick, and Michael Spinker (London: Verso Press, 1990), 1–82.

39. Gar Smith, "The *Ex-Chron*'s Big Bucks Stakes in YBC," *Media File*, December 1981.

40. " 'May God Punish You'—Threats to Skid Row Holdout," *San Francisco Chronicle*, 19 May 1971.

41. Lane Williams, "Clint Reilly Sues to Halt Purchase of Chronicle," *San Francisco Examiner*, 12 January 2000.

42. Seth Rosenfeld, "Chronicle Sale: The Deals behind the Deal," *San Francisco Examiner*, 3 May 2000.

43. Zachary Collins, " 'Troubling' Change in Editorials," *San Francisco Examiner*, 11 May 2000.

44. Felicity Barringer, "A Newspaper Experiment in San Francisco," *New York Times*, 20 November 2000.

45. Ibid.

46. Evelyn Nieves, "San Francisco Paper Struggles with the Printed Word," *New York Times*, 18 December 2000.

47. "San Francisco Examiner Fires Managing Editor," *New York Times*, 24 December 2000.

48. Reynolds Holding, "Mayor Pressured Hearst over Sale," *San Francisco Chronicle*, 28 April 2000; Seth Rosenfeld, "Examiner Purchase Plan Called a Sham," *San Francisco Examiner*, 28 April 2000.

49. Felicity Barringer, "Why the Old Math May Not Apply in San Francisco," *New York Times*, 26 March 2000.

CHAPTER 3. THE ASSAULT ON SOUTH OF MARKET

1. Quotations from Marsha Berzon, "Yerba Buena: A Case Study," *San Francisco Bay Guardian*, 17 April 1970, and interview quoted in John Emshwiller's paper "Yerba Buena: A New Colossus for San Francisco," submitted to Political Science 109 and Social Science 100BC, University of California, Berkeley, spring 1972.

2. "A War of Agencies: Planners v. Redevelopers," *San Francisco Examiner*, 25 June 1965.

3. Quoted in *San Francisco Chronicle*, 3 December 1965.

4. See Marsha Berzon, "Redevelopment: Bulldozers for the Poor, Welfare for the Rich," *San Francisco Bay Guardian*, 17 April 1970.

5. *San Francisco Chronicle*, 25 August 1965.

6. "Yerba Buena Center Public Facilities and Private Development," Environmental Impact Report (draft), submitted to the City and County of San Francisco (Arthur D. Little, Inc., and URS Research Company, May 1973), table A-4.

7. *San Francisco Chronicle*, 11 February 1966.

8. See, for example, Real Estate Research Corporation, *Land Utilization and Marketability Study*, prepared for the San Francisco Redevelopment Agency (Los Angeles, 1965); Roy Wenzlick & Co., *Land Utilization and Market Analysis*, prepared for the San Francisco Redevelopment Agency (St. Louis, 1963); Economic Research Associates, *Economic Performance of Public Facilities in Yerba Buena Center*, prepared for the San Francisco Redevelopment Agency (Los Angeles: 9 February 1970).

9. For accounts of the manipulation of consultants' reports by public bodies seeking to construct stadium complexes, see Charles G. Burck, "It's Promoters vs. Taxpayers in the Superstadium Game," *Fortune* (March 1973): 104–7, 178–82.

10. For a historical description of the supervisors, their financial support, and their links to the business community, see data compiled in *The Ultimate Highrise: San Francisco's Mad Rush toward the Sky*, ed. Bruce B. Brugmann and Greggar Sletteland (San Francisco: San Francisco Bay Guardian Books, 1971), 72–80. See also Carol Kroot, "Mayor, Sups Reveal Investments," *San Francisco Progress*, 15 February 1975; Jerry Burns, "S.F. Officials List Holdings," *San Francisco Chronicle*, 12 February 1975.

11. For a detailed discussion of HUD's role in YBC, see Richard LeGates, "Can the Federal Welfare Bureaucracies Control Their Programs?: The Case of HUD and Urban Renewal," *Urban Lawyer* (spring 1973): 228–63.

12. See also the 30 January 1966 *Examiner* for a statement by Robert Rumsey, the agency's assistant director, that the plan for a convention center and arena required a city bond issue.

13. Harold Kaplan, *Urban Renewal Politics: Slum Clearance in Newark* (New York: Columbia University Press, 1963), 29.

14. Leon E. Hickman, "Alcoa Looks at Urban Redevelopment," in *Urban Renewal: People, Politics, and Planning,* ed. Jewel Bellush and Murray Hausknecht (New York: Doubleday Anchor, 1967), 270.

15. See Mike Miller, "The Inscrutable Chinese Cultural Center—It's a Holiday Inn," *San Francisco Bay Guardian,* 28 March 1972; also the two-part series by John Burks, "Chinatown's Dream Delayed" and "Chinatown's Bridge of 1,000 Controversies," *San Francisco Examiner,* 26 and 27 July 1971. These sources illustrate the furor over the Chinatown Holiday Inn, built on the site of the old Hall of Justice under the auspices of the SFRA; as a "compromise" with Chinatown residents who wanted housing, not a tourist hotel, for their neighborhood, the developer agreed to dedicate one floor of the new hotel for a Chinese Cultural Center.

16. *San Francisco Examiner,* 11 May 1969.

17. The phrase "protected environment" appeared frequently in agency publicity about Yerba Buena Center. See, for example, the agency's brochure inviting developers to bid on the Central Blocks, "A Major Opportunity to Invest in Downtown San Francisco" (n.d. [1969]), which speaks of YBC being large enough to "guarantee a protected, quality environment."

18. *San Francisco Examiner,* 4 January 1966.

19. *San Francisco Examiner* and *San Francisco Chronicle,* 29 December 1965.

CHAPTER 4. THE NEIGHBORHOOD FIGHTS BACK

1. A more complete historical sketch of the South of Market area, from which this section was drawn, is provided in Alvin Averbach, "San Francisco's South of Market District, 1858–1958: The Emergence of a Skid Row," *California Historical Quarterly* (fall 1973): 197–223. References to the interviews and written sources on which this historical overview is based are provided therein. Averbach was part of the author's original research and writing group that produced the 1974 book *Yerba Buena: Land Grab and Community Resistance in San Francisco* (San Francisco: Glide Publications). For an early general history of the city, see William Issel and Robert Cherny, *San Francisco, 1865–1932: Politics, Power and Urban Development* (Berkeley and Los Angeles: University of California Press, 1986); also Gray Brechin, *Imperial San Francisco: Urban Power, Earthly Ruin* (Berkeley and Los Angeles: University of California Press, 1999).

2. Jack London, "South of the Slot," in *Jack London Short Stories,* ed. Earle Labor, Robert C. Leitz III, I. Milo Shepard (New York: Macmillan, 1990), 417–30.

3. See Starr's introduction to "South of Market and Bunker Hill: An Introduction to Neighborhood Histories," *California History* (winter 1995/96), prefacing Anne B. Bloomfield's valuable history of the South of Market area, "A History of the California Historical Society's New Mission Street Neighborhood."

4. E. M. Schaffran and Company, "Relocation Survey Report, South of Market Redevelopment Project" (December 1963 and July 1965).

5. "South of Market Turmoil: Rumors and Redevelopment Agency," *San Francisco Examiner*, 15 September 1965. For a moving book of photographs of YBC displacees, see Ira Nowinski, *No Vacancy* (San Francisco: Carolyn Bean Associates, 1979).

6. See, for example, the editorial in the 11 June 1971 *Examiner*: "Just Who Lives in Yerba Buena?"

7. E. M. Schaffran and Company, "Relocation Survey Report," table 12, "Highlights."

8. Housing Act of 1949, Chap. 338, Sec. 105. The Housing Act of 1964, Sec. 305(a)(1), gave to individuals displaced from renewal sites the same protection given to families under the 1949 Act.

9. E. M. Schaffran and Company, "Relocation Survey Report," appendix, table 7.

10. This estimate was made by Supervisor Roger Boas. See *San Francisco Chronicle*, 2 March 1971.

11. San Francisco Department of City Planning, *Issues in Housing, Housing Report II* (July 1969), 26.

12. "Review of Slum Clearance and Urban Renewal Activities of the San Francisco Regional Office, Housing and Home Finance Agency, 1959," Report to the Congress of the United States by the Comptroller General of the United States, July 1960, 32–43. See also Nathaniel Lichfield, "Relocation: The Impact on Housing Welfare," *Journal of the American Institute of Planners* (August 1961): 199–203.

13. The reasoning and methodology underlying the "turnover game" were to be found in their highest form in the E. M. Schaffran and Company, "Relocation Survey Report."

14. "The Shame of San Francisco: An Analysis of San Francisco's Housing Crisis and Defects of San Francisco's Proposed 'Workable Program for Community Improvement,' " prepared by The Citizens' Emergency Task Force for a Workable Housing Policy (n.d. [1969]).

15. "South o' Market Renewal Makes Little People Unhappy" (last of three-part series), *San Francisco Examiner*, 18 September 1965.

16. See the story on the Carmel Hotel (mistakenly identified as the "Canton Hotel") in "Displaced Persons Face Hardships," *San Francisco Argonaut*, 2 March 1968.

17. "U.S. Blasts Hasty S.F. Slum Ax," *San Francisco Chronicle*, 28 September 1967.

18. "Renewal Agency Gets a Talking To," *San Francisco Chronicle*, 6 March 1970.

19. "Furor in Pensioner's Hotel Slaying: Renewal Agency Security Issue," *San Francisco Chronicle*, 16 December 1970.

20. Carol Kroot, "George Woolf, 1889–1972," *San Francisco Bay Guardian*, 5 July 1972.

21. *San Francisco Examiner,* 19 June 1970.

22. Report to Court, by U.S. Dept of HUD, *TOOR* v. *HUD,* No. C-69 324 (N.D. Cal., filed 24 August 1971).

23. This survey was undertaken during the summer of 1971 and was based on interviews with a one-third sample of all persons officially relocated by SFRA since December 1969 whose current addresses could be found. The interviewers were university students working on a summer project through the San Francisco Neighborhood Legal Assistance Foundation, under the supervision of Melvin Mitnick and Chester Hartman. The interviewers were Andrea Ach, Travers Baer, Wendy Chaikin, Susan Chu, Jo Ann Majid, Gerry Palast, Christopher Peck, Alan Ramo, Stephen Wiman, and Kathy Zelinsky.

24. See draft copy of environmental impact report on the Yerba Buena Center project (Arthur D. Little, Inc., and URS Research Co.): part E, "Social and Displacement/Relocation Impacts," table E-9. Of the 654 displacees in the agency caseload during this three-year period, no rent information was available for 404, or 62 percent of the total. At least as many persons as were on the official agency caseload were displaced from the area without entering agency relocation statistics. Detailed information on rent increases was deleted from the report as released to the public (although TOOR had obtained a copy of the original draft, and its attorneys had submitted this draft as part of some legal papers filed with the federal court challenging HUD's approval of the Redevelopment Agency's relocation plan). According to the 2 May 1973 *San Francisco Progress:* "The Arthur D. Little report endured numerous rewrites before the company felt it was suitable for submittal. A segment of the rough draft on relocation submitted to Judge Stanley Weigel several months ago is barely recognizable. Most of the strong words and critical comments have been deleted. For example, the report no longer states that: elderly residents (most of the present population in YBC) do not adapt readily to change; adequate housing for those who will be relocated is lacking; community residents cannot expect jobs from the project; relocation may cause an instant skid-row downtown, in the Mission district or elsewhere South of Market." This is apparently not an unusual practice: An *Examiner* story from 1983 states, "Observers noted that EIRs frequently are edited to suit the developers" (Gerald Adams, "Praised High-rise Now Being Criticized," *San Francisco Examiner,* 25 February 1983).

25. On the importance of these local ties, see Marc Fried, "Grieving for a Lost Home," in *The Urban Condition,* ed. Leonard Duhl (New York: Basic Books, 1963), 151–72; and Marc Fried et al., *The World of the Urban Working Class* (Cambridge, Mass.: Harvard University Press, 1973).

CHAPTER 5. INTO THE COURTS

1. *Western Addition Community Organization* v. *Weaver* 294 F. Supp. 433 (1968).

2. For 1971 actions, see U.S. Department of Housing and Urban Development, "Findings and Determination of HUD Pursuant to Sec. 105(c)(3), West-

ern Addition A-2" (Cal. R-54, 1 April 1971). The A-2 project's legal troubles were not to end with the dissolution of the preliminary injunction, however. In 1971, the federal district court issued a temporary order barring SFRA from displacing anyone from the area unless HUD certified, on a case-by-case basis, that relocation housing met federal standards with respect to housing quality and tenants' rent-paying abilities—see *San Francisco Chronicle*, 2 April 1971; later that year HUD ordered the Redevelopment Agency not to relocate any more project area residents until new housing was available for them within the project area. A decade later, SFNLAF filed another suit, this one on behalf of thirty-two hundred former A-2 project area residents who held Certificates of Preference for occupancy of replacement housing in the project area, charging that no replacement housing had been built and asking the court to order HUD and the agency to provide this housing. The litigation—*Rogers et al. v. HUD et al.*, #C-81–3690 SC—was settled in 1987 with a Redevelopment Agency agreement to rehabilitate some units for large families and transfer the apartments to the Housing Authority, and giving the few displaced A-2 certificate holders (who could be located after so many years) preference for those units and for the units being built to replace the Yerba Buena Plaza public housing project in the A-2 area. (Letter to author, dated 1 September 1993, from Arnold C. Ellis, San Francisco Neighborhood Legal Assistance Foundation.)

The sad and protracted history of Western Addition commercial renewal around Fillmore Street and the many abortive development plans for the area are discussed in Gerald Adams, "Dormant Fillmore Shopping Area a Victim of Urban Undevelopment," *San Francisco Examiner*, 16 August 1978, and Marilyn Clark, "The Tragedy of the Fillmore," *San Francisco Bay Guardian*, 10 June 1981. The Fillmore Center commercial development was later characterized as "a redevelopment project where stores sit empty despite expectations that they would house minority-owned businesses" (John King, "S.F. Redevelopment Agency at Crossroads," *San Francisco Chronicle*, 25 January 1993). A recent attempt to create (or re-create) a Jazz District fell apart. The contrast between the two sides of Fillmore Street that abut Geary Boulevard is captured in this account: "Six lanes of Geary Boulevard divide Fillmore Street—a clear demarcation of prosperity and languishing possibilities. While the upper half of Fillmore sports trendy and fashionable shops, lower Fillmore is overwhelmed with a string of discount clothing stores, a check cashing store and fast food restaurants" (Venise Wagner, "Trying to Jazz Up the Fillmore," *San Francisco Examiner*, 9 July 2000). A ninety-minute film history, "The Fillmore," produced by Peter L. Stein of KQED, was released in mid-1999. It quotes a local barber saying, "We used to call it the Fillmore. Now we call it the No More." Local residents interviewed for the film make an intriguing connection between the loss of community caused by urban renewal and the fatal search for community by those involved in the People's Temple, whose headquarters building was centrally located in the Fillmore. (See chapter 11 regarding the People's Temple.)

3. For a review of judicial supervision of the urban renewal program before and after the WACO case, see Chester W. Hartman, "Relocation: Illusory

Promises and No Relief," *University of Virginia Law Review* 57 (1971): 745–817.

4. The general state of the San Francisco housing market was well analyzed in "The Shame of San Francisco: An Analysis of San Francisco's Housing Crisis and Defects of San Francisco's Proposed 'Workable Program for Community Improvement,' " prepared by the Citizens' Emergency Task Force for a Workable Housing Policy (n.d. [1969]).

5. Affidavit of Peter Bender, filed in *TOOR* v. *HUD* in support of a motion for a temporary restraining order, 23 November 1969.

6. Exhibition submitted in support of plaintiffs' successful motion for temporary restraining order against interfering with attorney-client relationship; motion heard in December 1969 before Federal Judge Stanley A. Weigel. See also "Redevelopment Agency Hotels: They Talk of Beatings," *San Francisco Chronicle*, 14 April 1970.

7. "Renewal Agency Gets a Talking To," *San Francisco Chronicle*, 6 March 1970.

8. Concerning the court's decision on pending motions, see statement accompanying Findings and Conclusions on Motion for Preliminary Injunction: Orders on Motions for Dismissal and Summary Judgment, No. C-69 324 (N.D. Cal., 29 April 1970). The TOOR decision is reported at 406 F. Supp. 1024 (N.D. Cal. 1970).

9. Notes of TOOR attorney Amanda Hawes, who was present at this session,

10. See G. William Domhoff, *Bohemian Grove and Other Retreats: A Study in Ruling Class Cohesiveness* (New York: Harper & Row, 1974).

11. Kline got to know Brown as a result of his Yale Law School friendship with Brown's son, Jerry, and regarded him as someone with "strong populist impulses, in the hope that that character make-up would outweigh Mayor Alioto's far closer relationship with the ex-governor." Letter to author, dated 10 August 1993, from J. Anthony Kline. Kline was a former speech-writer for Brown.

12. Walter H. Blum, *Benjamin H. Swig: The Measure of a Man* (San Francisco, 1968), 77.

13. Nationally, only 19 percent of all families displaced by urban renewal had, during the 1950s and 1960s, relocated into public housing (Hartman, "Relocation," 745–817).

14. "Judge Voices Misgivings on Yerba Buena Housing," *San Francisco Examiner*, 19 August 1970.

15. For a good discussion of these issues, see Gordon Fellman, in association with Barbara Brandt, *The Deceived Majority: Politics and Protest in Middle America* (New Brunswick, N.J.: Transaction Books, 1973). A parallel account of the conflicts between Legal Services attorneys and the community is contained in Harry Brill, *Why Organizers Fail: The Story of a Rent Strike* (Berkeley and Los Angeles: University of California Press, 1971), 112–39.

16. *San Francisco Chronicle*, 6 November 1969.

17. Ibid., 20 January 1970.

18. Ibid., 28 May 1971.

19. Interview quoted in John Emshwiller, "Yerba Buena: A New Colossus for San Francisco," paper submitted to Political Science 109 and Social Science 100BC, University of California, Berkeley, spring 1972.

20. *San Francisco Chronicle,* 22 June 1971.

21. Report to the Court, by U.S. Dept. of HUD, *TOOR* v. *HUD,* No. C-69 324 (N.D. Cal., filed 24 August 1971).

22. *San Francisco Chronicle,* 25 August 1971.

23. Letter dated 30 August 1972, from James P. Jacquet, Program Manager, San Francisco Area Office of HUD, to Robert Rumsey, Executive Director, SFRA.

24. Quoted in Herb Caen's column, *San Francisco Chronicle,* 23 July 1972.

25. Memorandum and Order, *TOOR* v. *HUD,* No. C-69 324 SAW (N.D. Cal., 11 July 1972).

26. See draft copy of the Arthur D. Little Environmental Impact Report on Yerba Buena Center, part E, "Social and Displacement/Relocation Impacts," table E-5.

27. *San Francisco Chronicle,* 29 February 1972.

28. Ibid., 3 November 1971.

29. Letter in 31 January 1972 *San Francisco Chronicle,* from Kenneth F. Phillips, National Housing and Economic Development Law Project, University of California, Berkeley.

30. *San Francisco Chronicle,* 4 July 1972.

31. See Kline's essay in Ira Nowinski's forthcoming updated photography book, *No Vacancy.*

32. "Yerba Buena Revisited: A 3-part Analysis of a Public Interest Case," Federal Judges Program, Earl Warren Legal Institute, University of California Law School, 8 February 1982; author's interview with Judge Weigel, 14 August 1982.

33. *San Francisco Chronicle,* 18 March 1972.

34. Judge Weigel died in September 1999 at the age of 93. His *New York Times* obituary (4 September 1999) noted that "he was . . . known for his independence and his courage to render decisions regardless of their popularity."

35. "Redeveloper Accuses Judge Weigel of Bias," *San Francisco Examiner,* 12 January 1972.

36. *San Francisco Examiner,* 25 January 1972; *San Francisco Chronicle,* 25 January 1972.

37. *San Francisco Chronicle,* 9 February 1972; *San Francisco Examiner,* 8 February 1972; 338 F. Supp. 29 (1972).

38. Letter from B. E. Bergesen, III, and Kenneth Hecht, Youth Law Center and Employment Law Center, San Francisco. An edited version of their letter appeared in the 27 January 1972 *Examiner.*

CHAPTER 6. THE REDEVELOPMENT AGENCY FLOUNDERS

1. Allan B. Jacobs, *Making City Planning Work* (Chicago: American Society of Planning Officials, 1978), 30–31.

2. Memorandum, dated 18 December 1967, from T. J. Kent Jr., deputy for development, to Mayor John F. Shelley: "In important ways, the Redevelopment Agency has become a government within a government. It already has too broad a range of responsibilities for effective control to be exercised by the Mayor and Board of Supervisors."

3. *San Francisco Chronicle,* 29 April 1971.

4. William Lilley, III, "Herman Death Ends an Era," *National Journal,* 18 September 1971.

5. "Yerba Buena Center Public Facilities: A Description of Scope, Characteristics, Financing and Leasing Plans for the Public Facilities," submitted by Thomas J. Mellon, chief administrative officer, 6 March 1972.

6. The method for computing tax losses is adopted from Edward J. Ford Jr., "Benefit-Cost Analysis and Urban Renewal in the West End of Boston" (Ph.D. diss., Boston College, 1971).

7. According to the 28 September 1972 *Chronicle:* "Before approving the half cent increase in the hotel tax, members of the [Finance] committee attempted to pacify unhappy hotel operators by moving to provide more funds for advertising the city as a convention and tourist attraction."

8. *San Francisco Progress,* 27 April 1973.

9. *Duskin* vs. *Alioto et al.,* Superior Court City and County of San Francisco, No. 641–688; *Williams* v. *City and County of San Francisco et al.,* Superior Court City and County of San Francisco, No. 644–426.

10. *Redevelopment Agency of the City and County of San Francisco* vs. *All Persons,* Superior Court City and County of San Francisco, No. 667–945.

11. Letter to author, dated 19 October 1982, from Gerald A. Wright, Esq., supplemented by letter of clarification, dated 7 September 1983.

Gerald Wright's sardonic account of how this came about is as follows: "The method of achieving the settlement was simple: I was sitting in Dianne Feinstein's living room together with representatives from the Redevelopment Agency and various attorneys. I was asked what my clients would accept in settlement of their lawsuit. I said that they would settle for a binding commitment by the City to build what it said it would, when it said it would. That statement caused a lot of confusion. I was asked, 'How much may we spend?' The answer was, 'I don't care, just tell me what it will cost.' After about one minute's thought someone said, 'How about $200 million?' I said, 'Fine.' After a brief huddle, the Redevelopment folks asked if they could raise that to $210 million, and I said 'Fine' to that as well. . . . After some more discussion, the Redevelopment Agency and City representatives also agreed that the project bonds would be sold no later than June 30 of the following year. These two concepts—a dollar limit (however extravagant) and a definite starting date (however far-distant)—were then embodied in a settlement agreement that was approved by enactment of a City ordinance. That was the end of the Yerba Buena project as it was then conceived, because public agencies are not in the habit of building things on budget and on time."

12. "Board Ok's Yerba Buena Settlement," *San Francisco Chronicle,* 1 October 1974.

13. Dan Borsuk, "U.S. Helps Save Yerba Buena Center," *San Francisco Progress,* 8 March 1975.

14. Peter Kaplan, "Toward a Replanning of San Francisco's Yerba Buena Center: September 1974–December 1975," paper submitted to Prof. Barry Checkoway, CP 237, Dept. of City and Regional Planning, University of California, Berkeley, 15 December 1975, 4–5.

15. "Statement by Alvin Duskin on a Resolution of the Yerba Buena Issue," 14 April 1975.

16. E. Cahill Maloney, "Proposition M: Who Sets Priorities?" *San Francisco Progress,* 12 October 1983.

17. Dick Nolan, "Sending in the Muscle," *San Francisco Examiner,* 14 April 1975.

18. Dick Nolan, "Seeing the Wheels," *San Francisco Examiner,* 15 April 1975.

19. Letter to author, dated 19 October 1982, from Gerald A. Wright, Esq.

20. Jackson Rannells, "Yerba Buena's Friends Gather—1500 Protest Its Delay," *San Francisco Chronicle,* 18 April 1975.

21. "Yerba Buena: Cut through the Smokescreen over Jobs and You Still Find a Half Billion Dollar Pricetag," *San Francisco Bay Guardian,* 19 April–2 May 1975.

22. Minutes, SFRA Commission meeting, 5 February 1980; letter to author, dated 14 October 1982, from Helen Sause, SFRA.

23. Letter to author, dated 12 December 1983, from Earl P. Mills, deputy executive director, SFRA; minutes, SFRA Commission meetings, 5 and 29 May 1979.

24. Dick Nolan, "Deals Big and Little," *San Francisco Sunday Examiner & Chronicle,* 27 April 1975; Donald Canter, "Labor Agrees to Yerba Buena Pact," *San Francisco Examiner,* 5 February 1975; Paul Shinoff, "Arrest of S.F. Official Puzzles His Supervisor," *San Francisco Examiner,* 11 January 1981; "He, 3 Pals Caught Near Castroville," *San Francisco Examiner,* 10 January 1981.

25. Kaplan, "Toward a Replanning of San Francisco's Yerba Buena Center," 18–19. The source Kaplan cites for the Duskin quote is "Yerba Buena: Why Won't City Hall Put This Chunk of Manhattan to a Vote of the People?" *San Francisco Bay Guardian,* 3–16 May 1975.

26. Chester Hartman, *Yerba Buena: Land Grab and Community Resistance in San Francisco* (San Francisco: Glide Publications, 1974).

27. An incomplete list of those attending one or both meetings included: Sue Bierman of Citizens for Representative Government (later to be appointed to the City Planning Commission by Mayor Moscone and still later to be elected to the Board of Supervisors); Terry Covert of the Neighborhood Environmental Caucus; Alvin Duskin; Jim Flack of Friends of YBC Park; Douglas Engmann of the Stanyan-Fulton St. Association (later to be appointed to the Mayor's Select Committee on YBC and the Board of Permit Appeals by Mayor Moscone); Anthony Gilbert, TOOR/TODCO's attorney; Richard Goldman of the Citizens Waterfront Committee; Richard Gryziec of San Francisco Tomorrow; Sue Hestor of the Eureka Valley Promotion Association; Bob Cuff of the Mission Planning

Council; Marsha Lindeen of the Inner Sunset Action Committee; Peter Mendelsohn of TOOR; David Fulton of the Bay Area Citizens Action League; Earl Moss of the Victorian Alliance; Glenn Omatsu of the Committee Against Nihonmachi [Japantown] Evictions; William Shapiro; Charles Smith and others of the International Hotel Tenants Association; Calvin Welch of 409 House; John Bardis of the Mt. Sutro Defense Committee (later to be elected to the Board of Supervisors); Tim Eichenberg of the Sunset-Parkside Education and Action Committee; Frances Brown of the Legislative Council for Older Americans; Lee Meyerzove of the San Francisco Coalition; Mary Moser of Fair Oaks Neighbors; and a representative of the League of Women Voters.

28. Among the plaintiffs were several who had attended the Goodman Building meetings; several of these attendees withdrew as plaintiffs when they learned the timing of the suit. Among the better known plaintiffs were Jack Morrison, John Bardis, and Charles Starbuck (later to be appointed to the City Planning Commission by Mayor Moscone).

29. District Court of Appeal, First Appellate District, Division 4, *C. Starr et al.* v. *City and County of San Francisco et al.*, 1 Civ. No. 40111.

30. Robert Bartlett, "Swig Takes Over a Commitment," *San Francisco Chronicle*, 29 November 1975; Jack Viets, "Joseph Alioto Testifies in Bitter Family Debt Suit," *San Francisco Chronicle*, 15 November 1982; Jack Viets, "Jury Rules on Alioto Shipping Lease," *San Francisco Chronicle*, 3 December 1982.

31. See Melvin Swig's "Other Voices" column, "City to Benefit from Entertainment Center," *San Francisco Examiner*, 29 December 1975.

32. In Swig's "Other Voices" column (see note above), Swig claimed, "It won't cost the City a penny!"

33. Larry Liebert, "Jee Rejects Swig Bid for Alliance," *San Francisco Chronicle*, 19 July 1975. A 23 July 1975 *Chronicle* story quotes Evans's concerns about "a Candlestick Park-type mediocrity."

34. See the humorously titled editorial "Reasonable Discussion Prevailed," *San Francisco Progress*, 30 July 1975. For further description of Alioto's headbanging, see Larry Liebert, "Swig and Jee Agree on Arena," *San Francisco Chronicle*, 24 July 1975.

35. "Yerba Fund to Ease Property Tax Burden," *San Francisco Chronicle*, 20 September 1975.

36. Letter, dated 5 December 1975, from Victor Honig and Chester Hartman, Citizens Committee on Yerba Buena Center, to Board of Supervisors president Dianne Feinstein and other members of the board. See also Chester Hartman, "Other Voices" column, "Making Sport with Taxpayers' Money," *San Francisco Examiner*, 15 December 1975.

37. George Christopher, "Review of the Acquisition of the San Francisco Giants Baseball Team: Decisions on location of the stadium; construction and financing; general comments pertaining to the Candlestick Park project and proposed new stadium," September 1982, 39.

38. For a good treatment of the dynamics and effects of intercity competition in the world of professional sports and owners' calculations and motivations, see

S. Prakash Sethi, *Up against the Corporate Wall,* "Corporate Decisions and Their Effects on Urban Communities—The Milwaukee Braves, Atlanta: Indiscriminate Moving of Sports Franchises" (Englewood Cliffs, N.J.: Prentice-Hall, 1971), 267–80.

CHAPTER 7. RESOLVING THE CONVENTION
CENTER DEADLOCK

1. Randy Shilts, *The Mayor of Castro Street: The Life and Times of Harvey Milk* (New York: St. Martin's Press, 1982), 100.

2. Stephen Barton kindly made available to me his notes on the Select Committee's meetings and hearings, from which much of this description is drawn.

3. See Stephen E. Barton, "The Neighborhood Movement in San Francisco," *Berkeley Planning Journal,* vol. 2, nos. 1–2 (spring 1985): 85–105.

4. "The N.Y. Convention Center—Too Big to Be Bad," *New York Times,* 30 April 1978.

5. Richard Gryziec, "A Proposal for a 'Tivoli Gardens' in Yerba Buena," *San Francisco Examiner,* 26 May 1976.

6. Allan Temko, "A Blueprint for S.F. Fun, Culture," *San Francisco Chronicle,* 15 August 1977.

7. Andy Friedman, "Power Politics and Hollow Formalism," *San Francisco Odalisque,* 2–15 September 1976.

8. Dan Borsuk, "Mayor Pushes YBC Theme Park," *San Francisco Progress,* 1 September 1976.

9. Interrogatories Nos. 50 and 51, Set 1, Trial Brief, *C. Starr et al.* v. *City and County of San Francisco,* Superior Court No. 9–631.

10. Editorial, *San Francisco Chronicle,* 17 January 1962.

11. Memorandum, dated 10 March 1977, from Chief Administrative Officer Roger Boas to Members of the San Francisco Hotel and Motel Industry.

12. Memorandum, dated 3 January 1978, from John Igoe (YBC Project Coordinator) to Richard Sklar, Subject: Utilization of Hotel Tax Revenues—Hotel Owners Meeting.

13. Dick Nolan, "Let Ben Do It," *San Francisco Examiner,* 30 March 1978.

14. Robert Levering, "Will Yerba Buena Be an $8 Million Hole in the Ground?" *San Francisco Bay Guardian,* 17–25 August 1978.

15. "Voter Approval Sought for Non-profit Bonds," *San Francisco Progress,* 28 July 1976.

16. Carol Kroot, "Non-profit Corporations: Millions for Public Works without Vote," *San Francisco Progress,* 2 April 1976.

17. Larry Hatfield, "Roger Boas: Free-Spender to Tightwad," *San Francisco Sunday Examiner & Chronicle,* 17 October 1976.

18. Ibid. See also Dave Farrell, "Mayor Picks Nothenberg for No. 2 S.F. Job," *San Francisco Chronicle,* 7 October, 1986; Bruce Brugmann, "Hurray! Boas the Buckler Is Back," *San Francisco Bay Guardian,* 22 October 1976, and its

reference to the earlier story about Boas, "A Profile in Courage," in the 30 September 1969 *Guardian*, on Boas's 1969 reelection campaign: "On the crucial September 1 Transamerica vote, Boas was off on a pack trip in the Sierras. Boas told *The Guardian* he had planned the trip for a year and that it had nothing to do with his vote. Well, how would you have voted if you were there? 'Frankly, I'd rather duck that one.' "

19. Gerald Adams, "CAO Boas's Moment of Pride and Exuberance," *San Francisco Examiner*, 16 December 1981.

20. Letter to author, dated 19 July 1982, from Michael S. McGill.

21. Walter Blum, "The City *Is* His Business," *California Living*, 18 September 1983. Emphasis in original.

22. Bruce Brugmann, "Only an Anti-Highrise Initiative Can Save SF!" *San Francisco Bay Guardian*, 18 January 1979.

23. "Moscone Center: How It Finally Was Accomplished," feature/background enclosed in press kit accompanying opening of Moscone Center, December 1981.

24. Gerald Adams, "A Hard Look: As Battlefield Shrinks, Yerba Buena Finally May Grow," *San Francisco Examiner*, 22 March 1978.

25. The City's "all persons" action was No. 740–623, Superior Court, County of San Francisco; the *Davis et al.* action brought by the CCYBC was No. 741–978, Superior Court, County of San Francisco.

26. Guy Wright, "When Labor Switched," *San Francisco Examiner*, 13 April 1975.

27. *San Francisco Examiner*, 28 April 1971.

28. Dick Nolan, "The Loose Numbers," *San Francisco Examiner*, 30 April 1975; "Whose Yerba Buena?" *San Francisco Examiner*, 16 January 1974. End runs around the voters are of course not confined to San Francisco and California. When New York State governor Nelson Rockefeller's opulent half-billion dollar Albany South Mall project ran into the reality that voters would not pass a bond issue to pay for it, the state and Albany County rigged a deal whereby the county would float the bonds and enter into a lease-purchase arrangement with the state to make the project technically "self-supporting," thereby avoiding the necessity to take the project to the voters. The ploy meant $44 million in additional interest payments by the state. See William Kennedy, "Everything Everybody Ever Wanted," *Atlantic Monthly* (May 1983): 77–82. Commenting on New York City's mammoth convention center project, then under construction and experiencing massive cost increases, delays, and technical defects, the *New York Times*'s Sydney Schanberg ("Befogging the Taxpayer," 9 April 1983) observed:

> One fundamental reason for the heavy fog and confusion that have descended is that, as with most grand-sized government projects, the public officials who conceived the center don't let the public in on the true costs and the potential for delays and overruns.
> You see, if you tell taxpayers from the start how deep they're going to reach into their pockets, maybe they'll holler so loud that you'll have to take their

views into account. But that, of course, might interfere with the grand schemes and with the principle that papa knows best what's good for his children. So now, four years later, the children—all of us—are greeted with surprise announcements and disclosures that things are not as they should be at the convention center, that it's going to cost more and take longer than our leaders promised.

Since the state officials who conceived the project were afraid that voters would reject a ballot referendum for issuing regular State bonds to build the center, they chose a back-door method—bonds issued by the Triborough [Bridge Authority] which don't require voter approvals.

On the New York convention center fiasco, see also Martin Gottlieb, "Convention Center Still Enmeshed in Uncertainty," *New York Times*, 1 July 1983; Martin Gottlieb, "Completion Date in Mid-'86 Seen for Convention Center," *New York Times*, 16 July 1983; Jane Perez, "A House Panel Votes to Allow Convention Center Lease Deal," *New York Times*, 28 July 1983.

29. Dick Nolan, "The High Rollers," *San Francisco Sunday Examiner & Chronicle*, 20 April 1975.

30. Larry Liebert, "The Secret Talks on Yerba Buena," *San Francisco Chronicle*, 25 June 1974.

31. "Private Builders Get YBC Warning," *San Francisco Progress*, 4 July 1975.

32. See Wallace Turner, "San Francisco Pins Big Hope on Convention Center," *New York Times*, 23 January 1981; Gerald Adams, "CAO Boas's Moment of Pride and Exuberance."

33. Dick Nolan, "The Button Pushers," *San Francisco Examiner*, 20 May 1975.

34. California Court of Appeals, No. 1 Civ. 45720.

35. Janice E. Kosel, "Municipal Debt Limitation in California," *Golden Gate Law Review* 7 (spring 1977): 645.

CHAPTER 8. SOUTH OF MARKET CONQUERED

1. Memorandum, dated 26 January 1982, from Director of Planning Dean Macris to City Planning Commissioners, subject: "South of Market Interim Controls."

2. Letter, dated 24 November 1980, from Roger Boas to the Redevelopment Agency commissioners. See also John Herbers, "The Convention Center Boom," *New York Times*, 7 May 1978, reporting that "there are signs that some cities may end up with white elephants as the competition increases."

3. Marshall Kilduff, "New Design for Yerba Exhibit Hall," *San Francisco Chronicle*, 26 July 1977.

4. Gerald Adams, "Boas Attacked in Yerba Buena Complex Dispute," *San Francisco Examiner*, 24 January 1980.

5. For both quotations, see letter, dated 24 November 1980, from Roger Boas to Redevelopment Agency Commissioners.

6. "Yerba Buena Advisor Quits over Spurning of Tivoli Idea," *San Francisco Chronicle,* 29 May 1981.

7. Gerald Adams, "S.F. to Award Its Top Prize Soon," *San Francisco Examiner,* 17 September 1980.

8. Gerald Adams, "4 of 10 Bidders out on Yerba Park Project," *San Francisco Examiner,* 30 July 1980.

9. Gerald Adams, "Yerba Buena Developers down to Two," *San Francisco Examiner,* 8 October 1980.

10. Allan Temko, "Decision Day on Developing Yerba Buena," *San Francisco Chronicle,* 20 November 1980.

11. Peter Pen, "Labor Strife for Marriott Looms in D.C.," *Washington Post,* 4 February 1984.

12. Marshall Kilduff, "Yerba Buena Bidder Is Blum's Friend," *San Francisco Chronicle,* 28 August 1980.

13. Gerald Adams, "City Link Is No Bar to Bid by Builder," *San Francisco Examiner,* 28 August 1980.

14. "The Yerba Buena Team: A Who's Who," *San Francisco Chronicle,* 21 November 1980.

15. "A Canadian Family Becomes Key Force in City Real Estate," *New York Times,* 24 March 1982.

16. Susan Goldenberg, *Men of Property: The Canadian Developers Who Are Buying America* (Toronto: Personal Library, 1982), 27–46. See also Anthony Bianco, *The Reichmanns: Family, Faith, Fortune and the Empire of Olympia & York* (New York: Times Books, 1997).

17. Gerald Adams, "New Yerba Buena Proposal a Whopper," *San Francisco Examiner,* 8 December 1979.

18. Cited in Marcelo Rodriguez and Alan Kay, "Is the S.F. Redevelopment Agency about to Give Yerba Buena Center Away?" *San Francisco Bay Guardian,* 5 August 1981.

19. *San Francisco Bay Guardian,* 4 November 1981.

20. Deborah Quilter, Marcelo Rodriguez, and Alan Kay, "How Could the Supervisors Have Approved YBC?" *San Francisco Bay Guardian,* 4 November 1981.

21. "Cost Analysis Summary," attachment to letter to author, dated 9 December 1982, from Joseph A. Sickon, Inspector General, General Services Administration.

22. "U.S. Agency Chief Admits Meeting on a Land Deal in San Francisco," *New York Times,* 24 July 1982. For a profile of the Marriott Corporation, see Walter Shapiro, "The Empire Builder," *Washington Post Magazine,* 19 September 1982.

23. Evelyn Hsu, "Talk of GOP Favoritism in a Yerba Buena Deal," *San Francisco Chronicle,* 24 July 1982.

24. "U.S. Agency Chief Admits Meeting on a Land Deal in San Francisco," *New York Times,* 24 July 1982.

25. Ibid.

26. Office of Audits, Office of the Inspector General, GSA, "Proposed Sale of the 49 Fourth Street Property, San Francisco, California," 3D-20876–00–23, 16 September 1982.

27. Myron Struck, "Levitas Would Delay GSA Land Sale," *Washington Post,* 6 January 1983.

28. John Fogarty, "Mayor Threatens Suit to Get Land for Hotel," *San Francisco Chronicle,* 29 January 1983.

29. "Some Tough Bidding by S.F.," *San Francisco Chronicle,* 31 March 1983.

30. "Lopsided Bid War for Disputed Hotel Site," *San Francisco Examiner,* 27 April 1983.

31. "Just Two Bids for Disputed S.F. Hotel Site," *San Francisco Examiner,* 26 April 1983.

32. "Lopsided Bid War for Disputed Hotel Site."

33. "August 4, 1982. Hearings on reported proposed sale of federal property declared excess in San Francisco by the GSA," Subcommittee on Public Buildings and Grounds, Subcommittee on Investigations and Oversight of the Committee on Public Works and Transportation, unedited, unprinted transcript.

34. Allan Temko, " 'People's Theater' of the Future," *San Francisco Chronicle,* 14 September 1988.

35. In "Radical Look Rattles S.F.'s City Planners: Federal Building Design Called Appropriate for Houston, L.A.," *San Francisco Chronicle,* 5 July 2001, John King notes, "[T]here has been such a hostile reaction to the proposed federal tower . . . that one might think the building would be topped with a statue of Jesse Helms."

36. *Hotel Employees and Restaurant Workers Union, Local 2, AFL-CIO* v. *Marriott Corporation,* No. C-89–2707, MHP, 23 August 1993, Memorandum and Order (rejecting Marriott's motion for summary judgment).

37. See Jonathan Marshall, "S.F. Marriott Concedes to Union," *San Francisco Chronicle,* 8 October 1996.

38. Jonathan Curiel, "Brown Leads Call to Boycott S.F. Marriott," *San Francisco Chronicle,* 5 September 2000; Nina Wu, "For Hotel Workers, It's All About Fairness," *San Francisco Examiner,* 12 July 2001.

39. Richard D. Hylton, "Real Estate Giant in Canada Enters Bankruptcy Filing," *New York Times,* 15 May 1992; Richard D. Hylton, "Big Canadian Developer Trying to Confine Bankruptcy Damage," *New York Times,* 16 May 1992; Steven Prokesch, "Developer Files for Bankruptcy for Huge London Office Project," *New York Times,* 28 May 1992; also, Anthony Bianco's cover article in the 20 January 1997 *Business Week,* "Faith and Fortune—Paul Reichmann: Talented, Pious, Driven—but Not Infallible."

40. Burton J. Wolfe, "The Candlestick Swindle," *San Francisco Bay Guardian,* 14 May 1968; David Johnston, "Found! $15 Million More for the City's General Fund," *San Francisco Bay Guardian,* 1 April 1981; Glenn Dickey, "Why Candlestick Isn't Working—a Lesson in Obsolescence," *San Francisco Chronicle,* 20 December 1982; see also the interesting but somewhat exculpatory

September 1992 memoir ex-mayor George Christopher issued when discussions of replacing Candlestick Park first began, "Review of the Acquisition of the San Francisco Giants Baseball Team: Decisions on Location of the Stadium; Construction and Financing; General Comments Pertaining to the Candlestick Park Project and Proposed New Stadium."

41. Carl Nolte, "Should San Francisco Scrap Candlestick?" *San Francisco Chronicle,* 20 December 1982.

42. See the "op-ed" by Smith College economist Andrew Zimbalist, "Take Me Out to the Cleaners," *New York Times,* 14 July 1992; also Zimbalist's book, *Baseball and Billions: A Probing Look inside the Big Business of Our National Pastime* (New York: Basic Books, 1992).

43. A useful review of the stadium controversy, through 1991, from which much of the following material is drawn, is contained in Richard Edward DeLeon, "Save Our Giants: Political Hardball in China Basin," in *Left Coast City: Progressive Politics in San Francisco* (Lawrence: University Press of Kansas, 1992), 107–22.

44. The Green Bay, Wisconsin, Packers football is the fascinating oddball exception to this observation—otherwise applicable to teams of all major league sports. In 1922, when the Packers almost went bankrupt, four fans organized the franchise into a nonprofit corporation whose directors would be elected by local shareholders. This nonprofit, with help from the city and school board, built the city's first stadium. When financial trouble hit again during the Depression, the new bailout plan involved convincing the chamber of commerce to sell twenty-five-dollar shares door to door. Today, some 110,000 fans— "cheeseheads"—more than half of whom live in Wisconsin, own shares in the team. The shares cannot be traded, pay no dividends, and never appreciate in value (investors can redeem their shares by selling stock back to the team). But shareholders are entitled to vote for the team's board of directors. The corporation's mission is to maintain the team in Green Bay (population: 97,000) in perpetuity. Any profits are reinvested in the stadium or players, or both. Direct benefits to the city of Green Bay are estimated at $60 million a year. The team provides a lovely example of community-owned enterprise—homegrown (and home-remaining) royalty, as it were. (See Michael Shuman, "Community-Ownership: Green Bay Packer Style," *Grassroots Economics Organizing Newsletter* 35 [January/February 1999]: 5.)

45. San Francisco Giants, "The Future of Candlestick Park," March 1982.

46. "Stadium Feasibility Analysis," Task Force Report to the Mayor, October 1983.

47. Jim Kelly, "Mayor, Renne at Odds over Stadium," *San Francisco Progress,* 14 October 1983.

48. "Review of the Report of the Mayor's Stadium Task Force," Report to the Board of Supervisors of the City and County of San Francisco, Budget Analyst for the San Francisco Board of Supervisors (February 1984); Scott Blakey, "Analyst Blasts Mayor's Study That Backed New S.F. Stadium," *San Francisco Chronicle,* 29 February 1984; Dave Farrell, "City Disputes Criticism of the Stadium Task Force," *San Francisco Examiner,* 29 February 1984.

49. Steve Wiegand, "Legal Problem Arises in S.F. Stadium Plan," *San Francisco Chronicle,* 15 October 1983.

50. See the April 1994 issue of the *San Francisco Tomorrow* newsletter, "The Giants' $93 Million Fraud," critiquing the January 1994 economic impact report by Economic Research Associates commissioned by the team. See also SFT's September 1995 newsletter for additional objections, and Edward Epstein, "Critics Sound Off on Giants' Plan for New Ballpark," *San Francisco Chronicle,* 18 April 1997.

51. A Seattle survey showed that "56 percent of the businesses near the Kingdome said the stadium had no effect on them, 20 percent said it had a beneficial effect, and 26 percent said it was bad for their business" (Carl Nolte, "A Great Domed Stadium—How It Would Change San Francisco," *San Francisco Chronicle,* 23 December 1982). Nor has the $100 million renovation of New York City's Yankee Stadium provided much economic benefit to the rundown Bronx neighborhood surrounding it. (See Michael Katz, "Stadium's No Hit with Bronx Residents," *San Francisco Chronicle,* 14 August 1976.)

52. There is some excellent literature on the topic. See, for example, Michael N. Danielson, *Home Team: Professional Sports and the American Metropolis* (Princeton: Princeton University Press, 1997); Joanna Cagan and Neil DeMause, *Field of Schemes: How the Great Stadium Swindle Turns Public Money into Private Profit* (Monroe, Maine: Common Courage Press, 1998); Roger Noll and Andrew Zimbalist, eds., *Sports, Jobs and Taxes: The Economic Impact of Sports Teams and Stadiums* (Washington, D.C.: The Brookings Institution, 1997); Kenneth L. Shropshire, *The Sports Franchise Game: Cities in Pursuit of Sports Franchises, Events, Stadiums and Arenas* (Philadelphia: University of Pennsylvania Press, 1995). Critiques come from the right as well as the left: See the unpublished 1999 paper of Heritage Foundation Senior Fellow Ronald Utt, "Edifice Wrecks: Are Cities Helped or Hurt by Funding Convention Centers and Stadiums?" and his op-ed in the 14 June 1999 *Washington Post,* as well as Tim Keyed, "The Stadium Shell Game," *Readers Digest* (November 1997): 153–56. See also Alan Abrahamson and Sam Farmer, "NFL Ledgers Reveal Profits Depend on New Stadiums," *Los Angeles Times,* 13 May 2001; the revealing data reported in this article derive from financial documents entered into evidence in the Raiders' suit against the NFL (referred to above).

53. Leslie Wayne, "Picking up the Tab for Fields of Dreams: Taxpayers Build Stadiums, Owners Cash In," *New York Times,* 27 July 1996.

54. Quoted in Richard Perez-Peña, "Economists Dispute Value of Spending on Professional Sports Stadiums," *New York Times,* 3 August 1997.

55. Danielson, *Home Team.*

56. See Holly Bailey, "Big League Lobbying," in the March 1999 issue of *Capital Eye,* the newsletter of the Center for Responsive Politics, for a chart of the 1997–98 soft money and individual campaign contributions of sports franchise owners.

57. Ryan Kim, "Giants Home, At Last Giants Home, At Last," *San Francisco Examiner,* 12 April 2000; Rob Morse, "A Day of Glorious Sensory Overload," *San Francisco Examiner,* 12 April 2000.

58. Erin McCormick, "Giants Turn a Profit," *San Francisco Examiner*, 1 October 2000.

59. Jonathan Curiel, "Giants' Parking Toughest Ticket in Town," *San Francisco Chronicle*, 30 March 2000.

60. Evelyn Nieves, "Opening Day for Big Wallets and New Stadium," *New York Times*, 12 April 2000.

61. McCormick, "Giants Turn a Profit." A recent controversy over financing plans for a new arena to bring the National Basketball Association Vancouver Grizzlies to Memphis led to abandonment of the original scheme to repay the bond issue with property taxes, following citizen protest and the threat of a voter referendum. See Emily Yelin, "For a Sports Bridesmaid, A Blissful Union," *New York Times*, 22 June 2001.

62. "Minn. Strikes Out in Stadium Probe," Associated Press, 15 November 1999 story.

63. See Edward Epstein, "Giants Ponder Building Arena," *San Francisco Chronicle*, 4 May 2001; Edward Epstein, "Privately Funded S.F. Arena Could Add Up," *San Francisco Chronicle*, 21 May 2001.

64. An earlier illustration: "[Feinstein] has a fund-raising dinner, hosted by 49ers owner Eddie DeBartolo, scheduled for the St. Francis Hotel on December 12, and hopes to raise another $300,000 to $400,000 through that event." John Jacobs, "Feinstein Fund Raising Tied to Husband's Role," *San Francisco Examiner*, 3 December 1989.

65. Abrahamson and Farmer, "NFL Ledgers."

66. For a description of the publicity campaign, as well as the by now expected "flak" role played by the city's daily newspapers in such situations, see Phyllis Orrick's "Unspun" column, *SF Weekly*, 16–22 April 1997.

67. Carla Marinucci, Gregory Lewis, and Erin McCormick, "Stadium Measures Win by a Whisker," *San Francisco Examiner*, 4 June 1997.

68. Kevin Sack, "N.F.L. Owner Ties Ex-Governor to Extortion," *New York Times*, 7 October 1998.

69. Kevin Sack, "Former Louisiana Governor Guilty of Extortion on Casinos," *New York Times*, 10 May 2000; Rick Bragg, "Ex-Governor of Louisiana Gets 10 Years," *New York Times*, 9 January 2001. Edwards's business and political activities had been investigated more than twenty times over the past two decades; in 1991, when running for governor against former Ku Klux Klan leader David Duke, Edwards's more liberal supporters sported bumper stickers saying, "Vote for the Crook—It's Important."

70. Ray Delgado, "DeBartolo Loses 49ers to His Sister," *San Francisco Examiner*, 20 March 2000. For additional details about the relationship between Governor Edwards and the DeBartolos (father as well as son), see Tyler Bridges, *Bad Bet on the Bayou: The Rise of Gambling in Louisiana and the Fall of Governor Edwin Edwards* (New York: Farrar, Straus & Giroux, 2001).

71. See Cassi Feldman, "Bayview Residents Are Getting Sick While the Navy Makes Excuses," *San Francisco Bay Guardian*, 4 October 2000.

72. Nina Wu, "EPA Fines Navy for Hunters Point Toxins," *San Francisco Examiner*, 8 June 2001.

73. Dan Evans, "Decade-Old Bayview Toxic Site to Be Cleaned Up—Finally," *San Francisco Examiner*, 13 June 2001.

74. See the lengthy feature by Lisa Davis, "Fallout," *SF Weekly*, 9 May 2001.

75. John Ross and Tim Redmond, "The Octopus Revisited," *San Francisco Bay Guardian*, 19 October 1983.

76. *Mission Bay Planning News* (newsletter of the Southern Pacific Development Company), July/August 1983.

77. "Stadium Feasibility Analysis," Task Force Report to the Mayor, October 1983.

78. David Willman and Dan Meyers, "Brown's Choice of Clients Invites Conflict Questions," *San Jose Mercury News*, 12 February 1984; Gale Cook and Steven Capps, "SP, Developers Top Brown's Clients," *San Francisco Examiner*, 6 March 1984.

79. James Finefrock, "SP's Tax Bill Cut in Half by City Panel," *San Francisco Examiner*, 3 February 1984.

80. "S.P. Wins Big Tax Cut on S.P. Land," *San Francisco Chronicle*, 4 February 1984.

81. Marshall Kilduff, "Bid to Take SP Land for Housing," *San Francisco Chronicle*, 7 February 1984.

82. "Judge Denies SP Tax Break for Mission Bay, *San Francisco Chronicle*, 27 November 1984; "A Back-room Deal for Mission Bay," *San Francisco Bay Guardian*, 28 November 1984.

83. Tali Woodward, "The Real Welfare Cheats," *San Francisco Bay Guardian*, 6 October 1999.

84. Gerald Adams, "Maher Has Radical Redesign Plan for Mission Bay," *San Francisco Examiner*, 23 January 1984; Dave Farrell, "Supervisor Launches Action to Take Over SP Land for Housing," *San Francisco Examiner*, 7 February 1984; "First Step toward Acquiring SP Land," *San Francisco Chronicle*, 6 March 1984.

85. "Mission Bay Plan Trimmed—Mayor Still Opposed," *San Francisco Chronicle*, 2 May 1984.

86. "Panel Oks Mission Bay Takeover Plan," *San Francisco Chronicle*, 3 May 1984; Maitland Zane, "S.F. Delays Action on SP Land," *San Francisco Chronicle*, 8 May 1984.

87. "Agreement on Scaled-down Mission Bay," *San Francisco Chronicle*, 3 August 1984.

88. "S.F. Drops Plan to Seize Mission Bay from SP," *San Francisco Chronicle*, 16 August 1984.

89. Allan Temko, "Fresh Start on Mission Bay Project," *San Francisco Chronicle*, 22 January 1985.

90. Marshall Kilduff, "Mission Bay Critics Win One Round," *San Francisco Chronicle*, 19 June 1986.

91. "Developer Reports Backtracking on Mission Bay Planning Costs," *San Francisco Chronicle*, 21 February 1986.

92. "Supervisors' Panel to Review Four Options for Mission Bay," *San Francisco Chronicle*, 11 June 1986.

93. "Mission Bay Plans Are Toned Down," *San Francisco Chronicle,* 19 September 1986.

94. "Flap Over Prices and Subsidies," *San Francisco Chronicle,* 28 December 1987.

95. "Nightmare-by-the-Bay," *San Francisco Bay Guardian,* 31 August 1988.

96. "A Real Alternative for Mission Bay," *San Francisco Bay Guardian,* 23 November 1988.

97. "Quake Put a Dent in Development Plans," *San Francisco Chronicle,* 6 November 1989.

98. "Agreement Reached on Mission Bay," *San Francisco Chronicle,* 17 January 1990.

99. "Financial Details of City's Deal on Mission Bay," *San Francisco Bay Guardian,* 31 January 1990.

100. "Mission Bay's Fatal Flaws," *San Francisco Bay Guardian,* 14 February 1990; "Issues of Contention at Mission Bay Project," *San Francisco Chronicle,* 31 January 1990.

101. "Make Way for Ducklings," *San Francisco Bay Guardian,* 18 July 1990.

102. "S.F. Planners Back Mission Bay," *San Francisco Chronicle,"* 24 August 1990.

103. Michael McCabe, "Mission Bay Foes Forced to List Drive's Sponsor," *San Francisco Chronicle,* 27 October 1990.

104. "Voters Put S.F. Back on Slow-growth Track," *San Francisco Chronicle,* 8 November 1990.

105. "S.F. Supervisors Give Final Ok to Mission Bay," *San Francisco Chronicle,* 26 February 1991.

106. "Mission Bay Startup Set for Next Year," *San Francisco Chronicle,* 16 October 1991.

107. See "Legislative Analysis" prepared for the 14 October 1998 hearing of the Board of Supervisors' Economic Development, Transportation and Finance Committee; John King, "Hotel, Highrise Part of Mission Bay Plan," *San Francisco Chronicle,* 10 July 1997; memo, dated 24 July 2000, from James B. Morales, executive director, to [San Francisco Redevelopment] Agency Commissioners; Tyche Hendricks, "Developers Ready Mission Bay Sites," *San Francisco Examiner,* 27 January 2000; Rachel Gordon, "S.F. Picked for Second UC Campus," *San Francisco Examiner,* 17 May 1996; Morris Newman, "A $4 Billion Mix of Uses in San Francisco," *New York Times,* 9 January 2000. See also, for general review of earlier Mission Bay politics and planning, Stephen J. McGovern, *The Politics of Downtown Development: Dynamic Political Cultures in San Francisco and Washington, D.C.* (Lexington: University Press of Kentucky, 1998), 170–79, and chap. 5; Elizabeth Morris, "The Mission Bay Project, San Francisco," chap. 7 in "Urban Redevelopment and the Emerging Community Sector," Ph.D. diss., Dept. of City and Regional Planning, University of California, Berkeley, 1998.

108. Lloyd Watson, "Counseling 'From Dirt to Dust,' " *San Francisco Chronicle,* 26 September 1988.

109. Rebecca Solnit and Susan Schwartzenberg, *Hollow City: The Siege of San Francisco and the Crisis of American Urbanism* (London: Verso, 2000), 75.

CHAPTER 9. MOSCONE CENTER DOINGS

1. Allan Temko, "Moscone Center's Splendor," *San Francisco Chronicle*, 3 December 1981.

2. Michael Taylor, "Leaks Found in Foundation of Moscone Center," *San Francisco Chronicle*, 11 May 1982.

3. Editorial, "Moscone Center: Trial and Triumph," *San Francisco Examiner*, 2 December 1982, referring to Tim Reiterman's story in the previous day's *Examiner*.

4. Taylor, "Leaks Found."

5. Michael Taylor, "Mayor Threatens Suit on the Leaky Moscone," *San Francisco Chronicle*, 12 May 1982.

6. Gerald Adams, "Moscone Center: Big Grab at Convention Bucks," *San Francisco Examiner*, 25 November 1981.

7. Taylor, "Mayor Threatens Suit."

8. Tim Reiterman, "Costly Flaws That Plague Moscone Center," *San Francisco Examiner*, 3 December 1982.

9. Tim Reiterman, "$50,000 Worth of Chairs Stolen from Moscone," *San Francisco Examiner*, 10 October 1982.

10. Tim Reiterman, "New Moscone Center Ripoff: $10,000 Piano," *San Francisco Examiner*, 22 October 1982.

11. "Mayor Raps Boas in Official's Firing," *San Francisco Chronicle*, 18 October 1982.

12. Tim Reiterman, "S.F. Convention Chief Steered Deal to Firm That Aided Him," *San Francisco Examiner*, 7 November 1982.

13. "Mayor Raps Boas."

14. Reiterman, "S.F. Convention Chief."

15. Tim Reiterman, "Moscone Center's Glitches," *San Francisco Sunday Examiner & Chronicle*, 11 December 1983.

16. Paul Liberatore, "Troupe's Bitter Skit at Moscone Center," *San Francisco Chronicle*, 14 December 1981. "Ghosts" has been published in *West Coast Plays 10* (Berkeley: California Theater Council, 1981), 31–39.

17. Both quotations are from " 'Political' Art Furor at Moscone Center," *San Francisco Chronicle*, 1 December 1981.

18. Letter to author, dated 12 August 1983, from Katherine Porter.

19. Scott Winokur, "Artist Defends Moscone Statue as 'A Piece for the People,' " *San Francisco Examiner*, 3 December 1981.

20. Letter to author, dated 16 March 1982, from Frederic Stout.

21. Paul Shinoff and Steven Capps, "To S.F. It's a Bust; to the Artist It's Finished," *San Francisco Examiner*, 4 December 1981.

22. The tax-exempt feature of such bonds, while resulting in considerable savings to the agency in terms of the lower interest rates they produce, at the

same time creates one of the income tax system's greatest loopholes. The recipients of state and local bond interest income (and hence of the tax shelter they provide) are persons in very high income brackets. See David J. Ott and Attiat F. Ott, "The Tax Subsidy through Exemption of State and Local Bond Interest" in *The Economics of Federal Subsidy Programs, A Compendium of Papers Submitted to the Joint Economic Committee,* Congress of the United States, Pt. 3, "Tax Subsidies," 15 July 1972, 305–16.

23. "Report on Yerba Buena Convention and Exhibition Center," submitted by Roger Boas, chief administrative officer, 9 May 1978, 28.

24. Don Wegars, "$10 Million Jump in Costs for Yerba Buena Center," *San Francisco Chronicle,* 23 December 1978.

25. Wallace Turner, "San Francisco Dedicates $126 Million George Moscone Convention Center," *New York Times,* 3 December 1981.

26. Letter, dated 30 November 1982, from Roger Boas, chief administrative officer, to Mayor Dianne Feinstein and Board of Supervisors. Subject: Moscone Convention Center: First Year Anniversary.

27. Evelyn Hsu, "Boas Reveals That Moscone Has a Deficit," *San Francisco Chronicle,* 1 December 1982.

28. "A Moscone Deficit Was Forecast," *San Francisco Chronicle,* 2 December 1982.

29. Hsu, "Boas Reveals That Moscone Has a Deficit."

30. "Conventions Are Getting Smaller, Less Extravagant As Firms Cut Back," *Wall Street Journal,* 20 July 1982; Hsu, "Boas Reveals That Moscone Has a Deficit," where Boas notes that "The Convention and Visitors Bureau recommends that we keep rents at absolute rock-bottom."

31. Reginald Smith, "$73 Million Plan to Double Size of Moscone Center," *San Francisco Chronicle,* 23 April 1986.

32. John Eckhouse, "S.F. Facing Convention Crisis," *San Francisco Chronicle,* 23 March 1987.

33. Paul Farhi, "Hard Times for Brooks Hall, Civic Auditorium," *San Francisco Examiner,* 14 July 1985.

34. Ibid.

35. "Santa Clara's $34 Million Piece of the Action," *Peninsula Times-Tribune,* 14 May 1983; Michele Munz, "Competition Builds for Bay Area Business. Cities Plan New Facilities, But Is There Enough Business for All?" *San Francisco Business Journal,* 30 March 1983.

36. Memorandum, dated 3 January 1978, from John Igoe, YBC project coordinator, to Richard Sklar. Subject: Utilization of Hotel Tax Revenues—Hotel Owners Meeting.

37. See, for example, the editorial "Yerba Buena Aborning," in the 21 February 1975 *San Francisco Chronicle:* "If development now proceeds as planned, it will promptly open up an estimated $51 million payroll for construction workers on the public facilities alone, with an eventual total of 36,000 permanent jobs."

38. Development Research Associates, *Transient Housing Study* (1970), prepared for the San Francisco Redevelopment Agency.

39. "What We Should Ask Ourselves Regarding the Convention Center," mimeographed text of remarks (delivered at a private meeting organized by Richard Goldman), by Howard G. Sloane, managing director, N.Y. Coliseum (n.d. [1973]).

40. "Final Environmental Impact Statement, Yerba Buena Redevelopment Area, California R-59, in San Francisco, California," HUD-R09-EIS-78–2F, prepared by San Francisco Area Office, U.S. Department of Housing and Urban Development (1978), VII-56d.

41. "Official Statement, The Redevelopment Agency of the City and County of San Francisco, Relating to $97,000,000 Lease Revenue Bonds, Series 1979 (George R. Moscone Convention Center)," 20 March 1979, table 9, p. 31; later figures supplied by the Convention & Visitor's Bureau.

42. Material in this paragraph is from a letter to the author, dated 21 August 1997, from S. Dale Hess, San Francisco Convention & Visitors Bureau and from documentation accompanying the letter.

43. David Owen, "Meet Me in St. Louis: The People People Have a Convention Convention," *Harpers* (September 1983): 8–16.

44. "Final Environmental Impact Report, Yerba Buena Center," published 25 April 1978, vol. 2, 254.

45. Interview quoted in John Emshwiller's paper, "Yerba Buena: A New Colossus for San Francisco," submitted to Political Science 109 and Social Science 100BC, University of California, Berkeley, spring 1972.

46. *San Francisco Examiner*, 31 January 1972.

47. Marybeth Branaman, *South of Market Commercial and Industrial Survey* (S.F. Redevelopment Agency, July 1963), 6.

48. Malcolm Glover, "Unions, Emporium Argue over Lost Warehouse Jobs," *San Francisco Examiner*, 31 August 1983; "Unions Map National Fight to Hold Warehouse in S.F.," *San Francisco Examiner*, 12 September 1983.

49. New York State Comptroller, Fiscal Research Department, "Financing Convention Centers" (October 1981).

50. "Conventions Are Getting Smaller, Less Extravagant As Firms Cut Back," *Wall Street Journal*, 20 July 1982.

51. Newsletter of San Francisco Medical Society, November 1978.

52. Michelle Munz, "Convention Groups Sound Off about S.F.," *San Francisco Business Journal* (30 May 1983).

53. Don Lattin, "Becoming a Place Where Only the Wealthy Can Meet," *San Francisco Examiner*, 29 July 1981.

54. Jeff Jarvis, "Moscone Center Opening to Be Starter for Others," *San Francisco Examiner*, 11 November 1981.

55. Ibid.

56. William E. Schmidt, "Fewer Overseas Tourists Visiting U.S. in '82," *New York Times*, 1 August 1982; Steven Rattner, "Lower Prices Draw More Americans to Europe," *New York Times*, 2 August 1982.

57. Research Dept., Security Pacific Bank, "Northern Coastal California, Economic Issues in the Eighties," (San Francisco: Security Pacific Bank, March 1982), 10.

58. Wallace Turner, "Cable Car Halt May Strand Tourism," *New York Times,* 5 August 1982.

59. "Farms Cancel 1982 Convention in S.F.," *San Francisco Chronicle,* 30 August 1979.

60. "Cost of Convention Boycott to States That Have Not Ratified Equal Rights Proposal Put at $100 Million," *New York Times,* 4 April 1978.

61. "S.F. Told of Lost Conventions," *San Francisco Chronicle,* 11 September 1973.

62. McCabe, 4 February 1974; 14 August 1974; 15 May 1979; and 24 June 1981. For an international study of tourism's destructive impact on the very properties that led a place to become a tourist attraction, and measures taken to counter this self-destruction, see Fred P. Bosselman, *In the Wake of the Tourist: Managing Special Places in Eight Countries* (Washington, D.C.: The Conservation Foundation, 1978).

63. Charles McCabe, "Tourist Blight (3)," *San Francisco Chronicle,* 24 January 1979.

64. Tim Reiterman, "Why Moscone Center Is Losing Conventions," *San Francisco Sunday Examiner & Chronicle,* 5 December 1982.

65. "Rooftop Exhibit Hall Urged for Moscone," *San Francisco Chronicle,* 14 December 1985.

66. Marshall Kilduff, "Moscone Ballot Measure Gets Committee O.K.," *San Francisco Chronicle,* 11 July 1986.

67. "Panel Named to Study Enlarging Moscone Center," *San Francisco Chronicle,* 13 February 1986.

68. Reginald Smith, "$73 Million Plan to Double Size of Moscone Center," *San Francisco Chronicle,* 23 April 1986.

69. Marshall Kilduff, "Moscone Addition Price Soars to $140 million," *San Francisco Chronicle,* 8 July 1986; "Boas Offers Third Plan for Moscone Center," *San Francisco Chronicle,* 9 July 1986.

70. "Moscone Center Sequel May Be a Costly Boondoggle," *San Francisco Chronicle,* 21 July 1986.

71. Marshall Kilduff, "Moscone Bonds Ok'd for Ballot," *San Francisco Chronicle,* 22 July 1986.

72. Dale Lane, "S.F. Has an L.A. Lawyer to Thank for Selection," *San Jose Mercury News,* 22 April 1983.

73. Michelle Munz, "Business Donates to Get Convention," *San Francisco Business Journal,* 7 March 1983; Mark Simon, "S.F.'s Bid for the Democratic Convention," *Peninsula Times-Tribune,* 11 March 1983.

74. Marshall Kilduff, "Democrats' Scouts to Size Up S.F.," *San Francisco Chronicle,* 10 March 1983.

75. "Report on the Yerba Buena Convention and Exhibition Center," submitted by Chief Administrative Officer Roger Boas, 9 May 1978.

76. Pamela Abouzied, "Democratic Conclave to Be Costly," *Oakland Tribune,* 20 May 1983; Bruce J. Adams, "Demo Security Will Cost S.F. $1 Million More," *San Francisco Chronicle,* 20 April 1983; Marshall Kilduff, "Pricetag for Sprucing Up Hall for Demos," *San Francisco Chronicle,* 20 May 1983.

77. David Johnston, "How Dallas Tops S.F. in Readying for Convention," *San Francisco Examiner,* 13 October 1983.

78. Tim Reiterman and Andrew Ross, "City Told Year Ago of Demo Cost Glitch," *San Francisco Examiner,* 22 March 1984.

79. Tim Reiterman and James Finefrock, "How Democratic Convention Will Benefit Moscone Center," *San Francisco Examiner* 23 March 1984.

80. Larry Liebert, "Baseball and Politics in 1984," *San Francisco Examiner,* 22 April 1983.

81. "Demo Convention Site Selectors SF-Bound," *San Francisco Progress,* 9 March 1983; Michelle Munz, "Business Donates to Get Convention."

82. David Johnston, "Dems Finally Will Sign Convention Contract with the City," *San Francisco Examiner,* 12 September 1983.

83. First part of quotation from Laurence McQuillan, "Why S.F. Won: The Dems Must Focus on the West," *San Francisco Examiner,* 22 April 1983; last part of quotation from Carl Cannon, "How S.F. Wooed, Won Demos," *San Jose Mercury News,* 22 April 1983.

84. Dick Nolan, "Pass the Quiche," *San Francisco Examiner,* 21 April 1983.

85. Jerry Roberts, *Dianne Feinstein: Never Let Them See You Cry* (New York: Harper Collins, 1994), 213.

86. Evelyn Hsu, "Feinstein's Status Still on the Rise," *San Francisco Chronicle,* 14 July 1984.

CHAPTER 10. YERBA BUENA GARDENS, TODCO'S HOUSING, AND THE SOUTH OF MARKET NEIGHBORHOOD

1. See Leslie Kaufman, "Sony Builds a Mall. But Don't Call It That," *New York Times,* 25 July 1999. A Metreon brochure contains this hype: "When you think of famous corners, what comes to mind? Haight and Ashbury? Forty-second and Broadway? Well, now add Fourth and Mission to the list."

2. Rebecca Solnit and Susan Schwartzenberg, *Hollow City: The Siege of San Francisco and the Crisis of American Urbanism* (London: Verso, 2000), 52.

3. Herman's more extensive account of his initial meeting with Elberling is contained in a short essay that will be part of Ira Nowinski's updated edition of *No Vacancy,* a collection of South of Market photographs.

4. "The New Gray Neighbor," *Progressive Architecture* (August 1981): 72–75. For the "user needs survey" undertaken to provide basic information on design criteria, which architect Herman commissioned as part of his contract with TODCO, see Chester Hartman, Jerry Horovitz, and Robert Herman, "Designing with the Elderly: A User Needs Survey for Housing Low-Income Senior Citizens," *The Gerontologist* (August 1976): 303–11, reprinted in Chester Hartman, *Between Eminence and Notoriety: Four Decades of Radical Urban Planning* (New Brunswick, N.J.: Rutgers Center for Urban Policy Research, 2002), 165–72.

5. Tom Kent, "The House that TODCO Built," *Metro,* December/January 1981.

6. Tom Kent, introduction to unpublished portfolio of photographs of Woolf House and its construction, by Sandra Marks, one of the original TOOR staff members.

7. See S.F. Redevelopment Agency, "South of Market Earthquake Recovery Redevelopment Plan," 11 June 1990.

8. A lovely feature on TODCO's housing appears in Gerald D. Adams, "Tenants Enjoy Affordable Rooms with a View: Low-Income Elderly Renters Are Right at Home in SoMa's Woolf House," *San Francisco Chronicle*, 7 January 2001.

9. Letter to author from Robert Herman, dated 13 July 1991.

10. See Elberling's "Remembrance of My 18 Years at TODCO," in Ira Nowinski's updated *No Vacancy*.

11. See also Dexter Waugh and Corrie Anders, "South of Market Land Values up—Low-income People Out," *San Francisco Examiner*, 2 June 1983.

12. Jean Fuller Anderson, "New Wave of Entrepreneurs Is Rejuvenating South of Market Showplace Square Area," *San Francisco Business*, 26 July 1982; Jack Miller, "New Owners Plan for Big Showplace," *San Francisco Sunday Examiner & Chronicle*, 22 May 1983.

13. See Gayle S. Rubin, "The Miracle Mile: South of Market and Gay Male Leather," in *Reclaiming San Francisco*, ed. James Brook, Chris Carlsson, and Nancy J. Peters (San Francisco: City Lights Books, 1998), 247–72.

14. See John McCloud, "Builders Bet on San Francisco High-Rises," *New York Times*, 29 August 1999.

CHAPTER 11. CITY HALL

1. Eugene C. Lee and Jonathan S. Rothman, "San Francisco's District System Alters Electoral Politics," *National Civic Review* 67 (April 1978): 173–78.

2. Dexter Waugh, "Community Congresses: The New Way to Carve a Consensus," *San Francisco Examiner*, 16 May 1977.

3. Duffy Jennings, "Group Seeks Repeal of District Elections," *San Francisco Chronicle*, 2 December 1976.

4. Ibid.

5. Jerry Burns, "He Says He's Fighting a Radical Takeover," *San Francisco Chronicle*, 26 May 1977.

6. Herb Caen, "View from the Middle," *San Francisco Chronicle*, 12 June 1977.

7. National League of Cities, "Types of Representation by Population Ranges and Forms of Government," database report, 31 July 1997.

8. Dick Nolan, "First You Lose Contact, Then You Lose Control," *San Francisco Sunday Examiner & Chronicle*, 12 June 1977.

9. "Prop. T: Should the Verdict Stand?" *San Francisco Business* (January 1977).

10. Jerry Burns, "How Two Politicians Soured on Each Other," *San Francisco Chronicle*, 18 July 1977.

11. Jerry Burns, "Moscone Angered by 'Radical Plot' Charge," *San Francisco Chronicle*, 27 May 1977.

12. Charles McCabe, "August 2, Last Hurrah?" *San Francisco Chronicle*, 6 June 1977.

13. Jerry Burns, "Coming Soon—Bitter City Election," *San Francisco Chronicle*, 7 May 1977.

14. Ibid.

15. "The Pettit Report on the Politics of San Francisco," 1, no. 2 (21 July 1980).

16. Herb Caen's 12 June 1977 *Chronicle* column, as quoted in Bob Levering, "The Back Room Plot behind Prop. B," *San Francisco Bay Guardian*, 16 June 1977.

17. Jerry Burns, "The Spending on Props. A & B," *San Francisco Chronicle*, 28 July 1977.

18. Charles McCabe, "The Last Hurrah," *San Francisco Chronicle*, 22 August 1977.

19. Lee and Rothman, "San Francisco's District System," 176, 178.

20. Ibid. Jerry Burns, "Winning Costs Less in S.F. District Elections," *San Francisco Chronicle*, 14 January 1978.

21. Material in this section comes largely from interviews with Mike Weiss, author of *Double Play: The San Francisco City Hall Killings* (Reading, Mass.: Addison Wesley 1984), and from his articles, "Black Monday," *San Francisco Magazine* (November 1982): 63–69, and "Trial and Error," *Rolling Stone* (12 July 1979): 47–49. A docudrama on these events, titled *The Dan White Incident*, written and directed by Steve Dobbins, premiered at the People's Theater, Fort Mason, San Francisco, 29 March 1983. The high drama of the event has led to other treatments as well: a documentary movie, *The Times of Harvey Milk*, produced by Richard Schmeichen, 1986; a docu-opera, *Harvey Milk*, music by Stewart Wallacer, libretto by Michael Korie, which premiered in Houston and was produced as well by the NYC Opera (see Bernard Holland, " 'Harvey Milk,' a Gay Opera as a Grand Coming Out Party," *New York Times*, 6 April 1995, and Tim Golden, "A Gay Camelot Comes Home to Find It's True," *New York Times*, 30 November 1996); and a musical, *The Harvey Milk Show*, by Dan Pruitt and Patrick Hutchinson (reviewed, quite negatively, by Lloyd Rose, "The Harvey Milk Show: A Wasted Opportunity," *Washington Post*, 1 May 1997).

22. Randy Shilts, *The Mayor of Castro Street: The Life and Times of Harvey Milk* (New York: St. Martin's Press, 1982), 200. According to Peter Wiley and Robert Gottlieb, "Simmons got his collection of shops and restaurants approved by the Planning Commission and Board of Supervisors through a judicious distribution of campaign funds and leases at his new enterprise to members of the Board and Commission" (*Empires in the Sun: The Rise of the New American West* [New York: G. P. Putnam's, 1982], 133).

23. Shilts, *The Mayor of Castro Street*, 200.

24. Weiss, "Trial and Error."

25. "Dan White Said Involved in Book-movie Deal," *Washington Post*, 16 February 1984.

26. "Dan White Suicide," *San Francisco Chronicle*, 22 October 1985.

27. Weiss, "Trial and Error."

28. Ibid.

29. See Shiva Naipaul, *Black and White: Journey to Nowhere, a New World Tragedy* (London: Abacus, Sphere Books, 1981); Deborah Layton, *Seductive Poison: A Jonestown Survivor's Story of Life and Death in the People's Temple* (New York: Anchor Books, 1998); Tim Reiterman and John Jacobs, *Raven: The Untold Story of Rev. Jim Jones and His People* (New York: Dutton, 1982).

30. Larry Liebert, "Feinstein Dined, Interviewed, Praised in N.Y.," *San Francisco Chronicle*, 5 April 1984.

31. Jeff Gillenkirk, "Feinstein in the Middle," *San Francisco* (December 1981): 76–79.

32. Jeff Gillenkirk, "Purse Strings Persuasion," *New West* (19 May 1980): NC20–22.

33. See Jerry Roberts, "New S.F. Try for District Elections," *San Francisco Chronicle*, 10 April 1987.

34. Venise Wagner, "Blacks Losing Clout in S.F.," *San Francisco Examiner*, 29 October 2000.

35. For a discussion of the G and H campaigns and their underlying issues and politics, see Richard DeLeon, Steven Hill, and Lisel Blash, "The Campaign for Proposition H and Preference Voting in San Francisco, 1996," *Representation*, vol. 35, no. 4 (winter 1998): 265–74.

36. Carl Irving, "Difficult, Principled Panthers Who Started It," *San Francisco Examiner*, 20 April 1983. See also Evelyn Hsu, "Roots of the Recall," *San Francisco Chronicle*, 4 April 1983.

37. Tim Redmond and Alan Kay, "Feinstein vs. Feinstein," *San Francisco Bay Guardian*, 6 April 1983.

38. Larry Liebert, "Feinstein's Big Bankroll in Recall Battle," *San Francisco Chronicle*, 18 March 1983; "Many Contributors Have Ties to City Agencies, Commissions," *San Francisco Examiner*, 3 April 1983; Reginald Smith, "Mayor's Friends Raised $441,543 for Recall Fight," *San Francisco Chronicle*, 15 April 1983; David Johnston, "Corporate Cash Swells Feinstein's Antirecall Coffer," *San Francisco Examiner*, 3 April 1983; David Johnston, "Feinstein Has Large Fund for Recall Battle," *San Francisco Examiner*, 18 March 1983.

39. Smith, "Mayor's Friends."

40. Johnston, "Corporate Cash."

41. Redmond and Kay, "Feinstein vs. Feinstein"; see also editorial, *San Francisco Bay Guardian*, 13 April 1983.

42. Larry Liebert, "Kopp's Ex-Campaign Chief Now Guiding Feinstein," *San Francisco Chronicle*, 10 February 1983.

43. Editorial, *San Francisco Bay Guardian*, 13 April 1983.

44. Wallace Turner, "San Francisco Politics Is Something Else," *New York Times*, 17 April 1983.

45. Larry Liebert, "*60 Minutes* and S.F. Recall," *San Francisco Chronicle*, 25 April 1983; see also Dick Nolan, "Blurred Images," *San Francisco Examiner*, 27 April 1983.

46. Wallace Turner, "Bid to Oust S.F. Mayor Polarizes Splinter Groups," *New York Times*, 26 March 1983.

47. David Johnston, "Feinstein: In or Out?" *San Francisco Examiner*, 20 April 1983.

48. Larry Liebert, "Feinstein's Foes Are Worried," *San Francisco Chronicle*, 23 April 1983.

49. Redmond and Kay, "Feinstein vs. Feinstein."

50. Marshall Kilduff, "Recall Fight Cost Mayor $600,000," *San Francisco Chronicle*, 14 July 1983.

51. Liebert, "Feinstein's Foes."

52. Johnston, "Feinstein: In or Out?" For a review of this technique, see Lisa Romano, "Growing Use of Mail Voting Puts Its Stamp on Campaigns," *Washington Post*, 29 November 1998.

53. David Johnston and Carl Irving, "80 Percent. Feinstein Looks to November: We'll Cream 'Em," *San Francisco Examiner*, 27 April 1983.

54. Liebert, "Feinstein's Foes Are Worried."

55. Jim Kelly, "Feinstein's Victory Receives Worldwide Coverage," *San Francisco Progress*, 29 April 1983.

56. Larry Liebert, "The Winners and Losers," *San Francisco Chronicle*, 28 April 1983.

57. Guy Wright, "Beyond Recall," *San Francisco Chronicle*, 1 May 1983.

58. For a review of Burton's career, see John Jacobs, *A Rage for Justice: The Passion and Politics of Phillip Burton* (Berkeley and Los Angeles: University of California Press, 1995).

59. Warren Hinckle, "Iron-heeled Justice," *San Francisco Chronicle*, 1 August 1983.

60. Jerry Roberts, *Dianne Feinstein: Never Let Them See You Cry* (New York: Harper Collins, 1994), 232, 234. A fairly balanced review of Feinstein's years in office can be found in the three-part series by Roberts and Dave Farrell, *San Francisco Chronicle*, 31 August, 1 September, and 2 September 1987.

61. Roberts, *Dianne Feinstein*, 219.

62. Larry Liebert and Reginald Smith, "Mayor Confident She'll Overcome Year of Surprises," *San Francisco Chronicle*, 6 December 1986.

63. See Andrew Ross and Dexter Waugh, "Feinstein Tarnished by Deficit," *San Francisco Examiner*, 28 February 1988.

64. Jerry Roberts, "Feinstein Won't Run for Sala Burton's Seat," *San Francisco Chronicle*, 12 February 1987.

65. The somewhat chaotic, disaligned state of San Francisco politics at the time was well captured in Jerry Roberts's, "When S.F. Politics Became a Free-For-All," *San Francisco Chronicle*, 26 March 1987.

66. See the editorial, "Give 'em Hell, Harry," *San Francisco Bay Guardian*, 25 March 1987.

67. See John Jacobs, "Feinstein Fund Raising Tied to Husband's Wealth," *San Francisco Examiner*, 3 December 1989.

68. See Robert B. Gunnison, "The Money Is Flowing to State's Gubernatorial Candidates," *San Francisco Chronicle*, 23 March 1990.

69. See "Maternity-Leave Law Found Illegal by Judge," *New York Times*, 22 March 1984; see also, Evelyn Hsu, "Feinstein's Stand on Issues—Some Feminists Are Wary," *San Francisco Chronicle*, 31 October 1983.

70. Roberts, *Dianne Feinstein*, 274.

71. See Marsha Ginsberg, "Bid for Senate Creates a New Feminist," *San Francisco Examiner*, 8 March 1992.

72. B. Drummond Ayres Jr., "California Race for Senate Seen as Costly Battle," *New York Times*, 11 March 1994; Todd S. Purdum, "California's Governor's Race: A New Height in Spending," *New York Times*, 13 February 1998.

The extraordinary financial requirements to run statewide in the country's most populous state were described as follows by California's other U.S. senator: " 'Let me tell you about the California race,' said Senator Barbara Boxer, a Democrat who described needing to raise $10,000 a day, 365 days a year, every year, in order to be financed for re-election." Francis X. Clines, "Senators Bemoan Unshakable Habit," *New York Times*, 20 March 1996.

73. Todd S. Purdum, "Feinstein to Stay Out of Race for Governor," *New York Times*, 21 January 1998.

74. "Mayor Agnos has taken steps to dismantle a Planning Commission that has presided over the biggest highrise office building boom in San Francisco's history." Gerald Adams, "Planning: Agnos Gets a Clean Slate," *San Francisco Examiner*, 12 January 1988.

75. Richard Edward DeLeon, *Left Coast City: Progressive Politics in San Francisco, 1975–1991* (Lawrence: University Press of Kansas, 1992), 158, 159.

76. Bill Mandel, "Goddess Politics in the City," *San Francisco Examiner*, 15 September 1991.

77. Raymond F. McLeod, "How Absentee Voting Changed Mayor's Race," *San Francisco Chronicle*, 13 December 1991, and "Asians Crucial for Jordan," *San Francisco Chronicle*, 12 December 1991.

78. "New Mayor's 'Shaky' Start Has San Francisco Puzzled," *New York Times*, 18 April 1992.

79. "Mayor's New Twist—the Dim Switch," *San Francisco Examiner*, 29 January 1992.

80. Stephen McGovern, *The Politics of Downtown Development: Dynamic Political Cultures in San Francisco and Washington, D.C.* (Lexington: University Press of Kentucky, 1998), 182.

81. See "Jury Finds San Francisco Police Violated Newspaper's Rights," *New York Times*, 18 September 1994; Lou Cannon, "Police Chief's Firing Is Focus of Noisy Protests in San Francisco," *Washington Post*, 22 May 1992.

82. See "S.F. Police Chief Is Dismissed," *New York Times*, 16 May 1992.

83. Cannon, "Police Chief's Firing."

84. See, for example, Gerald Adams, "Jordan Board Bucks Agnos Trend: Mayor Stocks Planning Board with Progrowth Members," *San Francisco Examiner,* 19 March 1992.

85. Richard E. DeLeon, "Progressive Politics in the Left Coast City: San Francisco," in *Racial Politics in American Cities,* ed. Rufus P. Browning, Dale Rogers Marshall, and David H. Tabb, 2d ed. (New York: Longman, 1997), 139, 155.

86. Brown's story-book life history has been told in many places—see, for example, James Richardson, *Willie Brown: A Biography* (Berkeley and Los Angeles: University of California Press, 1996).

87. Richard L. Berke, "California Term Limits: Political Musical Chairs," *New York Times,* 17 February 1994.

88. For a somewhat pessimistic broader view of this potential schism, see DeLeon, "Progressive Politics."

89. William Claiborne, "San Francisco Race Turns Out to Be a Contest, Not a Coronation," *Washington Post,* 4 November 1995.

90. B. Drummond Ayres Jr., "It's Official: Willie Brown Runs for Mayor," *New York Times,* 4 June 1995.

91. Cary Goldberg, "Willie Brown's Latest Performance Is a Hit," *New York Times,* 20 February 1996.

92. Steve Wiegand, "Willie Brown—Another Year of Money, Power," *San Francisco Chronicle,* 30 November 1985.

93. Marshall Frady, "An American Political Fable: How San Francisco's Mayor Willie Brown Became One Consummate Example of Democratic Inaction," *New Yorker,* 21–28 October 1996, 200.

94. "Nowadays [while in the assembly] Brown raises an average of $40,000 a day in campaign funds during election season" (Wiegand, "Willie Brown").

95. Neil Henry, "California's Ex-Speaker Still Making Waves," *San Francisco Chronicle,* 18 June 1995.

96. *San Jose Mercury News,* 14 February 1984.

97. Bill Wallace and Steve Wiegand, "Brown's Law Firm Serves Big Developers," *San Francisco Chronicle,* 13 February 1988.

98. Gale Cook and Steven Capps, "SP, Developers Top Brown Clients," *San Francisco Examiner,* 6 March 1984.

99. Marcelo Rodriguez, "Ten at the Top," *San Francisco Magazine* (September 1982): 60–71.

100. Steven Capps, "Brown Says He's Not Giving up Law Practice," *San Francisco Examiner,* 6 March 1984.

101. David Willman and Dan Meyers, "Brown's Choice of Clients Invites Conflict Questions," *San Jose Mercury News,* 12 February 1984.

102. "Willie Brown Is Ignoring the Whispers in Sacramento," *San Francisco Chronicle,* 13 February 1988.

103. Henry, "California's Ex-Speaker."

104. David L. Kirp, review of Richardson's *Willie Brown,* "The Black Kid Can Count," *The Nation* (25 November 1996): 30.

105. B. Drummond Ayres Jr., "California Speaker Frustrates G.O.P. One Last Time," *New York Times,* 6 June 1995. For other descriptions of this dizzying display of power and egotism, see William Claiborne, "California Speaker Hangs on by a Thread," *Washington Post,* 6 December 1994; "California Speaker Resigns," *Washington Post,* 15 September 1995; B. Drummond Ayres Jr., "California's Squabbling Legislature Just Stumbles Along," *New York Times,* 9 July 1995; William Claiborne, "Brown Surrenders the Speaker's Reins, but Pulls the Strings," *Washington Post,* 7 June 1995.

106. Quoted in Henry, "California's Ex-Speaker."

107. "Holding Willie Brown Accountable," *San Francisco Bay Guardian,* 21 March 1984.

108. Jim Balderston, "The Aquarium Conspiracy," *San Francisco Bay Guardian,* 31 May 1989; Greg Lucas, "New Probe of Willie Brown," *San Francisco Chronicle,* 11 August 1989.

109. Craig McLaughlin, "The Six Conflicts of Willie Brown," *San Francisco Bay Guardian,* 27 September 1987.

110. See John Boudreau, "Brides, Grooms and Partners," *Washington Post,* 26 March 1996.

111. "The Source" column, *Washington Post,* 28 February 1997.

112. Frady, "An American Political Fable."

113. Ibid.

114. Randy Shaw, "Wayward Willie," *In These Times,* 3 March 1997.

115. Frady, "An American Political Fable."

116. Rene Sanchez, "Booming City, Embattled Mayor," *Washington Post,* 26 October 1999.

117. Erin McCormick, "Money Isn't Kingmaker in S.F. Mayor's Contest: Reilly's Outlay Estimated at $140 Per Vote; Could Be a National Record," *San Francisco Examiner,* 4 November 1999.

118. Ilene Lelchuk, "Generation Gap in SF Mayor Race," *San Francisco Examiner,* 9 December 1999.

119. Carla Marinucci, "Clinton Collects Half-Million in S.F.: He Lends Support to Brown in Mayor's Re-election Bid," *San Francisco Chronicle,* 1 December 1999; Rachel Gordon, Zachary Coile, and Ilene Lelchuk, "Da Landslide," *San Francisco Examiner,* 15 December 1999.

120. Erin McCormick and Scott Winokur, "Tab for Mayor's Landslide: $5 Million," *San Francisco Examiner,* 16 December 1999; see also Erin McCormick, "Soft Money Floods Campaign for Brown," *San Francisco Examiner,* 9 December 1999.

121. McCormick and Winokur, "Tab"; McCormick, "Soft Money."

122. Robert Salladay and Lance Williams, "State Party Sending in Support Troops for S.F. Mayor's Re-election Campaign," *San Francisco Examiner,* 8 December 1999. The account notes that "some staffers . . . complained that their bosses were pressuring them to volunteer."

123. George F. Will, "Willie Brown Besieged," *Washington Post,* 7 November 1999.

124. For a review of Ammiano's record as a supervisor, see Erin McCormick, "Ammiano Has Mixed Success on Board," *San Francisco Examiner*, 8 December 1999.

125. Evelyn Nieves, "San Francisco Mayor Easily Wins Another Term," *New York Times*, 16 December 1999.

126. The quotation is from David Lee, executive director of the Chinese American Voter Education Committee, as reported in Zachary Coile and Rachel Gordon, "S.F. Mayoral Race Catches National Spotlight," *San Francisco Examiner*, 5 December 1999.

127. "Question Authority?" *San Francisco Examiner*, 12 December 1999.

128. William Booth, "Out Man's Odds: Tom Ammiano Turns the San Francisco Mayoral Race Upside Down," *Washington Post*, 13 December 1999.

129. "Election Changes Rules for Brown," *San Francisco Examiner*, 15 December 1999.

130. Rachel Gordon, "Incumbent Katz Throws Curve Ball in Supes' Race," *San Francisco Examiner*, 9 July 2000.

131. Rachel Gordon and Katherine Seligman, "Uproar over Supervisor's Eviction of Woman, 64," *San Francisco Examiner*, 6 April 2000; David R. Baker and Jonathan Curiel, "Evicted S.F. Tenant Sues Supervisor Amos Brown," *San Francisco Chronicle*, 14 September 2000.

132. Rachel Gordon, "Soft Money Lifts Supes' Spending Cap," *San Francisco Examiner*, 17 October 2000.

133. Ibid.

134. Phillip Matier and Andrew Ross, "Brown's Supervisor Picks Showered with 'Soft Money,' " *San Francisco Chronicle*, 1 November 2000. For additional detail on Brown's use of soft money, see Lance Williams and Chuck Finnie, "Gusher of 'Soft Money' a Bonanza for S.F. Mayor," *San Francisco Chronicle*, 2 May 2001.

135. Johnny Brannon, "Big $$$ No Influence in Runoff Results," *San Francisco Examiner*, 18 December 2000.

136. Brannon, "Big $$$." The writer is quoting David Lee, director of the Chinese American Voter Education Committee.

137. Ilene Lelchuk, " 'Call Me Matt': Eclectic, Informal Gonzalez Lends a Green Party Presence to Board," *San Francisco Chronicle*, 21 February 2001. For Mark Sanchez information, see http://www.sfgate.com/news/baycitynews, 20 December 2000.

138. Nina Wu, "City Likely to Face Redistricting," *San Francisco Examiner*, 3 April 2001.

139. Angela Previn, "Newsom Saw City Hall Battle in the Making," *San Francisco Examiner*, 3 April 2001.

140. Rachel Gordon, "Supervisor Apologizes to Brown for Spat," *San Francisco Chronicle*, 6 April 2001.

141. *San Francisco Examiner*, 7 December 1976.

142. Donald Canter, "Hamilton Wins Promotion to Top Redevelop Post," *San Francisco Examiner*, 2 March 1977; Redevelopment Agency Commission meeting

minutes of 21 December 1976, 4 and 11 January 1977; Marshall Kilduff, "A Bitter Split in S.F. Redevelop Agency," *San Francisco Chronicle*, 1 January 1977.

143. Marshall Kilduff, "Vocal Black Pastor Loses S.F. Post," *San Francisco Chronicle*, 28 September 1978.

144. Canter, "Hamilton Wins Promotion."

145. See "High-rent Senior Housing Ok'd," *San Francisco Chronicle*, 24 September 1986; "Controversial Japantown Project Ok'd," *San Francisco Chronicle*, 11 February 1987.

146. Gerald Adams, "The Bid Decision," *San Francisco Examiner*, 18 June 1980.

147. "L.A. Developer to Head S.F. Agency," *San Francisco Chronicle*, 20 May 1987.

148. "2 Nominated to Redevelopment Panel," *San Francisco Chronicle*, 10 September 1988.

149. San Francisco Redevelopment Agency, "Mission Statement: Housing and Economic Development Policies," adopted April 1989; see also San Francisco Redevelopment Agency, "A Redevelopment Report: 1991," especially the contributions by Art Agnos ("A New Era, a New Mission") and Buck Bagot ("The Decade for [Truly] Affordable Housing").

150. Steve Massey, "New City Hall Password Is 'Slow Growth,' " *San Francisco Chronicle*, 1 March 1989.

151. "S.F. Renewal Agency Builds New Image—'Affordable Housing' Replaces Bulldozers," *San Francisco Chronicle*, 20 August 1991.

152. John King, "Hom's Lawyer Calls Hearing A Farce," *San Francisco Chronicle*, 18 May 1993.

153. "Matier and Ross" column, *San Francisco Chronicle*, 15 October 1997.

154. David Pasztor, "The Redevelopment Sinkhole," *SF Weekly*, 4–10 February 1998.

155. Ibid.

156. Allan B. Jacobs, *Making City Planning Work* (Chicago: American Society of Planning Officials, 1978), 20–21. Revealingly, the index to Jacobs's book contains not a single entry to Yerba Buena.

157. Bruce B. Brugmann, "Mayor Moscone's Private 'Dear Dick' Letter to Chronicle Publisher," *San Francisco Bay Guardian*, 8 February 1979; emphasis in original.

158. Gerald Adams, "Mayor's Pro-Building Planners," *San Francisco Examiner*, 12 March 1981.

159. Susan Sward, " 'Conflict' Issue Forces 2 from S.F. Commission," *San Francisco Chronicle*, 16 August 1985; Marshall Kilduff, "Why the Mayor Moved Quickly on the Conflict Issue," *San Francisco Chronicle*, 17 August 1985.

160. "First Asian on S.F. Police Commission," *San Francisco Chronicle*, 2 February 1984.

161. Gerald Adams, "The Perpetual Crisis," *California Living*, 28 August 1983.

162. Moira Johnston, "The Political Odyssey of Dianne Feinstein," *Savvy* (September 1983): 38–42; Adams, "The Perpetual Crisis."

163. "What Goes Up," documentary produced by Bob Calo and John Roszak, KQED-TV, aired 22 and 26 December 1982.

164. Quoted in McGovern, *The Politics of Downtown Development*, 79.

165. Sharon Elise Dunn, "S.F.'s Planning Commission: Out of Control?" *San Francisco Bay Guardian*, 2 November 1983.

166. Gerald Adams, "Rezoning Proposed for Huge Sector of S.F.," *San Francisco Examiner*, 13 November 1981.

167. "Planning a Planning Commission," *San Francisco Examiner*, 17 January 1988.

168. Kilduff, "Why the Mayor Moved Quickly."

169. "Matier and Ross" column, *San Francisco Chronicle*, 15 October 1997.

170. Allan B. Jacobs, "Notes on Planning Practice and Education," in *The Profession of City Planning: Changes, Images, and Challenges, 1950–2000*, ed. Lloyd Rodwin and Bishwapriya Sanyal (New Brunswick, N.J.: Rutgers Center for Urban Policy Research, 2000), 48.

171. Chuck Finnie, "Ex- Planning Chief Calls Firing Political," *San Francisco Examiner*, 19 September 2000.

172. Chuck Finnie, "Newest Planner Is Robert Lurie Kin," *San Francisco Examiner*, 21 September 2000.

173. Edward Epstein and Dan Levy, "Ammiano Rips 49ers Mall Deal As a Boondoggle," *San Francisco Examiner*, 3 December 1999.

174. Duffy Jennings, "A Redevelopment Choice Questioned," *San Francisco Chronicle*, 22 October 1976; Carol Kroot, "Nominee Wexler Conflict?" *San Francisco Progress*, 24 October 1976.

175. Gerald Adams, "Wexler Resigns City Redevelopment Agency Post," *San Francisco Examiner*, 8 December 1980.

176. Marshall Kilduff, "$35 Million Van Ness Condo Plan," *San Francisco Chronicle*, 15 September 1982.

177. Marshall Kilduff, "Favoritism Denied: S.F. Attorney's Ties to Redevelop Agency," *San Francisco Chronicle*, 1 May 1985.

178. Marshall Kilduff and Evelyn Hsu, "It Was a Busy Commission Meeting," *San Francisco Chronicle*, 6 November 1982.

179. "Renewal Agency Aide Resigns Post," *San Francisco Chronicle*, 9 June 1981; Redevelopment Agency Commission meeting minutes of 7 February 1984.

180. Marshall Kilduff, "Height Exemption Is Okd for 12-Story Senior Tower," *San Francisco Chronicle*, 22 July 1987.

181. Kilduff and Hsu, "It Was a Busy Commission Meeting."

182. Chuck Finnie, "Brown Chastises Cronyism: Demands Disclosure from Commissioners," *San Francisco Chronicle*, 31 January 2001.

183. "New City 'Conflict' Problem," *San Francisco Chronicle*, 17 December 1974.

184. Redevelopment Agency Commission meeting minutes, 20 July 1982.

185. Gerald Adams, "City's Secret Switch on Yerba Buena," *San Francisco Examiner*, 12 April 1993.

186. See "He, 3 Pals Caught near Castroville," *San Francisco Examiner*, 10 January 1981; "Arrest of S.F. Official Puzzles His Supervisor," *San Francisco Examiner*, 11 January 1981. The agency's position: "The matter of Phillips's employment was 'between Morris Phillips and Mr. Tishman.' " See Reginald Smith, "Convicted Renewal Agency Executive on Developer's Payroll," *San Francisco Chronicle*, 3 May 1985.

187. Redevelopment Agency Commission meeting minutes, 5 October 1982; 11 May 1982; 25 May 1982; 25 January 1983; 19 October 1982; 7 April 1981; 31 January 1984.

188. Steve Oney, "The Skyline That Ate San Francisco," *California Magazine* (May 1983): 72–81.

189. Ibid.

190. Kilduff and Hsu, "It Was a Busy Commission Meeting."

191. Marshall Kilduff, "Gordon Lau Quits Port Commission," *San Francisco Chronicle*, 28 January 1986; "Another S.F. Commissioner Resigns over Mayor's Order," *San Francisco Chronicle*, 29 January 1986.

CHAPTER 12. HIGH-RISES AND THE ANTIHIGH-RISE MOVEMENT

1. Steve Oney, "The Skyline That Ate San Francisco," *California Magazine* (May 1983): 72–81, 137–43.

2. Bruce Brugmann and Greggar Sletteland, eds., *The Ultimate Highrise: San Francisco's Mad Rush toward the Sky* (San Francisco: San Francisco Bay Guardian Books, 1971).

3. A summary of these studies appears in the "Draft Environmental Impact Report, 222 Kearny Street," San Francisco Department of City Planning, 81.687E, publication date 11 March 1983, table C-3, 159.

4. San Francisco Planning and Urban Renewal Association, "Impact of Intensive Highrise Development on San Francisco," 1975.

5. Sedway-Cooke et al., "Downtown San Francisco Conservation and Development Planning Program, Phase I Study," October 1979.

6. Arthur Andersen and Company, "Downtown Highrise District Cost Revenue Study," November 1980.

7. San Francisco Tomorrow Newsletter, issue no. 89, January 1983, quoting article by Philip Hager in the *Los Angeles Times*, 18 May 1981.

8. Allan Temko, "A Plan to Let Sunshine into S.F.," *San Francisco Chronicle*, 18 July 1983.

9. Gerald Adams, "50 Skyscrapers Later, What Will Our Cities Look Like?" *San Francisco Examiner*, 6 January 1982.

10. "Draft Environmental Impact Report, 222 Kearny Street." Traffic/transit data are from table 9, 108.

11. See the articles by Michael Cabanatuan, Steve Rubenstein, Pia Sarkar, and Justino Aquila, *San Francisco Chronicle*, 28, 29, 30 January 2001. BART is not alone among the more recent subway systems in experiencing growing

pains: See the two-part series by Lyndsey Layton, "Metro at 25: Region's Subway System Begins to Show Its Age, Limits," on Washington, D.C.'s, problems, *Washington Post*, 25, 26 March 2001.

12. "Draft Environmental Impact Report, 222 Kearny Street." Traffic/transit data are from table 9, 109.

13. Ibid., table 10, 111; table D-5, 205.

14. Michael Cabanatuan, "Bay Area Ranked among Worst in Nation," *San Francisco Chronicle*, 17 November 1999.

15. "Draft Environmental Impact Report, 222 Kearny Street," table 11, 112; table D-4, 203.

16. Ibid., 119–22.

17. For a review of the impact of high-rise development in other cities, see the three-part series on Manhattan in the *New York Times*, 12–14 July 1982, "Building Boom Raises Questions on Life in a Denser Manhattan" (Paul Goldberger), "Manhattan in Change: Shaping Vital Services" (Deirdre Carmody), and "Manhattan in Change: The Future of the Economy" (Frank J. Prial); Sharon Feigon, *The Impact of Downtown Development on Seattle Housing Costs* (Scientists/Citizens Organization on Policy Issues, January 1982), and *The Downtown Boom: A Report on the Costs of Downtown Growth. Who Loses? Who Wins?* (Seattle: Freemont Public Assoc., n.d. [1980–81]).

18. A case study of the U.S. Steel controversy can be found in Frederick M. Wirt, *Power in the City: Decision Making in San Francisco* (Berkeley and Los Angeles: University of California Press, 1974), 197–204.

19. Ibid., 204–7, for a short case study of the first Duskin initiative.

20. From talk by Moscone at candidates' night before 250 members of the All People's Coalition in the Visitacion Valley area, and from a September 1975 interview with Moscone by *San Francisco Bay Guardian* reporter Jerry Roberts, as cited in David Johnston, "Was the Alleged $10,000 Hughes Bribe Merely a Downpayment to Influence Moscone on Airport Expansion?" *San Francisco Bay Guardian*, 5 October 1978.

21. Allan B. Jacobs, *Making City Planning Work* (Chicago: American Society of Planning Officials, 1978), 40. Moscone, by contrast, made a conscious attempt to place women and minorities on the City's boards and commissions; of 207 such appointments during his first two years, 82 were women, 63 of whom were nonwhite, and another 63 were nonwhite males (Carol Kroot, "The New Mayor's View . . . His First Two Years," *San Francisco Progress*, 1 January 1978; the figures are those offered by Moscone).

22. Personal communication to the author from Jack Morrison, 21 April 1983.

23. "Draft Environmental Impact Report, 222 Kearny Street," appendix A.

24. San Francisco Planning and Urban Research Association, "Managing Growth in San Francisco: A Highrise Initiative Forces Government Action," Report #157 (October 1979).

25. Paul Goldberger, "Limitation on Skyscrapers Urged in San Francisco," *New York Times*, 26 August 1983; Paul Goldberger, "San Francisco Plans a Coherent Future," *New York Times*, 2 October 1983.

26. San Francisco Department of City Planning, "The Downtown Plan—Proposal for Citizen Review" (August 1983). An environmental impact report on the Downtown Plan was released by the Planning Department on 16 March 1984.

27. *The Commonwealth*, 23 January 1984.

28. A skillful analysis of the realities of the plan and the City's tactics in publicizing it is to be found in Tim Redmond, "The Downtown Plan—A Highrise Developer's Dream," *San Francisco Bay Guardian*, 31 August 1983.

29. Harold Gilliam, "The Downtown Plan," *San Francisco Sunday Examiner & Chronicle*, 23 October 1983.

30. "So What's up with Downtown? The Downtown Plan: A Citizens Critique," prepared for Teach-In, 16 January 1984, by San Franciscans for Reasonable Growth in conjunction with the San Francisco Plan Campaign. Emphasis in original.

31. Bruce Pettit, "Prop. M vs. Downtown Plan," *San Francisco Examiner*, 3 September 1983.

32. Gerald Adams, "Downtown Blueprint Would Control Spread," *San Francisco Examiner*, 30 July 1982.

33. Allan Temko. "New S.F. Plan Bows to the Past," *San Francisco Chronicle*, 8 October 1983.

34. See Kirstin E. Downey, "Developer Payment to S.F. Citizen Group Likely to Stir Debate," *San Francisco Business Journal* (28 January 1985); "Payment Avalanche May Grow: Developers Angry," *San Francisco Business Journal* (11 February 1985), and editorial in same issue, referring to payments made to Hestor as attorney's fees and to SFRG as part of these settlements.

35. Reginald Smith and Larry Liebert, "D.A. Investigates Highrise Foes—at Mayor's Orders," *San Francisco Chronicle*, 18 April 1985.

36. *San Francisco Bay Guardian*, 13 February 1985.

37. This section draws largely on the detailed descriptions in Richard Edward DeLeon's "The Birth of the Slow-Growth Movement and the Battle for Proposition M," chap. 4 in *Left Coast City: Progressive Politics in San Francisco, 1965–1991* (Lawrence: University Press of Kansas, 1992), 57–83.

38. Ibid., 58.

39. See table 6.1, 136, in Stephen J. McGovern, *The Politics of Downtown Development: Dynamic Political Cultures in San Francisco and Washington, D.C.* (Lexington: University Press of Kentucky, 1998).

40. See John Jacobs and Gerald D. Adams, "S.F.'s Highrise Insiders: How They Work," *San Francisco Examiner*, 15 June 1986, first of a superb four-part series (see also the followup articles appearing in the next three days' *Examiner*).

41. DeLeon, *Left Coast City*, 56.

42. Christine Hanley, "San Francisco's Office Spaces Snapped Up at Breakneck Speed," *Associated Press*, 17 April 2000; Rachel Gordon, "Controversial Plan on Dot-Com Growth," *San Francisco Examiner*, 18 April 2000; Katherine Seligman, "Dot-Coms Dominate Space in SoMa," *San Francisco Examiner*, 26 March 2000; Matt Smith, "Make Room for Dot-Coms," *SF Weekly*, 16–22 February 2000.

43. Seligman, "Dot-Coms Dominate."

44. Lucia Hwang, "Planners Give Nod to Illegal Office Conversions," *San Francisco Examiner,* 17 January 2001.

45. Stephanie Salter, "Prop. L Is a Tourniquet; Prop. K Is a Post-it," *San Francisco Examiner,* 29 October 2000.

46. See Chuck Finnie, "Mayor's Pals Get a Prop. K Loophole," *San Francisco Chronicle,* 18 September 2000.

47. See David R. Baker, "Suit Asks Removal of Ballot Measure," *San Francisco Chronicle,* 31 August 2000.

48. David R. Baker, "Ballot Battle to Set Shape of S.F. Skyline," *San Francisco Chronicle,* 16 October 2000.

49. Salter, "Prop. L Is a Tourniquet; Prop. K Is a Post-it"; Rob Morse, "The Mayor Will Have L to Pay," *San Francisco Examiner,* 25 August 2000.

50. Ryan Kim, "Biggest Issue for S.F. Election Is Development," *San Francisco Examiner,* 6 November 2000.

51. Baker, "Ballot Battle."

52. See Jackie Spinner, "Bay Area Office Rents Rank No. 1," *Washington Post,* 30 August 2000; Baker, "Ballot Battle"; David Lazarus, "Demand High for Offices in SF: Real Estate Market Hot Despite Dot-Com Decline," *San Francisco Chronicle,* 31 October 2000. The story notes moves into downtown San Francisco and planned moves by Microsoft, Commerce One, Cisco Systems, and Sun Microsystems.

53. See also the 1991 volume, *Landmarks of San Francisco,* by Patrick McGrew (New York: Harry Abrams).

54. See "Assisting in the Rehabilitation of Affordable Housing," *San Francisco Heritage Newsletter* (September/October 1996).

55. E. Cahill Maloney, "Chamber of Commerce Target of Transit Fee Demonstrations," *San Francisco Progress,* 29 May 1981.

56. E. Cahill Maloney, "Annual Downtown Transit Fee Urged," *San Francisco Progress,* 25 February 1981.

57. Larry Liebert, "2 Sides Try to Reconcile on Fees," *San Francisco Chronicle,* 26 May 1981.

58. "Final Environmental Impact Report, 333 Bush Street," S.F. Department of City Planning, 81.461E, publication date 10 September 1982, 97.

59. Lewis Leader and Larry Hatfield, "War Declared on Muni Tax," *San Francisco Examiner,* 21 April 1981.

60. Larry Liebert, "Feinstein Hasn't Heard Transit Fee Grumbling," *San Francisco Chronicle,* 26 May 1981.

61. Liebert, "2 Sides Try to Reconcile."

62. Ibid.

63. Liebert, "Feinstein Hasn't Heard."

64. Interview with Richard Sklar by Art Silverman, *Metro* (April/May 1983): 8–10. As a serious steward of the city's public transit system, fully aware of the impact new office construction was having on his ability to run the system effectively, Sklar was using his ex-officio Planning Commission spot as a bully

pulpit to warn against development that ignored transit realities. See Gerald Adams, "Feinstein-Sklar Feud Is Now Out in Open," *San Francisco Examiner,* 5 July 1982.

65. Marcelo Rodriguez, "Ten at the Top of San Francisco," *San Francisco* (September 1982): 60–71.

66. Gerald Adams, "Going Gets Rocky for Rincon Point–South Beach Plan," *San Francisco Examiner,* 16 May 1983; San Francisco Tomorrow Newsletter no. 92, June 1983.

67. William Carlsen, "Top Court Rules for S.F. on Transit Fee," *San Francisco Chronicle,* 2 May 1987.

68. McGovern, *The Politics of Downtown Development,* 166.

69. Lucia Hwang, "Muni Misses Out on Millions in Developer Fees," *San Francisco Examiner,* 5 February 2001.

70. Alan Kay, "Feinstein Backs Down on Transit Assessment District," *San Francisco Bay Guardian,* 23 June 1982.

71. Peter Byrne, "Rewarding Failure," first of a two-part report, *SF Weekly,* 2 and 9 December 1998; see also "San Francisco's Mass Transit Faces Scrutiny," *New York Times,* 16 November 1997, reporting that, following a six-month investigation by the National Transportation Safety Board, "federal transportation officials warned this week that problems plaguing San Francisco's mass transit system could lead to a catastrophic accident."

72. An elaborate history of the initiative is provided in George Cothran, "Rescue Muni to the Rescue," *SF Weekly,* 23 June 1999.

73. Irene Lelchuk and Tyche Hendricks, "Activists Missing from Muni Board," *San Francisco Examiner,* 1 February 2000.

74. See Martin Gottlieb, "A Citywide Fund to Aid Housing under Study," *New York Times,* 11 July 1983; Martin Gottlieb, "Tax on Developers?" *New York Times,* 14 July 1983; John Perrotta, "Office Developers Hit D.C. Plan to Make Them Provide Housing," *Washington Post,* 11 June 1983; "Report to the Mayor on the Linkage between Downtown Development and Neighborhood Housing," Boston, October 1983; Bill Allen, "Dealing with Developers," *Shelterforce* (November 1982). See also "Linkage Programs: Employment and Affordable Housing," Current Topics from the Housing Trust Fund Project, March 1991.

75. Memorandum dated 22 January 1982, from Director Dean Macris, Dept. of City Planning, to Interested Parties; subject: OHPP Guideline Revisions.

76. The unreleased draft of the Downtown EIR, which Environmental Science Associates was carrying out for the Department of City Planning, reportedly put forth the figure that 56 percent of downtown office workers lived in San Francisco, a far higher figure than the 40 percent proportion resulting from the OHPP formula. See Gerald Adams, "The Perpetual Crisis," *California Living* (28 August 1983).

77. "Office Affordable Housing Program Annual Report," June 1998. For an early history of OHPP, see Laurie Share and Susan Diamond, "San Francisco's Office-Housing Production Program—Office Developers Finance Local Housing Costs," *Land Use Law and Zoning Digest* (October 1983): 4–10; Susan R.

Diamond, "The San Francisco Office/Housing Program: Social Policy Underwritten by Private Enterprise," *Harvard Environmental Law Review* vol. 7, no. 2 (spring 1983): 449–86.

78. See Tyche Hendricks, "Housing Funds Adrift at City Hall," *San Francisco Examiner*, 27 October 2000; Lucia Hwang, "$12 Million: Missing or Misplaced?" *San Francisco Examiner*, 27 March 2001.

79. See "San Francisco Updates Its Linkage Ordinance," *News from the Housing Trust Fund Project* (spring 2001): 6–7.

80. Marshall Kilduff, "San Francisco's Novel Scheme to Provide Affordable Housing," *California Journal* (May 1982): 169–70.

81. Ibid.

82. Ibid.

83. Diamond, "The San Francisco Office/Housing Program," 460–61, footnotes omitted. For a general discussion of linkage programs in San Francisco, see McGovern, *The Politics of Downtown Development*, 95–110. McGovern's interview with land-use attorney Zane Gresham, a longtime critic of linkage, reports that he

> acknowledged that overt business objections have subsided because many business people have simply "internalized" the policy. Furthermore, Gresham stated that some developers have actually used linkage to their advantage by bolstering their public image. He described how one developer told him that he thought child care linkage was the most "crazy ass thing I ever heard of," but he decided not to oppose it. "Instead what I'm going to do is figure out a way to cozy up to somebody who does child care and go parading around town that I'm a big child care advocate. It's politically attractive, it's a cheap buy, I'll do it." (159)

84. Corrie Anders, "State Rejects the City's Master Housing Plan," *San Francisco Examiner*, 22 January 1982.

85. E. Cahill Maloney, "Special Interest Protections Inserted into State Housing Bill," *San Francisco Progress*, 19 May 1982.

86. Marshall Kilduff, "Exception for S.F. Highrises Hits a Snag in Legislature," *San Francisco Chronicle*, 21 May 1982.

87. Alan Kay and Frank Clancy, "S.F. Developers, Officials Move to Block Anti-Highrise Lawsuits," *San Francisco Bay Guardian*, 26 May 1982.

88. William Carlsen, "Court Scolds S.F. on Planning Policy," *San Francisco Chronicle*, 25 January 1984.

89. See Rachel Gordon, "Developer Cuts Deal with Labor," *San Francisco Examiner*, 26 September 2000; Daniel Evans, "Suit Seeks to Lower Boom on Bloomies," *San Francisco Examiner*, 7 December 2000; "Bloomingdale's in the City! But at What Price?" San Francisco Tomorrow Newsletter, July–August 2000.

CHAPTER 13. THE HOUSING CRISIS AND THE HOUSING MOVEMENT

1. Gerald D. Adams, "S.F. Tenants Union Busy as Demand Overwhelms Supply," *San Francisco Examiner*, 20 November 2000.

2. Ilene Lelchuk, "Lucky Few Get Low-Cost Homes," *San Francisco Chronicle*, 2 February 2001.

3. San Francisco Planning Department, "1998 Housing Inventory" (June 1999), table 23, 29.

4. Pia Sarkar, "HUD Tells Us What We All Know: S.F. Rents Absurd," *San Francisco Examiner,* 13 June 2000.

5. Frank Ahrens, "A City Open to All.Comers," *Washington Post,* 27 November 2000. See also Corrie M. Anders, "Just 11% in City Can Afford a Home," *San Francisco Examiner,* 11 January 2000.

6. Ilene Lelchuk, "S.F. Approves Living Wage Law," *San Francisco Examiner,* 22 August 2000.

7. Diana Pearce, with Jennifer Brooks, "The Self-Sufficiency Standard for California" (prepared for Californians for Family Economic Self-Sufficiency and Equal Rights Advocates, November 2000); see also Carol Ness, "What It Really Costs to Live in The City," *San Francisco Examiner,* 20 November 2000.

8. Lelchuk, "Lucky Few."

9. Evelyn Nieves, "In San Francisco, Renters Are Supplicants," *New York Times,* 6 June 2000.

10. Sheila Mato, "Home Prices Are Beginning to Decline in Upscale San Francisco Neighborhoods," *Wall Street Journal,* 27 March 2001.

11. For a review of housing problems throughout the state, which of course are relevant to the local scene, see "Locked Out! California's Affordable Housing Crisis" (Sacramento: California Budget Project, May 2000).

12. "Housing Affordability Falls 4 Points to 32 Percent in December, C.A.R. Reports" (C.A.R. News Release, 1 February 2001).

13. "Springfield, Ill., Most Affordable Housing Market in Third Quarter 1999" (News Release, NAHB, 6 January 2000).

14. Angela Previn, "Housing Tops S.F. Voters' Worries," *San Francisco Examiner,* 2 February 2001.

15. Peter Fimrite, "Prosperity Brings Faceless Character to Cities: Throughout Bay Area, Residents See Negative Toll on Diversity Wrought by High Housing Costs," *San Francisco Chronicle,* 27 November 2000.

16. "Commercial Uses Eating Up Housing, S.F. Group Says," *San Francisco Chronicle,* 21 October 1986.

17. Gerald Adams, "City Housing Crunch Getting Worse," *San Francisco Examiner,* 18 November 1983.

18. "The Case for Vacancy Decontrol and for Tighter Control of Rents in Occupied Units," report prepared at the request of the office of Supervisor Harry Britt (n.d. [October 1983]).

19. Letter to author, dated 9 August 1993, from Ted Gullicksen, S.F. Tenants Union.

20. Wayne King, "Changing San Francisco Seen as Haven for the Elite," *New York Times,* 9 June 1981.

21. Evelyn Nieves, "In Old Mission District, Changing Grit to Gold," *New York Times,* 21 January 1999. See also the KQED-TV 1994 video, "The Mission" (executive producer Peter L. Stein), in their series, "Neighborhoods: The Hidden Cities of San Francisco."

22. "Activists, Police Clash at Hearing," *San Francisco Examiner*, 8 September 2000; see also Ryan Kim, "Mission Residents Lambaste Planners," *San Francisco Examiner*, 9 June 2000, reporting on a meeting of five hundred local residents with the City's planning director and two Planning Commission members. This event produced a reporter's nostalgic look back at the Mission Coalition Organization; see Ryan Kim, "Echos in the Mission," *San Francisco Examiner*, 10 July 2000.

23. See, for example, Emily Gurnon, "DA Won't Charge Yuppie Foe," *San Francisco Examiner*, 16 March 2000; see also the op-ed, "Robin Hood Didn't Do It," by Po Bronson, in the *New York Times*, 13 February 2000, on the overcommercialization of the Internet, likening the "denial of service" attacks on major Web companies that occurred the week before, by hackers, to the Yuppie Eradication Project.

24. Rachel Gordon, "Inner Mission Tech Offices Get Green Light," *San Francisco Examiner*, 27 June 2000.

25. Marianne Costantinou, "Specter of Eviction in the Mission," *San Francisco Examiner*, 29 November 1999.

26. David R. Baker, "Rent Increases Threaten to Kill S.F. Nonprofits," *San Francisco Chronicle*, 26 October 2000.

27. Dan Levy, "S.F. Arts Groups Face Tsunami of Rising Rents," *San Francisco Chronicle*, 4 October 2000.

28. See Neva Chonin and Dan Levy, "No Room for the Arts," *San Francisco Chronicle*, 17 October 2000, and the excellent set of related articles in the 18 and 19 October editions.

29. Chonin and Levy, "No Room."

30. Levy, "S.F. Arts Groups."

31. Rachel Gordon, "City to Subsidize Arts Groups' Rent," *San Francisco Examiner*, 31 October 2000.

32. Rachel Gordon, "More Funds to Help Save Nonprofits," *San Francisco Examiner*, 14 November 2000.

33. Zoë Mezin, "City Government Priced Out of S.F. Rentals," *San Francisco Examiner*, 18 December 2000.

34. Ryan Kim, "Largest-Ever City Live-Work Project OK'd for Fourth Street," *San Francisco Examiner*, 8 September 2000.

35. Debra Walker, "Response(s) to 'Live/Work: A Neighborhood Study' by the San Francisco Urban Institute," *SFUI Quarterly* (summer 1999): 41.

36. *Asian Neighborhood Design* (fall/winter 1998).

37. Peter Cohen, "Once Affordable Neighborhoods: San Francisco's Transforming Industrial Districts"; "Live/Work: A Neighborhood Study" (survey by the Public Research Institute, commissioned by the San Francisco Urban Institute at San Francisco State University), *SFUI Quarterly* (summer 1999): 34–40. See also Edward W. Lempinen, "Loft War Raging in SOMA: Live/Work Spaces Provide Housing but Displace Businesses, Artists," *San Francisco Chronicle*, 30 March 1998. The ever with-it San Francisco Mime Troupe's 1999 production, "City for Sale," dealt with this issue, portraying conflict between Agnes, a

twenty-seven-year-old website producer, "making $72K a year plus stock options and bonuses," and Xavier, also twenty-seven, who "clears $12K in a good year as a musician."

38. Ryan Kim, "Study Rips Office, Loft Trend in NE Mission," *San Francisco Examiner*, 1 November 2000.

39. Rachel Gordon, "6-Month Loft Ban Okd on 9–1 Vote," *San Francisco Chronicle*, 13 February 2001.

40. Bill Wallace, "Live-Work Blaze Ruled Arson," *San Francisco Chronicle*, 20 October 2000.

41. Lucia Hwang, "Ruling Gives New Definition to Lofts," *San Francisco Examiner*, 14 May 2001.

42. Nina Wu, "So Much for SoMa Boom," *San Francisco Examiner*, 2 April 2001.

43. Christopher Merrill, "Now Is the Time to Buy a House," *San Francisco Examiner*, 16 May 2001.

44. Nina Wu, "Home Sweet 2nd Home," *San Francisco Examiner*, 15 May 2001.

45. A nice feature on the Tenants Union and its increased workload in the current crisis can be found in Gerald D. Adams, "S.F. Tenants Union Busy As Demand Overwhelms Supply," *San Francisco Examiner*, 20 November 2000. Founded in 1970, its membership in the past decade has grown from nine hundred to thirty-five hundred. Among its major functions is advising persons facing eviction and steep rent hikes.

46. James Sobredo, "From Manila Bay to Daly City," in *Reclaiming San Francisco: History, Culture, Politics*, ed. James Brook, Chris Carlsson, and Nancy J. Peters (San Francisco: City Lights Books, 1998), 273–86.

47. For a full account of this struggle, up through the eviction, see Chester Hartman, "San Francisco's International Hotel: Case Study of a Turf Struggle," *Radical America* (May/June 1978): 47–58, reprinted in Chester Hartman, *Between Eminence and Notoriety: Four Decades of Radical Urban Planning* (New Brunswick, N.J.: Rutgers Center for Urban Policy Research, 2002), 134–43. A more recent account of the I-Hotel saga appears in Larry R. Solomon, *Roots of Justice: Studies of Organizing in Communities of Color* (Oakland: Chardon Press, 1998). See also Frank Clancy, "The Legacy of the International Hotel," *San Francisco Bay Guardian*, 22 September 1982; L. A. Chung and Reginald Smith, "Action on International Hotel Site," *San Francisco Chronicle*, 13 March 1984. A documentary film, "The Fall of the I-Hotel," directed by Curtis Choy and produced by the Asian American Media Center in San Francisco, was released in 1983; a feature film based on the residents' struggle, minus the politics ("Street Music," produced by Jenny Bowen and Richard Bowen), also was released in 1983. A San Francisco Mime Troupe play about the I-Hotel, "The Hotel Universe," was published in *West Coast Plays 10*, ed. Rick Foster (California Theatre Council, 1981), 3–30. An account of the I-Hotel saga, by Calvin Trillin, appeared in the 19 December 1997 *New Yorker* ("U.S. Journal—San Francisco").

48. L. A. Chung, "The I-Hotel Battle May Finally Be Over," *San Francisco Chronicle,* 9 July 1984.

49. "Housing Plan Ends 18-Year S.F. Battle," *San Francisco Chronicle,* 4 February 1987.

50. Teresa Moore, "New Plan for International Hotel Site," *San Francisco Chronicle,* 5 December 1991.

51. "Lest We Forget," *San Francisco Bay Guardian,* 29 July 1987.

52. For the Goodman building story, which deserves far more space than can be devoted to it here, see *Goodman Building: Research, Feasibility, Planning* (National Endowment for the Arts and Marquis and Associates, 1977); Chester Hartman, "Housing Struggles and Housing Form," in *The Form of Housing,* ed. Sam Davis (New York: Van Nostrand Reinhold, 1977), 113–37; Katy Butler, "San Francisco Artists Flee City in Search of Cheap Rent," *San Francisco Chronicle,* 15 August 1983, which notes that artists now "feel like an endangered species in a city that once prided itself as an artistic habitat."

53. Maitland Zane, "Artists' Colony Reblooms in S.F.," *San Francisco Chronicle,* 22 June 1996.

54. Dawn Garcia, "S.F. Supervisors Ban Demolition of Homes," *San Francisco Chronicle,* 2 February 1988.

55. See Jim Forbes, "The Birth of Rent Control in San Francisco," *San Francisco Apartment Magazine* (June 1999): 12–13.

56. *California Living, Sunday Examiner & Chronicle,* 23 April 1978, as quoted in David Brigode, "Elections for Sale," paper submitted for college course PA 899, San Francisco State University Urban Studies Dept., 17 December 1983.

57. Chester Hartman, "Landlord Money Defeats Rent Control in San Francisco," in *Rent Control: A Source Book,* comp. John Gilderbloom (Santa Barbara: Foundation for National Progress, Housing Information Center, 1981), 197–201; reprinted in Hartman, *Between Eminence and Notoriety,* 301–4.

58. Alan Ramo and Alan Kay, "Computerized Mailings Change the Face of Local Elections," *San Francisco Bay Guardian,* 17 November 1982.

59. Jeff Gillenkirk, "Target Practice: Their Aim Is True," *New West* (14 January 1980): 65–67.

60. Brigode, "Elections for Sale."

61. Alan Ramo, "San Francisco's Rental Mess," *San Francisco Bay Guardian* (two-part series), 1 and 8 December 1982.

62. Corrie Anders, "The Coming Battle over City's Rent Control Loopholes," *San Francisco Examiner,* 15 January 1982.

63. Marcelo Rodriguez, "The Landlords Move In at SF's Rent Board," *San Francisco Bay Guardian,* 10 December 1980; Marcelo Rodriguez, "Despite SF's Rent Control, Rents Are Going through the Ceiling!" *San Francisco Bay Guardian,* 6 January 1982.

64. Amy Linn and James Finefrock, "Developer Sued over Condo Sales," *San Francisco Examiner,* 28 November 1983; letter to author, dated 26 August 1993, from David Moon, assistant district attorney, San Francisco.

65. William Carlsen, "S.F. Tenants Sue City Attorney," *San Francisco Chronicle,* 14 March 1984.

66. Evelyn Hsu, "Supervisors' Truce with City Attorney," *San Francisco Chronicle,* 6 March 1984; see also Tim Redmond, "The Agnost Years: A Pattern of Pro-Development Opinions," *San Francisco Bay Guardian,* 14 March 1984.

67. Tim Redmond, "The Agnost-Barkley-Alioto Connection," *San Francisco Bay Guardian,* 8 February 1984. Agnost died in 1986, and Mayor Feinstein appointed Supervisor Louise Renne as his replacement until the next election, at which time Renne won a full term; she was subsequently reelected several times, but in 2001 announced that she would not run again.

68. People's Law School, "Evictions in San Francisco," January 1979; more recent data were supplied by Jim Faye of the San Francisco Tenants Union.

69. "The Case for Vacancy Decontrol."

70. David Brigode, "A Broad Overview—the San Francisco Housing Crisis: Data, Analysis, Evaluations, and Recommendations" (Masters thesis, San Francisco State University, 1983), 30.

71. "The Case for Vacancy Decontrol," 16.

72. Ibid., 4.

73. Corrie Anders, "Showdown on Rent Control," *San Francisco Examiner,* 8 January 1984.

74. Evelyn Hsu, "Board Votes Today on Rent Control," *San Francisco Chronicle,* 9 January 1984; see also Tim Redmond, "Cliffhanger Finish Expected in Tenants' Attempt to Strengthen S.F. Rent Control," *San Francisco Bay Guardian,* 4 January 1984.

75. "Feinstein Veto Upheld on Rent Control Law," *San Francisco Chronicle,* 27 June 1986.

76. A review of housing activism at the state level in California may be found in Allan David Heskin, *Tenants and the American Dream* (New York: Praeger Publishers, 1983), 39–65.

77. Quoted in Jerry Roberts, "Behind the Fierce Battle over Proposition 10," *San Francisco Chronicle,* 23 May 1980.

78. "The Election's Big Spenders," *San Francisco Chronicle,* 17 September 1980.

79. Frank Clancy, "L.A. Assemblyman Maneuvers Quietly to Outlaw Effective Rent Control," *San Francisco Bay Guardian,* 23 March 1983.

80. For examples of press coverage of these nearly annual Sacramento battles, see "Assembly Votes to Let State Set Rent Laws," *San Francisco Chronicle,* 4 May 1984; "Last-Minute Anti-Rent Control Effort Fails in State Senate," *San Francisco Bay Guardian,* 10 September 1986.

81. For a study challenging landlord claims of huge financial losses due to tenants fighting evictions, see Richard LeGates and Allan Heskin, "The Case against Pre-Trial Rent Deposits in California" (February 1992).

82. A similar effort in New York (another "hotbed" of rent control), requiring tenants facing eviction actions to deposit with the court any monies the landlord claims are owed before the tenant can even get a hearing, was defeated

in the state legislature in 1997. Billy Easton and Jeanne Finley, "Rent Deposit Bill Withdrawn," *Tenants & Neighbors* (winter 1997).

83. See "Vacancy Control Lacks Majority," *San Francisco Chronicle,* 15 October 1988; "Uphill Fight for Vacant Rent Controls," *San Francisco Chronicle,* 3 November 1988; Craig McLaughlin, "Out-of-Town Landlords Fund No on U Fight," *San Francisco Bay Guardian,* 26 October 1988.

84. Steve Massey, "Agnos to Propose Rent Controls on Vacant Apartments," *San Francisco Chronicle,* 6 July 1989.

85. On Nelder's protracted dance, see "Nelder Stalls Rent Vote," *San Francisco Bay Guardian,* 2 August 1989; "Waiting for Wendy," *San Francisco Bay Guardian,* 23 August 1989; "Vacancy Control Still Stuck," *San Francisco Bay Guardian,* 4 October 1989; "New Rent Measure Goes to S.F. Board," *San Francisco Chronicle,* 24 January 1989.

86. See "The Vacancy-Control Sell-Out," *San Francisco Bay Guardian,* 14 February 1990.

87. See "Vacancy Control I, Vacancy Control II," *San Francisco Bay Guardian,* 21 February 1990.

88. See Vince Bielski and Sara Catania, "Who's in Control?" *San Francisco Bay Guardian,* 6 March 1991; Craig McLaughlin, "Tenants Group Offers Deal," *San Francisco Bay Guardian,* 29 May 1991.

89. See "Tenant Groups Pushing S.F. to Enforce Rent Control," *San Francisco Bay Guardian,* 7 April 1991.

90. See "Ward Introduces Measure Activists Call 'Unacceptable,' " *San Francisco Bay Guardian,* 15 May 1991.

91. See Reynolds Holding, "Housing Group Sues to Halt S.F. Rent Law," *San Francisco Chronicle,* 12 June 1991; "Rent Control Challenge Tossed Out," *San Francisco Chronicle,* 24 August 1991.

92. Matthew C. Sheridan, "The Evolution of Residential Rent Stabilization and Arbitration Ordinance," *San Francisco Apartment Magazine* (June 1999): 15–20.

93. An account of the Proposition H campaign, by an attorney with the Tenderloin Housing Clinic who was intimately involved in it, can be found in Randy Shaw, *The Activist's Handbook: A Primer for the 1990s and Beyond* (Berkeley and Los Angeles: University of California Press, 1996).

94. San Francisco Tenants Union, "Analysis of Vacancy Decontrol Evictions and Displacement," July 1989; "Displacement in San Francisco: A Study of Renters Who Moved," July 1989.

95. Forced displacement consistently produces disadvantageous postrelocation results for tenants. For a historic review of such studies, see Chester Hartman, "The Housing of Relocated Families," *Journal of the American Institute of Planners* (November 1964): 266–86; reprinted in Hartman, *Between Eminence and Notoriety,* 74–104. Chester Hartman, "Relocation: Illusory Promises and No Relief," *Virginia Law Review* 57 (1971): 745–817; Chester Hartman and Richard Legates, "Gentrification-Caused Displacement," *The Urban Lawyer* (winter 1982): 31–55.

96. San Francisco Tenants Union, "An Analysis of Owner Move In Evictions: Data on 1996 Evictions; Characteristics of Tenants; OMI Numbers 1988–1997" (n.d.); also, Christopher Merrill, "Past Due," *San Francisco Bay Guardian,* 4 December 1996. See also the Tenants Union study, "Tenant Displacement in the 1990s: The Abuse of Owner Move In Evictions in San Francisco" (June 1996).

97. For a gruesome tale of injustices perpetrated under the OMI provisions, see Nestor Makhano (a pseudonym for a spokesman for the Mission Yuppie Eradication Project), "Disaster Courts the Mission," *SF Weekly,* 21 April 1999.

98. Evelyn Hsu, "How Buyers Beat the Condo Law," *San Francisco Chronicle,* 4 March 1985; Steve Heller and Jean Tepperman, "Tenants vs. 'Tenants in Common,' " *San Francisco Bay Guardian,* 26 December 1990. Extensive use of solicitation letters to landlords by realtors increased the knowledge and popularity of this gimmick.

99. Christopher Merrill, "More Renters Get Hickey Treatment," *San Francisco Examiner,* 6 February 2001. The headline reference is to one John Hickey, a San Francisco landlord whose outrageous greed in dealing with his tenants (a la Angelo Sangiacomo—see text above) "have been reprehensible enough to deny him [San Francisco Apartment Owners] association membership."

100. Matt Isaacs, "Supes May Cap Selling Rentals," *San Francisco Examiner,* 25 May 2001; see also San Francisco Tenants Union, "Ellis Evictions, 1999–2001."

101. Barbara Herzig, "Why Did the Real Estate Industry File a Lawsuit?" *San Francisco Apartment Magazine* (June 1999): 30–31.

102. Dan Evans, "Landlords: Where Do We Live?" *San Francisco Examiner,* 12 July 2001.

103. Ryan Kim, "Landlords Rush to Beat Eviction Deadline," *San Francisco Examiner,* 18 November 1999.

104. Christopher Merrill, "Board Holds Off Passing Costs on to Tenants," *San Francisco Examiner,* 12 February 2001. The article refers to a recommendation by a committee of the Board of Supervisors for a moratorium on such pass-throughs, given the continuing hold-up of implementation of Proposition H by the court—see text below.

105. Ibid.

106. Tyche Hendricks, "Two Renters' Propositions Split in S.F.," *San Francisco Examiner,* 8 November 2000.

107. Michael Stoll, "Supervisors Act to Head Off Mass Evictions," *San Francisco Examiner,* 12 June 2001; Christopher Merrill, "Down Goes Brown," *San Francisco Examiner,* 10 July 2001.

108. Merrill, "Down Goes Brown."

109. Gerald Adams, "City Agencies' Spat May Affect Condo Forms Changes," *San Francisco Examiner,* 13 July 1982; memorandum dated 8 March 1982, from Supervisor Harry Britt to Honorable Dianne Feinstein. Subject: 1982 Condominium Conversion Regulations; Amy Linn and James Finefrock, "Low-Cost S.F. Condos—A Dream That Failed," *San Francisco Examiner,* 7 November 1983.

110. Gale Cook, "3 Senators Feted at Muir Apts. Owner's Restaurant," *San Francisco Examiner*, 20 April 1983; Robin Clark and James Finefrock, "State Showdown on $40 Million Gamble," *San Francisco Sunday Examiner & Chronicle*, 8 May 1983; "Traweek Appears Beaten," *San Francisco Chronicle*, 29 June 1983.

111. See Larry Liebert, "Traweek Defends Political Ties," *San Francisco Chronicle*, 9 March 1986.

112. Leslie Guevarra, "Judge Quashes Condo Lawsuit against S.F.," *San Francisco Chronicle*, 31 December 1986.

113. See "Community Based Non-Profit Affordable Housing Development in San Francisco" and "San Francisco's Council of Community Housing Organizations, 1978–1991" (both published April 1991); Calvin Welch and Rene Cazenave, "San Francisco Council of Community Housing Organizations," *Shelterforce* (January/February 1994): 9–11. An exhibition on the accomplishments of San Francisco's community-based nonprofits—"Neighbors and Neighborhoods—Building Affordable Housing Together"—was shown at the San Francisco Main Library, May–June 1997.

114. Jim Balderston, "Hotel Ordinance Facing Stiff U.S. Court Challenge," *San Francisco Independent*, 14 April 1992.

115. See "Supervisors Ok 1-Year Ban on Chinatown Hotel Razing," *San Francisco Chronicle*, 24 April 1984.

116. Evelyn Nieves, "Homeless Defy Cities' Drive to Move Them," *New York Times*, 7 December 1999.

117. See Rob Waters and Wade Hudson, "The Tenderloin: What Makes a Neighborhood," in *Reclaiming San Francisco*, ed. James Brook, Chris Carlsson, and Nancy J. Peters, 301–16; Greg Hugunin, "Tender Box," *SF Weekly*, 21–27 July 1999.

118. Warren Hinckle, "The Tenderloin's Tarzan vs. His Tenants," *San Francisco Chronicle*, 4 April 1980.

119. Warren Hinckle, "Old Folks Get a Raw Deal in S.F. Hotels," *San Francisco Chronicle*, 11 April 1980.

120. See, for example, Jim Balderston, "Jail for Landlord," *San Francisco Bay Guardian*, 28 November 1990; Walt Gibbs, "Settlement in Astoria Eviction Suit," *San Francisco Examiner*, 30 March 1986; Kevin Leary, "S.F. Tenants Win Record Award against Landlord," *San Francisco Chronicle*, 18 June 1988.

121. Marshall Kilduff, "Board Approves Weaker Law on Tourist Rooms," *San Francisco Chronicle*, 9 June 1981.

122. Jim Balderston, "The Homeless Battle Comes Home," *San Francisco Bay Guardian*, 20 September 1989.

123. Frank Clancy and Alan Ramo, "Thousands of S.F. Residential Rooms Lost Despite Controls," *San Francisco Bay Guardian*, 2 February 1983; Sara Colm and Rob Waters, "Hotels Convert Despite Law," *Tenderloin Times*, March 1982.

124. Erik Shapiro, "City Plans: Rezoning or Redevelopment?" *Tenderloin Times*, May 1983; Sara Colm with Rob Waters, "Battle Lines Drawn on Union

Square West," *Tenderloin Times,* June 1983; Marshall Kilduff, "New Limits on Building Proposed for Tenderloin," *San Francisco Chronicle,* 5 April 1983; "North of Market Rezoning Study," S.F. Department of City Planning, March 1983.

125. Letter to author, dated 31 August 1993, from Kevin Carew, North of Market Planning Coalition.

126. See John King, "Tenderloin Showing Signs of New Hope," *San Francisco Chronicle,* 28 June 1993.

127. "Final Report, North of Market Planning Coalition, Tenderloin 2000 Survey and Plan" (July 1992). For a detailed, possibly overly hopeful, description of the many steps to resist development pressures on the Tenderloin, see Tony Robinson, "Gentrification and Grassroots Resistance in San Francisco's Tenderloin," *Urban Affairs Review,* vol. 30, no. 3 (January 1995): 483–513.

128. Kathleen Sullivan, "Hotel West, Drake in Tenderloin Promise Not to Evict Tenants to Evade Law," *San Francisco Examiner,* 11 May 2000.

129. Ahrens, "A City Open to All.Comers."

130. Kathleen Sullivan, "New Effort to Prevent Hotel Fires," *San Francisco Chronicle,* 12 June 2001.

131. Emily Gurnon, "City Fails to Enforce Hotel Safety Law," *San Francisco Examiner,* 18 November 1999.

132. On problems in San Francisco's public housing projects generally, see Public Housing Task Force, "Crisis in Public Housing: A Review of the Alternatives for Public Housing in San Francisco and Recommendations for the Future" (April 1982).

133. See Reginald Smith and Mark Z. Barabak, "Feinstein Warns Housing Agency to Shape Up," *San Francisco Chronicle,* 2 February 1985.

134. Reginald Smith, "Housing Chief's Unenviable Job," *San Francisco Chronicle,* 2 February 1985.

135. See "New S.F. Housing Chief Promises 'Safe' Projects," *San Francisco Chronicle,* 9 May 1989.

136. See Robert Collier, "New Mayor to Take Hard Look at Housing Authority," *San Francisco Chronicle,* 10 January 1992.

137. Vernon Loeb, "Resident Expert: DC's Housing Authority Was in the Dumps When David Gilmore Moved In," *Washington Post,* 7 May 1998; after going to Seattle, Gilmore in 1994 took over the District of Columbia public housing program.

138. Carey Goldberg, "San Francisco Housing Authority Serves As Model of Decay," *New York Times,* 24 May 1996.

139. See "San Francisco Housing Agency Taken Over," *New York Times,* 10 March 1996.

140. Bob Egelko and Lance Williams, "Housing Exec Guilty of Bribes," *San Francisco Examiner,* 27 September 2000.

141. Ilene Lelchuk, "Housing Chief's Big New Contract," *San Francisco Examiner,* 15 March 2000; Erin McCormick, "Midwest Audit Rakes S.F. Housing Chief," *San Francisco Examiner,* 5 August 2000.

142. Johnny Brannon, "Feds Slap S.F., Yank $20 Million in Housing Grants," *San Francisco Examiner,* 28 December 2000.

143. Patrick Hoge, "S.F. Housing Chief Charged With Funds Theft in Ohio," *San Francisco Chronicle,* 22 March 2001.

144. Net loss of low-income units as a result of HOPE VI activities is not just a San Francisco phenomenon. See the December 1998 report of HUD's Office of Inspector General, "Nationwide Audit HOPE VI Urban Revitalization Program, Audit Report No. 99-FW-101–0001."

145. "David Bryson of the National Housing Law Project . . . says he has noticed that in San Francisco many developments being demolished are predominantly minority, often in well-integrated, mixed-income neighborhoods. When given a portable [Section 8 housing] voucher [for use to relocate into privately owned housing], many tenants choose to move to more heavily minority neighborhoods with lower median incomes—often the only areas where they can afford rent" (Winton Pitcoff, "New Hope for Public Housing?" *Shelterforce,* March/April 1999: 18–21, 28; see also Evelyn Nieves, "Blacks Hit by Housing Costs, Leave San Francisco Behind," *New York Times,* 2 August 2001; and Ilene Lelchuck, "North Beach Project Residents Ready to Fight Eviction," San Francisco Chronicle, 9 August 2001).

146. See Jeff Chang, "Housing Divided: Tragic Failures & Hopeful Successes in Low-Income Project Integration," *RaceFile* (July/August 1997): 22–36; Venice Wagner and Michael Dougan, "Last Viet Families Quit Troubled S.F. Project," *San Francisco Examiner,* 9 June 1997.

147. For a general description of the problem, see Alfred M. Clark III, "Can America Afford to Abandon a National Housing Policy?" *Journal of Affordable Housing and Community Development Law* 6 (spring 1997): 185–206.

148. See California Housing Finance Agency Board of Director's Meeting, "California Preservation Outlook," presentation by Bill Rumpf, California Housing Partnership Corporation, 8 July 1999.

149. See Informational Memorandum, dated 24 July 1998, from James Morales, executive director, to [S.F. Redevelopment] agency commissioners, "Update on the Housing Preservation Program."

150. See "A Plan to Save Low-Cost Housing in S.F.," *San Francisco Chronicle,* 27 March 1990; "Agnos Warning on End of Aid for Housing," *San Francisco Chronicle,* 18 September 1990.

151. For a general social policy treatment of the issue, see Christopher Jencks, *The Homeless* (Cambridge, Mass.: Harvard University Press, 1994). See also Howard Schatz and Beverly J. Ornstein, *Homelessness: Portraits of Americans in Hard Times* (San Francisco: Chronicle Books, 1993).

152. Tim Redmond, "Do the Streets Belong to the Street People?" *San Francisco Bay Guardian,* 19 May 1982.

153. Bill Mandel, "Undesirable Elements," *San Francisco Examiner,* 12 August 1983.

154. Ibid.

155. Barney Jarvis, "ACLU Assails 'Street Sweeps' by S.F. Cops," *San Francisco Chronicle,* 17 December 1986. The attorney, John Crew, was subsequently awarded forty-nine hundred dollars in damages and got the police rule book amended.

156. Edward W. Lempinen, "Chief Jordan Raps Resolution on Homeless," *San Francisco Chronicle,* 27 October 1988.

157. See J. L. Pimsleur and Maitland Zane, "S.F. Police Clear Out Car Dwellers," *San Francisco Chronicle,* 26 July 1988. Evelyn Nieves's, "Living in a Bulky Van, Trying to Move Ahead," *New York Times,* 19 December 1999, details the life of a San Francisco woman living in her van.

158. Clarence Johnson, "Court Upholds S.F.'s Ban on Sleeping in Cars," *San Francisco Chronicle,* 8 August 1990.

159. Vince Bielski and Johan Carlisle, "Go to Sleep, Land in Jail," *San Francisco Bay Guardian,* 24 July 1991.

160. Kathy Bodovitz, "Agnos Offers Homeless Plan Deadline," *San Francisco Chronicle,* 20 April 1990.

161. Kathy Bodovitz, "How Quake Changed the Way S.F. Cares for Homeless," *San Francisco Chronicle,* 7 December 1989.

162. Sharon Waxman, "Keeping Focus on Homeless: San Francisco Activist Proves a Civic Embarrassment," *Washington Post,* 17 July 1996. This particularly inhumane practice did not end in 1996. A December 1999 *New York Times* account noted: "In recent weeks, the police have started arresting volunteers for handing out food to homeless people (without having a permit to do so) at United Nations Plaza. (The catch: the city will not grant them a permit.)"

163. See C. T. Lawrence and Keith T. McHenry, *Food Not Bombs: How to Feed the Hungry and Build Community* (Philadelphia: New Society Publishers, 1992); also, Jesse Drew, "Any Vegetable: The Politics of Food in San Francisco," in *Reclaiming San Francisco,* ed. James Brook, Chris Carlsson, and Nancy J. Peters, 317–31.

164. Andrew Ross and Andy Furillo, "Poll: Homeless S.F.'s No. 1 Problem," *San Francisco Examiner,* 7 January 1990.

165. See Edward Lempinen, "Society's Haves Getting Weary of Have-Nots," *San Francisco Chronicle,* 31 October 1988; Andy Furillo, "Homeless Face Growing Hostility in Nation's Cities," *San Francisco Examiner,* 15 July 1990.

166. Ingfei Chen, "Jordan Recommends Tightening Up on Homeless," *San Francisco Chronicle,* 10 July 1991.

167. Christine Spolar, "San Francisco's New Urban Outlaws Carry Bedrolls and Sleep Outdoors," *San Francisco Chronicle,* 24 November 1993.

168. April Lynch and Bill Wallace, "S.F. Sweeps Yield Few Convictions," *San Francisco Chronicle,* 22 October 1993.

169. Rachel Gordon, "Board Votes Down Alioto Amnesty for Homeless," *San Francisco Examiner,* 26 October 1993.

170. Ibid.

171. Sharon Waxman, "Keeping Focus on Homeless," *Washington Post,* 17 July 1996.

172. Quoted in Bill Mandel, "The City's Changing Image," *San Francisco Examiner,* 28 March 1983.

173. Evelyn Nieves, "Homelessness Tests San Francisco's Ideals," *New York Times,* 13 November 1998.

174. Kathleen Sullivan, "Homeless Say Shelters Lack Basic Amenities," *San Francisco Examiner*, 6 October 2000.

175. Carey Goldberg, "Homeless in San Francisco: A New Policy," *New York Times*, 20 May 1996.

176. Letter to author, dated 18 April 1997, from Alan L. Schlosser, managing attorney, ACLU Foundation for Northern California.

177. See Mary Curtius, "San Francisco Mayor Says City's Homeless Problem May Not Be Solvable," *Washington Post*, 13 October 1996.

178. Randy Shaw, "Wayward Willie," *In These Times* (3 March 1997).

179. Evelyn Nieves, "Homeless Defy Cities' Drives to Move Them," *New York Times*, 7 December 1999.

180. Curtius, "San Francisco Mayor."

181. William Claiborne, "San Francisco's Homeless Expected Compassion, but Got a Crackdown," *Washington Post*, 28 November 1997.

182. Nieves, "Homeless Defy"; Rene Sanchez, "City of Tolerance Tires of Homeless," *Washington Post*, 28 November 1998.

183. Ilene Lelchuk, "City's Homeless Count Shows Where Aid Needed," *San Francisco Examiner*, 4 May 2000.

184. Zoë Mezin, "Police Sweeps Aid Mid-Market Cleanup," *San Francisco Examiner*, 14 May 2001; the *Examiner* has done its part to stir up the pot, with a series of articles with such titles as "Mid-Market: It's an Awful Mess" (30 March 2001, by Matt Isaacs) and an accompanying two-part series of editorials (29–30 March 2001) titled "The Mess on Market Street," the first of which ends, "The mid-Market is an embarrassment, a civic disgrace. San Francisco deserves better. Will our leaders have what it takes?"

185. Sanchez, "City of Tolerance."

186. Nieves, "Homelessness."

187. Richard Cohen, "Homeless in San Francisco," *Washington Post*, 2 December 1997.

188. Sanchez, "City of Tolerance"; Nieves, "Homeless Defy."

189. "Fancy Shelter for Dogs Is Deemed Fit for Humans," *New York Times*, 22 March 1998; Evelyn Nieves, "A Campaign for A No-Kill Policy for the Nation's Animal Shelters," *New York Times*, 18 January 1999.

190. See these reports from the National Law Center on Homelessness and Poverty, "No Homeless People Allowed: A Report on Anti-Homelessness Laws, Litigation and Alternatives in U.S. Cities" (Washington, D.C.: 1994); "Mean Sweeps" (1997).

191. "Famed, and Spacious, Army Post Is Focus of Housing Fray," *New York Times*, 10 May 1998.

192. See Carl Nolte, "S.F. Will Fight Proposal to Shut Presidio Base," *San Francisco Chronicle*, 31 December 1988; "Boxer, Pelosi in S.F. to Lobby for the Presidio," *San Francisco Chronicle*, 7 January 1989; "Experts Say Presidio Makes Up 2% of S.F. Economy," *San Francisco Chronicle*, 31 December 1988.

193. See "1,001 Ideas on What to Do with It Now," *San Francisco Chronicle*, 11 January 1989; "Presidio Wish List Covers Gamut of Issues," *San Francisco Chronicle*, 23 April 1989.

194. "Presidio Takes First Steps to Become a National Park," *San Francisco Chronicle*, 1 May 1990; "Panel Named to Help Presidio Become a New National Park," *San Francisco Chronicle*, 2 July 1991; "First Presidio Building in Civilian Hands," *San Francisco Chronicle*, 29 May 1991.

195. See Larry Hatfield, "Medley of Bay Leaders to Run Presidio," *San Francisco Examiner*, 18 April 1997.

196. An early 1980s proposal by Ronald Reagan's Interior Secretary James Watt to have the Disney Corporation manage the Grand Canyon was roundly criticized and rejected.

197. See Elliot Diringer, "Toxic Hazards at the Presidio—Asbestos, Gas Leaks, PCB," *San Francisco Chronicle*, 6 January 1989; Mickey Butts and Saul Bloom, "The Presidio Is Leaking," *San Francisco Bay Guardian*, 16 August 1989.

198. Patricia Leigh Brown, "A Force in Film Meets a Force of Nature," *New York Times*, 30 March 2000.

199. Eric Brazil, "Critics Blast Lucasfilm Center Design," *San Francisco Examiner*, 25 October 2000.

200. Eric Brazil, "Lucasfilm Reveals Big Plans for Presidio," *San Francisco Examiner*, 18 June 2000.

201. Glen Martin, "Battle of the Presidio: Showdown over Development of S.F. National Parkland," *San Francisco Chronicle*, 4 May 2000.

202. Ibid. David R. Baker, "New Presidio Plan Opens Door to Hotels: Trust's Proposal Worries Neighbors of Sprawling S.F. Park," *San Francisco Chronicle*, 25 July 2001.

203. For a typical account, see Henry K. Lee, "4 Dozen Arrested at Presidio," *San Francisco Chronicle*, 19 May 1997.

204. See Gregory Lewis, "Housing Chief: Let Poor Live in Presidio," *San Francisco Examiner*, 12 March 1997; Edward Epstein, "Brown Says He Wants Low-Cost Housing at Presidio," *San Francisco Chronicle*, 21 April 1997. The Golden Gate National Recreation Area superintendent, no fan of having his facility used to house the homeless but recognizing the need, offered to ship these units by barge to another location, such as Treasure Island or Bayview–Hunters Point.

205. "Comments of Community Leaders on Plans of the National Parks [sic] Service to Demolish the Remaining 466 Wherry Housing Units" (n.d.).

206. See "Treasure Island: A Landfill Full of Possibilities," *New York Times*, 15 April 1996.

207. Johnny Brannon, "S.F. Has Island Homes for Rent," *San Francisco Examiner*, 27 December 2000.

208. See "Summary of Homeless Services Component, Draft Reuse Plan, Naval Station Treasure Island" (n.d.).

209. See Institute for Policy Studies Working Group on Housing, "The Right to Housing: A Blueprint for Housing the Nation" (Washington, D.C.: 1989); Chester Hartman, "The Case for a Right to Housing," *Housing Policy Debate* 9, no. 2 (1998): 223–46; reprinted in Hartman, *Between Eminence and Notoriety*, 280–97.

210. Calvin Welch, "What Housing Crisis?" *SFUI Quarterly* (summer 1999): 4–6.

211. Randy Shaw, "National Arena Holds Key to San Francisco's Future," *SFUI Quarterly* (summer 1999): 14–19.

212. Bay Area Council, *Housing: The Bay Area's Challenge of the '80s* (December 1980); from foreword by B. F. Began, chair, and Angelo J. Syracusa, president.

213. Ibid., 4.

214. Ibid., 5.

215. Ibid., 17.

216. Ibid.

CHAPTER 14. THE LESSONS OF SAN FRANCISCO

1. Letter dated 12 August 1982 from John Elberling to the Planning Commission and Planning Director Dean Macris, commenting on the draft environmental impact report to the Residential Element of the Comprehensive Plan for the City and County of San Francisco.

2. See Elizabeth Morris, "Urban Redevelopment and the Emerging Community Sector," Ph.D. diss., Dept. of City and Regional Planning, University of California, Berkeley, 1998.

3. Paulina Borsook, "How the Internet Ruined San Francisco," http://www.salon.com/news/feature/1999/10/28/internet/index.html.

4. Rebecca Solnit and Susan Schwartzenberg, *Hollow City: The Siege of San Francisco and the Crisis of American Urbanism* (London: Verso, 2000), 167, 168, 34, 122, 123, 124.

5. See John C. Bonifaz, " 'Not the Rich, More Than the Poor': Poverty, Race and Campaign Finance Reform," *Poverty & Race* (September/October 1999): 1–2, 6–8, reprinted in *Challenges to Equality: Poverty and Race in America*, ed. Chester Hartman (Armonk, N.Y.: M. E. Sharpe, 2001) 183–200.

6. An argument that San Francisco is losing its regional locational advantage, due to communications and information processing advantages in just those sectors that earlier valued centralization—finance, insurance, public utilities, communications—may be found in Michael J. Potepan and Elisa Barbour, "San Francisco's Employment Roller Coaster: A Report on the City's Employment Economy from 1980 to 2000" (San Francisco: San Francisco Urban Institute, March 1996).

7. Morris Newman, "High Density Rentals for Silicon Valley," *New York Times*, 17 September 2000.

8. On some important racial dimensions of regionalism and the newly emerging concerns about sprawl, see John A. Powell, "Race and Space," *Poverty & Race* (January/February 1999): 3–4, 6, reprinted in *Challenges to Equality*, 20–27. On the political and related economic dimensions, see Myron Orfield, "San Francisco Bay Area Metropolitics: A Regional Agenda for Community and Stability" (Urban Habitat Program, 1998) and "What If We Shared? A Report by the Urban Habitat Program" (May 1998).

9. Rebecca R. Sohmer and Robert E. Lang, "Downtown Rebound" (Fannie Mae Foundation and Brookings Institution Center on Urban and Metropolitan Policy Census Note, May 2001), 1.

Index

Text:	10/13 Aldus
Display:	Akzidenz Grotesk Bold Extended; Univers Condensed Light and Bold
Compositor:	Impressions Book and Journal Services, Inc.
Printer:	Edwards Brothers, Inc.